The Peru Reader,
Second Edition

The Latin America Readers, a series edited
by Robin Kirk and Orin Starn

Also in the series:

The Brazil Reader: History, Culture, Politics
Edited by Robert M. Levine and John J. Crocitti

The Argentina Reader: History, Culture, Politics
Edited by Gabriela Nouzeilles and Graciela Montaldo

The Mexico Reader: History, Culture, Politics
Edited by Gilbert M. Joseph and Timothy J. Henderson

The Cuba Reader: History, Culture, Politics
Edited by Aviva Chomsky, Barry Carr, and
Pamela Maria Smorkaloff

The Costa Rica Reader: History, Culture, Politics
Edited by Steven Palmer and Iván Molina

Praise for the first edition of *The Peru Reader*

"This book is as indispensable for the first-time visitor to Peru as for the serious student of Latin American history and culture." — Michael F. Brown, author of *Who Owns Native Culture?*

"Original and lively, with indigenous and vernacular voices richly represented, this book brings together an astonishing range of primary texts to introduce readers to the cultural and political history of what is now Peru. Nothing like it exists, in English or Spanish." — Mary Louise Pratt, author of *Imperial Eyes: Travel Writing and Transculturation*

"The introductory readings chosen by the editors provide excellent accounts of the ancient civilizations of the Andes, cover the conquest and colonial periods as well as republican Peru, and conclude with an extensive discussion of contemporary problems. . . . This fine initiative raises hopes for volumes on other Latin American countries for which historical material of this quality is not easily available to the general reader." — *Foreign Affairs*

"*The Peru Reader* is a joy both for Peru specialists and those seeking an introduction to the country's political and social development." — John Crabtree, *Journal of Latin American Studies*

"Readers well acquainted with Peru will find gems in [this] collection unfamiliar to them, and students of Latin American history and culture in general can mine *The Peru Reader* endlessly." — Henry A. Dietz, *Latin American Research Review*

"An excellent collection of essays about Peru." — Stephen M. Hart, *Bulletin of Hispanic Studies*

"A multi-faceted representation of this complex Andean country." — Sarah A. Radcliffe, *Bulletin of Latin American Research*

THE
PERU
READER

HISTORY, CULTURE, POLITICS

Second edition, revised and updated

Edited by Orin Starn, Carlos Iván Degregori, and Robin Kirk

DUKE UNIVERSITY PRESS   *Durham and London 2005*

© 2005 Duke University Press   All rights reserved
Printed in the United States of America on acid-free paper
Typeset in New Baskerville by Tseng Information Systems, Inc.
Library of Congress Cataloging-in-Publication Data appear
on the last printed page of this book.

CONTENTS

A Note on Style   xi

Introduction   1

PART I · THE ANCIENT CIVILIZATIONS   13
The Chavín Cult, *Brian Fagan*   17
Nazca Pottery, *Javier Sologuren*   28
The Huarochirí Manuscript, *Anonymous*   30
Moon, Sun, Witches, *Irene Silverblatt*   36
The Origins of the Incas, *Garcilaso de la Vega*   50
Cloth, Textile, and the Inca Empire, *John Murra*   56
Taxation and the Incas, *Pedro de Cieza de León*   71
Officials and Messengers, *Guamán Poma de Ayala*   76
The Search for Machu Picchu, *Hiram Bingham*   82

PART II · CONQUEST AND COLONIAL RULE   93
Atahualpa and Pizarro, *John Hemming*   97
In Defense of the Indians, *Bartolomé de las Casas*   119
Our House, *Marco Martos*   123
The Tragedy of Success, *Steve J. Stern*   124
Diary of Colonial Lima, *Josephe de Mugaburu y Honton*   149
Friar Martín's Mice, *Ricardo Palma*   154
The Rebellion of Túpac Amaru, *Alberto Flores Galindo*   159
"All Must Die!" *José Antonio de Areche*   169

PART III · REPUBLICAN PERU   175
The Battle of Ayacucho, *Antonio Cisneros*   179
Comas and the War of the Pacific, *Florencia E. Mallon*   181
Priests, Indians, Soldiers, and Heroes, *Manuel González Prada*   199

Women of Lima, *Flora Tristán*   207
Amazonian Indians and the Rubber Boom, *Manuel Córdova*   215

PART IV · THE ADVENT OF MODERN POLITICS   227
Tempest in the Andes, *Luis Valcárcel*   231
Water! *Juan Pévez*   235
Reflections, *José Carlos Mariátegui*   240
Human Poems, *César Vallejo*   246
The APRA, *Víctor Raúl Haya de la Torre*   253
The Massacre of Chan Chan, *Carleton Beals*   258
Lost to Sight, *César Moro*   266

PART V · THE BREAKUP OF THE OLD ORDER   269
The Pongo's Dream, *José María Arguedas*   273
"The Master Will No Longer Feed Off Your Poverty," *Juan Velasco*   279
The 24th of June, *Gabriel Aragón*   285
Villa El Salvador, *Cecilia Blondet*   287
Recipe for a House, *Mercedes Torribio*   293
Featherless Vultures, *Julio Ramón Ribeyro*   296
Peru's African Rhythms, *Nicomedes Santa Cruz*   305
A Guerrilla's Word, *Javier Heraud*   307
Liberation Theology, *Gustavo Gutiérrez*   309
A World for Julius, *Alfredo Bryce Echenique*   313

PART VI · THE SHINING PATH   319
"A Frightening Thirst for Vengeance," *Osmán Morote*   323
We Are the Initiators, *Abimael Guzmán*   325
The Quota, *Gustavo Gorriti*   331
Memories of a Cadre, *"Nicario"*   343
Oath of Loyalty, *Anonymous*   351

PART VII · MANCHAY TIEMPO   353
Vietnam in the Andes, *"Pancho"*   357
Death Threat, *Anonymous*   364
Women and Terror, *Raquel Martín de Mejía*   366
Chaqwa, *Robin Kirk*   370
Huamanguino, *Ranulfo Fuentes*   384
"There Have Been Threats," *María Elena Moyano*   387
Peasants at War, *Ponciano del Pino*   393
Time of Reckoning, *Salomón Lerner*   401

PART VIII · THE COCAINE ECONOMY 407
The Hold Life Has, *Catherine J. Allen* 411
My Little Coca, Let Me Chew You! *Anonymous* 424
The Cocaine Economy, *Jo Ann Kawell* 425
Drugs, Soldiers, and Guerrillas, *"Chanamé"* 438

PART IX · THE STRUGGLE FOR SURVIVAL 441
Soup of the Day, *Family Kitchen No. 79* 445
Nightwatch, *Orin Starn* 447
"A Momentous Decision," *Alberto Fujimori* 460
Choleric Outbreak, *Caretas* 468
Bribing a Congressman, *Alberto Kouri and Vladimiro Montesinos* 474
Simply Pascuala, *José María Salcedo* 477

PART X · CULTURE(S) REDEFINED 481
Chayraq! *Carlos Iván Degregori* 485
The Choncholí Chewing Gum Rap, *Nosequién y los nosecuantos* 489
Sarita Colonia Comes Flying, *Eduardo González Viaña* 491
Is Peru Turning Protestant? *Luis Minaya* 496
Interview with a Gay Activist, *Enrique Bossio* 502
Adrenaline Nights, *Carmen Ollé* 507
Reencounter, *Giovanna Pollarolo* 509
I Am the Bad Girl of the Story, *María Emilia Cornejo* 511
Conversation in the Cathedral, *Mario Vargas Llosa* 512
The Slave, *Jaime Bayly* 528
Aguaruna Adventures, *Anonymous* 553
Self-Images, *Workshop for Social Photography* 562

Suggestions for Further Reading 567
Acknowledgments 571
Acknowledgment of Copyrights 573
Index 577

A NOTE ON STYLE

This anthology contains works from many different periods, authors, and points of view. We have tried to keep our editing and abridgement to a minimum in the interest of preserving tone and reflecting the historical context in which each work was written. Those familiar with the changing history of Quechua orthography will notice variations in the spelling of commonly used words—among others, chacra and chacara, Inca and Inka, and Atahualpa and Atawalpa.

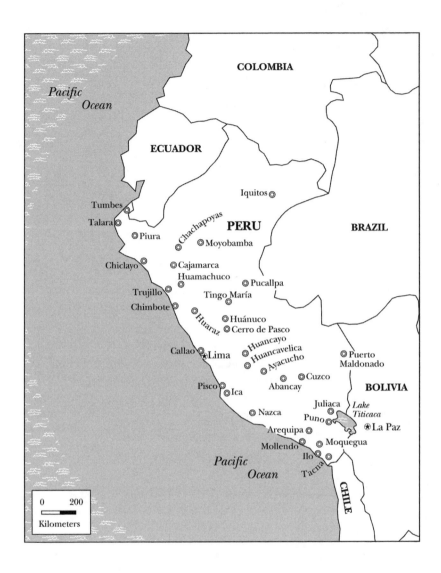

INTRODUCTION

I am of the opinion . . . that there is no kingdom in the world more rich in precious ores, for every day great lodes are discovered both of gold and of silver," asserted the Spanish soldier Pedro de Cieza de León in 1550.[1] Others told stories just as startling about the newly conquered land of Peru. In the account of Garcilaso de la Vega, the son of an Inca princess and a Spanish conqueror who wrote the famous *Royal Commentaries of the Incas and General History of Peru* from his adopted homeland of Andalusia, the great Inca ruler Huayna Capac, on the birth of his first son, ordered "a rope of gold to be made, which was so thick that more than two hundred Indian lords could barely lift it."[2] Still another chronicler described a simulated garden of "plants, trees, and flowers of gold and silver" on Lake Titicaca.[3] These accounts fueled the myth of El Dorado, a golden empire more fabulous than Cortés's recently discovered Mexico. The newest Spanish colony was not just a prime source of wealth for the Habsburg Dynasty in its quest for European supremacy over England and France. As a faraway land of tantalizing mystery, Peru also mirrored the dreams and desires of generations of Europeans in the seeming confines of the Old World.

The myth of El Dorado represents an early chapter in a long history of powerful images of Peru as a land of magical strangeness and fantasy. Inspired by the passions of European Romanticism of the nineteenth century, French and German travelers penned breathless accounts of soaring Andean peaks plunging into luxuriant Amazonian canyons of orchids, pythons, and jaguars.[4] The early-twentieth-century American adventurer Hiram Bingham, a future senator from Colorado, thrilled *National Geographic* readers with his odyssey across raging rivers and wild jungles to Machu Picchu, the "Lost City of the Incas." Seventy years later, news crews from ABC and CBS ventured down to report on murderous rebels, starving peasants, and Colombian drug runners in the "white gold" rush of the coca trade.

It seems safe to say that no country in this hemisphere outrivals Peru in its aura of mystery and exoticism. The bloodiest conquest. The richest treasures. The most poignant ballads. The most violent revolutionaries. As dramatic as Peru indeed can be, these extreme, sometimes exoticizing, depictions too often stand in for deeper understanding, and other viewpoints. Our aim with *The Peru Reader* is to offer a richer, more informed portrait of Peru and the astonishing complexity of its past and present. Here the reader holds an anthology of poems, short stories, colonial chronicles, interviews, song lyrics, speeches, essays, and much more.[5]

Of course, many others before us have wanted the world to see Peru with new eyes. It was in 1613, for example, that Guamán Poma de Ayala, in his 1,200-page letter to King Philip III of Spain, strove to shake the invaders from their disastrous assumption that Indians were inferior and urged that they be seen instead as able partners in building a prosperous colony. This at once impassioned, self-serving, and insightful tour de force lay forgotten until it was discovered in 1908 in a Copenhagen archive. The fate of Guamán Poma's *The First New Chronicle and Good Government* can be read as a metaphor for much compelling work passed over for the known, the easy read—for what leaves preconceptions unchallenged. In the tradition of Guamán Poma, we hope that the seventy-four pieces in this anthology will work to reveal the diversity and dynamism of Peru and its people.

What were our criteria for selecting material? Perhaps the most immediate was a desire to offer readers an opportunity to hear the views of Peruvians about their country. Much of what is available in the United States and Europe comes off the computers of Western journalists and scholars. Except for the novelist Mario Vargas Llosa, and before him, poet César Vallejo, no Peruvian has been translated with any regularity. Social critics and scholars like Manuel González Prada, Luis Valcárcel, and Alberto Flores Galindo; political figures like Víctor Raúl Haya de la Torre and General Juan Velasco; poets, fiction writers, and songwriters like Carmen Ollé, J. R. Ribeyro, and Nicomedes Santa Cruz are just a few among dozens of important Peruvian intellectuals and politicians included here, many of whom appear in English for the first time in this anthology. Even much of the writing of famous figures like the Quechua-speaking novelist and anthropologist José María Arguedas and the socialist critic José Carlos Mariátegui has not been published outside Peru.

A biting and hilarious Arguedas short story, "The Pongo's Dream," and some of the sharp-sighted Mariátegui's most trenchant reflections on Peru also appear for the first time in English in *The Peru Reader*. Decolonization and transnationalism have meant a greater visibility for modern-day writers, artists, scholars, and activists in Europe's former colonies. Our only regret is that this long book could not be even longer to include still more material from the likes of Arguedas and Mariátegui.

The anthology is not limited to the work of Peruvian politicians and intellectuals, however. Despite what anthropologist José Matos Mar calls the "desborde popular" (popular overflow) of recent decades, including political upheaval and rapid urbanization, large sectors of Peru's population have remained at the margins of this divided society. This internal colonialism privileges the needs of the white and the wealthy over those of peasants, street vendors, maids, soldiers, Amazonian Indians, African Peruvians, and Quechua and Aymara speakers, who find their views ignored or suppressed inside the country and barely circulated beyond its borders. To counter this invisibility, we have translated some of the best of the growing genre of testimonial literature, such as the autobiography of Juan Pévez, founder of the Ica Peasant Federation, first recorded and published by a Lima advocacy and research center. In addition, *The Peru Reader* draws on interviews of our own and transcriptions of those done by others. It would be naïve to imagine that these views "from below" are always noble. The lower-middle-class navy soldier "Pancho," now a drug addict in the decaying Lima neighborhood of Barrios Altos, gives a wrenching account of his involvement in rape and massacres in the campaign against the Communist Party of Peru–Shining Path. At the same time, however, the themes of struggle and vision, often against tremendous odds, stand out in the stories of many others, including the gay and lesbian leader Enrique Bossio, evangelical pastor Luis Minaya, rape victim and human rights advocate Raquel Martín de Mejía, and Lucanas peasant turned Lima squatter Mercedes Torribio. We include these remarkable first-person accounts in hopes of contributing to a shake-up of the unilateral privilege of journalists and scholars of any nationality to "speak for" the subaltern around the world.

Yet it would be disingenuous to present *The Peru Reader* as a transparent record of Peruvian "voices." For one thing, we have included what we believe to be some of the best writing about Peru by outsiders. Despite his hyperbole about Inca beneficence and wealth, the young Extremaduran Cieza de León was an extraordinary observer, and many consider him one of the Americas' first great ethnographers. The American journalist

Carleton Beals wrote a wonderful account in 1930 of the American Popular Revolutionary Alliance and the politics of socialism and Indian rights, as mass politics erupted in Peru in a climate of upheaval inspired by the Mexican and Russian revolutions. Readers will find not only Cieza and Beals in this anthology, but also present-day U.S. and European scholars. Since the end of World War II and with the interest in area studies in the wake of the cold war, research on the Andes has grown into a thriving enterprise. Here the reader will find, among others, pieces by historian Steve J. Stern on Indians who learned to manipulate the rules of their conquerors and anthropologist Catherine Allen on the ritual importance of coca in a contemporary Cuzco village. Talented observers such as these bring other perspectives to Peru, providing a fuller variety of understandings of the past and present.

Of course, we have edited, translated, and selected material, and inevitably our tastes and positions have played a role in the orchestration of what voices appear here. Yet, an attempt to cut across boundaries is reflected also in our own different interests and professions, which we believe enrich the selection: a U.S. anthropologist who worked for many years in the Andes, and now teaches at Duke University; a Peruvian researcher who has written about race, migration, and culture, directed the Institute for Peruvian Studies, and served on the national Truth and Reconciliation Commission charged with investigating the political violence of the 1980s; and a North American journalist and human rights activist who has specialized in issues concerning women, guerrilla war, and refugees. In addition, we have consulted an array of friends and colleagues from all walks of life. As a pan-American, multiprofessional collaboration, this book tries to break beyond the national and professional perimeters that can make for parochial, inbred views.

The result is a mixed-field, cross-disciplinary anthology. At present, scholars read mostly in their particular specialty. Journalists, development workers, human rights lawyers, and other professionals keep up with what seems most relevant to their jobs. By contrast, we believe a broad sampling of texts enriches even the narrowest of interests. Although it might seem irrelevant by traditional standards of scholarly professionalism and objectivity, the work of poets and fiction writers has a tremendous amount to teach about Peruvian society. By the same token, those in the arts or "practical" professions can learn a great deal from the wealth of fine work by scholars. Rather than promote a single "correct" understanding, we seek to step over standard boundaries to view Peru from a variety of perspectives, concurring wholeheartedly with anthropologist Renato Rosaldo's challenge to see "from a number of positions rather than being locked into any particular one."[6] We provide our more meticulous readers with an extensive list of suggestions for further reading at the end of the book.

For the sake of simplicity, sections were organized chronologically and under broad themes. The organization of some sections may appear to be self-evident—"The Ancient Civilizations," for instance; others reflect our attempt to distill the spirit of an era in a dramatic way that gave us room to include contemporary pieces. It would surprise no one versed in modern poetry to hear that surrealist César Moro had little interest in Peruvian politics. Yet we included his poem "Lost to Sight" in the section titled "The Advent of Modern Politics" because it reveals a break with poetic orthodoxies, a challenge to the status quo, that mirrors the break in Peru between a crumbling oligarchy and the mass political movements gathering at the grassroots. In keeping with our emphasis on Peru's global interconnections, it seems to us appropriate to spice a section heavily influenced by political developments in Europe and the Soviet Union with the wildly imaginative work of a Peruvian swept away by the repercussions of these changes in the arts. Because we believe history is a prerequisite to any understanding of the present, "The Advent of Modern Politics" is one of five sections devoted to pre-1980 Peru. Three sections follow on key themes of that turbulent decade: the Shining Path, political violence, and cocaine. We end with two sections devoted to the trends we believe will shape Peru well into this new century: the struggle for economic survival and political democracy in the new global order and the cultural reconfiguration of a multivocal polity.

The past few decades have brought tremendous uncertainty and hardship for millions of Peruvians. In 1980, the Marxist revolutionaries of the Shining Path launched their brutal campaign to overthrow the government. Seventy thousand Peruvians died in the war between guerrillas and government forces for mastery of the country, and poor, Quechua-speaking villagers suffered the brunt of the terror unleashed by both sides. More than six hundred thousand peasants were forced to flee their homes. Although the Shining Path was finally defeated a decade later, the plague of poverty is as widespread as ever. Almost 10 million people, a quarter of the population, live in extreme poverty, with households earning less than $50 a month. The rush of successive governments to embrace the free market, privatization, and multinational corporate investment hardened frightening contrasts between the haves and the have-nots. In Lima's exclusive white neighborhoods, you see Mercedes SUVs, businessmen in Dior suits, and high-end Silver Cross strollers pushed by Indian maids in the same country where tens of thousands of children die from malnourishment and disease every year.

In the United States and Europe, news of these travails can reinforce the impression of the perennial Otherness of Peru and the Third World. This was certainly the case in much of the coverage of the bloody turmoil of the late 1980s and early 1990s. "The unfolding tragedy of Peru's bloody history has taken this Andean country to the brink of total collapse," intoned the reporter in a 1992 documentary on British television.[7] Corruption. Disease. Violence. Misery. These labels turn into metonyms for a nation whose plight appears disastrous, yet also, for that same reason, distant and remote. In fact, ties have relentlessly tightened between Peru and the rest of the world. Peruvian exports, from alpaca sweaters to cocaine, flow north. Migrants from tiny Andean villages settle in Washington, Madrid, and Berlin. Meanwhile, a stream of journalists, missionaries, tourists, scholars, diplomats, and development workers still flows to cities from Cuzco to Iquitos to Lima, despite real and imagined dangers, and decisions on aid and loans in New York and Paris affect the lives of millions of Peruvians. Blurred, even, is the boundary between "us" and "them." Andean-born migrants become U.S. citizens and drive their kids in minivans to suburban New Jersey schools; European and North American expatriates make their lives in Lima with Peruvian tastes and friends and lovers, as the "foreign" becomes more of a home than their native countries. In all these ways, Peru locks into the world traffic of people and ideas, where, as anthropologist Arjun Appadurai puts it, "groups are no longer tightly territorialized, spatially bounded, historically unselfconscious or culturally homogenous."[8]

The closeness of these connections makes more pressing than ever a critical understanding in the United States and Europe of Peru's predicament. One of our goals is to give shape to the amalgamated quality of Peru's cultural visions and traditions and their dazzling regional variety. Many outsiders want to imagine the Third World as replete with primordial purity and authenticity. One travel company advertising on the Internet offers a Peruvian tour with the promise of encounters with "splendidly dressed traditional Quechua Indians" who maintain "a mystical attachment to the land" unchanged from the "glorious ancient empire of the Incas." In this exotic imagery, which circulates in Peru as well as abroad, the country appears to be beyond the flow of history.[9] Yet the readings we have selected underscore that there are no "pure" or timeless lifeways anywhere in this nation of "todas las sangres" (all the bloods), as Arguedas called it. From the legend of mulatto Saint Martín of Porres and a rap about a Lima woman in Miami to an Ayacucho ballad about army-led massacres in the Andes, an intricate mosaic of cultural visions has grown at the crossroads of tradition and transculturation from precolonial to contemporary times. Culture and tradition, as Mariátegui insisted already in 1927, turn out to be "alive and mobile . . . always remold[ing] themselves before our eyes."

Unlike, say, Meiji Japan or Iran of the mullahs, Peru has absorbed and often embraced the influences of a larger and sometimes hostile world. Already on the parapets of Ollantaytambo in 1539, the Spanish invaders found their technology thrown back at them as the young Manco Inca rallied his troops on a stolen stallion. Despite his impassioned defense of Indian customs, Guamán Poma was quick to acknowledge the benefits of many Spanish ways, including stone bridges, steel, and even Christianity. In the twentieth century, Arguedas wrote "Ode to a Jet Plane" in Quechua with the same passion as his poems to the *apus*, or mountain spirits, even as millions of Andean peasants abandoned the myth of the return of the Incas for the myth of progress through roads, bridges, schools, and the other markers of Western-style modernity. Much of Peru's history speaks of the attempt to define identity in the volatile interplay of the local, national, and global. While this interplay has brought the destruction of an untold wealth of visions and traditions, like the Moche statuary melted into gold bars for the Spanish treasury, it has also opened avenues for creation and invention, on display in the graceful lyrics of an Afro-Peruvian *décima* and images from the Workshop for Social Photography (TAFOS) made on Japanese cameras and German film by the members of the communities photographed. Even Vallejo, in his brighter moments, maintained an almost utopian optimism about Peru's possibilities in an ever-tightening world: "Mountains of my Peru, the Peru of the world. And Peru, at the cusp of the globe. I embrace it."[10] At the same time, however, the anthology examines the structures of privilege and power that underlie Peruvian society.

We don't want our readers to turn these pages expecting a blithe postmodern carnival of polyphony. Colonialism imposed the rule of a handful of white Spaniards over an indigenous population of more than 10 million. Black slaves and then indentured Asians were also made into European subjects. Today, the brown-skinned, or *cholo*, majorities continue to contend with poverty and racism. "On the coast they called me 'hick' . . . and denied me everything," laments a song by Los Shapis, the most popular purveyors of the hybrid of Colombian *cumbia*, Cuban *salsa*, and Andean ballads called *chicha*, after the fermented corn beer drunk in the mountains since before the Spanish.[11] Here readers will find selections underlining the inequalities that led some observers to compare Peru of the mid–twentieth century to South Africa under apartheid, like novelist Alfredo Bryce Echenique's cutting portrayal of the good life at a Lima golf club. Other readings explore how ideologies of male and heterosexual supremacy have interlocked with hierarchies of class and color, further belying the imagery of a united nation that is manufactured by nationalist mythology. Although First World oppression is seldom the only explanation for Third World poverty, a number of selections point to a troubling history of foreign intervention and exploitation, at times bolstered by alliances with national elites. From the British backing of the Chilean invasion in the War of the Pacific to the futile "Drug War" of the United States and the uncompromising demands of the International Monetary Fund, this history of imperial intervention has contributed to the country's impoverishment and the persistence of oppression and division.

As much as anything, we hope readers come away with a new appreciation for the stubborn initiatives Peruvians have launched to remake their world. It is commonplace to hear of the supposed fatalism and resignation of Latin America. But many of the pieces in this anthology burst apart this stereotype to show how Peruvians have aggressively cultivated and pursued their own visions. It would be wrong to fall into an uncritical celebration of "local agency" or "popular movements" (one need only think of the wide support for Alberto Fujimori's authoritarian regime to see that there is no guarantee that the politics of "the popular" will be benign). Even the most ostensibly admirable movements also have their share of internal divisions and contradictions, whether the eighteenth-century Indian rebellion of Túpac Amaru II or the land takeovers of Lima's deserts by poor squatters today. Yet, in the face of misery and want, the pursuit of an independent vision continues to characterize an array of individual and collective projects, from Andean village patrols to Lima soup kitchens. Not just the futile gestures of the powerless, what poet Czeslaw Milosz labels the "glory of slaves," these initiatives have contributed to a dramatic remaking of Peru in recent decades: the eruption of the informal economy and popular culture, the explosion of Lima into a labyrinthine megalopolis of almost 8 million, discontent with the traditional political parties, and the breakup of the oligarchical state. If Peru remains riven by exclusion and hierarchy, neither is it any longer what Manuel González Prada called a nation of "gentlemen and serfs." This is the direct result of the restless refusal of the majorities to accept the old order's terms.

It would be foolish to pretend to see very far into Peru's future. In addition to the raw scars of the bloody civil war, the problems of unemployment and lack of opportunity plague the country as much as ever. A pattern of new governments raising high expectations followed by catastrophic failure has put hope itself in short supply. The silver-tongued Alan García left Peru on the brink of collapse before fleeing the tax collectors at the end of his first presidency. Then the long, quasi-dictatorial reign of Alberto Fujimori ended in his exile to Japan and the jailing of his Rasputinesque advisor, Vladimiro Montesinos. Perhaps not altogether deservedly, Alejandro Toledo, Fujimori's successor, saw his approval ratings plummet below 10 percent. He became the butt of *Tolechistes*, or Toledo jokes, many measuring a jaded cynicism about politicians in general: "How do you know when Toledo is about to lie? When his lips start moving." Voters returned Alán García to the presidency in 2006 only as the lesser of two evils compared to his opponent, a former army officer with an unsavory past of his own.

Is Peru condemned to a permanent limbo of poverty, corruption, and lack of opportunity? Although it may never descend to the hellish famine or suffering of a Sudan or Congo, the danger is that Peru will be left to third-class global citizenship, the visa class pertaining to the picturesque but not particularly important, a vacation and research destination where misery is pushed beyond the walls of the tourist hotel and population sample. Without hope of making a decent living, thousands of young people abandon Peru every year, taking with them the country's most valuable resource. Today more than 2 million Peruvians live abroad in a diaspora from Tokyo to San Francisco and Sweden. For these expatriates, the delectable lime-and-ocean taste of a raw seafood salad, or *ceviche*, a Sunday expedition to watch rivals Alianza Lima and Universitario square off at the soccer stadium, and the other distinctive pleasures of their homeland are only a memory.

Even so, the struggle for a better life continues in Peru no matter the enormous, perhaps insurmountable, obstacles. We think of the villagers we have met from Purus in the cold, desolate moors of Iquicha forty miles north of the city of Ayacucho. Balanced on a saddle at 12,000 feet, their village was reduced to burned, stony ruins by the Shining Path in 1985. Some Pureños were hacked to death in the guerrilla attack; others fled to neighboring hamlets and gray shantytowns in Ayacucho and Lima. These survivors, many speaking only the Indian language of Quechua, never gave up hope of returning home. In 1994, nine years after fleeing for their lives, forty families braved the danger of new rebel assault to re-settle and rebuild their village. Today, as hard as life remains in the high-lands of Iquicha, the villagers live in peace, with their own school, health clinic, and main square with benches and flowers. From the writings of nineteenth-century priests to the present day, the Iquichans have been described as part of an "ancient archaic Peru" of "strange customs" and "incomprehensible enigmas."[12] From a different angle, we might view their journey as symbolic of Peru's broader predicament at the century's end: populated with ruins both ancient and new, which, far from for-gotten, provide the stone and mortar for visions of the future. "We are faced with a transitory landscape, where new ruins pile up on each other," concludes writer Celeste Olalquiaga, and "it is in these ruins that we look for ourselves."[13]

Notes

1   Pedro de Cieza de León, *The Incas of Pedro de Cieza de León*, edited with an introduction by Victor Wolfgang von Hagen, translated by Harriet de Onis (Norman: University of Oklahoma Press, 1959), p. 156.

2   Garcilaso de la Vega, *Royal Commentaries of the Incas and General History of Peru, Part I*, translated by Harold Livermore (Norman: University of Oklahoma Press, 1966), p. 316.

3   Francisco López de Gámara, quoted in ibid., p. 318.

4   See Mary Pratt, *Imperial Eyes: Travel Writing and Transculturation* (London: Routledge, 1992), for an introduction to this literature.

5   Some of these essays were written for *The Peru Reader*, and others are previously pub-lished articles or excerpts from books. The Acknowledgment of Copyrights section contains the full citations for all copyrighted materials. Unless otherwise noted, trans-lations are by the editors.

6   Renato Rosaldo, *Culture and Truth: The Remaking of Social Analysis* (Boston: Beacon Press, 1989), p. 169.

7   The program appeared as part of the series called *Dispatches* and was controversial for what many took to be its pro–Shining Path slant.

8   Arjun Appadurai, "Global Ethnoscapes: Notes and Queries for a Transnational An-thropology," in *Recapturing Anthropology: Working in the Present* (Santa Fe, N.M.: School of American Research Press, 1991), p. 191.

9   On the exoticizing tendency to view the Andes as a timeless, unchanging place beyond the flow of history and the modern world, see Orin Starn, "Missing the Revolution: An-thropologists and the War in Peru," in *Rereading Cultural Anthropology* (Durham, N.C.: Duke University Press, 1992).

10 As is true of much of Vallejo's poetry, it is difficult to capture in translation the exact flavor of the original Spanish of *Human Poems*: "Sierra de mi Perú, Perú del mundo. Y Perú al pie del orbe. Yo me adhiero."

11 Quoted in Steve Stein and Carlos Monge, *La crisis del estado patrimonial en el Perú* (Lima: Instituto de Estudios Peruanos, 1988), p. 149.

12 Mario Vargas Llosa, "The Story of a Massacre," *Granta* 9 (1983): 62–83.

13 Celeste Olalquiaga, *Megalopolis: Contemporary Cultural Sensibilities* (Minneapolis: University of Minnesota Press, 1992), p. 94. Olalquiaga was born in Chile and lives in New York, yet this phrase about the global predicament of late modernity seems especially poignant for both Purus and Peru.

I · THE ANCIENT CIVILIZATIONS

N one of Peru's ancient cultures used the written word. They depended on oral tradition, ceramics, painting, and, in the case of the Inca, the abacus-like strands of knotted string called *quipus* (which the curious are still attempting to decipher).[1] So most of what was initially known came from chroniclers of the conquest, who described ruins or noted down Inca custom and myth. Yet none can be considered a definitive source despite their various strengths, whether Pedro de Cieza de León, Garcilaso de la Vega, or a host of lesser-known figures like Cristóbal de Mena, Francisco Lópes de Gómara, and Juan de Betanzos. Most were Spanish. We have little direct testimony from the native side of the conquest. And all had personal and political agendas, like Garcilaso, who sought to validate the Incan side of his ancestry by painting an idyllic picture of Cuzco's empire.

Many Spanish chronicles were not even available until recently. As England promoted tales of Spanish iniquity, the so-called Black Legend, in the battle for imperial supremacy, the Council of the Indies banned manuscripts like Cieza's that referred to abuses (as Cieza's English-language editor points out, the manuscript "gather[ed] dust and dry rot in the Escorial . . . [for] three hundred years").[2] Even the scant writings of Inca survivors or their subjects, like Guamán Poma de Ayala, are problematic, as historian María Rostworowski has pointed out. "[In Inca history telling] the supposed *truth* or exact *chronology* of events wasn't required or considered necessary," she writes in her history of the Incas. "In many cases, this led to the extreme of ignoring certain Incas who had reigned, in order not to displease the reigning Inca."[3]

Modern archaeology has provided a second and more recent path to ancient societies. Many of the most spectacular sites—the Moche tombs at Sipán and the Nazca lines among them—were largely ignored until the twentieth century (and some foreigners then claimed to "discover" ruins that were in fact never "lost"—it was a local farm boy, after all, who guided Hiram Bingham to visit the crumbled walls of Machu Picchu). The West's appetite for antiquities has also fueled private plunder. To this day, this demand fuels a lucrative illegal market in antiquities, as economic crisis multiplies the number of *huaqueros*, poor Peruvians who dig up promising sites.

Only in 1905 did Peru's government ask German archaeologist Max Uhle to prepare the first national archaeology museum. By World War II, the work of Julio C. Tello, remembered as the "father" of Peruvian archaeology, established that Peru's ancient civilizations were not derivations of the Aztecs and the Mayas but developed on their own. Likely populated after the great push eastward over the Bering Strait, Peru's earliest hunter-gatherer sites are now dated at roughly 14,000 B.C. By 1500 B.C., a society had taken root that ruled from a labyrinthine temple known as Chavín de Huántar in modern-day Ancash. A theocracy, Chavín is considered one of the first major Andean civilizations, a complex and highly stratified society that maintained extensive trade networks and temples.

Regional kingdoms like the Moche, Nazca, and Tiahuanaco emerged around the birth of Christ. The Moche in particular left a stunning record. Preserved in ceramics, weavings, and metalwork is an exquisite portrait of ritual, daily life, and even unusual individuals, rivaling the art of the European Renaissance that came a thousand years later. Like their neighbors, the Moche were embroiled in frequent territorial wars. Eventually, scientists believe, they were absorbed by the Wari, Peru's first aggressively expansionist state, around A.D. 800. The Wari reign, however, was short-lived. "When colonized cities began to grow, or with the arrival of other rivals, the Wari, at their peak, began to decline," writes archaeologist Luis Lumbreras. "Everything happened quickly, and the empire fell."[4]

It wasn't until the Incas that another people succeeded in reconstructing the Wari empire, indeed doubling it in size. At the time of the conquest, the Inca had just reached Chile's Maule River and the borders of modern-day Colombia, an empire larger than imperial Rome. Although famed for their buildings and their gold, the Incas' greatest talent lay in statecraft, embodied in the supreme Inca, who symbolized not only civil government but a direct descent from the sun. Defeated peoples faced a stark choice: accept their rule in exchange for fixed tribute or risk annihilation.

Figure 1. This Moche vessel shows mastery of an astonishing realism in clay.
(Courtesy of Banco de Crédito)

The glamorization of ancient Andean civilization as made up of utopian societies is easily debunked by a close reading of historical texts, which, along with the glories of the Incas, recount how Cuzco's lords subjugated other groups with a brutality rivaled only by the Spanish. Indeed, the ubiquitousness of "trophy heads" in Andean art is mute testament to conflicts probably as desperate as any today. Yet, as contemporary poet Javier Sologuren illustrates in "Nazca Pottery," there is also much to prize in Peru's pre-Columbian past, from the mastery of the expressive arts to the raw ingenuity developed for survival in one of the world's most challenging environments.

Notes

1   See Frank Salomon, *The Cord Keepers: Khipus and Cultural Life in a Peruvian Village* (Durham, N.C.: Duke University Press, 2004).

2   Pedro de Cieza de León, *The Incas of Pedro de Cieza de León*, edited with an introduction by Victor Wolfgang von Hagen, translated by Harriet de Onis (Norman: University of Oklahoma Press, 1959), p. xxv.

3   María Rostworowski, *Historia del Tahuantinsuyu* (Lima: Instituto de Estudios Peruanos, 1988), p. 13.

4   Luis Lumbreras, *De los orígenes de la civilización en el Perú* (Lima: PEISA, 1988), p. 96.

THE CHAVÍN CULT

Brian Fagan

In a deep canyon in the central Andes, the stone fortress-temple of Chavín de Huántar was a tantalizing enigma until the work of Peruvian archaeologist Julio C. Tello placed it firmly at the epicenter of an emerging Andean civilization. Though later studies have identified more ancient sites, Chavín de Huántar—possibly the main temple of the Chavín culture—is unique for its labyrinthine construction and dramatic religious iconography, including the famous Raimondi Stone, named after an Italian explorer and now housed in Lima. As archaeologist Brian Fagan notes, one of Chavín de Huántar's most interesting features is the way it melds Amazonian with mountain imagery, reflecting its status as a busy crossroads between Peru's jungle and coast.

Chavín de Huántar stands high in the Peruvian Andes, dating back some 2,500 years and therefore one of the most ancient shrines in the Americas. Its U-shaped temple opens east toward the nearby Mosna River and the rising sun. The sacred precinct faces away from the nearby prehistoric settlement, presenting a high, almost menacing, wall to the outside world. The entire effect is one of mystery and hidden power, something quite alien to a Christian visitor. Worshippers entered the sacred precincts by a roundabout route, passing along the temple pyramid to the river, then up some low terraces that led into the heart of the shrine. Here they found themselves in a sacred landscape set against a backdrop of mountains. Ahead of them lay the hidden place where the axis of the world passed from the sky into the underworld, an oracle famous for miles around.

The Celestial River

The sky and the underworld—as in Mesoamerica the layers of the cosmos played a central role in Andean life from the very earliest times, especially in a world of harsh droughts and unpredictable rainfall. Life was especially risky in the mountains, where farming was an endless struggle. It was here that the changing seasons assumed great importance, where the movements of heavenly bodies provided a critical barometer for planting and harvest, for the cycles of farming life. For thousands of years, Andean astronomers used the heavens and jagged mountain ridges to measure the endless rhythm of their lives. The Maya used the sun and moon, the Andeans the Milky Way, *Mayu*, the "Celestial River." Their modern descendants use it to this day.

Like astronomers elsewhere in the Americas, the Andeans used sighting lines to track the movements of familiar heavenly bodies. Anthropologist Gary Urton has watched modern Quechua farmers near Cuzco use the corners of buildings and fixed points on mountain peaks to monitor the constellations. The silver tracery of the Milky Way is the fundamental reference point for defining time and space. The Milky Way divides the heavens, slanting from left to right for the first half of the year, in the opposite direction for the second half. The cloudy stream also forms two intersecting axes over a twenty-four-hour period. These NE-SW and SE-NW axes reflect the rotation of the galaxy during the day.

Ancient Andeans, like their twentieth-century descendants, divided the heavens into four quarters—*suyu*. Their astronomers used these four quarters to plot not only stars, planets, and sun and moon, but "dark clouds," the blank darkness between constellations. Even today, some Indian groups believe these are animals—foxes, llamas, snakes, and other creatures. All these phenomena form the basis of both the ancient and modern Andean calendar. The solstices of the Milky Way mark the wet and dry seasons, providing a way of predicting river floods. The movements of the sun and moon help in the planning of planting and harvest. A vast reservoir of astronomical knowledge was integral to Andean agriculture and to religious belief. It was also fundamental to the new beliefs that flowered with the Andean civilizations.

The roots of the religious ideology that centered on Chavín grew deep in Andean soil, among people who lived in harsh, demanding environments and depended on one another for survival. It was an ideology that borrowed from many sources, from tropical rainforest peoples, from primordial mountain farmers, and from fisherfolk at the mercy of the tides and unpredictable vagaries of the Pacific Ocean.

The first flowerings of these beliefs are lost in the remote past, but we are fortunate that the prehistoric Andeans themselves commemorated them on textiles, in clay, metal, wood, and stone, on artifacts preserved in the arid soils of the desert Peruvian coast. Flying over the desolate landscape, the casual observer would be astonished to learn that this was the cradle of some of prehistoric America's most elaborate and accomplished civilizations, a place where pyramids were first built as early as they appeared along the Nile. How did these remarkable states arise in such an unpromising environment? The answers come not only from the coast itself, but from excavations at archaeological sites high in the Andes inland.

Cotton: The Fabric of Civilization

In 3500 B.C., numerous fishing villages flourished along parts of the Peruvian coast. But despite its rich fisheries, the coast was no paradise. Sometimes a warm countercurrent known as El Niño, triggered by complicated pressure changes far offshore in the Pacific, reduced upwelling close inshore so much that anchovies and other fish migrated elsewhere. Even with all the technology of modern weather forecasting, El Niños are very unpredictable and can have a devastating effect on coastal communities. They bring torrential rains and trigger catastrophic flooding inland. Except perhaps locally, the coastal populations of 3500 B.C. were never large, partly because the fisherfolk lacked cotton for nets and lines and hollow gourds to use as net floats, two critical innovations for fishing on any scale.

Cotton and gourds are not native to the coastal desert. They were introduced in domesticated form around 3500 B.C., after many centuries of being grown in moist tropical environments to the north and east. Not that the coastal people were unaware of agriculture, for they grew small amounts of squash, beans, and chile peppers. Over the centuries, they developed strong reciprocal ties with inland communities, supplying them with fish meal and shellfish, also salt, all products essential for farming communities living on predominantly carbohydrate diets. In time, the coast and the highlands became interdependent, not only for food and other staple commodities, but for luxuries such as shiny mountain obsidian and ornamental sea shells. Doubtless, it was these ancient

YEAR	EPOCH and PERIOD			NORTH COAST	NORTH MTNS.	CENTRAL COAST	SOUTH COAST	CENTRAL MTNS.	LAKE TITICACA-ALTIPLANO
1 500	Centralized Urban Societies	Military States	Inka Empire	Inka Chimú Northern Wari	Inka Local Wari Kingdoms	Inka Chancay Pachacamac	Inka Ica-Chincha Southern Wari	Inka Chancas Wari	Inka Aymara Kingdoms
			Regional States						
1 000			Wari Empire						
500		Theocratic Kingdoms and Chiefdoms	Regional States	Moche and Gallinazo	Cajamarca and Recuay	Lima	Nazca	Huarpa	Tiwanaku and Pucara
A.D. –0– B.C.			Formative Period	Salinar Cupisnique	Huaras Chavín	Ancón	Paracas	Rancha Chupas Wichqana	Kalasasaya Chiripa Wankarani
1 000		Village-based Farmers	Archaic Period	Huaca Prieta	?	Paraiso Encanto	Otuma Chilca	Cachi Piki	?
5 000									
10 000		Hunter-Gatherers	Lithic Period	Paiján	Lauricocha Guitarrero	Canario Arenal Chivateros Oquendo	?	Jaywa Puente Ayacuchco Pacaicasa	Viscachani
20 000									

Figure 2. The Development of Andean societies from 20,000 B.C. to the conquest. (Courtesy of María Rostworowski)

trade networks that brought gourds, and, perhaps most important of all, cotton, to the coast.

Before 1492, cotton was an expensive rarity in the Old World, grown mainly in India and the Near East, used mainly for padding jerkins worn under suits of armor and to make coarse fustian. The Andeans were growing fine quality, long-stranded cotton for thousands of years before Columbus, creating fabric sometimes so fine that the Spaniards mistook it for Chinese silk. The dry environment of the Peruvian coast has preserved cotton cloth well over two thousand years old, much of it dyed in at least 109 hues in seven natural-color categories.

The Andeans not only domesticated cotton, but developed many strains that flourished at different altitudes. Such was their breeding expertise that it soon became a staple of coastal society, used for fishing nets and lines and as a substitute for textiles made of cactus and grass fiber. Cotton could be grown on a large scale in warm, lowland environments, so a lucrative trade in fabric developed with the highlands. This may have been the trigger that opened up large areas of desert valley land on the coast to irrigation and to large-scale cultivation of cotton. Organized irrigation works perhaps began with many minor projects involving individual families and neighboring villages. Coastal populations rose rapidly. By 2000 B.C., some settlements housed between 1,000 and 3,500 people living off a combination of fishing and agriculture.

The simple cotton weaving techniques resulted in symmetrical, angular decorative motifs that were to persist for many centuries, to be copied in clay, metal, and stone. Almost invariably, the weavers used familiar designs from popular ideology: anthropomorphic figures with flowing hair or snakes dangling from the waist, birds of prey, snarling felines, and two-headed snakes. Often the weavers would combine the forms of several creatures, such as crabs and snakes, in a single design. When fresh and brightly colored, the cotton textiles recreated familiar myths and spirit creatures that inhabited the cosmos. They were not emblems of rank, of social importance. They were symbols of popular belief in societies where the community came before the individual, where membership in an *ayllu*, the communal institution with its obligations to fellow kin and to the ancestors who controlled land and food resources, was all-important. Judging from the general similarities between early coastal textile designs and later Andean art styles, the same beliefs were very long-lived indeed.

Pyramids and a New Social Order

The strong sense of community felt by Andeans as early as 3000 B.C. expressed itself not only in textiles, but in a remarkable flowering of monumental architecture. More than one thousand years before the Olmec civilization flourished in Mexico, the people of the Peruvian coast built a series of ritual centers that rank among the most ambitious of all public works undertaken by the prehistoric Americans. One such was El Aspero on the central coast, a large settlement covering nearly 33 acres (13.2 ha.), complete with pyramid mounds, residential areas, terraces, and underground storage structures. The largest pyramid, Huaca de los Idolos, is 33 ft. (10 m.) high, measuring 131 by 98 ft. (40 by 30 m.) at the base. In about 2000 B.C., hundreds of people labored to build the pyramid in stages. During the quiet months of the farming year, teams of *ayllu* members constructed interconnecting room complexes, then filled them with hundreds of tons of rubble dumped in cane, fiber, or reed containers. Perhaps each person fulfilled his labor obligation by carrying a specified number of loads. Such a standard unit of measurement would have been invaluable for working out how many people were needed to build a mound. Once one layer of rooms was full, they built another, then filled that until an artificial mountain rose high above the valley.

Then they faced the pyramid with angular basalt blocks brought in from more than half a mile (0.8 km.) away. This pyramid building technique was used for more than two thousand years.

Why should such technologically unsophisticated people build such enormous structures, and who organized these massive public works? Archaeologist Richard Burger believes that monuments like El Aspero were public displays of prestige and economic power, in the same way that we build ever-taller skyscrapers or send spaceships to the Moon. The individuals who directed these building works were almost certainly descendants of earlier kin leaders who used their wealth and abilities to intercede with the ancestors and the spiritual world to control the labor of hundreds of fellow kin.

Throughout the centuries that followed, power was measured by an individual's ability to marshal large numbers of people for impressive public works in the name of the gods. By this time, too, maize had arrived from the highlands and was doing well in the irrigated lands. The coastal farmers were preadapted to grow it, having already transformed many valley landscapes with major irrigation works. Their highly productive fields often yielded several crops a year, creating large food surpluses that supported a growing population of farmers, artisans, and priests concentrated in villages and occasional large towns.

By 2000 B.C., ceremonial architecture on the coast had assumed several forms. There were mounds and pyramids, some, like that at Salinas de Chao on the north coast, more than 80 ft. (24 m.) high—dwarfed by the 481 ft. (146 m.) height of Egypt's Great Pyramid, but still a very imposing structure. And there were large circular pits or sunken plazas intended artificially to raise and lower sacred spaces relative to one another, an artifice that anticipates the design of the later shrine at Chavín de Huántar. The worshipper might enter the ceremonial precincts at ground level, then descend into a circular, sunken court, before climbing a rectangular platform mound to the temple on the other side.

Around 1800 B.C., at El Paraíso in the Chillón Valley near Lima, ceremonial architecture took another form, a distinctive U-shaped layout of platform structures that circumscribed a large plaza, leaving it open on one side. This vast site consists of at least six huge, square buildings constructed of roughly shaped stone blocks cemented with unfired clay. The builders painted the polished clay-faced walls in brilliant hues. A square building surrounded by tiers of platforms reached by stone and clay staircases dominated each complex. The largest is more than 830 ft. (250 m.) long and 166 ft. (50 m.) wide, standing more than 30 ft. (20 m.) above the plain. Roofs of matting supported by willow posts once covered the interior rooms.

The building of El Paraíso must have taken many years. About 100,000 tons of rock quarried from the nearby hills went into the site. There are few signs of occupation around the major buildings, as if they were shrines and public precincts rather than residential quarters. Why did the architects choose a U-shape? It may be a sacred metaphor for the dual opposing forces of left and right. By building a U-shape, archaeologist Donald Lathrap believes, the priests could focus sacred energy, create a shrine which formed a symbolic vertical axis between the living and spiritual worlds. This axis was to be of fundamental importance in Andean life for many centuries.

We know little or nothing of the religious beliefs of these coastal kingdoms, but the variations in temple architecture hint at a diversity of cults. In the highlands, where people lived off hunting and seasonal agriculture, populations rose more slowly. They built much smaller ceremonial centers at places like Kotosh on the eastern slopes of the Andes, mostly along major trade routes to the coast, places that maintained contacts with the tropical rainforest. Japanese archaeologists working at Kotosh even found the jaw of a voracious piranha fish from the humid Amazon lowlands, apparently prized as a woodworking tool. Highland shrines centered around small chambers where burnt offerings "fed" the gods, as they did in much later times. Although there were many common beliefs, there was, apparently, no pervasive doctrine that unified Andeans of many cultural loyalties. Then, after 900 B.C., a flamboyant, shamanistic ideology swept much of the highlands and lowlands, redefining many of the fundamental beliefs of Andean life.

The Chavín Phenomenon

In 1919, Peruvian archaeologist Julio Tello was exploring the remote Pukcha River basin in the foothills of the Andes. To his surprise, he came across the remains of a remarkably sophisticated, stone-built temple pyramid near the small village of Chavín de Huántar. Tello excavated part of the temple. He uncovered carved stelae, monoliths, and many potsherds adorned with a remarkable array of forest animals—felines, birds of prey, lizards, caymans, and mythical creatures, part human, part animal, all executed in a distinctive style. Later that year, Tello recognized the same animal motifs on pottery and goldwork from the north coast of Peru, far from Chavín de Huántar itself.

Like many early archaeologists, Julio Tello was a scholar with wide-ranging interests. Not for him the narrow, specialist approach that is the mark of professional archaeology today. He wandered all over coast and highlands, acquiring an encyclopedic knowledge of sites and artifacts throughout the Andean region. It was during these wanderings that he recognized Chavín-like motifs on the pottery and textiles buried with the dead on the arid Paracas peninsula on the south coast, and at other sites as far south as the shores of Lake Titicaca high in the Andes. But the animals in Chavín art were tropical creatures. From where did this inspiration derive? From the rainforests on the eastern slopes of the Andes was Tello's assessment. Chavín, he said, was the roots and trunk, the "mother culture" of Andean civilization. Today scholars know that those roots go much deeper and earlier than Chavín, but they remain fascinated by the puzzle that is the Chavín Phenomenon.

Chavín de Huántar lies in a small valley 10,000 ft. (3,100 m.) above sea level, midway between the Pacific coast and tropical rainforest. The local farmers had access to several distinct ecological zones within easy walking distance. There were irrigated maize fields in the valley bottoms, potato gardens on the slopes, and high-altitude grasslands for grazing llamas and alpacas. This was an environment capable of sustaining hundreds of people and a major ceremonial center.

Between about 850 and 460 B.C., Chavín de Huántar was but a small village and shrine, a strategic crossing point for access routes from the Andes to the coast. The entire site is scattered with marine shells, imported pot fragments, and a few bones of puma and jaguar. Richard Burger, a recent excavator of Chavín, believes that these animals were not indigenous to the area, that their bones were imported for making ritual objects. Then, between 460 and 390 B.C., the entire population concentrated in the temple area, along the riverbanks. This may have been a period when Chavín became a major center of pilgrimage, for many exotic objects testify to myriad contacts with other areas of the Andes. A century later, the town was growing rapidly, and eventually covered about 103 acres (42 ha.), four times its previous size, with a resident population of between two thousand and three thousand people. By now, Chavín de Huántar was a major religious shrine, probably famous over an enormous area of the Andes and coast, and a highly organized trade and production center where skilled artisans manufactured ceramics and all manner of ritual objects. Some pink *Spondylus* sea shells were of such ritual importance that they had been traded from as far away as the Ecuadorian coast, some 500 miles (800 km.) to the north. Some of these shells were decorated with feline motifs, others made into pendants or ornaments for the temple walls.

Chavín de Huántar's Old Temple is a group of rectangular buildings, some standing up to 40 ft. (12 m.) high. The U-shaped temple, inspired perhaps in outline by El Paraiso and other ancient architectural traditions of the coast, encloses a rectangular court on three sides, but is open to the east, the direction of sunrise, and of the forest. This original structure was subsequently rebuilt and extended with additional buildings and a new court. Inside, the buildings are a maze of passages, galleries, and small rooms, ventilated with numerous small shafts. Conspicuous, but inaccessible, the Old Temple was a mysterious, and powerful, focus of supernatural forces.

No one knows what rituals unfolded in the innermost sanctum of the Old Temple, in the presence of the white granite monolith in a cruciform chamber near the central axis of the oldest part of the shrine. The lance-like figure (hence its name, the "Lanzón") stands in its original position, perhaps erected before the building was constructed around it. Some 15 ft. (4.5 m.) high, it depicts an anthropomorphic being. The eyes gaze upward, the feline mouth with its great fangs snarls. The left arm is by the side, the right raised, with claw-like nails. Snarling felines stare in profile from the elaborate headdress. A girdle of small feline heads surrounds the waist.

The Lanzón was built into the floor and ceiling, as if symbolizing the deity's role as a conduit between the underworld, the earth, and the heavens above. Perhaps it was a powerful oracle, for Julio Tello found another, smaller cruciform gallery immediately above the figure, so close that one could reach the top of the monolith by removing a single stone block. Thus, divinations could be so arranged as to evoke responses from the Lanzón itself. There are early historical accounts that describe Chavín de Huántar as an important oracle many centuries after it fell into disrepair.

Chavín art is dramatic, strangely exotic, filled with mythical and living beasts and snarling humans. The imagery is compelling, some of the finest from prehistoric America, an art style with a strong Amazonian flavor. It is as if Chavín ideology has attempted to reconcile the dichotomy between high mountain and humid jungle, melding together primordial beliefs from the forests with those of farmers in remote mountain valleys.

Experts believe there were two major gods at Chavín. The first was the "Smiling God" depicted on the Lanzón stela, a human body with a feline head, clawed hands and feet. The second was a "Staff God," carved

Figure 3. The "Staff God" from the Raimondi Stone shows a figure with snarling mouth and serpent headdress grasping two staffs adorned with jaguar mouths. (Courtesy of Brian Fagan)

in low relief on another granite slab found in the temple. A standing man with downturned, snarling mouth and serpent headdress grasps two staffs adorned with feline heads and jaguar mouths. Both these anthropomorphic deities were supernatural beings, but may represent complex rituals of transformation that took place in the temple, according to Richard Burger. There are some clues from other Chavín reliefs. A granite slab from the plaza bears the figure of a jaguar-being resplendent in jaguar and serpent regalia. He grasps a powerful, hallucinogenic San Pedro cactus, a species still used today by tribal shamans peering into the spiritual world. The San Pedro contains mescaline, and has mind-altering effects, producing multicolored visions, shapes, and patterns. This powerful hallucinogen gives the shaman great powers, sends him on flowing journeys through the subconscious, and gives him dramatic insights into the meaning of life. Perhaps the Chavín jaguar-humans represent shamans transformed into fierce, wily jaguars by potent doses of hallucinogenic plants. Such shamanistic rituals, so common in South America to this day, have roots that go back deep into prehistory, to Chavín and probably beyond.

The shaman and the jaguar, and the complex relationship between them, were a powerful catalyst not only in the Andes, but in Mesoamerica as well. This was not because a compelling shaman-jaguar cult developed in, say, Olmec or Chavín society and spread far and wide to become the foundation of all prehistoric American civilization. It was simply because of the deep and abiding symbolic relationship between the human shaman and the animal jaguar in native American society literally wherever jaguars flourished.

Chavín ideology was born of both tropical forest and coastal beliefs, one so powerful that it spawned a lively, exotic art style that spread rapidly over a wide area of the highlands and arid coast. Chavín was the catalyst for many technological advances, among them the painting of textiles, many of which served as wall hangings with their ideological message writ large in vivid colors. These powerful images, in clay, wood, and gold, on textiles and in stone, drew together the institutions and achievements of increasingly sophisticated Andean societies. Such cosmic, shamanistic visions were Chavín's legacy to later Andean civilizations.

NAZCA POTTERY

Javier Sologuren

Among the regional kingdoms that flourished around A.D. 300 were the Nazca, remembered best for the elegant figures and geometric shapes built across miles of arid mesa near modern-day Nazca. Many of those images—a monkey, a humming-bird, a spider—are repeated in red and black Nazca pottery, some of the finest of ancient Peru. Writing in the 1960s, Javier Sologuren championed what was later called "pure" poetry, as distinct from the "social" verse of some of his con-temporaries. Although life in pre-Hispanic Peru was by no means easy or egali-tarian, including in Nazca the sacrifice of prisoners of war, his graceful poem reflects a nostalgia for ancient culture perhaps sharpened by modern-day tra-vails.

I recall that time when once I lived in your easy valleys of resonant spray,
the littoral of my land stretched out in memory.
From the burnished sea to the Andean wall
the eternal snows to the womb of the ocean
my countrymen worked and fished.
God of old Nazca, half-fish, half-cat,
elastic swift amphibian creature
evoked along the coast of my ancient Peru;
where the soft clay was shaped into the form
of a vivid and graceful bird by the dual kiss
of the warm sun and the craftsman's touch;
and in the colors of its thin skin are mixed
the common vegetables, subtle seasoning
and simple flowers, symbols of a mature wisdom.
Beautiful ceramics in which my eyes trace

a luminous whorl of leaves fresh with dew,
musical contours and frescos of dawn,
soft forms faithful to the hand's caress.

THE HUAROCHIRÍ MANUSCRIPT

Anonymous

The myth of Caui Llaca's flight from the trickster god Cuni Raya Viracocha plays on the favorite Andean theme of conflict and union between the sexes. Part of the Huarochirí manuscript, a unique seventeenth-century collection of indigenous and colonial mythology, this story may predate the Incas' arrival in the valleys above Lima. To defend himself against charges of abusing parishioners, priest Francisco de Avila apparently sponsored the collection of the myths to prove that Huarochirí's Indians were idolaters. Avila became one of the leaders in the destruction of indigenous religion, presiding in 1609 over a huge bonfire of sacred huacas, idols, and mummies in what anthropologist Frank Salomon has called a "giant auto-da-fé in Lima's great cathedral square."*

A long, long time ago, Cuni Raya Vira Cocha used to go around posing as a miserably poor and friendless man, with his cloak and tunic all ripped and tattered. Some people who didn't recognize him for who he was yelled, "You poor lousy wretch!"

Yet it was this man who fashioned all the villages. Just by speaking he made the fields, and finished the terraces with walls of fine masonry. As for the irrigation canals, he channeled them out from their sources just by tossing down the flower of a reed called *pupuna*.

After that, he went around performing all kinds of wonders, putting some of the local *huacas* to shame with his cleverness.[1]

Once there was a female *huaca* named Caui Llaca.

Caui Llaca had always remained a virgin.

Since she was very beautiful, every one of the *huacas* and *villcas* longed for her.[2] "I've got to sleep with her!" they thought.

But she never consented.

Once this woman, who had never allowed any male to fondle her, was weaving beneath a *lúcuma* tree.

Cuni Raya, in his cleverness, turned himself into a bird and climbed into the *lúcuma*.

He put his semen into a fruit that had ripened there and dropped it next to the woman.

The woman swallowed it down delightedly.

Thus she got pregnant even though she remained untouched by man.

In her ninth month, virgin though she was, she gave birth just as other women give birth.

And so, too, for one year she nursed her child at her breast, wondering, "Whose child could this be?"

In the fullness of the year, when the youngster was crawling around on all fours, she summoned all the *huacas* and *villcas* to find out who was the child's father.

When the *huacas* heard the message, they were overjoyed, and they all came dressed in their best clothes, each saying to himself, "It's me!" "It's me she'll love!"

This gathering took place at Anchi Cocha, where the woman lived.

When all the *huacas* and *villcas* had taken their seats there, that woman addressed them:

"Behold, gentlemen and lords. Acknowledge this child. Which of you made me pregnant?" One by one she asked each of them:

"Was it you?"

"Was it you?"

But nobody answered, "The child is mine."

The one called Cuni Raya Vira Cocha had taken his seat at the edge of the gathering. Since he looked like a friendless beggar sitting there, and since so many handsome men were present, she spurned him and didn't question him. She thought, "How could my baby possibly be the child of that beggar?"

Since no one had said, "The child is mine," she first warned the *huacas*, "If the baby is yours, it'll crawl up to you," and then addressed the child:

"Go, identify your father yourself!"

The child began at one end of the group and crawled along on all fours without climbing up on anyone, until reaching the other end, where its father sat.

On reaching him the baby instantly brightened up and climbed onto its father's knee.

When its mother saw this, she got all indignant: "Atatay, what a disgrace! How could I have given birth to the child of a beggar like that?" she said. And taking along only her child, she headed straight for the ocean.

And then, while all the local *huacas* stood in awe, Cuni Raya Vira Cocha put on his golden garment. He started to chase her at once, thinking to himself, "She'll be overcome by sudden desire for me."

"Sister Caui Llaca!" he called after her. "Here, look at me! Now I'm really beautiful!" he said, and he stood there making his garment glitter.

Caui Llaca didn't even turn her face back to him.

"Because I've given birth to the child of such a ruffian, such a mangy beggar, I'll just disappear into the ocean," she said. She headed straight out into the deep sea near Pacha Camac, out there where even now two stones that clearly look like people stand.

And when she arrived at what is today her dwelling, she turned to stone.

Yet Cuni Raya Vira Cocha thought, "She'll see me anyway, she'll come to look at me!" He followed her at a distance, shouting and calling out to her over and over.

First, he met up with a condor.

"Brother, where did you run into that woman?" he asked him.

"Right near here. Soon you'll find her," replied the condor.

Cuni Raya Vira Cocha spoke to him and said,

"You'll live a long life. You alone will eat any dead animal from the wild mountain slopes, both guanacos and vicuñas of any kind and in any number.[3] And if anybody should kill you, he'll die himself, too."

Farther on, he met up with a skunk.

"Sister, where did you meet that woman?" he asked.

"You'll never find her now. She's gone way far away," replied the skunk.

When she said this, he cursed her very hatefully, saying,

"As for you, because of what you've just told me, you'll never go around in the daytime. You'll only walk at night, stinking disgustingly. People will be revolted by you."

Next he met up with a puma.

"She just passed this way. She's still nearby. You'll soon reach her," the puma told him.

Cuni Raya Vira Cocha spoke to him, saying,

"You'll be well beloved. You'll eat llamas, especially the llamas of people who bear guilt. Although people may kill you, they'll wear you on their heads during a great festival and set you to dancing. And then when they bring you out annually they'll sacrifice a llama first and then set you to dancing."

Then he met up with a fox.

"She's already gone way far away. You'll never find her now," that fox told him.

When the fox said this, he replied,

"As for you, even when you skulk around keeping your distance, people will thoroughly despise you and say, 'That fox is a sneak thief.' When they kill you, they'll just carelessly throw you away and your skin, too."

Likewise he met up with a falcon.

"She's just passed this way. You'll soon find her," said the falcon.

He replied,

"You're greatly blessed. When you eat, you'll eat the hummingbird first, then all the other birds. When people kill you, the man who has slain you will have you mourned with the sacrifice of a llama. And when they dance, they'll put you on their heads so you can sit there shining with beauty."

And then he met up with some parakeets.

"She's already gone way far away. You'll never find her now," the parakeets told him.

"As for you, you'll travel around shrieking raucously," replied Cuni Raya Vira Cocha. "Although you may say, 'I'll spoil your crops!' when people hear your screaming they'll chase you away at once. You'll live in great misery amidst the hatred of humans."

And so he traveled on. Whenever he met anyone who gave him good news, he conferred on him a good fortune. But he went along viciously cursing those who gave him bad news.

When he reached the seashore, he turned back toward Pacha Camac.

He arrived at the place where Pacha Camac's two daughters lived, guarded by a snake.

Just before this, the two girls' mother had gone into the deep sea to visit Caui Llaca. Her name was Urpay Huachac.

While Urpay Huachac was away, Cuni Raya Vira Cocha seduced one girl, her older daughter.

When he sought to sleep with the other sister, she turned into a dove and darted away.

That's why her mother's name means "Gives Birth to Doves."

At that time there wasn't a single fish in the ocean.

Only Urpay Huachac used to breed them, at her home, in a small pond.

It was these fish, all of them, that Cuni Raya angrily scattered into the ocean, saying, "For what did she go off and visit Caui Llaca, the woman of the ocean depths?"

Ever since then, fish have filled the sea.

Then Cuni Raya Vira Cocha fled along the seashore.

When Urpay Huachac's daughters told her how he'd seduced them, she got furious and chased him.

As she followed him, calling him again and again, he waited for her and said, "Yes?"

"Cuni, I'm just going to remove your lice," she said, and she picked them off.

While she picked his lice, she caused a huge abyss to open up next to him, thinking to herself, "I'll knock Cuni Raya down into it."

But Cuni Raya in his cleverness realized this; just by saying, "Sister, I've got to go off for a moment to relieve myself," he made his getaway to these villages.

He traveled around this area for a long, long time, tricking lots of local *huacas* and people, too.

Notes

For complete references and footnotes see the original translation in *The Huarochirí Manuscript: A Testament of Ancient and Colonial Religion.* Translation from the Quechua by Frank Salomon and George L. Urioste (Austin: University of Texas Press, 1991).

1   A *huaca* is a local deity.

2   The exact sense of *villca* in the manuscript is uncertain but perhaps related to a con-
    temporaneous Aymara word meaning both "sun" and "shrine."

3   The *guanaco* (*Lama guanicoe*) is a large camelid that lives in the Andes. The *vicuña* (*Lama
    vicugna*) is a small camelid that lives at high altitude and is prized for its fine wool.

MOON, SUN, WITCHES

Irene Silverblatt

Anthropologist Irene Silverblatt describes ancient Andean societies as valuing men and women equally, but almost as separate species, "as if the world," she writes, "were divided into two interdependent spheres of gender." It was only with the fifteenth-century rise of the centralized Inca state, she argues, that male power began to expand, solidifying under Spanish rule. Ironically, much of the literature documenting "gender parallelism" was written by men determined to eradicate it — "extirpators of idolatry" and ecclesiastical courts of the Spanish Inquisition who presided over the repression of the supposed "witches" and "sorcerers" of Andean beliefs.

The social relations into which Andean women and men were born highlighted gender as a frame to organize life. Chains of women paralleled by chains of men formed the kinship channels along which flowed rights to the use of community resources. The material well-being of Andean men and women was attained through bonds with same-sex kin. Women and men acted in, grasped, and interpreted the world around them as if it were divided into two interdependent spheres of gender. Armed with this understanding of the workings of the world, and of the role of humankind in it, Andean mortals structured their cosmos with goddesses and gods whose disposition reflected these conditions of life.

Women and men conceptualized the functioning of the universe and society in terms of complex relations between sacred beings, grouped into sexually distinct domains, and between sacred beings and humankind. The majority contrasted the powers of the earth with powers embodied in the skies and mountains. Andean peoples populated their heavens with deities who took on a masculine cast when counterposed to the female images of earthly regeneration contained in the Pachamama (Earth Mother)[1] and her sacred "daughters." Resembling her human counterparts, Pachamama embodied procreative forces, while the gods represented political ones. It was agreed that their interaction—the dialectic between female and male forces—was essential for the reproduction of social existence.

Norms of reciprocity that governed interpersonal relations also shaped ties between Andean peoples and the supernatural. The gods bestowed life, and ultimately ensured the reproduction of the Andean world; Andean mortals owed this divine generosity products of labor as well as appropriate worship. Many (though not all) of the religious cults organized to honor the Andean divinities were divided along gender lines: women and men sponsored their own religious organizations dedicated to the appropriately gendered divine beings of the cosmos. Moreover, these organizations controlled rights to land and its produce which, following Andean custom, met the gods' due.

Structuring the Cosmos

The god of thunder and lightning, Illapa (or Rayo) dominated the heavens of many non-Inca Andean communities. Andean gender ideologies, encrusted in cosmology, knit two strands to tie this male deity to the goddess of the earth: as provider of rain and as god of conquest. Illapa could manufacture hail, clouds, lightning, and terrible storms in addition to much-needed rain. Polo de Ondegardo, who wrote one of the earliest chronicles of Andean life, describes him as a cosmological force:

> They called him by the three names Chuquiilla, Catuilla, Intiillapa; pretending that he is a man who is in the sky with a slingshot and pitcher, and that in his hand lies the power to cause rain, hail, thunder, and everything else that belongs to the region of the sky where clouds are formed. This *huaca* is worshipped by all Indians, and they offer him diverse sacrifices.

Bernabe Cobo, a Jesuit priest, elaborates:

> They thought he was a man who was in the sky, formed by stars. . . . They commonly held the opinion that the second cause of water which falls from the sky was due to Thunder, and that he was responsible for providing it when it seemed appropriate. They also said that a very large river crossed the middle of the sky . . . [which we call] the Milky Way. . . . They believed that from this river he took the water which was spilled over the earth. Since they attributed Thun-

der with the power to cause rain and hail and all the rest which refers
to clouds and the celestial regions where all these imperfect mixtures
were fabricated, under the name of Thunder . . . they adored the
lightning, the rainbow, the rains, hail, and even storms and whirl-
winds.

The Pachamama, who embodied the generative forces of the earth,
needed a male celestial complement to realize her procreative powers.
So Andean thought paired her to the god of thunder as bestower of rain.
Similarly, the Andean way of seeing the world would consider Illapa's
rain-causing powers meaningless if not tied to his capacity to generate
fertility in the earth. This was one dimension of the dynamics of Andean
thought which bound the god of heavens to the goddess of the earth.

Thunder was also a conqueror. And as the emblem of powers that allowed one portion of humankind to control others, Illapa was set off
against forces of natural fertility and bounty. Many Andean peoples conceived of Illapa as the ancestor-father of heroic founders of descent
groups whom myth had proclaimed as the conquerors of other native
kindreds. These mythic victories made sense of the internal ranking of
descent groups which together formed an *ayllu,* or community. They also
help explain why this divinity, as well as the descent groups claiming
his direct ancestry, could stand for all the social descent groups which
formed a political unit.

Rodrigo Hernández Príncipe, a priest who was sent to the northern
highlands to root out idolatry, was seized by the "pagan" displays of worship surrounding the god Thunder. He has left us the most detailed
portrait of how Illapa and his descendants were venerated. Each family
would establish a shrine to Thunder, on a mountaintop outside the village
center, which was attended by male heads of household. As representatives of their families to Thunder, these men were named *churikuna* (in
Quechua, *churi* is the way a father calls his son). In this manner, household heads were transformed into the descendants of Illapa. Each perceived himself as a knot on a genealogical thread which ultimately ema-
nated from this god. Note that the knots on this thread were male; for
the links connecting the deity of conquest to his mortal children were
made through men.

Andean gender norms might have conceived men to be the sons of
heroic conquerors, but the Pachamama had a special place in her heart
for women. This is not to say that men were not devoted to the goddess of
fertility. Spanish colonizers frequently commented upon the reverence

in which Andean peoples, regardless of gender, held her. She was, after all, the embodiment of the earth's regenerative powers. Women and men alike needed to honor her and be mindful of her; the Pachamama would allow only those who worshipped her properly to receive the benefits of the earth's fertility. Thus, as Cobo emphasized:

> All adored the earth, which they called Pachamama, which means Earth Mother; and it was common for them to place a long stone, like an altar or statue, in the middle of their fields, in honor of this goddess, in order, in that spot, to offer her prayers and invoke her, asking her to watch over and fertilize their fields; and when certain plots of land were found to be more fertile, so much greater was their respect for her.

The Pachamama disclosed other signs of her reproductive powers to the Andean universe: her daughters were emblems of the specifics of highland bounty—maize (Saramama), potatoes (Axomama), coca (Cocamama), even metals (Coyamama) and clay (Sañumama). Saramama and Axomama were sacred beings that reveal themselves through the "extraordinary" forms in which they appear. Possessing an outstanding quality or unusual characteristic, such plants housed divine powers to engender themselves in abundance. Polo de Ondegardo provides us with this description:

> May is the month when the corn is brought in from the fields. This festival is celebrated while the corn is carried in, during which they sing certain songs, praying that the corn lasts for a long time, and each one makes a *huaca* [shrine] from the corn in their house; and this Saramama, made from the maize from their fields which stands out the most because of its quantity, is put in a small bin they call *pirhua*, with special ceremonies, and they worship it for three days. . . . And this maize is placed in the finest shawls that each one has, and after covering and adorning it, they adore this *pirhua*, and they hold it in great esteem and they say it is the Mother of Corn of their fields and that by virtue of her, corn is given and preserved.

Seventy years later, an extirpator of idolatry extracted this testimony from Hacas Poma, the *curaca* [chief] of Otuco, who described his *ayllu*'s idolatrous practice of worshipping the Mother of Corn:

> And when they harvest the best ears of corn from their fields, those of five to a stalk, or if the corn is what is called *misasara* which has

rows of kernels that are brown, violet, white, and other colors, or other cobs that are called *airiguasara* which are half white and half brown, these ears of corn are placed in the middle of the field, and they are covered with corn silk, and they are burned in offering to the same field so that it be strong and provide a good crop for the coming year; and when they found this corn called *airiguasara* and *misasara* they made *chicha* out of the corn from the section of the field where it was harvested, and they drank it with much dancing and joy, and part of the *chicha* was offered to the idols. . . . And when corn stalks that were imbued with the fertility of the earth were found in their fields . . . they collected them and kept them in storage bins which were reserved for their idols and ancestors, where the corn was adored and reverenced because it was said that they were Sara-mamas, mothers and creators of maize; and when they made sacri-fices to and reverenced their ancestors, some of these Saramamas were burned and sacrificed to the idols and a portion was sown in their fields in order to increase their production.

Some of the corn that was imbued with the fertility of the earth was returned to it: that which was fertile would make for more agricultural fertility. Yet a portion of this sacred corn was given to the gods who em-bodied generative powers. Offerings were made to the earth. Offerings were also made to the ancestors, to Hacas Poma's forefathers who were Illapa's sons. José de Arríaga, a Spanish priest, tells us that after these holy stalks with many ears of corn were honored, danced to, and danced with, sacrifices were made to Lliviac—a name by which the god of thun-der and lightning was also known—to ensure a good harvest. Although celebrations of Saramama accentuated female powers, the interdepen-dent dualities of the Andean cosmos, metaphorized as male and female forces, were expressed and realized in this ritual of fertility.

Our most complete descriptions of the Pachamama's many manifes-tations are of Saramamas. However, Saramamas were but one emblem of the Pachamama's attributes. Just as "special" ears of maize were ven-erated as Mothers of Corn, so were unusual (in the Andean meaning of the word) potatoes, coca leaves, *quinoa* plants, and other crops essential to Andean life. But the Pachamama's generative powers were not limited to the creation of abundant harvests. Products of the earth herself also supported existence in the Andes and were reverenced for their contri-bution to social life. An *ayllu* of potters in Ancash worshipped the Sañu-mama, the Mother of Clay, for providing them with the means to create their pitchers, bowls, and pots. The metals of the earth which the Pacha-mama produced, molded into beautiful adornments and representations of gods, were also sacred manifestations of the Earth Mother's forces. Corn and clay, potatoes and gold were linked together as emblems of female powers of creation; as Albornoz, an extirpator of idols, pointed out:

> They chose the most beautiful fruit and kept it, and in its likeness they made others of different stones or of gold or silver, like an ear of corn or a potato, and these were named Mamasara and Mamapapa; and they did the same with the rest of their fruits and vegetables, and in like manner with all minerals, gold, silver, and mercury, which they discovered many, many years ago. They selected the most beautiful stones composed of these metals and they kept them and they still keep them and they reverence them, calling them the Mothers of these minerals. And before going to work [in the mines], on the day they are to work, they reverence and drink to that stone, calling it the Mother of that mineral on which they will labor.

If priests who hunted Andean idolatries in the seventeenth century did not uncover Pachamamas, they did find goddesses of like kind. The story of one of these heroines, Mamarayiguana, was related in the testimony of Hacas Poma, the *curaca* of Otuco in the highlands of Cajatambo. Mother Rayiguana had the *conopas* of all the fruits and vegetables that formed the basis of Andean subsistence in her power. *Conopas* were miniatures or models that could generate the items they represented. Some Sara-mamas and Axomamas, for example, were discovered in the form of *cono-pas*; the stone or metal images of corn and potatoes that Albornoz speaks of were called *conopas* by their Indian owners. These were in the posses-sion of Mamarayiguana; and, not surprisingly, it was a male divinity of the sky, the bird Yucyuc, who was instrumental in catalyzing her procre-ative powers. Hacas Poma recounts:

> When the fields were plowed in preparation for seeding . . . the bird [Yucyuc] was taken out in procession through the streets by the *pallas* [princesses] who played little drums, singing to him, "O Lord Bird Yucyuc . . . because you brought us the *conopas* of food and stole them from Mamarayiguana. . . ." For their ancestors held the tradition and belief that the bird Yucyuc implored the tiny bird Sacracha to carry a fistful of fleas and throw them in the eyes of Mamarayiguana, who was in the village of Caina, so that as she scratched the bites,

she would let loose her child *conopa* which she carried in her arms, and then the bird Yucyuc would steal it. . . . And Mamarayiguana begged him not to take her little child, that she would distribute all the foods; and thus she gave potatoes, *ocas, ollucos [ullucos], masuas,* [and] *quinoa* to the highland Indians, and corn, manioc, yams, and beans to the lowland Indians; and for that reason they adore Mamarayiguana as a goddess and creator of foods, and they worship the bird Yucyuc as an instrumental cause and because of whom Mamarayiguana distributed all of the foods.

The same logic that shaped the relationship between the Pachamama, her *conopa* manifestations, and the god of thunder is at the root of this legend. While Mother Rayiguana contains the sources of fertility and creation, food production can be carried out only if a male celestial deity intercedes. Each is incomplete without the other. Gender symbols, structured by a logic of mutuality, gave form to the ways in which Andean peoples construed their universe.

Andean peoples paired gender symbols with cosmological forces as they interpreted the world around them. The sacred beings of the Andes reached out, however, to the human beings of their own sex. Mother Earth, like Mother Rayiguana, smiled favorably on women. The goddess of fertility was close to them, just as they, in turn, held the Pachamama in special reverence. Native men and women both gave offerings to the Pachamama, but only women forged a sacred tie with her. The Andean division of labor had women put seeds in the earth as men broke the soil with their foot plows. Like anyone who was going to meet the gods, women had to purify themselves before sowing. They experienced this act as a holy one, the time to consecrate their bond with the Pachamama. Talking to her, invoking her, reverencing her, women placed seeds in the earth.

The Pachamama also embraced midwives, who parlayed the sacred forces of fertility into human reproduction. Their special role in community religious life has been hidden by the prejudices of the Spanish chroniclers. The chroniclers saw nothing special in midwives, whom they lumped together with other herbal curers and "doctors" of traditional medicine. Imposing norms of a righteous Catholicism, the Spaniards condemned all of these practitioners as sorcerers. In spite of themselves, however, chroniclers let slip that those native to the Andes viewed midwives in a special light. Garcilaso de la Vega, who defended traditional herbalists from the witchcraft charges levied against them by most of the Spanish establishment, was adamant that "women who served in this function [midwives] were more like witches than anything else." Perhaps they were "like witches" because as Cobo pointed out, women had to celebrate special rituals before being able to practice midwifery:

> There were also women midwives, some of whom said that in their dreams they had been given this office, and others dedicated themselves to this office when they had two babies at one birth; in which [i.e., in order to become midwives] they had to perform many ceremonies, fasts, and sacrifices.

Midwives, then, recognized their calling in dreams or by giving birth to children who were somehow special and unusual. "Extraordinary births" were signs of the Earth Mother; they were manifestations in human beings analogous to the many-eared corn stalk or the double potato, which marked the forces of fertility that blessed Mother Corn and Mother Potato. Dreams revealed a religious vocation in the Andes. Like others who were "called" into the service of Andean gods, midwives too were made aware of their mission in dreams. As representatives of the Pachamama, these women had to attend rituals that prepared them to commune with the sacred.

Dual Religious Organizations

The gods of the Andes seemed to favor mortals of like sex. Some of them even desired to be worshipped through religious cults whose members were exclusively of the appropriate gender. Or so many Andean peoples believed. It is not hard to see why. They were conceived into a culture that accented gender as a structure for the social relations of life. Men and women of the Andes attained material well-being through ties with family of the same sex. Kinship, the bedrock of *ayllu* organization, was conceptualized as parallel chains of men and women. The organization of religious life into two gendered worlds was a dimension of the Andean social experience segregating women from men. Andean mortals, then, populated their cosmos with gods whose predilections mirrored the conditions of human life.

Saramamas held an exceptional place in the life of women from the village of Pimachi. There women built a cult around them. Fields were set aside, and their produce was earmarked for the festivities which celebrated two *ayllu*'s Saramamas. Twice a year, at *pocoy mita* (time of the first rains) and *cargua mita* (time when corn turns yellow prior to the harvest), women hosted celebrations in their honor. In the early seventeenth century, Bernardo de Noboa, who had been sent by his Limeñan archbishop to uncover Pimachi's idols, found out that María Chaupis Tanta watched over the Corn Mothers' ceremonial clothing and silver offerings. Following Andean norms of cosmic gender relations, the Saramamas were sisters of Pimachi's two dominant gods.

Carrying out his mission to root out pagan and idolatrous traditions, Noboa levied charges against several women. The ecclesiastical tribunal convicted them for being "confessors, dogmatists, witches, and leaders of [idolatrous] ceremonies." Noboa's condemnations disclose that these "witches" and "female dogmatists" led a female constituency. Isabel Yalpay, Francisca Quispe Tanta, Francisca Quillay Tanta, María Chaupis Tanta (minister of the Saramama cult), and Francisca Nauim Carhua were sentenced for being the confessors of women: leading and instructing women in idolatrous practices, teaching them the traditions of their ancestors, insisting that they maintain the adoration of their native deities in defiance of colonial civil and ecclesiastic regimes. Noboa passed sentence:

> Be attentive to the charges and merits of this suit, because of the crime committed by the aforementioned women, whom I should condemn and do condemn — the aforesaid Isabel Yalpay . . . to go out with her hair shorn . . . and to be whipped one hundred times astride a colored llama through the public streets of this village, as the voice of the town crier makes known her crime, and to serve four years in the church in the town of Acas and to be for a period of ten years at the disposition of its priest . . . and because of our mercifulness we did not make her serve double the time in the Hospital of Charity in Los Reyes [Lima]; and Francisca Quispe Tanta for the same reason, for being a witch confessor who teaches rites and ceremonies to all the Indian women [receives the same sentence] . . . and María Chaupis Tanta for the same reason, for having been a witch confessor and for having exhorted all Indian women not to adore Christ our Savior, but the idols and *guacas* [*huacas*], I condemn her to be shorn and to go out in the manner of a penitent with a rope around her throat . . . and with a cross in her hands . . . and to be given one hundred lashings through the public streets astride a llama as the crier denounces her crime, and to serve in the church of Acas for ten years at the disposition of its priest, and if she breaks sentence, she will be

punished by serving twice the amount of time in the aforementioned Hospital of Charity . . . and Francisca Nauim Carhua for the same reason, for being the leader of [idolatrous] ceremonies and confessor, preacher of idolatry who commanded them no longer to adore Christ our Savior, but to return to the idols, *guacas*, and other rites and ceremonies of their pagan ways [receives the same sentence]. . . . And in addition to the sentences imposed on all the aforementioned women, [I order] that they never meet together in public or in private, nor when they pray with the boys and girls, and that they be isolated . . . and this is my definitive sentence, having acted with due kindness, piety, and mercy.

Other ecclesiastical suits brought against those who remained faithful to their pre-Hispanic religious traditions document the communal yet female-dominated devotion shown toward Saramamas. In several communities of the north-central sierra, Corn Mother was the central figure of cults presided over by women "witches and dogmatists." Saramamas were either the wives or, as in Pimachi, sisters of the principal gods of these *ayllus*. As in Pimachi, Saramamas were bestowed with fields and herds to maintain the cults devoted to their service. Followers showered them with sacramental objects and fine garments in deference to their powers to ensure bountiful harvests.

Andean women felt close to the goddesses of the cosmos for the ability they shared to reproduce life. Some even expressed this affinity as kinship, claiming the goddesses as their ancestors. Priests rooting out idolators in the village of Coscaya (Department of Arequipa) uncovered this relationship between women and Corn Mothers, or Mamayutas. The inquisitors, in the proceedings of ecclesiastical trials, described rites celebrating Mamayutas' generative powers. During one of the central rites, women presented Mamayutas with offerings of aborted fetuses and of children who died soon after birth. Hernández Príncipe witnessed a comparable ceremony in the north-central sierra; he was horrified upon discovering that the shrines constructed by male household heads, *churikuna*, to the thunder god contained similar kinds of offerings. These symbolized the kinship felt between men and Illapa and were a sign of the reverence with which they held the celestial founders of their descent groups. Similar offerings made by women to Mamayutas suggest analogous structures.

Coscayan women looked to Mamayutas as their ancestors, as the founders of a female line of which they were the living descendants. Daughters of Mamayutas were also the inheritors of her powers. A witness, Juan Carama, testified

> how Catalina Marmita had told this witness how in the heights of this village she guarded and cared for some earthen jars which were named Mamayutas, that one had breasts and the other was a man, and she kept them inside a trough, and for this purpose she had placed inside [the trough] coca, plumes of birds, and ears of corn and balls of colored wool; and these Mayutas were kept there in that trough as the Mother of the corn of their fields and of other things which they take to be in their [Mamayutas'] name. . . . And in like fashion, next to this trough they have another, and inside of it women place their newly born children who had died, whom they take there to offer to the Mayutas in order that they consume them; dead guinea pigs wrapped up in bits of cloth are also in the trough, all as offerings to the Mamayutas.

Two men, familiar with these rites, declared:

> Don Diego Ogsa and Don Pedro Cayo were directed [in these rites], in times long past, by Catalina Marmita, now dead, an old woman and very elderly. . . . In the heights of the village [there were] two troughs in which two figures of clay, like half-pitchers, one with breasts which they called Mamayuta, and the other the husband of this Mamayuta, were kept . . . and in [this trough] there were dead guinea pigs wrapped in bits of cloth and feathers . . . and two de-grained ears of corn . . . and the aforementioned corn was sent by the Inca of Cuzco to be adored. . . . And these two [Don Diego and Don Pedro Caya] were accomplices, and . . . the old woman instructed all the Indian men and women of this village in this adoration.

Like the thunder god, Mamayutas were worshiped by both men and women. Nevertheless, Andean kinship placed Illapa at the head of a chain of sons and grandsons, while Mamayutas narrowed their kin to daughters and granddaughters. Andean gender ideologies had Thunder, the god of conquest, share his powers of domination with men who, as heads of household, were formal representatives of household politics. At the same time, Mamayuta, goddess of fertility, was transmitting powers of procreation to women.

True to Andean "dialectical" tradition, Mamayuta had a masculine aspect as well as a feminine one, but clearly the latter predominated. For an elderly woman presided over her cult: Catalina Marmita, the priestess who instructed both men and women in the rites celebrating Mamayuta's divine powers, and who guarded the offerings presented by women's hands.[2]

Spaniards did not expect to find women presiding over their own religious organizations. Self-fulfilling prophesies saw to it that descriptions of cults to female ancestors or to goddesses are very scarce. This makes it hard to flesh out the structures of these cults—to learn which women joined them, who became leaders. It seems that women attained positions in these ritual organizations by several means. Some might have rotated through a series of ranked offices in a way similar to the *varayoq* systems or civil-religious hierarchies in contemporary communities. Some probably succeeded their mothers in office.

The Spanish chronicler Murúa tells us a legend about an elderly woman who was the proud possessor of a staff that had originally belonged to a female deity. Staffs are symbols of office in the Andes, and we can presume that this one was passed down through a line of women. Women were the inheritors of ritual staffs, an expression of the transmission from mother to daughter of posts in a religious organization.

Several testimonies recorded in the suits brought against heretics describe how rights to office in native religious structures were determined by parallel transmission. In the village of Caxamarquilla, for example, the renowned priestess Guacayllano passed down her position and authority to her daughter, Catalina Mayhuay. The celebrated creator of food, known as Mamaraiguay in the town of San Antonio de Lancha (Province of Cajatambo), was under the guardianship of María Catalina. This elderly woman inherited her ritual duties, obligations, and knowledge from her mother, María Cocha. She stated in her declaration:

> Asked why it was prohibited to eat meat or chili pepper [*ají*], or why married men could not sleep with their wives when yams were sown in her village . . . [she] answered that this was a custom that their elders had transmitted to them; and that she was taught this by her mother, María Cocha. . . . She declared that there were two idols in her village: one was called Auquilibiac, whose owner was Antonio Tapaojo, and the other was named Mamaraiguay, and [she] is the inheritor of this idol, because her mother had left it to her.

Parallel transmission bestowed María Catalina with her mother's authority in a religious organization that extolled a female sacred being, the fertility goddess, Mamaraiguay. Called Mamarayiguana in a neighboring village, she was heroine of the myth that explained how humankind received their subsistence. We discover in this testimony that Mamaraiguay was the divine object of a religious cult in which women held the pre-eminent ritual positions. Moreover, at least in Lancha, Mamaraiguay was cosmologically paired with Auquilibiac, whose name alone reveals his association with the thunder god. The cult to Auquilibiac, as María Catalina testified, was led by a man, Antonio Tapaojo. In Lancha, Andean gender ideologies grasped Mamaraiguay and Auquilibiac as the interdependent female and male forces of all creation. Favoring the mortals of their respective genders, this god and goddess chose to be celebrated in cults that mirrored the sexual division of the cosmos.

Gender parallelism was strikingly apparent in Andean ritual. During the ceremonies of *Oncoy llocsitti*, the two sex-specific worlds of the Andean community stood out. This festival was celebrated in Huamantanga, a village of the Lima highlands, when potatoes were prepared for processing into *chuño* (a kind of freeze-dried potato). During moonlit nights, men and women would make offerings to their shrines and ancestors, thanking them for allowing the potatoes to mature. The women and men of Huamantanga performed these rites in lines; the women all in one procession on one side, and the men together on the other.

Another telling ceremony was *Vecochina*, which was solemnized by descent groups from the village of Otuco. During this rite, they joined together to worship common ancestors and divinities. Everyone left their homes to honor their shrines and progenitors, singing and dancing through all the village streets. This procession was led by the ministers of the gods, who were counterposed by the "old women" who sang the songs of their gods' histories. According to one testimony:

> The *Vecochina* . . . meant that everyone from all the *ayllus* . . . left their houses, led by the priests and ministers of the idols and by the old women who accompanied them with their small drums, playing them through all the streets, chanting songs in their native language following their ancient custom, referring to the histories and ancient deeds of their ancestors and gods.

Whether women officiants were entrusted with the devotion of female deities or not, ties articulating women often prevailed, as women priests tended to be confessors of those whose gender they shared. Leonor Nabin Carhua, who devoted her life to the care of several of the principal divinities of Otuco (both male and female), nevertheless heard the confessions of the other women of her *ayllu*. When, in a dream, ancestors told Otuco's *curaca* that Leonor should be ordered into the service of its gods, they specified that her responsibilities included the confession of women. She testified:

> When her husband died, Hacas Poma told her not to marry because the *huacas* and ancestors told him that it was indispensable for her to become a minister, to make *chicha* for the offerings to the idols and ancestors, and that likewise, she had to become a confessor, in order to hear the confessions of the Indian women of her *ayllu*.

Women and men in the Andean *ayllu* apprehended a world crisscrossed by bonds of gender. Only later would the Incas make use of this dimension of Andean experience as *ayllus* were entrapped in an imperial web.

Notes

For complete references and footnotes, see the original version of this piece in Irene Silverblatt's *Moon, Sun, Witches: Gender Ideologies and Class in Inca and Colonial Peru* (Princeton, N.J.: Princeton University Press, 1987), pp. 20–39.

1   Although the domains of these divinities were viewed as interdependent and mutually defining, the nature of the relationship between them was always contextually determined. Andean dialectical logic would not accept the attribution of intrinsic or absolute qualities to perceived constituents of the social, natural, or supernatural universe.

2   I do not want to give the impression that all *ayllu* religious activity was structured by the model of gender parallelism. The parallel structure of the politico-religious organization in the *ayllu* was only one of several principles that shaped ritual life.

THE ORIGINS OF THE INCAS

Garcilaso de la Vega

Historian Harold Livermore has called Garcilaso de la Vega's Royal Commentaries of the Incas *"one of the first American classics." The Cuzco-born author belonged to Peru's first generation of mestizos, the son of a Spanish conqueror and an Indian princess who was a second cousin to Atahualpa, the last Inca ruler. The Incas began their meteoric expansion from small kingdom to massive empire in the fourteenth century. Here, Garcilaso, who left Peru as a young man never to return, offers an elaborate account of Inca origins and the founding of their capital, Cuzco. The incorporation of biblical images and the mistaken presentation of the Incas as the beneficent inventors of Andean civilization (which ignores the great accomplishments of earlier states) suggest why Garcilaso is regarded as one of the most unreliable chroniclers. Yet his graceful account also demonstrates the literary imagination that made him into one of the Americas' first great writers and a powerful voice in the cause of redeeming the value of Peru's pre-Columbian traditions.*

While these peoples were living or dying, it pleased our Lord God that from their midst there should appear a morning star to give them in the dense darkness in which they dwelt some glimmerings of natural law, of civilization, and of the respect men owe to one another. The descendants of this leader should thus tame those savages and convert them into men, made capable of reason and of receiving good doctrine, so that when God, who is the sun of justice, saw fit to send forth the light of His divine rays upon those idolaters, it might find them no longer in their first savagery, but rendered more docile to receive the Catholic faith and the teaching and doctrine of our Holy Mother the Roman Church, as indeed they have received it—all of which will be seen in the course of this history. It has been observed by clear experience how much prompter and quicker to receive the Gospel were the Indians subdued, governed, and taught by the Inca kings than the other neighboring peoples unreached by the Incas' teachings, many of which are still today as savage and brutish as before, despite the fact that the Spaniards have been in Peru seventy years. And since we stand on the threshold of this great maze, we had better enter and say what lay within.

After having prepared many schemes and taken many ways to begin to give an account of the origin and establishment of the native Inca kings of Peru, it seemed to me that the best scheme and simplest and easiest way was to recount what I often heard as a child from the lips of my mother and her brothers and uncles and other elders about these beginnings. For everything said about them from other sources comes down to the same story as we shall relate, and it will be better to have it as told in the very words of the Incas than in those of foreign authors. My mother dwelt in Cuzco, her native place, and was visited there every week by the few relatives, both male and female, who escaped the cruelty and tyranny of Atahualpa (which we shall describe in our account of his life). On these visits the ordinary subject of conversation was always the origin of the Inca kings, their greatness, the grandeur of their empire, their deeds and conquests, their government in peace and war, and the laws they ordained so greatly to the advantage of their vassals. In short, there was nothing concerning the most flourishing period of their history that they did not bring up in their conversations.

From the greatness and prosperity of the past they turned to the present, mourning their dead kings, their lost empire, and their fallen state, etc. These and similar topics were broached by the Incas and Pallas [female royalty] on their visits, and on recalling their departed happiness, they always ended these conversations with tears and mourning, saying: "Our rule is turned to bondage," etc. During these talks, I, as a boy, often came in and went out of the place where they were, and I loved to hear them, as boys always do like to hear stories. Days, months, and years went by, until I was sixteen or seventeen. Then it happened that one day when my family was talking in this fashion about their kings and the olden times, I remarked to the senior of them, who usually related these things: "Inca, my uncle, though you have no writings to preserve the memory of past events, what information have you of the origin and beginnings of our kings? For the Spaniards and the other peoples who live on their borders have divine and human histories from which they know when their own kings and their neighbors' kings began to reign and when one empire gave way to another. They even know how many thousand years it is since God created heaven and earth. All this and much more they know through their books. But you, who have no books, what memory have you preserved of your antiquity? Who was the first of our Incas? What was he called? What was the origin of his line? How did he begin to reign? With what men and arms did he conquer this great empire? How did our heroic deeds begin?"

The Inca was delighted to hear these questions, since it gave him great pleasure to reply to them, and turned to me (who had already often heard him tell the tale, but had never paid as much attention as then), saying:

"Nephew, I will tell you these things with pleasure: indeed it is right that you should hear them and keep them in your heart (this is their phrase for 'in the memory'). You should know that in olden times the whole of this region before you was covered with brush and heath, and people lived in those times like wild beasts, with no religion or government and no towns or houses, and without tilling or sowing the soil, or clothing or covering their flesh, for they did not know how to weave cotton or wool to make clothes. They lived in twos and threes as chance brought them together in caves and crannies in rocks and underground caverns. Like wild beasts they ate the herbs of the field and roots of trees and fruits growing wild and also human flesh. They covered their bodies with leaves and the bark of trees and animals' skins. Others went naked. In short, they lived like deer or other game, and even in their intercourse with women they behaved like beasts, for they knew nothing of having separate wives."

I must remark, in order to avoid many repetitions of the words "our father the Sun," that the phrase was used by the Incas to express respect whenever they mentioned the sun, or they boasted of descending from it, and none but Incas were allowed to utter the words: it would have been blasphemy and the speaker would have been stoned. The Inca said:

"Our father the Sun, seeing men in the state I have mentioned, took pity and was sorry for them, and sent from heaven to earth a son and a daughter of his to indoctrinate them in the knowledge of our father the Sun that they might worship him and adopt him as their god, and to give them precepts and laws by which they would live as reasonable and civilized men, and dwell in houses and settled towns, and learn to till the soil, and grow plants and crops, and breed flocks, and use the fruits of the earth like rational beings and not like beasts. With this order and mandate our father the Sun set these two children of his in Lake Titicaca, eighty leagues from here, and bade them go where they would, and wherever they stopped to eat or sleep to try to thrust into the ground a golden wand half a yard long and two fingers in thickness which he gave them as a sign and token: when this wand should sink into the ground at a single thrust, there our father the Sun wished them to stop and set up their court.

"Finally he told them: 'When you have reduced these people to our service, you shall maintain them in reason and justice, showing mercy, clemency, and mildness, and always treating them as a merciful father treats his beloved and tender children. Imitate my example in this. I do good to all the world. I give them my light and brightness that they may see and go about their business; I warm them when they are cold; and I grow their pastures and crops, and bring fruit to their trees, and multiply their flocks. I bring rain and calm weather in turn, and I take care to go round the world once a day to observe the wants that exist in the world and to fill and supply them as the sustainer and benefactor of men. I wish you as children of mine to follow this example sent down to earth to teach and benefit those men who live like beasts. And henceforward I establish and nominate you as kings and lords over all the people you may thus instruct with your reason, government, and good works.'

"When our father the Sun had thus made manifest his will to his two children, he bade them farewell. They left Titicaca and travelled northwards, and wherever they stopped on the way they thrust the golden wand into the earth, but it never sank in. Thus they reached a small inn or resthouse seven or eight leagues south of this city. Today it is called Pacárec Tampu, 'inn or resthouse of the dawn.' The Inca gave it this name because he set out from it about daybreak. It is one of the towns the prince later ordered to be founded, and its inhabitants to this day boast greatly of its name because our first Inca bestowed it. From this place he and his wife, our queen, reached the valley of Cuzco which was then a wilderness."

The Foundation of Cuzco, the Imperial City

"The first settlement they made in this valley," said the Inca, "was in the hill called Huanacauri, to the south of this city. There they tried to thrust the golden wand into the earth and it easily sank in at the first blow and they saw it no more. Then our Inca said to his wife: 'Our father the Sun bids us remain in this valley and make it our dwelling place and home in fulfillment of his will. It is therefore right, queen and sister, that each of us should go out and call together these people so as to instruct them and benefit them as our father the Sun has ordained.' Our first rulers set out from the hill of Huanacauri, each in a different direction, to call the people together, and as that was the first place we know they trod with their feet and because they went out from it to do good to mankind, we made there, as you know, a temple for the worship of our father the Sun, in memory of his merciful beneficence towards the world. The prince went northwards, and the princess south. They spoke to all the men and women they found in that wilderness and said that their father the Sun had sent them from the sky to be teachers and benefactors to the dwellers in all that land, delivering them from the wild lives they led and in obedience to the commands given by the Sun, their father, calling them together and removing them from those heaths and moors, bringing them to dwell in settled valleys and giving them the food of men instead of that of beasts to eat. Our king and queen said these and similar things to the first savages they found in those mountains and heaths, and as the savages beheld two persons clad and adorned with the ornaments our father the Sun had given them—and a very different dress from their own—with their ears pierced and opened in the way we their descendants have, and saw that their words and countenances showed them to be children of the Sun, and that they came to mankind to give them towns to dwell in and food to eat, they wondered at what they saw and were at the same time attracted by the promises that were held out to them. Thus they fully credited all they were told and worshipped and venerated the strangers as children of the Sun and obeyed them as kings. These savages gathered others and repeated the wonders they had seen and heard, and a great number of men and women collected and set out to follow our king and queen wherever they might lead.

"When our princes saw the great crowd that had formed there, they ordered that some should set about supplying open-air meals for them all, so that they should not be driven by hunger to disperse again across the heaths. Others were ordered to work on building huts and houses according to plans made by the Inca. Thus our imperial city began to be settled: it was divided into two halves called Hanan Cuzco, which as you know, means upper Cuzco, and Hurin Cuzco, or lower Cuzco. The king wished those he had brought to people Hanan Cuzco, therefore called the upper, and those the queen had brought to people Hurin Cuzco, which was therefore called the lower. The distinction did not imply that the inhabitants of one half should excel those of the other in privileges and exemptions. All were equal like brothers, the children of one father and one mother. The Inca only wished that there should be this division of the people and distinction of name, so that the fact that some had been gathered by the king and others by the queen might have a perpetual memorial. And he ordered that there should be only one difference and acknowledgment of superiority among them, that those of upper Cuzco be considered and respected as first-born and elder brothers, and those of lower Cuzco be as younger children. In short they were to be as the right side and the left in any question of precedence of place and office, since those of the upper town had been gathered by the men and those of the lower by the women. In imitation of this, there was later the same division in all the towns, great or small, of our empire, which were divided by wards or by lineages, known as *hanan aillu* and *hurin aillu,* the upper and lower lineage, or *hanan suyu* and *hurin suyu,* the upper and lower district.

"At the same time, in peopling the city, our Inca showed the male Indians which tasks were proper to men: breaking and tilling the land, sowing crops, seeds, and vegetables which he showed to be good to eat and fruitful, and for which purpose he taught them how to make ploughs and other necessary instruments, and bade them and showed them how to draw irrigation channels from the streams that run through the valley of Cuzco, and even showed them how to make the footwear we use. On her side the queen trained the Indian women in all the feminine occupations: spinning and weaving cotton and wool, and making clothes for themselves and their husbands and children. She told them how to do these and other duties of domestic service. In short, there was nothing relating to human life that our princes failed to teach their first vassals, the Inca king acting as master for the men and the Coya queen, mistress of the women."

CLOTH, TEXTILE, AND THE INCA EMPIRE

John Murra

Anthropologist John Murra has been a leading figure in Andean studies for four decades. He may be best known for coining the term "verticality" to describe how pre-Hispanic civilizations gained access to a maximum number of ecological "floors," managing the exchange of lowland produce like coca and fruits for high Andean crops like potatoes and quinoa. In this classic essay, Murra focuses on the crucial role of cotton cloth in Inca times, using it as a window to view the relations of reciprocity and redistribution that cemented Cuzco's rule.

Years of full-time devotion have been lavished by some students on the description and analysis of the variety and technical excellence of Andean textiles. As Junius Bird, a leading student of the craft, has indicated, "some of them rank high among the finest fabrics ever produced." Andean interest in cloth can be documented archaeologically to have endured for millennia, long before the coming of the Inca. Recent ethnohistoric studies show that this extraordinary imagination in creating a multiplicity of fabrics was functionally matched by the many unexpected political and religious contexts in which cloth was used.

The major textile fibers spun and woven in ancient Peru were cotton in the lowlands and the wool of llamas in the Andes. Cotton is found in some of the earliest strata (pre-2000 B.C.), long before the appearance of maize on the Coast. Its twining and later weaving reached excellence very early and throughout coastal history it remained the important fiber; Bird goes so far as to say that the whole "Peruvian textile craft is based on the use of cotton and not on wool or any other fiber." It is unfortunate that our sixteenth-century ethnohistorical sources said so little about cotton cultivation, and it is curious that coastal ceramics, which so frequently illustrate cultivated plants and fruits, rarely if ever show cotton.

In the mountains, archaeology tells us little, since textiles do not keep well in Andean conditions; this fact sometimes leads to neglect of the cultural significance and technical quality of highland fabrics, so evident from the chronicles. Although excavations show that *auchenidae* had been hunted for many thousands of years, it has been impossible so far to date the beginning of llama domestication. Judging by llamas as represented on pottery and by sacrificed llama burials found on the Coast as early as Cupisnique times, we can assume that these animals were already domesticated by 1000 B.C. Bird suggests that a growing interest in wool by coastal weavers was possibly the major incentive for the domestication of *auchenidae*, but at the present stage of highland studies, the taming of the guanaco and alpaca by those who had hunted them for five thousand years and who first cultivated the potato is still a possibility.

In time, the use of wool increased even on the Coast and it became widespread with Inca expansion, but apparently it had not penetrated everywhere, even in the highlands. The Spanish chronicler Santillán reported in the 1560s that some highlanders carried burdens on their backs as they had no llamas, and even in very cold country their clothes were woven "like a net" from maguey fibers. Garcilaso de la Vega also points to regions where maguey thread was woven into cloth, as wool and cotton were lacking. Although neither source localizes these regions, tradition recorded by modern folkloric research describes some of the early inhabitants of the Callejón de Huyalas as *karapishtu*, maguey leaf wearers. Huamán Poma, the seventeenth-century Andean petitioner to the king of Spain, who reports an ingenious four-stage evolutionary sequence for highland cultures, claimed that before people learned to weave they went through a period when they were dressed in "leaves" and later, through another period, wrapped in furs. While the wool of alpacas and vicuñas may have been used even before domestication, it was in Inca times that llama herding was deliberately expanded through the use of *mitmaq* colonists, in much the same way as the state encouraged the cultivation of maize.

The most systematic historical description of Inca looms and classification of fabrics has been given us by the Jesuit Bernabe Cobo. Although each fabric, weaving, or ornamenting technique must have had its own name, the chroniclers were content with a dual classification: (1) *awasqa*, the cloth produced for domestic purposes, which was rather rough, indifferently colored and thick, and (2) *kumpi*, a finer fabric, woven on a different loom. All early observers agreed that *kumpi* blankets and clothes were wonderfully soft, "like silk," frequently dyed in gay colors or ornamented with feathers or shell beads. The weave was smooth and continuous, reported Pedro Pizarro, "no thread could be seen." Comparisons in those early days of the invasion were all unfavorable to European manufactures; only eighteen years later does Spanish soldier Pedro de Cieza de León speak of it as a lost treasure.

Clothing was not tailored but left the looms virtually fully fashioned. The most detailed ethnohistoric description of peasant clothing appears in Cobo. According to Cieza there were no status differences in the tailoring of garments but only in the cloth and ornamentation used. This is easily noted in the quality of archaeological textiles, since some graves display elegant new garments which must have required considerable expenditure of time and effort, while others were buried in worn ordinary clothes. Ethnic and regional differences in clothing are predictable but cannot be documented from the sources beyond the variety of *llawto*, headdressess, the hairdo, and frequently the type of cranial deformation.

There is a standard, much quoted portrait of the never idle Andean peasant woman spinning endlessly as she stood, sat, or even walked. She spun the thread and made most of the cloth in which she dressed herself and her family and took the spindle into her grave as a symbol of womanly activity.

In practice, the sexual division of labor was less rigidly defined. Spinning and weaving skills were learned in childhood by both girls and boys. While wives and mothers were expected to tend to their families' clothing needs, all those who were "exempted" from the *mitta* [*mita*] labor services—old men and cripples and children—helped out by spinning and making rope, weaving sacks and "rough stuff" according to strength and ability. Modern ethnologic research confirms this impression: both sexes weave, but different fabrics. Specialized craftsmen tended to be, and still are, men.

In the Andes, all households had claims to community fibers, from which the women wove cloth. However, not all village communities had their own alpacas or cotton fields. In that case the housewives got their fibers through trade and barter. Iñigo Ortiz's wonderfully detailed description of Huánuco village life in 1562 records various transactions: potatoes and *charki* for cotton, peppers for wool.

The uses to which textiles were put by the Andean peasant family should not be taken for granted. People do have to keep warm at 10,000 feet, and clothes are always important psychologically and ornamentally, but in the Andes the functions of cloth went far beyond such universals. It emerges as the main ceremonial good and, on the personal level, the preferred gift, highlighting all crisis points in the life cycle and providing otherwise unavailable insights to the reciprocal relations of kinfolk.

Shortly after the child was weaned he was given a new name at a feast to which many relatives, lineal and affinal, were invited. An "uncle" acted as sponsor and cut the first lock from the child's hair. The relatives followed: all who sheared hair were expected to offer gifts. Polo de Ondegardo, an early chronicler, enumerates silver, cloth, wool, cotton, and "other things."

Initiation came at puberty for girls and at fourteen or fifteen for boys. The latter were issued a *wara*, a loincloth woven for the occasion by their mothers. This public loin-girding was known as *warachikoy*. Receiving new clothes woven with magic precautions and wearing them ceremonially was an important part of the change in status, but details of it for the peasantry have been neglected by the chroniclers who have concentrated on the initiation of the young from the royal lineages.

While most chroniclers and modern commentators have accepted some version of the story that marriage depended on royal sanction, late-seventeenth-century sources like chroniclers Román, Morúa, and Poma indicated that at the peasant, *ayllu*-level marriage took place on local initiative with textile bride-wealth presented by the groom and his kin. Román had mentioned llamas, but Morúa argued that only *señores*, lords, could offer these beasts; peasant marriages were preceded by gifts of food, guinea pigs, and cloth. One of the qualifications of a desirable wife was her ability to weave, and Román tells us that the several wives of a prominent man would compete as to who could "embroider a better blanket."

Of all life's crises and their association with cloth, death is the best documented in archaeology, the chronicles, and in ethnology. Polo points out that the dead were dressed in new clothes, with additional garments placed in the grave along with sandals, bags, and headdresses. This was not only an Inca custom, but a pan-Andean preference, going back thousands of years. Coastal archeology, which has at its disposal a fuller statement of the culture due to the marvelous preservation of all remains in the desert, reveals that the dead were wrapped in numerous layers of cloth. Confirming Polo's observation, many mummies enclosed scores of garments, some of them diminutive in size and woven especially as mortuary offerings. Yacovleff and his associates have tried to calculate the amount of cotton needed to make a single mummy's shroud from Paracas: it measured about 300 square yards, and we are told that this size was not unique; it required the product of more than two irrigated acres planted to cotton.

The wake and burial took as long as eight days; according to Morúa, the mourners wore special clothing. They took the garments of the deceased on a tour of the places where he dwelled. The widow and other relatives of the deceased went to wash the clothes at a specific place at the river bank or irrigation ditch. At periodic intervals, and annually in November–December, "anniversaries" were celebrated with new offerings of food, drink, and clothing. The anniversary gifts were needed because the souls were wandering about and in need of food and clothes.

Peasant and ethnic community worship in the Inca state has never been adequately studied, since no European bothered to describe it in the early decades after the invasion. Only at the beginning of the seventeenth century when idol-burners like Avila, Arriaga, Teruel, or Albornoz report on their vandalism do we get a hint of what local, ethnic religion may have been like, as contrasted with the activities of the state church. Arriaga, for example, is proud of having brought back to Lima and burned six hundred "idols, many of them with their clothes and ornaments and very curious *kumpi* blankets." They also burned the *mallqi*, bones of "ancestors who were sons of the local shrines . . . dressed in costly feather or *kumpi* shirts." If the ancestor was a woman, her shrine included her spindle and a handful of cotton. These tools had to be protected in case of an eclipse, when a comet was believed to threaten the moon (also thought of as a woman). The spindles were in danger of turning into vipers, the looms into "bears and tigers."

Sacrifices are another measure of a culture's values. Santillán tells us that the main offerings of the Inca were cloth and llamas, both of which were burned. Cobo says that the offering of fine cloth "was no less common and esteemed [than the llamas], as there was hardly any important sacrifice in which it did not enter." Some of these garments were male, others female; some were life size, others miniature, like those burned in offering to Pachamama, Mother Earth. Cobo copied Polo's information that at Mantocalla, near Cuzco, wooden reproductions of corncobs, dressed like men or women, were used to feed the sacrificial pyre on which llamas were burned at maize shucking time.

The economics of such offerings and sacrifices needs further clarification. Local shrines had access to lands and herds, and many of the textiles sacrificed were the product of labor invested by the community on such fields. There may also have been minor offerings in kind from the household economy of the believers, but this is uncertain.

Recent research has emphasized not only the contrast between the peasant community and the Inca state, but also the intermediary role of the ethnic ruler, the *koraka*. He was, at the lower echelons, so frequently a member of the community, his authority and expectations reinforced by so many kinship ties and obligations, that the weaving contributions to the *koraka* partake of the reciprocity arrangements which functioned at all levels of village economic life. As we would expect, access to cloth is frequently mentioned among a *koraka*'s privileges. The fullest, if still sketchy, picture of his weaving claims emerges from Iñigo Ortiz's questionnaires.

The Huánuco *koraka* had automatic access to community wool and cotton, but the report takes this for granted and does not elaborate. It emphasizes instead his claims to labor, by enumerating that he "received" shirts and sandals, headdresses and carrying bags, woven for him by "his Indians." Some of the garments were woven by women, others by men, and they did it, according to Ortiz's formula, when "he begged them." Neither the *minka* nor *mitta* reciprocal services are mentioned in this context, nor do we know who "his Indians" were who wove when "begged"—they may have been ordinary villagers whose ties to the *koraka* were "reciprocal," or retainers like one Liquira, who devoted full time to the service of Chuchuyaure, the lord of Yachas, or even his several wives, whom the Europeans, ignoring polygyny, called women "*de servicio.*" Some clarification is gained from the testimony of Polo and another Spanish chronicler, Falcón: it is true, claimed the first, that the chiefs "received" much cloth, but the weavers were their own wives. Falcón, quite independently, recorded somewhat later two contradictory versions: the *koraka* insisted that before 1532 they had "received" cloth, while the peasants interviewed denied it. Falcón thought that both told the truth: cloth, which was needed by the lord for varied purposes, was mainly woven for him by his many wives, but as the invaders had prohibited polygyny, there was in the 1570s a shortage of "working hands." All sources agree that the weaving was done with the *koraka*'s fibers.

There is less ambiguity when we come to peasant-state relations as expressed in cloth. In Inca thinking there were two main economic obligations which the citizen had toward the state, and to each of them corresponded an enduring pre-Incaic right guaranteeing subsistence and traditional self-sufficiency to the peasant community, a right which the Inca found convenient to respect:

Obligation to work the crown and church lands.	↔	Right to continue to plant and harvest one's own crops on *ayllu* lands.
Obligation to weave cloth for crown and church needs.	↔	Right to wool or cotton from community stocks for the making of one's own clothes.

This Andean definition of equivalence between weaving and food production as the peasantry's main obligations to the crown is confirmed by two independent but contemporaneous statements about tasks considered important enough by the state to give "the Indians time off." Polo indicates that such time off was granted only to work the peasant lands and to weave the family clothes; otherwise they were always kept busy "with one task or another." Spaniard Pedro Sarmiento is even more rigid and specific: only three months were "granted the Indians" and all the rest of the time was spent working for the Sun, the shrines, and the king; of the three months, one was for plowing and sowing, one for harvesting, and a third, "in the summer," for fiestas and "in order that they spin and weave for themselves." We need not accept as accurate these actual schedules; what matters are the implicit priorities; these are confirmed by later Andean writers. Garcilaso is categorical: the compulsory "tribute" consisted in delivering food from Inca lands and cloth from Inca wool. Juan Salcamayhua describes one of the kings as "a friend of cultivated fields and cloth making."

Much as the *koraka* had to provide the fibers which were worked up for him as cloth, the Inca state did not expect the peasantry to use its own raw materials for the weaving *mitta*. As Polo put it: "no Indian contributed (to the state) the cloth woven for his own garments from the wool given him by the community."

Such Andean continuity between the weaving obligations to the *koraka* and to the state is then confused by another statement of Polo's: "They were inspected to see if they had made it into cloth and they punished the careless and thus all went around dressed." Why would inspection be necessary to enforce the making of *one's own* clothes? Polo said, to insure that people went around dressed; but this was just the perennial European preoccupation with the nakedness of "savages." All Andean peoples wore clothes for the simple reason that it was cold, and archaeology tells us they did so long before the Incas, not to mention the difficulties of setting up a bureaucratic system large enough for so much "inspection and punishment." Given the compulsory nature of the allotment ("they never took into account if the person receiving wool already had some from his own llamas"), Polo's threat of "inspection" most likely refers to issues of state fibers made routinely to the housewife to be woven into garments for state purposes.

However, such distribution of state fibers to the citizenry does contribute to a misunderstanding of the Inca economy which has haunted Inca studies since the 1570s. Andean chroniclers like Blas Valera, in their nostalgia for ancient rights which contrasted so visibly with European exactions, interpret such compulsory issues of state wool and cotton as a welfare feature by a "diligent *pater familiae*." There *were* "welfare" measures in the Inca state, but they consisted in the pre-Incaic reciprocal duties and privileges incumbent on *ayllu* members.

The amount to be woven by each household is a matter of some controversy. Cieza claims that each household owed one blanket per year and each person, one shirt. Three of our sources, on the other hand, insist that there was no limit or account, "they simply wove what they were ordered to weave and were always at it." Interestingly enough, two of these very same sources insist elsewhere, somewhat like Cieza, that each household owed only one garment per year. They may be confusing different sets of obligations—one garment to the state, a uniform, verifiable quantity; an unspecified amount for the *koraka*, since this obligation was governed by tradition and local reciprocities.

In searching for an understanding of such a high interest in cloth, so obvious in both archaeological remains and ethnohistoric reports, it may be useful to parallel our study of the functional aspects of cloth in the peasant village with a survey of its uses by the state.

At this level, we have some quantitative impressions. At the time of the European invasion, state warehouses were located throughout the kingdom, and virtually every eyewitness has indicated his amazement at their number and size. Some contained food, others weapons and ornaments or tools, but the startling and peculiarly Andean aspect was the large number holding wool and cotton, cloth and garments.

Among the eyewitnesses of the invasion, Francisco Xerez reports that in Caxamarca there were houses filled to the ceiling with clothes tied into bundles. Even after "the Christians took all they wanted," no dent was made in the pile. "There was so much cloth of wool and cotton that it seemed to me that many ships could have been filled with them." As Pizarro's army progressed across the Inca realm, similar stores were found at Xauxa and in Cuzco. In the capital, it was "incredible" to see the number of warehouses filled with wool, rope, cloth both fine and rough, garments of many kinds, feathers, and sandals. Pedro Pizarro mused some forty years later about what he had seen as a youth: "I could not say about the warehouses I saw, of cloth and all kinds of garments which were made and used in this kingdom, as there was no time to see it, nor sense to understand so many things."

Later chroniclers added some information on the bookkeeping procedures by which the state administration kept track of all these textiles which had been "tributed" by the people or woven by the state's own craftsmen. Cieza reports that in each provincial capital there were *khipo kamayoq* who took care of all accounts, including textile matters. At Maracavilca in Xauxa, Cieza located one "gentleman," Guacarapora by name, who had kept full records of everything looted from the warehouse in his charge, including cloth, in the eighteen years which had elapsed since the invasion.

One gathers from the chroniclers that the army and warfare were major consumers of fabrics. The military on the move expected to find clothes, blankets, and tent-making equipment on their route. Spaniard Jerónimo Román was told that such warehouses were located close to the frontiers, where battles were expected. Poma reports that young men of eighteen to twenty, who acted as the army's carriers and messengers, would be issued some hominy and thick clothes as "a great gift." Soldiers who had distinguished themselves in battle were given cloth, and one chronicler was told that the vast storehouses of "new clothing" found at Atawalpa's encampment at Caxamarca were to be issued to his armies on his formal accession to the throne.

Even the royal kin were susceptible to offers of textiles. During the reconquest of Ecuador by Wayna Qapaq, the king was confronted with a rebellion of his relatives who resented the unprecedented gifts and privileges granted to the Kañari, an incipient standing army. Sarmiento reports that the king soothed his rebel relatives with clothes and food, in that order. In Salcamayhua's independent report of the same incident, the king had to offer "for grabs" much cloth and food and other, unnamed, valuable things. The much debated historical sequence of Spaniard Fernando de Montesinos may be imaginary, but his account that, during the reign of one Titu Yupanqui, the soldiers rebelled because they were hungry and had not received the two suits of clothing owed them annually has a culturally authentic ring. "The king ordered the granaries repaired and the clothing *mitta* revived"; only then were the soldiers satisfied.

There are other ways of indicating the extraordinary attachment displayed by the army toward cloth. In describing the occupation of Xauxa by the Europeans, one chronicler says that general Quizquiz's retreating army burned at least one and maybe several warehouses full of "many clothes and maize," in that order. In describing the same events, another tells us that when Quizquiz had to withdraw suddenly, he left behind 15,000 llamas and 4,000 prisoners, but burned all of the cloth which he could not carry. The enemy was not deprived of the men (who, according to Garcilaso, joined the European army) or of llamas, but of cloth. To the north, in Ecuador, Atawalpa's lieutenant, Rumiñawi, retreating before Sebastián de Benalcázar's invaders, similarly burned down a room-full of fine cloth kept there since Wayna Qapaq's time. When Pedro de Valdivia invaded Chile in 1541, he found that orders had reached the local population from Inca resistance headquarters to "hide the gold, as we were coming for no other reason . . . to burn the food and the cloth. . . . The execution was letter-perfect; they ate the llamas, pulled up all the cotton, burned the wool, their own clothing . . . and the sowed fields."

None of these attitudes can be understood as matter-of-fact clothing or ornamental needs. Here archaeology is more helpful than the chronicles, since we find evidence of the magico-military importance of cloth back in Mochica times, two thousand years ago. Battle scenes painted on North Coast pottery show prisoners being undressed and their clothes carried off by the victor. These attitudes endured beyond the fall of the Inca state: during the civil wars among the Europeans, their Andean troops believed that the enemy could be harmed or killed by getting hold of his clothes and using them to dress an effigy which was hanged and spat upon. When the Almagristas lost the battle of Salinas, the Indians who accompanied both armies proceeded to undress the dead and even the wounded. [Inca leader] Titu Cusi claims that during Manco Inca's withdrawal to resistance headquarters at Vilcabamba, in the 1540s, a skirmish took place in the highlands; even if the nature of the battle was distorted, his statement that the victorious Indians took all the Europeans' clothes is likely to reflect cultural norms. More than two centuries later, in 1781, the European dead were undressed during the Indian rebellions which culminated in the siege of Cuzco and La Paz.

Feather-ornamented cloth seems to have had a special association with soldiers and war. The feathers collected by children while herding were used in *kumpi* and "other military and imperial needs." In describing the military warehouses which he saw in the fortress near Cuzco, one Spaniard reports one containing 100,000 dried birds whose feathers were used for clothing. The sentences preceding and following this account discuss military stores. Salcamayhua, whose historical accuracy is doubtful, but whose sense of appropriate apparel, being unselfconscious, should be good, states that when Yawar Wakaq expected war, he ordered the preparation of feather garments and of armor. *Mitmaq* colonists, who sometimes acted as frontier guards, were "paid" in feathers as well as clothes.

Any commodity so highly valued is bound to acquire rank and class connotations. The king had certain fabrics reserved for his use alone and his shirts are reported to have been very delicate, embroidered with gold and silver, ornamented with feathers, and sometimes made of such rare fibers as bat hair. Morúa claims to have handled a royal garment so delicately made that it fitted into the hollow of his hand.

The main insignia of royalty was a red wool fringe which fell over the king's forehead and was sewn onto his headdress. Kings were quite fastidious and changed their clothing frequently. Morúa and Garcilaso tell us that royalty gave away their discarded apparel, but Pedro Pizarro claims to have seen hampers which contained all of Atawalpa's used clothing, along with the bones and corn cobs he had gnawed on. This is credible as we know from Pedro Sancho, another and independent witness of the invasion, that the mummies of deceased kings kept "everything"—not only vessels used for eating, but all hair, nail parings, and clothes.

The court, the royal lineages, and the state church shared in the status consumption and display of textiles. The initiation rites of royal youths are well described by the Spaniard Cristóbal de Molina: the ceremony lasted most of the month of November, but spinning and weaving preparations by the womenfolk in the initiate's immediate family began in September. At each step of this protracted initiation, the candidate changed clothes, and each garment was a gift from a particular relative, a ceremonial obligation expressing and strengthening kin ties. The colors, the fabrics used, the ornamentation, all had some relation with the legendary history of the twelve royal *panakas*.

Royal marriages shared in this symbolic use of textiles. In the Cuzco area the Inca himself sometimes solemnized the weddings of his kin. He ordered enough clothes to be brought from the warehouse and gave each bride and groom two suits of clothing, food, and llamas. Morúa is the only source to give us a fairly detailed description of a king's marriage. The Inca took a rich cloth and a *tupu*-pin to his bride and told her that "in the same way as she would be mistress of that cloth, so she would lord over all things, just as he did." On presenting the bride with the fabric, he asked her to put it on, and in return she offered him a garment woven by her own hands. After the wedding they went to the royal quarters, through streets "paved" with colored and feathered cloth. Among the grants made on this occasion by the king to his court were fabrics of all kinds according to status, also llamas and wool, even lands and servants.

Like life crises, religious activities are easier to document at the state level; the associations of church and cloth were manifold. Some of the images of Sun or Thunder were made of thick blankets, so tightly packed that the "idol" could stand by itself; others were made of gold and dressed in vestments of gold thread and wool. Most of the time the statues sat hidden behind a *kumpi* curtain of the finest and "subtlest" kind. On great holidays the images were brought out on the shoulders of priests and placed in public on a small seat, smothered in feather blankets. Pirwa, the first legendary human who had been sent by the Creator "to guard the Inca dynasty," is recorded to have stood watch over their clothes, "treasures," and warehouses in that order.

The ceremonial state calendar included many sacrifices, when fabrics as well as llamas were offered and burned. At Zithuwa time, in September, when illness was driven out by washing it down the river, the priests threw into the water eviscerated llamas, much cloth of all colors, coca leaf, and flowers. During Camay, in December–January, when ten llamas were sacrificed for the king's health, each royal lineage (*parcialidad*) contributed ten garments of very fine red and white cloth to be burned in honor of the Sun, Moon, Thunder, Wiraqocha, and Earth Mother. At Mayocati, on the nineteenth day of the same month, multicolored clothes, feathers, llamas, flowers, and the ashes of the whole year's sacrifices were again thrown in the river, to be carried off into the Amazon. Many of these sacrifices were made from the warehouses of the church, the several shrines, and sometimes even from those of the state.

The extraordinary value placed on cloth by Andean cultures and the existence of class differences allowed the manipulative use of this commodity in a variety of political and social contexts. We saw above the compulsory nature of peasants weaving for their *koraka* and for the state. The *koraka*, in turn, provided "gifts" for the Cuzco representatives, including clothes, from the populations to be enumerated and administered.

When Wayna Qapaq passed through Xauxa and organized one of the many wakes for his mother, he was impressed with gifts of fine cloth so well worked "that the king himself dressed in it."

Since traditional reciprocity was the model for Inca state revenues, an ideologic attempt was made to complement such massive textile exactions through a redistributive policy which exalted the institutionalized generosity of the crown. The simple fact that a fine cloth like *tokapu* or *kumpi* had come to be defined as a royal privilege meant that grants of it were highly valued by the recipient, to the point that unauthorized wear of vicuña cloth is reported to have been a capital offense. On important state occasions, like accession to the throne or at the death of a king, when large crowds gathered at Cuzco, the crown distributed among those attending as many as one thousand llamas, women, the right to be borne in litters, and, inevitably, cloth.

Everybody from a humble peasant working for his *koraka* to a lofty royal prince who was being removed from the succession race "considered themselves well rewarded" by a grant of garments, particularly if these had belonged to the chief or the king. Anybody who had carried "tribute" or an idol or had come to Cuzco on an official errand was given something "in return," depending on status, but always including cloth. Sons of *koraka*, who were hostages in Cuzco, had their exile sweetened by grants of clothes from the royal wardrobe, which they sent home, a sign of royal pleasure.

Administrators leaving Cuzco for the provinces and local *koraka* deserving the king's favor could count on grants of many kinds, including "women and servants," but always cloth. One of Wayna Qapaq's sons, Waman, who had done well at some administrative task, was granted "as a great favor" a gold-threaded shirt. The same source alleges that a *Wunu*, the highest regional administrator, would get land, two "rich" shirts, three hundred cloths of *kumpi* and *lipi*; even the officials in charge of the king's clothes were rewarded with fabrics. Conversely, those officials guilty of crimes against the state lost their "estate" (*hazienda*), their servants, and their cloth. There is nothing strange in the political use of prestige objects; the novelty consists in discovering that, in the Andean area, the artifact of greatest prestige and thus the most useful in power relations was cloth.

Exchanges of cloth were an integral part of diplomatic and military negotiations. When young Yawar Wakaq was held captive by the Anta, his father, Inca Roka, sent the kidnappers cloth as well as an offer of ritual kinship. In the early days of his succession dispute with Waskhar, Atawalpa sent his royal brother a delegation with a gift of clothing; "taking the clothes which his brother sent him, Waskhar threw them in the fire and said: my brother must think that we do not have this kind of cloth around here or he wants to cover his deceit with it."

When an area was incorporated into the kingdom, the new citizens were granted "clothes to wear . . . which among them is highly valued," according to Blas Valera. The local deity was included among the beneficiaries: in Huarochirí, Pariacaca received cloth of all kinds from the king. Some reciprocity prevailed: once defeated, the coastal king of Chimú sent the conqueror cloth, shell beads, and twenty girls. Sometime after the campaign was terminated, the king himself appeared in the dress of the local inhabitants, "much to their great pleasure."

Understanding the functions of cloth in such a military context may lead to a major new insight into Inca economic and political organization. The sources quoted hint strongly of the compulsory nature of these "gifts" of cloth to conquered ethnic groups. Several chroniclers, and particularly Garcilaso, have been greatly impressed with what they see as a campaign of peaceful penetration, the paradox of the gift-laden conqueror. They see in this a further example of the "generosity" of the Inca state.

There is another way of viewing such ceremonial gifts to the vanquished, at the moment of their defeat: the compulsory issue of culturally valued commodities in a society without money and relatively small markets can be viewed as the initial pump-priming step in a dependent relationship, since the "generosity" of the conqueror obligates one to reciprocate, to deliver on a regular, periodic basis, the results of one's workmanship to the Cuzco warehouses.

To the Andean peasant, the Inca "gift" could be stated as doubly valuable: as cloth and as a crown grant. The state was doubly served: the supply of cloth was ensured and the onerous nature of the weaving *mitta* could be phrased in terms of culturally sanctioned reciprocity. But one can also see in this textile "gift" the issuing of Inca citizenship papers, a coercive and yet symbolic reiteration of the peasant's obligations to the state, of his conquered status.

A primary source of state revenues, an annual chore among peasant obligations, a common sacrificial offering, cloth could also serve at different times and occasions as a status symbol or a token of enforced citizenship, as burial furniture, bride-wealth, or armistice sealer. No political, military, social, or religious event was complete without textiles being volunteered or bestowed, burned, exchanged, or sacrificed. In time, weaving became a growing state burden on the peasant household, a major occupational specialty, and eventually a factor in the emergence of retainer craft groups like the *aklla*, the weaving women, a social category inconsistent with the prevailing Cuzco claim that services to the state were no more than peasant reciprocity writ large.

Note

For complete references and footnotes, see the original version of this essay, "Cloth and Its Functions in the Inca State," published in the *American Anthropologist*, no. 4 (1962): 710–728.

TAXATION AND THE INCAS

Pedro de Cieza de León

As a fourteen-year-old boy, Cieza watched the ship loaded with Atahualpa's fabulous gold ransom dock in Seville. Within a year, he was soldiering in the Andes in search of fortune. But unlike many of his companions, Cieza was also keenly interested in where he was. After grueling marches, night would find Cieza noting down names, dates, customs, ruins, flora and fauna, culminating in an eight-volume firsthand account that remains one of the most empathetic portraits of pre-Hispanic civilizations and the toll of the conquest. In this excerpt, Cieza focuses on the Inca tax collection system, which typified the efficiency of their massive bureaucracy.

I t would be well to tell how the different nations under the Incas were taxed, and how the returns of this taxation were handled in Cuzco. For as is well known to all, not a single village of the highlands or the plains failed to pay the tribute levied on it by those who were in charge of these matters. There were even provinces where, when the natives alleged that they were unable to pay their tribute, the Inca ordered that each inhabitant should be obliged to turn in every four months a large quill full of live lice, which was the Inca's way of teaching and accustoming them to pay tribute. We know that for a time they paid their tax in lice until, after they had been given flocks and had raised them, and made clothing, they were able to pay tribute henceforth.

According to the *Orejones* of Cuzco and the other native rulers of the land,[1] the system of taxing was said to be this: the ruling monarch sent out from the city of Cuzco certain of the most important officials of his household on a visit of inspection over one of the four highways that lead out of the city, which, as I have said, are those of Chinchaysuyu, which crosses the provinces as far as Quito, including all the land lying to the north; Cunti-suyu, which includes the regions and provinces neighboring on the Southern Sea and many of those of the highlands; Colla-suyu, which runs through all the provinces lying to the south as far as Chile; and, finally, Anti-suyu, which is the route to the lands of the Andes Mountains, including the slopes and flanks of these.

Therefore, when the Lord-Inca wished to learn what all the provinces between Cuzco and Chile, such a vast extension, were to contribute, he sent out, as I have said, persons who enjoyed his confidence, who went from village to village observing the attire of the natives and their state of prosperity, and the fertility of the land, and whether they had flocks, or metals, or stores of food, or the other things which they valued and prized. After they had made a careful survey, they returned to report to the Inca about all this. He then called a general assembly of the principal men of the kingdom, and when the chieftains of the different provinces that were to be taxed had gathered, he addressed them with affectionate words, saying that inasmuch as they accepted him as sole sovereign and monarch of so many and such great lands, they would agree, without being distressed thereby, to give him the tribute due his royal person, which he wanted to be moderate and so unvexing that they could easily pay it. And when he had been answered to his satisfaction, certain of the *Orejones* set out with the native lords to fix the tribute they were to pay. In some regions this was more than that now paid to the Spaniards, but the system the Incas employed was so good that the people did not feel it, and prospered; but with the disorder and greed of the Spaniards the number of the people has fallen off to such a degree that most of them have disappeared, and they will be wiped out completely as a result of the covetousness and greed of most, or all of us here, unless God in His mercy remedies the situation, putting an end to the wars which can rightfully be considered the scourge of His justice,[2] and the taxation is carried out with moderation so that the Indians can be free and masters of their person and property, without other taxes or tributes than the levy on each settlement. I shall go into this later on in more detail.

On these visits of the envoys of the Incas to the provinces, as soon as they arrived they could tell from the quipus[3] the number of people, men and women, old folks and children, and gold or silver miners, and they ordered that so many thousand Indians be put to work in the mines, to dig the amount of those metals that had been set to be turned over to the inspectors assigned for that purpose. And as during the time the Indians appointed to work the mines were doing this they could not cultivate their fields, the Incas ordered those from other provinces to come and plant the crops at the proper season in lieu of tribute, so that they [the fields] would not lie fallow. If the province was a large one, it furnished Indians both to mine the metals and to sow and work the land. If one of the Indians working in the mines got sick, he was allowed to return home at once, and another came to take his place; but none was assigned to the mines unless he was married so that his wives could look after his food and drink, and, aside from this, it was seen to it that they were supplied with food in abundance. With this way of doing things, none of them considered it hard work even if they spent their whole life in the mines, and none of them died from overwork. Besides, they were permitted to stop work several days in the month for their feasts and recreation; and the same Indians were not continuously in the mines, but every so often they were sent away and others came in their place.

So well had the Incas organized this that the amount of gold and silver mined throughout the kingdom was so great that there must have been years when they took out over fifty thousand arrobas of silver, and over fifteen thousand of gold, and all this metal was for their use. These metals were brought to the capital of each province, and the same system of mining and delivering them prevailed throughout the kingdom. If in certain regions there were no metals to be mined, so that all should contribute their share, they set tribute of small things, and of women and children who left their villages without any sorrow, for if a man had only one son or daughter, they did not take the child, but if he had three or four, they took one in payment of his service.

Other regions paid as many thousand loads of corn as there were houses in it, which was done at every harvest, and was credited to the province. In other areas they similarly supplied as many loads of *chuño*[4] as the others of corn, and others *quinoa*, and others tubers. Some places gave as many blankets as there were married Indians in it, and others as many shirts as there were people. Others were obliged to supply so many thousand loads of lances, and others, slings and *ayllos*,[5] and the other arms they use. Certain provinces were ordered to contribute so many thousand Indians to go to Cuzco to work on the public buildings of the city and those of the Incas, supplying them with the necessary food. Others contributed cables to haul stones; others, coca. In this way all the provinces and regions of Peru, from the smallest to the most important, paid tribute to the Incas, and all this was accomplished in such orderly fashion that neither did the natives fail to pay what they owed and were assessed, nor did those who collected these tributes venture to take one grain of corn in excess. And all the food and articles necessary for making war which were contributed were expended on the soldiers or the regular garrisons that were established in different parts of the kingdom for its defense. When there was no war, most of this was eaten and consumed by the poor, for when the Incas were in Cuzco they had their *hatun-conas*, which is the name for a bondsman, and in such number that they sufficed to work their lands and care for their houses and sow the necessary food supplies, aside from that which was always brought for their table from the different regions, many lambs and fowls and fish, and corn, coca, tubers, and all the fruits they raise. And there was such order in these tributes which the natives paid and the Incas were so powerful that they never had a war break out again.

To know how and in what way the tributes were paid and the other taxes collected, each *huata*, which is the word for year, they sent out certain *Orejones* as supervisory magistrates, for they had no authority beyond visiting the provinces and notifying the inhabitants that if any of them had a complaint, he should state it, so that the one who had done him a wrong could be punished. And when the complaints were heard, if there were any, or it was learned that somewhere a debt was pending, they returned to Cuzco, from which another set out with authority to punish the culprits. In addition to this, there was another important provision, which was that from time to time the headmen of the provinces appeared on the day appointed for each nation to speak to bring to the knowledge of the Inca the state of the province and the shortage or abundance that existed in it, and whether the tribute was too large or too small, and whether they could pay it or not. After which they were sent away satisfied, for the Inca rulers were certain they were not lying but telling the truth. For if there was any attempt at deceit, stern punishment followed and the tribute was increased. Of the women given by the provinces, some of them were brought to Cuzco to become the possession of the Lord-Incas, and some of them were sent to the temple of the sun.

Notes

1   Literally, large ears, *orejones* was used by the Spanish to refer to the Inca nobility who wore disc-plugs in their ear lobes.
2   The "wars" were the civil wars which began in 1536 between those partners in the conquest of Peru, Diego de Almagro and Francisco Pizarro.
3   String-knot mnemonic devices.
4   Essentially dehydrated potatoes. To prepare it, the Indians used their worst agricultural

enemy, frost. *Chuño* properly made cannot be injured by either frost or damp. Potatoes are spread out, allowed to freeze, then trod upon to squeeze out all moisture.

5   *Ayllos*, which the Spaniards called *bola(s)*, is a sling, used to entangle the feet of warriors or animals. It consisted of two weights of stone varying in size from that of a pullet's egg to that of an orange. The weights were wrapped in rawhide and attached to the sling. It was used (and still is in Argentina by Gauchos) with extreme accuracy.

OFFICIALS AND MESSENGERS

Guamán Poma de Ayala

One of the most remarkable documents to come out of colonial Peru, Guamán Poma's 1,200-page letter to King Phillip III of Spain was probably never read and ended up in a Copenhagen archive until its discovery in 1908. Son of an Ayacucho curaca, or chief, Guamán Poma probably learned Spanish from a half-brother and traveled the country widely. To be sure, the Nueva Coronica y Buen Gobierno *was full of repetitions and a negative view of women, whom its author believed were witches and adulterers. Yet Guamán Poma ("falcon puma" in English) also offers an insider's view of the Inca state, here the system of administrators and messengers that knit the Inca empire. This excerpt ends with an impassioned denunciation of the Peruvians' treatment at the hands of the Spaniards, who kept "property, gold, and silver as their idols."*

The communications of the whole country were secured by the messengers, called *chasqui*, of whom some were called "higher messengers" and some "messengers with a shell trumpet." They were usually of good family and were famous for their loyalty. They wore a sun-bonnet of white feathers so that they could be seen from a long way off by other messengers. The purpose of the trumpet was similar: to alert the next runner at the relay station by a blast of sound from the approaching *chasqui*. They were armed with a cudgel and a sling and were maintained at the Inca's expense, being authorised to draw food and other stores from his warehouses all over the country.

The messengers with a trumpet worked in relays, one *chasqui* relieving another after a distance of just under two miles. In this way the rate of progress of the message could be kept astoundingly high. It was said that a snail picked off a leaf at Tumi in the north of the empire could be delivered to the Inca in Cuzco still alive. As for the higher messengers, their task was to carry heavy loads on a whole day's journey at a time.

All the messengers were under the authority of an official chosen from among the Inca's children. This person kept a keen eye open to detect any breakdowns in the system and remedy them when they occurred. Under the Inca's authority, he also regulated the issue of rations from the warehouses. The messengers were treated as a permanent force, the members of which were never moved to other employment. Reliance was placed on their fidelity, devotion to duty, and speed of travel. It was unheard of for a *chasqui* to let down his relief.

The wives and families of messengers were allowed to provide them with whatever comfort could be arranged. The messengers were also allowed to own land and beasts, but only in the vicinity of their work, which might require their presence at any moment of any hour of the day or night.

The roads trodden by these runners were under the control of an administrator who was always chosen from among the Anta Incas.[1] There were six important highways and a much greater number of interconnecting roads. The first highway went along the coastal plains and sandy beaches of the south. The second one led to Urupampa and the third one through Huayllacucho. The fourth passed through Huamanga on the way to Xauxa. The fifth penetrated into the jungles and the sixth followed the chain of the Andes up to the northern sea.

These highways were all carefully measured and marked with the distances to their destinations. They followed a straight course some eleven feet wide, the edges being contained by evenly placed curb stones. Their rectilinear form was so accurately carried through that no other authority on earth could have matched the achievement.

Control posts and inns were placed at intervals along the highways and administered by the province concerned. Travelers could find lodging, service and food there, important officials paused there on their journeys, and the messengers were always in a state of readiness. The highways were kept in perfect order. Where they passed through marshes, stone causeways were laid down to make a firm footing.

Long bridges over the river gorges existed at a number of places, and there were many smaller bridges. The strength of the construction varied with the size of the rivers. Sometimes fiber ropes and timbers were used and sometimes floating rafts. These last were contrived by the ferrymen of the Collao.

Under the Incas, all the bridges came under the control of a single official. When the Spanish viceroys took over, they ordered the construction of stone bridges, thus saving the lives of many poor Indians who used to be employed in mending our own hazardous contraptions. It would be a mercy for our people if all the bridges could be built of stone.

Two high officials presided over the placing of landmarks and boundaries in the Inca Empire. One of them, who was always a member of the Higher Cuzco nobility, had the responsibility for dividing the land into separate allotments. The other, who was an Inca of Lower Cuzco, had charge of the actual demarcation. Their writ extended to the whole area, both mountainous and littoral, which Túpac Inca Yupanqui had ordered to be parceled out. Even if there was only one Indian, or one woman or child, in any particular place there was still a division of the land and an allotment of pasture and water for irrigation. Straw and wood was also shared out and such tact and fairness was shown that there were seldom any grievances. Everybody, from the Sun and Moon down to the poorest Indian, received enough to live on, without disturbing the rights of the community which had been passed down from generation to generation. The decisions of the two officials, acting together, were obeyed without question because they were seen to be impartial and helpful.

Both the Inca and his Council of the Realm were served by secretaries, some of whom belonged to my family in past times, and my ancestor the *Incap rantin* or Viceroy also had his own secretary. Such people were highly esteemed because of their ability to use the *quipu*.[2] The secretaries calculated dates, recorded instructions, received information from messengers and kept in touch with their colleagues who used the quipu in all parts of the country. They accompanied the rulers and judges on important visits, recording decisions and contracts with such skill that the knots in their cords had the clarity of written letters.

There was a chief treasurer, who kept the accounts of the whole empire and received the Inca's share of the country's wealth. His ability was so outstanding that on one occasion, in order to try him out, the Inca is said to have ordered an exact count of the entire population of Tahuantinsuyu. Using grains of quinoa, an Indian cereal, the treasurer represented one Indian with each of these grains. Then he recorded the total on a special quipu which had cords made from the wool of three different animals, so that he was able to demonstrate the accuracy of his calculation as ably as any Christian clerk.

With the help of a colleague, the treasurer was able to do sums accord-

Figure 4. Guamán Poma de Ayala accompanied his letter to Philip III with hundreds of drawings, like this one of an Inca bureaucrat with a quipu.

ing to the decimal system. *Uc* was the name for the figure one; *chunga* for ten; *pachaca* for 100; *huaranga* for 1,000; *huno* for 1,000,000; and *pantacac huno* for infinity.

Inspectors used to be sent to all parts of the country to examine the inns and relay stations, check the level of the stores in the warehouses, and visit the communities, the shrines, and the houses of the sacred virgins. Some of these inspectors acted additionally as spies and tale-bearers for the Inca. They were commissioned to investigate alleged crimes, and if they could discover no proper evidence they sometimes went back to the Inca with a pack of lies and fabrications which they poured into his ear. For this reason, whenever the inspectors came on the scene, our people were careful to keep themselves to themselves. The saying went round among them: "Keep quiet and you won't get into trouble."

The Council of the Realm had its seat in the capital city of Cuzco in the middle of the empire. If ever one of the great nobles lost his place in the Council, all his relations were deprived of office at the same time. Only members of the hereditary ruling caste were eligible, for the eminence and majesty of the office could not be reconciled with mediocrity or humble birth. If these nobles had been of less than the highest rank, the Inca himself might have been brought into contempt.

Common Indians, of whichever sex, were never allowed direct access to the ruler, but had to submit their petitions for justice through an intermediary. But the Inca himself felt much sympathy for the poor and unfortunate. Sometimes he sent for one of them and said in a kindly way: "My son, tell me your story. . . ."

I, Guamán Poma, chief of Lucanas, have opened the secrets of the quipu to my readers. I have recounted what has been told me by descendants of the Incas and the other dynasties of rulers. I have traced our history from the arrival of the first Indian sent by God to these shores through the various ages which followed. Everything has been conscientiously set down in this book, and now I am able to proceed further and tell what I have personally observed and experienced from my years of service with the Christians.

Your Majesty, in your great goodness you have always charged your viceroys and prelates, when they came to Peru, to look after our Indians and show favor to them, but once they disembark from their ships and set foot on land, they forget your commands and turn against us.

Our ancient idolatry and heresy was due only to ignorance of the true path. Our Indians, who may have been barbarous but were still good creatures, wept for their idols when these were broken up at the time of the conquest. But it is the Christians who still adore property, gold, and silver as their idols.

Notes

1   Anta was a region north of Cuzco.
2   A mnemonic device of string and knots.

THE SEARCH FOR MACHU PICCHU

Hiram Bingham

The rise and fall of the Inca empire has fascinated legions of scholars, travelers, and adventurers over the centuries. In 1911, the young American explorer Hiram Bingham, a future politician and Yale professor, announced his discovery of the spectacular Inca ruin at Machu Picchu. As the intrepid American explorer searching for lost treasure and mysterious ruins in exotic places, Bingham was the real-life prototype for the Harrison Ford character in the Indiana Jones *adventure movies. The truth, however, is that many locals in the Urubamba Valley already knew of Machu Picchu's existence long before Bingham's expedition. A little farm boy, in fact, led the lanky American to the ruins. Bingham's real accomplishment was to recognize the full importance of Machu Picchu and to supervise the clearing away of the jungle that had enveloped the Inca citadel. Most archaeologists now believe that Machu Picchu was a country retreat for the Inca ruler Pachacuti in the fifteenth century. The ruin, rightly regarded as one of the seven wonders of the world, thrills tens of thousands of visitors a year with its wild orchids, superb Inca stonework, and spectacular views of the jungle and surrounding mountains. Ernesto "Che" Guevara, the Argentine doctor who helped mount the Cuban Revolution, called Machu Picchu "a place that drives any dreamer to ecstasy."*

It was in July, 1911, that we first entered that marvelous canyon of the Urubamba, where the river escapes from the cold regions near the Cuzco by tearing its way through gigantic mountains of granite. From Torontoy to Colpani the road runs through a land of matchless charm. It has the majestic grandeur of the Canadian Rockies, as well as the startling beauty of the Nuuanu Pali near Honolulu on Maui. In the variety of its charms and the power of its spell, I know of no place in the world which can compare with it. Not only has it great snow peaks looming above the clouds more than two miles overhead; gigantic precipices of many-colored granite rising sheer for thousands of feet above the foaming, glistening, roaring rapids; it has also, in striking contrast, orchids and tree ferns, the delectable beauty of luxurious vegetation, and the mysterious witchery of the jungle. One is drawn irresistibly onward by ever-recurring surprises through a deep, winding gorge, turning and twisting past overhanging cliffs of incredible height. Above all, there is the fascination of finding here and there under the swaying vines, or perched on top of a beetling crag, the rugged masonry of a bygone race; and of trying to understand the bewildering romance of the ancient builders who ages ago sought refuge in a region which appears to have been expressly designed by Nature as a sanctuary for the oppressed, a place where they might fearlessly and patiently give express to their passion for walls of enduring beauty. Space forbids any attempt to describe in detail the constantly changing panorama, the rank tropical foliage, the countless terraces, the towering cliffs, the glaciers peeping out between the clouds.

We had camped at a place near the river, called Mandor Pampa. Melchor Arteaga, proprietor of the neighboring farm, told us of ruins at Machu Picchu. The morning of July 24th dawned in a cold drizzle. Arteaga shivered and seemed inclined to stay in his hut. I offered to pay him well if he would show me the ruins. He demurred and said it was too hard a climb for such a wet day. When he found that we were willing to pay him a *sol*, three or four times the ordinary daily wage in this vicinity, he finally agreed to guide us to the ruins. No one supposed that they would be particularly interesting. Accompanied by Sergeant Carrasco I left camp at ten o'clock and went some distance upstream.[1] On the road we passed a venomous snake which recently had been killed. This region has an unpleasant notoriety for being the favorite haunt of "vipers." The lance-headed or yellow viper, commonly known as the fer-de-lance, a very venomous serpent capable of making considerable springs when in pursuit of its prey, is common hereabouts. Later two of our mules died from snake-bite.

After a walk of three quarters of an hour the guide left the main road and plunged down through the jungle to the bank of the river. Here there was a primitive "bridge" which crossed the roaring rapids at its narrowest part, where the stream was forced to flow between two great boulders. The bridge was made of half a dozen very slender logs, some of which were not long enough to span the distance between the boulders. They had been spliced and lashed together with vines. Arteaga and Carrasco took off their shoes and crept gingerly across, using their somewhat prehensile toes to keep from slipping. It was obvious that no one

Figure 5. Hiram Bingham in front of his tent at Machu Picchu, 1912.

could have lived for an instant in the rapids, but would immediately have been dashed to pieces against granite boulders. I am rank to confess that I got down on hands and knees and crawled across, six inches at a time. Even after we reached the other side I could not help wondering what would happen to the "bridge" if a particularly heavy shower should fall in the valley above. A light rain had fallen during the night. The river had risen so that the bridge was already threatened by the foaming rapids. It would not take much more rain to wash away the bridge entirely. If this should happen during the day it might be very awkward. As a matter of fact, it did happen a few days later and the next explorers to attempt to cross the river at this point found only one slender log remaining.

Leaving the stream, we struggled up the bank through a dense jungle, and in a few minutes reached the bottom of a precipitous slope. For an hour and twenty minutes we had a hard climb. A good part of the distance we went on all fours, sometimes hanging on by the tips of our fingers. Here and there, a primitive ladder made from the roughly hewn trunk of a small tree was placed in such a way as to help one over what might otherwise have proved to be an impassable cliff. In another place the slope was covered with slippery grass where it was hard to find either handholds or footholds. The guide said that there were lots of snakes here. The humidity was great, the heat was excessive, and we were not in training.

Shortly after noon we reached a little grass-covered hut where several good-natured Indians, pleasantly surprised at our unexpected arrival, welcomed us with dripping gourds full of cool, delicious water. Then they set before us a few cooked sweet potatoes, called here *cumara*, a Quichua word identical with the Polynesian *kumala*, as has been pointed out by Mr. Cook.[2]

Apart from the wonderful view of the canyon, all we could see from our cool shelter was a couple of small grass huts and a few ancient stone-faced terraces. Two pleasant Indian farmers, Richarte and Alvarez, had chosen this eagle's nest for their home.[3] They said they had found plenty of terraces here on which to grow their crops and they were usually free from undesirable visitors. They did not speak Spanish, but through Sergeant Carrasco I learned that there were more ruins "a little farther along." In this country one never can tell whether such a report is worthy of credence. "He may have been lying" is a good footnote to affix to all hearsay evidence. Accordingly, I was not unduly excited, nor in a great hurry to move. The heat was still great, the water from the Indian's spring was cool and delicious, and the rustic wooden bench, hospitably covered immediately after my arrival with a soft, woolen poncho, seemed most comfortable. Tremendous green precipices fell away to the white rapids of the Urubamba below. Immediately in front, on the north side of the valley, was a great granite cliff rising 2,000 feet sheer. To the left was the solitary peak of Huayna Picchu, surrounded by seemingly inaccessible precipices. On all sides were rocky cliffs. Beyond them cloud-capped mountains rose thousands of feet above us.

The Indians said there were two paths to the outside world. Of one we had already had a taste; the other, they said, was more difficult—a perilous path down the face of a rocky precipice on the other side of the ridge. It was their only means of egress in the wet season, when the bridge over which we had come could not be maintained. I was not surprised to learn that they went away from home only about once a month. Richarte told us that they had been living here four years. It seems probable that, owing to its inaccessibility, the canyon had been unoccupied for several centuries, but with the completion of the new government road settlers began once more to occupy this region. In time somebody clambered up the precipices and found on the slopes of Machu Picchu, at an elevation of 9,000 feet above the sea, an abundance of rich soil conveniently situated on artificial terraces, in a fine climate. Here the Indians had finally cleared off some ruins, burned over a few terraces, and planted crops of maize, sweet and white potatoes, sugar cane, beans, peppers, tree tomatoes, and gooseberries. At first they appropriated some of the ancient houses and replaced the roofs of wood and thatch. They found, however, that there were neither springs nor wells near the ancient buildings. An ancient aqueduct which had once brought a tiny stream to the citadel had long since disappeared beneath the forest, filled with earth washed from the upper terraces. So, abandoning the shelter of the ruins, the Indians were now enjoying the convenience of living near some springs in roughly built thatched huts of their own design.

Without the slightest expectation of finding anything more interesting than the stone-faced terraces of which I already had a glimpse, and the ruins of two or three stone houses such as we had encountered at various places on the road between Ollantaytambo and Torontoy, I finally left the cool shade of the pleasant little hut and climbed farther up the ridge and around a slight promontory. Arteaga had "been here once before," and decided to rest and gossip with Richarte and Alvarez in the hut. They sent a small boy with me as a guide.

Hardly had we rounded the promontory when the character of the stonework began to improve. A flight of beautifully constructed terraces, each two hundred yards long and ten feet high, had been recently res-

Figure 6. Machu Picchu, photographed in 1925 by the famous Peruvian photographer Martín Chambi. (Courtesy of Teo Allaín Chambi)

cued from the jungle by the Indians. A forest of large trees had been chopped down and burned over to make a clearing for agricultural purposes. Crossing these terraces, I entered the untouched forest beyond, and suddenly found myself in a maze of beautiful granite houses! They were covered with trees and moss and the growth of centuries, but in the dense shadow, hiding in bamboo thickets and tangled vines, could be seen, here and there, walls of white granite ashlars most carefully cut and exquisitely fitted together.[4] Buildings with windows were frequent.

Under a carved rock the little boy showed me a cave beautifully lined with the finest cut stone. It was evidently intended to be a Royal Mausoleum. On top of this particular boulder a semicircular building had been constructed. The wall followed the natural curvature of the rock and was keyed to it by one of the finest examples of masonry I had ever seen. This beautiful wall, made of carefully matched ashlars of pure white granite, especially selected for its fine grain, was the work of a master artist. The interior surface of the wall was broken by niches and square stone-pegs. The exterior surface was perfectly simple and unadorned. The lower courses, of particularly large ashlars, gave it a look of solidity. The upper courses, diminishing in size toward the top, lent grace and delicacy to the structure. The flowing lines, the symmetrical arrangement of the ashlars, and the gradual gradation of the course, combined to produce a wonderful effect, softer and more pleasing than that of the marble temples of the Old World. Owing to the absence of mortar, there are no ugly spaces between the rocks. They might have grown together.

The elusive beauty of this chaste, undecorated surface seems to be due to the fact that the wall was built under the eye of a master mason who knew not the straight edge, the plumb rule, or the square. He had no instruments of precision, so he had to depend on his eye. He had a good eye, an artistic eye, an eye for symmetry and beauty of form. His product received none of the harshness of mechanical and mathematical accuracy. The apparently rectangular blocks are not really rectangular. The apparently straight lines of the courses are not actually straight in the exact sense of that term.

To my astonishment I saw that this wall and its adjoining semicircular temple over the cave were as fine as the finest stonework in the far-famed Temple of the Sun in Cuzco. Surprise followed surprise in bewildering succession. I climbed a marvelous great stairway of large granite blocks, walked along a pampa where the Indians had a small vegetable garden, and came into a little clearing. Here were the ruins of two of the finest structures I have ever seen in Peru. Not only were they made of selected blocks of beautifully grained white granite; their walls contained ashlars of Cyclopean size, ten feet in length, and higher than a man. The sight held me spellbound.

Each building had only three walls and was entirely open on the side toward the clearing. The principal temple was lined with exquisitely made niches, five high up at each end, and seven on the back wall. There were seven courses of ashlars in the end walls. Under the seven rear niches was a rectangular block fourteen feet long, probably a sacrificial altar. The building did not look as though it had ever had a roof. The top course of beautifully smooth ashlars was not intended to be covered.

The other temple is on the east side of the *pampa*. I called it the Temple of the Three Windows. Like its neighbor, it is unique among the Inca ruins. Its eastern wall, overlooking the citadel, is a massive stone framework for three conspicuously large windows, obviously too large to serve any useful purpose, yet most beautifully made with the greatest care and solidity. This was clearly a ceremonial edifice of peculiar significance. Nowhere else in Peru, so far as I know, is there a similar structure.

These ruins have no other name than that of the mountain on the

slopes of which they are located. Had this place been occupied uninter-
ruptedly, like Cuzco and Ollantaytambo, Machu Picchu would have retained its ancient name, but during the centuries when it was abandoned,
its name was lost. Examination showed that it was essentially a fortified
place, a remote fastness protected by natural bulwarks, of which man took
advantage to create the most impregnable stronghold in the Andes. Our
subsequent excavations and the clearing made in 1912, to be described
in a subsequent volume, has shown that this was the chief place in Uilca-
pampa.[5] It did not take an expert to realize, from the glimpse of Machu
Picchu on that rainy day in July, 1911, when Sergeant Carrasco and I
first saw it, that here were most extraordinary and interesting ruins. Although the ridge had been partly cleared by the Indians for their fields
of maize, so much of it was still underneath a thick jungle growth—some
walls were actually supporting trees ten and twelve inches in diameter—
that it was impossible to determine just what would be found here. As
soon as I could get hold of Mr. Tucker, who was assisting Mr. Hendriksen,
and Mr. Lanius, who had gone down the Urubamba with Dr. Bowman,
I asked them to make a map of the ruins.[6] I knew it would be a difficult
undertaking and that it was essential for Mr. Tucker to join me in Arequipa not later than the first of October for the ascent of Coropuna. With
the hearty aid of Richarte and Alvarez, the surveyors did better than I
expected. In the ten days while they were at the ruins they were able to
secure data from which Mr. Tucker afterwards prepared a map which told
better than could any words of mine the importance of this site and the
necessity for further investigation.

With the possible exception of one mining prospector, no one in Cuzco
had seen the ruins of Machu Picchu or appreciated their importance. No
one had any realization of what an extraordinary place lay on top of the
ridge. It had never been visited by any of the planters of the lower Urubamba Valley who annually passed over the road which winds through
the canyon two thousand feet below. It seems incredible that this citadel,
less than three days' journey from Cuzco, should have remained so long
undescribed by travelers and comparatively unknown even to the Peruvians themselves. If the *conquistadores* ever saw this wonderful place, some
reference to it surely would have been made; yet nothing can be found
which clearly refers to the ruins of Machu Picchu. Just when it was first
seen by a Spanish-speaking person is uncertain. When the Count de Sartiges was at Huadquiña in 1834 he was looking for ruins; yet, although so
near, he heard of none here. From a crude scrawl on the walls of one of
the finest buildings, we learned that the ruins were visited in 1902 by Liza-

rraga, lessee of the lands immediately below the bridge of San Miguel. This is the earliest local record. Yet someone must have visited Machu Picchu long before that; because in 1875, as has been said, the French explorer Charles Wiener heard in Ollantaytambo of there being ruins at "Huaina-Picchu or Matcho-Picchu." He tried to find them. That he failed was due to there being no road through the canyon of Torontoy and the necessity of making a wide detour through the pass of Panticalla and the Lucumayo Valley, a route which brought him to the Urubamba River at the bridge of Chuquichaca, twenty-five miles below Machu Picchu.

It was not until 1890 that the Peruvian Government, recognizing the needs of the enterprising planters who were opening up the lower valley of the Urubamba, decided to construct a mule trail along the banks of the river through the grand canyon to enable the much-desired *coca* and *aguardiente* to be shipped from Huadquiña, Maranura, and Santa Ana to Cuzco more quickly and cheaply than formerly. This road avoids the necessity of carrying the precious cargoes over the dangerous snowy passes of Mt. Veronica and Mt. Salcantay, so vividly described by Raimondi, de Sartiges, and others. The road, however, was very expensive, took years to build, and still requires frequent repair. In fact, even to-day travel over it is often suspended for several days or weeks at a time, following some tremendous avalanche. Yet it was this new road which had led Melchor Arteaga to build his hut near the arable land at Mandor Pampa, where he could raise food for his family and offer rough shelter to passing travelers. It was this new road which brought Richarte, Alvarez, and their enterprising friends into this little-known region, gave them the opportunity of occupying the ancient terraces of Machu Picchu, which had lain fallow for centuries, encouraged them to keep open a passable trail over the precipices, and made it feasible for us to reach the ruins. It was this new road which offered us in 1911 a virgin field between Ollantaytambo and Huadquiña and enabled us to learn that the Incas, or their predecessors, had once lived here in the remote fastnesses of the Andes, and had left stone witnesses of the magnificence and beauty of their ancient civilization, more interesting and extensive than any which have been found since the days of the Spanish Conquest of Peru.

Notes

1   Carrasco was a Peruvian policeman whom the authorities in Cuzco had assigned to help Bingham's expedition.
2   O. F. Cook was the botanist in Bingham's expeditions.

3   The full names of these men were Torribio Richarte and Anacleto Alvárez; a plaque at
    the entrance of Machu Picchu today acknowledges their role in discovering the ruin.

4   An ashlar is a squared block of smooth, neatly trimmed stone.

5   Bingham wanted to believe that Machu Picchu was the city of Vilcabamba ("Uilca-
    pampa" in his spelling), the fabled final refuge of the Incas. Subsequent investigation
    has strongly suggested that this was not the case. Most contemporary scholars believe
    that Espíritu Pampa, farther down in the jungle, was the city where the last Inca, Túpac
    Amaru, ruled until his capture and execution by the Spaniards in 1572.

6   Tucker, Hendriksen, Bowman, and Lanius were, respectively, the engineer, geologist-
    geographer, topographer, and assistant to the expedition.

II · CONQUEST AND COLONIAL RULE

The first encounter of Tawantinsuyu's subjects and Spanish expeditionaries under Francisco Pizarro apparently took place off the coast of present-day Ecuador in 1527. Only five years later the fateful events unfolded that transformed the history of those lands known from then on as "Peru," probably after the "Virú" tribe thought by Mexico's Spanish conquerors to live to the south. In the Andean city of Cajamarca, the Spaniards met, ambushed, and captured the Inca ruler Atahualpa, slaughtering thousands of his warriors, in a sequence of cinematographic improbability and drama.

The tremendous trauma of 1532 would be reenacted in Andean festivals through the centuries and analyzed by dozens of social psychologists and historians. It also generated an array of myths. Until quite recently, one of the most prevalent was that of the "vanquished race." The Indians defeated in a single afternoon by a handful of white adventurers had shown themselves lacking "the ability to make their own decisions and . . . incapable of taking individual initiative," in the words of novelist Mario Vargas Llosa.[1] From this perspective, they could or should be exterminated, "civilized," instructed, or saved, depending on the narrow-mindedness or empathy of the particular observer.

The conquest also spawned the Inkarrí myth. Here Atahualpa's capture melded with the death of Túpac Amaru, the last Inca rebel against the Spaniards, and for his presumption beheaded in Cuzco's Plaza de Armas forty years later. The myth asserts that the Inca's buried body, beginning with the head, has begun to reconstitute itself. With his return would come a golden age, idealized to be sure, of the Inca empire.

The Inkarrí myth nourished the dreams of the vanquished for an "inversion of the world" and fueled colonial insurrections. Even as they con-

verted to Christianity and acknowledged the Spanish king, Cuzco's Indian aristocracy emphasized its descent from Peru's ancient rulers and
developed a strong sense of what anthropologist John Rowe called "Inca
nationalism."[2] A series of uprisings of *curacas*, or Indian chiefs, in the
seventeenth and eighteenth centuries culminated in the great late eighteenth-century rebellions of Túpac Amaru II and Túpac Katari in what
is today southern Peru and highland Bolivia.

Besides myths, the colonial order radically transformed Andean societies. After an initial period of indirect rule through curacas, who supervised the collection of tribute and labor services from the *encomiendas*,
or "grants" of Indians, given by the Crown to the conquerors, the ener-
getic and methodical viceroy Francisco Toledo implemented a sweeping
reform in the 1570s. Natives were "reduced" into Spanish-style towns;
the colonial *mita* of tribute and forced labor was imposed; a prosperous
mining economy was established, supplied with labor by the *mita* system; and a huge body of legislation suppressed Andean customs and religion. The reaction to colonial rule went from resignation to radical rejection, reflected in the messianic insurrection launched in 1742 by Juan
Santos Atahualpa in the central jungles that was a forerunner of Túpac
Amaru II's rebellion half a century later.

But most responses fell in between, in the broad category of what one
observer has called "resistant adaptation."[3] This led to status and economic differentiation within the Spanish-imposed category of "Indian"
and syncretism and reinvention in culture and religion. From the old pre-
Columbian *ayllus* and Spanish *cabildos*, or municipalities, came the "indigenous communities" that lasted into the twentieth century. Andean
and European traditions fused in Cuzco's baroque art and the Indian festivals of Inti Raymi and Q'oylluriti. But colonial rule was disastrous for
the majority of the conquered, reflected in the cataclysmic collapse of
the indigenous population from roughly 9 million to just 600,000 in the
century after the conquest.[4] Even the lives of those who learned to play
by the colonial rules and climb the economic ladder were fraught with
irony and paradox. As historian Steve J. Stern asserts, "The tragedy of
Indian success stemmed ultimately from the way it secured the participation of a defeated people in its own oppression."

But colonial rule also changed the lives and customs of the peninsu-
lar Spaniards who settled in Peru. The new viceroyalty was finally con-
solidated after four decades of wars between Spaniards and Indians and
then the conquerors themselves, divided between Pizarro and Diego de
Almagro. Bankrolled by Potosí's silver after 1570, these Europeans and

their descendants turned Lima into what historian Luis Miguel Glave terms a capital of "opulent decadence . . . [with its] wealthy merchants, pompous clerics, grave doctors and endless ceremonies both sacred and profane."[5] Under colonial rule, however, the descendants of the conquerors also differentiated. An elaborate edifice of "castes" grew from the intermingling of Europeans, Indians, and African slaves, who by 1636 already made up more than a third of Lima's population, and conflict developed between creoles, the American-born of European descent, and peninsulars from Spain.[6] As historian Alberto Flores Galindo has observed, the distinction between colonizers and colonized blurred over time. The growing number of mestizos and creoles meant that "the hegemony of Spain over its colonies turned less transparent, as did the dependence of the colonies on Madrid."

At the end of the eighteenth century, creoles joined the Spanish royalists to put down Indian rebellions. Most preferred European rule to a Peru under the "heathen" and "savage" majorities in the Andes. Just a few decades later, however, they won independence from Spain without sacrificing the privileges of race and status, thanks to the arrival of the creole armies of Gran Colombia and Río de la Plata. Far from a real liberation for Peru's majorities, this new republic was to be in many ways even more unequal and divided than the colonial system that had prevailed since Toledo more than three centuries before.

Notes

1   Mario Vargas Llosa, "Questions of Conquest," *Harper's*, December 1990, pp. 45–53, quote on p. 49.
2   John Rowe, "El movimiento nacional inca del siglo xviii," *Revista universitaria* 107 (Cuzco, 1954): 14–47.
3   Steve J. Stern, "New Approaches to the Study of Peasant Rebellion," in *Resistance, Rebellion, and Consciousness in the Andean Peasant World, 18th to 20th Centuries*, edited by Steve J. Stern (Madison: University of Wisconsin Press, 1987), p. 9.
4   David Noble Cook, *Demographic Collapse: Indian Peru, 1520–1620* (Cambridge, England: Cambridge University Press, 1981), offers a good discussion of the complicated questions involved in trying to calculate Peru's pre-Columbian population.
5   Luís Miguel Glave, "Lima a principios del siglo XVII," unpublished manuscript, p. 1.
6   Frederick P. Bowser, *The African Slave in Colonial Peru, 1524–1650* (Stanford: Stanford University Press, 1974), p. 339.

ATAHUALPA AND PIZARRO

John Hemming

An almost surreal combination of wild luck, single-minded greed, and resourceful-ness enabled the conquistador Francisco Pizarro and his band of 150 Spaniards to conquer the Inca empire. Poma, Cieza de León, Garcilaso de la Vega, and other first chroniclers of the New World were fascinated by the tale. The blind Boston lawyer William H. Prescott wrote his History of the Conquest of Peru *in 1847 from these accounts, without ever visiting Peru. Yet no one has told the story of the conquest better than historian John Hemming, whose magisterial* The Conquest of the Incas *has become a must-read book on this period of Peruvian history. This vivid chapter recounts Pizarro's capture of the Inca Atahualpa in the Andean city of Cahamarca, triggering the empire's collapse.*

On 25 September 1513 a force of weary Spanish explorers cut through the forests of Panama and were confronted by an ocean: the Mar del Sur, the South Sea or Pacific Ocean. This expedition was led by Vasco Núñez de Balboa, and one of its senior officers was a thirty-five-year-old captain called Francisco Pizarro. Six years after the first discovery, the Spaniards established the town of Panama on the Pacific shore of the isthmus. Panama became a base in which to build ships to explore and exploit this unknown sea. It was the threshold of a vast expansion.

Spain was developing with explosive force during these years. Throughout the Middle Ages the crusading knights of Castile had been driving the Mohammedans out of the Iberian peninsula. The final victory of this reconquest came in January 1492, with the surrender of Granada to the Castilians under King Ferdinand of Aragon. A few months later in that same year Christopher Columbus sailed westwards into the Atlantic and made a landfall in the Caribbean. The ensuing years were spent establishing a Spanish presence in the islands of the West Indies and exploring the northern coast of South America. Francisco Pizarro took part in many of these explorations, tough and unrewarding raids on the tribes of the American forests.

The European conception of the Americas—or Indies, as they were called—changed dramatically when in 1519 Hernán Cortés discovered and invaded the mighty Aztec empire in Mexico. Cortés led only some five hundred men and sixteen horses, but he skillfully won the alliance of rebellious subject tribes. By adroit diplomacy and the endurance and ruthless courage of his men, Cortés conquered an empire of exotic brilliance. Spain, a country of under ten million inhabitants, had seized a land with a population and wealth as great as its own. Cortés's achievement fired the romantic Spanish imagination. Younger sons of feudal families and Spaniards of all classes sailed eagerly to seek adventure and riches across the Atlantic.

While Cortés was conquering Mexico, Spaniards were beginning to explore the Pacific coast of South America. In 1522 Pascual de Andagoya sailed some two hundred miles along the coast of Colombia and ascended the river San Juan. He was seeking a tribe called Virú or Birú; and the name of this tribe, altered to "Perú," came to be applied to a country lying far to the south.

Three partners acquired Andagoya's ships and succeeded in raising money to finance another voyage. The three were Francisco Pizarro and Diego de Almagro, both citizens of Panama and holders of quotas of Indians there, and Hernando de Luque, a priest who was apparently acting as agent of the trio's financial backer, Judge Gaspar de Espinosa. Pizarro sailed in November 1524 with eighty men and four horses. This first expedition was not a success: it reached a place that the Spaniards called, for obvious reasons, Port of Hunger, and Almagro lost an eye in a skirmish with primitive natives at "Burned Village." No riches were found along the coast, and the adventurers had difficulty persuading Espinosa to finance a further attempt.

The three partners entered into a formal contract on 10 March 1526, and Pizarro sailed eight months later. He took some 160 men and a few horses in two small ships commanded by the able pilot Bartolomé Ruiz. The expedition divided: Pizarro camped at the river San Juan, Almagro returned for reinforcements, and Ruiz sailed on southwards. Ruiz's ships crossed the equator for the first time in the Pacific, and then, suddenly, came the first contact with the Inca civilization.

The Spanish ships encountered and captured an ocean-going balsa raft fitted with fine cotton sails. No one who saw that raft was in any doubt that it was the product of an advanced civilization. The vessel was on a trading mission to barter Inca artifacts for crimson shells and corals. A breathless report of the raft was sent back to King Charles I, who was also Holy Roman Emperor Charles V. "They were carrying many pieces of silver and gold as personal ornaments . . . including crowns and diadems, belts and bracelets, armour for the legs and breastplates; tweezers and rattles and strings and clusters of beads and rubies; mirrors decorated with silver, and cups and other drinking vessels. They were carrying many wool and cotton mantles and Moorish tunics . . . and other pieces of clothing colored with cochineal, crimson, blue, yellow, and all other colors, and worked with different types of ornate embroidery, in figures of birds, animals, fish, and trees. They had some tiny weights to weigh gold. . . . There were small stones in bead bags: emeralds and chalcedonies and other jewels and pieces of crystal and resin. They were taking all this to trade for fish shells from which they make counters, coral-colored scarlet and white." Eleven of the twenty men on the raft leaped into the sea at the moment of capture, and the pilot Ruiz set six others free on shore. But he shrewdly kept three men to be taught Spanish and trained as interpreters for a conquest of this mysterious empire.

Ruiz rejoined Pizarro and ferried the expedition south to explore the coast of Ecuador. They returned to the uninhabited Isla del Gallo, Island of the Cock, in the Tumaco estuary. These coasts are humid, barren of food and often infested with noxious mangrove swamps. The Spaniards suffered terribly. Three or four a week were dying of hunger and disease. When the expedition had lost a large part of its men, a desperate appeal from the survivors reached the Governor of Panama. He opened a full-scale enquiry on 29 August 1527, and ordered that any men who wished to return should be evacuated. The expedition had been maintained largely by the fanatical determination of Francisco Pizarro. He now drew a line across the sand of the Isla del Gallo and challenged his men to cross it and remain with him. Thirteen brave men did so. They stayed with Pizarro on the island and ensured the continuance of the expedition.

Pizarro's perseverance was rewarded the following year. He sailed south in a voyage of true exploration, with only a handful of soldiers and none of the baggage of an invasion. The expedition entered the Gulf of Guayaquil, and sighted its first Inca city at Tumbez. An Inca noble visited the ship and a Spaniard, Alonso de Molina, landed with a present of pigs and chickens. A tall and dashing Greek, Pedro de Candía, also landed to confirm Molina's description of Tumbez as a well-ordered town. Here at last was the advanced civilization that the adventurers had been seeking so ardently. Candía astounded the inhabitants by firing an arquebus at a target, but this first contact between Spaniards and subjects of the Inca was very cordial.

Pizarro sailed on down the coast of Peru as far as the modern Santa River. Two further landings confirmed the magnitude of the discovery and the sophistication of this mysterious empire. The expedition returned with evidence: llamas, pottery and metal vessels, fine clothing, and more boys to be trained as interpreters. Pizarro's men had glimpsed the edges of a great civilization, the product of centuries of development in complete isolation from the rest of mankind.

The explorers were excited by their discoveries and the potential for conquest, but they could not arouse the enthusiasm of the governor of Panama. They decided to send Pizarro back to Spain to win royal approval, and to raise more men and money. Pizarro was well received by King Charles at Toledo in mid-1528. He was fortunate that his visit coincided with the return of Cortés, who charmed the court ladies with lavish presents of Mexican treasure, and was rewarded with a marquisate and other honors. Cortés encouraged Pizarro; but it was the brilliant inspiration of the conquest of Mexico that made it easy for Pizarro to recruit keen young adventurers in his native Trujillo de Extremadura. King Charles had to leave Toledo, but on 26 July 1529 the queen signed a Capitulación authorizing Pizarro to discover and conquer "Peru." Pizarro was named Governor and Captain-General of Peru, Almagro became commandant of Tumbez, and Luque was appointed Protector of the Indians, with a promise of becoming Bishop of Tumbez.

Pizarro sailed from Seville in January 1530 with a flotilla full of would-be conquerors, including his younger half-brothers Hernando, Juan, and Gonzalo Pizarro and Francisco Martín de Alcántara. In Panama, Diego de Almagro was understandably disgusted with his meager appointment in the Toledo agreement. He was persuaded to continue the enterprise only by being promised the title Adelantado (Marshal) and a governorship of territory beyond that of Pizarro.

Pizarro's third voyage sailed from Panama on 27 December 1530, but inexplicably chose to land on the Ecuadorean coast long before reaching Tumbez. Months of hardships followed: a wearisome march along the tropical coast, an epidemic of buboes, a stay on the dreary island of Puná in the Gulf of Guayaquil, and many skirmishes with primitive natives. The most serious battle took place when the expedition attempted to cross on rafts from Puná to the mainland of Inca Peru. The conquistadores were finally beginning to invade the Inca empire, but they were in a remote corner, far from its fabulous cities and treasures. Tumbez, the site of the promised bishopric, was in ruins and there were no signs of a Spaniard who had chosen to remain there. The natives said that this destruction was the result of a civil war within the Inca empire.

The year 1531 and part of 1532 had elapsed since this third expedition left Panama, but Pizarro advanced cautiously. He left Tumbez in May 1532 and moved to the district of Poechos on the Chira River. He spent the ensuing months exploring the arid northwestern corner of Peru. Weeks were spent ferrying some of the men from Tumbez to Tangarara, 120 miles to the south. Various reinforcements sailed down the coast to raise the spirits of Pizarro's men: the seasoned conqueror Sebastián de Benalcázar brought thirty men from Nicaragua, and the dashing Hernando de Soto came with another contingent. Pizarro killed a local chief called Amotape, apparently to intimidate the natives of this outlying province. He then selected a site for the first Spanish settlement in this strange new country: in mid-September a small ceremony marked the foundation of San Miguel de Piura near Tangarara. Some sixty Spaniards were left as the first citizens of San Miguel, and Pizarro struck out into the Inca empire with a tiny army: 62 horsemen and 106 foot soldiers. The months of hesitation were over.

Pizarro's force marched out of San Miguel on 24 September 1532. It spent ten days at Piura, paused at Zarán (modern Serrán), Motux (Motupe), and reached Saña on 6 November. Up to now the Spaniards had remained on the coastal plain, a narrow strip of desert between the Pacific and the Andes Mountains, but on 8 November they decided to turn inland and march up into the sierra. The Incas were mountain people, with lungs enlarged by evolution to breathe rarefied air. Although they had conquered the many civilizations of the hot coastal valleys, the true Inca empire lay along the ranges of the Andes, and it was here that any conqueror must confront them.

With striking good fortune, Pizarro's Spaniards marched into Peru precisely at a moment of great passion in a war of dynastic succession. When Pizarro first sailed down the Pacific a few years earlier, the Inca empire was ruled in tranquility by one venerated supreme Inca, Huayna-Capac. His possessions stretched for almost three thousand miles along the Andes, from central Chile to the south of modern Colombia—a distance greater than that across the continental United States, or Europe from the Atlantic to the Caspian. With the Pacific Ocean to the west and the Amazonian forests to the east, the Incas were confident that they had absorbed almost all civilization.

Huayna-Capac had for many years been leading the empire's professional army against tribes in the extreme north, Pasto and Popayán in Colombia. The fighting was stubborn and the campaigns dragged on. The Inca and his court had long been absent from the imperial capital Cuzco, and Huayna-Capac was considering establishing a second capital in the north at Quito or Tumibamba. It was during these campaigns that Huayna-Capac was first informed of the appearance of tall strangers from the sea. He was destined never to see any Europeans. His army and court were struck by a violent epidemic that killed Huayna-Capac in a delirious fever, at some time between 1525 and 1527. The disease may have been malaria, but it could have been smallpox. The Spaniards brought smallpox with them from Europe, and it spread fiercely around the Caribbean among peoples who had no immunity. It could easily have swept from tribe to tribe across Colombia and struck the Inca armies long before the Spaniards themselves sailed down the coast. The epidemic "consumed the greater part" of the Inca court including Huayna-Capac's probable heir, Ninan Cuyuchi. "Countless thousands of common people also died."

The premature deaths of the great Inca Huayna-Capac and his heir left an ambiguous situation. The most likely successor was the Inca's son Huáscar, and he succeeded as ruler of the capital city Cuzco. Another son, Atahualpa, was left in charge of the imperial army at Quito. He was probably acting as provincial governor of the area on behalf of his brother, although a number of chroniclers said that the dying Inca had decided to divide the vast empire into two sections, one ruled from Cuzco, the other from Quito. We shall never know the exact nature of the legacy. What we do know is that, after a few years of quiet, civil war broke out between the two brothers. Different chroniclers gave different versions of the origins of this conflict, depending on the sympathies of their native informants. Being Europeans, most chroniclers were at pains to discover which brother, Huáscar or Atahualpa, had the best "legitimate" claim to the throne. This was irrelevant, for the Incas did not stress primogeniture. They were concerned only that the new Inca should be of royal blood and fit to rule. If the eldest or favorite son designated as heir by his father proved weak or incompetent, he was soon deposed by a more aggressive brother in a civil war or palace revolution. Most of the eleven Incas who had ruled up to this time had succeeded only after some such struggle, and the result was a line of remarkable rulers.

When the civil war broke out, Atahualpa had possession of the professional army, which was still fighting on the northern marches under its generals Chalcuchima, Quisquis and Rumiñavi. Huáscar had the loyalty of most of the country. It took only a few years for relations between the two brothers to degenerate into open conflict. Huáscar's militia army attempted to invade Quito, but after initial success was driven south through the Andes by the seasoned forces loyal to Atahualpa. A series of crushing victories by the Quitans culminated in the defeat and capture of Huáscar in a pitched battle outside Cuzco. Many peoples of the empire regarded the victorious Quitans as hostile invaders, and the professionals responded with the brutality they had learned in the northern campaigns. Atahualpa ravaged the province of the Cañari tribe as punishment for its chief's intrigues. Quisquis, the general who conquered Cuzco, set out to exterminate all members of Huáscar's family to dispose of any other pretenders. He sent the captive Inca northwards under strong escort. Chalcuchima, Atahualpa's supreme commander, held the area of the central Andes with another army at Jauja, while Rumiñavi was the general left in command of the Quitan homeland. Atahualpa himself marched triumphantly southwards in the wake of his generals.

Pizarro started his march down the Peruvian coast just as this fierce civil war was ending. His men saw ample evidence of the recent fighting. Tumbez was in ruins. When Hernando de Soto rode inland on a reconnaissance, he reached a town called Cajas, which was "in considerable ruin from the fighting that Atahualpa had waged. In the hills were the bodies of many Indians hanging from trees because they had not agreed to surrender: for all these villages were originally under Cuzco [Huáscar], whom they acknowledged as master and to whom they paid tribute."

When Pizarro learned about the civil war, he immediately grasped how useful it could be for him. Cortés had brilliantly manipulated rival factions during the conquest of Mexico twelve years before. Pizarro hoped to do likewise.

By another extraordinary coincidence, the victorious Atahualpa happened to be camped in the mountains at Cajamarca, not far from Pizarro's line of march. Reports reached Atahualpa as soon as the Spaniards landed on the mainland, and he was told that they were pillaging the countryside and abusing the natives. But Atahualpa was too engrossed in the civil war to be particularly concerned with the movements of the 150 strangers. He was fully occupied in leading his army, arranging the occupation of the newly won empire, planning his own journey to Cuzco, and awaiting reports from his commanders to the south. When Pizarro and his men marched out of San Miguel, Atahualpa did not yet know whether Quisquis had won or lost the battle for Cuzco. But he sent one of his close advisers to investigate the strangers. This Inca noble reached Cajas while Soto's reconnaissance was there, and at once impressed the Spaniards with his authority. They noted that the local chief "became greatly frightened and stood up, for he did not dare remain seated in his presence." And when the envoy reached Pizarro's camp, "he entered as casually as if he had been brought up all his life among Spaniards. After having delivered his embassy . . . he enjoyed himself for two or three days among us." Atahualpa's messenger brought presents of stuffed ducks and two pottery vessels representing castles. The more suspicious Spaniards assumed that the ducks, which had been skinned, were intended to represent the fate that awaited the intruders, while the model castles were to indicate that many more fortresses lay ahead.

The envoy had also been ordered to report on Pizarro's force. During the two days he was in the Spaniards' midst, he went about examining every detail of their horses and armor and counting their numbers. He asked some Spaniards to show him their swords. "He happened to go up to one Spaniard to do this, and put his hand on his beard. That Spaniard gave him many blows. When Don Francisco Pizarro heard of this, he issued a proclamation that no one should touch the Indian, whatever he did." The envoy invited Pizarro to proceed to Cajamarca to meet Atahualpa. Pizarro accepted, and sent the Inca a present of a fine Holland shirt and two goblets of Venetian glass.

The small force of invaders turned inland, away from the Pacific coast and up into the Andes. The Spaniards probably marched up an Inca trail ascending the Chancay stream past the town of Chongoyape. From the sands of the coastal desert they would have passed through plantations of sugar and cotton. As they climbed through the Andean foothills, the valley narrowed into a canyon whose sides would have been covered in fields and terraces. At the source of the Chancay, Pizarro's force probably swung south along the watershed of the Andes, crossing treeless savannah at some 13,500 feet. They were apprehensive, excited by the rapid change of altitude, and disquieted by the sight of Inca forts and watchtowers overlooking their route. But Atahualpa had decided to allow the strangers to penetrate the mountains, and his warriors did nothing to impede their advance.

The Spaniards were fortunate that Atahualpa had decided not to oppose their march into the mountains, for they were moving across difficult country, a region rarely penetrated to this day. Hernando Pizarro wrote: "The road was so bad that they could very easily have taken us there or at another pass which we found between here and Cajamarca.

For we could not use the horses on the roads, not even with skill, and off the roads we could take neither horses nor foot soldiers." This assessment was reasonable: less professional Inca armies destroyed a force as large as this in similar mountainous country four years later.

Finally, on Friday 15 November, the Spanish force emerged from the hills and looked down onto the valley of Cajamarca. This is a beautiful, fertile valley, only a few miles wide but remarkably flat—a very rare distinction in the vertical world of the Andes, where most rivers rush through precipitous canyons, and the only flat ground is on the high, infertile savannahs. The valley today has cows grazing beneath eucalyptus groves, and boasts a chocolate factory—all imported and unusual sights. The ground is strewn with millions of potsherds, painted with elaborate geometric designs of the pre-Inca Cajamarca civilizations, and on the desolate hills above the town are weird watercourses and incomprehensible designs cut into rock outcrops. Modern Cajamarca is a charming red-roofed Spanish town, with fine colonial monasteries and a lovely cathedral.

Pizarro halted his men at the edge of the valley to await the rear guard, and then rode down in three squadrons in careful marching order. Atahualpa had the tents of his army's camp spread out across a hillside beyond the town. "The Indians' camp looked like a very beautiful city. . . . So many tents were visible that we were truly filled with great apprehension. We never thought that Indians could maintain such a proud estate nor have so many tents in such good order. Nothing like this had been seen in the Indies up to then. It filled all us Spaniards with fear and confusion. But it was not appropriate to show any fear, far less to turn back. For had they sensed any weakness in us, the very Indians we were bringing with us would have killed us. So, with a show of good spirits, and after having thoroughly observed the town and tents, we descended into the valley and entered the town of Cajamarca."

Cajamarca itself proved to contain only four or five hundred of its normal two thousand inhabitants. There was a sun temple in an enclosure at its edge, and a series of buildings full of holy women. These chosen women formed part of the empire's official sun religion, but were also one of the privileges of the ruling Inca hierarchy. They were chosen as girls, for either their noble birth or outstanding beauty, and were then moved to cloistered colleges in the provincial capitals such as Cajas or Cajamarca. These chosen girls, *acllas*, spent four years weaving fine cloth or brewing *chicha* for the Inca and his priests and officials. Some then became *mamaconas*, remained in perpetual chastity, and spent their lives in the service of the sun and shrines. Others were given as wives to Inca nobles or tribal chiefs, and the most beautiful became concubines of the Inca himself.

The Spaniards first saw a "nunnery" of *acllas* and *mamaconas* when Hernando de Soto led a reconnaissance inland to Cajas. It is easy to imagine the effect of this building full of beautiful girls on men who had been without women for months. Diego de Trujillo recalled that "the women were brought out onto the square and there were over five hundred of them. Captain [Soto] gave many of them to the Spaniards. The Inca's envoy grew very indignant and said: "How dare you do this when Atahualpa is only twenty leagues from here. Not a man of you will remain alive!'"

Francisco Pizarro assembled his men in the square of Cajamarca, which was surrounded on three sides by long buildings each of which had a series of doors onto the open space. It began to hail, so the men took shelter in the empty buildings. The Spaniards were apprehensive but eager to behave correctly. Francisco Pizarro therefore sent Hernando de Soto to visit Atahualpa with fifteen horsemen and Martín, one of the interpreters acquired on the second voyage. They were to ask him how he wished the strangers to lodge. Shortly after Soto's departure, Hernando Pizarro grew alarmed. As he explained: "I went to talk to the governor, who had gone to inspect the town in case the Indians should attack us by night. I told him that in my view the sending of fifteen of the best horsemen was a mistake. . . . If Atahualpa decided to do anything, [the fifteen] were not enough to defend themselves; and if some reverse befell *them* it would be a very serious loss to him. He therefore ordered me to go with a further twenty horsemen who were in a fit state to go, and once there to act as I saw fit." Fortunately for us, the contingents sent to visit Atahualpa on that first evening included some of the chroniclers who left eyewitness accounts: Hernando Pizarro, Miguel de Estete, Juan Ruiz de Arce, Diego de Trujillo, and possibly Cristóbal de Mena and Pedro Pizarro.

A paved road ran for the few miles between Cajamarca and the Inca's residence. Atahualpa was in a small building close to some baths, the natural hot springs of Kónoj that still hiss and bubble out of the ground to this day. The Spaniards advanced with trepidation through the silent ranks of the Inca army. They had to cross two streams, and left the bulk of the horsemen at the second stretch of water while the leaders rode in to find Atahualpa. "The pleasure house . . . had two towers [rising] from four chambers, with a courtyard in the middle. In this court, a pool had been made and two pipes of water, one hot and one cold, entered it. The two pipes came from springs . . . beside one another. The Inca and his women used to bathe in the pool. There was a lawn at the door of this building, and he was there with his women." The moment had finally come when the first Spaniards were to confront the ruler of Peru. Here was "that great lord Atahualpa . . . about whom we had been given such reports and told so many things." "He was seated on a small stool, very low on the ground, as the Turks and Moors are accustomed to sit," "with all the majesty in the world, surrounded by all his women and with many chiefs near him. Before arriving there, there had been another cluster of chiefs, and so forth with each according to his rank."

Atahualpa was wearing the royal insignia. Every important Peruvian wore a *llautu*, a series of cords wound round the head. But the Inca alone had a royal tassel hanging from the front of this circlet. It consisted of "very fine scarlet wool, cut very even, and cleverly held toward the middle by small golden bugles. The wool was corded, but below the bugles it was unwound and this was the part that fell onto the forehead. . . . This tassel fell to the eyebrows, an inch thick, and covered his entire forehead." Because of the tassel, Atahualpa kept his eyes downcast and Soto could get no reaction from him. "Hernando de Soto arrived above him with his horse, but he remained still, making no movement. [Soto] came so close that the horse's nostrils stirred the fringe that the Inca had placed on his forehead. But the Inca never moved. Captain Hernando de Soto took a ring from his finger and gave it to him as a token of peace and friendship on behalf of the Christians. He took it with very little sign of appreciation." Soto delivered a prepared speech to the effect that he was a representative of the governor, and that the governor would be delighted if he would go to visit him. There was no reaction from Atahualpa. Instead, one of his chiefs answered for him and said that the Inca was on the last day of a ceremonial fast.

At this point Hernando Pizarro arrived and delivered a speech similar to Soto's. Atahualpa apparently gathered that the new arrival was the governor's brother, for he now looked up and began to converse. He told of the first report about the Christians that he had received from Marcavilca, chief of Poechos on the Zuricari River (the modern Chira) between Tumbez and San Miguel. This chief "sent to tell me that you treated the chiefs badly and threw them into chains, and he sent me an iron collar. He says that he killed three Christians and one horse." Hernando Pizarro responded hotly to the latter claim. "I told him that those men of San Miguel were like women, and that one horse was enough [to conquer] that entire land. When he saw us fight, he would see what sort of men we were." Hernando Pizarro warmed to his subject and became more ex-

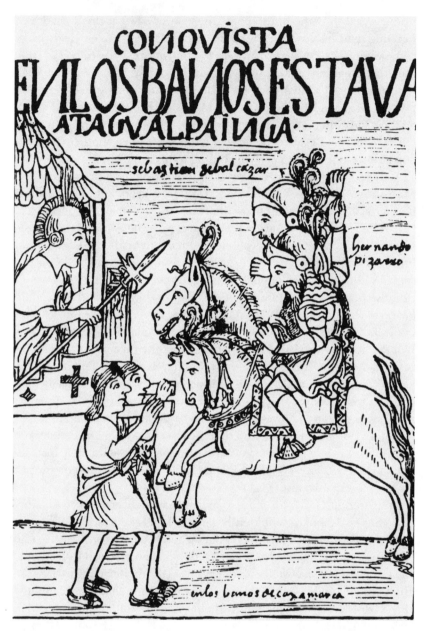

Figure 7. Atahualpa meets Hernando de Soto at Kónoj, now called Baños del Inca. (From Guamán Poma de Ayala, *Nueva Coronica y Buen Gobierno*)

pansive. He told Atahualpa that "the governor [Francisco Pizarro] loved him dearly. If he had any enemy, he should tell [the governor] and he would send to conquer that person. [Atahualpa] told me that four days' march away, there were some very savage Indians with whom he could do nothing: Christians should go there to help his men. I told him that the governor would send ten horsemen, which was enough for the entire land. His Indians would be needed only to search for those who hid. He smiled, as someone who did not think much of us."

Atahualpa invited the Spaniards to dismount and dine with him. They refused, and he offered them drink. After some hesitation for fear of poison, they accepted. Two women immediately appeared with golden jugs of the native maize beverage, *chicha*, and ceremonial drinks were exchanged with the Inca. The sun was now setting, and Hernando Pizarro asked permission to leave. The Inca wanted one Spaniard to remain there with him, but they claimed that this would be contrary to their orders. So they took their leave, with Atahualpa's instructions that they were to make their quarters in three houses on the square, leaving only the main fortress for his own residence. He also gave them the assurance they most wanted: he himself would go to Cajamarca the following day to visit Pizarro.

During the meeting, Atahualpa had been "closely examining the horses, which undoubtedly seemed good to him. Appreciating this, Hernando de Soto brought up a little horse that had been trained to rear up, and asked [the Inca] whether he wanted him to ride it in the courtyard. He indicated that he did, and [Soto] maneuvered it there for a while with good grace. The nag was spirited and made much foam at its mouth. He was amazed at this, and at seeing the agility with which it wheeled. But the common people showed even greater admiration and there was much whispering. One squadron of troops drew back when they saw the horse coming toward them. Those who did this paid for it that night with their lives, for Atahualpa ordered them to be killed because they had shown fear."

The Spaniards now had time to ponder the seriousness of their situation. "We took many views and opinions among ourselves about what should be done. All were full of fear, for we were so few and were so deep in the land where we could not be reinforced. . . . All assembled in the governor's quarters to debate what should be done the following day. . . . Few slept, and we kept watch in the square, from which the campfires of the Indian army could be seen. It was a fearful sight. Most of them were on a hillside and close to one another: it looked like a brilliantly star-studded sky." Cristóbal de Mena recalled how the danger broke down class differences among the Spaniards. "There was no distinction between great and small, or between foot soldiers and horsemen. Everyone performed sentry rounds fully armed that night. So also did the good old governor, who went about encouraging the men. On that day all were knights."

The Spaniards now realized, for the first time, the sophistication of the empire they had penetrated. They found themselves isolated from the sea by days of marching over difficult mountains. They were in the midst of a victorious army in full battle order, which Soto and Hernando Pizarro estimated at forty thousand effectives—"but they said this to encourage the men, for he had over eighty thousand." Added to this was the fear of the unknown, "for the Spaniards had no experience of how these Indians fought or what spirit they had." From what they had seen of Atahualpa himself, his well-disciplined army, and the brutality of the recent civil war, they had no reason to hope for a friendly reception of any long duration.

The men Pizarro was leading were skilled and seasoned soldiers. Many had gained experience in the conquests in and around the Caribbean, Mexico, and Central America. Pizarro himself had first arrived in the Indies in 1502 and was now, in his mid-fifties, one of the richest and most important citizens of Panama. Although he could not read and was a poor horseman, his command of the expedition was never in question for a moment—any friction that occurred was between his captains, Diego de Almagro, Hernando de Soto, Hernando Pizarro, and Sebastián de Benalcázar. Other members of the expedition had gained experience in the battles of northern Italy and north Africa that were making Spain the leading nation in Europe and the Spanish tercios its most dreaded soldiers. Even the youngest members—for most of the Spaniards were in their twenties—compensated for any lack of fighting experience by skill in military exercises and by courage and dash. In the feudal structure of Spanish society an ambitious man could rise only by marrying an heiress or by warfare. There was the spirit of a gold rush about this expedition, fortified by some of the conviction of a crusade.

Despite their experience, Pizarro's 150 men had marched into an impasse and were now thoroughly frightened and desperate. All that they could decide during that anxious night was to employ the various tactics and advantages that had proved successful in the Caribbean. They could use surprise, attacking first without provocation, and take advantage of the novelty of their appearance and fighting methods. Their weapons—

horses, steel swords, and armor—were far superior to anything they had encountered so far in the Indies, although they were not so sure about the Incas. They had in mind the tactic that had succeeded so well in the conquest of Mexico: the kidnaping of the head of state. They could also try to make capital of the internal dissensions within the Inca empire—Hernando Pizarro had already offered the services of Spaniards to help Atahualpa in his intertribal fighting. Possibly their greatest advantage lay in the self-assurance of belonging to a more advanced civilization and the knowledge that their purpose was conquest: to the Indians, they were still an unknown quantity of uncertain origin and unsure intentions.

It was agreed that Governor Pizarro should decide on the spur of the moment the course of action to be adopted when Atahualpa was in Cajamarca the following day, Saturday 16 November. But careful plans were made for a surprise attack and capture of the Inca. "The governor had a dais on which Atahualpa was to sit. It was agreed that he should be enticed onto it by kind words and that he should then order his men to return to their quarters. For the governor was afraid to come to grips when there were so many native warriors and we were so few." The attack was to be made only if success appeared possible or if the natives made any threatening move. There were two more peaceful options. Atahualpa might be persuaded to make some act of political or spiritual submission. Or, if the natives seemed too powerful, the Spaniards could maintain the fiction of friendship and hope for a more favorable opportunity in the future.

The square of Cajamarca was ideally suited to the Spaniards' plan. Long, low buildings occupied three sides of it, each some two hundred yards long. Pizarro stationed the cavalry in two of these, in three contingents of fifteen to twenty, under the command of his lieutenants Hernando de Soto, Hernando Pizarro, and Sebastián de Benalcázar. The buildings each had some twenty openings onto the square, "almost as if they had been built for that purpose." "All were to charge out of their lodgings, with the horsemen mounted on their horses." Pizarro himself, being a poor horseman, remained in the third building with a few horse and some twenty foot. His contingent was "charged with the capture of Atahualpa's person, should he come suspiciously as it appeared that he would."

Roads ran down from the town and entered the square between these buildings. Groups of foot and horse were concealed in these alleys to close them. The lower side of the square was enclosed by a long wall of tapia, compacted clay, with a tower in the middle that was entered from the outside; beyond this lay the open plain. At the middle of the square, apparently on the upper side, was a stronger stone structure that the Spaniards regarded as a fort. Pizarro had the remainder of the infantry guard the gates of this, possibly to preserve it as a final refuge. Inside he stationed Captain Pedro de Candía with "eight or nine musketeers and four small pieces of artillery." The firing of these arquebuses was the pre-arranged signal for the Spaniards to charge into the square.

Atahualpa was in no hurry to make the short journey across the plain to Cajamarca. He had just finished a fast, and there was drinking to be done to celebrate this and the victory of his forces at Cuzco. The morning went by with no sign of movement from the native encampment. The Spaniards became increasingly jittery. The familiar noble envoy arrived from Atahualpa saying that he intended to come with his men armed. "The governor replied: 'Tell your lord to come . . . however he wishes. In whatever way he comes, I will receive him as a friend and brother.'" A later messenger said that the natives would be unarmed. The Spaniards "heard mass and commended ourselves to God, begging him to keep us in his hand." Atahualpa's army finally began to move at midday and "in a short while the entire plain was full of men, rearranging themselves at every step, waiting for him to emerge from the camp." The Spaniards were concealed in their buildings, under orders not to emerge until they heard the artillery signal. The young Pedro Pizarro recalled: "I saw many Spaniards urinate without noticing it out of pure terror."

Atahualpa had clearly decided to turn his visit to the extraordinary strangers into a ceremonial parade. "All the Indians wore large gold and silver discs like crowns on their heads. They were apparently all coming in their ceremonial clothes." "In front was a squadron of Indians wearing a livery of checkered colors, like a chessboard. As these advanced, they removed the straws from the ground and swept the roadway." "They pointed their arms toward the ground to clear anything that was on it— which was scarcely necessary, as the townspeople kept it well swept. . . . They were singing a song by no means lacking grace for us who heard it."

As the tension mounted, Atahualpa paused on a meadow half a mile from the town. The road was still full of men, and more natives were still emerging from the camp. There was another exchange of messengers. Atahualpa started to pitch his tents, as it was by now late afternoon: he said that he intended to stay the night there. This was the last thing Pizarro wanted, for the Spaniards were particularly frightened of a night attack. In desperation, Pizarro sent one Hernando de Aldana "to tell him to enter the square and come to visit him before night fell. When the messenger reached Atahualpa, he made a reverence and told him, by signs, that he should go to where the governor was." He assured the Inca "that no harm or insult would befall him. He could therefore come without fear—not that the Inca showed any sign of fear."

Atahualpa complied. With the sun sinking low, he continued his progress into the town. He left most of the armed men outside on the plain, "but brought with him five or six thousand men, unarmed except that they carried small battle-axes, slings and pouches of stones underneath their tunics." Behind the vanguard, "in a very fine litter with the ends of its timbers covered in silver, came the figure of Atahualpa. Eighty lords carried him on their shoulders, all wearing a very rich blue livery. His own person was very richly dressed, with his crown on his head and a collar of large emeralds around his neck. He was seated on the litter, on a small stool with a rich saddle cushion. He stopped when he reached the middle of the square, with half his body exposed." "The litter was lined with parrot feathers of many colors and embellished with plates of gold and silver. . . . Behind it came two other litters and two hammocks in which other leading personages traveled. Then came many men in squadrons with headdresses of gold and silver. As soon as the first entered the square, they parted to make way for the others. As Atahualpa reached the center of the square, he made them all halt, with the litter in which he was traveling and the other litters raised on high. Men continued to enter the square without interruption. A captain came out in front and went up to the fort on the square which contained the artillery" and "in a sense took possession of it with a banner placed on a lance." This stiff banner was Atahualpa's royal standard, with his personal coat of arms.

Atahualpa was surprised to see no Spaniards. He later admitted that he thought they must have hidden from fear at the sight of his magnificent army. "He called out, 'Where are they?' At this Friar Vicente de Valverde, of the Dominican order . . . emerged from the lodging of Governor Pizarro accompanied by the interpreter Martín," "and went with a cross in one hand and his missal in the other. He advanced through the troops to where Atahualpa was."

The various chroniclers who were present gave slightly different versions of the conversation that ensued between Valverde and Atahualpa. Most agreed that the priest began by inviting the Inca to advance into the building to talk and dine with the governor. Ruiz de Arce explained that this invitation was made "in order that he would emerge more from his men." Atahualpa did not accept. He told Valverde that he would not move forward until the Spaniards had returned every object that they had stolen or consumed since their arrival in his kingdom. He may have been establishing a *casus belli* with this difficult demand.

Valverde began to explain his own function as a minister of the Christian religion, and launched into an exposition of "the things of God." He also mentioned that he, a friar, had been sent by the emperor to reveal this religion to Atahualpa and his people. In effect, Valverde was delivering the famous Requirement, an extraordinary document that the royal council had ordered to be proclaimed in any conquest before resorting to bloodshed. The priest said that the doctrine he was describing was contained in the breviary he was holding. "Atahualpa told him to give him the book to examine. He gave it to him closed. Atahualpa did not succeed in opening it, and the friar extended his arm to do so. But Atahualpa struck him on the arm with great disdain, not wishing that he should open it. He himself persisted in trying to open it and did so." He was "more impressed, in my opinion, by the writing itself than by what was written in it. He leafed through [the book], admiring its form and layout. But after examining it, he threw it angrily down among his men, his face a deep crimson." "The boy who was interpreter and was there translating the conversation went running off to fetch the book and gave it to the priest."

The critical moment had come. Xerez and Hernando Pizarro wrote that Atahualpa stood up on his litter, telling his men to make ready. The priest Vicente de Valverde returned to Pizarro, almost running, raising a call to battle. According to Mena, he shouted: "Come out! Come out, Christians! Come at these enemy dogs who reject the things of God. That chief has thrown my book of holy law to the ground!" According to Estete, he cried to Pizarro: "Did you not see what happened? Why remain polite and servile toward this overproud dog when the plains are full of Indians? March out against him, for I absolve you!" And for Trujillo it was: "What is Your Honor going to do? Atahualpa has become a Lucifer!" For Murúa: "Christians! The evangels of God are on the ground!" Juan Ruiz de Arce wrote, simply, that Valverde returned "weeping and calling on God."

Pizarro launched the ambush with the prearranged signal. He "signaled the artilleryman [Pedro de Candía] to fire the cannons into their midst. He fired two of them but could not fire more." The Spaniards in armor and chain mail charged their horses straight into the mass of unarmed natives crowding the square. Trumpets were sounded and the Spanish troops gave their battle cry "Santiago!" "They all placed rattles on their horses to terrify the Indians. . . . With the booming of the shots and the trumpets and the troop of horses with their rattles, the Indians were thrown into confusion and panicked. The Spaniards fell upon them and began to kill." "They were so filled with fear that they climbed on top of one another—to such an extent that they formed mounds and suffocated one another." "The horsemen rode out on top of them, wounding and killing and pressing home the attack." "And since the Indians were unarmed, they were routed without danger to any Christian."

"The governor armed himself with a quilted cotton coat of armor, took his sword and dagger and entered the thick of the Indians with the Spaniards who were with him. With great bravery . . . he reached Atahualpa's litter. He fearlessly grabbed [the Inca's] left arm and shouted "Santiago," . . . but he could not pull him out of his litter, which was on high. All those who were carrying Atahualpa's litter appeared to be important men, and they all died, as did those who were traveling in the litters and hammocks." "Many Indians had their hands cut off but continued to support their ruler's litter with their shoulders. But their efforts were of little avail, for they were all killed." "Although [the Spaniards] killed the Indians who were carrying [the litter], other replacements immediately went to support it. They continued in this way for a long while, overpowering and killing the Indians until, becoming exhausted, one Spaniard stabbed [at the Inca] with his dagger to kill him. But Francisco Pizarro parried the blow, and from this parry the Spaniard trying to strike Atahualpa wounded the governor on the hand. . . . Seven or eight [mounted] Spaniards spurred up and grabbed the edge of the litter, heaved on it and turned it onto its side. Atahualpa was captured in this way and the governor took him to his lodging." "Those who were carrying the litter and those who escorted [the Inca] never abandoned him: all died around him."

Meanwhile the terrible carnage continued in the square and beyond. "They were so terrified at seeing the governor in their midst, at the unexpected firing of the artillery and the irruption of the horses in a troop —which was something they had never seen—that, panic-stricken, they were more concerned to flee and save their lives than to make war." "They could not flee in a body because the gate through which they had entered was small. They therefore could not escape in the confusion. When those at the rear saw how far they were from the sanctuary and safety of flight, two or three thousand of them flung themselves at a stretch of wall and knocked it to the ground. [This wall] gave onto the plain, for on that side there were no buildings." "They broke down a fifteen-foot stretch of wall six feet thick and the height of a man. Many horsemen fell on this." "The foot soldiers set about those who remained in the square with such speed that in a short time most of them were put to the sword. . . . During all this no Indian raised a weapon against a Spaniard."

The cavalry jumped the broken curtain wall and charged out into the plain. "All were shouting, 'After those with the liveries!' 'Do not let any escape!' 'Spear them!' All the other fighting men whom the [Inca] had brought were a quarter of a league [a mile] from Cajamarca and ready for battle, but not an Indian made a move." "When the squadrons of men who had remained in the plain outside the town saw the others fleeing and shouting, most of them broke and took to flight. It was an extraordinary sight, for the entire valley of four or five leagues was completely filled with men." "It was a level plain with some fields of crops. Many Indians were killed. . . . Night had already fallen and the horsemen were continuing to lance [natives] in the fields, when they sounded a trumpet for us to reassemble at the camp. On arrival we went to congratulate the governor on the victory."

"In the space of two hours—all that remained of daylight—all those troops were annihilated. . . . That day, six or seven thousand Indians lay dead on the plain and many more had their arms cut off and other wounds." "Atahualpa himself admitted that we had killed seven thousand of his Indians in that battle." "The man [killed] in one of the litters was his steward (the lord of Chincha), of whom he was very fond. The others were also lords over many people and were his counselors. The cacique lord of Cajamarca died. Other commanders died, but there were so many of them that they go unrecorded. For all those who came in Atahualpa's bodyguard were great lords. . . . It was an extraordinary thing to see so great a ruler captured in so short a time, when he had come with such might." Atahualpa's nephew wrote that the Spaniards killed Indians like a slaughterer felling cattle. The sheer rate of killing was appalling, even if one allows that many Indians died from trampling or suffocation, or that the estimates of dead were exaggerated. Each Spaniard massacred an average of fourteen or fifteen defenseless natives during those terrible two hours.

Atahualpa had been hustled away from the slaughter of his subjects and placed under strong guard in the temple of the sun at the edge of Cajamarca. Some of the cavalry continued to patrol the town in case five or six thousand natives on the hill above might attempt a night attack. Meanwhile, with the bodies of thousands of natives lying in heaps on the square, the victors were paying extraordinary attention to their prisoner. "The governor went to his quarters with his prisoner Atahualpa. He disposed of his clothes, which the Spaniards had torn to pull him from the litter . . . ordered local clothing to be brought, and had him dressed. . . . They then went to dine, and the governor had Atahualpa sit at his table, treating him well and having him served as he was himself. He then ordered him to be given the women he wished from those who had been captured, to serve him, and ordered a bed to be made for him in the room where the governor himself slept."

All this solicitude was accompanied by speeches of amazing condescension. "We entered where Atahualpa was, and found him full of fear, thinking that we were going to kill him." "The governor . . . asked the Inca why he was sad, for he ought not to be sorrowful. . . . In every country to which we Christians had come there had been great rulers, and we had made them our friends and vassals of the emperor by peaceful means or by war. He should not therefore be shocked at having been captured by us." "Atahualpa . . . asked whether the Spaniards were going to kill him. They told him no, for Christians killed with impetuosity but not afterwards."

Atahualpa asked as a favor of the governor to be allowed to speak to any of his people who might be there. "The governor immediately ordered them to bring two leading Indians who had been taken in the battle. The Inca asked them whether many men were dead. They told him that the entire plain was covered with them. He then sent to tell the troops who remained not to flee but to come to serve him, for he was not dead but in the power of the Christians. . . . The governor asked the interpreter what he had said, and the interpreter told him everything."

The Spaniards immediately asked the glaring question: Why had a ruler of Atahualpa's experience and power walked into such an obvious trap? The answer was quite clear. The Inca had totally misjudged and underestimated his opponents. Marcavilca, chief of Poechos, and the noble envoy who had spent two days with the invaders had both seen the Spaniards at their most disorganized. According to Atahualpa, they "had told him that the Christians were not fighting men and that the horses were unsaddled at night. If he [the noble] were given two hundred Indians, he could tie them all up. [Atahualpa said] that this captain and the chief . . . had deceived him."

The Inca admitted the fate he had planned for the strangers. "He answered half smiling that . . . he had intended to capture the governor but the reverse had happened, and for this reason he was so pensive." "He told of his great intentions: what was to have been done with the Spaniards and the horses. . . . He had decided to take and breed the horses and mares, which were the thing he admired most; and to sacrifice some of the Spaniards to the sun and castrate others for service in his household and in guarding his women." There is no reason to doubt this explanation. Atahualpa, flushed with victory in the civil war, could afford to play cat-

and-mouse with the extraordinary strangers that had marched from some other world into the midst of his army. He could not conceive that, with the odds so completely in his favor, the Spaniards would be the first to attack. Nor could he imagine that an attack would come without warning or provocation, before he had even held his meeting with Governor Pizarro.

The Spaniards themselves had acted in terror and desperation, and could scarcely believe the crushing success of their ambush. "Truly, it was not accomplished by our own forces, for there were so few of us. It was by the grace of God, which is great."

Note

References for all quotations can be found in the original version of this piece, in John Hemming's *The Conquest of the Incas* (New York: Harcourt Brace Jovanovich, 1970), pp. 23–45.

IN DEFENSE OF THE INDIANS

Bartolomé de las Casas

Contrary to the stereotype of their monolithic wickedness in the subjugation of the Americas' indigenous peoples, some Spaniards protested the brutality of conquest and colonial rule. None was more influential than Bartolomé de las Casas, the long-lived Dominican bishop of Chiapas in Mexico. Although later to be blamed for supposedly exaggerating his countrymen's cruelty and advocating the enslavement of Africans instead of Indians as a "lesser evil," the aristocratically born Andalusian was a tireless champion of Indian rights. His writings were widely read in colonial Peru. These excerpts from "In Defense of the Indians," a passionate response to court theologian Juan Ginés de Sepúlvedas's assertion of Indian inferiority, give a flavor of his forthright criticism of Spain's role in the New World.

And so what man of sound mind will approve a war against men who are harmless, ignorant, gentle, temperate, unarmed, and destitute of every human defense? For the results of such a war are very surely the loss of the souls of that people who perish without knowing God and without the support of the sacraments, and, for the survivors, hatred and loathing of the Christian religion. Hence the purpose God intends, and for the attainment of which he suffered so much, may be frustrated by the evil and cruelty that our men wreak on them with inhuman barbarity. What will these people think of Christ, the true God of the Christians, when they see Christians venting their rage against them with so many massacres, so much bloodshed without any just cause, at any rate without any just cause that they know of (nor can one even be imagined), and without any fault committed on their [the Indians'] part against the Christians?

What good can come from these military campaigns that would, in the eyes of God, who evaluates all things with unutterable love, compensate for so many evils, so many injuries, and so many unaccustomed misfortunes? Furthermore, how will that nation love us, how will they become our friends (which is necessary if they are to accept our religion), when children see themselves deprived of parents, wives of husbands, and fathers of children and friends? When they see those they love wounded, imprisoned, plundered, and reduced from an immense number to a few? When they see their rulers stripped of their authority, crushed, and afflicted with a wretched slavery? All these things flow necessarily from war. Who is there who would want the gospel preached to himself in such a fashion? Does not this negative precept apply to all men in general: "See that you do not do to another what you would not have done to you by another"? And the same for the affirmative command: "So always treat others as you would like them to treat you." This is something that every man knows, grasps, and understands by the natural light that has been imparted to our minds.

From the fact that the Indians are barbarians it does not necessarily follow that they are incapable of government and have to be ruled by others, except to be taught about the Catholic faith and to be admitted to the holy sacraments. They are not ignorant, inhuman, or bestial. Rather, long before they had heard the word Spaniard they had properly organized states, wisely ordered by excellent laws, religion, and custom. They cultivated friendship and, bound together in common fellowship, lived in populous cities in which they wisely administered the affairs of both peace and war justly and equitably, truly governed by laws that at very many points surpass ours, and could have won the admiration of the sages of Athens. . . . Now what belief will be placed in the Spaniards—greedy, violent, and cruel men who put unarmed and harmless Indians to the sword and rob them with extraordinary avarice? From this we conclude that the Indians, seeing their wicked deeds, commit no sin and do not deserve punishment if they do not accept the gospel. Nor would any nation have been guilty for not accepting the faith of Christ if, supposing the impossible, the Apostles had behaved like the Spaniards. In this regard we have the Lord's statement: "If I had not performed such works among them as no one else has ever done, they would be blameless."

War is not a suitable means for spreading Christ's glory and the truth of the gospel, but rather for making the Christian name hateful and detestable to those who suffer the disasters of war. So war against the Indians, which we call in Spanish *conquistas*, is evil and essentially anti-Christian. For that is not a reason why we may pursue them by war, nor have they ever, even in past centuries, committed any crime against us that would

Figure 8. Indian kicked at an inn. (From Guamán Poma de Ayala, *Nueva Coronica y Buen Gobierno*)

call for war. They have been totally unknown in our regions. Therefore, since war should not be waged unless there has first been a provocation by the person against whom warfare is being prepared toward the one who is waging the war, it follows that war against the Indians is unlawful.

Finally, let all savagery and apparatus of war, which are better suited to Moslems than Christians, be done away with. Let upright heralds be sent to proclaim Jesus Christ in their way of life and to convey the attitudes of Peter and Paul. The Indians will embrace the teaching of the gospel, as I well know, for they are not stupid or barbarous but have a native sincerity and are simple, moderate, and meek, and, finally, such that I do not know whether there is any people readier to receive the gospel. Once they have embraced it, it is marvelous with what piety, eagerness, faith, and charity they obey Christ's precepts and venerate the sacraments. For they are docile and clever, and in their diligence and gifts of nature, they excel most peoples of the known world.

OUR HOUSE

Marco Martos

*Even into the twentieth-century conservative regimes of Benavides and Prado, offi-
cial history celebrated the role of the Spanish in Peru. Francisco Pizarro's bones still
lie in state in Lima's cathedral, just across the Plaza de Armas from an equestrian
monument to the capital's founder. Spain's language, religion, and music—these
imports were seen as the defining pillars of Peruvian culture. Yet the memory of
the conquest as the country's downfall also persisted in the thinking of many Peruvians. The view of a "house divided in spoonfuls" as Spain's legacy to Peru prevails
in this poem from contemporary poet Marco Martos, whose work is characterized
by the sense of irony and moral outrage evident here.*

In galleons, on war-horses, with their lances
and helmets—illiterate the first lot—
they arrived in waves
and in this house which was ours,
right here, they laid down the law.
They were the kings,
they had the weapons.
And when in the end they went
after some deaths, shootings and treaties,
as a legacy, they left us
their blood and the cross, a language and nothing;
the house divided
in spoonfuls.
Now neighbors, invited guests,
starving beggars, all claim us as their own.

THE TRAGEDY OF SUCCESS

Steve J. Stern

Colonial rule meant impoverishment and death for millions of indigenous Peru-
vians. The conquest's trauma fueled the Taki Onqoy (literally, "dancing sickness")
movement of the 1560s, where Indians possessed by Andean deities prophesied the
expulsion of the Spaniards and their Christian God. Yet as historian Steve J. Stern
underscores in this excerpt from his book on the south-central Andean province of
Huamanga, there was also economic and social differentiation within the "republic
of Indians." In addition to his emphasis on the very different experiences of Indian
commoners and elites under Spanish rule, Stern shows the bustling and conten-
tious vigor of Huamanga's colonial society, forcing us to reassess the common view
of the supposed isolation and "timelessness" of Peru's Andean interiors.

In Huamanga, if one saw a gallant figure dressed in rose velvet breeches
with fine gold trim, bright doublet beneath a dark velveteen cape from
Segovia, broad felt hat, and a pair of good shoes, one probably expected
to see the face of a wealthy colonial, or perhaps even a mestizo. Sometimes, however, the face belonged to an Indian. The growing poverty of
Andean peoples by the early seventeenth century could lead us to overlook the rise of natives who escaped severe burdens imposed upon most
Indians, in some cases climbed the social ladder, and accumulated considerable wealth.

Several studies of colonial Peru have suggested the historical importance of privileged strata within the "republic of Indians." There was an
embryonic potential for class divisions among Huamanga's societies before Spanish conquest, but certain institutions stifled their further development. After conquest, the strategic position of Hispanizing *kurakas,* or
chiefs, as mediators between natives and colonials intensified incipient

contradictions in native society; the post-Incaic alliances caught native elites between traditional roles as protectors of *ayllu* [communal] interests, and new opportunities and demands as "friends" of the conquistadores. During the crisis of the 1560s, the Taki Onquoy movement pressured collaborators of the colonial regime to purify themselves and renew exclusively Andean loyalties, but the tenuous and guarded relationship of Indian elites to the uprising mirrored their ambivalent, contradictory position. A decade later, Toledo's reforms organized a network of state power to coerce a surplus out of a self-sufficient *ayllu* peasantry; the system worked in part because its power groups incorporated Indian as well as Hispanic lords.

The Indians eventually undermined Toledan *mitas* [forced labor] and tributes, but not the emergence of multiracial power groups. Indeed, judicial politics encouraged mutually beneficial arrangements among native elites and Hispanic patrons who sometimes profited by subverting state-sponsored extractions. The economic boom of the late sixteenth century integrated local societies into a highly commercialized economy; local commodity-circulation patterns induced internal differentiation even further, concentrating Indian resources in fewer hands, and privatizing a proportion of *ayllu* lands. From the first years of conquest, but with increasing force in the seventeenth century, *ayllu* society lost migrants to cities, mines, commercial centers, Spanish patrons, and foreign Indian communities. Some of the migrants learned skills or developed connections that saved them from the fate of poor Indians and enabled them to join the ranks of those who profited from the commercial economy.

The personal strategies and achievements of successful Indians, who assimilated in important ways to Hispanic-mestizo society, bear a close relationship to the broader history of European exploitation and Indian resistance. Their achievements stimulated a process of class differentiation within native society, inserted European-style relationships, motivations, and culture more directly into peasant life, and furthered the shrinkage of traditional Andean rights and resources. The tragedy of Indian success lay in the way it recruited dynamic, powerful, or fortunate individuals to adopt Hispanic styles and relationships, thereby buttressing colonial domination. The achievements of native individuals, in the midst of a society organized to exploit indigenous peoples, educated Indians to view the Hispanic as superior, the Andean as inferior.

Paths to Success

Despite conditions that severely impoverished most natives by the early seventeenth century, a minority managed to accumulate sufficient funds to buy or rent valuable rural and urban property. A sample of fifty-two transactions shows that many Indians who bought or rented lands and homesteads spent sums far beyond the economic horizons of most natives. Fully half (50.0 percent) the purchases cost 40–90 pesos (of 8 *reales*); another fourth (28.3 percent) required 100 pesos or more. These represented large sums for an Indian. The state's annual tribute, a heavy burden for many, amounted to less than ten pesos; an unskilled *asiento* Indian earned perhaps twenty pesos for an entire year's service; an expenditure of thirty pesos to rent a *mitayo* replacement was unrealistic for a poor peasant.[1]

Even by Hispanic standards, some Indian purchases represented significant accumulations. One woman bought part of a fine city lot owned by a distinguished *encomendero* family.[2] The 300 pesos she spent equaled eight or nine months of the profit expected by a master who rented out a skilled slave artisan. Juana Payco and Don Pedro Pomaconxa each bought valuable lands from foreign *ayllus* for 600 pesos. That amount of money sufficed, in most years, to buy a prime African slave. Some transactions, especially purchase or rental of city residences by Indians whose economic base remained in the countryside, fulfilled prestige desires. To establish a respectable residence in Huamanga, one *kuraka* shunned a site in the city's Indian parishes; instead, he rented homes in the finer, more expensive Spanish section.

Even as monetary obligations and debt became increasingly oppressive forces in the lives of poor Indians, an emerging sector of natives accumulated enough liquid wealth to become creditors. The wills of prosperous Indians recorded lists of uncollected petty debts. Native artisans and other "credible" figures served as bondsmen of Indians in debt or in trouble. Some loans were more than petty in size. Lorenzo Pilco, born to a wealthy Indian family in the city of Huamanga, and owner of valuable lands in rural Angaraes, loaned 300 pesos to an impoverished *kuraka*. Pilco eventually had the chief jailed for lack of payment. Significantly, even Spaniards turned to wealthy Indians for credit on occasion. One Spaniard secured a one-year loan of 140 pesos from Doña Juana Méndez; another paid 50 pesos of interest a year on a long-term loan of 700 pesos from Catalina Reinoso, an Indian gentlewoman who owned a vineyard in the Nazca Valley descending from Lucanas to the Pacific coast.

The historical question we must ask is how an emerging sector of wealthy Indians earned such funds and protected themselves from expropriations that confined most natives to a meager existence. The economic and political means by which a minority of Indians achieved success, in a society that had despoiled most *ayllus* and peasants of the capacity to produce and market a surplus, warrant close examination.

In a thriving commercial economy heavily dependent on artisanal or craft technologies, those who sold skilled services might earn substantial incomes. Experienced mine workers commanded handsome wages in the seventeenth century. Inflated prices controlled by outside merchants, respites from a harsh existence in drinking and gambling, and fraudulent abuses by mine owners often consumed wages quickly. But some Indians probably managed to accumulate savings, by setting aside significant amounts of wages or stealing valuable ores. More attractive than mining were artisanry and transport, relatively independent forms of work for which there was high demand. Huamanga's economy relied heavily on skilled trades and crafts for construction and manufactures, and Indian artisans assumed a prominent role in all kinds of "Hispanic" occupations, as silversmiths, painters and gilders, masons, stonecutters, carpenters, joiners, tanners, tailors, shoemakers, and the like. Martín de Oviedo, a Spaniard with a strong reputation as a "master sculptor" and architect, was hired in 1609 to refurbish the interior of the Dominican church for 4,600 pesos; Oviedo, in turn, subcontracted for Indian carpenters, painters, and gilders to work on the project. An independent Indian craftsman could earn a very respectable income. In two months, a stonecutter could fashion a water wheel worth sixty pesos. Juan Uscamato, a carpenter, earned 150 pesos by agreeing to build a flour mill in six months. His expenses were low, and he probably did not have to work full time on the mill, since the contractor agreed to supply needed materials, including carved stone and iron tools, and six Indian laborers to work under Uscamato.

The *asiento* labor contracts of Huamanga show a dramatic income gap between skilled Indians and unspecialized laboring peons. Artisans hired in *asientos* earned double or triple the wages promised for general service, some 40–60 pesos a year besides subsistence. *Arrieros* (muleteers, drivers of animal trains) earned at least twice as much again, some 80–130 pesos a year. The nonmonetary components of the compensation often included special rights which widened the gap further. One tanner received ten semifinished hides that, in effect, subsidized his independent work. *Arrieros* received a few extra yards of cloth to stock their wares.

More important, the drivers' work helped them consolidate independent trading connections and lower their own business costs by transporting commodities on employers' animals, as in the case of the employer who formally agreed that his hired *arriero* could make "all the trips he wants with [the employer's] animal train."

Concessions such as these mattered because those who engaged in substantial trade or commercial production could accumulate great wealth. Indian merchants, like Spaniards, speculated in commodities. Artisans, unlike *arrieros*, could not pursue commerce full time, but ambitious craftsmen engaged in varied mercantile transactions on the side. Indians, like Spaniards, carved out private landholdings for commercial production of coca, wine, maize, wheat, vegetables, wool, meat, hides, cheese, and the like. Indeed, Indian entrepreneurs tended to focus their accumulations of private property in the very zones that attracted their Spanish counterparts: the well-located and fertile valleys of the Angaraes-Huanta district, the city of Huamanga and its surrounding valleys, the coca *montaña* [jungles] of eastern Huanta, and, to a lesser extent, fertile pastures and farmlands along the road that cut across Vilcashuamán to Cuzco and Potosí.

Marketable skills and services, commercial production, and trade itself earned Indians considerable revenues, but they do not explain how a successful minority protected its wealth from expropriation. *Ayllus* too had earned very impressive incomes in the sixteenth century, but colonial control made such accumulation increasingly difficult, if not impossible, for most *ayllus* in the seventeenth century. The economic function of the colonial power structure was, after all, to usurp Indian resources and to siphon the surplus of a native society reduced to bare subsistence. *Kurakas* enjoyed greater access to revenues than common households, but redistributive obligations presumably limited the capacity of chiefs to accumulate personal resources while kinfolk slid deeper into poverty. Indeed, the chiefs' personal liability for community obligations, especially tribute and *mita*, sometimes forced them to sell valuable lands or animals, and subjected their wealth to confiscation by *corregidores* [magistrates]. The periodic *composiciones de tierras* permitted colonial judges to award title to "surplus" Indian lands requested by Spanish petitioners.[3] In practice, the land inspections made *ayllu* land tenure a precarious proposition. To avoid dependence on a European overlord, a *forastero* might seek a livelihood in a new Indian community setting.[4] But earning the acceptance of foreign *ayllus* might entail new kinship bonds, or payments of rent for land-use rights, which limited accumulation.

Under these circumstances, earning a respectable income did not, by itself, insure one against impoverishment. Indians could achieve lasting economic success only if their socioeconomic "strategy" shielded them, in part at least, from colonial expropriations and from redistributive obligations to poorer Indians. A key shielding device involved "privatizing" property rights. Individual title to land, recognized by Spanish law, protected the owner from legal confiscations that befell *ayllu* property. Private ownership of property also provided a weapon against overlapping or collective claims by *ayllus* and ethnic groups, especially if the owner accumulated lands in "foreign" zones, i.e., outside the domain traditionally claimed by the Indian's *ayllu* or ethnic relatives. But even within a given *ayllu* or ethnic domain, a process of privatization transferred a proportion of property rights to powerful or wealthy local Indians, and to wealthy outsiders of all races. During the first *composición de tierras*, held in 1594, some of Huamanga's *kurakas* secured private title to extensive land-use rights traditionally allotted them by *ayllus*. A *kuraka* who wished to protect his prestige or to work the lands by calling upon traditional *ayllu* relationships probably could not alienate such lands from collective claims in an absolute sense. But we know that *kurakas* sold or rented some of these lands to outsiders, and that in later generations, children who "inherited" lands from deceased chiefs defended their property rights against Indian relatives. Even if a chief (or his heirs) did not privatize *ayllu* property for his own use, he held authority to sell community lands in order to pay tributes or to hire *mitayo* replacements. Such sales alienated property from ethnic and *ayllu* domains in a more permanent sense. Fertile lands once held by *ayllus* circulated as commodities on a surprising scale in the seventeenth century, especially in dynamic commercial zones of northern Huamanga, and the buyers of valuable property included Indians as well as Spaniards and mixed-bloods.

Another form of protection lay in escaping tribute and *mita* obligations. A household continually drained by contributions to pay *ayllu* tributes or hire *mitayo* replacements could hardly expect to accumulate money sufficient to buy lucrative property, even if it earned a significant monetary income. The colonial regime, however, exempted certain natives from *mita* and tribute, and Spanish law failed to incorporate the large *forastero* population systematically until the eighteenth century.

The evidence suggests that the privilege of exemption brought considerable benefits. Tributary status did not apply to independent women heads of household, and women accounted for over a third (35.8 percent) of Indian purchases or rentals of property. *Forasteros* and artisans also played a conspicuous role in private accumulations of property. The *forasteros'* ill-defined legal status freed them from *mita* and tribute as long as they escaped tax collectors sent from their original communities; artisans, both village and urban, held legal exemption from the *mita.* Finally, major *kurakas*, municipal functionaries (mostly officers of the Indian *cabildo*, or town council), and lay assistants of Catholic priests all enjoyed exemptions from *mita* and some of them, from tribute. A few earned modest salaries as well. Within *ayllu* society, therefore, appointments to municipal and church posts distributed privileges which allowed some people to accumulate resources while others eked out a bare existence or fell into debt.

A third form of shielding, and one that increased opportunities for economic gain dramatically, exploited privileged ties to the colonial power structure. Within *ayllu* society especially, access to power often proved a decisive determinant of revenues and obligations. Powerful *ayllus* and favored relatives of *kurakas* paid lighter tributes than others, and the *kurakas* themselves levied extra tributes. The Toledan regime had reorganized the countryside by establishing a series of multiracial power groups, with a Spanish *corregidor* at the center, but including a contingent of Indian functionaries and assistants. The revamped Indian power structure drew its members from important *kuraka* families, socially mobile commoners eager to benefit by association with Hispanic power, and (in the seventeenth century, at least) a few *forasteros* integrated into local *ayllu* societies. Judicial politics further cemented alliances between Indian elites and Hispanic patrons. The assistance of Hispanic patrons brought with it a quid pro quo: loyalty to the interests of "friends," cooperation in local schemes of extraction. In effect, local alliances assimilated an elite fraction of *ayllu* society to the Hispanic power structure, and thus to the conversion of political advantage into private wealth. The liability of *kurakas* for community tribute and *mita*, for example, theoretically subjected chiefs to confiscations of wealth that might have impoverished them in the seventeenth century. Some confiscations did indeed occur, but often *kurakas* enlisted the aid of *corregidores* and priests to "prove" that *mita* and tribute quotas had been set too high. Instead of losing resources to pay for tributes in arrears, a *kuraka* could earn thousands of pesos by joining Hispanic friends in mutually profitable schemes, such as putting-out systems to sell cloth or rope woven by *ayllus.* The burden of such schemes and the reduced quotas of legal *mitas* and tributes fell most heavily on the least powerful and poorest segments of native society.

The differentiation of native society into rich and poor reflected the ability of a minority to free itself from constraints that bound most Indians. We ought not underestimate the difficulty of such achievements, especially for natives who did not inherit advantages by birth into powerful or wealthy Indian families. For the great majority the road to success was closed. Daring decisions did not guarantee prosperity. Emigration from the society of one's relatives, perhaps the boldest step an Indian might take, led some individuals to success, but prosperous emigrants were a minority. Most *forasteros* lived a more modest existence as *yanaconas*, day laborers, petty producers, community peasants integrated by marriage into foreign *ayllus*, vagrants, and the like.[5] Artisanry exerted a special appeal precisely because it offered the surest path to economic improvement and independence. Prospective apprentices flocked to cities to find artisans willing to teach them a trade in exchange for their labors.

Those who earned relatively high incomes, of course, did not automatically accumulate "private" resources shielded from overlapping or redistributive claims by poorer relatives. Women heads of household, for example, enjoyed legal exemptions from *mitas* and tributes, and participated heavily in commercial production and trade. But ties of kinship and obligation meant—in some cases, at least—that apparently "private" resources in fact helped to shore up the faltering economic base of poorer kinfolk, including male tributaries. In these cases, "success" was less individualized, more subject to a web of overlapping rights that redistributed accumulations.

By the seventeenth century, however, an emerging strata of ambitious Indians superseded such obstacles and accumulated impressive personal wealth. As we shall see, the success of these natives changed the very texture of Indian life.

The Social Significance of Indian Hispanism

Above all else, Indian success rested upon one's capacity to imitate Hispanic strategies of accumulation or to develop close ties with Hispanic-mestizo society. The material well-being of these Indians no longer depended, as it had for their ancestors, on their ability to mobilize traditional forms of property, reciprocal obligation, and loyalty within an ancient family of *ayllu* and ethnic relatives. Their economic welfare came to depend primarily upon their capacity to privatize interests in a commercial setting: to accumulate private property, exploit commercial opportunities, and convert political influence, service, or privilege into liquid wealth. For these Indians, rural commodity circulation and a certain monetization of obligations represented an opportunity, not a burden or a symptom of declining self-sufficiency. The penetration of commercial capital into the countryside created opportunities to buy lands, to extend commercial networks, to consolidate influence as creditors to those trapped in a quagmire of tributes, corvées, subsistence problems, and debts.

A certain Hispanization of property and relationships, linked to the emergence of successful natives, thus began to remold the internal structure of Indian society. The process of Hispanization, like the internal differentiation it mirrored, was only partial or incomplete. *Ayllu* reciprocities and property rights still constituted an important resource for many Indians. But those who continued to depend exclusively upon "traditional" rights were condemned to poverty, and by the early seventeenth century, relations between rich and poor Indians began to take on a more "Hispanic" tonality and texture. Wealthy Indians no longer depended upon the collective claims of *ayllus* and ethnic groups for access to property; they acquired private title to the best Indian lands, both in *ayllu* homelands and among foreign Indians. Commercial transactions and debt forged new bonds and dependencies superseding those of kinship and reciprocal obligation. Wealthy and powerful natives looked beyond traditional Andean reciprocities for access to labor, and resorted to Hispanic methods of labor exploitation. Indian miners, coca planters, and *hacendados* attached dependent laborers to their properties and hired temporary workers for wages. On occasion, a prominent Indian even secured an official *mita* allotment! In 1598, Viceroy Luis de Velasco granted the Indian Doña Isabel Asto, a rich miner and widow of a Spaniard, sixty *mitayos* to work her mines in Huancavelica. In one of ten (10.3 percent) *asiento* labor contracts in Huamanga, the hired Indian worked for an Indian master. The employers, some of them artisans hiring apprentices, were clearly men and women of considerable means. One Indian merchant could afford to pay a hired *arriero* 100 pesos a year in wages. Another employer, Catalina Cocachimbo, recruited a *yanacona* by lending an Indian 150 pesos. Adopting both the form and content used by Hispanic colonials, she contracted the peon to work for her at 20 pesos a year to repay the debt; after one year, he would receive a plot of land to grow his own food.

In June 1630, for example, the Indians and chiefs of Guaychao had to sell valuable community lands to an outsider to raise funds. Yet in the very same month Pedro Alopila, a local *ayllu* Indian, bought for himself some twelve hectares of irrigable maize lands from a Spanish landowner. Internal differentiation opened the door to new relationships far removed from traditional bonds among *originarios*.[6] Consider, for example, the career of Juana Marcaruray, a woman who retained her *ayllu* presence and identity until her death. Within the region of her *ayllu* homeland, she accumulated seven private properties (including two coca fields), indebted various members of the community, and collected rent from Indian tenants on her property.

The case of Don Juan Uybua and Sebastián Cabana, *ayllu* Indians of the same village, is also revealing. Uybua, a local *kuraka*, paid a debt of 90 pesos owed by Cabana, who was accused of losing four cows and three horses. But Uybua's act hardly represented the traditional generosity expected of a chief bound by long-term reciprocities with kinfolk. The two Indians apparently belonged to different (though related) *ayllus*, and Uybua used the debt to make a typically "Hispanic" arrangement. To "repay" the loan, Cabana had to agree to a labor *asiento* binding him to Uybua for almost seven years! Uybua would placate the indebted peon's *kurakas* by paying them the annual tribute owed by Cabana.

The emerging Indian elite of the seventeenth century thus embraced strategies and relationships drawn from the dominant, exploiting sector of society. Increasingly, Hispanic models of advancement offered the only way out of confines that shackled most Indians. Those whose personal success required a Hispanization, however partial, of their economic lives included *originarios* as well as *forasteros*, socially mobile commoners as well as *kurakas*, permanent city dwellers as well as Indians who maintained homes and bases in both city and countryside. Not surprisingly, the material culture and technology of Indian production bore witness to the process of Hispanization. Artisans used Spanish tools and materials in their shops; ranchers raised herds of cows and sheep; farmers harnessed plows to oxen to till wheat fields. To a certain extent, the spread of Hispanic material culture was more generalized than that suggested here, particularly as growing numbers of Indians produced "Spanish" commodities such as eggs or beef, or served as peons to Spanish overlords. But the material "Hispanization" of Indian production was more closely associated with wealthy Indians, including chiefs.

The spread of Hispanic "culture," moreover, was not confined to resources used in material production. Wealthy Indians bought and used the accoutrements of cultured Spanish folk. They wore fine clothes (made in Europe), traveled on horse and saddle, bought furniture, jewelry, and trinkets for their homes, enjoyed wine with meals, and owned Span ish firearms and swords. The successful (or pretentious) appropriated the Spanish titulature of Don or Doña, and acquired urban predilections. Even if their livelihood kept them in the countryside much of the time, wealthy Indians established second homes in which to live and do business in Huamanga or other cities. A few cultured natives even read and wrote Spanish. In 1621, the Jesuits opened the Royal School of San Francisco de Borja, a boarding school in Cuzco that taught Spanish language, religion, and culture to sons of major *kurakas* from Huamanga, Cuzco, and Arequipa. The new school represented a small part of a much broader educational process, formal and informal, long underway, which created a growing sector of *ladino* Indians. The *ladinos* were people of Indian parentage whose culture, demeanor, and lifeways took on a more mestizo or even Spanish character. They knew the ways of Spanish-mestizo society, dressed in nontraditional garb, understood and spoke Spanish, and in some cases even cut their hair. In cities and mining centers especially, *ladino* traits spread through the Indian population far beyond the successful, prospering elite. But the most "Hispanic," least "mestizo" or "Indian," of the *ladinos* were those whose socioeconomic stature allowed them to buy fine clothes, mix in Spanish circles, get an education, and the like.

Apparently, the successful valued their Hispanism highly. Juana Hernández, owner of at least eighty-five hectares of wheat and corn fields near Julcamarca (Angaraes), proudly called herself "a *ladina* Indian, and very intelligent in Spanish language." Indians spent considerable sums —200 pesos for a suit of clothes, 50 pesos for a gun—to collect Spanish items. Don Fernando Ataurimachi of Huamanguilla (Huanta), descendant of the Inca Huayna Capac, related by kinship to Spaniards, and owner of urban property and irrigated corn lands, collected Spanish guns, lances, halberds, and swords. The proud Ataurimachi made a point of showing off his collection at great public festivals.

Some of the Hispanizing Indians took Christian religion quite seriously. The defeat of Taki Onqoy, of course, made plain that all Indians needed to avoid the wrath of powerful Christian gods. To placate the gods and their priests, peasants submitted to a thin overlay of Christian ritual. Catholicism might have enjoyed somewhat greater acceptance among city Indians cut off from rural kin networks and ancestor-gods. But the evidence suggests a striking enthusiasm on the part of wealthy Indians in both city and countryside. Ataurimachi of Huamanguilla married his Indian wife in a Christian ceremony supervised by a Catholic priest. Successful Indians led the native *cofradías* [Catholic lay associations], sought Christian burial in places of honor—"inside the church next to the pulpit"—and had masses said for their souls. Some donated lands, animals, and money to the church, or set up ecclesiastical benefices to look after their souls. Some Indians, of course, had good reason to profess Christianity; they had climbed in social and economic station by serving Catholic priests as sextons (*sacristanes*), choir leaders (*cantores*), and the like.

But others, too, developed close bonds with Christian gods and their representatives on earth. Catalina Pata, a city Indian of Huamanga, bought a huge crucifix that stood a yard and a half tall in her home. Her son, a wealthy artisan, donated lands to the Augustinians "on the condition that the day I die they accompany me . . . and give me a burial inside their church and sing a mass [for my soul]." The will of Don Diego Quino Guaracu, a minor chief of Andahuaylas, named Friar Lucas de Sigura executor of the Indian's estate. Quino gave the priest, apparently a close friend, control of a handsome ecclesiastical benefice of lands sufficient to support nine or ten peasant families. In addition, Quino ordered that his daughter be raised in Huamanga's convent of Santa Clara, "where she might grow up civilized and Christian." For these Indians, Christianization—which by no means excluded continuance of traditional paganisms—constituted far more than a superficial overlay. Like the secular symbols of Hispanism, Christian religion expressed relationships and aspirations that deeply touched their lives.

In a society where "cultural" and "economic" dimensions of life interpenetrated one another deeply, Indian Hispanism had profound symbolic importance. Andean culture esteemed cloth highly as a ritual article and as an emblem of ethnic affiliation and social position. Natives who wore fine Hispanic clothes vividly expressed an aspiration to move beyond a condemned Indian past and merge into the upper strata of colonial society. Andean thought interpreted "religious" relationships as a mutual exchange that provided material reward to those who served the gods. Christian devotion by wealthy Indians symbolized their attempt to nurture a mutually beneficial interchange with the Hispanic world, its gods (including saints) as well as its people.

Symbolically, then, cultural Hispanism expressed the socioeconomic orientation of an emerging Indian elite whose acquisition of private property, pursuit of commercial gain, and social relationships tended to differentiate them from the Andean peasantry and to assimilate them to an exploitative class of aristocrat-entrepreneurs. Even in the case of modestly successful Indians (small farmers, urban artisans, and the like) who did not develop direct relationships with *ayllu* peasants, dependent retainers, or contracted laborers, their differentiation as a class of small independent producers represented a drain on the resources and labor-power available to *ayllu* society. And the most impressive success stories tended to create a strata of "Europeans" with Indian skin and faces, a provincial elite whose Andean heritage and connections enabled it to inject Hispanic-style relationships, motivations, and culture all the more deeply into the fabric of Indian life.

But the ties between Hispanism and Indian success were sometimes more direct than those implied by mere imitation of European models, or a reproduction of Hispanic styles and relationships within native society. One recalls that Doña Isabel Asto, Don Fernando Ataurimachi, and Don Diego Quino Guaracu all had Spanish relatives or friends. As we have seen, ambitious Indians sought Spanish allies or benefactors for protection or advancement; Spanish individuals and power groups, in turn, enhanced their authority and economic potential by cultivating a clientele of Indian allies and functionaries. Success drew an Indian into Hispanic-mestizo circles, and oppression created desires to find a better life by associating with non-Indian sectors of society. A minority of Indians developed close social bonds outside native society. They bought Indian lands on behalf of colonials, donated or willed property to non-Indian friends, and appointed Spaniards executors of their estates. In a number of cases, the bonds between Indians and Spaniards even included marriage and kinship.

To the Spanish elites, marriage to native women from influential or wealthy families brought social connections and dowries. Even a high elite family consented to such arrangements if the Indian woman enjoyed a sufficiently noble background. The descendants of Antonio de Oré, an esteemed pre-Toledan *encomendero*, proudly documented their aristocratic Spanish genealogy. The Oré pride, however, did not prevent Antonio's son Gerónimo from marrying an Inca noblewoman.

More often, lesser or aspiring elites sought to gain or extend footholds in the countryside of Huanta, Angaraes, and Vilcashuamán by marrying Indian women. Juan Ramírez Romero had a notoriously exploitative reputation when he served as lieutenant of a rural *corregidor* from 1601 to 1606. This ambitious *hacendado* and "citizen" of Vilcashuamán, owner of extensive ranches, farms, and sugar fields, probably made his first inroads by marrying Doña María Cusiocllo. Ramírez observed that "my father-in-law," a local *kuraka*, had given him much of the property as dowry. Not far away, an Indian-white couple, Doña Beatriz Guarcay Ynquillay and

Don Cristóbal de Gamboa, owned sixty hectares of land donated by her brother, chief *kuraka* of Vischongo, "to cancel his sister's rights . . . in the property of their father Don Juan Pomaquiso."

For some Indian women, marriage or informal conjugal relations with outsiders had its attractions. The daughters of Indian chiefs may have had little choice in the matter, but wealthy or ambitious women shared the Hispanic orientation of their male counterparts. María López, an Indian, acquired several urban properties in Huamanga during her marriage to a respectable Spanish resident. When her husband died, she established an informal relationship and had a child with Gaspar de Arriola, a wealthy "citizen" of Huamanga "to whom I am much obligated for good works." Arriola contributed valuable lands to the support of López and their illegitimate son. More humble Indian women, too, had reason to pursue relations with outsiders. Young males seemed to experience a kind of life crisis on the threshold of marriage and tributary responsibilities; some fled and swelled the *forastero* population. Young women facing the grim burdens of *ayllu* life must have experienced crises and tensions of their own, especially if they had a chance to "escape" by marrying outsiders —*forastero* Indians, free blacks, mixed-bloods, or Spaniards. Among the *originario* population, women usually outnumbered men anyway. Some women made the jump and did well. Juana Curiguamán, for example, married a free mulatto, Alonso de Paz; not far from her homeland in Soras, they bought a modest hacienda worth 600–700 pesos. Describing the situation, Felipe Guamán Poma de Ayala of Lucanas complained that Indian women "no longer love Indians but rather Spaniards, and they become big whores." His remark expressed male resentment; it underestimated the importance of force and sexual assault in many Indian-white relationships and ignored the women whose lives and resources remained bonded to Indian kinfolk (of both sexes). Nevertheless, Poma's exaggeration corresponded to a very real social pattern, to a Hispanic allure that attracted both female and male.

At its highest levels, Indian success signified a fuller emergence of class relationships within seventeenth-century native society. Hispanism was a path to success for a small minority, but it also tended to transform the prosperous into foreigners—people whose economic relations, social bonds, and cultural symbols differentiated them from poorer, more "Indian" counterparts and imparted a Hispanic-mestizo dimension to their identities. In any given rural terrain, the emerging provincial elite included a strong component of "outsiders" anyway—*forastero* Indians, Spanish colonials and officials, mestizos (some of them heirs of Indian-white marriages among local elites), occasionally a black or mulatto. But even a local *ayllu* Indian acquired a more alien character if success violated community norms or assimilated the native to outside exploiters. Poma observed an erosion of major *kurakas'* legitimacy among kinfolk; social climbers who had usurped chieftainships from rightful heirs, and chiefs whose social and economic activities allied them with hated colonials "are no longer obeyed nor respected." Consider also the will of Juana Marcaruray, a wealthy *ayllu* Indian with no children. Marcaruray left her considerable estate to her friend Doña Mariana de Balaguera, wife of the municipal standard-bearer of Huamanga, "in view of [my] having received very many good works, worthy of greater reward, from her household." Traditionally, property rights would have reverted to *ayllu* relatives if the deceased left no spouse or children.

Success tended to draw the most dynamic and powerful members of native society—*originarios* as well as *forasteros*, villagers as well as city folk—into the world of aristocrat-entrepreneurs, and thereby widened the social basis of colonial exploitation. The question we may ask is whether this tendency met with any kind of resistance. As we shall see, considerable tension and conflict marred the achievements of successful Indians.

Strife, Tension, and Purification

In a society where ethnic loyalties continued to set communities against one another, *forasteros* who intruded on *ayllu* domains contended with hostilities that sometimes flared into open conflict. Catalina Puscotilla, an "Indian hacendada," held 130 hectares of prime land near the village of Espíritu Santo, midway between the urban markets of Huancavelica and Huamanga. The zone's waters, ecology, and location made it especially important for commercial agriculture, and Puscotilla's Indian husband had agreed in 1625 to pay the Crown 298 pesos for legal title to the land. The local Quiguares Indians bitterly disputed the award of valuable property to outsiders, however, and a classic hacienda-community conflict festered for decades. In the 1640s Puscotilla, now a widow, was still fending off the Quiguares, as well as a mestizo rival who had entered the fray. Lorenzo Pilco, a wealthy city Indian and "master shoemaker," encountered similar problems in the countryside. To end litigation with the Angaraes Indians of Pata, Pilco resorted to an expedient well known to Spanish entrepreneurs. He simply paid the Indians, who could ill afford protracted legal struggles anyway, seventy pesos to withdraw their suit.

Outsiders could gain more acceptance by integrating themselves into community life and responsibilities, but such integration gave local Indians a means to exert pressure for redistribution of wealth. In 1642 Clemente de Cháves, a *ladino* from Huamanga, spent thirty pesos to buy a modest amount of land from a wealthy *ayllu* Indian of Huanta. The fact that Cháves married and settled in the area, and "helps [the community] serve the mitas of Huancavelica" undoubtedly stabilized his presence. A wealthier *forastero*, Don Diego de Rojas, married Teresa Cargua of Lucanas Andamarcas. Rojas apparently won the esteem of his new kinfolk, for he served as chief of their small *ayllu*. Acceptance of Rojas's leadership probably derived from his willingness to submit to local reciprocities that demanded "generosity" on the part of chiefs. An Indian as wealthy and powerful as a Lorenzo Pilco, who had a *kuraka* jailed for failure to pay a debt, might shun obligations that limited one's capacity to accumulate or privatize wealth. But if he did, the intruder risked the same conflicts and litigations that afflicted Spanish entrepreneurs.

Conflict between *ayllu* Indians and wealthy *forasteros* is readily understandable, but Poma's observation that *kurakas* lost "respect" as they were integrated into the colonial political and economic structure suggests the development of more precarious, forced relations between chiefs and "their" people. At times, loss of confidence in the reciprocal exchanges that bound chiefs and *ayllu* peasants erupted in outright refusals to obey an "illegitimate" request. In Vilcashuamán, for example, some Papres and Chilques *kurakas* and Spanish priests decided that *ayllus* ought to plant nearly 300 hectares of wheat to earn funds for local churches and *cofradías*. When the peasants discovered that they would not be paid for their work, resistance grew so fierce that the project had to be abandoned. A chief who lost legitimacy among kinfolk faced serious problems beyond those of simple disobedience. Emigration of *ayllu* Indians might increase; complaints to Spanish officials might undermine ethnic or *ayllu* authority; rivals to a chieftainship might secure a following and embroil local society in a civil war.

A new tension thus entered the relationship of major chiefs and *ayllu* peasants. To shore up the legitimacy that made *ayllu* households responsive to their requests, chiefs had to demonstrate loyalties and perform services for *ayllus* and ethnic groups. Probably such services included skillful leadership in judicial politics and other defenses against extractive relations; "generosity" in redistributing wealth to poorer kinfolk; enforcement of a "fair" distribution of burdens and rights within the community of producer-relatives; and symbolic expressions of solidarity with *ayllu* and ethnic relatives. These services enhanced prestige among kin, but they also limited the degree to which a chief could privatize resources and interests, or function as a reliable partner of colonial power groups. The structural position of ambitious chiefs thus embodied a deep contradiction. To operate effectively, with minimal force, required that chiefs earn the confidence of kin, but too zealous a defense of *ayllu* interests handicapped their ability to accumulate wealth or pursue private gain. *Kurakas* were conspicuous among the Indians whose "Hispanic" success differentiated them from the seventeenth-century peasantry, but their success eroded some of the "influence" associated with traditional reciprocity relationships. The result was a more strained, suspicious relationship in which conflict, coercion, and economic power acquired added importance.

Similar tensions probably accompanied the success of *originarios* who never held an important chieftainship. In the final analysis, *ayllu* Indians did not readily accept the legitimacy of a complete alienation of resources from the fabric of community life and authority. Wealthy *ayllu* Indians, *kurakas* or not, faced a network of relatives, *ayllus*, and ethnic groups who claimed overlapping rights to "private" lands and revenues. Indeed, *kurakas* sometimes used their position as spokesmen of the community to expropriate or redistribute the "private" property of wealthy *ayllu* rivals, including women. *Ayllu* enemies countered with legal suits to protect their resources. Such conflicts exacerbated the erosion of the chiefs' moral authority and hardly lessened resentments created by networks of private interest and wealth, much of it beyond the control of *ayllu* society. Beyond a certain point, privatization of resources alienated not just the resources attached to the owner, but the owner too, from *ayllu* Indians.

By the early seventeenth century, then, the success of a minority amidst growing pauperization created new strains in native Andean life. Indian Hispanism—as a socioeconomic strategy and as a set of cultural symbols —constituted for some a path to economic success and at least the pretense of social respectability. But to those left behind, especially the *ayllu* peasantry, it represented a powerful, oppressive force in the very heart of rural society. Hispanism symbolized the conversion of Indian society's foremost figures into partners of colonial rule and exploitation, a widening split of interests, loyalties, and orientations that accompanied differentiation into rich and poor. It symbolized, too, a loss of "confidence" that touched all sectors of Andean society. Poor Indians understood very well the temptation to escape or soften burdens by allying with the world of the colonials, in a search for personal gain that weakened community solidarity and confirmed the superiority of the Hispanic over the Andean.

At moments of crisis, these tensions exploded in nativist outbursts that sought to purge Andean society of Hispanic-Christian influence. The data available on these internal convulsions are extremely scarce, but the Jesuits recorded one such instance in 1613 when an epidemic swept western Huamanga (the Castrovirreyna-Huancavelica zone settled by the Huachos and Yauyos peoples). In this case, at least, Indian nativism generated fierce loyalties and violence. Indians not only killed two Catholic priests, but also one of their own chiefs. Quickly, Catholic *extirpadores* [extirpators] of the idolatry dragged 150 pagan priests to the city of Castrovirreyna for the standard public spectacle and proceedings: whippings and haircuts for the worst offenders, a bonfire to destroy Andean articles of worship (including the *huacas*, or idols, themselves), "confession" and eventual rehabilitation of the idolaters. But some of the offenders refused to submit and staged a spectacular show of defiance. Within five days, thirty of "the most obstinate" leaders, "exasperated and desperate," had killed themselves "with poison that they took by their own hand."

As in the 1560s, when millenarian upheaval inflamed Huamanga, the *huacas* served as a medium of popular protest and calls for change. In the Taki Onqoy movement, the Andean gods had literally "seized" the bodies of Indians, transforming previously uninfluential natives into authoritative voices of angry gods. This time, the *huacas* voiced popular impulses by appearing to a variety of people in visions and dreams. "Three times they appeared in public to many people, and preached and taught them what to do." The *huacas* rebuked the Indians for supposed disloyalty and neglect of the native deities, who had taken vengeance by sending disease and hard times to the land. And they issued a series of anti-Christian "commandments." The Indians "should not recognize any other god except their *huacas*" and should know "that everything that the Christians teach is false." The natives should perform the traditional rites and services owed to ancestor-gods and should avoid any collaboration with Spaniards, who were "enemies of the *huacas*." The Indians "ought not go to serve the Spaniards, nor deal with them, nor communicate, nor ask [their] advice . . . unless forced to."

The qualification "unless forced to" conceded a harsh fact of life. In the context of the early seventeenth century, the colonial power structure was too secure to be smashed or challenged overtly. But the Indians should not collaborate willingly. Instead, they should close ranks around a purifying hatred of colonials and Christian influence. "The day that a cleric or priest leaves town," ordered the *huacas*, "[the Indians] should catch an all-black dog and drag him along all the streets and spots where the priest had walked." Afterwards, the natives should kill the animal at the river, "and where [the river parts into] two branches they should throw in [the body], in order that . . . they purify the places walked by the priest." In Andean culture, the juncture of two streams had special ritual significance as a symbol of perfection or the achievement of "balanced" social relationships.

What distinguished the religious turmoil of 1613 was not its "idolatrous" nature, but rather its intense nativism—an attempt to wipe village society clean of Hispanic-Christian influence. Idolatry itself was neither exceptional nor especially anti-Hispanic. Huamanga's Indians had long adhered to traditional religious practices, sometimes concealed beneath an overlay of Christian symbols and holidays. From an Andean point of view, "pagan" traditions balanced relationships with ancestor-gods who vitally affected the material welfare of the gods' children. Most Indians, therefore, could scarcely abandon their service to Andean gods. At crucial moments in the ritual calendar or life cycle, alcohol and coca lowered inhibitions and "the most Christian [Indian], even if he [could] read and write, [chant] a rosary, and dressed like a Spaniard," reverted to Andean paganisms. Indeed, successful or Hispanized native elites, including lay assistants of Catholic priests, often led traditional religious practices. This form of idolatry, though it sometimes expressed a muted hostility to Christian gods, tended to encourage coexistence and eventual interpenetration of Andean and Hispanic gods, symbols, and practices. In this sense, it promoted a syncretic religious culture through which Hispanizing Indian elites could maintain traditional sources of prestige and influence among kinfolk, while pursuing strategies and relationships drawing them ever more tightly into the world of Hispanic exploiters.

The nativist idolatry that erupted in 1613, on the other hand, promoted fiercely aggressive anti-Hispanic sentiments, and spoke directly to the internal crisis symbolized by Indian Hispanism. For syncretism or coexistence, it substituted internal purification. For tradition led by a native elite, it substituted visions and dreams beyond the control of local authority. Before affirming the prestige of Hispanized Indians, it first put their loyalties on trial. At bottom, nativist currents and outbursts represented a protest against internal trends that sapped the strength and unity of Andean society. The message of anti-Hispanism, we ought to remember, was directed at Indians, not Spaniards. The *huacas'* commandments called upon all natives to reject the temptation to forsake the Andean for the Hispanic, in a quest for personal success that weakened community solidarity and confidence in the adequacy of Andean tradition. The most pointed targets of such "commands," however, were those who had already made such a choice. To regain the favor of the *huacas*—and of poor peasants—successful natives would have to drop Hispanic aspirations that converted them into willing partners of colonial enemies. By reaffirming a purer loyalty to native Andean relationships, successful natives could demonstrate solidarity with the more "Indian" peasantry. Those who rejected the call of the *huacas* risked extreme alienation from local Indian society, and even violence. Nativists turned against ethnic elites who shied away from religious purification and in one case poisoned "a *kuraka* of theirs, a good Christian, for not coming to their rites nor wanting to worship their idols."

But murder remained the exception rather than the rule. Among the *originarios*, at least, a good many elites responded to the pressure of local sentiment and participated in the condemnation of their Hispanic-Christian ways. The threat of social alienation could become a tool of resistance that conditioned social and economic behavior. Indeed, to the extent that *ayllu* peasants could mobilize such a tool to redistribute the resources of successful Indians, they placed limits on the process of privatization and internal differentiation reshaping rural life. But why, we may ask, should a notable fraction of the successful Indians adopting "Hispanic" strategies and relationships prove so vulnerable to the threat of alienation from Andean gods and peoples?

Between Two Worlds

One answer, at first sight adequate, lies in the realm of physical safety and material interest. Indians feared antagonizing Andean gods who ruled over one's health, economic well-being, and the like. Equally important, many successful Indians retained important economic ties in the *ayllu* countryside. Presumably, they could pursue those interests and protect their persons more effectively if they built loyalties and cooperative relationships, or at least avoided gratuitous antagonisms. Social isolation, beyond a certain point, invited violence, disruptive conflicts, and perhaps expulsion from valuable property. Even *forasteros* assumed relationships and obligations that stabilized their presence. Successful *originarios* depended upon "traditional" rights and obligations for some part of their access to resources and labor. A *kuraka* who enjoyed prestige among "his" people could set up a lucrative putting-out system with little trouble. A chief who had lost the "respect" or confidence of *ayllu* households, on the other hand, contended with uncooperative, resistant people. By this logic, those Indians who depended upon a certain esteem among *ayllu* peasants to maintain or enhance their material well-being could not afford to ignore pressures to participate in the nativist idolatries of an aroused peasantry.

Yet this answer is true only up to a certain point. After all, the direction of change limited the material vulnerability of wealthy Indians to declining esteem. An Indian elite that controlled considerable wealth and had integrated itself into provincial power groups enjoyed the same weapons of coercion and economic domination held by colonial aristocrat-entrepreneurs. They had powerful friends and relatives, and sufficient wealth to contract laborers, recruit dependent clients and retainers, accumulate property independent of *ayllu* control, invest in commerce, indebt (and jail) poor Indians, and the like. Indeed, deteriorating self-sufficiency and commercial penetration of their communities left peasants dependent on wealthy superiors of all races for money, subsistence, credit, and protection. As wealthy Indians developed "Hispanic" patterns of accumulation, they emancipated their *economic* lives from the esteem of kinfolk. The wealthiest Indians could indeed afford to withdraw themselves from the traditional burden of prestige and reciprocal obligation, and some in fact did.

But others did not. The structural position of successful Indians, as a group, was laden with a deep contradiction that inhibited their social acceptance among Spaniards and Indians alike, and generated ambivalent loyalties and identities. As an emerging class, the successful Indians held interests and aspirations joining them to the colonial Hispanic world whose social, economic, and cultural patterns they emulated. But the stain of their racial origins linked them to the Indian peasantry and generated social barriers that normally prevented their complete merger into Hispanic society and culture. Ruling classes tend to consider those whose labor they exploit as "lazy" or inherently inferior. In a colonial situation, where class relationships have their genesis in the conquest of one people by another, this characterization applies to entire castes defined by their racial and cultural origins, in this case the "republic of Indians." The achievements of an Indian minority, judged by the Spaniards' own standards, flew in the face of the natives' supposedly inherent degradation. Dynamic Indians competed with Spaniards for land, labor, and profits; they recast themselves in the trappings of Hispanic culture and found Spanish suitors, allies, and friends. In some cases, they even mastered reading and writing skills known by only a minority of Spaniards. These wealthy and acculturated Indians flagrantly violated the worldview and psychology of colonialism.

The Spanish response to *ladinos*, elites, and social climbers was, therefore, highly contradictory. On the one hand, colonial entrepreneurs and officials pursued the contacts they needed to exploit or control the Indian countryside. Their natural allies and friends were powerful, wealthy, and ambitious Indians. But dynamic Indian figures also disturbed the racial hierarchy that legitimated colonial exploitation and entitled all whites—even those who could not break into high elite circles—to a respectable social and economic position. Hence acculturated or wealthy natives also aroused the hostility and contempt heaped upon pretenders who deny their "true" origins. (It is true that money or wealth could help one surmount racial barriers, but the economic success of many Indians, even if impressive and disturbing to racial hierarchies, was nonetheless modest when measured by the standards of high elite circles of Spanish colonial society.)

In general, then, successful Indians could not simply abandon their racial origins and find social acceptance and identification in a Hispanic world. But strong ambivalences also colored relationships with the bulk of Indian society. On the one hand, poor Indians "needed" wealthier, more acculturated counterparts. Their wealth could shore up deteriorating household and *ayllu* economies or save an Indian debtor from jail. Their cultural knowledge of Hispanic society could strengthen juridical and other defenses against European enemies or establish contacts that might serve the community. In addition, poor Indians probably looked upon successful natives with a certain amount of pride; like Spaniards, they understood that Indian dynamism provided a symbolic counterpoint to stereotypes condemning natives to inferiority and subordination. In certain respects, then, a wealthy *ladino* whose loyalties and commitments joined him or her to Indian society could prove to be an exceptionally valuable and popular leader.

But there, alas, was the rub—in the question of loyalties and commitments. A widening gulf of suspicion, tension, and conflict accompanied the differentiation of Indian society into rich and poor, and for very good reason. Success assimilated the most powerful and dynamic fraction of Indian society to an exploitative class of aristocrat-entrepreneurs; the more modest success stories often represented a drain from *ayllu* society of needed people, skills, and resources, and weakened its internal solidarity. The cultural Hispanism of ambitious Indians expressed their weakening commitment to an onerous Andean heritage and their conspicuous aspiration to blend into the dominant sectors of colonial society. Thus even as poor Indians "needed" their more Hispanized counterparts and might take some pride in their achievements, they lost confidence in the loyalties of a new, more alien Indian elite. One response, especially against *forasteros*, was open conflict. But another, probably more widespread, was more subtle. Social pressure forced wealthy Indians to demonstrate their loyalties to the people to whom they "belonged," or else suffer an awkward, alienated relationship governed by colonial rules of coercion and economic domination.

The Indian elite, especially its poorer and more rural segments, was vulnerable to the pressure of social ostracism precisely because contradictions of class and race blocked their fuller acceptance into Spanish society. The structural position of *ladinos* suspended them between two social worlds, Hispanic and Andean, without fully welcoming them into either. Somewhat ill at ease in Spanish circles, yet estranged or suspect in peasant society, at least some acculturated Indians endured considerable psychic strain and inner conflict. We know, for example, that Andean *huacas* haunted "Christian" Indians in dreams and visions, sometimes for years. Often the native gods first presented themselves to both men and women as attractive sexual partners luring the unfaithful to return to Andean loyalties. Indians whose "Hispanic" wealth, socioeconomic strategies, and aspirations tended to differentiate them from the peasantry nevertheless found that they could not make a final break from Indian society. At least some continued to search for esteem or social acceptance among Indians and responded to pressures to demonstrate loyalty to Andean society.

And on occasion, a popular hero emerged from the ranks of the fortunate and powerful. Don Cristóbal de León, son of a middle-level *kuraka* in Lucanas Andamarcas, was a cultured *ladino*: Spanish in dress and hairstyle, Christian in religion, and known for his learning and ability. Given his political and economic privileges and his acquired culture, León was in a position to integrate himself into the provincial power group exploiting the local peasantry or to leave for a respectable life in a Spanish city. But León departed from conventional patterns and incurred the wrath of local colonials. León continued to live in his *ayllu* homeland, opposed drafts of peasant laborers to transport wine from Pacific coastal valleys across Lucanas to Cuzco, and condemned putting-out arrangements run by *kurakas* and *corregidores* to sell cloth in lucrative markets. At one point, he even set out to Lima to denounce local abuses before the viceroy. The local *corregidor* imprisoned León, "punished" him, and threatened to end the matter by hanging him. The incident marked the first of several confrontations between León and local *corregidores*. In 1612, a *corregidor* and visiting priest finally killed the persistent troublemaker. Significantly, other chiefs and notables had avoided helping León out of his scrapes.

The tragedy of Indian success stemmed ultimately from the way it secured the participation of a defeated people in its own oppression. The colonial regime rewarded Indians whose advantages, skills, or luck enabled them to adopt Hispanic forms of accumulation, and punished those whose identification with the peasantry was too strong or aggressive. The political implications were profound. The lure of success and the threat of loss recruited Indian allies to the colonial power structure, discouraged overt challenges that invited repression, and fragmented the internal unity of Andean society. The economic implications, too, were far-reaching. Success stimulated class differentiation within the "republic of Indians," dividing it into the rich and more acculturated on the one side, the poor and less acculturated on the other. The achievements of an Indian minority accelerated the erosion of traditional resources and relationships, while implanting Hispanic property, relationships, and culture deeply within the "internal" fabric of Indian life. The emergence of a colonial Indian elite generated new sources of social conflict, tension, and protest in native society. Yet here, too, was an element of tragedy. For in pressuring Indian elites to demonstrate their loyalties and service to the community, peasants acknowledged that they needed "Hispanic" wealth and skills to survive and defend themselves against colonial exploiters. And in the end, though peasant pressure placed certain limits, at given times and places, on the differentiation of Indian society into rich and poor, it could not reverse the overall trend.

For many of those left behind by Indian success, the only escape was escape itself, flight in search of a better life. Among the fugitives, a small fraction would themselves join the ranks of the successful Indians. As they rebuilt lives in a more Hispanic-mestizo mold, they would gain distance from a condemned Andean heritage left to the peasantry. But they could not escape entirely. A welter of memories, habits, relationships—and snubs—would bind them and their children to their Indian origins.

Notes

For complete references and footnotes, consult the original version of this piece, in Steve J. Stern, *Peru's Indian Peoples and the Challenge of Spanish Conquest* (Madison: University of Wisconsin Press, 1982), pp. 158–183.

1   An *asiento* was a labor contract in which the hired party agreed to settle with and serve a master and employer for a specified length of time. A *mitayo* was an Indian laborer forcebly drafted to work for selected beneficiaries of the state.

2   An *encomendero* owned an *encomienda*, a land grant from the Spanish king.

3   The *composición de tierras* was the inspection and legalization of land title.

4   A *forastero* is literally a stranger, someone from a different *ayllu* or ethnic group.

5   A *yanacona* was a native retainer or serf bound to a colonial overlord.

6   *Originarios* were local *ayllu* Indians descended from common ancestor-gods, as distinguished from immigrant *forasteros* descended from foreign *ayllus* and ancestors.

DIARY OF COLONIAL LIMA

Josephe de Mugaburu y Honton

Lima was named the "City of Kings" for the Magi, since it was founded by Pizarro on Epiphany in 1535. But for Spanish soldier Josephe de Mugaburu y Honton, who filled his seventeenth-century diary with balconied palaces, bullfights, and religious and military processions, the true kings were the archbishops and viceroys of Lima high society. Mostly absent are the underclasses — Indians and slaves — upon whose backs the prosperity that bankrolled this display rested. By the seventeenth century, the capital's 30,000 inhabitants made it the largest city in South America and the hub of official business, trade, military activities, and religious affairs for the immense viceroyalty of Peru, stretching from Panama to Argentina.

Entrance of the Viceroy

On Saturday, the 19th of September [of 1648], [the count] left Callao, and without stopping at any *chácara* he went directly to the hermitage of Nuestra Señora de Monserrat, while the countess came to the palace where she slept.[1]

On Sunday, the 20th of that month, on the eve of the day of the apostle Saint Matthew, the new viceroy entered Lima under a canopy. Several troops of Indians went to [the hermitage of] Monserrat as well as numerous infantrymen on duty, along with two captains, Don Marcos de Lucio and Don Francisco de Flores, and with Colonel Don Antonio de Mogollón y Ribera. Not having continued to the university as had the city councilmen, they did not pass before His Excellency. They took his oath and then he rode on horseback under the *pallium* [canopy], as was the custom, with the aldermen as *pallium* bearers, and the justices holding the reins of the horse. At the bronze marble [memorial stone] they showered him with many flowers and silver. And in Mercaderes Street there was another arch where they also showered him with many flowers and with silver. All the area encompassed by the arch was paved with ingots of silver; there were almost 300 bars of silver.

There was also a squadron in the plaza with many people present, and the company guard of the Marquis of Mancera turned out. The palace company did not go out into the plaza because they always flanked inside until His Excellency entered. Ten pieces of artillery in the plaza fired three times after his entrance into the palace, which was at dusk.

On Tuesday, the 28th of the month, he called on the gentlemen of the Inquisition.

On Wednesday he went to visit the monastery of Santo Domingo; he called on the father provincial and visited there at great length. He then went to [the monastery of] San Francisco where they received him with the cross raised and a canopy. He visited the cell of the commissary general and, after having prayed, visited all of the cloister.

On Thursday, the 1st of October, he visited the other religious orders in the same way, with which he concluded his official calls.

On Tuesday, the 6th of the same month, the Marquis of Mancera with his son Don Antonio de Toledo, and Don Bartolomé de Salazar, justice of the court, went to visit the Viscount of Portillo, Don Agustín Sarmiento de Sotomayor.

At dusk on the same day the Count of Salvatierra with Don Andrés de Vilela, president of this royal *audiencia*, also went to visit the viscount, and there were many offerings on the part of the Count of Salvatierra, who treated him as his second cousin.

On the night of Thursday, the 15th of the month of October, the Count of Salvatierra presented his brother, Don Alvaro, as his lieutenant, with the staff of command of general of Callao, first rendering with great solemnity the honors that such cases require. Present were Battalion Commander Don Antonio Mogollón de Ribera, Adjutant Don José Ferrer, and many captains of the battalion of this city in units with their cavalrymen. Many *caballeros*, or knights, of this city were also present. Don José de Cáceres, as secretary of the government of this City of Kings, read the titles of all the favors granted by the viceroy.

The Armada

The armada left Callao for Tierra Firme [Panama or northern South America] with the treasure of His Majesty on Thursday, the 29th of October 1648. It was the first that the Count of Salvatierra personally dispatched, and it left under the command of General Melchor Polar and Admiral Don Juan de Quesada, treasurer of the royal funds. On the sixth day of navigation General Melchor Polo died and [his body] was cast to sea.

Royal Celebrations

On Thursday, the 17th of December of 1648, there were royal celebrations wherein many *caballeros* of this city appeared in grand uniforms, something very spectacular and much admired because of the high cost of livery. There were also *cañas* [jousting games] and the bulls were the bravest ever run in the Plaza [de Armas] of Lima.

On Tuesday, the 22nd of this month, there were bulls, and the same *caballeros* came out in great splendor to the plaza for [jousting] games of *alcancías*. There were many that pricked the bulls with a *garrocha* [iron-pointed pole]. On both days Don Lucas de Almeida came out with many of these pointed weapons, and he used them much to the satisfaction of those who were watching, because there were many *caballeros* in the plaza who had come from all over the kingdom upon the arrival of the Count of Salvatierra.

Dispatch Ship

Thursday, the 31st of December of 1648, the dispatch ship arrived at this city bearing news of the arrival of the galleons [from Spain] at Panama, and it brought some letters which said that the Marquis of Mancera would be going to Mexico as viceroy.

Damiana, my [step-]daughter, was selected by lot for the sodality of the Pure and Immaculate Conception of Our Lady at [the church of] San Francisco on Monday, the 30th of November of 1648, day of the glorious Apostle Saint Andrew. She came out in the procession the 8th of December of that year with eleven other maidens, which made a total of twelve. The sponsor who took her by the hand was Martín Velasco, twenty-fourth of the sodality, and the superior was Juan López de Utrera. She has a dowry of 450 patacoons [pesos] for such time as she enters the state of matrimony or the religious life. My daughter came out in the lots drawn the second year after I had made the petition; the day she appeared [in the procession] she was thirteen years, two months and eleven days old.

In the year 1648 I gave Matheo de Zamacola seven hundred patacoons to take to Tierra Firme [Panama]; he will use them for my account. The

Figure 9. Native artists contributed to what became known as the Cuzco School of Baroque painting, already renowned in Josephe de Mugaburu y Honton's time. This portrait of the Archangel Gabriel by an anonymous artist exemplifies the Cuzco School. (Courtesy of Banco Latino)

contract was executed before Martín de Ochandiano, public notary, and a comrade of Zamacola was secondary trustee.

The Holy Lignun Crusis

On Sunday, the 19th of September of 1649, the great relic of the holy *lignun crusis* [fragment of authentic cross of Jesus] which His Holiness donated to this holy church was placed in the cathedral. It had been brought by the Count of Salvatierra, viceroy of these kingdoms, and it was carried in a very solemn procession from the monastery of San Francisco to the cathedral, in which the religious orders, the councils of this city, the viceroy, and the *audiencia* participated.[2] They also brought out six white banners with green crosses which were carried by six priests named by the archbishop as *visitadores* to visit all the archbishopric and preach the faith of Our Lord Jesus Christ to the Indians and do away with their idolatry, and to punish such [idolatrous] Indians.

On this day it was announced that the celebrations which His Holiness had ordered eliminated were not to be observed. And this day Father Fray Blas de Acosta of the order of Predicators gave a sermon at the cathedral.

Procession

Sunday, the 17th of October of the year 1649, a holy crucifix was taken in great solemnity from [the church of] San Agustín to that of La Encarnación. It was the greatest procession ever held in this city, with [statues of] all the saints of that [Augustinian] order adorned as for the procession of Corpus [Christi] which the convent of San Agustín celebrates with great splendor. All the streets and all the altars along the way were decked with hangings. The Count of Salvatierra, viceroy of these kingdoms, all the *audiencia*, and a great number of infantry preceded the procession, and a squadron was formed at the small Encarnación plaza.

Notes

1 A *chácara* is a modest-sized farm; also spelled *chacra*.
2 The *audiencia* was the administrative-judicial court for the viceroyalty and its provinces.

FRIAR MARTÍN'S MICE

Ricardo Palma

An amazing 2,500 of the 6,000 Spanish men in Lima in the early seventeenth century were friars, an indication of the central role of the Catholic Church in Peru's early history. Among them, Martín de Porres, a lay brother in the Dominican monastery, stands out. Son of a Spanish noble and a Panamanian slave, one of the more than ten thousand enslaved blacks brought to Peru in the first hundred dred years after the conquest, he is still one of Peru's most popular saints. This tale of Martín's exploits comes from the nineteenth-century folklorist Ricardo Palma, whose Peruvian Traditions, *despite a detached irony about colonial foibles, came to define the creole elite's nostalgia for the intrigues and opulence of Spanish society in Peru.*

A dog, mouse, and cat ate
Together from the same plate.

This couplet ends a printed list of miracles and virtues circulated in Lima about 1840, when our devout and sophisticated capital solemnly celebrated the beatification of Friar Martín of Porres.

This saintly man was born in Lima on December 9, 1579, the illegitimate son of the Spaniard Don Juan of Porres, knight of Alcántara, and a Panamanian slave. Little Martín's father took him as a young boy to Guayaquil, where he learned to read and write at a school where the teacher made much use of the cane. Two or three years later, his father brought Martín back to Lima and apprenticed him to learn the useful trade of haircutting and bloodletting in a barbershop on Malambo Street.

Martín did not take to the razor and lancet even though he quickly learned the knack of them, and opted instead for a career as a saint, which in those days was a profession like any other. At twenty-one, he donned the habit of lay brother at the Dominican monastery, where he died on November 3, 1639, with the smell of sainthood.[1]

Our compatriot Martín performed miracles by the bundle, both in life and after his death. He performed miracles with the ease with which others write verse. One of his biographers (I don't remember whether it was Father Manrique or Doctor Valdés) relates that the Dominican prior had to forbid Martín from continuing to miraclify (please excuse the verb). And to show the dutiful, obedient spirit of this servant of God, the biographer relates how, just as Martín was passing by a scaffolding, a bricklayer fell from thirty or forty feet above. Our lay brother stopped in his tracks, and yelled—"Wait a second, brother!" And until Martín got back with permission from the prior, the bricklayer was suspended in mid-air.

A really good miracle, right? Well, it goes from good to better.

The prior ordered the marvelous lay brother to buy a pound of sugar for the infirmary. Perhaps he didn't give him quite enough money to get the fine, white kind, and Martín came back with unrefined sugar.

"Are you blind, brother?" said the prior. "Didn't you notice by its murky color that it looks more like dirty syrup than sugar?"

"Don't worry, father," said Martín. "I'll wash the sugar now. That'll fix everything."

And without giving the prior time to argue, he stuck the sugar in a fountain, and took it out dry and white.

Hey! Don't make me laugh, I've got a split lip.

Believe what you want. But be assured that I'm not holding a knife to the reader's throat to make him believe any of this. Freedom must be free, as a journalist from my hometown once said. And I note here that, having promised only to talk about Martín's mice, the story of the saint was getting away from me. Enough fooling around, I say, and let's get down to the business of the mice.

Friar Martín of Porres had a special affection for mice. These pesky animals were unknown in Peru until 1552, annoying guests who arrived just after the conquest. They came from Spain aboard one of the shipments of dried cod sent to our ports by one Don Gutierre [*sic*], Bishop of Palencia. Our Indians baptized the mice as *huchucas*, arrivals-by-sea.

In Martín's barbering days, a mouse was still almost a curiosity, since, relatively speaking, the mouse clan was just beginning to multiply. Maybe

SAN MARTIN DE PORRES

Figure 10. San Martín, in the hospital infirmary with his trademark broom and one of his many miracles, on a votive card sold today in front of Lima churches.

that was when Martín started to develop a fondness for rodents. And, seeing in them the work of the Lord, it may be presumed that he might have drawn a comparison between himself and those tiny beings, as in the words of the poet:

When God was wasting his time on me
he might have created a mouse, or even three.

When our lay brother worked as a nurse in the monastery, the mice frisked about in the cells, kitchen, and refectory like marauding Moors. Cats were scarce in Lima, arriving only in 1537. It's a known historical fact that the first cats were brought by the Spanish soldier Montenegro, who sold one in Cuzco for 200 pesos to the Don Diego de Almagro the Elder.

The friars were sick of the rodent invasion, and invented different traps to catch them, though they rarely worked. Friar Martín also set a mouse trap in the infirmary, and one unsuspecting big mouse got caught, attracted by the smell of cheese. The lay brother let it go, putting it in the palm of his hand, and saying:

"Go on your way, little brother, and tell your friends not to be a pest in the cells. Have them go live in the garden, and I'll be sure to bring them food every day."

The diplomat took care of this diplomacy, and from that moment the mouse army left the cloisters and moved to the garden. And of course Friar Martín visited them every morning, carrying a basket of provisions or leftovers, and the mice came as if summoned by a dinner bell.

Our good lay brother kept a dog and a cat in his cell, and had succeeded in getting both animals to live together in harmonious brotherhood. So much that they ate together from the same bowl or plate.

One afternoon he was watching them eat in healthy peace, when all of a sudden the cat arched its back and the dog growled. A mouse, attracted by the food's smell, had dared to stick its nose out of its hole. Friar Martín saw it, and turned to the dog and cat, saying:

"Calm down, creatures of God, calm down."

Right away he went over to the wall and said:

"Advance without fear, brother mouse. It seems to me that you must be hungry; come forward, no one will hurt you."

And looking over to the other two animals, he added:

"Come on, children, make a little room for the guest from now on, since God gives enough for all three of you."

And the mouse, without having to be asked twice, accepted the invitation, and from that day he ate in fellowship and love with the dog and cat.

And . . . And . . . And . . . Still you don't believe! Well, I have to leave.

Note

1   In other words, Martín was not a full priest, but rather a member of the so-called third order of lay brothers under the Dominicans.

THE REBELLION OF TÚPAC AMARU

Alberto Flores Galindo

More than a hundred Indian rebellions rocked the Andes of Peru and Bolivia between 1720 and 1790. The largest was led by José Gabriel Condorcanqui, a prosperous trader and Indian noble who took the name of Túpac Amaru II after the last Inca executed by the Spaniards, from whom he claimed direct descent. While the rebel chief professed loyalty to Christianity and the Spanish king, testifying to heavy European influence on the native elite, he also wanted to build what historian Alberto Flores Galindo calls an "Andean utopia" through a restoration of Inca rule. The threat of this Indian nationalism to white supremacy was reflected in the violence of the final suppression of the rebellion by the colonial authorities.

On November 4, 1780, the Indian leader Túpac Amaru II captured the Spanish *corregidor*, or administrator, Antonio de Arriaga; he would execute him two days later. This took place in Peru's southern Andes in a village called Tinta with a population of about two thousand. It was in Tinta that Indian rebel leaders from Cuzco, Puno, and other villages in the region would gather to come up with a plan not only to end exorbitant taxation by the Spaniards, but to drive out the Europeans and restore an Inca monarchy.

Túpac Amaru's decrees and proclamations would reach across Peru's highland cities. Later, his followers would destroy Spanish estates (*haciendas*) and textile mills (*obrajes*) all the way to Cuzco itself. Nevertheless, five months after Arriaga's execution, the rebel chief and eight other leaders would be arrested and put to death in Cuzco's main square.

But the Great Rebellion—as the colonial authorities called it—did not end with their deaths. It continued in Puno under the leadership of Diego Cristóbal Túpac Amaru, and in parts of present-day Bolivia, northern Argentina, and Chile. The city of La Paz was taken twice by Julián

Apasa Túpac Katari (first for 109 days, then for 64 days). Confronted with the difficulty of subduing the revolt and the tremendous cost of mobilizing troops (against Túpac Amaru alone they sent 17,500 soldiers), the Spaniards negotiated peace with the rebels. Still, conflicts continued. In June 1781, Felipe Velasco Túpac Inca, who regarded himself as Túpac Amaru's brother, tried to organize a rebellion in the mountains of Huarochirí, near the capital of the viceroyalty in Lima. Only the execution of Diego Cristóbal in August 1783 ended this convulsive period of Andean rebellion, which lasted more than three years.

The upheaval covered the entire southern Andes, roughly 200,000 square miles of strategically vital territory. At the very center of Spain's South American dominion, this area included cities such as Arequipa, Cuzco, and La Paz, mining centers such as Potosí, and ports such as Arica, an expanse that cut across key lines of communication between Lima and Buenos Aires. With a dense indigenous population, it was economically varied. Coca was grown in both the upper Amazon valley of Cuzco and the Bolivian lowlands, or *yungas*. Abancay had sugar; Arequipa, wines and liquor; Cochabamba, wheat; Ollantaytambo, corn. Textile mills operated in Cuzco's upper provinces. Trade knit these cities with mule trains, trading posts, and great annual markets like Copacabana, Tungasuca, and Cocharcas.

According to historian Boleslao Lewin, about 100,000 Indians participated in the rebellions, some 40,000 rebels in La Paz alone.[1] If we take into account that insurgent peasants were usually accompanied by their entire families, and if we add to this the people living in rebel-controlled areas, then the number is even higher. To be sure, one should not exaggerate. In Cuzco, for example, there were both rebel and loyalist towns. Divided allegiances sometimes fractured even neighborhoods within towns, as appears to have been the case in Chucuito. The reasons for disunity are complicated. Although there were earlier plans for a rebellion dating from 1770 and the leaders appear to have known each other (Túpac Amaru and Túpac Katari, both muleteers and traders, traveled from one extreme of the southern Andes to the other), the events were not synchronized and each revolt had its own character.

Everyone referred to Túpac Amaru as the Inca. But while in Cuzco, his proclamations were interpreted to call for respect for the property and lives of mixed-bloods (*mestizos*) and creoles (*criollos*); in La Paz it was believed that the Inca wanted all non-Indians put to death in a kind of ethnic cleansing. Some leaders in Atacama held the same opinion. In Arequipa in 1789 and in Oruro in 1781, by contrast, rebel leaders were actually creoles with urban followers composed of a mix of Indians and mixed-bloods. There was not just one, in short, but many faces to the rebellion.

At the moment when these rebels attempted, any way they could, to transform their world, the Bourbon dynasty under the reign of Charles III (1759–1788) was looking for a way to reorganize the imperial state and to streamline an antiquated colonial system. Andean colonial rule in the mid-eighteenth century followed the same model as that employed in other parts of the hemisphere by both the British and the Spanish. The metropolitan center siphoned off colony surpluses through commercial monopolies, the mining of precious metals, and heavy taxes. It was a system, as one observer has concluded, set up "to obtain the greatest amount of precious metals with the smallest investment possible."[2]

The distinction between colonizers and colonized, at first strictly drawn around the concept of separate "republics" of Spaniards and Indians, blurred with time. After all, unlike the Portuguese colonists in Africa and Asia, the Spaniards did not stay on the coast. To the contrary, they made their way into the interiors of the American continent. There they established mining centers, cities, and estates. Along with colonial administrators came merchants, landlords, and people who simply wanted to "do the Americas." These Spaniards often intermarried with Indians, creating the racial category of *mestizos*. There were also the creoles, of Spanish descent yet born in the Americas. As the lines between colonizers and colonized became less clear, so did the colonies' relation to Madrid. Initially, both Spaniards and creoles could occupy public office. By the first half of the eighteenth century, however, creoles were the majority in municipalities, religious orders, and even in the viceregal administration. Peru was part of the Spanish polity, just like any other imperial province. Together with its European aristocracy, a parallel aristocracy—that of the supposed descendants of the Incas—helped to maintain an illusory image of Peru's equal status within the empire.

To understand Spain's American rule, historian Richard Morse has adopted Max Weber's concept of "patrimonial society."[3] The king occupied the apex of multiple hierarchies whose counterbalances checked secessionism, yet muddled the system's operation. His authority was based on a civil supremacy sealed by church backing. In Peru, this political demarcation divided territory into parishes (*curatos*), magistries (*corregimientos*), and chieftainships (*curacazgos*). Thus Indians had over them a magistrate (*corregidor*), a priest (*cura*), and a chief (*curaca*), and none of them had clearly defined functions. A magistrate might also be a merchant and a priest own lands, the same as a chief, who also might be a merchant. Not surprisingly, conflicts were frequent—often ending in a crossfire of accusations about who exploited Indians worst.

But the advent of the Bourbon dynasty to Spain's crown in the eighteenth century threw the patrimonial system into crisis. Divided was the immense viceroyalty of Peru. The viceroyalties of New Granada (1740) and then Río de la Plata (1776) were created. The Jesuits, who had achieved economic autonomy through their numerous estates and urban properties, were expelled in 1767. The state seized their holdings. In addition, the Bourbons tried to regulate access to public office to streamline bureaucracy. New administrators came from the Iberian peninsula. Creoles began to be displaced from government positions. Crown-appointed inspectors (*visitadores*) were sent to the colonies to limit the power of the viceroys. New taxes were instituted, including a 12.5 percent tax on alcohol. Other taxes increased. The sales tax (*alcabala*) on produce and merchandise, for example, jumped from 2 percent in 1772 to 6 percent in 1776. Customs controls were established, and the accounting system reformed. The government also clamped down on contraband and, in general, on the corruption so common under the patrimonial system. Historian John Lynch calls the Bourbon reforms a "second conquest" of America.[4] Indeed, this was how they must have been viewed by local merchants, artisans, and even Indian tributaries, subjected to a new head count to crack down on tribute evasion. The reforms affected everyone. "Finally," writes historian Timothy Anna, "Spain was exercising a classic commercial imperialism."[5]

The reforms opened an irreparable breach between colonial society and the Crown. Understanding the outbreak of rebellion, however, requires an attention to the particularities of the southern Andes. Among other transformations, mining in Potosí had begun to recuperate in 1740 after a long decline. Together with the development of other mining centers and a gradual demographic recovery after the cataclysmic conquest, trade intensified across the southern Andes, reflected in the growing number of muleteers. A number of cases illustrate this process. For example, the Cuzco estates of Pachaca, which produced sugar, and Silque, which produced corn, stepped up production. So did textile mills. Increased production and commerce, however, soon overwhelmed the markets of a society ill-equipped to absorb new wealth because of continuing poverty.

Between 1759 and 1780, as historians Enrique Tandeter and Nathan Wachtel explain, "the Indians found themselves in a flooded market and had difficulties in obtaining the money needed to pay taxes and for *repartos* (forced purchases of commodities from the government)."[6]

Fully a third of the viceroyalty lived in the southern Andes, and the region's indigenous population was more concentrated than in other colonial territories. Depending on the place, Indians were anywhere from 60 to 100 percent of the population. By the 1780s, as we have seen, they were left to face the ill-fated encounter of economic crisis and political changes. All of this occurred in a space articulated in a manner that almost guaranteed a regional response. The mines of Potosí and cities like Cuzco and La Paz were not just scattered points on the long route between Lima and Buenos Aires. To the contrary, the mercantile economy fostered regional interdependence. Together with peasants and artisans were local merchants like the Ugartes, the La Madrids, and the Gutiérrezes as well as Indian traders, some as prosperous as Túpac Amaru and others as poor as Túpac Katari. Many of these traders' names surface in the trials opened against the rebels in 1780. Listed in these records as among Túpac Amaru's closest collaborators, for example, were eight other muleteers. So, too, were some government administrators in Chuquisaca and Cuzco, among them some of the creoles who accompanied the rebels as scribes.

In short, conditions allowed an alternative to colonial domination to emerge in the southern Andes. For this to happen, however, the image of the absolute authority of the Spanish king and the monarchy had to shatter. Inadvertently, the Bourbons had prepared the way for the breakup of Spanish authority through their rapid reforms, but in the southern Andes the process occurred faster than in other places because this was precisely the region where a major sector of the population held to the concept of continuity with a different dynasty: the Incas, not the Bourbons. As the mixed-blood Ramón Ponce, one of Túpac Amaru's main commanders, declared in his confession: "He said that the kingdom belonged to him, because in the titles and decrees he was the fourth grandson of the last Inca."[7]

At the start of the rebellion, Túpac Amaru had his portrait painted holding the symbols of Inca royalty. Peasants who came to see him treated him as an Inca; and he was received under a canopy in the towns he visited, supervised by a Spanish priest in Andahuaylillas. His orders were to be obeyed because he was the heir to the Inca empire and thought by some even to possess divine powers like the ability to resurrect those who died in his service.

From the beginning, Túpac Amaru was surrounded by a clique of close followers, including his wife Micaela Bastidas, their children, and cousins. This made up the core of an authority structure to supplant the Spaniards. Within the hierarchy were colonels and captains around whom Túpac Amaru hoped to organize an army like that of the Spanish, though various difficulties were to develop with this effort.

The Indians drafted for this new army were summoned by Túpac Amaru himself, or through the intermediacy of his chiefs or newly appointed authorities. As they arrived, sometimes with their wives and children, two immediate problems arose: how they were to be armed and how they would be fed. In addition, according to the European model, soldiers were to be paid a salary as well as provided with coca and alcohol. But the uprisings interrupted trade routes and blocked roads. As months passed, these logistical problems led to desertions, which were severely punished. At one point, León Ponce—Túpac Amaru's lieutenant—was told "to return to his province and bring back as many deserters as could be found there, Indians and Spaniards alike."[8]

Túpac Amaru's army replicated the hierarchy of colonial society. In fact, this restoration of the "authentic" Inca monarchy demonstrated the influence of European concepts on the indigenous aristocracy. Besides the regular army, however, there were also spontaneous uprisings and a multitude of small confrontations. These became more common with the passing months, as the revolution spread south, becoming widespread in the high moors, or *altiplano*. When the followers of Túpac Amaru arrived in Pucara near Lake Titicaca, for instance, they found that an insurrection had already erupted. In places like this, there was a local dynamic to organizing and decision making.

The Spaniards found it difficult to believe that someone like Túpac Katari would assume the title of viceroy without possessing aristocratic blood, all the more so since he was poor, dressed in worn clothes, and spoke no Spanish. Truly, the world seemed to have turned upside down. They were, however, better able to understand Túpac Amaru. Some colonial officials were certain that the name of the Incas was itself enough to unite the multitudes. During the rebellion, royal treatment was afforded Túpac Amaru not just by Indians, but also by the Spaniards who followed him. This treatment makes it easier to understand the particular cruelty of the final sentence against the rebel leader. The executions of Túpac

Figure 11. Túpac Amaru II triumphant at the Battle of Sangarará, from a painting on goatskin by an anonymous early-nineteenth-century artist. (Courtesy of Pablo Macera)

Amaru and eight of his followers—the "show," according to a document from the time—lasted from 10:00 a.m. to past 5:00 p.m. on the afternoon of May 18, 1781. The spectacle was meant as a lesson to the Indians. It was supervised by the Crown's new representatives, including Visitor General (Visitador General) José Antonio de Areche and Judge Benito de la Mata Linares, the same people who wanted to reform the region's bureaucracy and increase revenues. The execution occurred within a society where rule would be increasingly based on brute coercion. From 1780 onward, military budgets increased as did the number of soldiers and militiamen. From 4,200 in 1760, the militia in particular grew to 51,467 immediately after the rebellion and finally to 70,000 by 1816. The militarization of the colonies resulted from Túpac Amaru's uprising.[9]

In justifying the sentence, José Antonio de Areche not only mentioned the "horrendous crime" of plotting against the monarchy, but also condemned the fact that many, especially Indians, had treated Túpac Amaru as "his excellence, highness, and majesty." This is why his execution had to be public and the remains spread across the mountains to prove Túpac Amaru was really dead, countering "the superstitions that led the people to believe that it was impossible to kill him because of the nobility of his character, which made him the inheritor of the Incas."[10]

For those who viewed Túpac Amaru as an Inca, however, the body was not that of a prisoner. Rather, it stood for the Indian nation. To quarter and then burn Túpac Amaru's body was to destroy symbolically the Inca empire. Years later, when Diego Cristóbal made peace with the Spaniards, Cristóbal assembled the supposed remains of Túpac Amaru and with great pomp buried them in Cuzco's San Francisco church. Shortly thereafter, however, the Spanish judge Mata Linares had Cristóbal arrested and condemned him to be hanged. After the execution, his body was also quartered and his houses sacked and destroyed.

On Túpac Amaru's death, the colonial authorities prohibited Inca nobility from using titles, ordered the destruction of paintings of the Incas, and forced the Indians to dress in Western clothes. According to Areche, these practices would eventually wipe out hatred toward things European. But the effect was the opposite: the measures accentuated the division between Spaniards and Indians. For Areche, the rebellion's defeat was part of the reorganization of the colonial system. Inca nobility and the Quechua language obstructed political centralization. Yet the rebellion had destabilized hopes for a return to the integration of the Andean population under Spanish rule. The massacres of Spanish immigrants, especially of those who had lived among the Indians, further widened the gap between the colonizers and the colonized. Old images of imperial authority and king had begun to dissolve.

The German baron Alexander von Humboldt journeyed across America about twenty years after the rebellion of Túpac Amaru. From the northern extreme of the viceroyalty, Humboldt made his way to Lima, remaining for several days. There, the renowned biologist and traveler spoke with local aristocrats and both creole and Spanish intellectuals. Interested in colonial government and ethnic relations, he was fascinated by the Great Rebellion of 1780. Humboldt felt sympathy for the Indians and was critical of the Spanish magistrates. Yet after careful study—he even claimed to possess documents signed by Túpac Amaru—he ended up backing the Spaniards' position in the conflict.

Humboldt believed that Túpac Amaru's initial aim of Inca restoration had devolved into a vicious caste war with no middle ground. The battle of Americans against Europeans, in other words, slid into a struggle of Indians against whites. Spaniards and Americans of Spanish descent were ultimately brought together on the same side, supported by Humboldt because, he believed, they stood for "civilization" against "barbarism."

Civilization and barbarism. These terms also appeared in the "Report of the Government of Viceroy Jáuregui," which sought an explanation for the rebellion deeper than a hatred of colonial magistrates. Ultimately, the report attributed colonialism's failure to the fact that "it is common among the Indians to have an inclination toward their ancient barbarous customs and also to venerate the memory of the Incas."[11] The same language appears in another report that recommended Spanish schooling for the children of the revolt's "principal Indians" in order to "civilize them." An entire literature by intellectuals and colonial functionaries writing in a mix of self-reflection and defense of the system grew up after the rebellion.

In the juxtaposition of civilization and barbarism, historian Charles Minguet sees the entire problem of the colonial world, where Western minorities dominated an indigenous and mixed-blood majority, looking down on their traditions.[12] Imagining history in terms of European superiority characterized the Spanish response to the rebellion of Túpac Amaru and would stubbornly recur even after independence from Spain in the early eighteenth century, into the modern history of Latin America.

Notes

1   Boleslao Lewin, *La revolución de Túpac Amaru y los orígenes de la independencia americana* (Buenos Aires: Editorial Americas, 1967), p. 102.

2   Tulio Halperin Donghi, *Historia contemporánea de América Latina* (Madrid: Alianza Editorial, 1967), p. 58.

3   Richard Morse, "The Heritage of Latin America," in *The Founding of New Societies: Studies in the History of the United States, Latin America, Canada and Australia*, edited by Louis Hartz (New York: Harcourt, Brace and World, 1964), pp. 201–236.

4   John Lynch, *Las revoluciones hispanoamericanas* (Barcelona: Ariel, 1984), p. 13.

5   Timothy Anna, *España y la independencia de América* (Mexico City: Fondo de Cultura Económica, 1986), p. 37.

6   Enrique Tandeter and Nathan Wachtel, *Precios y producción agraria: Potosí y Charcas en el siglo XVIII* (Buenos Aires: CEDES, n.d.), p. 91.

7   Luis Durand Flórez and Juan Manuel Mosco y Peralta, eds., *Colección documental del bicentenario de la rebelión emancipadora de Túpac Amaru*, vol. 3, no. 1 (Lima: Comisión Nacional del Bicentenario de la Rebelión de Túpac Amaru, 1980), p. 594.

8   Ibid., p. 650.

9   Leon Campbell, *The Military and Society in Colonial Peru, 1750–1810* (Philadelphia: American Philosophical Society, 1978), p. 17.

10 Ibid., p. 269.

11 Agustín de Jáuregui, *Relación de gobierno* (Madrid: Consejo Superior de Investigaciones Científicas, 1982), p. 193.

12 Charles Minguet, *Alexandre von Humboldt, l'historien et géographe de l'Amérique espagnole, 1799–1804* (Paris: Institut des hautes études de l'Amérique latine, 1969), p. 25.

"ALL MUST DIE!"

José Antonio de Areche

Spanish magistrate José Antonio de Areche supervised the gruesome execution of Túpac Amaru II, his wife, Micaela Bastidas, and seven other coconspirators in Cuzco's main square in 1781. Interestingly, however, Areche's language betrays a degree of fascination with the traditions of the Indian elite even as he advocates the destruction of the symbols of Inca rule, in what anthropologist Renato Rosaldo calls the "imperialist nostalgia" of European colonizers for the cultures they sought to destroy. Despite Spanish attempts to erase memory, the Inkarrí myth, with its promise of the recomposition of the Inca's body and the restoration of Indian rule, circulated in the southern highlands for decades, even centuries, to come.

I must and do condemn José G. Túpac Amaru to be taken out to the main public square of this city, dragged out to the place of execution, where he shall witness the execution of the sentences imposed on his wife, Micaela Bastidas; his two sons, Hipólito and Fernando Túpac Amaru; his uncle, Francisco Túpac Amaru; and his brother-in-law, Antonio Bastidas, as well as some of the principal captains and aides in his iniquitous and perverse intent or project, all of whom must die the same day.

And once these sentences have been carried out, the executioner will cut out his tongue, and he will then be tied or bound by strong cords on each one of his arms and feet in such a way that each rope can be easily tied or fastened to others hanging from the saddle straps of four horses so that, in this position, each one of these horses, facing opposite corners of the square, will pull toward his own direction; and let the horses be urged or jolted into motion at the same time so that his body be divided into as many parts and then, once it is done, the parts should be carried to the hill or high ground known as "Picchu," which is where he came to intimidate, lay siege to, and demand the surrender of this city;

and let there be lit a fire which shall be prepared in advance and then let ashes be thrown into the air and a stone tablet placed there detailing his main crimes and the manner of his death as the only record and statement of his loathesome action.

His head will be sent to the town of Tinta where, after having been three days on the gallows, it shall be placed on a stake at the most public entrance to the town; one of his arms will go to the town of Tungasuca, where he was chief, where it will be treated in like manner, and the other in the capital of the province of Carabaya; one of the legs shall likewise be sent for the same kind of demonstration to the town of Libitaca in the province of Chumbivilcas, while the remaining one shall go to Santa Rosa in the province of Lampa along with an affidavit and order to the respective chief magistrates, or territorial judges, that this sentence be proclaimed publicly with the greatest solemnity as soon as it arrives in their hands, and on the same day every year thereafter; and they will give notice in writing of this to their superiors in government who are familiar with the said territories.

Since this traitor managed to arm himself and form an army and forces against the royal arms by making use of or seducing and leading with his falsehoods the chiefs who are the second in command in the villages, since these villages, being of Indians, are not governed by such chiefs but rather by mayors who are elected annually by the vote or nomination of the chiefs: let these same electoral communities and the chief magistrates take care to give preference to candidates who know Spanish, and who are of the best behavior, reputation, and customs so that they will treat their subjects well and lovingly, honoring only those who have demonstrated honestly their inclination and faithfulness, eagerness, respect, obedience, submission, and gratitude to the greater glory of our great Monarch through the sacrifice of their lives, properties, or ranches in defense of their country or religion, receiving with brave disdain the threats and offers of the aforesaid rebel leader and his military chiefs, yet taking care that these elected leaders are the only ones with the right to the title of chief or governor of their *ayllus* [communities] or towns, and that they cannot transmit their position to their children or other family members.

To this same end, it is prohibited that the Indians wear heathen clothes, especially those who belong to the nobility, since it only serves to symbolize those worn by their Inca ancestors, reminding them of memories which serve no other end than to increase their hatred toward the dominant nation; not to mention that their appearance is ridiculous and very little in accordance with the purity of our relics, since they place in different parts images of the sun, which was their primary deity; and this prohibition is to be extended to all the provinces of this southern America, in order to completely eliminate such clothing, especially those items which represent the bestialities of their heathen kings through emblems such as the *unco*, which is a kind of vest; *yacollas*, which are very rich blankets or shawls of black velvet or taffeta; the *mascapaycha*, which is a circle in the shape of a crown from which they hang a certain emblem of ancient nobility signified by a tuft or tassel of red-colored alpaca wool, as well as many other things of this kind and symbolism. All of this shall be proclaimed in writing in each province, that they dispose of or surrender to the magistrates whatever clothing of this kind exists in the province, as well as all the paintings or likenesses of their Incas which are extremely abundant in the houses of the Indians who consider themselves to be nobles and who use them to prove their claim or boast of their lineage.

These latter shall be erased without fail since they do not merit the dignity of being painted in such places, and with the same end in mind there shall also be erased, so that no sign remains, any portraits that might be found on walls or other solid objects; in churches, monasteries, hospitals, holy places or private homes, such duties fall under the jurisdiction of the reverend archbishops or bishops of both viceroyalties in those areas pertaining to the churches; and in their place it would be best to replace such adornments with images of the king and our other Catholic sovereigns should that be necessary.

Also, the ministers and chief magistrates should ensure that in no town of their respective provinces be performed plays or other public functions of the kind that the Indians are accustomed to put on to commemorate their former Incas; and having carried out the order, these ministers shall give a certified account to the secretaries of the respective governments. In like manner shall be prohibited and confiscated the trumpets or bugles that the Indians use for their ceremonies and which they call *pututos*, being seashells with a strange and mournful sound that celebrate the mourning and pitiful memorial they make for their antiquity; and there shall also be prohibited the custom of using or wearing black clothing as a sign of mourning, a custom that drags on in some provinces in memory of their deceased monarchs and also of the day or time of the conquest which they consider disastrous and we consider fortunate since it brought them into the company of the Catholic Church and the very loving and gentle domination of our kings.

With the same goal it is absolutely forbidden that the Indians sign themselves as "Incas," since it is a title that anyone can assume but which makes a lasting impression on those of their class; and it is ordered, as is required of all those who have genealogical trees or documents that prove in some way their descent, that they produce them or send them certified and without cost by mail to the respective secretaries of both viceroyalties so that the formalities may be observed by those persons responsible to their excellencies the viceroys, consulting His Majesty where necessary according to each case; and the chief magistrates are charged to oversee the fulfillment of such requirements, to seek out and discover anyone who does not observe them correctly, in order to have it done or to collect the documents with the aim of sending them to the proper authorities after giving their owners a receipt.

And so that these Indians renounce the hatred that they have conceived against the Spaniards, and that they adhere to the dress which the laws indicate, adopting our Spanish customs and speaking Castilian, we shall introduce more vigorously than we have done up to now the use of schools, imposing the most rigorous and fair penalties on those who do not attend once enough time has passed for them to have learned the language; the duties and responsibilities involved in this plan going to the very reverend ecclesiastical prelates so that, in the opposition between parishes and doctrines, they take care that those candidates bring affidavits from the provincial judges as to the numbers of people who speak the said Castilian in those provinces, noting in the tribunal that they send to the vice-protectors the particulars with relation to each position; and there will be established a term of four years for the people to speak fluently or at least be able to explain themselves in Castilian, the bishops and chief magistrates being required to report on all this to their respective superior governing body, and it being left up to the sovereign discretion of His Majesty to reward and honor those towns whose inhabitants have rendered, under the present circumstances, their due loyalty and faithfulness.

Finally, the manufacture of cannons of all kinds shall be prohibited under the penalty that any noble found manufacturing such items will be sentenced to ten years of prison in one of the presidios in Africa and any commoner will receive two hundred lashes as well as the same penalty for the same time period; reserving for a future time a similar resolution with regards to the manufacture of powder. And since there are in many ore-crushing mills and timberyards in these provinces cannons of almost

every caliber, they will be gathered up by the magistrates once the pacifi-
cation of this uprising has been completely terminated, in order to give
account of them to the respective captaincy general so that he may determine whatever use he deem proper for them. Thus have I visualized,
ordered, and signed: this is my final judgment. José Antonio de Areche.

III · REPUBLICAN PERU

Independence was more the work of armies than of the people," wrote historian Jorge Basadre.[1] Peru was the last bastion of Spanish rule in South America. Colonialism's demise came only when the forces of the Argentine José San Martín and then the Venezuelan Simón Bolívar converged on South America's oldest viceroyalty. Although the charismatic San Martín garnered the wild cheers of a huge crowd in Lima when he declared Peruvian independence on July 28, 1821, many in the conservative elite had hoped until the last moment for a royalist victory. Very few in Peru's indigenous majority identified with this cause of the continent's wealthy creoles. Far from an eternal touchstone of solidarity or pride, "Peru" began as a shaky fiction with a limited grasp on the imagination of any major sector of the population of this new nation.

In the period between the Independence Wars (1820–1824) and the War of the Pacific (1879–1883), the colonial legacy of hierarchy and division foreclosed a shared sense of national identity. A tiny minority of European descent controlled land, power, and capital. The lower and bottom tiers of society were filled by the brown majorities. To be sure, neither the elite nor the underclasses were monolithic. Black slaves in Ica's vineyards and orchards were descendants of West Africans brought in chains to Peru in the seventeenth century. Chinese laborers were indentured in the 1850s to dig guano, bird dung, from the rocky islands of Paracas to ship as fertilizer to Europe. German colonists arrived at the century's close in the coffee-growing jungles of the Chanchamayo valley. Astute visitors, like French feminist Flora Tristán, understood that republican Peru was crosscut by differences along lines of political and religious conviction, gender, and ethnicity. In general, however, the society pivoted on the privilege of the wealthy and the European over the poor and "uncivilized" races. The sharp-tongued nineteenth-century critic Manuel González Prada compared the treatment of Peru's Indian majorities to that received by serfs under the boot of feudal lords.

Instability prevailed after independence. At least twenty-four regime changes erupted between 1825 and 1841, as fierce disputes raged between rival warlords, or *caudillos*.[2] From the late 1840s to the early 1870s, the Age of Guano brought a precarious consolidation. Exports of the bird dung from coastal islands reached more than $20 million a year by the mid-1850s, tightening Peru's links to the world economy.[3]

Especially strong was the connection to the main imperial power of the age, Great Britain. Peru of the nineteenth century was marked by the arrival of a stream of British as well as French, Italian, and German travelers, officials, and investors. Foreign businessmen partnered the coastal oligarchy in Andean mines, railroads, and cotton and sugar plantations, as the cheap labor of blacks, Chinese, and Indians generated the enormous profits that filled the coffers of British and German companies and bankrolled the magnificent estates and European excursions of the creole elite.

The Independence Wars were waged under the Enlightenment principles of equality of rights and economic man. Yet old colonial prejudices intersected with new "scientific" doctrines of racial "types" and hierarchies. Not all of these classifications were as virulent as that of the Lima intellectual who in 1891 decried the Andean Indians as "a degenerated, old branch of the ethnic trunk from which all inferior races emerged . . . with almost no mental life, apathetic, without aspirations."[4] Plenty of Peruvians found their own means to challenge the regnant order, whether in sly jokes or angry revolts. Yet interlocking hierarchies of class, gender, sexuality, ethnicity, and color retained a persuasive power, the ideological foundations of a country where the denial of political representation and economic rights to the majorities reflected their effective exclusion from the "imagined community" of national citizenry.[5]

The depth of division was laid bare by the War of the Pacific. Although guano deposits were a bonanza in the 1850s and 1860s, they were almost exhausted even before the conflict, and the mismanaged government went bankrupt in 1874. In 1879, Peru and Bolivia folded before the Chileans, who had British backing to seize nitrate fields in the southern Atacama desert. Chinese joined the invaders to loot the northern plantations of their Peruvian masters, and poor blacks in the southern provinces of Capeweed and Chincha attacked both Chinese bondsmen and white owners.[6] Meanwhile, a number of prominent Lima families collaborated with the Chileans on their arrival in the capital in 1881. General Andres Avelino Cáceres rallied a resistance movement in the central highlands, but even the history of these *montoneros*, or guerrillas, turned into another example of social conflict and division as the movement boiled over into the breakaway peasant republic of Comas that remained a thorn in the side of the Peruvian government until the century's end.

The War of the Pacific left Peru in shambles. Under a more utopian scenario, the crisis might have led to the transformation of Peruvian society. Fragments of a vision of a better order circulated in unlikely places in the years during and after the conflict, for instance, in the shaky scrawl of a letter by Comas guerrillas claiming "reason and justice" for the defense of their homeland against the alliance of local landlords and the Chilean army or even in the Indian rebellion of Atusparia in the alpine Huaraz valley in 1884.[7] Yet in the short run, at least, the more common pattern proved to be the repression of social unrest, the seizure of the lands of highland communities by big landowners, and an updated version of the top-down control by foreign companies and coastal elites that had prevailed in the decades before the war. As Peru headed toward the new century, the possibility of a nation grounded in the needs of the majority seemed as distant as ever.

Notes

1 Jorge Basadre, *La multitud, la ciudad, y el campo en la historía del Perú* (Lima: Mosca Azul, 1980), p. 142.

2 Paul Gootenberg, *Between Silver and Guano: Commercial Policy and the State in Postindependence Peru* (Princeton, N.J.: Princeton University Press, 1989), pp. 11–12.

3 Ibid., p. 14.

4 Quoted in Jo-Marie Burt and Aldo Panfichi, *Peru: Caught in the Crossfire* (Jefferson City, Mo.: Peru Peace Network, 1992), p. 8.

5 "Imagined community" comes from Benedict Anderson's influential *Imagined Communities: Reflections on the Origin and Spread of Nationalism* (London: Verso, 1983).

6 Heraclio Bonilla, "The War of the Pacific and the National and Colonial Problem in Peru," *Past and Present*, no. 81 (1978): 109.

7 Quoted in Florencia Mallon, *The Defense of Community in Peru's Central Highlands: Peasant Struggle and Capitalist Transition, 1860–1940* (Princeton, N.J.: Princeton University Press, 1983), p. 90.

THE BATTLE OF AYACUCHO

Antonio Cisneros

Spain's decisive defeat in South America came in December 1824. Now an enormous monument marks the plain above the village of Quinua where the Ecuadoran General José Antonio de Sucre led his forces to victory in the battle of Ayacucho. But poet Antonio Cisneros undercuts the aura of glory and sacrifice usually associated with the Independence Wars in this contemporary verse. One of Peru's best-known poets, Cisneros uses a characteristically dry, unadorned style to focus on the poor majorities who gave their lives as soldiers but reaped few benefits from victory or its aftermath.

From a Soldier

After the battle
there was nowhere to pile up
the dead,
so dirty and hollow-eyed, scattered
over the grass like leavings
from this tough fight,
the swollen and yellowed heroes
littered among the stones
and disembowelled horses
were stretched out beneath the dawn.

I mean that dead comrades
are the same
as any other edible meat
after a battle, and soon
a hundred brown birds

flocked upon their corpses
until the grass was clean.

From a Mother

Some soldiers who were drinking brandy
have told me that now this country
is ours.
They also said
I shouldn't wait for my sons.
So I must
exchange the wooden chairs
for a little oil and some bread.

The land is black as dead ants,
the soldiers said it was ours.
But when the rains begin
I'll have to sell
the shoes and ponchos
of my dead sons.

Some day I'll buy a long-haired mule
and go down to my fields
of black earth
to reap the fruit
of these broad dark lands.

From a Mother
again

My sons and the rest of the dead still
belong to the owner of the horses
and the owner of the lands, and the battles.

A few apple trees grow among their bones
and the tough gorse. That's how they fertilize
this dark tilled land.
That's how they serve the owner
of war, hunger, and the horses.

COMAS AND THE WAR OF THE PACIFIC

Florencia E. Mallon

After Lima's collapse before the Chileans in 1881, the future Peruvian president Andrés Avelino Cáceres led the resistance in the central highlands of Junín. Historian Florencia E. Mallon describes the poor peasants who were the backbone of these montoneras, *or guerrilla bands. Wealthy estate owners turned out to be more afraid of a unified, armed peasantry than of the Chileans. Cáceres himself supervised the repression of rural mobilization after his victory. This conflict led to the establishment of the independent peasant republic of Comas that lasted for twenty years until it was put down by the central government.*

We will make rifles from wood, bullets from hard stone.[1]

On the morning of April 15, 1881, Andrés Cáceres, colonel in the defeated Peruvian army, surreptitiously boarded the train at Viterbo, near Lima, and headed for the central highlands. He left behind him an occupied city, and the memory of a two-year military campaign during which the Peruvian forces had been slowly, almost inexorably, pushed back from the sandy wastes of the Atacama desert to the very doors of Lima. Fought over the huge nitrate deposits discovered in this desert in the mid-nineteenth century, the War of the Pacific had ended in complete disaster for Bolivia and Peru. Unable to obtain credit in Europe, Peru had not acquired sufficient armaments. In order to raise funds internally, the Congress—made up of the most powerful *hacendados* [estate owners], mineowners, bankers, and guano consignees—would have had to tax itself. The members refused, even in the face of an imminent Chilean invasion, indulging instead in a long series of debates on free trade, censuring ministers and rejecting all economic plans that attempted to tap their personal fortunes. Council upon council of ministers had been forced to resign, unable or unwilling to take the necessary measures. And as the treasury emptied out, the Peruvian army had begun to lack not only small arms, artillery, and ammunition, but also salaries, clothes, shoes, and food.

As many of his compatriots had done during the past two years, Cáceres was about to make one more sacrifice for his *patria*: a nation that existed in barely more than name, and whose defeat was due much more to this fact than to problems of military strategy. After the final battle at Miraflores on January 15, the wounded Cáceres had hidden himself, with the help of friends, in various hospitals and private homes, frustrating a concerted Chilean search. When the occupation forces had required that officers of the defeated army give their addresses, Cáceres had not complied. While his wound healed, he had nursed a plan to retire to the highlands and organize a new army:

> As a result of the disaster at Miraflores, there arose in me the idea of escaping to the highlands and continuing the resistance against the invader, since I thought that, taking advantage of the defensive possibilities the region offered, it would be feasible to mount an obstinate resistance that would force the enemy to waste his energies and moderate his ambitions, limiting him to the area of the coast that he already occupied.

Between 1881 and 1883, Cáceres organized three different armies in the central highlands, each composed mainly of merchants, smaller *hacendados*, and peasants from the region. He and his representatives toured the provinces of Jauja and Huancayo, speaking in Spanish and in Quechua, requesting money, men, and arms. They spoke to the merchants and wealthier peasants from the area's villages, encouraging the formation of guerrilla forces in the peasant communities. With the aid of peasant guerrillas, Cáceres's army then managed to foil two separate Chilean expeditions, earning a considerable reputation among the area's inhabitants.

Yet no measure of heroic exploits or symbols could compensate for the lack of unity and national purpose of the Peruvian elite. Unable to unite effectively around either negotiation or resistance, various elite factions fought against each other, seeming to forget that Peru was an occupied country. And this confusion was mirrored in the central highlands. Although Cáceres received support from most groups in the early months of his campaign, the realities of protracted resistance and the actual presence of the Chilean army soon eroded his base among the larger mineowners, *hacendados*, and merchants. With their properties suffering the brunt of wartime exactions, this group was soon eager to seek peace at any price. Some collaborated actively with the Chileans, hoping to accelerate negotiations or even profit from speculation. All looked with trepidation at the mobilization of peasant guerrillas, wondering if the peasants might not turn on them after repelling the invaders.

For the peasants, the Chilean invasion of the central highlands marked their sudden and brutal initiation into the intricacies of international politics. Threatened in their homes by a foreign invader, encouraged by their political authorities, priests, and merchants to fight against him, they carried out a bold and tenacious rear-guard campaign against the Chilean army, both alone and in alliance with the Cacerista regular troops. They developed an elementary sense of nationalism which was grounded, above all else, in their love for the land and in a fierce sense of territoriality. And in the heat of battle, they discovered in themselves a unity and strength that was to take them far beyond the initial purpose that Cáceres had envisioned for them.

The Resistance of La Breña

When the Chilean occupation army entered Lima on January 17, 1881, they did not find a government able to negotiate the Peruvian surrender. Nicolás de Piérola, who as dictator had organized the defense of Lima, had fled to the highlands with a small entourage. In the next two years, Peru would once again be embroiled in a struggle among caudillos, as various leaders attempted to establish a sufficiently wide territorial base to be recognized as the legitimate Peruvian government. The Chileans, for their part, would throw their support behind one faction and then another, attempting to find one with which they could successfully negotiate a peace treaty.

When Cáceres retired to the highlands, the Civilista party, composed mainly of progressive *hacendados*, bankers, and guano consignees, received initial recognition from the Chileans and attempted negotiation until the prospect of territorial losses caused an impasse in the discussions. On the other side, a loose coalition of military officers initially gathered around Piérola, refusing to negotiate and preaching continued resistance. By retreating to the sierra, where Piérola had his camp, Cáceres placed himself squarely in the latter faction. Only a few days after Cáceres's arrival on April 26, Piérola named him political and military leader of the central highlands resistance.

Cáceres's choice of the central sierra also exhibited a shrewd under-standing of military strategy and local politics. As previous nineteenth-century conflicts had shown, the central highland area was an ideal loca-tion for a resistance campaign. Access to the region depended upon a few easily guarded mountain passes. The abundant agricultural and live-stock production could maintain an army for long periods of time. But most important for Cáceres, the central highlands provided him with a strong political base. As the descendant of a prestigious family from Aya-cucho, Cáceres was related by blood or marriage to some of the more prominent elite families in the central sierra. Thus he could expect help and personal friendship from a number of the region's powerful patrons, and hoped to have at his disposal their clientele networks.

Cáceres also knew that the central sierra elite had participated ac-tively in defending Lima from the Chileans. The Concepción Battalion of the National Guard, composed of Juan Enrique Valladares, his brother Manuel Fernando, his brother-in-law Luis Milón Duarte, and many more prestigious merchants and *hacendados*, had distinguished itself in battle at Miraflores. The Jauja Battalion, led by an important merchant and in-cluding within its ranks a number of smaller *hacendados* from the Jauja region, had fought beside it. Together with the forces under Cáceres's command, these two battalions had beaten back the Chileans in a brave counterattack, and Cáceres hoped that they would continue to fight as tenaciously once the battle shifted closer to home.

In contrast to the elite, the central sierra peasants had not partici-pated actively in the war's coastal campaigns. Some of the merchants who lived in or traded with the villages had volunteered for the Na-tional Guard battalions, and so had several smaller *hacendados* and owners of medium-sized commercial properties. Don Pedro Remusgo and don Carlos Villanes, for example, owners of small haciendas in the northern part of the Yanamarca valley, were officers in the National Guard's Jauja Battalion. Among the region's wealthier peasant families, a few had sent their sons to fight at Miraflores. Thus Fidel Crespo, related by marriage to the Ortega family of Acolla, was a sublieutenant. In other cases, vil-lagers had been victims of forced conscription for the makeshift forces organized to defend Lima. But for most peasants, the war was far away, and they had other, more immediate, concerns.

The resistance of La Breña, as Cáceres's campaign in the central high-lands came to be called, radically changed this situation. No longer were the battles fought on a distant battlefield. Even in the central sierra, where peasants were accustomed to seeing caudillos pass through with their troops on their way to and from the presidential palace, no one could remember having seen anything like it. In the nine months between May 1881 and February 1882, the region's inhabitants withstood two separate Chilean invasions. They were forced to support both the Peruvian and Chilean armies, a task that decimated supplies very quickly. For an army that numbered fifteen hundred men at its highest level, Cáceres decreed that each province of the department of Junín should provide a monthly quota of 26 head of cattle, 3,790 head of sheep, 663 *quintales* (66,300 pounds) of potatoes, 24 *quintales* of wheat, and 48 *quintales* of corn. And this was the most reasonable exaction. The much more numerous Chilean troops took whatever they could find, wherever and however they could find it. It is not surprising, therefore, that when Cáceres's representatives came to the villages to tell the peasants about their "patriotic duty to combat the Chilean invader," they usually found a receptive audience.

The village of Comas, to the east of Jauja, was a case in point. Especially after a Chilean detachment passed through the community on February 24, 1882, demanding food for immediate consumption and ordering additional supplies for their return within several days, municipal officials decided that it was time to resist. They wrote to Ambrosio Salazar y Márquez, a wealthy peasant who had passed through their community on February 8 urging the immediate organization of guerrilla bands, and asked for his help in organizing a *montonera*.[2] As they explained, they had been particularly irritated by a letter from Jauja's parish priest, who had demanded provisions for the Chilean garrison in that city and threatened reprisals if the orders were not obeyed.

As peasant enthusiasm for the resistance effort increased, however, so did elite ambivalence. When Cáceres first arrived in the central highlands, most *hacendados* welcomed him warmly as one of their own. During the first Chilean invasion in May 1881, the Valladares gave Cáceres and his wife a place to stay on their retreat from Jauja to Concepción, presenting them with some of the famous butter made on the haciendas Laive and Runatullo. The Peñalosas, a prestigious *hacendado* family in Huancayo, also opened their doors. But the realities of a protracted Chilean occupation tended to change elite attitudes. Even during the first invasion, when the leader of the Chilean expedition sent a message to Huancayo threatening to burn the city unless a heavy exaction was met within forty-eight hours, a fraction of the area's merchants and *hacendados* quietly decided to meet Chilean demands. They raised 60,000 *soles*—the price of a medium-sized hacienda—and thirty horses, commissioning Manuel Zevallos, a prominent *hacendado*, to take the goods to the Chileans under cover of night. Cáceres discovered the plan, however, and arrested the mayor of the city, confiscating the goods to use them for his own army. And although the Chilean forces were soon ordered to retreat toward Lima, leaving Huancayo intact, the elite's alternatives were already clear. Either they gave in to Chilean demands, hoping to limit the destruction of their property and investments; or they took a patriotic stand, knowing that Cáceres's minute force could not effectively defend them from Chilean reprisals. No matter how bravely they had fought at Miraflores, many hacendados were increasingly ambivalent about continuing the battle in their own backyard.

In January 1882, the arrival of a second Chilean expedition, commanded by Colonel Estanislao del Canto, marked an important watershed in the campaign of La Breña. In contrast to its predecessor, the del Canto expedition was not only an invading force: it was a true army of occupation. Having forced Cáceres to retreat to Ayacucho, del Canto established headquarters in the southern part of the Mantaro valley. The houses of several prominent citizens in Huancayo were requisitioned to serve as lodgings for the officers of the various Chilean battalions. In both Huancayo and Concepción, del Canto put pressure on local officials and demanded contributions from merchants and *hacendados*. Troop detachments combed the area's villages and haciendas, looking for supplies to maintain the three thousand enemy soldiers.

Faced with a prolonged occupation and unable to rely on immediate help from Cáceres's regular army, the region's inhabitants were forced to take matters into their own hands. Throughout the early months of 1882, the peasants of the area's villages met in community assemblies to organize guerrilla bands and fight the Chileans. They elected merchants, parish priests, and noncommissioned officers—usually from outside the community—as leaders of the *montoneras*. In the village of Comas, Ambrosio Salazar y Márquez, a prestigious *vecino* from San Gerónimo de Tunán who owned property in the village of Quichuay and was a graduate of the prestigious Colegio de Santa Isabel in Huancayo, answered the peasants' request for aid by organizing and financing a guerrilla force. On the west bank of the Mantaro River, the parish priest of Huaripampa, Father Mendoza, organized a guerrilla band composed of peasants from the villages of Huaripampa, Muquiyauyo, Llocllapampa, Ullusca, and others. José María Béjar, from an important Jauja family, organized peasant resistance in the village of Sincos, slightly to the south of Muquiyauyo. And at the southwestern limit of the Mantaro area, Corporal Tomás Laimes, a veteran of Miraflores and originally from Huanta, Ayacucho, fomented and centralized guerrilla activity in the villages of Chongos Alto and Huasichancha.

While Cáceres's army, decimated by battles and forced marches, was recuperating in Ayacucho, the peasant guerrillas executed a number of successful rearguard actions against the Chileans. The first of these was the ambush of a Chilean detachment in Comas. On February 24, 1882, a patrol of approximately forty soldiers, under the command of Captain Fernando Germain, passed through Comas on their way to pillage the hacienda Runatullo. The Comas *montonera*, led by Ambrosio Salazar, decided to ambush the patrol upon its return. Organized in a double line, with thirty rifles and fifty *galgueros*,[3] the *Comasinos* attacked the Chileans at Sierra Lumi on March 2. When the battle was over, 35 of the 40 Chileans lay dead on the field, and the peasants had captured 800 head of cattle and 100 horses from the hacienda Runatullo, as well as 35 horses and as many Winchester rifles belonging to the Chileans.

The *montoneras* continued their resistance in April and May. Along the west bank of the Mantaro River, a Chilean patrol met stiff opposition in Chupaca on April 19, but was finally able to beat back the guerrillas and burn the village. Three days later, the *montonera* in Huaripampa, under the leadership of Father Mendoza, engaged another Chilean patrol in fierce combat. Fighting with ten shotguns, five rifles, and numerous sticks, lances, and slingshots, the guerrillas held off the Chileans to the last man. And on the eastern side of the river, the *montoneras* from Tongos, Pazos, and Acostambo fought the Chileans on May 21 and 22. In the latter village, two peasants were surprised by a Chilean soldier while they attempted to push a boulder down the hill onto an enemy column. The Chilean charged one of the peasants, plunging his bayonet into the guerrilla's chest. The Peruvian, in turn, plunged his knife into the Chilean. The second peasant then used his machete to cut off the Chilean's head. When Cáceres arrived in Acostambo two months later, he found the Chilean soldier's head impaled on a lance and exhibited in a public place.

In addition to inflicting notable casualties, loss of weapons, and loss of morale on the Chilean army, the peasant *montoneras* greatly worried the regional elite. Although the guerrillas had been organized by wealthy or prestigious outsiders in touch with Cáceres's general guerrilla command, the need to rely on an armed and mobilized peasantry had imbued the La Breña campaign with a democratic flavor that most elite members found distasteful. It was one thing to resist the invader, but to create an armed, mobilized, and relatively autonomous peasantry and, even worse, to respect them as citizens—that was an entirely different story. The most dangerous part of it, moreover, was that the peasants were beginning to believe in their equality as soldiers. Not only did they keep the booty and ammunition they obtained from the Chileans, but they also entered haciendas asking for provisions.

For an elite whose regional dominance had been shaky in time of peace, the threat of an armed peasantry in time of war seemed more dangerous than the presence of a foreign army. Some elite members succumbed to pressure from the Chilean high command and collaborated openly. Juan Enrique Valladares, for example, mayor of Concepción and previously the organizer of the Concepción Battalion, wrote a letter to the guerrilla leader Ambrosio Salazar in Comas, asking him to put down his weapons, return the body of the Chilean captain, and give back the horses and rifles captured in the Sierra Lumi ambush. Others were unable to accept that they and the guerrillas were fighting on the same side. Thus Jacinto Cevallos, a prominent *hacendado* from Huancayo, sent a note to the administrator of his hacienda Punto after a *montonera* from the village of Acobamba had stopped there and asked for provisions. The letter called the peasants barbarians, and promised revenge. Of course, some of the area's citizens collaborated with the Chileans out of simpler motives. Guillermo Kirchner, for example, was able to make a neat profit by helping to market the booty obtained from many of the Mantaro valley communities and haciendas. But whether they were motivated by fear or by profit, an important fraction of the regional elite began to look increasingly like traitors to the peasant guerrillas.

The peasants were extremely angered by elite collaboration. When Ambrosio Salazar wrote back to Valladares, he violently refused to come to terms, even if the Chileans returned to Comas and burned the village to the ground. But perhaps the most indicative reaction came from the Acobamba guerrillas. Having intercepted the note Cevallos sent to his administrator, they decided to send a letter to Cevallos on April 16, 1882. "To Mr. Civilista Don Jacinto Cevallos," they wrote,

> You would think that under the Sun and the earth they would not know that you were a traitor to the homeland where you were born, well they do know, and we know that you with all your friends traitors to our amiable [*sic*] homeland are in this province communicating and giving explanations on how they can ruin the Peruvians, to those treacherous Chilean bandits invaders [and] like you traitors to their homeland. Also you would think that we couldn't grab the

communication that you were passing to your Administrator, well we have it in our hands informed of its contents we must tell you: that all the Guirrillas [*sic*] that are in the valleys of these hills led by the Commander Gonzales Dilgado [*sic*] are with the express orders of the General Don Andres Abilino [*sic*] Caseres [*sic*] and we have orders to punish the deceitful actions of the traitors of the homeland: and you don't put us in the group of the barbarians like you told your Administrator because we with reason and justice unanimously rose up to defend our homeland we are true lovers of our homeland where we were born. I [*sic*] don't know what people you call miserable and want to revenge yourself over the course of time: don't you think that we until the present coccasion [*sic*] even though you call us barbarians we still don't walk around committing revenge and other barbarous things, instead we proceed with all loyalty all the Guirrillas even though we know that you are one of the closest associates of the infamous Dr. Giraldez. It's true that the other day since we passed through your Hacienda after having made an advance across these places to fight those Chilean bandits while we were passing through we asked your administrator to give us about eight cattle for our food to give their rations to two thousand men that are at our command: this is all we have done in relation to your hacienda and you think we have committed barbarous acts, but any hacendado should be able to tolerate us as patriotic soldiers.

God keep you—[signed] Mariano Mayta, Lieutenant Governor —Faustino Camargo, Captain—Martin Vera, Captain, Lieutenant Governor—Mariano Campos, Lieutenant Governor—Domingo Mercado.

This letter, written in uneducated, shaky, almost illegible handwriting, bears witness to the intense process of ideological growth undergone by the peasants of the central highlands during the La Breña campaign. After suffering a year of Chilean occupation and seeing their homes and fields looted by a foreign invader, the peasants of the region were forced to confront a very basic fact: that the intricacies of national and international politics had an important effect on their daily lives. Out of this confrontation, they developed both an understanding of national politics and a strong sense of nationalism, though neither would be recognized as such by modern or upper-class standards. Their nationalism, for example, was not a general or symbolic sense of nationhood, but a feeling founded very concretely on their love for their homeland—for the place where they were born, "under the Sun and the earth"—for the land they planted. Thus the Chileans were not enemies because they were Chileans, but because they invaded and destroyed the homeland, the peasants' most precious resource, their source of subsistence and life. In a similar vein, the guerrillas' understanding of national politics was not an abstract analysis of political parties, but a clear grasp of the implications of political debates for developments in their own villages. When they addressed Cevallos as Civilista, therefore, they did not mean that he belonged to that party, but that he was acting as they had heard a Civilista acted: talking to the Chileans, collaborating with them, prolonging their occupation of the Peruvian homeland.

Yet what is most important about this letter, and what must have frightened Cevallos even more than the idea of two thousand peasants passing through his hacienda, is the way in which peasant nationalism and class consciousness fed into one another. Throughout the letter, the guerrillas return to the same theme—how angry they are that Cevallos should consider them barbarians. They knew full well that if a group of regular soldiers under the command of a prestigious officer had entered his hacienda asking for provisions, Cevallos would not have considered them in the same light. It was only because the guerrillas were peasants that the *hacendado* could not see them as his allies. He would rather collaborate with the Chileans, with the invaders, than with Peruvian peasants. And this was the ultimate treachery; for, as the guerrillas stated, "any *hacendado* should be able to tolerate us as patriotic soldiers."

Thus the letter from the Acobamba guerrillas was both a statement of outrage and a warning. As they saw it, while the *hacendados* and merchants had stood idly by, paying the Chilean exactions, lodging the Chileans in their houses, it was the peasants who had risen up to fight the invader, even if they only possessed boulders and slingshots. Yet the elite had the audacity, the nerve, to treat the peasants as barbarians and common criminals. But they would pay in the end: as soldiers of Cáceres, the peasants not only had orders to punish "the deceitful traitors of the homeland," they also had the legitimate right to decide who the traitors were.

When Cáceres renewed his efforts against the Chilean forces in July 1882, it was the peasant guerrillas, not the regular army, who formed the vanguard of the struggle. On July 8, for example, the Comas guerrillas, under the command of Ambrosio Salazar, led an attack on Concepción. In a nocturnal battle lasting seventeen hours, these guerrillas, with the help of a small detachment of Cáceres's regular army and scarcely eleven inhabitants of Concepción, exterminated the seventy-nine men that made up the Chilean garrison and appropriated all remaining rifles and ammunition. And the *Comasinos* were not alone. All along the Mantaro valley, from Marcavalle in the south, through Jauja and on to Tarma, the peasant *montoneras* proved decisive in defeating the occupying army.

Cáceres was extremely impressed by the enthusiasm of the peasant guerrillas. After confirming the enemy's retreat from the department of Junín, he sent an official report of the campaign to the Peruvian authorities in Lima in which he praised the actions of the region's peasants. "The Supreme Government's attention should be especially directed to the spontaneous mass uprising of all the Indians in the Departments of Junín and Huancavelica," he wrote, "with which they have given a most valuable service. This event foreshadows a unanimous movement that will soon transform the nature of the present war." And to ensure the continued support of the peasants, Cáceres issued a decree exonerating all guerrillas from the payment of the Indian head tax.

Cáceres's prediction that peasant participation would change the nature of the war proved a great deal better founded than he realized. Although by September 1882 the central sierra was once again free of the foreign invader, it was also on the threshold of a class war that, hidden among the folds of national resistance, could explode at any moment. Yet the underlying struggle was not simply one of the peasants against the regional elite. While the increasing penetration of commercial capital into the peasant community had created a particularly high level of class tension before the war, it was in the context of the La Breña campaign that the tension worked itself out. Nationalism, class conflict, and class alliances were thus articulated in a complex pattern, having a great deal to do with the way the guerrillas had been organized in the first place, and with the way that different fragments of the elite had reacted to the Chilean invasion.

In organizing the guerrillas, the Caceristas had relied on smaller merchants, priests, and noncommissioned officers who, through local networks of patronage and clientele, had forged alliances with the wealthier peasants and political authorities in the villages. In this way, the leaders could arm, mobilize, and incorporate the poorer peasants while still controlling the *montoneras* from the top down. The merchants and wealthy peasants, moreover, served as intermediaries between the regional elite and the peasant community, helping to bind the two classes together for a common nationalist cause. But the intermediaries could only be successful if both the peasants and the regional elite continued to support the resistance effort. While this support was still strong in the northern part of the Mantaro valley, it was eroding rapidly in the south.

The Chilean occupation had polarized the elite along both regional and economic lines. The southern part of the valley had been the main center of Chilean operations, and the central highlands' wealthiest and most prestigious *hacendados*, who lived and had their properties between Huancayo and Concepción, had been forced to bear the brunt of the invasion. Their haciendas suffered the repeated incursions of Chilean patrols. The peasant guerrillas in this area, particularly from Acobamba, Acostambo, Canchapalca, and Comas, fought fiercely and also took supplies from the haciendas. Because the southern merchants and landowners, wanting to protect what was left of their investments and extremely wary of the mobilized peasants, took an increasingly accommodating attitude toward the Chileans, they forced the guerrilla leaders and intermediaries to choose between a collaborationist upper class and a peasantry willing to push forward with the national resistance. Rather than give in to the enemy, the leaders continued the resistance and relied more completely on peasant support, giving the struggle a more popular base and a stronger class dynamic.

In the north, on the other hand, the Chilean presence was more sporadic. Elite fortunes, smaller and more concentrated in commerce, suffered less directly from Chilean exactions. The guerrillas, faced with a more intermittent Chilean threat, were not as independent and militant as they were in the south. The northern elite, therefore, at the margin of the Chilean occupation and less threatened by peasant mobilization, could more easily give Cáceres their continued support. As a result, the northern *montoneras* remained within the confines of the patron-client and multiclass alliances initially forged by the Caceristas.

The north-south dichotomy in the Mantaro valley illustrates two possible ways in which class tensions and incipient nationalism could interact. Though peasants developed nationalist feeling in both cases, in the south they experienced nationalism in opposition to the collaborationist elite. This deepened hostility between the classes and pushed them toward open confrontation. National unity was therefore undermined at the same time as nationalist feeling began to emerge. In the north, in contrast, peasants discovered nationalism in the context of a common struggle with the elite against the Chileans, and this common front did not break down in the heat of battle. Thus a more genuine nationalist front, which successfully subsumed class interests, could grow.

What the two cases have in common is the importance of the elite's actions in defining the strength or weakness of national cohesion. Nationalist feeling would have exercised a broader appeal for the lower classes if the elite itself had taken a united nationalist stand, actively defining and controlling nationalism from above. Evidence from the coast, however, as well as from most areas of the highlands, indicates that the majority of the elite was more concerned with the dual threat of lower class mobilization and loss of property than with the invasion of the Chilean army. In this context the northern Mantaro valley, especially the area around Jauja where landowners, merchants, and peasants remained united in their support for Cáceres, seems to have been the exception rather than the southern Mantaro area.

The elite's inability to unite around nationalism was borne out once again on August 31, 1882, when Miguel Iglesias, an *hacendado* from Cajamarca and previously a follower of Piérola, issued the "Cry of Montán." In this proclamation, Iglesias indicated his willingness to negotiate with the Chileans. By offering a viable alternative to the resistance campaign, he drew to his side a number of disaffected officers, politicians, and *hacendados* who were tired of the war, and he thereby posed a direct threat to Cáceres. In the first months of 1883, a number of towns began to declare their support for the "Cry of Montán," and the ideological war between Iglesistas and Caceristas extended into the central sierra. Cáceres met Iglesias's challenge head on, issuing proclamations to his army and to the towns of the central highlands and, at the end of January, marching against Canta, the first town in the region to declare itself in favor of Iglesias.

At different points during the month of April three Chilean divisions, with a total of 6,500 men, marched into the highlands with orders to defeat Cáceres and wipe out all guerrilla resistance. After fighting the Chileans courageously in several limited engagements, Cáceres was finally forced to regroup at Chicla, leaving Canta to the enemy. Knowing that his retreat facilitated the renewed occupation of the Mantaro valley, he sent a letter to the subprefect of Jauja on April 30, urging the independent organization of guerrilla forces in each of the area's towns and villages and warning the inhabitants against Peruvian "traitors." "Since despite the sanctity of the cause that we defend," he explained,

> there is no lack of perverted Peruvians who, allying with the Chileans, offer their services as spies or guides, or give them cattle, grain, money or other resources to help them with their wicked work of

devastation, and others who with false news and other methods dishearten the citizens and oppose the taking up of arms in defense of our country, it is necessary that you persecute and denounce these traitors and impose upon them the punishment that their infamous conduct deserves. Advising the inhabitants of this province that those who not only as private citizens, but also as political or municipal authorities, provide any help whatsoever to the enemy shall suffer the penalties that a traitor deserves.—You shall inform the villages of this idea through their governors, who should read to the communities the content of this letter. Telling them also that they should never, for any reason, obey authorities who in any way collaborate with the enemy.

Cáceres was right to warn against Peruvian "collaborators," for Iglesias's position appealed to several of the *hacendados* in the Mantaro valley. Luis Milón Duarte, related to the Valladares brothers by marriage and owner, with his wife Beatriz Valladares, of some of the richest haciendas in the central sierra, became Iglesias's political and military governor for the central highland provinces. In a statement he issued from his camp at Chocas on May 6, he summarized the feelings of many elite members when he said that the conditions for peace accepted by Iglesias were the best that could be expected, and that the most important thing was to end the destruction and work hard to reconstruct the country. "Fellow citizens," he began,

Inspired by patriotism, I did my duty during the war, both in the administration of General La Puerta and the dictatorship of Mr. Piérola, and after our disasters, having acquired the conviction that we were unable to continue the struggle to a successful conclusion, I employed my energies in searching, through peace, for the end to our national troubles, something which is desired by all.

I have been one of the few who has had faith and has persevered in the supreme attempt to redeem our country, and thus the arrows of injustice, calumny, and factionalist passions have wounded me. My modest person has suffered all kinds of hostilities; my properties have been sacked and burned, as much by the external enemy as by the internal enemies of peace.

Duarte continued his campaign against the "internal enemies of peace," combining threats and bribes in an effort to render ineffectual Cáceres's guerrilla support. In two further proclamations from Chocas, he ordered the disarmament of all private citizens within three days and the declaration of loyalty to Iglesias by all military and political personnel within eight days. Those not complying with the orders would be judged in civil and criminal court, but those who complied would receive amnesty. And, perhaps most interesting, all the guerrillas who left the *montoneras* would be rewarded and declared exempt from further military service.

Duarte's campaign did not have the desired effect. Although the Chilean division under the command of León García forced Cáceres to retreat to Tarma, they encountered fierce guerrilla resistance all along the road. Then on May 21, protected from the Chileans by the Tarmatambo guerrillas, the Cacerista army began its retreat to the north. Guided by Duarte, two of the three Chilean divisions gave chase. The third division, under the command of Colonel Urriola, was ordered to remain in the Mantaro valley and, having occupied Huancayo, to clean up the remaining pockets of guerrilla activity.

Urriola's invasion of Huancayo brought class tensions to the boiling point. Many among the city's elite, seconding Duarte's desire that the war be rapidly ended, received Urriola well. But the peasants, veterans of previous occupations, loyal to Cáceres, and still heavily mobilized, did not take kindly to Iglesista "treachery." From this point on, guerrilla activity took on a particularly violent and menacing tone, with the murders of several collaborationist Peruvians in the area being attributed to the *montoneras*. And on July 4, after Urriola had been ordered to march north to Jauja, the guerrillas from Huari took advantage of the Chilean army's absence to invade the city of Huancayo, killing a prominent citizen who attempted to calm them down.

From the point of view of the peasants, the Urriola expedition provided the final proof that local *hacendados* were traitors to the nation. This was the case because, despite the fact that Urriola's division was Chilean, the elite was willing to use its backing to repress the *montoneras* and ultimately to strip the peasant guerrillas of whatever legitimacy they still maintained as nationalist soldiers. The end result was simply that there was no longer any common ground for negotiation between the two classes. The elite viewed all action by the peasant guerrillas as race- or class-motivated pillage, whereas the peasants perceived elite attempts to protect their property as treachery to the national resistance. It is in this context, with class and national concerns intermingled and reverberating against each other, that the various land invasions and other actions in the area must be viewed.

By the time the war was completely over in early 1886, more than fifteen haciendas in the Huancayo area alone had been invaded by the peasants. Most of these properties belonged to people who had collaborated with the Chileans or with Iglesias: three to Luis Milón Duarte, four to the Valladares brothers, two to Jacinto Cevallos, and several to other "collaborators." Both Duarte and Giráldez had been assassinated. And in the Cerro de Pasco area, where the elite had also cooperated with the Chileans, the peasants had invaded a total of sixteen municipal properties and ten private haciendas.

While the actual mechanics of many of these actions are not known, the general context in which they occurred is fairly clear. In the course of the various resistance campaigns against the Chileans (1882–1883) and against Iglesias (1884–1885), the peasants gained de facto control of the countryside. In the same way as the regular armies, the peasant guerrillas lived off the land, taking cattle and other supplies from the haciendas to feed themselves or, in some cases, to finance the purchase of arms. Whenever they were faced with a superior force, the *montoneras* would retire to the high *puna* regions, which served as a nearly impenetrable defense. But it was precisely in the high *puna* that most of the large properties were located. Since the *hacendados* were forced to remain in the cities throughout these campaigns, whether or not the peasants actually held the entire land surface of the various haciendas, they were the only force in the countryside with the power to control hacienda resources. Motivated by their newly developed combination of nationalist outrage and class hostility, they used the existing balance of power to expand and consolidate their hold over the elite's property.

Yet it is important to emphasize that the land invasions were not indiscriminate. For the most part, they occurred in areas where the elite had collaborated openly with the Chileans or with Iglesias. The victims were mainly the individual landowners known to have been the worst offenders in this regard. In areas where the Cacerista alliance had been maintained, in contrast, most notably in the northern part of the Mantaro valley, there were no invasions at all. Thus it seems necessary to take the testimony of the *hacendados* and other sources close to them, such as the Chilean commanders, foreign consular officers, or political authorities, with a rather large grain of salt. While violent and racially motivated actions did occur, the generalized peasant mobilization in the central highlands was far from being an all-out racial war or the unleashing of some form of savage, atavistic barbarism. Quite the contrary, it was the Indian and mestizo peasants, rather than the elite, who were willing to subsume their class interests to a national resistance effort. They stopped doing so only once they realized that the elite was unable to accept them as patriotic soldiers.

But the heaviest blow to the peasant guerrillas' legitimacy was to come when Andrés Cáceres accepted the Treaty of Ancón. Signed in October 1883, the treaty changed the balance of power in the country as a whole by getting the Chilean army out of Lima and the Iglesistas into the presidential palace. Though it took Cáceres until June 1884 to acquiesce to the Ancón treaty, once he did so his entire view of the balance of forces in the central sierra underwent a transformation. Since the war with Chile was officially over, it was no longer necessary to fashion the broadest possible coalition to resist a foreign invasion. Indeed, given the broad and unpopular territorial concessions made to Chile by Iglesias, the issue became what type of alliance would be most successful in the impending and probably inevitable internal conflict between Iglesistas and Caceristas. And in that context the peasant guerrillas, with their control of elite property and their democratic pretensions, began to look increasingly less attractive to the leader of the La Breña campaign.

On July 2, 1884, a mere month after he accepted the Ancón treaty, Cáceres ordered the execution of four peasant guerrillas in the Plaza Huamanmarca in Huancayo. Their leader Tomás Laimes, a noncommissioned officer from Huanta, Ayacucho, confessed to sacking the haciendas of Tucle, Laive, and Ingahuasi, and distributing the booty among his men. He also admitted that his followers had killed Giráldez, among others, but insisted this was because the victims were traitors to the *patria* and Chilean spies. It is clear that, despite their recognition of guilt, the peasant guerrillas were confused and disoriented by what was happening to them. After all, the main reason they had entered Huancayo was to receive a supposed decoration from Cáceres in reward for their patriotism.

The execution of Laimes and his men marked the beginning of a concerted campaign by the Cacerista authorities to repress peasant mobilization. Several weeks after that first incident, Cáceres's representative in Huancayo sent a letter to the governor of Comas urging that the *montoneros* return to Manuel Fernando Valladares the cattle, sheep, horses, and llamas that they had taken from his haciendas Runatullo, Pampa Hermosa, Curibamba, and Ususqui. "This . . . general command gives the individuals from those communities every guarantee," he said,

> that they will not be persecuted or molested for the mistakes they have made; but [if they do not return what they have taken] . . . this office will dictate the most decisive and urgent measures in order to

capture those delinquents, as the most excellent General [Cáceres] has ordered, and impose upon them the severe and exemplary punishment that their grave crimes deserve.

Thus the Comas guerrillas, who only a short time before had been the backbone of Cáceres's resistance, were suddenly defined as a group of common criminals. This change was not due to any particularly barbarous acts they had committed, however, but simply to the fact that, if Cáceres wished to make a bid for national power, it was no longer possible to leave the countryside in the hands of independently armed peasants.

As Luis Milón Duarte, Juan Enrique Valladares, Jacinto Cevallos, Dr. Giráldez, Manuel Fernando Valladares, and many other *hacendados* had known from the beginning, to base a resistance campaign on an armed, mobilized, and increasingly autonomous peasantry was a risky proposition. But Cáceres and his followers had made an even more dangerous mistake. Because the La Breña campaign did not have the support of the entire regional elite, the Caceristas had in effect given the peasants the power to decide which *hacendados* were traitors to the cause. Yet long before the civil war was over, it became clear to the hero of La Breña that, in order to build an alliance that would carry him to the presidential palace, he had to mend fences with the *hacendados* as a class, including those who had collaborated with the Chileans. The only way to do so was to give the *hacendados* what they wanted and repress the very guerrillas who had made the La Breña campaign possible in the first place. What was not clear until much later was that it would take the government twenty years to bring the countryside under control.

Notes

For complete references and footnotes, see the original version of this piece in Florencia E. Mallon, *The Defense of Community in Peru's Central Highlands* (Princeton, N.J.: Princeton University Press, 1983), pp. 80–101. For a more recent interpretation of these events, see Florencia E. Mallon, *Peasant and Nation: The Making of Postcolonial Mexico and Peru* (Berkeley: University of California Press, 1994), especially chapters 6, 7, and 8.

1   From a *huayno*, or popular folk song, quoted in Adolfo Bravo Guzmán, *La segunda enseñanza en Jauja*, 2d ed. (Jauja, 1971), p. 286.

2   *Montoneras* refers generally to bands of armed men organized informally in the countryside to support a particular political cause. This term was already used to refer to armed bands in the central highlands during the Wars of Independence.

3   *Galgueros* refers to peasants in charge of pushing *galgas*, or large boulders, down on the enemy from the top of surrounding hills.

PRIESTS, INDIANS, SOLDIERS, AND HEROES

Manuel González Prada

Peru's disastrous defeat in the War of the Pacific in 1881 prompted soul-searching about the troubled relations of state and society. No one was more scathing than Manuel González Prada, a brilliant turn-of-the-century cultural critic and poet. Besides barbs against the clergy and the military, he wrote passionately about Peru's racial divisions, which he believed obstructed national progress, prefiguring the pro-Indian intellectuals of the indigenista *movement of the 1920s in his call for attention to the plight of the indigenous majorities. Yet González Prada also had a weak spot for army colonel Francisco Bolognesi and navy admiral Miguel Grau, feeding the national obsession with martyr-heroes who die terrible deaths for honor and country, and, perhaps above all, maintained a utopian faith in Western science and Peru's future generations.*

The Saber

A general, an empty barrel; an army on the march, the plague.
—Jonathan Swift, *Gulliver's Travels*

No one is so sensitive to the influence of authority as the soldier. The habit does not make the friar; but the stripes figure a great deal in the schooling of the tiger. Just stuffing a man into military uniform infuses him with servility toward his superiors and despotism toward his subordinates. How insolent the colonel's arrogance in his rebuke of the humble recruit! But how repugnant that same colonel's lowliness in the presence of a vain general! The army hierarchy is like a mountain of men who kiss the behinds of those above them and are kissed in the same place by those below.

And nevertheless, many sociologists extol military service as the most

Figure 12. "Wherever you push, pus comes out," said Manuel
González Prada of late-nineteenth-century Peru. (Courtesy of
Biblioteca Nacional del Perú)

rapid and sure means to civilize nations. Thus: instead of a teacher with
his primer, the corporal with a hickory cane; instead of the classroom
that sharpens the intelligence, the marching field or barracks yard where
the brain atrophies to the point of turning into the simple propellent of
automatic maneuvers. To see the civilizing quality of the barracks, one
has only to compare the conscript at the moment of enlistment with the
same man after years of service. The one who left honest, compassionate,
and hardworking comes back bribe-hungry, inhuman, and slothful. Indeed, there abounds in the population a lazy and knavish kind of person,
a composite of all vices and uselessness: the old soldier. The Peruvian who
becomes a military man offers us a metamorphosis in reverse, a butterfly
turned into a caterpillar.

The friar has served for many years as a target for satirical poets and
maniacal heretics. But does not the soldier deserve just as much derision
and scorn? A battalion does not differ much from a brotherhood. A prior
and a colonel differ in that the first mumbles prayers and the second
vomits blasphemies. If one translates the Latin in his breviary into hard
penance, the other only half understands the gibberish of his strategy.

The wearers of the uniform and the habit match each other in their low morals, equally degrading the barracks and the monastery, it being the same to obey the drumbeat as the bell's clatter, submitting oneself to army commands and the rules of the order. If friars and soldiers share the same obeisance to authority, they differ in many other ways. The friar stuffs his gut, drinks, gambles, and seduces women; but the soldier not only partakes in all this mischief, but also robs, burns, rapes, and kills. The friar covers himself with wine stains and grease spots from thick soup; the soldier appears with mud stains and spattered with blood. Priapus returns in the tonsure wearer, Cain in the saber carrier.[1] Priapus entertains us. Cain horrifies us. Tonsured pigs will never cause the same horror as epauletted beasts.

True, the inquisitor and the warrior spring forth from the friar, as shown by Saint Domingo of Guzmán and Carlist monks;[2] but from the soldier comes the Jesuit, as demonstrated by Saint Ignatius of Loyola. If the habit errs, the uniform backs it up. Without the support of brute or military force, neither the great religious persecutions nor the auto-dafés would have taken place. The soldier was always with the inquisitors and the executioners on guard by the bonfire. Even today, the saber supports the cross.

Only a perverse morality can make us regard as bandits six shirtless men who hang about the outskirts of a city and as heroes six thousand uniformed outlaws who invade the neighboring country's territory to steal away lives and property. What is bad in the individual we judge to be good in the collectivity, reducing good and evil to a simple question of numbers. The enormity of a crime or vice transforms it into a praiseworthy action or into virtue. We call the robbery of a million "business" and the garroting of entire nations "a glorious deed." The scaffold for the assassin; apotheosis for the soldier. And, nevertheless, the obscure laborer who kills a fellow worker, whether in revenge for some injury or to take his money or his wife, does not deserve so much ignominy or punishment as the "illustrious soldier" who kills twenty or forty thousand men to gain glory or to win the field marshal's baton.

Examining this closely, free from the usual prejudices: who are Alexander, Caesar, Napoleon, all the official heroes whose examples we cite to youth in civics books? Throat-slitters of human cattle. But we revile the practitioner of animal sacrifice and glorify the butchers of men. . . .

When man leaves behind his atavistic ferociousness, war will be remembered as a prehistoric barbarity, and famous and admired warriors of today will figure in the sinister gallery of the devil's children, by the side of assassins, executioners, and butchers. Napoleon's skull will be stacked next to that of a gorilla. Kuropatkin's sword will lie next to the arrows of a savage Indian.

The barracks have never been a civilizing school. And they never will be. They are a chunk of primitive jungle encrusted in the heart of modern cities.

Military science always reduces to the art of turning men into brutes and savages. To civilize with the saber, then, amounts to the same as to whiten with soot or to put out a fire with sulfuric acid.

Speech at the Politeama Theater

. . . With the freed, if undisciplined, masses of the Revolution, France marched to victory;[3] with armies of disciplined and unfree Indians, Peru will always go down to defeat. If we make Indians into servants, what nation will they defend? Like medieval serfs, they will only fight for a feudal lord.

And, although it may be hard and even cruel to repeat it here, do not imagine, ladies and gentlemen, that the spirit of servitude is peculiar only to the Andean Indian. We coastal mestizos also have in our veins the blood of the subjects of Phillip II mixed with the blood of the subjects of Huayna Capac. Our spine tends to bend.

The Spanish nobility left its degenerate and wasteful traits; the winners of the Independence Wars left their progeny of soldiers and bureaucrats. Instead of sowing wheat and mining metal, the youth of the last generation preferred to atrophy their brains in the barracks and rot behind the desk in state offices. Men suitable for the rough labors of the countryside and mines sought after the leftovers from the banquets of the bureaucracy, sucking insatiably the juices of the national treasury, and placed the caudillo who provided bread and honors above the nation that demanded money and sacrifices. For this reason, although Peru always had liberals and conservatives, there was never a true liberal or conservative party, but rather three great divisions: the rulers, the conspirators, and the indifferent by reason of egoism, imbecility, or disillusion. This is why, at the supreme moment of struggle, we did not confront the enemy as a bronze colossus, but as a pile of lead filings; not as a strong and united nation, but as a series of individuals attracted to the war by personal interests and divided among themselves by a factionalist spirit. When the most obscure soldier in the invading army had no other words on his lips but

Chile, we, from the highest general to the humblest recruit, repeated the name of a caudillo, like medieval serfs invoking a feudal lord.[4]

Indians of the moors and mountains, mestizos of the coast: all of us were ignorant and servile. We did not win, nor could we win.

If the ignorance of those who govern and the servitude of the governed were our conquerors, then let us turn to Science, that redeemer that teaches us how to soften Nature's tyranny and to adore Liberty, that engendering mother of strong men.

I am not speaking of the mummified science that is crumbling to dust in our retrograde universities. I am speaking of Science invigorated by the blood of the century, of Science with ideas of a gigantic radius, of Science that transcends youth and tastes like honey from Grecian beehives, of positivist Science that in only a century of industrial application has produced more good for humanity than thousands of years of theology and metaphysics.

I speak, ladies and gentlemen, of freedom for all, and especially for the least powerful. The cliques of creoles and foreigners who inhabit the strip of land between the Pacific Ocean and the Andes do not form the real Peru; the nation is made up by the Indian masses spread across the Eastern slopes of the mountains. The Indian has dragged along at the bottom level of civilization for three hundred years, as a hybrid with the vices of the barbarian without the virtues of the European. Teach him only to read and write, and you will see whether or not in a quarter of a century he will rise to the dignity of a man. To you, schoolteachers, falls the task of galvanizing a race that sleeps under the tyranny of the justice of the peace, magistrate, and priest, that trinity that brutalizes the Indian. . . .

In this labor of vengeance and reconstitution, we cannot depend on men of the past. The aged and worm-eaten trunks already produced their poisonous flowers and sour fruits. Let new trees be planted to give new flowers and new fruit! The old to the grave, the young to the work ahead!

Grau

Epochs exist in the history of every people that are personified by a single individual: Greece in Alexander, Rome in Caesar, Spain in Charles V, England in Cromwell, France in Napoleon, America in Bolívar. In Peru of 1879, it was not Prado, La Puerta, or Piérola.[5] It was Grau.

When the Huáscar [an iron-clad ship] weighed anchor in search of adventure, always risky and sometimes unfruitful, everyone turned their

Figure 13. Miguel Grau, one in Peru's pantheon of
military heroes, was celebrated by Manuel González
Prada as "human to a fault." (Courtesy of Biblioteca
Nacional del Perú)

eyes upon the ship's commander, everyone followed him with the wings
of the heart, everyone was with him. Everyone knew that triumph bordered on the impossible, given the superiority of the Chilean fleet; but
the sight of the Huáscar flattered national pride, a knight on the seas, an
echo of the legendary paladin who never counted his enemies before the
battle, because he expected to count them once they were conquered or
dead.

We, the legitimate inheritors of Spanish chivalry, inebriated ourselves
in the perfume of heroic actions; so much so that others, less innocent
than we and more imbued with the century's maxims, scorned the smoke
of glory and sated themselves with the butterscotch of cheap and easy
victories.

And we deserved an apology!

The Huáscar broke blockades, chased transport ships, snuck up on
fleets, escaped from ambushes and chases, and, more than a ship, seemed

a living being with the wings of an eagle, the vision of a lynx, and the wiles of a fox. Thanks to the Huáscar, a world that loves winners forgot our disasters and burned incense to us. Thanks to the Huáscar, hearts less open to hope gained enthusiasm and felt the generous impulse of sacrifice. Thanks to the Huáscar, in sum, the enemy was upset in his plans, he felt a vacillating uncertainty, and swallowed the exasperation of humiliated vanity. For the monitor, watching over the southern coasts, appearing at the most unexpected moment, seemed to say to Chile's ambition: "You will not pass here." All of this we owe to the Huáscar, and the soul of the monitor was Grau. . . .

He was human to a fault, exercising a generosity that in war's din ended up rousing our anger. Even today, remembering the cruelty of the Chilean conquerors, we deplore the exaggerated clemency of Grau on the night of Iquique.[6] To understand and forgive, one must make an effort, quiet the searing pain of an open wound, consider what happened from a more impartial distance. Then we can recognize that tigers that kill for the sake of killing or wound for the sake of wounding do not deserve to call themselves great, but rather men who in combat's madness know how to save pain and lives. . . .

As the flower of his virtues, Grau rejected resignation. No one knew more about danger, yet he marched to the front, eyes open, with a serene countenance. In him, there was nothing comic or faked; he personified naturalness. On looking at his loyal and open face, on shaking his weathered and calloused hand, one could feel that the blood of this body beat from a noble and generous heart.

This was the man who, in a boat of scant artillery, with inexpert sailors, found himself surrounded and attacked by the entire Chilean fleet on October 8, 1879.

In the heroic combat of one against seven, Grau could have surrendered to the enemy; but he understood that he was condemned to die by the nation's will, that his fellow citizens would not have pardoned his begging for life on the deck of conquering ships.

Yes. If the admirers of Grau had been asked what they demanded from the Huáscar's commander on October 8, all would have responded like Corneille's Horace: "That he die."[7]

Everything might have been suffered with stoic resignation, except the Huáscar afloat with its commander alive. We need the sacrifice of the good and humble to erase the opprobrium of the bad and haughty. Without Grau at Angamos Point, without Bolognesi at the bluff of Arica, would we have the right to call ourselves a nation?[8] What cause for embarrassment have we not shown the world, from the ridiculous skirmishes to the inexplicable mass desertions, from the treacherous flight of the caudillos to byzantine seductions, from the underground machinations of those of vulgar ambition to the sad burlesque of rope-dancing heroes!

In the war with Chile, we did not just shed blood. We were lepers. One forgives the grounding of a frigate with an inexperienced crew and flustered captain. One pardons the defeat of an undisciplined army with cowardly or inept officers. One comprehends people's cowering fear after continuous calamities on land and at sea. But one does not forgive, or pardon, or comprehend the upending of moral order, the complete destruction of public life, the macabre dance of buffoons disguised as Alexanders and Caesars.

Nonetheless, in the grotesque and somber drama of defeat, now and then luminous and likable figures step forward. War, with all of its evils, did us the favor of proving that we still know how to produce men of manly temper. Let us take heart, then. The rose does not flower in the swamp. The nation in which a Grau or a Bolognesi is born must be neither dead nor completely degenerate. . . .

Notes

These writings come from Manuel González Prada, *Pájinas Libres* (Lima: Fondo de Cultura Popular, 1966) and *Horas de Lucha* (Lima: Peisa, 1989), translation by the editors.

1   González is referring to the Greek god Priapus, a symbol of sex, and to Cain, the Old Testament character who murders his brother.

2   These were the fierce partisans of Charles IV in Spain.

3   In 1793 the revolutionary government in France established the first mass draft.

4   González means General Andrés Avelino Cáceres, the leader of resistance against the Chileans in the Andes.

5   These were other Peruvian leaders and politicians of the time.

6   In this battle, Grau's navy defeated the Chileans, killing their admiral. Grau returned the admiral's belongings to his widow along with a letter of condolence.

7   The reference is to a character in a play by the seventeenth-century French playwright Corneille about war in classical Rome.

8   Francisco Bolognesi was a Peruvian officer killed by the Chileans in the battle of Arica.

WOMEN OF LIMA

Flora Tristán

The daughter of a French mother and an Arequipan aristocrat father, Flora Tristán was plunged by her father's early death into a life of poverty in Paris. This background and an abusive husband fueled Tristán's lifelong commitment to economic justice and feminism. Her Peregrinations of a Pariah, *written about a voyage to Peru in the 1830s, pictured Lima as what literary critic Mary Pratt calls a "feminitopia" of independent, mysterious women, exemplified by the allure of the epoch's distinctive fashion: a black veil and wrap, or saya. Tristán returned to France in 1834 and devoted her life to women's and workers' rights.*

There is no place on earth where women are more *free* and have more influence than in Lima. They reign there uncontested. They are the instigators of everything. It seems that the women of Lima absorb for themselves alone the little bit of energy that this warm, intoxicating temperature leaves to its happy inhabitants. In Lima, the women are generally taller and better constituted than the men. They are mature at eleven or twelve years of age; nearly all of them marry at that age and are very prolific, usually having from six to seven children. They have fine pregnancies, give birth easily, and recover quickly. Almost all nurse their babies, but always with the help of a wet nurse who supplements the mother and, like her, suckles the child. That is a custom that comes to them from Spain, where in well-to-do families the babies always have two nurses.

In general the women of Lima are not beautiful, but their pleasing faces seduce with irresistible charm. There isn't a man whose heart does not beat with pleasure at the sight of a Liménienne. Their skin is not swarthy, as is believed in Europe; on the contrary, for most it is very white. The others, according to their various origins, are dusky, but with a

Figure 14. Socialist and feminist Flora Tristán
saw traces of a "feminitopia" in nineteenth-
century Lima.

smooth, velvety skin and a warm, vivid complexion. All the Lima women
have fine coloring, bright red lips, beautiful, naturally curly black hair,
dark eyes, admirably shaped, with a brilliant indefinable expression of
spirit, pride, and languor. In this expression lies all the charm of their
person. They speak with great fluency and their gestures are no less elo-
quent than their words. Their dress is *unique*.

Lima is the only city in the world where this costume has ever appeared.
Men have tried in vain to find its origin, even in the oldest chronicles,
but no one has yet discovered it. It does not resemble the various Spanish costumes at all, and what is most certain is that it was not brought
over from Spain. It was found when Peru was discovered, although, as is
well known, it never existed in any other city in America. Called a *saya*,
this costume is composed of a skirt and a kind of sack called a *manto* that
covers the shoulders, arms, and head. I hear our elegant women protest-
ing the simplicity of this costume; they are far from suspecting its coquetry. Made in different materials according to rank and fortune, that
skirt is of such extraordinary workmanship that it deserves a place in mu-

seums as a curiosity. This type of costume can only be made in Lima, and the Liméniennes claim that one must be born in Lima to be a maker of *sayas*; that a Chilean, an Aréquipénien, a Cuzquénien could never succeed in *pleating the saya*. This claim, whose truth I am not anxious to verify, proves how different from all known costumes this dress is. I am now going to try, by citing some details, to give an idea of it.

To make an ordinary *saya* one must have twelve to fourteen ells of satin; it is lined in a soft, thin silk or in very light cotton; the dressmaker, in exchange for your fourteen ells of satin, brings you a little skirt of three-quarters length that, from the waist, measured as two fingers above the hips, goes down to the ankles; it is so close-fitting that at the bottom it is only wide enough to permit one foot to be put before the other as one walks with tiny steps. Thus one is held as tightly by this skirt as by a corset. It is pleated from top to bottom in very narrow pleats and so evenly that it would be impossible to find the seams; these pleats are so firm and give such elasticity to this sack that I have seen *sayas* that had lasted for fifteen years and still kept enough elasticity to show off the figure and respond to all movements.

The *manto* is also artistically pleated but made of a very light material; it cannot last as long as the skirt nor can the pleating resist the continual movements of the wearer or the humidity of her breath. High society women wear *sayas* of black satin; elegant women also have them in fancy colors such as violet, brown, green, dark blue, or striped, but never in light colors because the prostitutes have adopted these by preference. The *manto* is always black, entirely covering the bust; only an eye is left visible. The Lima women always wear a small blouse, of which only the sleeves are visible; these sleeves, short or long, are of rich materials— velvet, colored satin, or tulle. But most of the women have bare arms in all seasons. The footwear of the Lima women is of an attractive elegance. They have pretty satin shoes in all colors, decorated with embroideries; if they are all of one color, the ribbons are in a contrasting shade. They wear silk stockings in various colors with richly embroidered clocks. Everywhere Spanish women are noticed for the rich elegance of their footwear, but there is so much coquetry in the shoes of the Lima women that they seem to excel in even that aspect of their apparel. The women of Lima have their hair parted in the middle; it falls in two perfectly made braids, ending in a large bow of ribbon. This style, however, is not exclusive. There are women who wear their hair curled *Ninon* style, hanging in long locks of ringlets on their bosoms, which, according to the custom of the country, are almost always bare.

Figure 15. For many Europeans, the so-called *tapadas*—upper-class women who veiled themselves in a distinctive black wrap, or *saya*—seemed to symbolize the exoticism and allure of the "City of Kings." Here they appear in Lima's Torre Tagle Palace in a 1911 photograph by Alphonse Dubreuville. (Courtesy of Biblioteca Nacional del Perú)

A Liménienne in a *saya* or dressed in a pretty gown coming from Paris is no longer the same person; one searches in vain, in the Parisian gown, for the seductive woman one encountered in the morning in the church of Sainte Marie. So, in Lima, all foreigners go to church, not to hear the monks chant the Holy Office, but to admire in their national costume these so different women. Everything about them is, in fact, seductive; their posture is as delightful as their walk; and when they kneel, they bend their heads archly, revealing their pretty arms covered with brace-lets, and their little hands whose fingers, resplendent with rings, caress a large rosary with voluptuous agility, while their furtive glances turn in-toxication into ecstasy.

One must, however, call attention to the extent to which the dress of the Lima women favors and assists their intelligence in acquiring the great liberty and dominating influence that they enjoy. If they should ever abandon this costume without acquiring new moral values, if they did not replace the means of seduction furnished them by this disguise and acquire instead talents and virtues directed toward the happiness and improvement of others, virtues for which until then they had not seen the need, one can predict without any hesitation that they would immediately lose all their power, and that they would even fall rather low and would be as unhappy as human creatures can be; they could no longer enjoy that incessant activity that their incognito favors and would be prey to bore-dom and without any means of compensating for the loss of esteem gen-erally suffered by beings accessible only to sensual pleasures. In proof of this point I am going to offer a little sketch of the habits of Lima society, and the reader may judge by this exposé the correctness of my observa-tion.

The *saya*, as I have said, is the national costume; all the women wear it, no matter what their rank; it is respected and is a part of the country's cus-toms, like the veil of Moslem women in the Orient. From one end of the year to the other, Lima women go out disguised thus, and whoever would dare to take from a woman in a *saya* the *manto* that entirely hides her face, except for an eye, would be indignantly pursued and severely punished. It is accepted that any woman *may go out alone*; most of them are followed by a negress servant, but that is not obligatory. This costume changes the person so much—even her voice, whose inflections are altered (the mouth being covered)—that unless the person has something remark-able about her, such as being very tall or very short, or is lame or hunch-backed, it is impossible to recognize her. One can easily imagine, I think, the many consequences resulting from a state of continual concealment, which time and habit have established and the laws have sanctioned or at least tolerated. A Lima woman breakfasts in the morning with her husband, in a little dressing gown in the French manner, her hair tucked up just like that of our Parisian women. If she wants to go out, she puts on her *saya* without a corset (the girdle of the lower part holding her figure sufficiently), lets her hair down, covers herself, that is to say, hides her face with her *manto*, and sets out for wherever she wishes. In the street she runs into her husband, who doesn't recognize her, leads him on with the eye, flirts with him, provokes remarks, enters into a long conversation, is offered ices, fruit, cakes, gives him an appointment, leaves him, and immediately gets into another conversation with a passing officer. She can push this new adventure as far as she wishes without ever removing her *manto*. She goes to see her friends, takes a walk, and returns home for dinner. Her husband doesn't ask where she has been for he knows perfectly well that if she wants to hide the truth, she will lie, and since there is no way to keep her from it, he takes the wisest course of not asking her. Thus these ladies go alone to the theater, to bull fights, to public meetings, balls, promenades, churches, go visiting, and are much seen everywhere. If they meet people with whom they want to chat, they speak to them, leave them, and remain free and independent in the midst of the crowd, much more so than the men, whose faces are uncovered. This costume has the tremendous advantage of being at once economical, very neat, convenient, and always ready without ever needing the least care.

From what I have just written about the costume and manners of the Lima women, one can easily see that they must have a set of ideas quite different from those of their European sisters who from childhood are slaves to laws, values, customs, prejudices, styles, and everything else; whereas under the *saya*, the Lima woman is *free*, enjoys her independence, and relies with confidence on that true force that every being feels is within him when he can act according to the needs of his nature. The woman of Lima, whatever her position in life, is always *herself*; never is she subject to constraint. As a young girl, she escapes from the domination of her parents through the freedom given her by her costume. When she marries, she does not take her husband's name but keeps her own, and always remains her own mistress. When household cares annoy her too much, she puts on her *saya* and goes out just as the men do when they pick up their hats—acting with the same independence in everything. In their intimate relationships, whether frivolous or serious, the Lima women always keep their dignity, although their conduct in this respect is very different from ours. Like all women, they measure the strength of the love they inspire by the extent of the sacrifices made for them; but because since its discovery their country has drawn Europeans to such a great distance from their homes only for the sake of its gold, and because *gold alone*, to the exclusion of talents or virtue, has always been the sole object of consideration and the motive for all actions, and it alone has led to everything, talents and virtue leading to nothing, the Lima women, consistent in their behavior to the order of ideas that follows from this state of affairs, see proof of ardor only in the quantities of gold offered them. It is by the value of his gift that they judge the sincerity of the lover; and their vanity is more or less satisfied according to the sums, large or small, or the prices of the objects they have received. When one wishes to give an idea of the intensity of the love of Monsieur Such-and-such for Madame So-and-so, only this phraseology is used: "He gave her a sack full of gold; he bought for her at enormous prices the most precious things he could find; he completely ruined himself for her." It is as if we said, "*He killed himself for her!*" So the rich woman always takes money from her lover, though she may *give it to her negresses* if she cannot spend it; for her it is *a proof of love*, the *only* one that can *convince her that she is loved.* The vanity of travelers has led them to disguise the truth, and when they have told us about the women of Lima and the good luck they have had with them, they have not boasted about how these women cost them a small fortune right down to the souvenir given by a tender friend at the moment of departure. These customs are very strange but they are real.

The women of Lima concern themselves very little with household affairs, but since they are very active, the little time that they devote to them is enough to keep everything in order. They have a definite liking for politics and intrigue; it is they who concern themselves with positions for their husbands, their sons, and all the men who interest them. To attain their objective, there is no obstacle or dislike that they do not know how to surmount. Men do not meddle in this sort of business, which is just as well; they wouldn't extricate themselves with the same cleverness. The women love pleasure and fetes, seek out meetings, gamble, smoke cigars, and ride horseback, not in the English style, but wearing wide trousers like the men. They have a passion for sea bathing and swim very well. As social accomplishments they play the guitar, sing rather badly (however, there are some who are good musicians), and dance their native dances with indescribable charm.

In general the women of Lima are uneducated, do not read, and remain unaware of what is happening in the world. They have much natural wit, quickness of comprehension, good memories, and surprising intelligence.

I have described the women of Lima such as they are and not according to what certain travelers say; that has certainly been difficult for me, for the pleasant and hospitable manner with which they have received me has made me very grateful to them; but my role as *conscientious traveler* has made it my duty to tell the whole truth.

AMAZONIAN INDIANS AND THE RUBBER BOOM

Manuel Córdova

Rubber tappers, or caucheros, *fanned out across the jungles of Brazil, Bolivia, and Peru in the late nineteenth and early twentieth centuries to collect the milky latex that was the latest in the cycle of booms and busts in Peruvian exports to the industrial north. The tropical port of Iquitos became one of the richest cities in Latin America, even as native Amazonians were ravaged by forced labor and disease. Fifteen-year-old mestizo Manuel Córdova was kidnaped from a rubber camp on the Peru-Brazil border in 1907 by the Amahuaca Indians. His tale of life with the Amahuaca, recorded years later by the American timber surveyor Bruce Lamb, offers a vivid view of the customs and mythology of one of the dozens of indigenous groups in Peru's rain forests and the rubber boom's tremendous impact.*

O nce, we were watching the boys shoot arrows at one another in the open area beside the village. It was a pleasant, cool afternoon. A group of young men were batting a cornhusk ball back and forth, trying to keep the ball from touching the ground. The game broke up and they started target practice with bow and arrow.

It had been several months since our raid on the invaders, and firearms had not been seen nor mentioned. Now Xumu asked me to demonstrate the rifle again and sent one of the men to get one. My first shot demolished a small target on a distant tree. Some of the men showed less reluctance toward the gun than before, and the chief encouraged one or two to handle it, which they did with considerable awe. Then Xumu turned and asked me if they could learn to shoot it.

Now all eyes were upon me; no one breathed. I felt somehow that this was a crucial turn of events. Deliberately, calmly, I answered, "Yes, but it will use up many bullets. We might need this ammunition to defend ourselves against invaders if they come back."

The rifle changed hands carefully among the group, but there was no more comment, and with dusk coming on everyone drifted back toward the houses. I was walking slowly along beside the chief. After some moments of silence he paused and turned toward me. "Could you not get for us more guns and more bullets?"

A bomb burst in my brain and for a moment I could not control the racing chains of thought—buy guns, where, with what? I was careful to let none of these disturbing questions show on my face, and after a brief pause I answered slowly, "Well, it depends on producing caucho rubber to trade."

"Can you not train a group of men to make caucho?"

And my answer, a simple "Yes, I can, if they will follow my instructions."

We went on slowly toward the houses. My mind was seething with the implications of this exchange. Uppermost was a feeling that I might after all have some power over my future, which I had not had in all my time with the Huni Kui [Amahuaca]. I had simply gone along from day to day, blotting out the future. Now perhaps I could have some influence on that future. There might be alternatives. Dangers, too, but risks mean little to a seventeen-year-old.

The next day the chief brought the matter up again. "To produce caucho, tools are needed. What are they?"

"Good sharp axes and machetes," I answered.

"We have some, but the people do not know how to use them."

"Show them to me," I said.

Xumu ordered all the axes and machetes brought to him. The tribe still used Stone Age axes and did not know that a steel ax must have a sharp edge to cut effectively. The few axes they brought out had the cutting edges worn down to the kind of blunt edge found on their stone axes. The machetes were largely fragments, except for a few which I thought probably came from the raid on our caucho camp on the Jurua and which the chief had kept, unused.

We found a piece of sandstone that would do for a grinding stone, and I began to sharpen one of the axes to show the sharp tapering edge the tools must have. The chief ordered the men to sharpen the axes and the machetes my way. I asked him to tell all the hunters to locate the caucho trees in their territories, so we would know where to begin.

In a few days the equipment was ready—the axes, machetes, and some heavy wooden mallets made to my specifications. Meanwhile the hunters had located many caucho trees in the forest surrounding the village. Now the chief picked a group of men to learn how to cut caucho.

I was not an experienced cauchero, but I knew how it was done. It was mostly hard, tedious work and I wondered how the Indians would take to it. As for me, the new enterprise gave a new meaning to life and I was inwardly greatly excited. I knew this must not show and I think it did not, although Xumu was undoubtedly aware of how I felt.

The caucho tree, one of the large forest trees, has a smooth gray bark filled with the milky latex which forms rubber. It is not easy to extract the latex. First all of the large surface roots of the tree must be traced along the ground and the underbrush cleared around them. Then small saucer-shaped depressions are dug with a machete at three-foot intervals along the roots, and these are lined with green leaves.

While other men are building a pole and vine platform around the main trunk of the tree above the low-buttressed roots, the ground roots are tapped. This is done by taking a machete and heavy wooden mallet and cutting inch-wide grooves in the bark at intervals along the root so that the latex will flow into one of the leaf-lined depressions.

When the platform around the trunk is finished the axemen start felling the tree. This is done in such a way as to leave the bottom of the tree trunk resting on the stump, forming a triangle with stump and ground. Thus the trunk is up off the ground and may easily be tapped. This kind of tree-felling control is not easy to develop. Once the tree is felled, excavations to receive the latex are made at intervals beneath the trunk and are lined with leaves. When these are ready, rings are cut in the bark around the trunk just above each depression in the ground. All of this must be done in one day, because the latex flows most freely just after a tree is felled. Two trained caucheros can finish the work on a tree in a day, but we were far from this.

In the leaf-lined depressions the latex collects and the moisture drains into the ground from the naturally coagulating latex, so that in three days the chunks can be gathered. These are then put in a crude press near the next tree to be worked. When the press, made of four rough slabs of wood and a primitive lever, is closed, fresh latex is poured on the rubber chunks to hold it all together in a compact block. These blocks are made the size a man can carry on his back.

What a mess we had at the beginning! Teaching the men the various tasks involved was complicated by the fact that they alternated the caucho producing with hunting. Even the most willing of them could not be kept at this kind of hard sustained work day after day; it was too different from their usual way of life. However, they were eager to learn when I told them about some of the things I could buy for them when the rubber was ready.

With their good muscular coordination the men learned quickly to use the sharp axes and machetes and to cut into the bark without going too deeply. However, a great many caucho trees were felled improperly before they learned the skill needed to get one to fall exactly right. After the first group of Indians were relatively good at the caucho-cutting I had them teaching other Indians and before long had a good rotating labor force. There was no labor shortage, for the chief assigned the men to work just as he appointed hunting areas and agricultural plots. At any rate, it was many weeks before we had twenty blocks of rubber weighing nearly half a ton altogether.

Xumu determined that this number of blocks—one-man loads—would be best for the first trip to the trading post. Any discussion of the trading post was always vague. I was unable to find out anything about how far away it was or in which direction.

When the rubber blocks were ready, the chief began to pick the men for the trip. Each packer was assigned his block of caucho and set about preparing his pack harness and back pad for it. The chief made a careful selection, choosing the strongest and most reliable men. By this time I knew the men fairly well myself from working so closely with them in producing the caucho, and I was pleased at his selection.

My own equipment consisted of one of the rifles, a machete and a small back pack containing a rolled-up pair of pants and a shirt which the chief dug up from his store of captured goods from past raids. When I tried this outfit on, the Indians looking on laughed and poked one another. I felt strange, too, and the clothes were not a very good fit. They would get me by, though—I could hardly go into a trading post naked.

In a few days we were off through the trackless forest, moving toward the northeast. This was completely unfamiliar territory to me, and I still had no idea where we were going. It was obvious though that the Indians were heading for a specific location.

For several days we traveled overland in the same general direction, without crossing any major streams. One day at mid-afternoon we came to a large stream. I wondered what its name was, and my companions told me they called it Hono-Diri-Ra, river with rapids. This did not help me in trying to locate myself.

Beside this river we stopped and made a camp of sorts. Nixi was the leader and I found out he knew that the blocks of rubber would float. While we were busy making camp, he sent scouts out ahead along the riverbank. They came back during the night and reported all clear. In the morning we tied the blocks of rubber together with vines and made two small rafts of logs from the riverbank forest. The men worked at this eagerly, for it meant relief from the tedious packing of a heavy load.

Scouts and hunters went out ahead on foot, and we launched our flotilla of rafts, all tied together. We could control navigation somewhat with long rafting poles which we pushed against the river bottom, but this was mainly to keep us in the main current. We were content to float downstream at the river's speed. After several days, we began to travel on the river only at night. The rafts were hidden and we rested during the day while the scouts were out.

As we floated downriver there was time for me to consider the situations and problems I might run into at an unknown trading post where I would be a stranger. I thought it unlikely the Indians were taking me to a place that would provide easy means of escape. Actually, escape was not foremost in my thinking at this time. I was for the moment purposefully occupied with the Indians, learning much of their jungle medicine, and, as I think back on it, I was perhaps under the thought control of the old man through the trances. At least he felt confident enough in me to send us off to a trading post. No doubt my companions had instructions to see that I had minimum exposure to the outside world.

One day we pulled our flotilla up onto the riverbank and separated the caucho blocks, which we put out on the riverbank to dry. The rafts were broken up and the logs scattered. I noticed that the Indians were edgy, and I thought we must be coming to the end of our journey. We camped here and the men assembled their packs again. At dawn the following morning we were off through the forest. Late that night we came to a stop again on the riverbank, and the men started threading the rubber blocks on a long vine.

Off in the distance I thought I heard a dog bark. In the light of a descending moon and the first streaks of dawn, the men drew around for a conference. Nixi was spokesman, since he had worked most with me. I distinctly heard a cock crow off down the river. I was sure then what this gathering was all about.

Nixi said, "We have tied all the blocks loosely together and put them in the water. There is also a three-log raft, big enough for one man. If you go down along the bank and avoid the deep water you will come to a Brazilian trading post around the next point. It is small, two or three houses, only a few people. Take the caucho down and trade it for guns. Be back here not later than sunset, sooner if possible. We will have the village surrounded. In case of serious emergency, signal us with the whistle of the eagle that we have taught you, and we will come. We outnumber those in the village two to one, and the men there are few. We have studied the place well."

I put on the pants and shirt from my pack. They felt incredibly strange on my body. Nixi gave me a long rafting pole, and he and a couple of the others held the log raft while I climbed onto it. With the pole I gently pushed the raft into the shallow water, and the string of blocks on the vine rope followed.

Now I had time to think of what I would say at the trading post. I tried to remember the few words of Portuguese I had learned when I had come through Brazil with my Peruvian companions; that was at least two years ago now. I had lost track of time, except as the Indians marked its passage. It seemed it would be a good strategy to talk as little as possible, in spite of my curiosity about many things.

As I came around the point the sun was just coming up over the horizon. There in a cove was the small village on the riverbank just as Nixi had told me. It was merely a small clearing with a group of several small palm-thatched houses. Smoke was rising out of the roof of two. On the bank a man was drawing water with a bucket. He looked up and saw me, then rushed up to one of the houses with his bucket of water.

By the time he was back I was tying up my raft at the canoe landing.

"*Bom dia*," he called as he approached.

"*Bom dia*," I responded.

"Caucho for sale?" he asked.

"Yes."

"Where from?"

"Upriver."

"You can trade it here—no need to go farther down."

"Good. You have rifles?"

"Just got a shipment in."

"Winchester?"

"Yes, of course!"

I began to pull up the string of rubber blocks to tie it securely.

"Well-made blocks," he said. "Must be nearly a ton. I will send a man down to help you bring them up to the scales."

It took the two of us until mid-morning to carry all the blocks up to a deposit where the weighing scale stood. Then, with the trader, we started weighing each block. I tested the beam scales for balance before we started, and the trader noticed this.

"What price?" I asked. From his reply and my memory it seemed the price had gone up since I had entered the forest on the Rio Jurua.

It was nearly noon before we finished weighing. I had to fend off a thousand questions with a one-word reply—where my caucho camp was, how many people, all Peruvians, etc. I was anxious for the tally and to start making my purchases. We went into the store and I checked the tally— over a thousand pounds.

First I bought a box of rifles and had to check each of the six it contained, then two shotguns and a big load of ammunition, ten axes, twenty machetes, new pants and shirt, mirrors, knives, and beads.

Lunch was brought in by a middle-aged Brazilian woman, and I thought of my mother. How was she? Did she consider me dead?

We ate Brazilian bean stew, *feijoada completa*, a complete meal with farina to mix with the rice, bans, and meat. All this was followed by sweet black coffee. The food tasted good, and it reminded me of my past.

As we ate there were a thousand more questions.

"When would I be back with more caucho?"

"Soon."

"Seen any Indians?"

"A few."

"Any trouble with them?"

"No."

"Well, be careful, they are notorious around here."

"So . . ."

I noticed by a marked calendar that it was June 15, 1910. Then I had been gone over two and a half years. I had a thousand questions of my own I wanted to ask, but didn't because of the complications that might develop. However, it came out in conversation without my having to ask that the trading post was on the Purus River near the border between Peru and Brazil, and the trader was Antonio Rodrígues.

It was the middle of the afternoon before I could get everything tallied up. I asked, "You interested in more caucho if it comes out on the river above here?"

"Of course, any time."

There was a considerable balance of money after my purchases and I was not sure how to handle it. Money had no use where I was going, but

Figure 16. Rubber trader and Yaguas Indians, ca. 1900.
(Courtesy of the Aliaga family)

I thought I might be able to leave a deposit here as the men did at the trading posts I knew in Peru.

Finally Rodrígues himself suggested it. "Look, if you are coming back, I can open up a book for you and hold your balance for future purchases. What's your name for the account book?"

He wrote down the balance, and I signed it in a halting, unpracticed hand.

"Can your man take me around the point upriver with my purchases, in a canoe?"

"But of course, if that's what you want."

Another hour to load the canoe and shove off. It was close to sundown when I finally arrived back where I had started from in the morning. There was not a whisper nor the slightest evidence of my companions, but I heard a familiar birdcall and knew they were there.

The Brazilian and I unloaded the canoe, and as the man turned the point returning downriver to the village, the Indians swarmed out around me, and there was a rush to get my load out of sight and to get moving before we could be discovered or followed.

I had been careful to have things packaged in convenient-sized loads for back packing. Of course the packs going back were small and light in relation to the rubber blocks that had been packed out. Soon we were ready, and as we melted into the forest I felt tension go out of me. I removed shirt and pants and belonged to the forest again.

As we moved through the forest I became increasingly aware of distress in my stomach. When we stopped at midnight I was in trouble with diarrhea. For over two years I had eaten nothing seasoned with salt and felt that this and the unaccustomed food must have caused my upset. My companions were immediately suspicious of poison, but I assured them there was no reason to be.

In the morning they prepared an herbal concoction for me to drink, and it helped my distress. We went on, but I was weak. After my system cleared completely of salt and my food was again limited to smoked meat and fruit from the forest, my condition improved.

Going back, we stayed away from the river. It took us ten days at a forced pace, but we did not travel at night. On this trip I made an effort to observe natural features of the forest and terrain. I was sure this would not be the only trip we would be making over this route. From my companions' talk, I sensed that the general route had been scouted out in advance of our trip.

On the last day our pace picked up, and one of our party went on in advance to advise the chief of our arrival. As we entered the clearing there was a shout from the assembled villagers, a shout that we answered. The chief came directly to me for the greeting, and the whole tribe gathered around us. Xumu ordered the pack loads put in front of us in the large circle of onlookers. The new guns were unpacked first and there was a gasp from the crowd at the sight of them.

The chief made a speech. "These will defend us from our enemies," he said. "You have seen what happens when they speak with the voice of thunder. We will dominate the forest and live without fear. You know who obtained these things for us." The Indians shouted as he put his hand on my shoulder. "We can get more if they are needed. Other things can be obtained with caucho. Let me show you." He opened the packages.

Next were the axes and machetes, which were unwrapped. The chief told the crowd, "With these we will produce more caucho to buy more guns, and these tools will make it easier to clear our plantations."

Another shout of approval went up from the crowd.

Then the knickknacks were opened up—mirrors, beads, fishhooks and other small items. The women screamed with delight at sight of the vari-colored beads. But the real sensation came when the men and women both realized they could see themselves in the dozen small mirrors I had brought.

Everything was community property and all was passed around for inspection. Finally it all came back to Xumu for his final disposal of the items among the various houses of the village.

Our return was cause for a big celebration, and body painting got under way in preparation. The use of the mirrors to inspect and modify the facial decorations soon became an exciting diversion. In addition to the broad band of black painted from one ear across the mouth to the other ear, intricate combinations of small dots and fine lines were used to decorate the rest of the face. A great deal of care was taken to produce an original design, and the effects were often striking. Of course the whole expanse of the body provided space for additional artistic effort. With various combinations of red and black colors and design motifs of large and small dots, wavy and zigzag lines, and various geometric forms, a great variety of effects was produced. The painting was done with great care, and the men and women were proud of the impact of the final overall effect.

In addition, the women wore wide necklaces and armbands of beads and animal teeth. The men wore headbands of flaring, brightly colored feathers that gave an effect of wearing a brilliant crown. The men also often placed bright feathers in their perforated earlobes, nose septum, and lower lip. Some also wore feathered arm and leg bands. When the tribe was assembled, fully decorated, for a celebration, they filled the village with a gay, strikingly colorful menagerie.

Large jars of fermented beverages had been prepared by the women in our absence; large piles of firewood were ready. At sundown several small fires were started to light the dancing area between the houses.

Chief Xumu appeared from his house dressed in his ceremonial shirt decorated with brilliant feathers woven into the cotton fabric. In one hand he had the dance leader's baton—a whisk of feathers and coarse animal hair on a string, tied to one end of a short stick. He gave orders for the women to pass around gourd cups of fermented drink. The men tied strings of rattles around their ankles, and soon the chants started.

The actual dancing began in a casual way after the chanting had been in process for some time. At a signal from Xumu the men and women formed in a line, alternating men and women, joining arms. At the beginning the chief led the line in a slow chanting snake dance, but as the pace and animation picked up he handed the baton to a younger man.

The tribe had a large and varied repertory of chants. The dance itself changed in tempo with the mood of the chant, but there was little variety in the dance. At times the men and women would form separate lines with hooked elbows and dance in opposition or form two concentric circles, moving and changing direction on signal from the leader.

Every two or three hours there would be a pause to cool off and the drinks would be passed around again. By morning some showed the effects of alcoholic intoxication, but the drinking and the dancing went on. Disorders among the men began to show up by the afternoon of the next day. These were drunken brawls or pushing contests which the chief stepped in to settle before serious bodily damage was done. He received instant response and respect, even from the drunkest and most disorderly of the participants.

I found out later that the chief used these dances and drinking bouts to relieve harmlessly the aggressions and tensions of personal and inter-family rivalries. Xumu took care to see that differences were settled to the apparent satisfaction of all who were concerned. His word on any settlement was final. If some latent rivalry or misunderstanding remained, it had to wait for the next dance. No fighting or disorder among the men was permitted during the routine daily life of the tribe, even though personal conflicts and differences did develop. The chief had the means and the power to eliminate those few that could not control themselves and conform, and the tribe realized this. A demonstration of his control had been provided the day I was brought to the village by my captors when the old woman went into a frenzy of rage and tried to club me. I still wondered why.

After two days and nights of dancing, there was a day of rest. Then the village went back to the usual routine of food gathering from the forest, hunting, and gardening. Use of the new axes and machetes made the preparation and tending of the family garden plots much easier than when there had been only stone tools. I had to show them how to sharpen and use these tools and insist that they be kept in good condition. Grinding stones were brought from rock deposits I had seen along the river on our trip to sell the first lot of rubber.

In addition to hunting, it was the work of the men to clear patches in the forest for new planting areas each year. This was done in the dry season so the brush that was gathered up could dry and be burned. These operations were all done at the direction of the chief so as to be properly timed. The burning and the planting had to be done at the very end of the dry season, just before the rains started, for best results. Xumu was an excellent weather prophet. He would announce the beginning and end of the dry season within a few days of its occurrence.

I vividly remember the people sitting around Xumu in the village clearing under the clear dry-season night sky, with the brilliant stars shining on a black velvet backdrop. The tribe had many complicated legends and myths about the stars and their meaning, but I cannot now, after these many years, recall them in any detail.

The moon, they believed, was a man's head in the sky. It got there this way. A man named Yobo, a sorcerer, argued with the others until they were furious. One grabbed his axe and cut off Yobo's head. The body fell to the ground and the head went rolling down the trail.

The people dug a hole and buried both the body and the head, but the head found a way out and rolled after them. They were surprised and ran home and closed their houses. A great sky-blue buzzard flew down and took the head up into the sky, and it shouted back, "Goodbye my people. I am going up into the sky."

Up there high in the heavens the buzzard tore out the eyes and they became stars. The blood that spilled out became the colors in the rainbow. And the head now is the shining moon.

The stars became many. Some formed the outline of the body of *txaxo* the deer, others *xoko* the alligator. And now if you look closely you can see many shapes in the sky made by the stars.

IV · THE ADVENT OF
MODERN POLITICS

Q*ueremos Patria*—We Want a Nation," proclaimed historian Víctor Andrés Belaúnde at the turn of the century.[1] Like Argentina's "generation of 1880" and Mexico's *científicos*, Belaúnde and other technocrats believed Peru could develop into a modern country only under the "democratic caesarism" of a progressive oligarchy. What Francisco García Calderón called an "aristocracy of the spirit," united in its faith in Western science and economic liberalism, would supervise the civilizing of the Indian masses into a real "citizenry," bridging the gap between the "legal country" and the "real country," and the cultural and racial divisions that had riven Peru in the first century after independence.[2]

The world economy was rapidly expanding after the 1890s, and the demand for sugar, cotton, rubber, wool, and silver fueled an economic recovery from the devastating War of the Pacific. Foreign companies invested heavily, controlling the giant Cerro de Pasco Corporation and Northern Peru Mining. Andean peasants left their mountain homes for seasonal or even permanent labor in the mines and northern plantations, where families like the Leighs and Gildermeisters formed the backbone of a coastal plutocracy of bankers, entrepreneurs, and landowners. As part of "modernization" under the top-down paternalism of the oligarchical state, the Piérola government (1895–1899) launched a campaign to build hospitals, schools, highways, and railroads. "Centralization" and "national integration" grew into the watchwords of the times. Despite this progressive veneer, however, the "Aristocratic Republic" reinscribed the familiar logic of control by a white elite, and the divide between brown and white, mountains and coast, and poor and rich remained a dominant feature of the social topography of the nation.

Figure 17. Workers march in Lima, 1912. (Courtesy of TAREA)

Nevertheless, by the first decades of the twentieth century a series of political alternatives challenged the very premises of oligarchical rule. One was the so-called *indigenista* movement. Apostles like historian Luis Valcárcel and lawyer Hildebrando Castro Pozo attacked racist assumptions of Indian inferiority and degradation. They contended that the path to national renewal lay in "indigenous" principles of reciprocity and cooperation. *Indigenismo* was never a mass movement, but was fractured into regional schools and afflicted by the sometimes condescending romanticism of its mostly mestizo and creole protagonists about "the Indian." Still, it left a lasting mark. *Indigenista*-organized Indian leagues were forerunners to the peasant federations of the 1950s and 1960s. Some *indigenistas* also briefly worked for the Leguía government (1919–1930) to promote the legal recognition of peasant communities and against the expropriation of their lands by powerful *hacendados*, or estate owners. Most broadly, *indigenismo* cleared ground for visions of Peru's future that might build on the traditions and interests of the national majorities.

Socialism was a contemporary and sometimes complementary influence. The working classes had multiplied in the plantations, mines, and factories. Already by the turn of the century, anarchists had formed some of Peru's first trade unions in slaughterhouses, bakeries, and textile mills. A worker culture of ballads, newspapers, meetings, and strikes flowered. News of the 1910 Mexican Revolution and Russia's Bolshevik Uprising fanned peasant and worker organizing, and José Carlos Mariátegui emerged as the leader of Peru's socialist movement. At odds with the rigid orthodoxy of the Soviet-line Marxism of the Third International, the young writer and activist believed in building on Peru's Andean traditions, and developed close ties with *indigenista* intellectuals like Valcárcel and José Uriel García along with his later antagonist Víctor Raúl Haya de la Torre. Mariátegui died at thirty-five of a crippling bone disease, and his infant Socialist Party divided. Socialism did not disappear completely, however. Later groups as different as the Shining Path and the United Left fought to lay claim to Mariátegui's legacy and the trade union movements of the century's first decades.

The most cohesive of the new political forces was the Popular Revolutionary Alliance of America (APRA). Founded in Mexico in 1924 by the Trujillo-born Haya, and with strong support among the plantation workers and middle classes on the northern coast, the party featured a religious-military flavor that combined a personality cult around its leader with a faith that "sólo el APRA salvará al Perú" (only the APRA will save Peru). The APRA called for an "anti-imperialist front" to redeem "Indo-America." Yet it also premised that planned capitalism under a corporate state was the key to popular prosperity and Latin American freedom from northern hegemony. In its appeals to both the poor and middle classes under the rubric of national and regional destiny, and in its nucleation around a charismatic leader, the APRA was a harbinger of the populism that marked Latin American politics for the rest of the twentieth century.

Augusto Leguía's *oncenio,* or eleven-year rule, blocked radical change. The former treasury minister promised to detain "the advance of Communism . . . [and its] dreadful consequences" and opened the country to further investment by U.S. companies.[3] Opposition leaders were deported, including the young Haya. To back efforts to expand public works, urbanization, and the middle classes, Leguía mixed armed repression, electoral gerrymandering, and savvy stagecraft, like his appeal to popular religiosity through the showy dedication of the republic of Peru to the Sacred Heart of Jesus. His rallying cry was a "New Fatherland." Yet the country continued to rest on the unstable foundation of the export of raw materials to the wealthy northern countries. The lucrative profits filled the coffers of foreign companies and their allies in the national elite under this neocolonial brand of capitalism.

The crash of 1929 shattered the Peruvian economy. As demand for Peruvian exports plummeted in Europe and the United States, and protest and strikes erupted in Lima and on the northern coast, some observers claimed that a revolutionary transformation approached. An "Indian Lenin," Valcárcel predicted, would lead a "tempest in the Andes" to liberate the masses. Although these utopian hopes were never fulfilled—Leguía was replaced by strongmen Luis Sánchez Cerro and Oscar Benavides, the first in an assortment of twentieth-century military presidents—neither was Peru to make a smooth return to the supremacy of the "gentlemen's clubs" of the creole oligarchy.[4] Radical ideologies and mass movements along with economic transformation and dislocation had sparked a growing sense of entitlement among the nation's majorities. The contradictory and sometimes violent logic of these powerful forces would tear and reweave the fabric of national life for the rest of the century.

Notes

1   Quoted in Julio Cotler, *Clases, estado y nación en el Perú* (Lima: Instituto de Estudios Peruanos, 1978), p. 98.
2   Quoted in ibid., p. 99.
3   Quoted in Thomas E. Skidmore and Peter H. Smith, *Modern Latin America* (New York: Oxford University Press, 1984), p. 206.
4   There were major differences between the regimes of the modestly born and unmistakably mestizo populist Colonel Luis Sánchez Cerro (1931–1933) and the more staid and creole General Oscar R. Benavides (1933–1939), with his pro-Franco, right-wing prime minister José de la Riva Agüero. However, the rule of both strongmen was characterized by a crackdown on political opposition, especially the APRA, and military backing.

TEMPEST IN THE ANDES

Luis Valcárcel

Indigenismo was strongest in Cuzco, where it was linked not just to a call for dignity for Indians and social justice, but also to the ancient Incan city's claim as the true capital of Peru. Along with writer José Uriel García and photographer Martín Chambi, the Cuzco-born Valcárcel was one of Peru's most influential twentieth-century artists and intellectuals, and, as the founder of the Institute of Ethnology at Lima's public university of San Marcos, the "father" of Peruvian ethnology. These excerpts from Tempest in the Andes *reflect a strong romanticism about the noble purity of the "Indian race," yet they also demonstrate the impassioned energy of the* indigenista *demand for justice for Peru's Andean majorities.*

Culture will radiate once again from the Andes.

From the Andes will flow, like rivers, the currents of renovation that will transform Peru.

For ten thousand years, the Indian has been the only worker in Peru. He raised with his hands the gigantic fortress of Sacsahuamán, the Sacred City of the Sun, the Incan temples and palaces, the great continental roads, the canals, the water tanks, the colossal aqueducts, the innumerable terraces, the subterranean galleries, the colonial cities with their massive cathedrals and granite-cloistered convents, the bridges, the factories, the railroads, the ports, the infernal shafts of the deep, multi-million-dollar mines.

The Indian did it all, while the mestizo idled and the white gave himself over to his pleasures.

All of the timeless virtues of the Indian still pulse through his blood.

We possess one of the planet's most beautiful regions. The Andes and the jungle are prodigiously brilliant, with their riches and diverse products and climates.

We can live in well-being and plentitude. No abysmal anxieties torture us. The land, abundant and maternal, more than meets our present and future needs.

The modern virus of elegant parasitism penetrates Peru through the open door of its Europeanized capital.

Inca culture is an original organism. It appears in the pre-Columbian world with all the traits of a sublime product of that perpetually renewed union between man and the earth.

Isolated from other continents, it developed by a self-nourishing process, growing on its own, with no influence from other races or groups. It arrived to splendor and greatness, with a luxuriant vitality found only in those cultures that have not slashed the umbilical cord that unites them to the earth.

The Andes are an inexhaustible fountain of vitality for Peruvian culture. Neither the Incas nor the Indians of today have lost their telluric balance. They live with the mountains and rivers, linking their society to nature and mixing themselves with it, in a nebulous pantheism with the world around them.

Four centuries of implacable destruction of a race. For four centuries the white invaders have struggled to uproot a culture. Our history is the tragedy of this struggle. The man from across the seas and the aborigine square off in this gigantic duel, never backing away from affirming their being or bending before destiny's deadliness. Crazed with presumptuousness, the conqueror wants to wipe away the entire past of ten thousand years of indigenous culture. One by one, all the old institutions fall under the hammer of the destroyer. The barbarous victor smashes down the sumptuous temples gloriously erected by the Incas in their eagerness for immortality. The solar pedigree of the empire perishes with the last lords of Vilcabamba. The head of the last prince of Tahuantinsuyu rolls off the gallows. But it is in vain! The Indian soul cannot be torn from the essence of its culture!

Figure 18. Although born in a Puno village, photographer Martín Chambi was also part of Cuzco's *indigenista* school, and his pictures, like this stunning 1941 still of the ruin of Wiñay Wayna, asserted the value of Peru's Inca heritage. (Courtesy of Teo Allaín Chambi)

We went beyond the Spanish oppressor in the torpid detour of the republican period, uncomprehending of historical reality. The final glimpses of autonomy, the simulation of Indian authorities, the conservation of communal property, the refuge in ornamental celebration where the insignias of the Inca still reappeared on some of his descendants as a relic of his greatness: all, all had disappeared in the name of a burlesque and somberly ironic equality. More blind, more ignorant than the conquerors, we discard all the wise protective laws of the ancient kingdom, which in those distant times were issued with such great knowledge of juridic virtue. There has been no emancipation for the American race.

The tremendous tragic silence of which Peru has been the theater for four hundred years is the denial of a cardinal truth: this is a nation of Indians.

But once the truth is proclaimed, and dignity is granted to the Indian, that lord of the land, creation of the Andes, granite symbol of an immortal culture, the Quispes and the Huamáns will be proud to sign their names, and it will no longer be a disgrace for Doctor Crisanto Condori that his old parents—who sacrificed themselves for him—continue to love him as an offspring of the race, just as they did when he tended the lambs on the *ayllu*'s [community] hills.

We must measure and weigh the enormous transcendence of this sensational discovery, of this happy invention that Peru is a nation of Indians. This fact means the rehabilitation of the majority of the country's inhabitants. It means real liberty from their extended slavery. It means—above all and before all—that a national conscience has been born, that Peru is no longer a nation in chaos and without destination.

WATER!

Juan Pévez

Born on a small farm in the sun-drenched southern department of Ica, Juan Pévez spearheaded one of the first efforts to organize a peasant union, the still-existing Peruvian Peasant Federation. This excerpt from his autobiography describes a 1915 struggle with an estate owner for water. In his account, Pévez exemplifies the combination of firm respect for written documents and legal protocol with the aggressive desire for economic justice that characterized the growing worker and peasant movements of the early twentieth century and remains a prominent motif in Peru's agrarian politics to this day.

One night in December 1915, my father heard noises. He always went out to check whenever there was a noise or the dogs barked, so he left to see what was happening. He came back happy, and said to my mother:

"María, I just heard the bells from the Tacama estate [*hacienda*]."

"You know you can't hear those bells just like that. We hear them only on still nights without wind," replied my mother.

"Dad, there's water, there's water!" I said, getting out of bed immediately. "The bells mean that water's coming [down the irrigation canal]. . . ."

Everyone rose. Not thirty minutes passed before the church bells of Parcona began to ring, letting everyone know that water was coming. Let's go, let's go! We all left in a parade because it was great that water was arriving so early in the year. Seldom was there water in December. It usually arrived only in January, sometimes not until the middle of the month. Other times it came in February, or in dry years not at all or just a bit in March that dried up quickly. Those were terrible years for the farmers of the Ica valley. When there was no water for irrigation, there was no work . . . nothing to eat. Those were drought years.

When we got to La Achirana, the water was already flowing. Everyone was happy, and I said to my father:

"Dad, why don't we make the most of this and open the sluice gates to irrigate our fields? It could be that the estate owners don't yet realize that the water has arrived. Because the Picassos live in Ica, sleep in Ica, they probably haven't realized it yet."

"While I open the sluice, you and Genaro go and fix what needs to be done to start," he replied.

That's exactly what we did. But it was almost daylight. It was just before 5:00 A.M., and we saw that the water was flowing through the sluice off to the Picassos' Vista Alegre estate. I told my brother:

"Genaro, go and see if we can 'steal' a bit of the water. I don't think the serfs [*peones*] of the estate are here, because they generally don't start quite yet."

That was how we had to put it: "steal" water from the estate owner, because he didn't let anybody get water until he had first irrigated his own estate. Our miserable little canal ran off the main channel to his property. The small farmers of Parcona were always waiting at the sluice gates in hopes of being allowed some water.

I went running to the head of the canal, where my father was. I found him together with a lot of peasants, almost all with very small landholdings. The village elders were talking as they watched the water stream toward the estate.

"What do you think of our luck? Even though God sends the water for everyone, the rich, the *hacendados*, are always first."

"And pity those who try to contradict them or make them change their abusive ways!"

As they were saying all of this, they looked at me as if waiting for an answer. Of course, it was because I was the only one in Parcona who had finished high school and was then studying in the School of Agronomy. In spite of my young age, they regarded me as something of an authority. I said:

"There's a law that prohibits estate owners from doing whatever they want. The government has issued a law that regulates the distribution of water for agriculture."

"That doesn't seem right to us. None of us have heard of such a law."

"It's that we don't even read the newspapers to find out what's happening, and the estate owners aren't going to tell us anything that doesn't suit them. So if we want, we can begin irrigating our lands right now, but first we need to get up our nerve and roll up our pants! If you want to try it, let's open our sluices and start irrigating the land."

Don Pedro Castillo, then the lieutenant governor of our village, said to me:

"Look, Pévez, I'm going to give the order to open our two sluices, but only on account of the law you are talking about. . . ."

"Let them open the sluices, Don Pedro. Nothing will happen."

"I'll go with you. I have faith in what Juan Hipólito says," said José Gómez.

And at that moment, our elders proceeded to open the gates. The water that was flowing into the big canal of Vista Alegre began to switch into our smaller ones. Genaro and I ran to make sure the water was getting into our fields. My dad and five other men stayed to guard our sluice, because when the workers at the estate noticed the flow of water slowing down they would come to investigate.

That's what happened. Less than thirty minutes had gone by before the foreman at Vista Alegre, Don Manuel Pacheco, arrived with eight serfs from the estate. From far away, everyone could hear the shouts of Picasso's faithful servant. On arriving, he ordered two of his men:

"Shut the gates!"

Pedro Ramos, José Gómez, Aurelio Escate, and my father objected forcefully, and the struggle began. All were shouting at the top of their voices, trying to break the morale of the other side. When I heard all the commotion, I went running to the gate, bringing with me a heavy club of carob-tree wood as a precaution. When I got there, I saw my father on the ground getting beaten by two men. I flattened one with the club; the other came at me, but I backed off when I saw that he was much stronger than I. I ran into the grape arbor, and he couldn't catch me. More of our men began to arrive and started to attack. Seeing that his men were being beaten to a pulp, Pacheco shouted:

"Let's go, boys. These cowards will now have to deal with Mr. Picasso. They'll see where they are going to end up!"

"And you'll see what we're going to do to you!" we yelled back.

Our people continued to irrigate our land without worrying about the incident. The flow of water stopped a few minutes later. We had to wait until the next day. Some went home happy, but others were concerned.

Close to where the fight had occurred, people gathered to talk:

"What are we going to do now?" said someone.

"Picasso can take us to court," my father said.

"Don't be afraid. I know there's a law that regulates the distribution of irrigation water. Besides, there's a Technical Commission in Ica to make sure the law is obeyed. It's been functioning since last year. Tomorrow, let's form a delegation to go to Ica and talk with the person in charge of the office."

That's what I said. But our good neighbor José Gómez said:

"Why don't we go right now?"

"Very good. Let's go right now."

A delegation of eight was formed, and half an hour later we were on the path to Ica to look for the Technical Commission. The office was on the corner of Bolívar and Independencia streets. The director, engineer Ezequiel Gago, listened to us attentively and asked for all the details about what had happened, the canal location, and so forth. And he told us:

"In the afternoon one of our employees will come to verify the location of the canals and the details of the brawl. You wait at La Achirana and come back tomorrow at 10:00 A.M. with a delegation of only four men. This very afternoon I will let Mr. Picasso know that he should be here at the same time to clear up the water rights."

My father, I, José Gómez, Pedro Ramos, and Aurelio Escate made up the delegation. We arrived at the set time, just before Mr. Picasso's representative, Don Francisco Lorenzi, the estate administrator. Lorenzi presented documents and petitions, as did our delegation. I had prepared them with engineer Alejandro Barrios, my teacher at the School of Agronomy, who reread to me the law about irrigation rights.

Engineer Gago invited me to present the reasons for our complaint, and then did the same with Mr. Picasso's representative. Lorenzi maintained:

"The Indians of Parcona have turned their backs on an old commitment, an old, established custom. They have dared to open the gates to their fields, unlawfully taking advantage of water belonging to Mr. Picasso. As we all know, custom is law. But these people have trampled the law and appropriated most of the water."

"What you have just told us has passed into history," engineer Gago replied. "Today, there is a law that regulates the distribution and use of water for irrigation. It says that irrigation will follow the order of the smaller channels that branch off from the main canal, from top to bottom. There are no exceptions, no privileges or preferential treatment."

That is what this government official told us. In accordance with the new law, we drew up a document in triplicate, which was signed by both parties. The meeting ended, and the engineer Gago told both sides not to fight anymore. Our committee thanked the head of the Technical Commission for this act of justice in favor of the indigenous peasants of Parcona.

The people of Parcona were intensely happy. This was the first time in the history of the valley that a group of peasants had won a case against a powerful landowner like Picasso.

REFLECTIONS

José Carlos Mariátegui

Son of a mestiza seamstress in coastal Moquegua, Mariátegui was a self-taught intellectual who began writing for a newspaper in his teens and never went to the university. After returning from Europe in 1923, he embarked on a meteoric career as a political organizer and cultural critic, writing on topics as varied as the Inca empire and Surrealism. The young socialist often reflected the prejudices of his times (note, for instance, his sarcasm about "cute flirts," as if only women sought the company of wealthy foreigners). An obdurate materialism underlay his barbs against Haya de la Torre's advocacy of anti-imperialism across lines of income and status. However, there was also a fresh originality to Mariátegui's thinking about the heterodoxy of tradition, and a larger desire for a flexible socialism that would build on Peru's distinctive customs and history. Although he died prematurely in 1930 of a crippling bone disease, Mariátegui was still one of the most insightful socialist theorists in twentieth-century Latin America.

The Heterodoxy of Tradition

Tradition is alive and mobile, quite the opposite of what the traditionalists would like to imagine. It is created by those who renovate and enrich it precisely in their resistance to it. It is suffocated by those who want it dead and inert, who want to stretch the past into an exhausted present.

There need be no real conflict between revolution and tradition, save for those who imagine tradition to be a mummy or a museum. The problem is really only with the traditionalists. Revolutionaries embody society's will not to petrify itself in a particular moment, not to freeze in a single position. Sometimes society loses the will to create, paralyzed by a feeling of exhaustion or disenchantment. Then it begins, inexorably, to age and decay. . . .

As long as the colonial mentality has dominated this country, we have been a people that imagined itself born of the Spanish conquest. Lazily, the creole national consciousness obeyed this prejudiced conviction of Spanish descendance. The history of Peru, in this view, began with Pizarro, Lima's founder. The Inca empire was felt only to be a prehistory. Everything autochthonous was considered outside of our history and, by extension, outside our tradition. This traditionalism impoverished the nation, shrinking it to mestizos and creoles.

More recently, the national tradition has been stretched to reincorporate a sense of the Inca past. But this should not swing to the other extreme of denying that other factors or values have also decisively shaped our being and personality as a nation. With the conquest, Spain's language and religion entered permanently into Peruvian history, connecting and joining it to Western civilization. The gospel, whether one takes it as truth or as religious ideology, came to weigh more than indigenous mythology. And, later, with the Independence Wars, the concept of the Peruvian republic also entered forever into our tradition.

When told about the "national tradition," then, we must first establish which "tradition" is being talked about, because we have a triple tradition [i.e., Spanish, Indian, African]. And also because tradition always remolds itself before our eyes, which so frequently insist on imagining it as motionless and exhausted.

Myths and Men

Reason and science have corroded and dissolved the prestige of the old religions. In his book on the meaning and value of life, Herman Eucken correctly and clearly explains this process of corrosion.[1] Scientific discoveries have given man a new feeling of power. Once awed by the supernatural, man has suddenly discovered an extravagant capacity to change and correct nature. This feeling has pushed the old metaphysics out of our souls.

But man, as philosophy defines him, is a metaphysical animal. He does not live productively without a metaphysical life vision. Myth propels men through history. Without myth, human existence has no historical meaning. Indeed, history is made by those who are possessed and illuminated by higher beliefs, by superhuman hopes; the rest are the drama's anonymous chorus. The crisis of bourgeois civilization was exposed at the very moment that it discovered itself to lack a myth. During the time of pride in positivism, Ernest Renan used to speak with melancholy about

Figure 19. José Carlos
Mariátegui, shortly
before his death in
1930. (Courtesy of
Biblioteca Nacional
del Perú)

religion's decline and to worry about the future of European civilization.[2]
"The devout," he wrote, "live in shadow. What will those who come after
us live in?" There is still no answer to this bleak question.

In this era, myth is what most sharply and clearly distinguishes the
bourgeoisie from the proletariat. The bourgeoisie no longer have any
myth. They have turned incredulous, skeptical, nihilist. The old liberal
faith of the Renaissance has become anachronistic. The proletariat possesses a myth: social revolution. They move toward that vision with a vehement and active faith. The bourgeoisie denies; the proletariat affirms.
Bourgeois intelligence entertains itself with rationalist criticism of revolutionary method, theory, and action. What a misunderstanding! The force
of revolutionaries lies not in science, but in faith, passion, and will. It is
a religious, mystical, and spiritual force. It is the force of myth. Revolutionary spirit, as I once wrote about Gandhi, is a religious spirit. Spiritual

values have moved from heaven to earth. They are not divine; they are human, social.

The same [rationalist] philosophy that teaches us the necessity of myth and faith generally turns out to be incapable of understanding the myth and faith of the new times. "The poverty of philosophy," as Marx used to say. The professional intelligentsia will not discover the path of faith; but the multitudes will. Later on it will fall to the philosophers to codify the thinking that emerges from the great initiatives of the masses. Did the philosophers during the decline of imperial Rome understand the language of Christianity? Philosophers of the decline of the bourgeoisie will have no better luck.

An Anti-Imperialist View

The national bourgeoisie sees cooperation with imperialism as a great source of benefits. It is sure enough of its own mastery of political power so as not to worry seriously about the question of national sovereignty. In general, the South American bourgeoisie, which has not yet experienced, except in Panama, U.S. military occupation, has no desire to admit the necessity of a second struggle for independence. The state, or rather the ruling class, has no wish for a wider and truer national autonomy. The Independence Wars are still too close in the past, and their myths and symbols too alive in bourgeoisie and petty bourgeoisie consciousness. The illusion of national sovereignty maintains most of its efficacy. To imagine that a feeling of revolutionary nationalism will develop among the middle and upper classes, similar to the kind that was a factor in the anti-imperialist struggles in Asian nations subjugated by imperialism over the last few decades, would be a serious mistake.

The creole aristocracy and bourgeoisie do not feel a bond of solidarity with the common people by ties of common history and culture. In Peru, white aristocrats and the bourgeoisie look down on popular traditions, on national traditions. They feel themselves before anything else to be white. The mestizo petty bourgeoisie imitates this example. The Lima bourgeoisie fraternizes with North American capitalists, even with the simple employees of their companies, at the country club, tennis club, and in the streets. The North American weds the creole girl across lines of race and religion, and she feels no scruples of national or cultural loyalty in preferring marriage with an individual of the invader race. The same goes for those from the middle classes. The cute flirt who can entrap a North American employee of the Grace Company does so with the satisfaction of one who feels herself to be improving her social status.[3] For these objective reasons from which no one easily escapes, nationalism is neither decisive nor fundamental in the anti-imperialist struggle in our social climate. Only in countries like Argentina, where the pride of the large and wealthy bourgeoisie in its own prosperity and power gives clearer and sharper contours to national personality, can anti-imperialism (perhaps) easily gain a foothold among the higher sectors of society.

In my view, anti-imperialism does not constitute, nor can it by itself constitute, a political platform, a mass movement to seize power. Even if it were admitted that anti-imperialism might mobilize the worker and peasant masses along with the bourgeoisie and nationalist petty bourgeoisie (and we have already firmly denied this possibility), the ideology of anti-imperialism does not annul antagonism along class lines, it does not overcome different class interests.

Once in power, neither the bourgeoisie nor the petty bourgeoisie will pursue an anti-imperialist policy. We have the case of Mexico, for example, where the petty bourgeoisie has just made a pact with North American imperialism. A "nationalist" government can use, in its relations with the United States, stronger language than Peru's Leguía government. This is a frankly and unabashedly pan-American and Monroeist government;[4] but, in truth, any other bourgeois government would follow the same pattern of little favors and concessions. Foreign investment in Peru grows in close and direct proportion to the nation's economic development, to the exploitation of its natural resources, to the population, and to expanded communications routes. How, then, can even the most demagogic of the petty bourgeoisie oppose capitalist penetration? Not at all, except in words. Not at all, except in a fleeting nationalist drunkenness. An assault on power under the banner of anti-imperialism, in the shape of a demagogic populist movement, even if it were possible, would never bring the conquest of power by the proletarian masses, by socialism. Once it assumed power, socialist revolution would discover its most savage and dangerous enemy in the petty bourgeoisie, dangerous for the confusion and demagoguery of its sloganeering.

While not foreclosing anti-imperialist agitation or any method to mobilize any social sector that might eventually join in the struggle, our mission is to explain and demonstrate to the masses that only socialist revolution will raise a definite and real barrier against imperialism's advance. In sum, we are anti-imperialists because we are Marxists, because we are revolutionaries, because we oppose socialism against capitalism as an antagonistic system, destined to succeed it, and because in the fight against foreign imperialisms we fulfill our obligations of solidarity with Europe's revolutionary masses.

Notes

1   Eucken was a late-nineteenth-century German philologist.
2   Renan was a late-nineteenth-century French philosopher.
3   W. R. Grace and Company was one of the largest North American firms in Peru at the time.
4   A supporter, in other words, of the 1814 Monroe Doctrine that claimed the right of the United States to intervene at liberty in Latin America.

HUMAN POEMS

César Vallejo

One of the twentieth century's great poets, César Vallejo was born in the dry mountains of the Andean town of Santiago de Chuco in 1892 and supported himself as a newspaperman in Paris until his death in 1938, with an interlude in Madrid during the Spanish Civil War. Vallejo, nicknamed "El Cholo," is famous for dazzling technical innovation and the sheer brilliance and provocation of his verse. An admiring Pablo Picasso painted his portrait. Vallejo was also a socialist. Themes of suffering and anguish infuse these four poems from his final collection, Human Poems, *which retain a painful immediacy a half-century after his death. The English edition of* Human Poems *became the first book of translated poetry to win the prestigious National Book Award.*

(Untitled)

A man passes with bread under his arm.
Will I write afterwards of my double?

Another sits, scratches, extracts a flea from his armpit, kills it
Of what value is a discussion of psychoanalysis?

Another has pierced my heart with a stick in his hand
To speak later to the doctor of Socrates?

A cripple passes, lending his arm to a child
Will I, afterwards, read André Breton?

Another shivers with cold, coughs, spits blood
Will there ever be room to allude to the deep I?

Another searches in the mud for bones, peels
How to write, afterwards, of the infinite?

A mason falls from a roof, dies, and eats no more lunch
To innovate, later, the trope, the metaphor?

A store owner robs a gram of weight from a client
To speak, afterwards, of the fourth dimension?

A banker falsifies his balance
With what affrontery to weep in the theater?

A pariah sleeps with his foot against his back
To speak, afterwards, to no one of Picasso?

Someone goes sobbing in a funeral procession
How to enter the Academy later?

Someone cleans a rifle in a kitchen
Of what value is speaking of the hereafter?

Someone passes counting his fingers
How to speak of the not-I without giving a scream?

Considering Coldly, Impartially . . .

Considering coldly, impartially,
that man is sad, he coughs and, nevertheless,
takes pleasure in his ruddy chest;
that the only thing he does is array himself
in days;
that he is a gloomy mammal and combs himself . . .

Considering
that man proceeds smoothly from work
and reverberates chief, sounds subordinate;
that time's diagram
is a constant diorama with its medals
and, half-open, his eyes studied,
since far-away times
his famished mass formula . . .

Understanding without effort
that man pauses, sometimes, to think,
as if he wants to cry,
and, prone to laying out as an object,
makes of himself a good carpenter, sweats, kills
and then sings, lunches, buttons up . . .

Considering also
that in truth man is an animal
and, notwithstanding, when he turns strikes me on the head with his
sadness . . .

Examining, to end,
his found fragments, his inner room,
his desperation at the end of his atrocious day, erasing it . . .

Understanding
that he knows I love him
that I hate him with an affection and to me he is, in sum, indifferent . . .

Considering his overall documents
and reviewing with my glasses on that certificate
that proves he was born exceedingly small . . .

I signal him,
he comes,
and I embrace him, thrilled.
What more is there! Thrilled . . . Thrilled . . .

Stumble between Two Stars

There are people so wretched they don't even
have a body; quantitative is the hair
by inches brilliant grief sinks
and manners, rise;
don't look for me, grindstone of oblivion
they seem to come from air, to mentally add up sighs, to hear
the bright lash in their words.

Leaving their skin, clawing at the sarcophagus in which they are born
they rise through their death hour by hour,
and fall, the length of their frigid alphabet, to the floor.
Oh from so much! oh from so little! oh from these females!
Oh in my room, hearing them with eyeglasses on!
Oh in my thorax, when they buy outfits!
Oh from my white grime, in their united scum!

Beloved be Sánchez's ears,
beloved the people who sit down,
beloved the stranger and his wife,
the fellow creature with sleeves, a collar, and eyes!

Beloved be the one with bed-bugs,
the one who has worn-out shoes in the rain,
the one who mourns with two matches a roll's cadaver,
the one who slams a finger in a door,
the one who has no birthday,
the one who lost his shadow in a fire,
the animal, the one that looks like a parrot,
the one that looks like a man, the poor rich one,
the one of pure misery, the poor poor!

Beloved be
the one who thirsts or hungers, but who doesn't have
hunger to satiate all his thirst,
nor thirst to satiate all his hungers!

Beloved be the one who works by the day, the month, by the hour,
the one who sweats with grief or with shame,
that one who goes, ordered by the hands, to the cinema,
the one who pays with what he lacks,
the one who sleeps on his back,
the one who no longer remembers childhood; beloved be
the bald man with no hat,
the just man without thorns,
the thief without roses,
the one who wears a watch and has seen God,
the one who has an honor and does not die!

Beloved be the child who falls and still cries
and the man who has fallen and no longer cries.
Oh from so much! Oh from so little! Oh from them!

The Nine Monsters

And unfortunately, pain grows in the world every moment
it grows thirty minutes to the second, step by step
and the nature of pain is twice the pain
and a martyr's condition, carnivorous, voracious,
is pain, two times
and the use of the pure herb, pain
two times
and the goodness of being, to hurt us doubly.

Never, human men,
has there been so much pain in the chest, on the lapel, in the
    handbag
in the glass, the butcher shop, in arithmetic!
Never so much painful affection,
never did what is far rush so close,
never ever did the fire
play better its role of deadly cold!
Never, Mr. Health Minister, was health
more fatal
and did the migraine wrench more fore from the forehead!
And in the pine box the piece of furniture had it, pain,
the heart, in its pine box, pain,
the lizard, in its pine box, pain.

Wretchedness grows, brother men,
faster than any machine, than ten machines, and it grows
with Rousseau's steer, with our beards;
evil grows for reasons we are not aware of
and is a flood of its own liquids
with its clay and its solid cloud!
Suffering reverses positions, it makes
the aqueous humor vertical

to the pavement,
the eye is seen and this ear heard,
and this ear gives nine bell-tolls at the hour
of lightning, and nine grins
at the hour of wheat, and nine female sounds
at the hour of weeping, and nine canticles
at the hour of hunger, and nine thunderclaps
and nine whipstrokes, minus one scream.

Pain grasps us, brother men,
from behind, in profile,
and it crazes us in cinemas,
nails us up on record players,
pries us loose on couches, falls perpendicular
on our tickets, on our letters;
and it is very serious to suffer, one can pray . . .

Well, as the product
of pain, there are some
who are birthed, others grow, others die,
and others that are born and do not die, and others
without having been born die, and others
are neither born nor die (They are the most.)
And as for the outcome
of suffering, I am sad
up to my head, and sadder to the ankle,
from seeing bread, crucified, from the turnip,
bloodied,
crying, from the onion,
from the grains, in general, flour,
from the salt, made dust, from the water, fleeing,
from the wine, a wretch,
so pale to the snow, to the sun what a blaze!
How, human brothers,
not to tell you that I can no more and
I can no more with so many pine boxes,
so many minutes, so many
lizards and so many
reversals, so far and so much thirst for thirst!
Mr. Health Minister: what to do?

Ah! Unfortunately, human men,
there is, brothers, so much to be done.

Note

These poems come from César Vallejo's *Poemas Humanos* (Barcelona: Laisa, 1989) and were translated by the editors.

THE APRA

Víctor Raúl Haya de la Torre

From his days as a student leader at Lima's San Marcos University to his death in 1980, Haya was one of twentieth-century Peru's most influential politicians. This famous speech was delivered on August 23, 1931, to a crowd of more than 40,000 packed into Lima's bullfighting coliseum, the Plaza de Acho. As enthused apristas waved their voting cards over their heads in a vigorous sign of the irruption of lower and middle classes into national politics, the APRA's founder wove together the themes of party ideology: anti-imperialism and pan–Latin Americanism; an alliance of the poor and the middle classes; the establishment of a corporate "technical" state based on a "scientific politics"; and, above all, an almost mystical faith in the APRA's ability to save Peru. The disastrous presidency of party leader Alán García (1985–1990) severely weakened the APRA, but it has been resurrected with García's surprise victory in the 2006 presidential election.

Party comrades, fellow citizens all:

Finally, Peru is reaching the advent of democracy, of good democracy, renovated under *aprismo*'s flag. It is no longer the old democracy of words that so many tyrants predicted. Now, it is authentic democracy forged by the people and defending the people willing to make the ultimate sacrifice to see it affirmed and transformed in our country, which so needs it. I have said that *aprismo* renews democracy because for the first time *aprismo* incorporates into national politics new ideas, new men, new methods, and above all because *aprismo* maintains that it is necessary to be responsible in politics. Our political life has lacked responsibility. That is why it has lacked prestige, it has lacked action, it has lacked authentic force from the grassroots. A politics based on graft, based on threats, based on trickery cannot be a politics of responsibility.

The guiding platform of *aprismo* has continental significance, yet does not exclude programs meant to be applied nationally. We believe Peru cannot separate itself from the problems of Latin America and that Latin America cannot separate itself from the problems of the world. If we live within an international economic system and economics plays a decisive role in a people's political life, it would be absurd to think that Peru, whose economy depends in part on this international economic organism, could live isolated, violating all scientific precepts and rejecting every type of alliance that would guarantee progress.

Our guiding platform for the continent is nothing more than the modern crystallization of the old ideal of Bolívar. In our platform of Latin American economic and political unity, we have synthesized Bolívar's immortal phrase: "Union, union adored America, or else anarchy will devour you!"

Why is the link between the concepts of economics and politics so fundamental to *aprismo*? Until today, only the heroic, fleeting, and empirical face of politics has prevailed in our country. We have yet to experience a scientific form of politics based on economics. Rather than invent reality, [scientific politics] discovers the space the people inhabit and attempts to organize and govern them. The link between the concepts of economics and politics is fundamental in *aprismo* so that we develop a wise mastery of the state. We all know that in this country, the science of economics, above all within government, has not been incorporated except in its most elemental form. In addition, Peru has never been governed economically because we lack statistics. This is a country where we don't even know the size of the population.

Before going into an analysis of the national economy, permit me to demonstrate another facet of this complex problem. As a people—and it is important to repeat this because it is part of our party's fundamental theory—we are not homogeneous. Our lack of economic and social involvement is not like that of European peoples, who have passed from one period to another in a perfectly clear progression. Unlike the peoples of Europe, we have not experienced a period of barbarism followed by feudalism, mercantilism, the rise of the bourgeoisie, and then industrialism. In our country, all of these world economic and social development stages coexist, live together. Within our borders, we have everything from the cannibal and the barbarian to the little lord living his civilized life. We are citizens with the *campa* and fellow countrymen of the feudal mountain lord.[1] Once, I said that anyone wanting to travel history has only to

Figure 20. Víctor Raúl Haya de la Torre giving his famous speech at Lima's bullfighting ring, the Plaza de Acho, in 1931. (Courtesy of TAREA)

make the trek between Lima and the eastern jungle. Given this kind of reality, what could a state be in a legal sense?

Comrades: if we are a democracy, democracy must assist the ambitions and necessities of the majority and the proletarian, peasant, and middle classes.

Today, the state does not reflect the interests of Peru's majority or its material or spiritual needs because it has never attempted to develop what is authentically Peruvian about Peru. Even after 110 years of independence, forgotten are the true inheritors and masters of this land, the three million indigenous people who know neither how to read nor how to write; we have never had an exemplary or a scientific politics; and we have never had a policy of educating and preparing the masses to participate democratically in the life of the state. This is why we have created a falsely constituted state that makes it possible for authoritarian governments, cruel tyrannies, and arbitrary liberators who later turn into tyrants to appear periodically. That is why we must fight for the "Peruvianization" of the state and the economic incorporation of our majorities, the nation's vital force and the ones who have a right to take part in the direction of our destiny because of their great number and ability.

Consequently, we are a political force that means to rescue for the nation's majorities the mastery of the state. We are a political organization that represents the interests of three classes that today are withdrawn from the state. Our party is a unified front, formed to solve the problems of these three classes, which draw together in what they share and unite around truly collective and national problems. These classes sacrifice their differences, of no immediate importance before the great problem of the salvation of the nation's majorities. Our party has formed so that these majorities can take over the state and make from it an instrument that will truly govern and rescue us from the economic inequalities in which we live, the determining factor in our political and social disequilibrium.

We want a state in which each person can participate without abandoning his or her vital function as a worker; and we want a state in which the technician and the expert direct state activities in order to put them on the correct path of solving our great problems. We propose the organization of a technical state; we propose moving toward a functional democracy. This is *aprismo*'s fundamental principle for state organization.

We wish to demonstrate that *aprismo* is not just an economic concept but also a political thesis and an ideology. Above all, however, *aprismo* is a moral force made up of intelligence and national culture. In this truly sacred cause, in this battle, which has no precedent in this nation, we must draw together as a true group or a true organization, showing the way not only to run government but also to capture government, without forgetting the country's fundamental problems.

I understand perfectly that our undertaking is heavy, our task difficult. And that it is not only necessary to speak clearly about the national problems we have included in our national platform, but to have faith, optimism, and strength so that this gigantic plan provides solutions. I understand perfectly that among a people whose political passions carry them to extremes our task is difficult; all energy appears extinguished; and it is difficult in a place where violence and grudges respect nothing and leave truly denigrating examples for young generations; difficult in a place where it is necessary to start by forming the very foundation of state organization. But *aprismo* is a new moral force that in the full sense of public service seeks to assume the management of public business.

Aprismo, then, is not just a political banner. In all ways, *aprismo* is a force that answers a national yearning. It is a force that answers an old wound in Peru. *Aprismo* means a new Peru arising, one wanting its proper place, to "Peruvianize," as our motto attests. *Aprismo* means the mobilization of all those who have remained at the margins of the business of the state and who now demand their rights and that their rights be respected.

ONLY *APRISMO* CAN SAVE US!

Note

1   *Campa* refers to the Asháninka people, an Amazonian group that lives in the central jungle.

THE MASSACRE OF CHAN CHAN

Carleton Beals

A pivotal event in the APRA's *early history was the 1932 Trujillo insurrection, a response by* apristas *to an attempt by populist dictator Luis Sánchez Cerro to wipe out the party. Brutally crushed, the insurrection ended with the execution of hundreds of militants in the ruins of the ancient Chimú fortress of Chan Chan, just north of Trujillo. Globe-trotting U.S. journalist Carleton Beals described Peru's political upheaval in* Fire in the Andes, *which was illustrated by the great Cajamarcan painter José Sabogal. This excerpt combines a fine evocation of the hot northern coast of desert, scrub brush, and ancient pyramids with the dramatic story of the massacre.*

I

Chan Chan, near Trujillo, is a vast conglomeration of crumbling adobe walls, which in its heyday, perhaps A.D. 1200, probably harbored several hundred thousand people. It and Pachacámac, near modern Lima, were the two great pre-Inca Chimú coast metropolises.[1]

Between Trujillo and Moche, close to the mountains, are the much older bulky Moon and Sun pyramids; deep under the high drifting sands, where even before the Christian era went Mochican [Moche] irrigation ditches, are still found Peru's finest ceramics. There, Father Calancha claimed, was discovered a gold sacerdote [priest] in mitre, woolen robe, ear-spreaders, and surplice; there he saw moulded figures of bearded men with forked tongues.

But Chimú consolidation of the north coast made Chan Chan the new center, though quite possibly it stretched clear to the distant Mochican hill city. Chan Chan's former importance in a great economic zone is still evident. In far sands from Chimbote to Chicama are found signposts

Figure 21. Among the dozens of illustrations by the Cajamarcan painter José Sabogal that accompanied *Fire in the Andes* were these classic scenes of Peru's northern coast: a pelican, a fisherman on a reed raft, a woman doing the *marinera* dance.

of the old roads; near Paiján, from the sea to Hacienda Salamanca, a great wall; near Pampuesto and Ascope, vast aqueduct remains; ruins of a dozen towns—Fachén, Rosario, Chiquitoy, El Brujo; the castles of Virú, the fortress of Cartavio.

Chan Chan ruled supreme until Inca Yupanqui's 50,000 warriors subjugated the coast and the bulk of its unappeasable inhabitants were sent as colonists to other parts of the empire. The Spaniards found the place nearly abandoned.

Yet Chan Chan's history embraces the entire Christian era, perhaps longer. It is still the scene of vivid events.

I made two trips to Chan Chan, one in the company of a specialist,

Señor José Eulogio Garrido, director of Trujillo's conservative daily *La Industria*, to learn about its ancient splendors; the other, with APRA revolutionists, to learn about its modern tragedy.

At first glance merely a chaos of crumbling walls, the more one penetrates into the shattered tangle, the more clear becomes the definite plan of the place. It spreads out from the bas-relief Palace of the Great Chimú in a series of quadrangles with high, thick, triple walls containing fortresses, temples, community centers, sport fields, schools, dwellings. Aqueducts brought water from the Moche River to large cobblestone reservoirs; adobe steps lead down to the surface. For miles along the beach a sea wall protected irrigated meadows, now overgrown with reeds and peat-like plants.

Picking our way through these forlorn bogs, we came to the hut of a lone fisherman—a survivor in physique and customs of the old Mochicas. The *enea*, the local reed, he uses for almost everything: walls, roof, bed, and his boat, the *caballito*, "little horse"—two bundles firmly tied, cut to leave a little kneeling place in the bow and tapering up to the high curving prow. With half of a thick Ecuadorian bamboo for a paddle, he ventures out in the stormiest weather many miles from shore and hundreds of miles along the coast; a journey to far Ecuador is nothing to him.

Fish, potatoes, oca root, and *chicha* form his diet. He markets fish only occasionally to supply petty needs, a few yards of cotton goods, leather for sandals, a new fish-hook. Independent, unresentful, contented, he lives peacefully among the ruins of his forefathers.

On my second trip leaders of APRA (the people's party seeking political renovation) took me to numerous crosses over dozens of crumbling *huacas*. These crosses are white with buzzard droppings—for under them lie the half-buried bodies of over a thousand people lined up and shot after the failure of the 1932 APRA revolt which shook this whole region from Trujillo up into the Cajamarca Sierra.

Bloody sergeant-major of Arequipa, Sánchez Cerro, had overthrown Leguía. My friend, APRA leader Víctor Raúl Haya de la Torre, was then held in Lima's big brick penitentiary. Sánchez Cerro was scourging the *apristas* with blood and fire everywhere. His repressive tactics precipitated the three-day Trujillo revolt.

We drove out the tree-shaded country road. At the edge of town the cobbles were broken by a strip of earth—the site of *aprista* trenches now covered over. "In this trench are buried half a dozen defenders."

Beyond the stadium—"APRA" painted in big letters on its roof—another trench with many crosses. "At least thirty are buried here!"

We penetrated on into the tangle of Chan Chan. There people, taken out on trucks, had been lined up alongside of ancient holes, ditches, and reservoirs and shot into their graves. Weeks passed before the townsfolk dared sneak out to cover over the bones, by then picked clean by vultures, rodents, and town curs which had repaired here by hundreds to snarl over the unburied remains. For months Chan Chan was a charnel house. Its pestiferous stench rose to high heaven for miles about, even to Trujillo.

Many bones are still uncovered. Beside a chauffeur's cap, tennis shoe, and rusted buckle we found a skull, cleft open by a machete blow, hair still clinging to it.

After suppressing the revolt, Sánchez Cerro soldiers ran amuck, entered homes, dragged people out on merest suspicion, hustled them to Chan Chan. Hundreds of peasants from the revolting Casa Grande and Cartavio estates were killed. In Cajabamba, the prisoners were bayoneted in their cells.

One Indian, Gregorio Piscoya—whose cross the *apristas* keep eternally fresh with flowers—charged like a mad bull against his executioners. He survived two volleys, a miracle that so unnerved his aggressors he managed to disarm one of them before dropping dead.

At the foot of one of the largest *huacas* Colonel Jiménez and three others, who also rebelled shortly after against Sánchez Cerro's tyranny, were similarly shot.

As we jumped from wall to wall, young Enrique Tello told me of those exciting days. In the first barracks attack, the three APRA leaders had been shot down. Confusion was spreading. Tello tightened up his belt, leapt into leadership, directed rebel forces during three days of furious combat.

After defeat, many who had participated took to the hills. Most were seized on the road and shot. Tello hid right in Trujillo, then one night walked out across country to the remote Sierra. For six months he lived utterly alone off wild game and the milk of a companion cow.

Trujillo still remains ardently *aprista*. Frequent pilgrimages are made to martyr graves and to niche 44 of the cemetery to which Jiménez's corpse has been transferred—the word "Hero" is scratched crudely upon the cement. The *apristas* control one of the leading dailies, *El Norte*, edited by Haya de la Torre's brother and by Antenor Orrego. Pérez Treviño edits a weekly magazine. Propaganda is active. Everywhere houses are daubed with signs; even high Andean precipices have been carved with gigantic letters: APRA. Desert plants, set out on high arid sands, spell APRA. On the Argentine beach I saw a lean dog branded on the side: APRA. Propaganda enthusiasm can go no further.

From the Mochicas to the Chimú kings, from Spaniards to Republicans, from dictatorship to Apra revolt, the course of Chan Chan's history unrolls its scroll. Chan Chan, older than New York, young when London was a mudhole, already ancient when Madrid was founded, now crumbles into the cemetery of bloody tyranny.

Once light-footed runners went forth over great highways carrying royal tidings; once the tall pikes of Chimú guards held the noble gates; now its forgotten streets are prowled by a few lone fisherfolk and guarded only by vultures perched on Christian crosses.

2

Accustomed to comfort, paved streets, electric lights, automobiles, you probably won't like [the town of] Moche.

Moche merely watches occasional autos, on the way from the pest-hole port of Salaverry to Trujillo, bump over its narrow cobbled streets, dodging ruts and open drains. Trujillo, Peru's third largest city, has feeble electric lights, several rattle-trap hotels, a few hundred automobiles, but no paved streets either. It does have a great granite statue of liberty surmounted by a gilded figure carrying a gilded torch far too big for it, bastard art perpetrated by some forgotten German artist, who these later Hitler days probably could execute a more feeling symbol of liberty.

But Moche is just Moche—unpretentious, indifferent, only a few cubby-hole stores, at first glance merely the typical nondescript Indian-mestizo town ever encountered halfway between more important points. Its multitinted flat-roofed buildings—dark adobe rooms with high ceilings and few windows—glow somnolently in the dusty haze and fierce sun of the dry coast under a sky of pale blue silk. Fields stretch here and there, adobe fences, banana trees, corn plots; cows moo; half-starved curs bark.

Life is simple in Moche. People don't read many books, most are busy about their crops, petty sales, families, children, love affairs. Moche, quite plain-spokenly, vegetates. For two thousand years it has vegetated, a longer time than any place in the United States has had a chance to vegetate.

But I like Moche. I like it if for no other reason than that my friend Garrido lives there. Garrido, slightly lame, slightly bald, is reclusive, not easy to cultivate; his silences are long and portentous. But he is gentle, considerate, his speech wise. Besides being a practical Trujillo newspaper editor, he is a poet whose soul is partly in the high sierras where he was born, partly here in Moche, where he wanders about in blue overalls. His beautiful Andean prose poems, mostly about his native Huancabamba, are vibrant with rich remembered emotions: every flower, every rock leaps into the eye with fresh sacred affection.

Though I visit the Andes out of curiosity, I will never love them. They are too brutal, too vast, too remote. They have lifted me to frightful agony of body and soul, to grand awe, but I always want to escape quickly. Unlike the harsh mountains of Mexico or California or New England's wooded hills, they do not pull me on and on with irresistible fresh delight. But from Garrido I learned at least to understand them better, to discover even in that rugged vastness, minor delicate notes, human life there, sad yet also rich and hopeful. But perhaps, since for so many centuries the Andean people have quite forgotten the inner meaning of the Andes and of themselves, even Garrido had to go to the lowlands, to Moche, to discover them. However much this bland little town on the open starry-sky plain differs from the stark bitter Andes, both are places of ancient Indian soil wisdom.

Garrido lives near the railway station, in a vast colonial house, surrounded by ample verandas, fronted by majestic wind-whipped palms. Enormous rooms ramble endlessly. Endlessly the sea breeze whips through those long ancient corridors.

Garrido lives there. The old wooden floors, knotted, eaten by time, are scattered with Indian rugs; few chairs, but many divans, cozy corners with Indian sashes hanging down in colorful fringes, many bookcases in odd places, lofty walls covered with paintings by Sabogal, Camilo Blas, and others, Peru's best artists. The big roominess, at times gloomy, forlorn, nevertheless conduces to peaceful meditation. I have sat there alone, thoughts inevitably tinged with melancholy, of something lost in life, a peace never found. In such a place as this would I have found some unshakable architecture of philosophy and conduct? Since I left Trujillo and Moche I have wanted much to know the whole history of that house. I never asked Garrido. And we both dislike writing letters.

Twilight dips over the world. Garrido lights a little lamp and reads those deeply moving poems of the far Andes, so remote, yet so near.

Garrido was one of that rare group of which Haya de la Torre was a member—students who came out of Trujillo University about fifteen years ago, most of whom have formed the nucleus of the APRA movement. But Garrido edits a Conservative newspaper, and his old comrades consider him a renegade. But not a politician or a lover of the immediate battle, his real life is in Moche. There he is patiently seeking something, seeking it in the dim boyhood past in the Andes, in the most rooted part of all Peruvian life, that which has survived more centuries than the Christian era, which had its glories in the days of Greece—the Indian community, where men live in such social cooperation that individualism seems a sickly disease.

One afternoon, laden with gifts, we walked out through sandy adobe walled lanes, crossed over half a dozen irrigation ditches bridged by fallen trunks, to the home of Don Sergio, descendant of the ancient Mochicans who built the Sun and the Moon *huacas* and did other glorious things.

Formal greetings. The cloth was promptly spread on a table under the trees and a great terra cotta vat of *chicha* brought out and blessed by the sign of the cross.

A very definite ritual rules *chicha* drinking. The host dips the half gourd into the frothy brown beer, greets his *compadre* with whom he wishes to drink, drains nature's goblet at one long draft, refills it, hands it to the chosen one. He in turn repeats the process. As a guest of honor, I received more than my share of greetings.

Plates of little crabs cooked with seaweed in rich greasy brown sauce and mellow boiled potatoes—I ate crabs till my fingers dripped from the brown sauce. Plop them whole into the mouth, shell and all, crunch on them, suck out the edible portions, then spit out the bits of shell. Hands and mouth are wiped on a big communal rag in the center of the table.

Music came—a guitar, a box to hammer on—survival of the Mozambique tom-tom, to dance the *tondero*—a Spanish-negro-Indian survival. A "captain" first danced in pantomime with his silver-topped staff as partner. Then he picked the next pair.

> De nuevo y acomodarse,
> dicen los mozos de cuerda . . .
> Once again and get comfortable
> the guitar boys say . . .

Though I had never tried the *tondero*, I was called on first to dance with the barefoot grandmother of the house, an agile though portly lady. She carried her skirt well lifted in her right hand between index finger and thumb, her arm and body arched; in her left hand, at the height of her shoulder, a kerchief. The man keeps his left hand behind his back, body curved graciously, hips outward to the right, the weight ever on the left foot. In his right hand he waves a loose kerchief to the compass of the movement. Backward, forward, circle around, in a series of quick stamp-jumps. The guitar twangs ever swifter; the beats come faster with an occasional guttural "*Ora!*" With tiny stamping steps, bodies vibrating, the eyes are fixed on the partner's eyes, mouths smiling; the dance quivers to a panting climax. . . .

Slowly the day melted away. The fine gold of the sun sifted in under orchard trees, glinted on bare brown skin, on white skirts and white trousers, color tones growing softer, ever softer, quietly fading.

Late twilight; we came back through the lanes, now smelling of burning brush and cooked food and cows. In the hushed odorous peace of a rural Peruvian night, we reached Garrido's roomy dark house and told over forgotten tales in the flickering shadows of a kerosene lamp on ancient walls.

Note

1   The Chimú reigned around A.D. 1200 along Peru's northern coast.

LOST TO SIGHT

César Moro

César Moro was the pen name of Alfredo Quíspez Asín, a Lima-born painter and poet, who, like a number of Peru's early-twentieth-century artists and intellectuals, lived in the Paris of Breton and Picasso. Novelist Mario Vargas Llosa has called Moro an exiliado interior, *an internal exile, for his avant-garde sensibility and pioneering openness about his homosexuality. The wild juxtapositions and excesses of "Lost to Sight" exemplify his unique brand of surrealism.*

I shall never renounce impudent luxury the sumptuous debauchery
of skins like the finest fasces hanging from ropes and sables
The immense landscapes of saliva with small canyons of fountain-pens
The violent sunflower of saliva
The word designating the object proposed by its opposite
The tree as a minimal night taper
The loss of faculties and the acquisition of insanity
The aphasiac language and its intoxicating perspectives
Logoclonia tic rabies interminable yawning
Stereotype tedious thought
Amazement
Amazement of glass accounts
Amazement of vapor of glass of branches of coral of bronchial
       tubes and of feathers
Smooth submarine amazement sliding fiery pearls impassive at
       laughter like a duck's plumage before one's eyes
Left-leaning amazement blazing at the right tattered and smoking
       columns in the center behind a vertical staircase on a swing

Mouths with sugar teeth and reborn dying tongues of petrol let down
       crowns over opulent breasts bathed in honey and variable acid
       bunches of saliva
Amazement theft of stars clean chickens worked in stone and tender
       terra firma measures the land across one's eyes
Young amazement outcast of lucky light
Amazement women asleep on mattresses of fruit peelings crowned
       with fine naked chains
Amazement evening trains gathering the eyes scattered over the
       meadows when the train flies up and the silence can no longer
       follow the trembling train
Amazement like a burglar demolishing mental doors breaking down
       the watery glance and the glance that is lost on the
       threshold of the dry timber velvet Tritons watch over the
       slip of a woman sleeping naked in the wood and traverses
       the meadows bounded by obscurely defined mental processes
       enduring questions and answers put by fierce unshackled
       stones taking into consideration the last dead horse at the
       early dawn of the intimate underclothes of my grandmother
       and my grandfather's grumbling as he faces the wall
Amazement chairs fly around on meeting an empty barrel covered
       with ivy poor neighbor of the flying attic requesting
       furnishings and plumbing for the lilies of the first shawl
       while a violent woman tucks in her skirts and shows an
       image of the Virgin accompanied by pigs wearing three crowns
       and two-colored chignons
Midnight decorates the left shoulder above the right shoulder
       grows the pestilential pasture rich in conglomerations of
       tiny prophesying rams and vitamins painted with freshly
       shadowed trees with wigs and bowls
Forget-me-nots and other vexatious geraniums spit out their
       wretchedness
The grandiose boreal light of schizophrenic thought
The sublime delirious interpretation of reality
I shall never renounce the primordial luxury of your precipitous
       fallings o diamond madness

V · THE BREAKUP OF THE OLD ORDER

At the beginning of the 1930s, Leguía's regime became a victim of the Great Depression, and the challenges of socialism and the APRA were bloodily put down. The oligarchy returned to power through an almost uninterrupted succession of dictatorial governments until free elections in 1956. For two decades, official Peru took on a conservative and Hispanicist flavor, reflected in the solemn celebration of the quatricentenary of Pizarro's death and the loud enthusiasm over Franco's victory in the Spanish Civil War.

These were the times when intellectuals from the oligarchy, like José de la Riva Agüero, saluted fascism in Italy and Germany, even as philosopher Alejandro Deustua affirmed that "Peru owes its misfortunes to the indigenous race, whose psychic degeneration has taken on the biological rigidity of a being that has definitively stopped evolving, and which has failed to contribute to the mestizo the virtues of a progressive race. . . . The Indian is not, and cannot be, anything but a machine."[1] For those of Quechua, Aymara, and Amazonian origin, Peru was truly a "broad and foreign world," as writer Ciro Alegría titled his most famous novel.

Nevertheless, under an apparently still surface, the new forces of mass communication and the market—along with the state's own measures of modernization through highways and schools—drew the majorities more firmly into national life. Between 1956 and 1964, Peru witnessed the largest peasant movements in South America. In invasions of estate lands, what José María Arguedas called "The Pongo's Dream" turned fleetingly into reality. At the same time, the great migrations began to remake the face of the coastal cities, especially Lima, the symbol of oligarchical power and creole pride. "We have arrived in the enormous town of the masters, and we are shaking it up. . . . We are squeezing this immense city that hated us, that despised us like the excrement of horses," Arguedas concluded.[2]

The Popular Action and Christian Democrat parties won the elections of 1963. Their victory marked the rise of an urban professional class that felt a strong affinity with the United States and its Kennedy-era Alliance for Progress, for them a path to development and modernity. The growing political clout of the middle classes also signaled the decline, if not the defeat, of the creole elite, whose foibles were so brilliantly chronicled by Alfredo Bryce Echenique in *A World for Julius*.

New president Fernando Belaúnde's government was obstructed by conservatives in the parliament. Unexpectedly, they won the once-radical APRA's backing for this last stand. On October 3, 1968, however, came another surprise. The military overthrew Belaúnde not to restore the oligarchical order, but to carry out the reforms promised by the civilian president. Six days after the coup, the self-appointed "Revolutionary Government of the Armed Forces" nationalized the oil wells of the International Petroleum Company, a subsidiary of Standard Oil of New Jersey. In 1969, it promulgated a sweeping agrarian reform, which abolished the old Andean estates as well as newer coastal plantations.

In retrospect, the first period of military government under General Juan Velasco (1968–1975) was fraught with contradictions. Velasco led a corporate and authoritarian regime, restricting freedom of expression and political parties. Over time, this state-centered model of development became an Achilles' heel. The foreign debt ballooned as the government turned to international lenders to finance grand public works. At the same time, the aggressive populism of the *chino* Velasco, nicknamed for his "Oriental" eyes, went along with an ideology of social democracy and mass mobilization, opening the gates for a greater protagonism of the *cholo* majorities in political and economic life.

Velasco was deposed in 1975 by a military coalition that implemented a series of counterreforms. A cluster of teacher and worker walkouts and regional autonomy movements broke out in response to these measures, culminating in 1977 and 1978 in the first truly national strikes in Peru's history. Small Marxist parties grew. So did "Christian base communities," linked to the liberation theology elaborated by the Peruvian Gustavo Gutiérrez, among others, after the reforms of the Second Vatican Council in 1963. Perhaps more strongly than at any time since Leguía's fall, room seemed to have opened for ideologies and parties that might represent the interests of Peru's dispossessed. "Our time," wrote Gutiérrez, "bears the imprint of those who in fact used to be 'absent' from our society and from the church."

Pressure from within and abroad forced the return of democracy. In 1978, the military government convoked a Constitutional Assembly. Fernando Belaúnde was reelected in presidential elections two years later. Peru seemed finally on track toward democracy and economic stability. To the contrary, however, unexpected developments were to redirect the country's history once again. The 1980s and early 1990s were to prove the most difficult times since the War of the Pacific.

Notes

1 Alejandro Deustua, *La Cultura Nacional* (Lima: Author, 1937), p. 68.
2 José María Arguedas, "To Our Creator Father, Túpac Amaru," translated by Jan Mennell, unpublished ms., p. 3.

THE PONGO'S DREAM

José María Arguedas

Arguedas learned Quechua as a boy from servants in the household of his step-mother and his father, an itinerant lawyer. Until his suicide in 1967, the novel-ist and anthropologist was perhaps more responsible than any other Peruvian for the impassioned defense of the Incan tongue and cultural autonomy for millions of Quechua speakers, challenging the powerful ideologies of "modernization" and "na-tional integration" predicated on the erasure of Peru's indigenous past. Although there was a strong utopian strain in Arguedas, he was not just interested in indige-nous traditions. He also wrote about the challenges of migration and modernity, and proclaimed himself an "hombre Quechua moderno," a modern Quechua man, reflecting his desire for a cultural pluralism for Peru that would go beyond a retreat into a narrow traditionalism. An adaptation of a story Arguedas heard from a Cuzco peasant, "The Pongo's Dream" captures the rigidity of the feudal order that still prevailed in many parts of the Andes in the mid-twentieth century. But the denouement, where the world turns upside down as in the Inkarrí myth, sug-gests the existence of a spirit of independence and opposition, which was to fuel the peasant movements of the 1950s and the breakup of the landlords' rule.

A little man headed to his master's mansion. As one of the serfs on the lord's estate, he had to perform the duty of a pongo, a lowly house servant. He had a small and feeble body, a meek spirit. His clothes were old and tattered. Everything about him was pitiful.

The great lord, owner of the mansion and lands surrounding it, could not help laughing when the little man greeted him in the mansion's cor-ridors.

"What are you? A person or something else?" the lord asked the little man in front of all the other serfs.

The pongo bowed his head and did not answer. He stood frightened, eyes frozen. "Let's see!" the lord said. "With those worthless little hands, you must at least know how to scrub pots or use a broom. Take this garbage away!" he ordered.

The pongo knelt to kiss his master's hand and followed him to the kitchen hanging his head.

The little man had a small body but an average man's strength. Whatever he was told to do he did well, but he always wore a slight look of horror on his face. Some of the serfs laughed at him, while others pitied him. "The most orphaned of all orphans," a cook of mixed blood once said upon seeing him. "His frozen eyes must be children of the moon wind, his heart must be all sadness."

The little man rarely talked to anyone. He worked and ate quietly. Whatever they ordered him to do was done obediently. "Yes, *papacito*, yes, *mamacita*," were the only words he uttered.

Perhaps because of the little man's frightened look and his threadbare, filthy clothes, or perhaps because of his unwillingness to talk, the lord regarded the pongo with special contempt. He enjoyed humiliating him most at dusk, when all the serfs gathered to say the Hail Mary in the mansion's great hall. He would shake him vehemently in front of the serfs like a piece of animal skin. He would push his head down and force him to kneel, and then, when the little man was on his knees, slap him lightly on the face.

"I believe you are a dog. Bark!" he would tell the pongo.

The little man could not bark.

"Stand on all fours," the lord would order him next.

The pongo would obey and start crawling on all fours.

"Walk sideways like a dog," the lord would demand.

The little man had learned to run like the small dogs inhabiting the high moors.

The lord would laugh heartily. His whole body shook with exhilaration.

"Come back here!" he would yell, when the servant reached the end of the great hall.

The pongo would return, running sideways, arriving out of breath.

Meanwhile, some of the other serfs would quietly say their Hail Marys, as if their voices were a wind hidden in their hearts.

"Perk up your ears, hare! You are just an ugly hare!" the lord would command the exhausted little man. "Sit on your two paws. Put your hands together."

The pongo could sit in the exact same prayerful pose that these animals take when they stand still on the rocks, looking as if he had learned this habit while in his mother's womb. But the one thing he could not do was perk up his ears. Some of the serfs laughed at him.

With his boot, the lord would then knock him to the brick floor.

"Let us say the Our Father," he would then say to his Indians as they waited in line.

The pongo would get up slowly, but he could not pray because he was not in his place, nor did any place belong to him.

In the darkness, the serfs would leave the great hall for the courtyard and head to their living quarters.

"Get out of here, offal!" the master would often order the pongo.

And so, every day, in front of the other serfs, the master would make his new pongo jump to his demands. He would force him to laugh, to fake tears. He would hand him over to the other workers so that they would ridicule him too.

But . . . one afternoon, during the Hail Mary, when the hall was filled with everyone who worked and lived on the lord's estate and the master himself began to stare at the pongo with loathing and contempt, that same little man spoke very clearly. His face remained a bit frightened.

"Great lord, please grant me permission. Dear lord, I wish to speak to you."

The lord could not believe his ears. "What? Was that you who spoke or someone else?"

"Your permission, dear master, to speak to you. It is you I want to talk to," the pongo replied.

"Talk . . . if you can."

"My father, my lord, my dear heart," the little man began. "Last night, I dreamt that the two of us had died. Together, we had died."

"You with me? You? Tell all, Indian," the master said to him.

"Since we were dead men, my lord, the two of us were standing naked before our dear father Saint Francis, both of us, next to each other."

"And then? Talk!" ordered the master, partly out of anger and partly anxious with curiosity.

"When he saw us dead, naked, both standing together, our dear father Saint Francis looked at us closely with those eyes that reach and measure who knows what lengths. He examined you and me, judging, I believe, each of our hearts, the kind of person we were, the kind of person we are. You confronted that gaze as the rich and powerful man that you are, my father."

"And you?"

"I cannot know how I was, great lord. I cannot know my worth."

Figure 22. Peasants from Paucartambo, Cuzco, the area where "The Pongo's Dream" takes place. Photograph by Martín Chambi, 1928. (Courtesy of Teo Allaín Chambi)

"Well, keep talking."

"Then, our father spoke: 'May the most beautiful of all the angels come forth. May a lesser angel of equal beauty accompany the supreme one. May the lesser angel bring a golden cup filled with the most delicate and translucent honey.'"

"And then?" the master asked.

The Indian serfs listened, listened to the pongo with a limitless attention, yet also afraid.

"My owner, as soon as our great father Saint Francis gave his order, an angel appeared, shimmering, as tall as the sun. He walked very slowly until he stood before our father. A smaller angel, beautiful, glowing like a gentle flower, marched behind the supreme angel. He was holding in his hands a golden cup."

"And then?" the master asked once again.

"'Supreme angel, cover this gentleman with the honey that is in the golden cup. Let your hands be feathers upon touching this man's body,' ordered our great father. And so, the lofty angel lifted the honey with his hands and glossed your whole body with it, from your head down to your toenails. And you swelled with pride. In the splendor of the heavens, your body shone as if made of transparent gold."

"That is the way it must be," said the lord. "And what happened to you?"

"When you were shining in the sky, our great father Saint Francis gave another order. 'From all the angels in heaven, may the very least, the most ordinary come forth. May that angel bring along a gasoline can filled with human excrement.'"

"And then?"

"A worthless, old angel with scaly feet, too weak to keep his wings in place, appeared before our father. He came very tired, his wings drooping at his sides, carrying a large can. 'Listen,' our great father ordered the angel. 'Smear the body of this little man with the excrement from that can you brought. Smear his whole body any way you want and cover it all the best you can. Hurry up!' So the old angel took the excrement with his coarse hands and smeared my body unevenly, sloppily, just like you would smear mud on the walls of an ordinary adobe house. And in the midst of the heavenly light, I stank and was filled with shame."

"Just as it should be!" crowed the master. "Keep going! Or is that the end?"

"No, my little father, my lord. When we were once again together, yet changed, before our father Saint Francis, he took another look at us, first at you, then at me, a long time. With those eyes that reach across the heavens, I don't know to what depths, joining night and day, memory and oblivion. Then he said: 'Whatever the angels had to do with you is done. Now, lick each other's bodies slowly, for all eternity.' At that moment, the old angel became young again. His wings regained their blackness and great strength. Our father entrusted him with making sure that his will was carried out."

"THE MASTER WILL NO LONGER
FEED OFF YOUR POVERTY"

Juan Velasco

Unlike other Latin American dictators, the humbly born General Juan Velasco viewed himself as a defender of the poor. He announced in 1968 that his "Revolutionary Government of the Armed Forces" would forge a "third way" of state-directed national development between capitalism and socialism. His reforms included the selective nationalization of foreign enterprises, the creation of a state-run system of mass organizations called the National System of Social Mobilization (SINAMOS), and, most important, the massive agrarian reform, handing over the estates of big landowners to their former serfs and employees. The Velasco government was hindered by disorganization and mismanagement. Yet this period of raised hopes and upheaval accelerated the weakening of the old order in Peru and fueled the forces of political mobilization, dislocation, and desire for full citizenship that wrenched the country over the next two decades. Velasco delivered this famous speech on television on June 24, 1969, the Day of the Peasant, to announce the agrarian reform.

Peruvians:

This is an historic day. And it's important that we all be aware of its full significance. Today, the Revolutionary Government has issued the Agrarian Reform Law, thereby giving the country its most vital instrument of transformation and development. History will remember this June 24 as the beginning of an irreversible process that will lay the groundwork for true national greatness, founded on social justice and the real participation of the people in the wealth and future of our motherland.

Peasant Day

Today, for the Day of the Indian, the Day of the Peasant, the Revolutionary Government honors them with the best of tributes by giving to the
nation a law that will end forever the unjust social order that impoverished and oppressed the millions of landless peasants who have always
been forced to work the land of others. Far, then, from an empty homage,
with an instrument of unassailable judicial action the Revolutionary Government has given shape to a national goal of justice fought for in our
Motherland. From this day forward, the Peruvian peasant will no longer
be a pariah or disinherited and living in poverty from the cradle to the
grave, powerless to make a better future for his children. As of this lucky
June 24, Peruvian peasants will truly be free citizens whose motherland
has finally recognized their right to the fruits of the land they work and a
position of justice within a society where nevermore will they be second-
class citizens, men to be exploited by other men.

When we assumed the government of the country, the armed forces
also made the solemn promise to carry out the vast task of national reconstruction. We were always aware of the immensity of this responsibility. Ours could not be just another government. It emerged with the
unforsakable mission to be the government of national revolution.

Armed Forces and Renovation

Moreover, we announce that the country's transformation is the historic
mission of the Armed Forces Government. To put it another way, the work
of government was never understood by the armed forces to be the banal
exercise of power, without direction or purpose; nor was it ever understood, under this regime, as a way to maintain the basic and unjust social
order, under which the majority of our people have been an exploited
majority, a majority in misery, a majority dispossessed. We did not assume
political power to plunder the treasury or to perpetuate injustice. To the
contrary, we assumed political power to make the state into a productive
instrument for the transformation of the motherland.

Today, Peru has a government dedicated to conquering the country's
development with the definitive cancellation of old social and economic
structures that no longer have any validity in our times. The far-reaching
reforms that so many of our fellow citizens have fought for are on the
march. And among them, without any doubt, the highest priority per-
tains to the country's agrarian system.

Figure 23. General Juan Velasco promulgated Peru's first sweeping
land reform. (Courtesy of *Quehacer*)

In place of large and medium-sized plantations, the law establishes
measures that guarantee that property as a unit of production will not
be divided. The law affects ownership, not the concept of agricultural
production or ranching. In the case of agro-industry, the law will make
holdings into cooperatives owned by the workers, while guaranteeing
that each new business functions as a single unit. In this sense, the law
considers land and the physical plant as an indivisible whole subject to
the agrarian reform. The processing plant for the raw materials of the
countryside is linked firmly to the land. Within these new cooperatives,
the law guarantees job stability, salaries, and the social rights of the man-
agers, administrative, and technical personnel and workers.

By rationalizing the use and ownership of land and creating incentives
derived from broader access to property, the agrarian reform will also
tend to produce more and better agricultural owners, that is, a more robust agricultural production that will benefit not the few but society as a
whole. The best guarantee of the country's accelerated, harmonious agricultural development is a peasantry every day more prosperous, organized, and unified.

In addition, it is essential for the nation's investors to understand fully the significance of the Agrarian Reform Law as a stimulant for our country's industrialization. In effect, the law opens new perspectives for investment in an industry built on riches and strengthened by work. New and diverse possibilities for economic development challenge the business acumen and dynamism of Peru's young industries, whose future will in great part depend on the tenacity of those who dedicate all their energy and talent. Industrialization is a centerpiece of our country's economic development. Efforts by those in industry can and must be a part of the transformation of Peru's traditional structure.

The new Agrarian Reform Law will also limit the right to own land in order to guarantee that land serves its social function in a new system of justice. In this sense, the law contains limits on land sales based on the regulation that land must be for those who work it and not for those who charge rent without tilling. Land should be for the peasant, for the small and medium-sized landowner; for the man who sinks his hands into it, creating wealth for all, the man who in the end fights and sinks the roots of his destiny into the fertile rows, the givers of life.

Finally, those who see their property reduced by the application of this law will receive a fair price from the state. But in full conscience, it is necessary to recognize that this agrarian reform is for our country, an imperative for justice that cannot be postponed. And just as it is true that this is a government for all Peruvians, so is it true that the government must be, above all else, a government for the majority and also for the most needy. The Revolutionary Government trusts that those who feel adversely affected by the Agrarian Reform Law will understand, above and beyond their perhaps understandable self-interest, the profound justice it encompasses and makes into reality. We will act fairly in applying this law. And we will respect the legitimate rights of those who fall under its mandate. But we will also be inflexible in demanding that the agrarian reform be applied completely.

For all these reasons and in response to the cries for justice and rights from Peru's neediest people, the Agrarian Reform Law gives its support to the great multitude of peasants who today belong to indigenous communities and from this day forward—abandoning unacceptable racist habits and prejudices—will be called Peasant Communities [*Comunidades Campesinas*]. The hundreds of thousands of farmers who are a part of them will have from this day forward effective support from the state in order to get credit and the technical assistance that is indispensable for converting their land into dynamic and productive cooperatives.

Adversaries and Detractors

The Agrarian Reform Law will have adversaries and detractors. They will come from a privileged group of political elites and economic monopolies. This is the traditional oligarchy, which will see its antipatriotic dominance of Peru in jeopardy. We do not fear them. To this oligarchy we say that we are determined to use all the energy necessary to crush any sabotage of the new law and any attempt to subvert public order.

The Agrarian Reform Law will also have defenders and friends. They will be those patriots who understand the decisive importance that this law will have for national development, and they will be men of the people, peasants, workers, students, all those who have always fought for social justice in Peru. They will understand that finally they can put into practice their ideals. It is not important that some of us are soldiers and others civilians. The motherland is one and belongs to all. What is important is that the social and economic transformation is carried out and from it is created a free, just, and independent nation. We are not alone. In the work of the agrarian reform, we have at our side peasants, workers, students, the immense majority of intellectuals, priests, industrialists, and Peruvian professionals. And this is what counts. These are the authentic people of our motherland. The armed forces stand at their side because they rise from the people, whose cause we back with unbreakable resolve.

Invocation to Youth

For this reason, I want to make a sincere invocation to Peruvian youth, for whom we want to forge a better motherland. Those of us now living out our adult years have received a world full of imperfection and injustice. For those who come after us, we want a free and just society. The legacy of a nation with no room for clamorous inequalities and the disapproval of the rest of the world we live in, this is our greatest challenge: to construct for our people and our youth a social order where man can live with dignity, knowing that he lives on land that is his and in a nation that owns its destiny.

Fellow Countrymen: I repeat, this is an historic day, whose transcendence will grow with the passage of time. Today, the Revolutionary Government feels the deep emotion of a mission and a duty fulfilled. Today, on the Day of the Peasant, we look to the citizenry with faith, pride, and hope; and we say to all of Peru that we owe the inspiration of our acts to the people and to them we today deliver a law that will forge greatness and justice as its destiny.

To the men of the land, we can now say in the immortal and liberating voice of Túpac Amaru:

Peasant: the Master will no longer feed off your poverty!

THE 24TH OF JUNE

Gabriel Aragón

Much of the agrarian reform did not measure up to Velasco's grand promise to "lay the groundwork for true national greatness." Coastal cooperatives established from expropriated cotton and sugar plantations were plagued by mismanagement, and members often became a new elite that also exploited poor migrants. In the Andes, less than half of landless and smallholding peasants actually received land. Still, as this ballad demonstrates, the breakup of the estates and the delivery of lands into the hands of "those who work it" contained a startling symbolism. For many in the countryside, Velasco remained the great emancipator who liberated peasants from tyranny, even enshrined in this Quechua ballad by schoolteacher Aragón from Canchis, Cuzco.

I

Vincticuatro junio p'unchay hatun qillqa dicritacum
llapa Perú campisinuq
hallpan riscatanankupaq

II

Manaraq iskay watapi
marzu killa qallriypi
Reforma Agraria liyinwan
hallpakuna rakirkunña

III

Lauramarca hacindapi
isqun pachak runakuna

qunqurchaki muchaykuspa
hallp'ankuta chaskiyunku

IV

Perú kamachiq Amawta
Juan Velasco Alvarado
Sutiykitas q'illkanqaku
llapa suyu campisinu

I

On the twenty-fourth of June
a great law was decreed
that all Peru's peasants
might recover their land.

II

All the lands have already been divided
by the Agrarian Reform
now, at the beginning of March [of 1971],
it has happened in less than two years.

III

Nine hundred men from
the estate of Lauramarka
have received their lands
kissing it on their knees.

IV

Juan Velasco Alvarado
teacher president,
your name will be remembered
by peasants of every region.

VILLA EL SALVADOR

Cecilia Blondet

Until 1971, Villa El Salvador was empty desert south of Lima. By 1990, African-Peruvians from Lima's decaying center and first- and second-generation migrants from the Amazon and Andean interiors had converted it into a bustling munici-pality of more than 300,000, recognized internationally as the best organized of Lima's shantytowns. This excerpt from feminist historian Cecilia Blondet's history of Villa El Salvador offers a detailed reckoning of its founding, focusing on the role of women, the church, and the Velasco government and the fierce persistence that has characterized the struggle for rights to housing and dignity.

On the night of April 27, 1971, about two hundred poor families from different run-down Lima slums and nearby shantytowns pre-pared to seize fallow land owned by the state in Pamplona, eight miles south of the city.[1]

For several days, the leaders, mostly young people from the provinces who rented apartments in the old slum of La Victoria, had been prepar-ing the takeover. Prospective squatters secretly bought the straw mats and poles needed for the new houses, kerosene stoves and kerosene, a bit of food, liquor, water, Peruvian flags, and blankets to cover themselves. In meetings, the duties and responsibilities each would assume during the takeover had already been decided.

While it was still dark, the scared, rushed, and nervous squatters began arriving one by one. The leaders' slogans and spirited shouts countered the atmosphere of tension and anxiety, caused as much by the action's audacity as by their uncertainty about how things would turn out. That same night, people lodging with area residents joined the takeover. Their participation augured the neighbors' consent and support, fundamen-tally important in the days to come. With their approval, the defense of the invaded area as well as food and water supplies would be assured. By dawn, the camp had been raised and everyone awaited the city and police's reaction.

Overcrowding and high rent had made their lives unbearable. The takeover could end their suffering, just as similar actions had helped thousands of other provincial families in Lima. But a decision such as this also brought serious risks. The squatters knew that at any moment the police could arrive and without warning unleash a battle. Judging by previous experience, the state would not easily bow to this show of popular pressure. Only with on-the-spot resistance coupled to public statements by politicians and support in the press could some sort of negotiation between the government and the group's leaders be contemplated. The possibility of success was slim and uncertain. The squatters knew this beforehand, but still they staked their claim.

During the first day, neighbors, friends, and others from the provinces passed the word. That night, 150 new families joined the takeover. The leaders watched this increase in numbers with concern. Although it was helpful to involve the greatest number of people in order to withstand police repression, it also made the takeover more of a challenge to public order.

Nervousness, anxiety, and uncertainty grew over the following days. Most squatters had to leave to work or study and could no longer wait for a battle with police. The fierce combatants who had guarded the initial camp were replaced by wives, grandparents, and nephews. During these days, all sorts of tall tales were woven about the takeover's future. "They say this president is a real *cholo* and isn't afraid of the rich," "they say that Sarita Colonia has returned again to earth and is among us to perform a miracle, since she was also from the provinces,"[2] and "they say the army is preparing to attack, what will happen?"

On Monday, May 3, the first police detachments arrived for the eviction. But besides a few tear gas bombs, there was little violence that day. To the bafflement of the squatters, the police attitude was more even-tempered than belligerent. Meanwhile, the squatters offered to begin negotiations with government authorities with the assistance of the local parish priest. A commission began negotiations with Housing Ministry authorities and reached an agreement whereby the squatters would sign up with the authorities and withdraw from the land in exchange for reassignment to a different place. The miracle appeared to be at the door.

The government's willingness to negotiate was easily explained. At this moment, the president, General Juan Velasco Alvarado, was inaugurating in Lima an important Inter-American Development Bank (IDB) conference on aid to developing countries. He needed a calm social and political climate to demonstrate to the world the broad support his regime enjoyed. But although Velasco, Sarita Colonia, and the IDB coincided for various reasons in easing tensions, less high-minded forces intervened to complicate the panorama.

While the commission of squatters argued with Housing Ministry authorities, the number of families joining the takeover grew by the hour. From all Lima and even some neighboring provinces, thousands of men and women who had just heard the news packed their bags, hoping to take advantage of the opportunity for a housing lot. In no time, the original area overflowed with successive waves of squatters, who advanced to seize neighboring lands. They took over land for the new La Inmaculada high school, run by Jesuit priests, entered areas owned by construction companies and developers, and settled on the skirts of the hills that surrounded one of the most exclusive residential neighborhoods of that period: Las Casuarinas. The threat was palpable for the country's upper class, which had seen all of the government's reforms as vicious attacks against private property. With terror, they watched the fulfillment of their own prophecy: the poor, the mountain hicks, the resentful and angry *cholos* were taking *their* city and were at the point of invading their very homes.

The national and international media gathered to cover the IDB conference gave front-page coverage to the events of that May. Different social and political sectors distributed press releases and pronouncements urging the government to exert authority and take immediate action to bring the chaos under control. The impudence of these young provincials was becoming a nightmare for many military leaders in government. Rapid and effective action to end the stand-off was required. On the afternoon of May 4, Interior Minister General Armando Artola gave orders to police to evict the squatters.

That night, when a general assembly of original squatters had been called to discuss the talks with the government and consider the problem posed by new arrivals, a massive police contingent occupied the settlement violently and battled the population. The night before, police had tried to carry out the eviction, but like the first time, they chose to withdraw. In contrast, the dawn of May 5 was different. One invader remembered: "First, a squad of riot police surrounded us and began to fire tear gas bombs until we vomited. All the women defended themselves with sticks. One began throwing stones, others joined in, and the plain erupted. It seemed like hell on earth or as if the night would never end."

But from the police viewpoint, things weren't much better. Battle fronts multiplied by the instant, since both old squatters and new arrivals were ready to take up the fight rather than retreat. When it appeared that the police were surrounded, they were given the order to shoot. Bullets forced the disorganized squatters to call off the offensive. Many were injured, and Edilberto Ramos, a young man from the provinces who had participated in the takeover from the start, was killed. "They also say that another young man, Vicente Salvador, was killed and it was he who gave the settlement our name, but this isn't confirmed because some say he didn't die."

When the news spread that a young man had died, an enraged mob reinitiated the assault and took as hostages a policeman and a police major. They stripped and beat them, took their badges, and forced them to climb to the top of the hill, kiss the cross, and shout in praise of the takeover and the people. In the crowd's exhilaration, the humiliation and beatings suffered by their captured aggressors was not enough. The people cried, "Crucify them, crucify them!" Local leaders apparently found no way to halt the widespread chaos that overtook Pamplona at dawn on May 5, 1971. As the wounded moaned, the cries and entreaties of the hostages could be heard: they too were fathers, they were only carrying out orders, they were also poor, *cholos*, it was their job. These were a few of the desperate pleas they babbled. Their appeals momentarily calmed the mob. The leaders took advantage of the moment to regain control. Just then, another police contingent arrived. Faced with this bloody, confused scenario, the police commander decided to wait rather than negotiate. As rocks flew, the local leaders agreed to hand over the hostages in exchange for the troop's withdrawal. Before leaving, the released major looked back at the crowd and thanked them for sparing his life, promising as an exchange to intercede on their behalf with the interior minister. The riot police withdrew in the midst of shouts of long life to General Velasco Alvarado and the revolution.

The lives of two naked police officers had been saved because they were *cholos* and workers just like most squatters. At the same time, they protected the government from a crisis: a massacre that night would have seriously tarnished the government's revolutionary image. The shouts for Velasco, identified by the multitude as a *cholo* and a hard worker, too, strengthened his new image of a grassroots leader.

But the problem didn't end there. The Catholic Church had become deeply involved. On the one hand, lands belonging to the Jesuits remained in the squatters' hands. On the other, the reform spirit of the Medellín Conference (1968) was very much present among an important group of national ecclesiastical authorities. In light of Latin American reality, the church's social doctrine was expressed in a mission to preach the gospel of the poor, resuscitating the image of a Christ weighed down by social injustice and searching for peace and equality. Influenced strongly by these beliefs, the Peruvian church leadership intervened. Monsignor Luis Bambarén, the auxiliary bishop of Lima, vicar of the zone and a Jesuit, expressed solidarity with the squatters by agreeing to a request by the Ciudad de Dios Parish Council, made up of area residents and parish priests, to cocelebrate a memorial mass in honor of the dead and wounded. In an open letter to the president of the republic, council members also protested police behavior during the battle; the statement later led to the council members' arrest.

On the morning of May 9, bishops Bambarén and Schmitz, together with four priests, held a "Mass of Solidarity" before a crowd consisting of squatters, the wounded, and the body of the man killed in Pampa de La Inmaculada. Recalling Christ's words on the cross in his homily, Monsignor Bambarén alluded directly to the aggression they had suffered, the injustice suffered by landless Peruvians, and the need to end hunger and misery and give dignity and opportunity to the poor.

While the church offered these words, the IDB conference met and journalists reported on it and Peru's serious situation. Traditionally dominant groups protested openly against the government, the church's political stance, attacks on private property, and general disorder.

In this context of rising tension and social protest, the government ordered Bambarén's arrest. The bishop had added his name to the letter sent to the president by the Ciudad de Dios Parish Council, whose members had been arrested a day earlier. With this move, the interior minister complicated the situation even further. The uproar in the country was complete, especially once news spread of the especially aggressive arrest as well as the minister's uncompromising attitude before such a high-ranking church official. Church support was massive. The bishop was released the following day with the president's apologies and the interior minister's resignation.

At this moment the church operated like a "hinge" between competing sectors within the government. Cardinal Juan Landázuri met with the president. Both agreed that mistakes had been made on both sides;

that the conflict was provoked by "enemies of the regime" who wanted to take advantage of the situation to "sow chaos and disorder"; that an attack such as this against private property could not be tolerated and property was to be respected while there was a search for a solution to the housing problems of the city's poor; and, lastly, that the church and the government would continue working together for the country's benefit.

As a result, on May 14 the daily newspapers announced that as proof of its commitment to the revolutionary process begun in 1968, the government ordered the relocation of 2,300 families to an area known as the Tablada de Lurín, twelve miles south of Lima. There, a great city for the poor would be built, a "model city" that would be called Villa El Salvador. The parish priest assigned to the new settlement brought with him a massive image of Christ the Savior, which was placed on a hill where the parish church would eventually be built.

Army trucks helped transport the squatters to their new settlement, a desolate sand dune lacking all basic public services. Everything needed to be done. The people had conquered a place they would have to begin domesticating that very day. The government's willingness to help at this stage would prove to be key, as would the church's support through the priests who pitched in like neighbors to construct the dwellings. But just as strong was the religious fervor contained in the hope placed in the miracles of Sarita Colonia and San Martín de Porres, as important in warding off evil spirits and scorpions as in protecting children from bites, envy, and the "evil eye." In the same way, the new homeowners kept the faith so that the shacks wouldn't crumble and with them faith and the strength to continue in their quest to put down roots in the capital.

Notes

1 More detailed information about the invasion is offered by Manuel Montoya Ugarte, "Pamplona: Un caso de movilización social a partir de la base" (thesis, Universidad Nacional Mayor de San Marcos, 1973); and Pedro Ferradas, *Villa El Salvador: De arenal a distrito municipal* (Lima: CELADEC, 1983). Testimonies taken during fieldwork form part of the bibliographic material.

2 Sarita Colonia was a young girl from Huaraz who migrated to Lima with her family in the 1930s. After her death, she became known in Lima as the folk saint of taxi drivers, hairdressers, recluses, and street vendors. For more on her life, see Part 10.

RECIPE FOR A HOUSE

Mercedes Torribio

Lima's population exploded from 645,000 to 4.6 million between 1940 and 1981 in what José María Arguedas described as the Andean "reconquest" of the Spanish conquerors' capital. These new arrivals built from scratch, squatting on unoccupied desert lands to establish pueblos jóvenes, *or young towns, now home to the majority of Lima's inhabitants. Ayacucho-born Mercedes Torribio's matter-of-fact account of her role in a 1968 land takeover exemplifies the stubborn quest of thousands of migrants for a house of their own, in addition to the increased prominence of women in the new sphere of shantytown politics.*

I was twenty years old in 1968. My family came originally from Lucanas province in Ayacucho, but I lived with my brother in a rented house in the Lima district of San Martín de Porres. One day my brother heard that a land takeover had begun the night before in the Payet neighborhood, a vacant lot that was going to be turned into a cemetery. We decided to join, and went right away to buy all the necessary materials. Four *esteras* for the walls.[1] Four wood posts for the corners. Five longer posts for the beams. Cardboard for the roof. And wire to tie everything together. We scraped together money to hire a truck and had it take to Payet the materials for the house and all of our possessions: a bed, clothes, a couple of chairs, and some pots. We set up our house of straw mats on the hillside with the other squatters, because the flat part of the lot was too thick with loose dirt and dust. All of us flew little red-and-white Peruvian flags over our houses. On the third day, we made a list of all of us who had invaded and elected a steering committee. It was decided to name the settlement the Pueblo Joven "José Olaya."[2]

Three months passed. One day a truckload of policemen arrived to evict us. They came with a bulldozer and engineers who were going to

Figure 24. Huddling in makeshift *iglus*, squatters begin a takeover
in El Agustino, Lima. (Courtesy of Daniel Pajuelo)

take the measurements for the cemetery. But we had all agreed to carry
a whistle to blow if anyone came to evict us. When the police arrived,
one woman saw them and started to blow. We all came charging out with
our broom handles, rocks, and Peruvian flags. The women went first, because the police were not so likely to fire on us. There were a lot of us,
250 families, and we had all come out yelling. The kids started to pull up
the stakes of the engineers and throw rocks at the bulldozer. When they
saw our numbers, the police and the engineers turned and ran.

The landowners filed charges against us for trespassing. But we scraped
together money to hire a lawyer to block the case. Around that time, we
hired a company to level out the ground. Then we divided up the land
into square lots and distributed the lots by a lottery to build more permanent houses. We also started all the applications for water, electricity,
and sewage, and formal recognition of the settlement from the Lima
municipality, the congress, and the president of Peru. The Lima municipality formally recognized our settlement in 1984, under Mayor Alfonso
Barrantes. Since water did not come for many years, we needed to pay
cistern trucks to haul it up to us every month. The truckdrivers never
wanted to come to our settlement, because it was so high up in the Lima

hills. So the prettiest girls used to go down to talk to them, to persuade them to come. It took six years to get electricity and seventeen years for the water finally to arrive, in 1985. We also built a primary school during the 1980s, and a medical post. All the money and labor for everything came from us, without any help at all from the government.

My house has two rooms of brick and concrete. I want to build more, but with the economic crisis none of us has money for anything, sometimes not even for food. The settlement has new projects, too. Right now only Twentieth of December Avenue is paved, but we want to pave other streets. We also want to start a day care center for working mothers. All in all, though, considering we started with nothing, everyone is proud of what we have done for ourselves.

Notes

1   An *estera* is a straw mat roughly six feet square used for walls and roofing in Lima shanty-towns.

2   *Pueblo joven,* or "young town," was then the most common name for new settlements in Lima. Sailor José Olaya was a hero of the Independence Wars against Spain.

FEATHERLESS VULTURES

Julio Ramón Ribeyro

*Partly influenced by romantic stereotypes of the nobility of the poor, some schol-
ars and journalists have stressed only the communal spirit and fortitude of Lima's
shantytown dwellers. But poverty also takes a toll in anxiety, suspicion, and domestic violence. One of Peru's finest twentieth-century writers, J. R. Ribeyro captures
the Hobbesian side of want in this classic short story, adapted by Peruvian director
Francisco Lombardi for his prize-winning 1989 movie* Caídos del cielo *(Fallen
from Heaven). Although the tale is set in Lima of the 1950s, scarcity continues to
prevail, and today the desperate and impoverished still fan out to search for garbage in the chilly darkness of Lima's dawn.*

At six in the morning, the city rises on tiptoe and begins to take its
first steps. A fine mist dissolves the outlines of objects and creates
an enchanted atmosphere. The people who traverse the city at this hour
seem to be made out of a different substance, belonging to a spirit world.
Devout women shuffle sorrowfully until, under the arches of churches,
they melt into darkness. The night owls, wasted by the dark hours, return to their homes wrapped in scarves and melancholy. The garbage
men begin their sinister sweep along Pardo Avenue, armed with brooms
and carts. At this hour, workers walking to the trolley are visible. Police
officers yawn as they lean against trees. Paperboys are purple with cold.
And servants bring out the garbage cans. Lastly, the featherless vultures
appear, like a kind of mysterious sign.

At this hour, Old Don Santos attaches his wooden leg and sits up on the
mattress, where he begins to bellow. "Get up! Efraín, Enrique! It's time!"

Rubbing their bleary eyes, the two boys run to the ditch in the yard. The
peaceful night has made the water fill in, and on the bottom one can see
weeds and minute organisms slipping by. After rinsing their faces, each

one grabs a pail and shoots into the street. Meanwhile, Don Santos makes his way to the pigsty and with his long cane smacks his pig's haunches as it rummages through refuse.

"You still have to wait a bit, hog! But just wait, your turn will come."

Efraín and Enrique take their time on the way, climbing trees to pick blackberries or picking up rocks, the sharp kind that cut through the air and wound when the back is turned. It is still starry dawn when they reach their domain, a long street adorned with elegant homes that empty onto a boardwalk.

They aren't the only ones around. In other yards, in other slums, someone has given the wake-up call and many have gotten up. Some carry pails, others cardboard boxes. Sometimes, an old newspaper is enough. Without realizing it, they make up a clandestine organization that has the whole city divided. There are those who wander public buildings while others have elected parks or garbage dumps. Even dogs have acquired habits and schedules, which misery has made them choose wisely.

After a short rest, Efraín and Enrique begin their work. Each one chooses a sidewalk. The garbage cans are lined up in front of the doors. Each has to be entirely emptied before the search can begin. A garbage can is always a grab bag of surprises. One finds sardine cans, old shoes, bits of bread, dead rats, filthy cotton. They are only interested in leftovers. In the pigsty, Pascual accepts anything, but prefers slightly decomposed vegetables. Each of their small pails fills with rotted tomatoes, pieces of fat, strange sauces that don't appear in any cookbook.

It isn't unusual, however, to make a valuable find. One day, Efraín found some suspenders that he used to make a slingshot. Another time, it was an almost perfect pear, which he devoured on the spot. Enrique, on the other hand, is lucky with medicine boxes, shimmering bottles, used tooth brushes, and similar knick-knacks that he collects avidly.

After a strict selection, the boys return the garbage to the can and move to the next. It isn't wise to dally because the enemy is always waiting to pounce. Sometimes they are surprised by the servants and must flee, dropping their treasures. More frequently, the garbage truck rolls around the corner and the day is lost.

As the sun crests above the hills, the starry dawn comes to an end. The mist has dissolved, the devout women are submerged in ecstasy, the night owls sleep, the paperboys have handed out the newspapers, the workers climb their scaffolding. Light dispels the magical dawn world. The featherless vultures have returned to their nest.

Don Santos waited for them with the coffee ready.

"Let's see, what have you brought me?"

He smelled the two pails and, if the provisions were good, always made the same comment: "Pascual will feast today."

But most of the time he exploded. "Idiots! What did you do today? You probably played! Pascual will starve to death!"

They ran off toward the arbor, ears stinging from slaps, while the old man dragged himself to the pigsty. From the depths of the pen, Pascual would start to grunt. Don Santos tossed in food.

"My poor Pascual! Today you'll go hungry because of those two brats. They don't spoil you the way I do. I'll have to beat them so they learn!"

With the beginning of winter, the pig had become an insatiable monster. Nothing satisfied him, and Don Santos took vengeance on his grandsons for the animal's hunger. He forced them to get up earlier to invade other territories in search of more refuse. Finally, he made them go to the garbage dump at the sea's edge.

"There you'll find more things. It will also be easier because everything is together."

One Sunday, Efraín and Enrique arrived at the cliff. Following tracks in the earth, the trucks of the garbage men were unloading garbage on a rock slide. Seen from the boardwalk, the dump formed a dark and steaming cliff, where vultures and dogs swarmed like ants. From a distance, the two boys threw rocks to scare off their enemies. A dog backed off howling. As they got closer, a nauseating stench overwhelmed them, reaching deep in their lungs. Their feet sank into a swelling of feathers, of excrement, of rotting or burned waste. Plunging in their hands, they began the exploration. Every so often, under a yellowing newspaper, they would find a half-eaten piece of carrion. From nearby outcroppings, vultures spied on them impatiently and a few closed in, hopping from rock to rock as if to encircle them. Efraín screamed to scare them off and his yells echoed off the narrow banks and loosened pebbles that rolled into the sea. After an hour of work, they returned to the yard, pails full.

"Bravo!" shouted Don Santos. "You'll have to repeat this two or three times a week."

From then on, every Wednesday and Sunday, Efraín and Enrique made their way to the dump. They quickly became part of the strange fauna of such places. The vultures, accustomed to their presence, worked at their side, squawking, beating their wings and scratching with their yellow beaks, as if to help the boys discover clues to the precious filth.

It was on the way home from one of these excursions that Efraín felt a pain in the sole of his foot. A glass shard had sliced open a small wound. The next day, his foot was swollen, but he went about his chores anyway. When they returned, he could hardly walk, but Don Santos paid no attention because he had a visitor. Don Santos watched the pigsty next to a fat man whose hands were stained with blood.

"In twenty or thirty days, I'll come by," the man said. "By then, I think he'll be just right."

When he left, Don Santos had fire in his eyes.

"Get to work! Get to work! From now on, we'll have to increase Pascual's rations. Our business is right on track."

The next morning, however, when Don Santos woke his grandsons, Efraín couldn't get up.

"He cut his foot," Enrique explained. "He cut it yesterday on a piece of glass."

Don Santos examined his grandson's foot. The infection had already spread.

"This is a fake! Have him wash his foot in the ditch and wrap it in a rag."

"But it hurts him!" interrupted Enrique. "He can't walk."

Don Santos thought for a moment. From the pigsty, you could hear Pascual's grunts.

"And what about me?" he asked, slapping his wooden leg. "You think my leg doesn't hurt me? I'm seventy years old and I work. . . . Stop all this fooling around!"

Efraín left for the street with his pail, supporting himself on his brother's shoulder. They returned about a half hour later with their pails almost empty.

"He couldn't get more!" Enrique told his grandfather. "Efraín is half crippled."

Don Santos looked at his grandsons as if he were contemplating a prison sentence.

"All right, all right," he said, scratching his sparse beard. He grabbed Efraín by the neck and propelled him into the bedroom. "The sick to their beds! To rot on a mattress! And you will do your brother's work. Get to the dump this instant!"

Enrique returned to the house around noon with two loaded-down pails. He was followed by a strange visitor: a scabrous, half-emaciated dog.

Don Santos grabbed his cane.

"Another mouth to feed!"

Enrique pulled the dog to his chest and ran toward the door.

"Don't hurt him, grandpa! I'll give him some of my food."

Don Santos drew closer, his wooden leg sinking into the mud.

"No dogs here! I have enough to worry about with you kids!"

Enrique opened the gate to the street.

"If he goes, I go too."

The old man stopped. Enrique took advantage of the moment to insist.

"He eats almost nothing. . . . Look how thin he is. Since Efraín is sick, he will help me. He knows the dump well and has a good nose for garbage."

Don Santos thought for a minute, looking to the sky where a fine drizzle was beginning to fall. Without saying anything, he put down his cane, grabbed the pails, and went limping to the pigsty.

Enrique smiled with happiness and, with his new friend clutched to his heart, ran to his brother.

"Pascual, Pascual. . . . Little Pascual!" sang the old man.

"I'll call you Pedro," said Enrique, petting the dog's head as they went to see Efraín.

His happiness was short-lived. Drenched with sweat, Efraín was tossing with pain upon the mattress. His foot was swollen like a rubber ball filled with air. His toes had all but lost their shape.

"I've brought you a gift. Look," he said, showing off the dog. "His name is Pedro. He's for you, to keep you company. . . . When I go to the dump, I'll leave him here with you and the two of you can play all day long. You can teach him how to fetch rocks."

"And grandpa?" asked Efraín, stretching out his hand to the animal.

"Grandpa didn't say anything," whispered Enrique.

The two of them looked at the door. A heavy mist had descended. They could hear their grandfather's voice.

"Pascual, Pascual. . . . Little Pascual!"

That same night, there was a full moon. The two boys were concerned because at such times their grandfather was impossible. Since sundown, they had seen him pacing the yard, talking to himself and smacking the arbor with his cane. At times, he walked over to the room, looked inside, and on seeing his silent grandsons would launch a spitball loaded with bitterness. Pedro was afraid of him. Every time he saw the old man, he cowered and stood as motionless as a rock.

"Scum! Nothing more than scum!" Don Santos repeated all night long, glaring at the moon.

The next morning Enrique woke with a cold. The old man, who heard him sneezing at dawn, said nothing. In truth, however, it was a disaster.

If Enrique got sick, who would take care of Pascual? The pig's voracity grew with its tremendous weight. In the afternoons, he grunted with his snout buried in mud. People came from as far as Nemesio's yard a block away to complain.

The next day, the inevitable happened: Enrique couldn't get up. He had coughed all night. Morning found him shivering, burning with fever.

"You too?" asked the grandfather.

Enrique pointed to his chest, which rasped. The old man stormed out of the room. Five minutes later, he returned.

"It's cruel to fool me like this!" he cried. "You torment me because I can't walk. You know very well that I'm old and lame. Otherwise, I'd send you to hell and take care of Pascual myself!"

Efraín woke up complaining, and Enrique began to cough.

"But it doesn't matter! I'll take care of him. The two of you are trash, nothing more than trash. A couple of poor, featherless vultures! You'll see how I'll get the better of you. Your grandfather is still strong. But one thing is for sure. Today there'll be no food for you! There won't be anything to eat until you get up and work!"

Through the doorway, they saw him lift the pails in the air and turn for the street. Less than half an hour later, he was back, crushed. Lacking his grandsons' agility, he was easily overtaken by the garbage men. And the dogs had tried to bite him.

"Pieces of scum! You know, you'll go without food until you work!"

The next day, he tried to repeat his effort with the pails, but was forced to give up. His wooden leg couldn't adjust to the asphalt roads, the hard sidewalks, and each step sent a spear of pain into his groin. At dawn on the third day, he collapsed on his mattress with energy only to insult his grandsons.

"If he dies of hunger," he screamed, "it will be your fault!"

The anguished, interminable days began. The three spent the day closed up in the room, without talking, suffering a kind of forced imprisonment. Efraín tossed and turned, Enrique coughed. After running around the yard, Pedro returned with a stone in his mouth to drop in his master's hands. Don Santos, half asleep, played with his wooden leg and sent them fierce looks. At noon, he dragged himself to a corner of the yard where vegetables grew and prepared his lunch, devoured in secret. At times, he circled the bed where his grandsons were sleeping, holding a piece of lettuce or raw carrot, trying to provoke their appetites to make their punishment even harsher.

Efraín no longer had the strength to complain. Only Enrique felt a strange fear growing in his heart. When he looked into his grandfather's eyes, he felt that he no longer knew him, as if his grandfather had lost any human feeling. At night, when the moon was full, he grabbed Pedro and held him as close as possible until the dog began to moan. At the same time, the pig began to grunt and grandfather complained as if he were being strangled. Sometimes, Don Santos fastened on his wooden leg and went out into the yard. In the moonlight, Enrique watched him move from the pigsty to the garden, his fists raised, stumbling into everything in his path. Finally, he would return to the room and stare at the boys, as if they were to blame for Pascual's hunger.

The last night of the full moon, no one could sleep. Pascual growled fiercely. Enrique had heard people say that when pigs were very hungry, they went just as crazy as men. Grandfather remained awake all night, without even turning off the lantern. This time, he didn't go into the yard or utter curses between clenched teeth. Sunk low in his mattress, he stared fixedly at the door. He seemed to be preparing within himself an old hatred, toying with it and getting ready to unleash it. When the sky began to fade above the hills, he opened his mouth, turned its dark hollowness toward his grandsons, and yelled.

"Up, up, up!" Blows began to rain down. "Get up, you loafers! How long are we going to be like this? It's over! On your feet!"

Efraín began to cry. Enrique got up, flattening out against the wall. His grandfather's eyes so fascinated him that he no longer seemed to feel the blows. He saw the cane lift and strike his head as if it were made of cardboard. Finally, he was able to react.

"Don't hit Efraín! It isn't his fault! Let me go alone. I'll leave, I'll go to the dump."

Grandfather stopped, panting. It took him a while to catch his breath.

"Right now . . . to the dump . . . take two pails, four pails."

Enrique pulled away, grabbed the pails, and left at a run. The fatigue of hunger and his convalescence made him stumble. When he opened the gate, Pedro wanted to follow him.

"Not you. Stay here to take care of Efraín."

He took to the streets sucking the morning air deep into his lungs. On the way, he ate weeds and was about to chew dirt. He saw everything as if through a magic cloud. Weakness made him light, ethereal. He almost flew like a bird. At the dump, he felt like another vulture among vultures. When the pails were overflowing, he started home. The devout women, the night owls, the barefoot newspaper boys, and all the other dawn secretions dispersed in the city. Enrique, returned to his world, walked happily among them, among dogs and ghosts, touched by the celestial hour.

When he entered the yard, he was struck by an oppressive, resistant air, which forced him to stop. It was as if at the door, the world ended and there began another made out of mud, growls, and an absurd penance. The surprising thing, though, was that this time there was a calm laden with bad omens reigning in the yard, as if all of the violence were in equilibrium, on the verge of explosion. Standing at the edge of the pigsty, his grandfather looked into its depths. He looked like a tree growing from his wooden leg. Enrique made a noise, but the old man didn't move.

"Here are the pails!"

Don Santos turned his back but remained immobile. Enrique dropped the pails and ran to the room. The moment Efraín saw him, he began to moan.

"Pedro . . . Pedro . . ."

"What happened?"

"Pedro bit grandpa . . . grandpa grabbed his cane . . . then I heard him howl."

Enrique left the room.

"Pedro, come here! Where are you, Pedro?"

There was no answer. His grandfather remained immobile, staring at the wall. Enrique felt a bad premonition. In one leap, he was next to the old man.

"Where is Pedro?"

His stare moved into the pigsty. Pascual was devouring something in the mud. All that was left were legs and a dog's tail.

"No!" screamed Enrique, covering his eyes. "No! No!"

Through his tears, he looked for his grandfather's gaze. But the old man avoided him, turning sluggishly on his wooden leg. Enrique began to dance around him, grabbing his shirt, screaming, kicking, trying to see his eyes to find an answer.

"Why did you do it? Why?"

The grandfather said nothing. Finally, impatient, he slapped his grandson aside, knocking him to his knees on the ground. Enrique saw how his grandfather, raised like a giant, stared obstinately at Pascual's banquet. Stretching out his hand, Enrique grabbed the cane, its tip dirtied with blood. With it, he rose on tiptoe and moved toward the old man.

"Turn!" he screamed. "Turn around!"

When Don Santos turned, he saw the cane cutting through the air until it struck his cheek.

"Take this!" yelled Enrique, raising his arm anew. But suddenly, he stopped, afraid of what he was doing. Throwing down the cane, he looked at his grandfather with regret. The old man took a step back, hands clutching his face. His wooden leg landed on wet earth. He slipped. With a cry, he fell over backwards into the pigsty.

Enrique took several steps back. At first, he tried to hear what was happening, but there was no noise. Little by little, he moved closer. His grandfather, the wooden leg splintered, was on his back in the mud. His mouth was agape. He was looking for Pascual, who had taken refuge in a corner and sniffed the mud suspiciously.

Enrique moved back with the same caution with which he had approached. His grandfather probably saw him because as Enrique ran to the room, he thought he heard the old man call his name, with a tone of tenderness that he had never before heard.

"To me, Enrique. To me."

"Quickly!" yelled Enrique, jumping onto his brother. "Quickly, Efraín! The old man has fallen into the pigsty! We have to get out of here!"

"But to where?" Efraín asked.

"Wherever—the dump—where we can eat something, where the vultures are."

"But I can't stand!"

Enrique picked up his brother with both hands and pulled him against his chest. Embraced as if they were one person, they slowly crossed the yard. When they opened the gate, they realized that the starry hour had passed and the city, awake and alive, opened before them its huge jaws.

From the pigsty came the rumble of a fierce battle.

PERU'S AFRICAN RHYTHMS

Nicomedes Santa Cruz

Known as pioneers of the rediscovery of African-Peruvian culture, Nicomedes Santa Cruz and Victoria Santa Cruz, his wife, began in the 1950s to collect, write, publish, and perform music, poetry, and dance based on the vigorous traditions of black Peruvians. In his book The Décima in Peru, *Nicomedes Santa Cruz recounts the colonial roots of this elegant melding of poetry and song, where the initial refrain contributes the final line to each verse, in this case in an A-B-C-D pattern. Santa Cruz's innovation was to blend this Spanish form with African rhythms and themes, well within the history of hybridity of the European and the African that lies at the root of what is known as* criollo *music, popular along the coast, and performed in the 1960s and 1970s by African-Peruvian artists like Santa Cruz and Lucha Reyes.*

Rhythms of slavery
against bitterness and pain.
To the beat of the chains
black rhythms of Peru.

1

My grandmother came from Africa adorned in shells,
Spaniards brought her
in a caravel ship.
They marked her with fire,
the branding iron was her cross;
and in South America,
between blows of pain
they gave blacks drums,
rhythms of slavery.

2
For a single coin
they sold her in Lima
and in the La Molina Hacienda
she served the Spanish.
She and other blacks from Angola,
earned so much from their work:
mosquitoes to suck their blood
hard ground to sleep upon
and nothing to console
against bitterness and pain.

3
On the sugar plantation
the sad *socabón* was born,
and at the rum press
black people sang the *zaña*.[1]
The machete and scythe
cut at brown hands;
and Indians with flutes
and blacks with timbrels
sang unhappy fortunes
to the beat of the chains.

4
The old died,
but in the cane fields
the sound of the *zamacueca* could be heard
and the *panalivio*, far in the distance.
And one hears the courting songs
my mother sang in her youth:
from Cañete to Timbuktu,
from Chancay to Mozambique,
clear notes carry
black rhythms of Peru.

Note

1   The *socabón, zamacueca, panalivio,* and *zaña* are different kinds of African Peruvian songs
that grew out of slave culture.

A GUERRILLA'S WORD

Javier Heraud

With the Cuban Revolution in 1959 and decolonization in Asia and Africa, guerrilla movements formed in many Latin American countries. In Peru, the Movement of the Revolutionary Left, under the rebel former aprista *Luis de la Puente Uceda, and the Army of National Liberation were short-lived, reflecting a fatal miscalculation by these mostly light-skinned intellectuals, who wrongly assumed that peasants and Indians would rally around them to overthrow the old order. Born to an upper-middle-class Lima family, the young poet Javier Heraud, killed in the Amazonian river town of Puerto Maldonado in 1963, came to symbolize this combination of commitment and romanticism of Latin America's Marxist guerrillas of the 1960s and 1970s.*

Because my country is beautiful like a sword in the air
and bigger now and even
still more beautiful,
I speak out and defend it
with my life.
I don't care what traitors
say
we've blocked the way
with thick tears
of steel.
The sky is ours.
Ours our daily bread.
We've sown and harvested
the wheat and the land,
ours too

and always ours
the sea,
the jungles
and the birds.

LIBERATION THEOLOGY

Gustavo Gutiérrez

In their famous Medellín declaration of 1968, the Conference of Latin American Bishops announced their commitment to a "preferential option for the poor," countering the church's centuries-old alliance with the Latin American oligarchy. No single figure was more influential in this break with the past than theologian Gustavo Gutiérrez, who grew up in the town of Huánuco in Peru's central mountains. Influenced by the example of his Dominican forerunner Bartolomé de las Casas and the new currency of Marxism in the 1960s and 1970s, Gutiérrez's 1971 book A Theology of Liberation *sought to transform Christ from the colonial Spanish figure of blood and suffering to a militant symbol of protest and to press Catholic "base communities" to trade in resignation for action on social justice.*

What we have often called the "major fact" in the life of the Latin American church—the participation of Christians in the process of liberation—is simply an expression of a far-reaching historical event: *the irruption of the poor.* Our time bears the imprint of the new presence of those who in fact used to be "absent" from our society and from the church. By "absent" I mean: of little or no importance, and without the opportunity to give expression themselves to their sufferings, their camaraderies, their plans, their hopes.

This state of affairs began to change in Latin America in recent decades, as a result of a broad historical process. But it also began to change in Africa (new nations) and Asia (old nations obtaining their independence), and among racial minorities (blacks, Hispanics, Amerindians, Arabs, Asiatics) living in the rich countries and in the poor countries as well (including Latin American countries). There has been a further important and diversified movement: the new presence of women, whom

Figure 25. Cartoonist Juan Acevedo captures the rift between traditional Catholics and the progressive wing inspired by Gustavo Gutiérrez. It reads: "Jesus belongs to all . . ." "Yes, to all the poor." (Used by permission of Juan Acevedo)

Puebla described as "doubly oppressed and marginalized" among the poor of Latin America.[1]

Liberation theology is closely bound up with this new presence of those who in the past were always absent from our history. They have gradually been turning into active agents of their own destiny and beginning a resolute process that is changing the condition of the poor and oppressed of this world. Liberation theology (which is an expression of the right of the poor to think out their own faith) has not been an automatic result of this situation and the changes it has undergone. It represents rather an attempt to accept the invitation of Pope John XXIII and the Second Vatican Council and interpret this sign of the times by reflecting on it critically in the light of God's word. This theology should lead us to a serious discernment of the values and limitations of this sign of the times.

An option for the poor is an option for the God of the kingdom whom Jesus proclaims to us; this is a point that I myself have developed and discussed in depth on various occasions. The entire Bible, beginning with the story of Cain and Abel, mirrors God's predilection for the weak and abused of human history. This preference brings out the gratuitous or unmerited character of God's love. The same revelation is given in the evangelical Beatitudes, for they tell us with the utmost simplicity that God's predilection for the poor, the hungry, and the suffering is based on God's unmerited goodness to us.

The ultimate reason for commitment to the poor and oppressed is not to be found in the social analysis we use, or in human compassion, or in any direct experience we ourselves may have of poverty. These are all doubtless valid motives that play an important part in our commitment. As Christians, however, our commitment is grounded, in the final analysis, in the God of our faith. It is a theocentric, prophetic option that has its roots in the unmerited love of God and is demanded by this love. Bartolomé de las Casas, who had direct experience of the terrible poverty and decimation of Latin American Amerindians, explained it by saying: "God has the freshest and keenest memory of the least and most forgotten."

The rich, troubled, and creative life that the Latin American church is living as it tries to respond to the challenge set for it by the new presence of the poor calls for a deeper understanding of its own faith in the Lord Jesus. For a long time, as a result of a Latin American cultural tradition imposed by colonization, theology as practiced among us simply echoed the theology developed in Europe. Latin American theologians had recourse to European theology without any reference to its intellectual and historical context, with the result that their theology easily became a set of abstract propositions. Or else they made a painful effort to adapt European theology to a new reality, but were unable to explain the reasons for its themes and priorities or for the development of this kind of thinking, as long as the effort was undertaken in a North Atlantic framework.

The praxis on which liberation theology reflects is a praxis of solidarity in the interests of liberation and is inspired by the gospel. It is the activity of "peacemakers"—that is, those who are forging shalom. Western languages translate this Hebrew word as "peace" but in doing so, diminish its meaning. Shalom in fact refers to the whole of life and, as part of this, to the need of establishing justice and peace. Consequently, a praxis motivated by evangelical values embraces to some extent every effort to bring about authentic fellowship and authentic justice. For faith shows us that in this commitment the grace of Christ plays its part, whether or not those who practice it are aware of this fact.

The historical womb from which liberation theology has emerged is the life of the poor and, in particular, of the Christian communities that have arisen within the bosom of the present-day Latin American church. This experience is the setting in which liberation theology tries to read the word of God and be alert to the challenges that faith issues to the historical process in which that people is engaged. Revelation and history, faith in Christ and the life of a people, eschatology and praxis: these are the factors that, when set in motion, give rise to what has been called the hermeneutical circle. The aim is to enter more deeply into faith in a God who became one of us, and to do so on the basis of the faith-filled experience and commitment of those who acknowledge this God as their liberator.

The major challenges to which theology must respond will come, therefore, from the demands of the gospel as seen today in the development of an oppressed but Christian people. Since liberation theology is a critical reflection on the word of God received in the church, it will make explicit the values of faith, hope, and love that inspire the praxis of Christians. But it will also have to help in correcting possible deviations on the part of those who reject the demands for participation in history and the promotion of justice that follow from faith in the God of life, and also on the part of those who run the risk of forgetting central aspects of Christian life, because they are caught up in the demands of immediate political activity.

Because liberation theology takes a critical approach, it refuses to serve as a Christian justification of positions already taken. It seeks to show that unless we make an ongoing commitment to the poor, who are the privileged members of the reign of God, we are far removed from the Christian message.

Note

1   Puebla refers to the 1977 Conference of Latin American Bishops meeting at Puebla, Mexico.

A WORLD FOR JULIUS

Alfredo Bryce Echenique

Despite twentieth-century upheavals, Lima's elite maintained a life of luxury in enclaves like Miraflores and San Isidro, with imported cars, servants, and an invisible yet powerful social code of belonging and exclusion. Connections with the United States became especially strong after the massive expansion of post–World War II investment by American companies under General Manuel Odría, known as the "Happy General" for his lavish parties for foreign dignitaries. Published in 1969, Alfredo Bryce Echenique's A World for Julius *is a sympathetic satire of the Peruvian oligarchy. In this excerpt from the novel, now a fixture of Peru's literary canon, the sentimental protagonist Julius, his mother Susan, her husband Juan Lucas, brothers Santiago and Bobby, and their chauffeur spend an afternoon at San Isidro's Lima Golf Club.*

Julius spent the summer between kindergarten and grade school at the Golf Club. They would all go in the station wagon, except for Santiago who was preparing for entrance exams to study agriculture at the university. The poor guy had a lot of tutors; they were young and most of them were in their last years of college. They always came around in pickups, offering those strong Inca cigarettes. The university qualifying examination was like the garage door of the mansion: behind it was Juan Lucas' antique Mercedes sports car. If Santiago gets accepted, he'll have transportation to the university and wheels for picking up easy girls in Lince, for instance. "Poor Santiago, he sure studies a lot!" Susan commented, sitting at the edge of the Club swimming pool. Bobby, on the other hand, was taking life easy, springing a thousand times off the diving board in order to impress the Canadian ambassador's daughter, a thirteen-year-old gringa. Julius didn't have a nanny anymore, and when Juan Lucas finished a round of golf in the morning and came in for lunch, which was always prefaced with *gin and tonics*,[1] he would take Julius with him to the table. Sometimes Carlos would take Santiago to the Club for lunch so he could get away from the books for a while.

That summer Juan Lastarria became a member of the Club. The family was in Ancón, but he spent most of his time in Lima taking care of the import and storage business and everything else; hence he took advantage of the situation to become a member of the Club and to go there without his wife. The poor guy almost went crazy hurrying all the time to finish his morning golf game so he could make a beeline to the pool and hover around his *duchess*. Still dressed in his golfing attire, he would kiss her hand ridiculously and sit there telling her he was a happy man, golfing had transformed him, it was rejuvenating him. Juan Lucas and his buddies named him Bulletproof because he would stick out his little chest when he appeared immaculate and pudgy in his bathing suit in order to take a dip in the pool. They made fun of him as he swam to keep fit. Susan felt sorry for him and begged them in English not to make her laugh anymore, and she told Julius not to listen to *those horrible things* they were saying about his uncle. But Juan Lucas insisted on explaining what his aunt Susana looked like in a bathing suit which precipitated a lot of manly laughter, and then they ordered more *gin and tonics* brought out from the bar of the Club by waiters scurrying along statuelike among so many women in bathing suits, so many girls, so many gringas. No one in the group paid; they would gamble for the bill in the bar later in the afternoon; they would ask for the dice and, while the women waited out on the terrace, they rolled the dice, accompanied by a round of late afternoon drinks. As they threw the dice, they would comment on the day's round of golf, the final scores, who shot what, and the roll of the dice would determine the one among them who would blurt out Damn it! not showing any anger but just manly enough for the occasion, and then sign the check that sooner or later would reach his office. Lastarria always got sidetracked in the middle of the dice roll because he would be watching the Club professional. The Argentine had been giving lessons to him at a very expensive hourly rate. He was good-looking and seemed fairly sophisticated, but stood out nevertheless like a tango singer in his hair style, a good player and tanned; hence, Lastarria didn't know whether to treat him like an employee of the Club or as a Señor.

It may seem strange but Julius began to detest the headwaiter who waited on them at lunch. He was the one who brought them the menus and then treated the waiters like dirt whenever they made mistakes. And the amazing part is that the headwaiter began to dislike Julius, as if he were the son of some Club member whose financial ruin was already well known by everyone. Something odd would occur every time that head-waiter came to their table; undoubtedly, he must have felt superior to the other waiters because his jacket was finer. But what about those dispar-aging glances at Julius? . . . Maybe it's because the other day Julius bent down and picked up a piece of bread from the floor that the waiter should have done or maybe it's because he isn't forceful enough when he deals with the caddies and the other waiters. There wasn't a logical explanation. What could explain this incipient hatred between a fiddling, ass-kissing waiter and a young boy who was about to turn seven years old? Whatever the case, Julius was able to ignore it by the time the food had arrived: shrimp cocktails, stuffed avocados, sole in white sauce, or crêpes au coin-treau, with flames leaping off the table that didn't even faze Juan Lucas.

The golfers and their wives would enter the dining room, looking tanned—in fact, elegantly tanned—and one could tell they were agile and in excellent economic shape. They would greet each other even if in the world of business they hated each other and there it wasn't a sin if someone had been divorced. Lovers, for instance, were accepted de-spite the gossip. And, of course, there were always those women whose names were more aristocratic, refined, and conservative than the others, but often these same people no longer had that much money and per-haps for that reason they didn't protest; in fact, many of them who came for lunch were merely invited: poor things, it was their proper social set-ting but there was the problem of the membership fee; frankly, they were in no position to judge vulgarities or immoralities. The drinks brought equality, the dining room became alive and, looking out the windows at the golf course, it was as if they were sailing over a sea of green, a pleasure trip on an ocean that unfortunately had its limits—the high walls enclos-ing the Club so that poor people couldn't get inside to steal the golf balls.

Lunchtime was always a problem for Lastarria. Even though he had spent a bunch of money outfitting himself to play golf, he had a hard time making friends at the Club. Everyone there, of course, knew who Juan Lastarria was, but that was precisely the problem: they knew what he was. They knew the same about others, but those were something: handsome, drunks, fun, friendly, or they simply managed to fit in easily. Lastarria, on the other hand, was still boorish and missed the point on just about everything. If Juan Lucas wouldn't invite him over to their table, the poor dummy would have to flee to another and, naturally, end up paying the bill; he would sign for it which is the one thing he had learned to do quickly. Susan became aware of the problem and many times she would be the one to invite him over to their table. She felt so sorry for him, dressed up like a golfer but not really looking like one. And that stupid sweater?

Once lunch was over there was lots of table talk. Then the men left to play another round of golf in order to complete the daily eighteen holes that they had begun in the morning. Susan also played, accompanied by several friends who were the wives of diplomats or people like Juan Lucas. There was always someone from England, a few Americans, and maybe a German woman as well. They would speak in English or Spanish, but no matter which language they used they always added delicious foreign words. Also they would occasionally speak French, whenever the ambassador's wife was along, but that's when many of the Peruvian women didn't say a word all afternoon. Needless to say, they all represented the latest in fashion: Aaaaahhhhh! and it's all very expensive. The men would walk on ahead in a group and blurt out Damn it! Bastard! or both, well said, appropriately timed, and manly. The caddies wouldn't dare to think that their refined ways were in any way queerish. If, for instance, you were on the outside looking in over the wall at the scene I'm describing, you'd be convinced that life couldn't be happier or more beautiful; moreover, you would have seen very good golfers. They were men who didn't show their age and had strong and sprightly arms; their women were lousy at hitting the ball but were beautiful. Spying over the wall a little longer and with keen sight, you could have also recognized Juan Lastarria and the Argentine professional, who knew how to deal with that kind of world, both walking after the little ball and all that it represented.

The children, meanwhile, would be in Ancón, at Herradura Beach, or in the pool at the Club. Julius played in the pool until the pressure of the water from diving started to hurt his eardrums. Bobby had nothing to do with him and he continued to jump off the diving board, always getting out of the pool near the Canadian ambassador's daughter. Naturally, rather than use the steps he would leap up onto the side of the pool in acrobatic fashion, adjust his bathing suit in order to let his belly button show, and trot over to the steps of the diving board to repeat the scene all over again. He would go up the steps, make sure she was watching, and take off running. Aunt Susana wouldn't have ever permitted her children to do this. When he got to the end of the board, he would fly off, transformed first into a gull, next into a plane nosediving into the sea, and then a round tire. But at the last moment he would straighten out gracefully and penetrate the water without a splash. A fantastic, daring jump. And he was ready to risk his life for the young Canadian girl. She was so pretty! . . . She, too, was attracted to him and, while she remained seated on her stool and watched, she soon smiled at him. Finally one day they met each other and started to swim together. Tarzan and Jane, that's the way he felt, and they dove down side by side from one side of the river to the other as if they were going to run into crocodiles on the way. Then one day a crocodile did appear: Julius. He approached them to ask the time and to tell Bobby that Mommy was about to call them to get ready to go home. For being a little brat and a crocodile, he received a tremendous swat from Tarzan, who was very embarrassed in front of the girl.

The golfers would return late in the afternoon. Some of the men took showers and others cooled off in the pool. Afterward they went to the locker rooms where, wrapped in a towel or naked depending on their masculinity or their stomachs, they would talk. The voices of Juan Lucas and his friends resounded throughout the numbered lockers of the Club while they got dressed and commented on that day's golf game. One day Lastarria undressed in front of everyone and his physique became the butt of a joke; everyone would laugh, he more than anyone else, and he finally started to feel like he had become a member of the Club. This was his favorite time. As soon as they were dressed they moved to the bar, this was their moment, the manly thing to do, roll the dice and there they accepted him and even commented on the progress he was making with the help of the Argentine golf pro. Little by little he became an insider and, if they kept on patting him on the back, soon he would feel right at home; in fact, he practically felt right at home, even though disagreeable things kept happening to him, like the other afternoon, for instance, when he thanked God for not being seen by anyone but feeling, just the same, so out of it. Poor guy. It was that ne'er-do-well count, that Peruvian Spaniard, the queer, so snobbish, a cretin, so broke but so elegant, so admired, and always getting himself invited everywhere. Well, that worthless count pushed him out of the way and beat him to the door, didn't even say hello, almost spit on him, the wise guy was drunk. And he, without even wanting to, blurted out excuse me, Count, and now that little incident didn't let him rest in peace; after all, I'm rich, important, a hard worker, a family man. What a stupid thing to say to the guy! and he would wake up in the middle of the night reliving the incident. Juan Lastarria had his dignity too, you know. Something else happened . . . ah, if it wasn't for these incidents he would feel like a real Club member . . . they had introduced him to the Japanese consul—Juan, the Japanese consul—and immediately he didn't like him. He debated between using diplomacy or talking as if to any old Chinaman down at the corner grocery store. But he couldn't decide, he took too long, and he didn't know what to do when the other put out his silky, cold hand, the consul was very oriental, overflowing with reverence. They looked at him as if he were a total idiot, Chinese people can be very refined, too. Things like that happened to poor Juan and they almost gave him heart attacks. Then everyone will say he had one because of economic problems, too much work, too many worries, the standard heart attack because of the typical tensions of the well-minded *business man*. . . .

They stayed in the bar until nightfall while the women waited outside on the terrace and the children, wanting to go home, began to get on people's nerves. The business deals came up in the bar also, but in general they simply used elegance to discuss the country's political situation or the current state of the fishing industry. Of course, they never forgot to crack the latest joke or to comment on the day's golf game. Once the "Damn it, today I have to pay" was heard, the golfers would begin to leave. Juan Lucas would go out to the terrace looking for Susan, kiss her, and they would adore each other. He would sit down next to her and they would remain there for a few minutes in silence, contemplating how the trees on the golf course would start to disappear as night came on, interrupting momentarily that enjoyable golden green summer. It produced a momentary imbalance in the organized equilibrium of their lives, but they didn't let it bother them. They would just round up the boys and point them to the station wagon in order to go home and, as they would leave, they said good-bye to a few Club members who were still there stretched out in lounge chairs: See you tomorrow, adiós! The caddies were leaving about that time as well and would pass by the station wagon. Juan Lucas was one who never missed the opportunity to make a sarcastic remark: "Well, they're letting the convicts out of jail," for instance, as he started the motor. "Good evening, Señor," said the headwaiter, opening the door to an old Oldsmobile that probably belonged to a Club member some ten or twelve years ago and was laden with chrome that squeaked, an obese Oldsmobile that took a while for its motor to warm up.

Note

1 Italicized text appeared in English in the Spanish original.

VI · THE SHINING PATH

On May 18, 1980, Peru held elections for a civilian president after twelve years of military rule. Few paid much attention to reports that, just the day before, five masked members of the Communist Party of Peru–Shining Path had burned ballots in the Ayacucho village of Chuschi. But Chuschi was the opening salvo in a revolutionary assault on the Peruvian state. As it continued into the 1990s, the Shining Path became the largest insurgency on Peruvian soil since Túpac Amaru's rebellion two centuries before and one of the most violent in late-twentieth-century Latin America.

Contradictory theories abounded about the Shining Path at the start. Some Lima intellectuals postulated that it was an Indian revolt to restore the Inca empire.[1] Conservative generals warned that the rebels were part of an international communist conspiracy. In the Peruvian press, they appeared as demented, or even drugged-up criminals. Later, U.S. policymakers and experts proclaimed them "narcoterrorists" in cahoots with Colombian drug lords. For much of the 1980s, this band of Maoist rebels served as a blank screen for anyone to project their theories, hopes, and even worst fears about the Andes and Latin America.

Better understandings have emerged in recent years. Far from an indigenous uprising, the Shining Path was founded in 1970 by white philosophy professor Abimael Guzmán, and its class-based Marxism is notable for a complete absence of appeals to Indian or Andean pride. An admirer of Stalin and Mao, Guzmán toured China during the Cultural Revolution. But he and a handful of other provincial intellectuals built the tightly organized party on their own in the Andean city of Ayacucho, announcing their contempt for the Soviet Union's "social imperialism" and, later, Deng Xiaoping's China. Children of peasant and poor urban families were packing the local university, and the Shining Path offered the chance to join a revolutionary vanguard whose triumph seemed guaranteed by this self-confident professor's explication of the "laws of historical materialism." Perhaps more than any other recent Latin American guerrilla movement, the Shining Path also sought to draw women into its ranks. One of the party's first "martyrs" was the *ayacuchana* Edith Lagos, killed in a police ambush in 1982.

The Shining Path was just one group, and not even the largest, in the alphabet soup of Marxist parties on Peru's campuses in the 1960s and 1970s. It was distinguished by followers' religious devotion to Guzmán (who took the nom de guerre of "President Gonzalo") and armed revolution. "We will be the protagonists of history" and the masses will "rise in revolution to put the noose around the neck of imperialism and the reactionaries, seizing and garroting them by the throat," Guzmán promised his young followers in his 1980 "We Are the Initiators" speech.

This fierce sense of destiny made the Shining Path a formidable force. Militants swore to die and kill for the revolution. They bombed electrical towers and factories, killed mayors, and massacred villagers to cross what Guzmán called the "river of blood" to destroy the "old state" and build a Maoist utopia in its place. Far from horror at violence, their poems and songs celebrate the human costs of the armed struggle in what might be called a "poeticization of death." "The blood of the people has a rich perfume, and smells like jasmine, violets, and daisies" are the lyrics to "Flor de retama," or "Broom Flower," an Ayacucho ballad they adopted as their unofficial anthem. So certain were Guzmán's followers of their cause that they imagined their party as the protagonist not just of a struggle to overthrow the Peruvian state, but of a "world proletarian revolution" to topple capitalism worldwide.[2]

Through the 1980s, the party maintained a presence in the south-central Andes and the shantytowns of Ayacucho, Huancayo, and Lima. It also carved a lucrative niche in the Huallaga valley as self-appointed defender of coca-growing peasants (though not, as suggested by the "narcoterrorist" neologism, as allies of Colombian buyers). Yet the Shining Path failed to build broad support among Peru's poor majorities, and resistance erupted in fashions as diverse as self-defense committees in Andean villages and Lima peace marches. Most Peruvians of all backgrounds rejected the Maoists' violent authoritarianism, more likely to be attracted by the "other paths" of the informal economy, social organizations like Lima soup kitchens and the peasant patrols of the northern Andes, or the search for a better life in Europe or the United States. Although party propaganda insisted on "the brilliant incorporation of the masses into the revolution," the Shining Path never had more than a few thousand militants. The chance of a guerrilla victory vanished with the 1992 capture of Guzmán, the man historian Nelson Manrique calls the "queen bee" who founded and dominated the Shining Path. These revolutionaries took up arms as Peru's other Marxist parties withered and socialism fell in Eastern Europe and the Soviet Union. Their "people's war" will go down as a gripping yet historically doomed anachronism.

A few scattered remnants of the Shining Path can still be found in Peru's back country even today. But the imprisoned Guzmán requested peace talks in a series of letters to the Peruvian government in 1999, while repentant third-in-command Oscar Ramírez Durand, "Comrade Feliciano," denounced the Shining Path leader for having made "cannon fodder" of Peru's people with his revolutionary ambitions. Even so, a bitter rage at poverty, racism, and corruption still attracted a trickle of Peruvians to the promise of purification through armed struggle. In late 1993, just as a number of Lima pundits began to announce the beginning of a postwar era in Peru, a column of fifty rebels descended on the Ayacucho village of Matucana Alta to murder twelve Quechua-speaking farmers, including six children, on charges of collaboration with the army. "The battle will be hard, arduous, cruel, long, and difficult," predicted Guzmán in 1980. In this prediction, at least, the bespectacled prophet of the Shining Path was entirely correct.

Notes

1   The same exotic view of the Shining Path as an indigenous uprising was later advanced in the British journalist Simon Strong's *Shining Path: the World's Deadliest Revolutionary Force* (London: HarperCollins, 1992).
2   See the interview with the now-jailed Shining Path leader Laura Zambrano in *El Diario*, March 14, 1988, p. 9.

"A FRIGHTENING THIRST FOR VENGEANCE"

Osmán Morote

The heart of the Shining Path's original leadership in Ayacucho was known as the "Sacred Family," provincial elites linked by intermarriage and political conviction: the Morotes, the Casanovas, the Carhuas, the Durands. Osmán Morote was the son of the rector of Ayacucho's university and eventually became the group's second-in-command. Written in 1971, just a year after Guzmán led the intra-Maoist split that ended with the Shining Path's founding, Morote's poem captures the rebellious spirit that characterized the Peruvian left in the 1960s and 1970s. Yet the intensity of the last verse can also be read as a chilling announcement of the Shining Path's particular vision, not just of justice, but of the vengeance necessary to completely destroy the old order.

The dictator
shifts his gaze
  and a rose
  acclaimed as fragrant
  falls, in a slice,
  from just one
  beheading.

The dictator
swivels his hands
  and
  one worker
  falls, the wife of a
  worker
  falls, the children of a
  worker
  fall.

Oh!
what a frightening thirst
for vengeance
devours me.

Note

This poem appeared in Catalina Arianzén, ed. *Nueva Poesía de Ayacucho* (Ayacucho: Universidad Nacional de San Cristóbal de Huamanga, 1971) and was translated by the editors.

WE ARE THE INITIATORS

Abimael Guzmán

As a child in the coastal town of Mollendo, south of Lima, Abimael Guzmán received the education typical of middle-class, provincial families, gaining a reputation for studiousness and reserve. It was in several visits to China, though, that he was exposed to the charged atmosphere of Maoist struggle of the Cultural Revolution as well as training in explosives and military tactics. By the middle of the 1970s, Guzmán believed the time was ripe for armed struggle and left his post at Ayacucho's university. On April 19, 1980, he delivered the famous "We Are the Initiators" speech to close the Shining Path's First Military School and open a new era. It prefigures the war's violence in its baroque vision of the "black filth" of the "rotten old order," even as it locates the Shining Path at the fiery center of the inevitable rumble of human history toward communist revolution, giving party militants the lead role in a world drama. While framing the violence as a "scientific certainty" guaranteed by the "laws of history," the man regarded by his followers as "the greatest living Marxist-Leninist" also borrows liberally from the Bible to underscore the imperative of seizing "guns and cannons" to make a classless utopia.

We are the initiators. We must recognize this deep in our souls. This is an historic meeting.

Comrades, we are the initiators. This is how we will be remembered in the history that the Party has been writing for many years, pages that no one will be able to erase.

We are the initiators. This First Military School of the Party is at once an ending and a beginning, it finishes and starts. It ends the time of peace. And begins the time of war. Comrades, our unarmed labors have concluded. Today our armed struggle begins: to lift up the masses, to lift up the peasantry under the infallible banners of Marxist-Leninist-Mao Zedong Thought. One era has ended. The preparations for a new one have been completed. We close what has been done to now; we open to the future. The key is action. The objective is power. This is what we will do. History demands it. The masses demand it. The people have foreseen and want it. We must fulfill our duty and we will do so. We are the initiators.

Centuries of hard exploitation have passed. The masses have been hit hard. They have been exploited, subjugated, implacably oppressed. But the exploited masses have always fought back through the ages. They have no desire besides class struggle. Nonetheless, the masses were always history's orphans. They had no leadership. Their words, protests, actions, and rebellions ended in disaster and defeat. But they never lost hope. The oppressed classes never lose it. The masses are the light of an emergent new world. With their own hands, they will bring about a transformation, forge tools. They are the fiber, the timeless heartbeat of history, generating the highest in ideas and science.

But the laws of history generated by the development of class struggle create the ultimate class: the international proletariat. This class grows in combat out of capitalism: a sinister system that sweats blood and filth from all its pores. A system where the proletariat fights to build unions, strikes, resistance, and revolutions. All of this struggle has concentrated in Marxism; and the proletariat, provisioning itself with a Party, turned into a fully developed class, with its own interests. And, at last, the Party provides the masses of the world with their long-desired liberator. In olden times, the masses awaited a liberator, placing their hopes in the hands of false saviors, until the powerful proletariat appeared, invincible and capable of creating a truly new order. The proletariat organized itself politically, and from then on a new history has begun to be woven, to mold itself into reality. . . .

Over a hundred years of combat, setbacks, and triumphs, the proletariat has learned to fight and to take power by force of arms. It efficiently seized power once in the Paris Commune, only to be smashed down in blood and fire. Still, we remember the Paris Commune, and those once slandered have today become heroes and their example lives while their executioners will be remembered by no one. With Lenin, this same class seized power in Russia to build a powerful state. It continued the fight with President Mao Zedong. He gave us a new path, resolving stubborn problems. And the proletariat began to battle under the banner of Marxist-Leninist-Mao Zedong Thought.

The revolution entered into a strategic equilibrium during World War II. Left behind were the formerly unchallenged sacred alliances

Figure 26. Abimael Guzmán, as he appeared in a party pamphlet from the late 1980s.

of the reactionaries, executioners, and class enemies. Marxism, reaching the great pinnacle of Mao Zedong Thought, has brought us a new moment: the powerful international workers' movement, the foaming waves of national liberation movements, the development of communist parties. We are entering the strategic offensive of the World Revolution. The next fifty to a hundred years will bring about the sweeping away of imperialism and all oppressors. History cannot be turned back. It is in the hands of the working class, the leadership of communist parties, and the force of the poor peasantry, the foundation of the people's war that will grow each day until it topples the old order. The world is entering a new moment: the strategic offensive of World Revolution. This is a fact of transcendental importance.

President Mao says: "The storm approaches, the wind roars in the tower." That is how it is: the storm approaches. The storm is taking shape, and the invincible flames of the revolution will grow until they turn to lead and steel, and from the din of battle and ceaseless fire will come the light. From the darkness will come the light, and there will be a new world. The reactionary order creaks, the old ship springs leaks, and it desperately sinks. But, comrades, no one should expect the old order to retire peacefully. Marx warned us: even sinking it throws the flailing blows of the drowning, desperate slashes to see if it can defeat us. This is impossible. The reactionaries dream of hyena blood: the agitated fantasies of their somber nights. Their hearts beat in sinister hecatombs. They arm themselves to the teeth. But they will not prevail. Their destiny is weighed and measured. Judgment day has arrived.

The imperialist superpowers—the United States, the Soviet Union, and other powers—invade, penetrate, undermine, destroy, and seek to bury their fear. But, as President Mao says, by attacking, aggressing, and launching attacks, they squander their energy and tangle themselves in the people's powerful clutches. The people rear up, arm themselves, and rise in revolution to put the noose around the neck of imperialism and the reactionaries, seizing and garroting them by the throat. They are strangled, necessarily, necessarily. The flesh of the reactionaries will rot away, converted into ragged threads, and this black filth will sink into the mud, and that which remains will be burned and the ashes scattered by the winds of the earth so that only the sinister memory will remain of that which will never return, because it neither can nor should.

Comrades, this is the way of the world today. We live in an extraordinary epoch. Never before have men had such a heroic destiny, so it is written. It has fallen to these men of today, these men that breathe, toil, and combat, the task of sweeping the reactionaries from the face of the earth. It is the most luminous and glorious mission ever entrusted to any generation. This is our situation. The World Revolution has entered the strategic offensive. No one can stop it. Infinite legions of iron are rising, and more will rise, more and more. They will multiply inexhaustibly to encircle and annihilate the reactionaries. The reactionaries, by tearing at the people's flesh, by unleashing their bloody slashes, will only tangle themselves, muddle themselves all the more. They will seek to satiate themselves with the blood of the people. But this blood will rise like pulsing wings, and that bruised flesh will turn into the powerful whips of vengeance, and muscles and action will turn into a steel battering ram to destroy the oppressors, who will be irretrievably smashed.

The reactionaries, comrades, have no chance. The revolution will triumph. The hour has sounded. The battle will be hard, arduous, cruel, long, and difficult. But triumph is ours. The masses will win. The peasantry will rise, and the proletariat will lead it. The communist parties will be in command, and red flags will be raised for eternity. The reactionaries have entered their last chapter. This is the world in which we find ourselves. . . .

Comrades, we are entering the great rupture. I have said many times that we are entering the rupture and that there are many chains to break, since the rotten old order still binds us. If we do not break these chains, we will not be able to demolish the old order. Comrades, the hour has arrived. There is nothing to discuss. Debate has ended. It is time for action. It is the moment of rupture, and we will not proceed by slow and delaying meditations, or in quiet rooms or hallways. We will enter the breach through the din of armed action. This is the way to proceed. The appropriate and correct way. The only way. There, in action, as we have learned, consciousness intensifies, will is stronger, passion more powerful, energy more charged. Comrades, there, in action, we will find the necessary energy, force, and ability to make the great rupture. This is the task we have assumed. The trumpets begin to sound. The roar of the masses grows and will continue to grow. It will deafen us. It will take us into a powerful vortex, to a single note. We will be the protagonists of history: responsible, organized, and armed. And this is how there will be a great rupture, and we will be the makers of the last new dawn. This is the task we have assumed.

I want to conclude. This school, this First Military School of the Party, is the ending and the beginning. The ending of everything accomplished until today. The beginning of tomorrow. What we have done until now is positive. It has borne good fruits. Ye shall know him by his works, it is written. The works are finished, before our eyes. There is nothing left to prove. That done until now has been good. The beginning, that which we must accomplish, will be even better. And, certainly, it will be the one great thing that we must do in our lives. It will come by force of arms, out of the cannon, out of the guns, out of the direct action of the Party over the masses. The people's war will grow. . . .

Marxist-Leninist-Mao Zedong Thought, the international proletariat and the peoples of the world, the working class, and the people of the nation, the Party with its committees, cells, and leaders: all of the great actions of the centuries have culminated at this moment in history. The promise unfolds, the future unfurls: ILA 80.[1]

We are obligated to live up to this promise. What has been given to us as a future must be fulfilled with our lives, for the sake of the people, the proletariat, and Marxist-Leninist-Mao Zedong Thought.

Comrades, the effort invested will reward itself by its accomplishments. It will need no other recompense.

The future lies in guns and cannons! The armed revolution has begun!

Glory to Marxist-Leninist-Mao Zedong Thought!

Let us initiate the armed struggle!

Notes

This speech appears in Luis Arca Borja, ed. *Guerra Popular en el Perú* (Brussels: Author, 1989) and was translated by the editors.

1 ILA is an acronym for Inicio de la Lucha Armada, or the "Initiation of the Armed Struggle," on May 17, 1980.

THE QUOTA

Gustavo Gorriti

From the beginning, the need to die and kill for the party and the revolution was an explicit part of the Shining Path's mystique. "Blood," wrote one militant, "makes us stronger . . . and if it is flowing, it is not harming us but giving us strength." Peruvian journalist Gustavo Gorriti is a leading analyst of the Shining Path, writing for the Peruvian press, El País *of Madrid, and the* New York Times. *This chapter from his history of the group explains the roots of "the quota," a condition of membership in the Shining Path.*

Marx, Lenin, and principally Mao Zedong have armed us. They have taught us about the quota and what it means to annihilate in order to preserve. . . . If one is persistent, maintains politics in command, maintains the political strategy, maintains the military strategy, if one has a clear, defined plan, then one advances and one is able to meet any bloodbath. . . . We began planning for the bloodbath in 1980 because we knew it had to come. —Interview with Abimael Guzmán, *El Diario,* July 24, 1988

When Abimael Guzmán referred to the "bloodbath" in 1988, the insurrection's history was already stained by it. The proverbial meat grinder had processed enough people to make the Shining Path uprising one of Latin America's bloodiest since the 1960s, with clear signs of becoming one of the cruelest wars in the continent's history.

Nevertheless, as of early 1981, extravagance, not violence, was the idiosyncrasy of the Shining Path rebellion. As yet, there were few victims, and a certain consensus persisted that as long as the Shining Path's fury remained transoceanic (that is, killing dogs and hurling insults at Deng Xiaoping and Enver Hoxha), the group's presence in Peru would be basically innocuous. It was, of course, a view as erroneous as it was distorted, although it reflected the low level of violence at the time.

The Shining Path's central committee held its fourth plenary session in May 1981. It was a thinly documented meeting, where in addition to analyzing and refining a plan to "develop the guerrilla war, opening guerrilla fronts as a function of the bases of support," the issue of "the quota" was broached.

This was a principal theme of the meeting and perhaps of those first war years. Not just the subject of heated debate, the quota became a solemn agreement, made with all the ceremony usually accorded rituals. Later, the quota and its practical consequences were mythified and adorned with symbols and metaphors as much by Shining Path commissars as by some leading pundits. Nevertheless, the heart of the debate had eminently practical, military concerns: transform the war into the central preoccupation of all Peruvians through a radical increase in violence, to raise the stakes and turn the blood trickle into a flood. To this end, Shining Path militants had to be convinced of two things: the need to kill in a systematic and depersonalized way as part of an agreed-upon strategy; and, as a necessary premise, not just the willingness but the expectation of giving up their own lives. This second concept is known as "the quota."

In the following years, the quota's very concept and the feverish, fulminating fervor of its expression gave the Shining Path the reputation (and to some degree the appearance) of being a death cult rather than a Marxist party. This charge was repeated from the ranks of the legal left, especially after the 1986 prison massacres.[1] According to these horrified accusations, the Shining Path's inspiration was not found in Marx or Lenin or even Mao, but in Reverend Jones and the Guyana cyanide pail.

In the face of such accusations, the Shining Path reacted with indignation, but without debating the heart of the issue: the relation between war and its costs, especially in blood. To what degree is the latter—in their view—not just the result of the former but its cause, fuel for the blaze? Since 1981, this had been a central issue, and the debate over "the quota" aimed at facing it squarely.

According to available documentation, the debate was conducted as a rigorous yet fundamentalist development of orthodox Marxism-Leninism-Maoism. Beginning in 1979, in its moment of "defining and deciding," the Shining Path had discussed the struggle's social cost. The essential tension in revolutionary movements between philanthropic intention and objectives and brutal means had been resolved according to Bolshevik and Stalinist tradition. And they had taken up arms. But even though the insurrection had begun, tension had not dissipated, nor

Figure 27. The quota demanded the blood price from militants, and the prison massacre in June 1986 became a major Shining Path holiday. Here the so-called Day of Heroism is commemorated in a party pamphlet from the late 1980s.

would it. Abimael Guzmán knew well and understood—as did Stalin in his time—that the conflict would only end when the paradox was driven home and the philanthropists ended their days by serving the commissars, now convinced that to kill gave life, that war brought peace, that the most extreme tyranny brought the greatest freedom. If this twisted thinking once took hold of Europe's most brilliant minds from the years between the world wars until the 1960s, why shouldn't it achieve something similar or better in Peru?

First, the idea's roots. One of the central themes in the development of orthodox Marxism is to direct violence with dispassionate energy and without hesitation. Marx tackled the problem with characteristic intensity in "The French Civil War," written immediately after the fall of the Paris Commune. The Commune's defeat, added to the experience of 1848, showed Marx that moderation led to catastrophe. "The state apparatus and its structural supports in society cannot simply be conquered; out of necessity they must be destroyed to be later rebuilt based on revolutionary principles."[2] In the introduction to the 1891 edition, Engels lamented the "reverent attitude" with which the Commune members "stood respectfully at the doors of the Bank of France" while Versailles' troops prepared to retake Paris. In his comments, Lenin went even further. Not only was it necessary to destroy the enemy so as not to be destroyed; it was necessary to destroy the state that represented its interests and the social organizations that shored it up. As developed by Lenin and his Soviet cast and later by Mao, Marxist social engineering begins with a demand for general demolition. Sentimentalism, dreams of harmony, and instantaneous justice are, in this school of thought, dangerous weaknesses that have to be fought constantly. In the permanent ethical discussion on valid tactics in a revolutionary struggle, the orthodox Marxist line presents itself as guided by the hardened philanthropy of a surgeon who does not hesitate to cut, to chop off a piece if necessary, to bathe himself in blood, to save the patient in the long run.

This hard realism was useful in the design of various strategies for the taking and maintenance of power during the reign of orthodox Marxism. The common thread uniting them (Leninism, its Trotskyist variant, the development of the Comintern, and Maoism) is found as much in the emphasis on the demolition of the "bourgeois" state as in the creation of the demolition machine: the communist party constructed on a Leninist model (professional revolutionaries, clandestine or semiclandestine, a relatively small core). One cannot forget, however, that in the heart of almost every manager and administrator of destruction, driven to achieve maximum dialectic efficiency and for whom sentimentality is close to pornographic, beats a romantic philanthropism, repressed but intense. The goal was utopia, society built on unparalleled justice: communism. The means to achieve it were supposedly "scientific" and included previous destruction, justified along with about anything else.

The adoption of extreme means for extreme ends, with an apparatus organized to carry out those means methodically, step by step, represented a considerable advantage for communist parties over their opponents or competitors throughout seventy years of struggle, beginning with the Russian Revolution of 1905. In most cases, communist parties began their struggle as a weak minority, and as a result emphasized strategies and tactics that depended on the patient accumulation of strength and its cautious preservation. At the same time, however, communist parties at war were willing to accept (or induce) dreadful social costs that other organized forces recoiled at or capitulated before. This was evident, for example, in World War II resistance movements.

As Franz Borkenau has pointed out, the communist partisans in Europe during World War II had an incalculable advantage over the noncommunist resistance movements, for the former, having a vested interest in social disruption, were prepared to face drastic reprisals, while the latter were constantly restrained in their tactics both by moral considerations and by the desire to avoid extreme civilian losses.[3] The paradox of the Soviet situation lies in the fact that a guerrilla movement enjoying the support of the established government of the country could be used for ruthless, unlimited action.[4]

This was also one of the principal reasons (the others were better organization and strategy) why almost all the communist organizations competing or in a clash with a noncommunist movement triumphed. This not only happened in Nazi-occupied Europe but also in China and later in Indochina and Vietnam. Mao's well-known quotes about "the omnipotence of the revolutionary war" and the need to "oppose war with war" arose from one of the most costly armed conflicts in this century in terms of suffering and human life.

If the acceptance of extreme social costs was part of orthodox Marxism's revolutionary engineering, it took place as part of a permanent tension and search for equilibrium with the principle of gaining and conserving strength. In practical terms, this meant that most losses in various wars were suffered by the noncombatant population.

Nevertheless, the eventual need for self-sacrifice, immolation in the struggle, has been highlighted since the very beginnings of the doctrine of orthodox Marxist insurrection. After criticizing the Paris Commune for not going far enough, Marx applauded the last decision to continue resisting when all hope was lost.

To forge fighting morale to strengthen militants' commitment was thus sanctified as sufficient reason to encourage cadres' self-denial, including self-sacrifice. This principle could be reconciled with the principle of preserving strength and the refusal to engage in unfavorable battles if such sacrifices lent more force to the party than was lost. The calculus was a permanent source of fierce internal dispute, but its usefulness was rarely doubted. Again, it was Mao who put this principle in lay terms:

> Is it contradictory to fight heroically and then abandon the territory?
> . . . If one eats first and then defecates, has one eaten in vain?

This disposition to self-sacrifice has certainly not been a communist monopoly throughout decades of wars and revolutions. But in comparison with other groups, the communist parties that emerged victorious were superior not only in strategy and organization, but also in three other areas: patience, willingness to self-sacrifice, and leadership.

Beginning with the Bolshevik Revolution and the subsequent civil war, the struggles fought by communist parties have been among the most ferocious humankind has lived. During the Soviet Union's civil war, more than 3 million people died. A few years later, during the convulsions created by massive collectivization and the 1930s purges, there were about 10 million victims. In World War II, the Soviet Union lost 20 million people. In the three and one-half years it took Tito to defeat the Germans and take power, more than 2 million died in Yugoslavia. There are no approximate figures for the number of deaths in China during the endless succession of battles from the 1920s until 1949, but it must have been in the millions. Between 2 and 4 million people were killed in the battles of Indochina and Vietnam before 1975.

From within the ruins of a destruction that would have frightened Tamerlane, the communist parties emerged—in each of the aforementioned cases—stronger than before the beginning of the conflict. They sailed, then drove the tempest. And all of these parties had the common features detailed above. Stalin, Tito, Mao, Ho directed an astonishingly efficient and devout organization, with lieutenants capable of leading army units with a skill history's great captains would have applauded (Zhukov and Koniev; Lin Biao and Peng Dehuai; Giap and Tran Van Tra, among others, are prominent figures in any military history), while at the same time following their leaders like adolescents captivated by a severe, wise teacher.

Today, after the fall of the Soviet Union and Eastern Europe's communist regimes, it is difficult to visualize the spirit and conviction that motivated communist cadres to carry out and endure some of history's stormiest enterprises. Both the old Bolsheviks who Stalin ordered shot, yet who died praising his name, as well as the cadres who undertook clandestine tasks in occupied territory knowing that the possibility of survival was minimal acted out of an intense faith in communist utopia, which they viewed as a scientific possibility yet felt with religious emotion. This secular fervor allowed its believers not only to explain self-sacrifice but to desire it, and made not just understandable but permissible crimes and excesses. The concept and use of "the quota" was a central element of orthodox Marxism during its development and domination.[5]

The above digression was meant to lay the groundwork for a fuller understanding of the Fourth Shining Path Plenary in May 1981 and its decidedly lethal consequences for Peru. Out of context, the discussion and agreement on the quota appear to be no more than arbitrary homicidal emotion. But in perspective, they should be understood as the entire praxis of the Shining Path, which is to say, a rigorous development of orthodox Marxism.

And it was not merely theoretical, but practical. Against the worldwide consensus formed in the latter part of the 1970s on the excesses of orthodox Marxism—especially under Stalin—Guzmán and his movement not only did not consider the costs excessive, but held up this period as the pinnacle of humankind. They were thinking along the same lines as many of the European and American intelligentsia of the 1920s and 1960s, despite the testimonies that emerged from behind the walls and an abundant and wrenching dissident literature. By the 1980s, the faith and hope in transcendental good that moved so many arms and loyalties, blinded so many eyes, and silenced so many consciences no longer moved anyone in the West or in the communist world. But it did move Guzmán and his party. In contrast to the great majority of Marxists in the 1970s and 1980s, who looked back with a growing feeling of embarrassment and alienation or at least considered what was done to be excessive, Guzmán and his party insisted that what was done was very good but did not go far enough.

Peru was to be the place where what went unfinished in other places would be carried out. Guzmán was well aware that the contagion of fanatical violence takes root slowly in peaceful countries and more slowly still if they are democratic. Peru was both in 1981. When the fourth plenary met, the insurrection was a year old. Until then, only one person had died. And Peruvian society, living the diverse possibilities of risk-free expression, of a partial role in government, of the irony and humor pent up after years of military government, was not only impermeable to violence but refracted it. The almost-sweet face of José María De la Jara, the interior minister, his obvious kindness, made building the hate necessary for fanatical violence difficult. Even within Shining Path ranks, a considerable percentage of militants continued to reject killing, the blood threshold, despite the conscious effort made at fostering indignation.

But without blood, the Shining Path's insurrectional strategy was without content. Without hate, they could not shepherd the energy necessary for the immense work of material and moral destruction and then the reconstruction of the alternative world as planned by the Shining Path.

Once initial plans for the "development of the war of guerrillas" were made, the fourth plenary session agreed to radically intensify violence. The bellicose warm-up had been completed the previous year, and firing up the troops would be easier. An increase in violence was geared to initiate the complicated game of action and reaction, where the goal was to provoke blind, excessive reactions from the state. The greater the success, the easier it would be to transfer the weight of blame to the state—the central objective of war propaganda—and the harder it would be for the regime to maintain a democratic image. Blows laid on indiscriminately would also provoke among those unjustly or disproportionately affected an intense resentment of the government. Most important, however, was that the exaggerated response of the state contribute to the dissolution of peace and help push the nation toward violence.

Escalation presumed a price for the Shining Path. One that could be very high. The party had to be prepared to take crushing blows and not only survive but finally emerge stronger. Measures had already been studied from an organizational and military viewpoint: to set up a double or triple underground network in key locations; to report, analyze, and evaluate each experience, so that the entire organization would learn from actions and a collective memory would emerge; and to concentrate or disperse cadres according to need. The only thing left to be defined was the moral attitude, both personal and in terms of the organization, once this Pandora's box of violence was opened.

As far as we know, during the fourth plenary Guzmán painted with emphatic strokes the personal consequences of war. Many of those at the plenary and many party militants would die, trapped by the same events they were setting in motion. And they would die in the worst possible ways. Their families would be destroyed, those dear and close to them would be jailed and tortured, others would be killed simply because they were relatives. There was nothing new in this, all of it had already happened in other parts of the world not long ago. But there was very little in Peru's history that prepared it to confront the level of violence that would eventually be unleashed. Dozens, hundreds of thousands of dead. Blood would flow in rivers and the only way to triumph would be by "crossing the river of blood." Guzmán then gave them the choice of deciding if they were determined to persist in the struggle, knowing what the future held. From his point of view, the "people's war" meant a long journey that had to be joined. A bloody Sinai, as inevitable as it was historically necessary. On the other side lay the promised land.

No direct record of the debate survives. Apparently, opposition was minimal. The Shining Path decided, with predictable solemnities, for "the quota": the willingness, indeed the expectation, of offering one's life when the party asked for it. The way in which the decision was taken, as a vote, a vow, took the Shining Path further than other communist parties, which always attempted to maintain the fiction that self-sacrifice was confined to certain situations.[6]

From then on, preparing for death became a central preoccupation for each militant as well as a way to indoctrinate cadres. After agreeing to the quota, militants no longer owned their lives. Manuscripts read and memorized in meetings, the notes taken in the margins began to repeat and hammer home this idea. To be prepared for death, to renounce life. Paraphrasing Guzmán, a manuscript captured in Lurigancho Prison in 1985 criticizes those who "fear making mistakes": "Others are careful, afraid to make mistakes, therefore are not sincere, they make excuses, they try to save their skin, what are they protecting? If you have nothing, if you've given everything to the P[arty], your life is not your own, it belongs to the P[arty]. Too much jeremiad, too much saving your skin."

The same manuscript includes decisions taken during the fiercest months of combat in 1984. After reaffirming the party's actions, it continues: "There is no construction without destruction, these are two sides of the same contradiction." The author accuses the government "of acting worse than the Spaniards who hacked Túpac Amaru to pieces": "The cruel form the war is taking is nothing more than the bloodbath we had proposed [sic] and the decision to go with it. We've made the irrevocable decision to cross [the river of blood] and conquer the far bank."

The quota, the ultimate sacrifice, took on even more weight because it was not only offered to the Peruvian revolution but to the cause of world communism, "whose millennium is opening," as Guzmán would say. Another Shining Path manuscript, written in 1985, explains the quota to the faithful:

> About the quota: the stamp of commitment to our revolution, to world revolution, with the blood of the people that runs in our country. . . . The quota is a small part of the Peruvian revolution and of world revolution. . . . Most [of the deaths] are caused by the reaction [of the state] and fewer by us. They fill lakes while we only soak our handkerchiefs.

Still another document, apparently copied by a mid-level leader in Ayacucho near the end of 1984, summarizes Guzmán: "Blood makes us stronger and if it's this 'bath' that the armed forces have made for us, the blood is flowing, it's not harming us but making us stronger."

As the war became more pitiless, the death vow took different forms. For many Shining Path militants, hunted and anguished, the idea of dying "snatching laurels from death" took on the intense attraction of an experience both mystical and sensual. It was the perfect escape from unbearable anxiety, ceaseless work, and the ever imminent threat of capture, with its horrific consequences.

This vision of death as an ardent surrender to the cause, a kind of sublimated sensual possession, opened unknown horizons in the militants' self-love. Combined with their millenarian vision and the personality cult of Guzmán, this created ephemeral, fevered, and mythic forms. Manuel Granados, an anthropologist who has studied the Shining Path, attempted this formula:

—Mao = a spark can *ignite* the meadow.
—A Shining Path militant = I am willing to cross the "*river of blood.*"
—Declaration of the PCP-SL [Communist Party of Peru–Sendero Luminoso] = the leadership is with you at the supreme moment of total release into the *purifying fire* of the A[rmed] S[truggle].
—Shining Path motto = *death* to invent the great subjective myth.
—Blaze–Invincible Fire–River of Blood–Death–*Subjective Myth*–Purifying Fire.[7]

Although its militants fell frequently into the ecstatic death-wish anticipation not uncommon in warrior-monk orders, and with the metaphors of bonfires and the flaming forest common to prophetic visions, in general terms the Shining Path tried to maintain its disposition to self-sacrifice within the constraints of political and military utility:

> Their being is to comply, willing to fight anywhere. There are no restraints and a challenge to death and to snatch laurels from death is forged, war is our daily life, to be willing to die, no one mourns.[8]

Death worship could be paralyzing. But it had the counterbalance of exhausting work, the concrete tasks the Shining Path imposed on its militants. In the end, from those conspirators who combined extreme overwork with the fondling of death fantasies emerged the phrase "holding your life in your fingertips," ready to give it up for the struggle. This expression was repeated by Guzmán in the 1988 interview and before him in interviews with other Shining Path leaders.

At its core, there was a clear strategic advantage to inducing a disposition to sacrifice: excellent troop control. To be able to do with their lives what war demanded, without protest. To get, for example, what Napoleon achieved, "[that] supreme egoist, who sent hundreds of thousands to their deaths cheering."[9] In Peru, a much greater egoism was needed, which Guzmán certainly did not lack.

But death and its strange and fascinating attraction held more sway in the Shining Path's course during a greater number of years than possibly even Guzmán calculated. Written by an anonymous Shining Path militant from the Upper Huallaga valley in 1984, this sad ballad ends with a defiant rhythm:[10]

> On the way out of Aucayacu
> there's a body, who could it be?
> Surely it's a peasant
> who gave his life for the struggle.
> . . . Today the quota must be filled
> If we have to give our blood
> for revolution, how good it will be.

Notes

1 In 1986, the government's plan to transfer some prisoners accused or convicted of belonging to the Shining Path ended with uprisings in three Lima prisons. The state's reaction was ferocious. When the dust settled, well over two hundred inmates and four guards were dead, and the island prison of El Frontón had been bombed into rubble.

2 John Shy and Thomas Collier, "Revolutionary War," in *Makers of Modern Strategy*, edited by Peter Paret (Princeton, N.J.: Princeton University Press, 1986), p. 826.

3   Franz Borkenau, *European Communism* (New York: Harper Brothers, 1953).

4   John Armstrong, ed., *Soviet Partisans in World War II* (Madison: University of Wisconsin Press, 1964).

5   The need for self-sacrifice was also understood by some noncommunist leaders. In his introduction to Charles W. Thayer's book, Fitzroy MacLean, a British officer who understood guerrilla warfare during World War II, quotes T. E. Lawrence: "We knew that we had won over a province when we were able to teach the civilians to die for our idea of liberty." Charles W. Thayer, *Guerrilla* (New York: Harper and Row, 1963).

6   From the fourth plenary forward, all Shining Path militants have had to make the "promise." Although the language may vary, the content is the same. "I commit myself to Comrade Gonzalo, leader of the Communist Party of Peru and the world revolution. I commit myself to the Central Committee of the Communist Party of Peru. I commit myself to Marxism-Leninism-Maoism, the Guiding Knowledge of Comrade Gonzalo, to accept my responsibility as a member of the Communist Party of Peru and never betray the party or the people. I commit myself with bravery, decision, and courage to fight against imperialism and feudalism until the liberation of the oppressed peoples of the world is achieved. I commit myself to struggle and offer my life to the world revolution."

7   Manuel Jesús Granados, "Ideology of the Communist Party of Peru–Shining Path," in *Socialismo y Participación* 37 (March 1987): 30–31.

8   Shining Path manuscript, written in Lurigancho in 1985.

9   Martin Van Creveld, *Command in War* (Cambridge, Mass.: Harvard University Press, 1985).

10 In Spanish, "un triste con fuga de tondero." A *triste* is a kind of sad lament, sometimes also known as a *yaravi*. Ending with a *tondero*, a lively beat popular in the north that dancers stamp their feet to, the *triste* would take on a defiant, rebellious tone, determined to survive despite the odds.

MEMORIES OF A CADRE

"Nicario"

For all of the seeming absurdity of Guzmán's millenarian vision of his handful of followers as the vanguard of "World Proletarian Revolution," the Shining Path had a degree of appeal to the disenfranchised in the impoverished Andean depart- ment of Ayacucho. Like "Nicario,"[1] a young peasant who joined, many were disen- chanted with the corruption and inefficiency of the Peruvian state and attracted by the party's sense of discipline and mission. This on-the-ground account of how the Shining Path functioned in Ayacucho villages centers on the destruction of the uni- versity experimental station in Allpachaka in 1982 and the arrival a year later of the armed forces. Eventually, Nicario takes the path of entrepreneurial capitalism rather than Marxist revolution, starting a small business in Lima.

In those days, the Shining Path still didn't exist. Sure, you might have heard about it. But not much. They just painted graffiti, or put stones in the roads. No one took it seriously. The first members were University of Huamanga students, who began to organize in different communities. But only three or four people came to meetings, mostly young students. This was about 1981.

In my community, there were three or four students. But they were real close-mouthed. Sure, other young people knew they were caught up in this, but we didn't pay it any mind, more likely we would insult them: op- portunists, adventurers, no? They would look at us and smile. When I was in my second year of high school, I was the first of my contemporaries to attend their meetings. One of the University of Huamanga students in- vited me. I accepted right away . . . because by then, in 1982, the Shining Path was very active. So all the young people were talking about it. We wanted to attend, but no one said let's go to a meeting.

A military leader led the assembly. He had belonged for some time, since 1979. He had rank, so he came with his machine gun. I timidly approached him. He introduced himself and his voice was coarse: yes, comrade, just so, with his boots.

When we began, there were about twelve of us. Only two were from Rumi. The leader explained Mao to us, how he had started and risen in the ranks and also how they were carrying out actions and how many more people had joined over these months and what Comrade Gonzalo thought about the Shining Path's growth.

Afterwards, they asked for opinions. Those who had attended before already knew how to express themselves, how to greet the comrade. Meetings began with a greeting to Comrade Gonzalo, a combative salute. This was the slogan. But because this was my first time, I said, "Comrades, forgive me, I am not yet capable of presenting myself." No, he said, you can speak. All we want is your decision to join or to see if you've just come to spy. That's how he said it. Others said they were ready at any moment to fight for the Party. Everyone said this. So did I when they insisted. If I had said that I wasn't ready yet, maybe they would have begun to criticize me, because there were criticism and self-criticism sessions. They gave us a task in this first meeting, to bring one or two trusted friends. I brought a friend, my mother's godson, to the next meeting.

Meetings were continual, sometimes twice a week in different communities. They gave us tasks. And they talked about the ideology, that there was a lot of bureaucracy in Peru and many criminals, many thieves, rapists, and that the Shining Path's objective was to make all of this disappear.

They were fulfilling the promise, no? For example, whenever you went to a meeting, you always brought your list of cattle rustlers, thieves. This person was first warned. The comrades in the armed group took care of this. We would take them to the corner, see? They would knock on the door and talk. If the person continued to rob, the next time they would be killed.

My first action was for the People's Anniversary in August. They had sworn in a couple of us as leaders of groups in different communities. In my community at that time, there were about fifteen or sixteen of us. In just three months, almost all the young people had joined.

We arrived at the plaza just as they were serving lunch and shouted, "Long live the armed struggle!" "Long live the guerrilla war!" The women and peasants remained silent. One of my comrades spoke, saying we defended peasants. Some women said maybe we were going to kill them. At that moment, some comrades were raising the flag in the plaza.

Others hung dummies with signs that read, "This is how we will kill the snitches." Others handed out a pamphlet called "Guerrilla War." When we asked the peasants, they all said they agreed with us and would co-operate. We also read a list of snitches who had spoken out against the Party and warned them not to open their mouths again.

Those of us from the village went with hoods. We were different from the [armed] group, we were a people's militia. When there was an action, the ones responsible for the community would meet with the military and political commanders and later with the militants to set a date and plan. There were many of us, two hundred and more, mainly high school students. Let's say that the group leader would meet with us and say that on such and such date we should raise a flag, paint slogans in a community, put rocks in the road, and set off dynamite. That night, all the communities would carry out actions. We would plan for the same hour, right? In Cangallo, they would detonate a charge at 7:00 on the dot. So just when we heard the dynamite explode, we would light ours and everything would be set in motion.

An assault was made on the University of Huamanga's experimental farm, Allpachaka. They planned for two months. Some comrades studied how many people worked there and if there were police officers. Afterwards, they told us they needed the support of all the communities and militants. Even if people weren't militants, they had to come.

On the appointed morning, we gathered in A. There, the comrades walked about freely with their weapons. It was practically a liberated zone. People arrived from all over. Each one of us had our bit of food, dried corn, cheese, potatoes. We had asked the peasants to prepare a lunch. Together, we collected three roomfuls of grain. There were about 500 of us, 600. More came from other communities, and we gathered about 1,400 people.

We entered Allpachaka at 5:00 A.M. It was surrounded so no one could leave. The peasants were brought into the plaza. If they remained in their houses, they would be punished, threatened. So people left their houses immediately. In the plaza, the political commander from Cangallo and Huancapi spoke. At that time, I didn't understand how much money Peru owed to the United States, the debt. He told us that in Lima, high officials lived like bulls that produce nothing, young bulls. A young bull has no value in the mountains, while an older bull does. A young bull is just a lot of fat, not even good for plowing. The Shining Path's goal was to take power through the guerrilla war: from the countryside to the city. We would stop selling what we cultivated so that people in the capital,

Figure 28. Guerrillas destroyed not only military targets, but development projects, municipalities, and church-sponsored research centers, like this one in Ayaviri, Puno. (Courtesy of Gabino Quispecondori)

people who don't work, would die of hunger, that is what he said. We the peasants are the only ones who give the fat cats what they need to eat, the millionaires. Four or five years from now, he said, we won't let food into Lima. But what of the poor? we asked. They told us that the poor would return to the countryside to fight with us.

We took over Allpachaka because the workers couldn't even afford the cheeses that were made there. The Party found out that the cheeses weren't even eaten in Peru, but went straight to Holland, I think. We learned that while the farm had the university's name, the university received no profits.

There were four bulls, all huge. The first thing we did was kill them and cut them up. Since we had pots, we cooked the meat with potatoes for soup. Everyone ate. There was food left over. People in other communities learned what was happening and came. Little old women asked us to give them meat, potatoes, whatever there was. We told them to take whatever they could carry. There were beds, carts, tables, cheeses, wines. Everything you could imagine. We gave it away, and whatever people couldn't carry we broke up. We arrived on a Saturday and the next Monday the cheeses were scheduled to be shipped, so we destroyed the stock-pile. We set fire to the grain, broke down doors, destroyed walls. We also freed the pigs and guinea pigs.

We killed as many cattle as we could. But while we were killing, the female peasants began to cry: the poor cattle, why kill them that way, it isn't their fault. When the women began crying, we stopped, but we had already killed one-fourth of them, about eighty head of cattle.

When we left, a man on horseback went straight to Ayacucho to report what had happened. The next day, we heard a report about Allpachaka on little radios some of the comrades carried with them and were content.

In those days, the Party named new authorities in the countryside. The old ones didn't complain because even the [community] president's son was a firm Party supporter, and he had convinced his father.

The new authorities carried out executions. There hadn't been any executions in my community, but there were in others. An execution began when the comrades would capture the person at home before he caught on. If the person said bad things about the Party or did bad things against it, he or she was executed. For example, if someone gave the police in Cangallo a list of comrades, that was a crime against the Party.

Of course, the relatives always felt bad. But they were caught by surprise. Executions happened from one moment to the next. Various ones were carried out in C., D., and E. People watched and said, well, if we see someone doing something for the Party, it's best to keep quiet. If the police come, they have to take our word: we don't know, we don't know. The people themselves said this. Some didn't agree, but didn't say a word. Some farmers left crying. It was scary and painful to kill in front of people.

The new authorities called communal work sessions to sow barley, wheat, potatoes, and corn for the Party. We planted on community land. What was planted was no longer for the community, but to supply the comrades in the field or for people who had nothing to eat. The sowing was done together, with flags placed in the field's four corners. The new system took hold best in Chuschi. The community had about eight hectares of land. The land was prepared with sixty teams of oxen, which had never been brought together before. It started at 7:00 in the morning and went on until 6:30 in the afternoon. When the work began, twelve sticks of dynamite were set off, six more at noon, and another twelve in the afternoon. It was the first time the Party and the people of Chuschi had done this kind of work. But the Party didn't get to harvest the crops because the army arrived.

Figure 29. Village woman in Cochas, Ayacucho, grieving relatives murdered in a Shining Path attack, 1986. (Courtesy of Alejandro Balaguer)

The women were most afraid the day the army arrived. Above the community, the road curves, and about fifty army trucks moved down at about 8:00 one morning. Female peasants gathered and began to cry. They said that they were sure to kill us all. But the trucks went straight to Cangallo.

Our idea was that the army would give the guerrillas more support, because the soldiers were sons of the poor, raised in poverty and misery. In meetings, we would say that this was in our favor. That's what the leaders told us, that the soldiers would also join the Party.

We tried to call a peasant meeting. But many were more concerned about leaving Rumi. They took their clothes and bags, and left for Ayacucho. Helicopters and war planes flew over, and all the peasants were frightened and no longer wanted to take part. Maybe, they thought, the army would catch us in a meeting and we had few defensive weapons. We told them not to worry, that we would defend them. But we lost support, and that's how the Shining Path lost support. All we had were grenades and dynamite, but nothing like machine guns, pistols, or FALS [automatic weapons]. There was a clash between us and the army. Four comrades with four weapons were lost. Afterwards, all the militants and guerrillas in Cangallo met. We thought we might mount an attack on the army along the road, but it wasn't possible. The guerrillas were ready, but the community militias were terrified.

After that, there was combat in G., from 6:00 A.M. until 4:00 P.M. Twelve Shining Path members fell, most principal leaders. The army lost five or six. It wasn't like fighting with the police, it was more difficult. Afterwards, a meeting was called for the entire province of Cangallo, and commissions came from Vilcashuamán, Huancapi, Huanta, San Miguel. I didn't attend but was told later that they decided to send four guerrillas from each group to different departments. The rest would remain in Ayacucho, meeting with peasants and carrying out actions. But it wasn't like before because there were so few of them. The army had already begun to patrol in the communities, committing massacres and abuses and even taking cattle and pigs to eat. They would break down doors, tear down houses, beat men and women, take them prisoner, and make them "disappear." All the peasants were afraid.

Nothing happened to me because I had a hole I slept in. It was just below my house, in a canyon. My mission was to keep the community involved, but they no longer wanted to attend meetings. Only the militants attended. Since the moment the army came, we worked by day as farmers and by night as guerrillas, day and night. Then the moment came for us to decide who would go with the Party and who would remain with the farmers. The Party needed thirty-four people. About fifty volunteered. Since the Party never rejects those with strong desire, all went. I remained, and there were only four or five of us. We had contact with the guerrillas, who stayed up on the heights. When they passed, we gave them food.

But by then, I had lost heart. It was too difficult. I couldn't go on. My brothers in Lima asked me to come. A brother visited me in 1982, the last time he came, and said, let's go. Eventually, I did.

I didn't like Lima, especially the dirty streets. Later, I got used to it. I arrived at my uncle's house, where my brothers and cousins lived. I worked in construction, then painted plaster saints and worked in a restaurant until my brother recommended me to a man who had a metal-working shop. He made kerosene and electric stoves. I started with the most basic things, like painting stoves, then learned more complicated tasks. A friend would tease me, saying, hey mountain hick, terrorist, why don't you go back to your town, sell your llamas, and with your savings buy yourself a metal-working machine?

So I began buying the basics and didn't even eat lunch with so much work. By 1987, I had my own equipment and along with my brother Alcides set up a stove shop. We had so much work that we expanded to include my other brothers. Now we can make all sorts of things, toasters for restaurants, fryers, and much more.

I can't return to my community because the police are looking for me. I don't know what the Shining Path has to say to me. Probably, they'll say that I'm a spy for the reactionaries, because I left without permission. After I left, my case was discussed in an assembly. They said clearly I didn't agree with the armed struggle, since I left without warning. But they haven't bothered me. When I arrived here, another militant from Macabamba called me to a meeting because he knew I had been involved there. But I didn't go. After about three months, the comrades in the countryside sent me a letter from my community with an address so that I could answer. I didn't, for fear I would be killed. After that, there were no more contacts. But if the Shining Path grows here in Lima, I'll have to get involved.

I think they can win, but the war will last a long time. The comrades made a mistake. They said that in 1990 there would be a Republic of the New Democracy. I think it will be more like 1995, or perhaps 2000.

Note

1 Most names in this piece have been changed for security reasons.

OATH OF LOYALTY
Anonymous

This remarkable paragraph opens a letter from a party member to the central com-
mittee, probably in 1989 or 1990. The growth of the personality cult to Guzmán
stands on display in the initial declaration of total loyalty to "our beloved and re-
spected President Gonzalo," even as the list of congresses and committees suggests
the gray institutionality of communist bureaucracy. More broadly, the mantralike
repetitions capture the ethos of unconditional surrender of individual will to the
cause of Gonzalo, the Party, and the "world proletarian revolution," opening a view
of the unbending commitment and centralized organization that made the Shining
Path such a formidable force in the 1980s and into the early 1990s.

Central Committee of the Communist Party of Peru
　Dear Comrades:
　I give you my greeting and my full and unconditional submission to
the greatest living Marxist-Leninist-Maoist on earth: our beloved and respected President Gonzalo, chief and guide of the Peruvian revolution
and the world proletarian revolution, teacher of Communists and party
unifier. I give you my greeting and full and unconditional submission
to the scientific ideology of the proletariat: Marxist-Leninist-Maoist and
Gonzalo Thought, especially Gonzalo Thought, all-powerful and infallible ideology that illuminates our path and arms our minds. I give you
my greeting and full and unconditional subjection to the great, glorious,
correct, and victorious Communist Party of Peru: the great instrument of
the armed revolution, having magisterially directed the popular war in
our country for eight years. I give you my greeting and full and unconditional submission to the Permanent Committee, Political Bureau, Central
Committee, and the entire system of Party leadership. I give you my greeting and full and unconditional submission to the First Marxist Congress

Figure 30. From behind bars, Guzmán still predicted victory in 1992. (Courtesy of Gilmar Pérez, *Caretas*)

of the Communist Party of Peru and the decisions and tasks that grow from it: a Marxist-Leninist-Maoist and Gonzalo Thought Congress, a brilliant historical achievement, an achievement of the victory that Gonzalo Thought has given us and the foundation of Party unification.

After giving you my greeting, dear comrades, let me turn to the business of this letter: as the Party leadership knows, I traveled to Bolivia on February 14 of this year, on the orders of the local committee of the Party in Puno in order to . . .

VII · MANCHAY TIEMPO

Manchay tiempo—a hybrid of Quechua and Spanish meaning "time of fear"—properly applies not to the first months of war from 1980 to 1982, but to the period beginning with its escalation in 1983 to the decade's end.[1] By the end of 1982, the Shining Path had gathered enough strength to mount effective attacks against police stations in the southern highlands. Militants were killing mayors, teachers, and civic leaders, most, as journalist Gustavo Gorriti has pointed out, "people of modest means" whom they identified with a corrupt state.[2] Convinced that military intervention would quickly end the insurgency, President Fernando Belaúnde ceded to them control of nine provinces in the departments of Ayacucho, Apurímac, and Huancavelica.

Most Peruvians woke to this change only in 1983, with the massacre of eight journalists and their guide in a hamlet known as Uchuraccay, northwest of Ayacucho's capital. The journalists were investigating rumors that the navy had killed members of a Shining Path band the week before in nearby Huaychao. Uchuraccay villagers detained and executed the reporters, believing them to be guerrillas. The massacre made the newspapers around the world, and a commission headed by novelist Mario Vargas Llosa produced a controversial investigation. The events in that tiny Andean village at last brought the war in the Andes into the spotlight in Lima and abroad.

Uchuraccay became a ghost town like hundreds of others. Between 1983 and 1985, the emergency zone grew from nine to twenty-seven provinces. More than five thousand people fell victim to political violence in the emergency zone, over 1 percent of the population, terror on a mass scale.[3] In 1985, Amnesty International released a report documenting 1,005 cases of "disappearance" attributed to the security forces, the majority of them poor peasants. "The scale of killing could be estimated in part by the high number of clandestine graves or cemeteries, and of places where numerous cadavers are thrown to the side of the road."[4]

The ferocity of the armed forces, although tragically misguided, did have an effect. Villages that aided guerrillas were wiped out. Even a hint of sympathy, which in the military's mind might be an affinity for leftist politics or a too strident insistence on human rights, condemned many, complicating the guerrillas' hunt for new converts. And many in Huanta's highlands had already grown disenchanted with the guerrilla demand to close markets and the murder of those who disagreed. To compensate, guerrillas used increasingly harsh measures to force support, including attacks on hostile villages and more public executions. The murder of a local leader had an impact well beyond the confines of a town: other officials would resign or leave; whole areas would be dubbed "red zones" and avoided, implicitly ceding victory to the Shining Path.

Instead of withering, as President Belaúnde had hoped, the Shining Path flourished. By 1986, militants had opened up new fronts in Junín, the central jungle, and Lima. In each region, guerrillas showed an uncanny ability to exploit local conflict to their advantage: cocaine in the Upper Huallaga, a dispute between peasant communities and Velasco-era cooperatives in the Mantaro valley, land takeovers in Lima. To a few, their reign meant a sudden end to delinquency and graft as thieves and corrupt officials were summarily killed. A new president, Alan García, even publicly admired their *mística* and commitment in a secret address to APRA youth in 1987, perhaps nostalgic for his own party's turbulent past.

To the majority, however, such ruminations bordered on the obscene. Devastation, loss, grief: these are the words that punctuated the stories of thousands of internal refugees, spouses, parents, and children who lost loved ones and livelihoods to political violence. As the war waned in the mid-1990s, survivors began to return to rebuild ruined villages in an obdurate refusal to abandon the hope of home. Though justice remains elusive, a government-appointed Truth and Reconciliation Commission has collected the testimonies of more than fifteen thousand people who had suffered political violence.[5] In its final report, the commission estimates that more than sixty-nine thousand people perished between 1980 and 2000. As was true at the war's beginning, most were poor, brown-skinned, Quechua-speaking, and far from Lima's power centers.

A few of the crimes may one day be prosecuted. But most of those who survived this time of fear have only memories and a shared sense of loss to mark those years. "Months and years have passed / Where could he be?"

goes the ballad "Huamanguino" by Ayacucho master songwriter Ranulfo Fuentes about one of those kidnapped and killed. "Perhaps under the stony ground / becoming earth / or among the thorns / budding like wild-flowers."[6]

Notes

1   Nelson Manrique, "La década de la violencia," *Márgenes* (Lima) 3, nos. 5/6 (December 1989): 137–180.

2   Gustavo Gorriti, *Sendero: Historia de la guerra milenaria en el Perú* (Lima: Apoyo, 1990), p. 376.

3   *Comisión Especial del Senado sobre las Causas de la Violencia y Alternativas de Pacificación en el Perú, Violencia y pacificación* (Lima: DESCO/Comisión Andina de Juristas, 1989), p. 375.

4   Amnesty International, *Peru Briefing* (London: Amnesty International, 1985), p. 21.

5   The final report of the Truth and Reconciliation Commission is available in Spanish and Englist at http://www.cverdad.org.pe/.

6   Chalena Vásquez Rodríguez and Abilio Vergara Figueroa, *Chayraq: Carnaval Ayacuchano* (Lima: CEDAP/TAREA, 1988), p. 182.

VIETNAM IN THE ANDES
"Pancho"

"Pancho" is the pseudonym of a navy veteran of the early years of the war on the Shining Path in Ayacucho. A native of the grimy port of Callao and a cocaine addict, he tells his story with an emptiness that will remind many of stories told by American veterans back from Vietnam. Although Peruvians fought within their own borders, soldiers raised on the coast arrived in the poverty-stricken southern Andes like foreigners, believing the worst of its Quechua-speaking inhabitants: they were considered not only ignorant and dirty, but also willing converts to a violent Maoist doctrine. The result of this encounter was thousands of dead and "disappeared," and a generation of young servicemen scarred by the atrocities they perpetrated.

Ayacucho

At the end of 1982, the admiral told us that we were going to Ayacucho, that they had formed a contingent of professional soldiers. It was an excellent mission. Still, I pissed in my pants with fear. Whoever said he wasn't afraid was an idiot. Fear? Every single second. But I liked the situation. In the end, whoever is going to die dies, goes to shit. We told jokes to pass the time during the flight. When we arrived, they put us into "Los Cabitos" for four or five days.[1] We were pioneers for the navy and would establish a presence there. I guarded the commander, and I felt calm because I thought he was the tops. He was very prudent.

We had olive-green uniforms. The Sinchis wore one like it,[2] and were used to doing things then dumping the blame on us. It was the navy, they would say. What we did was get rid of the helmet and use a wool cap. They called us *yanaumas*,[3] but at least they could tell us apart by the clothes, because the Sinchis were very abusive.

Ayacucho was in deplorable shape. There was so much poverty because the government has never helped there. So an idiot who is a communist arrives and begins to introduce the only political consciousness that has ever come to the place. You don't know anything, but already they have imparted something political like communism and, well, you turn into a communist.

Death

The first time we wasted someone was a little hard. On one patrol, we stopped a truck. It was night, and we asked all the occupants for their documents, we searched everything until we found some brushes and ramrods, tools used to clean shotguns. Whose is this? I screamed. No one answered. In another truck, we found a *cholo*. We asked for his documents. Afterwards we searched him and we found another ramrod. We arrested him immediately. He didn't talk at all. I reacted and I kicked him in the nuts. So you've turned out to be a *terruco*, I shouted.[4]

We had already fixed up a little room that we called the intensive care room. That was where we gave our war treatment, but not torture. Unless he didn't spill, then I'm lying to you. But if they talked, from there we sent them to Los Cabitos. There they would decide to off them or leave them alive.

The first time you waste someone is real tough. There was a really tough sergeant. He grabbed them and tortured them. These are errors all of us commit, but this guy went too far. Afterwards, we asked among ourselves: how do we finish him off? They tied the *cholo* to a tree, broke his neck, and he didn't die. A couple of shots finished the *cholo* off, may he rest in peace. Well, and where were we going to stash him? Any place is fine, so what, the *puna* (high-altitude desert) is so huge. But somebody had to do it. If the mucky-muck is screwing up, somebody's got to do it. I've always been the one. So when we went to deposit the guy, he already stunk and he was stiff. It gave us the shivers, but afterwards it went away.

Combat

The most difficult moment for me was an ambush they laid for us. Three guys died. I mean, forget it, have you seen the movies? That's what it was like. We were pinned down in the spot called the "death zone." The only thing you can do is look for cover and throw your body to the ground, quickly look for where they are firing at less and try sliding over there.

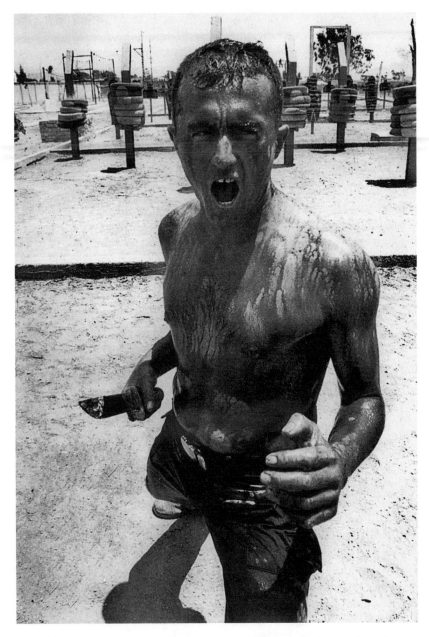

Figure 31. Government commando training to fight the Shining Path, 1982.
(Courtesy of Vera Lentz, *Caretas*)

You fall or get through. As I was telling you, they ambushed us, but we were lucky and we broke the ambush and counterattacked. We wasted a couple of them. Our error was afterwards. We were looking over the dead to see if there was still one alive. If there was, we offed him on the spot. One was just wounded and we didn't realize it. He squeezed off just one shot, but our luck was so bad that it hit a backpack filled with grenades, touching them off. Our sergeant flew apart in bits. The other guy standing close by had his legs destroyed, the guy began to beg us to kill him. I don't have feet, he screamed, kill me, buddy, please. . . . We put tourniquets everywhere so that he wouldn't bleed to death. . . . It was horrible, we called on the radio and nothing, the damn helicopter didn't come. The air force is a bunch of damn idiots. . . . They didn't care. . . . The army, though, did have balls.

Combat is combat, buddy. I respect those guys, those *terrucos*, because I believe you should respect the enemy, never under any circumstances underestimate him. They die for their ideas just like us.

Afterwards we began to do things for the community. For example, we distributed powdered milk, cooking oil, oatmeal too—everything was to win the people over. They sent this type of aid because the people suffered real poverty. For every three families a sack of milk, a barrel of cooking oil.

Smoke

Sometimes we lit up some dope. It was the tension. Once we found some guys in a gorge. We detained them and then searched them. We found nothing. So we took off their clothes and at about stomach-level we found a kind of pack. It was *pasta básica*.[5] These guys were carrying nothing less than eleven pounds. They were mules. Well, we're *criollos*.[6] I'd already smoked up my stash. Along with me was a black guy from Callao, so we stood them on their heads to see if there was money, but there wasn't. . . . We were pissed, angry because we hadn't found any green. You know, for some cigarettes, some beers, or a drink. We gave them back their merchandise, but not before I cut my share. We lit up at night, sometimes the black guy and I would go out on a mission and on the way we would light up. A short time later, we found out that the officers had only turned in a few ounces of the eleven pounds and had let the little mules go. There, the *pasta* is the purest and that's why it does you no harm. Here no, here it kicks you. You have to know where to buy.

Sex, Racism, and Death

When I searched women, the first thing I did was undress them. Old or young, I stuck my fingers in them just the same. You may not believe me, but there was one time when I found one explosive, pardon me, two. It's because they have big cunts. It was while I was searching her, I parted her legs and the explosive stuck out a little. And this? I asked. I continued searching her and in the skirt hem I found fuses and detonators. There they were, incredible but true. So from this moment I began to search all the *cholas*. Of course, they all weren't all dumb. There were some who wanted prick, and of course I let them have it. Sometimes little girls thirteen years old. They were sluts. I'm also going to tell you that if you get involved with a *chola*, she stays with you. Maybe it's because they see you as a *criollo* and it's different. To be straight with you, the *cholo* is like an animal for me. . . . He does it, then he sleeps. I remember that at first I rejected them because I didn't like them. Get out of here, you shitty *chola*, then fifteen days would go by and . . . please come in, young lady. A month and a half later . . . hot mama! . . . In the end, you understand, don't you? This happens the world over. In Vietnam, for example, for centuries and centuries, amen.

I'm going to tell you an anecdote. One day we had been on patrol for fifteen days. The patrol leader was a complete asshole, an imbecile, an idiot who had been a desk jockey his whole life, but they made him leader because he had seniority. One day, they gave us a *chola* to waste. Great, so where can we do it? We looked for and found a deserted house. But it had all the conveniences, furniture, a television. That's because we were in a drug zone. We installed ourselves there, and one by one we gave it to the poor *chola*. I remember that beforehand the guys had dressed her well with her little dress, and they made everything just right. I remember too that the patrol leader didn't want us to touch her, and I told him, "You are really fucked, the order's been given, we've got to waste this *chola* and nothing more." I remember her saying: "I'm a virgin, I'm a virgin." Get out of here, *chola*. Of course she wasn't a virgin. Here one learns to be a shit. Afterwards, the boys played her like a yo-yo. Then we wasted her.

Dirty War

Look, when the *terrucos* attack you, they send the *cholos* at you, they put them out front. The *cholos* who carry the slingshots load up a "Russian

Figure 32. Bodies of victims massacred by government forces, Huanta, 1984. (Courtesy of Abilio Arroyo)

cheese," light it, and begin to swing and shoot it toward their objective.[7] They have great aim! From 500 feet, they hit the target. I have a scar on my ankle. And the leaders are behind, well, waiting, out of fifty there are three or four, and these guys do have guns, machine guns or a rifle. The rest have slingshots, Russian cheeses, or old shotguns.

You maybe think, well, so Peruvians are killing each other. We're taking down our people. But what can we do, buddy, they're going to take us down, no question. It's ideology that they have, you know, they don't know the meaning of democracy. The only thing they know is communism and the Shining Path, nothing more.

We weren't defending Belaúnde,[8] we were defending the people. Sometimes, we would go to lands devastated by the *terrucos*, women burned alive, pregnant women, they cut them open, slashed their throats. Kids just like my son, dead, throats slit. It's because the leaders would tell them: attack this zone, and they attacked, they attacked and killed everyone. One, they killed about forty people, and we saved about twelve of the wounded. There was a fifteen-year-old *cholo* who had two lung punctures, from the back. Two lung wounds, how horrible.

Sometimes we would wonder what we were doing killing each other off. Sometimes you go nuts, start to scream at them. Some of the new kids [soldiers] went crazy. Went crazy. I baptized one of them. When it's your turn to waste someone, well, you give first dibs to the one who has never iced a person, so they feel this experience and gel a little more, because some people can't bear to do it. But sometimes if you're led along by others, in this case me, no? I said to him: drill him. He grabbed and raised his rifle. No, stab. With the knife. This bastard didn't know where to put it, he wanted to put it in the spinal column. He stuck it there and his hand folded over. Come here, kid, take your bayonet, finish him off. Like this, I told him, pow, I gave him a bayonet stroke and to shit, because I gave it to him in the lungs, in the ticker, and then I blew him to pieces. They themselves beg you, kill me with bullets. But not with bullets, no, because we had reporters after us.

The press is a double-edged sword. This is an unconventional war, it's an undeclared war, so it's a dirty war, do you understand me? Guerrilla wars are always this way, give it to him in the head, all over the world, in a dirty war anything goes.

Notes

1   Los Cabitos is the Ayacucho army base.
2   The Sinchis are a specialized antiterrorism unit within Peru's National Police. The name comes from the Quechua word for warrior-chief used in precolonial times.
3   *Yanauma* means "black head" in Quechua, referring to the black wool ski masks used by Peru's security forces and some civil defense patrols.
4   *Terruco* is a Quechua version of the Spanish word for terrorist.
5   Raw cocaine, about 90 percent pure.
6   *Criollos* are Peruvians of European as opposed to Andean descent.
7   Andean peasants have long used slingshots, or *huaracas*, to kill small birds and animals. Shining Path militants adapted them to grenades and homemade explosives, like "Russian cheeses" (*queso ruso*).
8   Then-president Francisco Belaúnde Terry.

DEATH THREAT

Anonymous

Terror in Lima's poor neighborhoods had intensified in the mid-1980s with Shining Path assassinations of community leaders and army rastrillajes, or sweeps. This Shining Path death threat was slipped into the briefcase of a leader of the Túpac Amaru neighborhood in El Agustino, Lima, in 1991. It reflected the Maoists' appeal to a strict morality and their frank willingness to use intimidation and death to force compliance. Hundreds of community leaders received similar threats throughout the 1980s and into the 1990s, and many were murdered, accused of not cooperating with rebel demands.

Mr. President [of the shantytown neighborhood committee]:

We have the great honor of greeting you to inform you of the following:

After this greeting, we want to let you know of our concern for our neighborhood, full of criminals seen every day in the parks, at the corners, hanging around to commit mischief, gambling at cards; all are criminals, but our leaders say nothing, they do nothing to combat them; [the criminals] are under their noses every day and they know it and don't say that they don't, so now, sirs it's time that we organize by forming a Defense Committee, and this is urgent.

Also, irresponsible parents who set a bad example should be severely punished for their lack of responsibility for their children. They should be punished in the central square to teach a lesson to others, because these bad examples and the tacit consent they give to disobedience gives birth to drug addiction and the robbery that is seen every day.

Sirs: This Defense Committee should function by coordinating neighborhoods to eliminate crime definitively, and a mass grave is already built for all of those bad elements that are not useful to society.

Madams: No one has confidence in the authorities because all criminals are arrested then set free, and want to steal even more.

Mr. President, this mandate gives you at most one week to work and if you use it to liquidate all types of criminals there will be no more people who live by seizing poor people's belongings, from those who don't know that "the cunning live off fools."[1]

Mr. President, this is not a game, because if you don't carry out our orders, you will be hung in the central plaza so that you will in this way learn how to carry out and respect, because we also know what you are up to. Sirs, we have a list of everyone, including their daily routines and if it isn't clear yet, we will let you know who should be liquidated; *fiestas chichas* should be banned,[2] and walks late at night for no reason; bars should be closed by 9:00 P.M. This message should be read aloud in a public assembly so that everyone will be aware of it. We hope that this will be done and will be there listening to the announcement.

NOTE: If you don't carry this out, we will make you carry it out, and we will sweep every one of you away.

Notes

1 "*El vivo vive del zonzo*" is a common Peruvian *dicho*, or saying.
2 *Fiestas chichas* are dance parties.

WOMEN AND TERROR

Raquel Martín de Mejía

Women were a target of terror from both sides in Peru's dirty war. The Shining Path assassinated dozens of female shantytown leaders, while the armed forces turned rape into common practice. Raquel Martín de Mejía, a special education teacher, was raped in 1989 by the head of the same army squadron that kidnapped and murdered her husband, a respected political activist and lawyer, in their hometown of Oxapampa in the central mountains. After fleeing Peru because of death threats, Martín bravely spoke about the rape in the hopes of bringing this rarely acknowledged human rights violation to public awareness. She now lives in Sweden with her daughter.

On Thursday, June 15, 1989, I spent a restful afternoon at home with my husband. We were asleep when at about 11:00 P.M. they knocked at the door to our house, yelling: "Mejía! Mejía!" My husband woke up, startled. He opened the bedroom curtain and peered outside. I was still half asleep.

My husband, barefoot and in a T-shirt and pajamas, went to the living room. He switched on the light before opening the door. When I got to the living room, I saw they were beating him up and that he was holding his head. One man was standing next to him, ready to smash him again with the butt of his machine gun. Six others stood in the living room with their machine guns—four of them in a half-circle blocking the bedroom door. They wore black ski masks and army uniforms—black sweaters, black combat boots, green pants.

I tried to go to my husband, to give him his shoes. But one of the masked men moved toward me, pointing his machine gun. The man in charge was tall—about 6′1″—and big.

The armed men took my husband out the front door to a yellow pickup truck, where a few others in hoods and army uniforms were waiting. The moon was bright, and with the porch light from the neighbor's house I could see the kidnapers make my husband take off his T-shirt and use it to blindfold him. They made him get onto the pickup's flatbed and then left. I returned to the house, afraid and not knowing what to do.

About fifteen minutes later, I heard another knock at the door. I thought it was my husband. So I opened the door. Six or ten armed and hooded men in army uniforms were waiting outside. The tall commander entered alone, and he quickly switched off the living room light. He asked for my husband's ID papers. His voice was slurred and his breath smelled of alcohol.

When I went to the bedroom to look for the papers, he followed and said I was also wanted as a subversive. Then he pulled out a list on a sheet of white paper. I couldn't read the names without my glasses. I put them on, but he had covered all but the first two names. My husband's was first. The name of Aladino Melgarejo, a teacher, was next.

I said he had the wrong man and should ask the local police about my husband—about his life, work, and honesty. He didn't listen and started to spray himself with some of my perfumes. Then he pulled down my pants and raped me in the bed where I had been sleeping with my husband.

After, he took me outside to see the man he said had given them my husband's name. Another subversive, he said. There was a man face down in the back of the pickup, but I had never seen him before. Hooded men in army uniforms sat on the tailgate. All of them left, and I went into the house to wash myself.

About 11:45 P.M., I heard another knock. When I opened the door, the same man who had raped me pushed into the house. He said that my husband would be taken by helicopter to Lima. Then he raped me again and left. I washed myself and sat in silence in my bedroom, terrified for my safety and the life of my husband.

My husband did not reappear. Three days later, on Sunday, I sent my nephew to look for the leader of an Amuesha community, a client of my husband's, to ask for his help.[1] A little later, the Amuesha leader came to say that the body of the teacher, Aladino Melgarejo, had been found near Oxapampa by the Santa Clara River, and there was another body nearby.

I tried to find some of Oxapampa's municipal officials to accompany me to the place where they had found the bodies. The mayor, the judge, and the director of the hospital were away. The judge's secretary and two policemen accompanied me to the riverbank.

Figure 33. Raquel Martín de Mejía, shown here with her daughter, has fought to bring to justice the soldiers who assaulted her and killed her husband in 1988. She now lives in exile in Sweden. Photograph by Robin Kirk.

We found the bodies of my husband and Aladino Melgarejo half-buried near the river, next to one of the bridge's pillars. The pillar was spattered with blood and pocked with bullet marks. The teacher had been decapitated. It looked like dogs had eaten off his face. The body of my husband was face down. He still had his eyes blindfolded with the T-shirt. There were torture marks, punctures on his arms and legs that looked like they were made by an awl or a pick. He also had an open wound on his skull, apparently from a bullet. The body was taken to the municipal hospital, where they did an autopsy.

Four days later I left Oxapampa to stay with relatives in Lima. I began to go to the police and congress to ask for an investigation, and spoke to the press about the case. Toward the end of the month, I received three anonymous phone calls threatening to kill me if I didn't "keep my mouth shut." One of the callers was a woman. I was afraid, and did not leave the house.

In July 1989, afraid for my life, I asked for the help of the Pro–Human Rights Association (APRODEH) in Lima. I made a statement on video, describing everything. In August, with the help of APRODEH and Amnesty International, I fled to Sweden.

Since I left Peru, I have continued to work for an investigation of the crimes committed against my husband and me and the punishment of those responsible. Someday, I hope, there will be justice.

Note

1   The Amuesha are an indigenous group in the upper Amazon below Oxapampa who had been defended in various disputes by Raquel Martín's husband, Fernando Mejía.

CHAQWA

Robin Kirk

*No international covenants protect internal refugees, those who flee political vio-
lence but cross no international borders. When thousands of families began to abandon their homes in the southern highlands in 1983,* desplazados, *as they are
known in Spanish, discovered that neither society at large nor humanitarian aid
groups recognized their plight. Instead, as Robin Kirk points out, they were invisible, the human cost of a war few were willing to recognize. As war spread, their
ranks were increased by Amazonian native communities, coca growers, and even
state officials and local intellectuals. Whole areas were abandoned in the war's devastation, as the violent disorder Quechua peasants called* chaqwa *gripped large
parts of Peru's territory. Even today, those driving south on the Pan-American
highway toward Ica will pass Nuevo Ayacucho, a settlement of shacks in the middle
of the desert. That thousands of poor refugees must make their homes in this god-
forsaken spot testifies to the desperation of those fleeing the war in the Andes.*

Peru's long history of internal migration is the essential context for
understanding the new, forced migration that began in 1983. Until
the 1940s, more than half of Peru's population lived in the Andes. After
World War II, industrialization and land reform were just some of the
forces behind the massive exodus to coastal cities, especially Lima, where
there were jobs, universities, and a higher standard of living. Families
often migrated in stages—first the head of household or working-age
sons, then the rest of the family. The first arrivals built precarious homes
of straw mats, cardboard, and junk wood in squatter settlements that were
labeled "young towns," *pueblos jóvenes,* currently home to more than half
of Lima's residents.[1]

The tendency to head for areas already settled by others from the
same district meant that many young towns maintained a unique regional

identity. Southern migrants, for instance, settled near factories along the southern arm of the Pan-American highway, connected by a busy flow of trucks and buses to their mountain homes. They often returned to their villages to harvest or plant, and local celebrations, such as the anniversary of a patron saint, were celebrated in Lima with dances and song.

By 1981 the proportion of Peruvians living in the Andes had fallen to 36 percent. The poorest states—Ayacucho, Apurímac, and Huancavelica—sent the most migrants. Their sense of loss and nostalgia for an old way of life enriched the ballads of folk musicians like the Jilguero of Huascarán and the Trío Ayacucho, whose lyrics mix the pain of leaving, coastal racism, and poverty with the hope that came with building a new life in the big city.

The First Refugees: 1983–1985

The new phenomenon of violence-provoked migration began with the declaration of the first "emergency zone" in 1983.[2] Entire families hid in their fields or slept in trees until it was safe to escape. The first to leave were peasants from the Ayacucho provinces of Victor Fajardo and Cangallo, where Shining Path recruitment and military repression were strongest. Poorer peasants from the highest, most isolated valleys and the highland desert, or *puna*, came to provincial capitals like Huanta. Peasants from lower valleys tended toward state capitals like Huamanga and Huancavelica.

Not all *desplazados* were peasants. A significant number, including artisans, shopkeepers, and professionals, came from small towns. Many town dwellers with family in Lima went to the coast, where they congregated in shantytowns settled by earlier economic migrants from their regions.[3]

Many of the displaced were young, prime targets for Shining Path recruitment. At the same time, the military considered young people to be potential guerrillas, especially if they studied at the University of Huamanga. Many authorities, especially mayors and local officials, fled, threatened by the Shining Path. Community organizers, journalists, and the legal left escaped when they saw that the military made few distinctions between their work and guerrilla organizing.

Hundreds of testimonies gathered by the Catholic Church's Episcopal Conference for Social Action (CEAS) showed that many *desplazados* fled their homes in the space of a night, leaving behind clothes and animals, the equivalent of a life's savings. Others tried to weather repeated guer-

Figure 34. A *desplazado* from Ayacucho, next to his home in Lima, 1986.

rilla and military incursions before fleeing. "This was an involuntary and, in many cases, compulsive migration, without any premeditation," Elsa Ballón of CEAS told me.

Ghost Towns

An OXFAM survey of thirty-two communities in northern Ayacucho found that the population decreased dramatically, from 6,067 families in 1981 to 2,940 in 1985. At an average of five persons per family, those figures represent a decrease of 15,600 people. Communities like Accomarca, Umaru, Huambalpa, and Caipara became ghost towns, completely abandoned or with only the elderly and orphans.[4]

The sharp rise in *desplazados* was most obvious in Ayacucho, until 1981 a provincial capital of seventy thousand. *Desplazados* built precarious huts on the barren hills surrounding the city. By 1985, then vice mayor Jaime Urrutia estimated, the population had grown to well over one hundred thousand. "Although no reliable numbers exist, we can calculate this growth with various indirect factors," Urrutia noted, "the growth of street selling, the rise in begging and common street crime to levels never before seen." This was how one reporter described the route from Ayacucho City to Tambo, Ayacucho, in 1986: "Where before there were crops—

primarily potatoes, corn, and beans—today grow weeds. Construction, granaries, cattle, corrals, all have been abandoned. Even machinery, useless now because of the ravages of time, was left behind as people were forced to flee."

The Second Wave: 1987–1991

In his inaugural speech on July 28, 1985, President Alan García promised to usher in new respect for human rights. At first, the drop in reports of violations was notable. In 1986, the attorney general's office received 108 reports of "disappearance," many fewer than in the three preceding years. García's minister of defense, Army General Jorge Flores, claimed that 80 percent of the Emergency Zone was "pacified" and promised a new counterinsurgency policy that would combine military force with projects that attacked "Ayacucho's misery, which feeds the spread of subversion."

Social workers in touch with *desplazados* noted that the number of displaced families arriving in Lima and Ayacucho decreased in 1985. For families already in exile, return became a more than tenuous hope. A 1987 survey of 280 *desplazado* families done by an independent research center found that most professed a strong desire to return.

Cesareo Ayala, president of the Sons of Huambalpa Association, fled to Lima after a series of violent attacks in Huambalpa, Ayacucho, first by soldiers and Sinchis on January 26, 1983,[5] and then by the Shining Path. The attacks made Huambalpa into a ghost town of children and the elderly too weak to travel. Ayala explained to journalists that one of the main reasons they chose to return to Huambalpa was their experience in Lima:

> Our arrival in Lima was filled with sadness. Our first attempts to forcibly settle unused land were repressed, and when we thought we had found a place, Army soldiers began to follow us and threaten us. Many of our fellow Ayacuchans had to beg to survive. Others worked as street vendors and a few in construction. We were accused of being terrorists in a very dismissive way by Lima people.

He and seventy-nine others returned to Huambalpa in 1986. Soon, more returned, until there were a total of eight hundred returnees.

But within months, they were once again forced to flee. Scant weeks after their arrival, the Shining Path assassinated a Huambalpa schoolteacher who had supported the return. Returnees risked being seen as traitors and informers by both sides.

By 1987 political violence was again on the rise. In contrast to earlier years, however, the Shining Path was able to maintain a strong presence over a much wider area. Guerrillas were active as far north as Huaraz, south to Puno and the Bolivian border, and increasingly in Lima. The government responded by declaring new states of emergency in Junín, Ucayali, San Martín, Huánuco, and Lima itself. However, human rights groups noted that areas declared emergency zones quickly became the scenes of repeated human rights violations by the security forces and brought little real advance against guerrilla activity.

The Case of Junín

The state of Junín bears special mention. Directly east of Lima, Junín provides the bulk of food and hydroelectric power for the capital. It is also an important mining center and transportation corridor, linking Lima to the central Andes and the jungle.

Junín was key to the Shining Path's plan to choke the capital by restricting the flow of goods from the countryside. The Shining Path began organizing in the highest, poorest parts of the Junín Andes, taking advantage of long-standing disputes over the huge agricultural cooperatives (Sociedad Agrícola de Interés Social [SAIS]) set up after Velasco's reform. These cooperatives employed a relatively small number, leaving many families still without land.

Historian Nelson Manrique theorized that once the first cadres won support, a second, more authoritarian group would arrive and impose a harsher regime. At that point, he said, the first forced migrations to Huancayo began. "The driving idea was that only the Shining Path and peasants be left in the countryside, until the counterinsurgency forces intervene, forcing the migration and the expulsion of vast sectors of the peasantry, as has happened in Ayacucho and elsewhere."[6]

In the jungle province of Satipo, the Shining Path touched off an ethnic and tribal war among native peoples and highland colonists. Manipulating local conflicts, guerrillas managed to divide some communities into pro- and antiguerrilla factions. By 1993, approximately thirty thousand Asháninkas were displaced, many fleeing to jungle communities where their numbers swelled formerly small villages.

Low Intensity/High Casualty

This second wave of displaced civilians fled in comparatively worse shape than those who left early in the war. Peru's economic collapse paired with the spread of the war meant that new *desplazados* faced unprecedented levels of malnutrition and disease and fought for living space in ever more crowded, underserviced, and violent *pueblos jóvenes*.

In the countryside, little effort was made to rebuild villages destroyed by the Shining Path—none to areas devastated by military operations, bombings, or attacks by civil defense patrols. President Garciá's short-lived attempt to direct public investment to the "Andean Trapezoid," made up primarily of southern Emergency Zone states, sank under mismanagement and corruption. Ayacucho was singled out as an "agricultural disaster zone" by 1987.

By the decade's end, Ayacucho, once the rich heart of modern Andean culture, was a society modeled on war. Many of its weavers, painters, sculptors, and musicians had left. For instance, the painters of Sarhua were forced to abandon their workshop in 1981, after the Shining Path burned it. They moved to Lima, where artists painted their elegant, brightly colored panels in a shantytown.

Limamanta Pacha *("From Lima")*

Most *desplazados* fled to Lima. For them, the vast metropolis seemed like a good place to hide and work until return was possible. Families took buses that connect provincial capitals to the coast or flagged down cargo trucks with space in the back for children and bundles of clothes.

Few, however, were prepared for what awaited them in the capital. Added to the long-standing prejudice against highlanders, Peru's poverty put *desplazados*, many speaking only Quechua and without marketable skills or the small capital necessary to start a business, at a sharp disadvantage when compared to the mass of Peru's poor.

Lima-based Ayacucho, Huancavelica, and Apurímac federations helped some *desplazados*. But demand quickly overwhelmed the traditional networks set up by these earlier, economic migrants. And political violence sowed distrust between the two groups. Established migrants were suspicious that *desplazados* had guerrilla ties. At the same time, the federations were under the scrutiny of the security forces as potential centers of guerrilla organizing.

"As the displaced population arrived in Lima, it began its peregrination at a much greater disadvantage than common, everyday migrants and had to confront not only the restricted and marginal conditions offered in the settlements, but also the marginality and hostility that comes from being Ayacuchan," explained Isabel Coral of the Center for Population Study and Development, which works with the displaced.

New Shantytowns

Most *desplazado* families concentrated in areas already settled by migrants from the southern Andes: Pamplona, San Juan de Lurigancho, Ate-Vitarte, and Villa El Salvador. Initially, the families stayed with relatives or others from their regions. Others, without such resources, slept in churches, alleyways, and empty lots until they found more permanent shelter.

A new phenomenon, refugee *asentamientos humanos* (human settlements), took shape in 1984, with the establishment of Huanta I. Forty-five Huanta *desplazados* made an agreement with the Huanta-born mayor of San Juan de Lurigancho, a municipality in northeast Lima, to build housing on a tract of municipal land. Another five hundred families, including two thousand children, made a similar arrangement to found Huanta II next door. Other settlements with a majority of *desplazados* include Juan Pablo II, Las Galeras, Cruz de Motupe, and Enrique Montenegro, all in San Juan de Lurigancho.

At first little distinguished the poverty in these settlements from a thousand others. Straw shacks clustered together on a bare stretch of hill. Foot trails connected door to door. Children, dogs, and chickens crisscrossed the beaten-dirt yards. The occasional water truck climbed a dirt track to fill a communal cistern or old oil drums.

Yet in these settlements, Quechua, not Spanish, was the first language. Everyone had a story of grief, fear, and loss stemming from political violence. Unlike other shantytown dwellers, who eventually convert their shacks into brick houses, many *desplazados* resisted settling in. For them, Lima was temporary shelter until they could return home.

Inside the shacks, whole families slept on a single bed or stretched out on blankets on dirt floors. Cooking was done in evaporated milk cans beaten flat, over fires made of junk wood. Many *desplazados* had open sores, eye infections, and chronic bronchitis, and complained of "nerves" and the "anguish" that kept them from sleeping at night.

A significant number of *desplazados* worked as laborers on farms just outside Lima. Some preferred the rural atmosphere over dirty, crowded Lima. But their labor was exploited by landowners unwilling to pay a decent wage. Although an entire family might work the fields, often only the male head of household was paid. Some families were paid only in "leftovers," the right to collect the crop left after harvesters were finished.

Severina lived in a *desplazado* settlement in south Lima.[7] She was a small, compact woman, her black hair neatly braided. She and her husband lived in a farming village in Huancavelica. They survived repeated attacks by the military and civil defense patrols. The end came when the Shining Path burned the village. She and her husband fled to Lima with their three children: "When we came, we didn't have water or lights or beds, and we missed home, we cried, we weren't used to life here. In the mountains, we ate from our fields, wheat, potatoes, corn, barley. But when we came here, there was nothing, and everything takes money. We've gone hungry here." With other *desplazados*, Severina and her family took over unoccupied land at the farthest reach of one of Lima's oldest shantytowns. While Severina raised the children in a one-room straw shack, her husband worked as a temporary construction worker and night watchman. He was paid the equivalent of $45 a month. Most was deducted for meals and lodging. He gave Severina the rest—$2 a week.

At first the family ate little. Her children suffered severe malnutrition. The only way to survive was to form an *olla común* ("common pot") with other displaced women. To receive food donations from Caritas-Lima, they obtained official recognition as a soup kitchen. The kitchen itself was a ramshackle hut, just big enough for two wood fires and the metal pots used to cook rice and soup: "We serve lunch and a small dinner, and for breakfast herb tea or water boiled with greens. Fifty-seven families eat here, including people from the neighborhood [not refugees]. But we have just two pots, and it's not enough to meet the demand. We need more pots, more capital. People come crying, but we can't feed everyone."

Living Fear
Fear—that a *batida* (police roundup) will start, or a cadre will appear with a blacklist, or a job will end, or food will run out—was also an ever-present part of *desplazado* life in Lima. "The fact of being an internal refugee in your own country means that you live with the constant fear that the precarious safety you have won could be taken away at any moment," said Caleb Meza, director of an evangelical social assistance program.

The case of Antonio was typical. From Huanta, Ayacucho, Antonio came to Lima with his three young daughters after his wife was killed by soldiers. He is an *arrepentido*, a former Shining Path collaborator who chose to leave the group. He said he abandoned Huanta because cadres had been pressing him to participate in armed attacks.

Antonio explained to a CEAS psychologist that he felt responsible for his wife's death. At first, he had to lock his daughters in their shack while he worked, and two of them suffered malnutrition. Although a social worker helped him place the girls in a temporary shelter, the separation

Figure 35. Painted by the Association of Popular Artists (ADAPS), this detail from a work in the town of Sarhua, Ayacucho, shows the destruction by the Shining Path of the municipality and its archives in 1982. Most villagers subsequently fled the terror of the guerrillas and the army. Photograph of painting owned by Robin Kirk and Orin Starn.

and guilt at not being able to care for them caused Antonio new anguish. It was expressed physically, by various parts of his body "going to sleep" and bad headaches. He was also plagued by repeated nightmares about his wife's death. Antonio also lived with the constant fear that the Shining Path would locate him and punish him as a deserter.

Ana María Rebaza, who headed the CEAS psychology team that works with *desplazados*, explained that they experience often crippling grief, depression, and feelings of guilt, nostalgia, and loss of identity. Sharp cultural differences separate country and city, highland values and coastal survival. Parents worried that children would be corrupted by crime and drugs.

"These are people who never had any intention of leaving their homes or having to deal with the very different and hostile world that is Lima," Rebaza said. She noted that organizations that work with the internally displaced devoted little time to treating the psychological effects of war.

"The highest barrier to dealing with the psychological trauma is the overwhelming material need for food and shelter."

The Shining Path

Until the Shining Path's defeat in the mid-1990s, it was the primary force behind Peru's later displacement. In many areas, the group dedicated itself to punishing communities for resisting their control, especially by forming civil defense patrols. In one of the bloodiest engagements of thirteen years of war, a guerrilla incursion near Mazamari, Junín, in 1993 cost the lives of sixty-two Ashaninkas and colonists, provoking the mass displacement of seven hundred people.

Typically, guerrillas waited until the men were on patrol to act. In darkness, they would surround a sleeping village and cut off escape routes. With a crash of explosives and the thunder of automatic weapons fire, they would attack, killing people in their homes or as they ran. In repeated cases, only those who managed to hide survived. Even when communities were able to grab their government-donated Winchesters, these rifles were no match for automatic weapons.

Another reason for flight was forced recruitment by guerrillas. Eduardo and his brother cared for their two younger sisters in a Lima shantytown. Repeatedly, guerrillas came to their mountain community with lists of children as young as nine to take, train in combat, and deploy:

> The guerrillas come recruiting to our village often, looking for children, boys and girls, as young as ten. When they come to a town, they already know who is who, they have a list, and they call children by their names. All the children in my family have been called. Often, my parents are working in the fields, so the girls were alone in the house and easy to snatch. They take them, and maybe the family never sees them again. So we decided to bring the girls here. They kill the family or the children if they don't appear.

The Coup and Its Consequences

For internal refugees, the consequences of the 1992 coup that placed quasi-dictatorial powers in the hands of President Alberto Fujimori were both direct and implicit. Perhaps the most noticeable change was an increase in the number of security force sweeps through poor shantytowns, precisely where many internal refugees lived. Whereas in previous years

Figure 36. Funeral of two brothers killed by the Shining Path in Puno. Relatives hold a picture of the grave of their father, also murdered by the guerrillas. (Courtesy of TAFOS)

sweeps were occasional occurrences, they began to occur almost daily, part of the government's new get-tough strategy.

For *desplazados*, who often fled their villages because of police and army incursions, a sweep was a terrifying, brutal experience. In darkness, it would begin with the rumble of vehicles and the quick thud of booted feet. Suddenly, there is a rap at the door and a rain of powerful flashlights. Usually, no warrants were necessary for police or soldiers to burst in, waving their weapons and hurling insults at the inhabitants. The house would be searched, often with intentional violence. Common household items—an opened bucket of black paint, a stash of empty evaporated milk cans—could be seized as "suspicious material."

Desplazados who had lost their national identity cards were automatically considered suspicious and risked arrest. In repeated cases, police forced people to sign fraudulent search results under threat of death or the arrest of a wife or child. If someone was held for further questioning, frequently the next stop was a torture room. Torture was an everyday occurrence in Peru. Detainees were beaten, threatened with death, subjected to near-drowning in filthy water, and given electric shocks.

Once a detainee was formally charged with supporting or belonging to a guerrilla group, a legal nightmare began in which the most basic rights were suspended. One of the most troubling decrees promulgated by President Fujimori was known as the antiterrorism law. It defined the crime of terrorism and established stiff penalties for certain acts, from participating in an armed attack to appearing to make excuses for insurgents, known as "apology for terrorism." The latter clause was used to threaten and imprison human rights activists, journalists, and other government critics, particularly in areas still under emergency legislation. For instance, Angélica Mendoza, the founder of the Ayacucho-based Families of the Disappeared and a defender of *desplazados*, was charged as a supposed "Shining Path ambassador" in France, a country she visited once for three days in 1985 as a guest of Amnesty International.

For internal refugees, already at a disadvantage because of poverty and the hardships of flight, these laws were an especially serious threat. To have a chance at acquittal, access to decent legal representation and money—both out of reach to most—was crucial. Also, internal refugees tended to be already "suspicious" in the eyes of the security forces because of their origin, accent, and status as *desplazados* living in shantytowns considered "red zones."

Prospects for Return

Although the idea of return was, for most desplazados, a distant, impossible dream, for a significant number it remained the object of constant thought, planning, and coordination. Committees of *desplazados* would make brief visits to their villages to assess the possibilities of return.

Figure 37. Cartoonist Alfredo satirized the human rights policy of the Fujimori government. The cartoon reads: "Fujimori promises to pacify the country before ending his term." "Pacify . . ." "Leave silent . . . without a sound . . . without a murmur." "Shhhhhh." (Courtesy of *La República*)

Through family networks, they kept abreast of recent developments, while never forgetting the volatility of any "apparently peaceful" period.

Return was tremendously complicated, though. This testimony from one internal refugee from Huancavelica laid out the obstacles in detail:

> We left our village in 1986 because the Shining Path came in and said we had to give them our children or face death. Although we recently sent a commission back to see about the possibility of return, it is impossible. The army base demands one sheep a month from each family, and where are we, arriving with nothing, to get a sheep? They do not respect civil authorities. One officer swaggered through the village while we were there, vowing to kill a local official because he had supposedly criticized that [demand]. The army gave the community five rifles for every hundred people. With that, they expect us to defend ourselves against the terrorists, who have automatic weapons? Forming a patrol just brings trouble, because then for sure the Shining Path will attack.

Within this grim panorama, however, there were positive changes worth noting. Prime among them was the success in some areas of civil defense patrols. In Huanta, Ayacucho, for example, patrols managed to force the Shining Path to the thinly populated *puna*, where their ability to mount attacks and force compliance was greatly reduced. A relative calm returned, halting further forced displacement and prompting some *desplazados* to consider return. With the backing of the army, one hundred families from the war-torn village of Iquicha began rebuilding in July 1993.

The hope of return remained powerful for thousands of refugees in the time of violence. "These are productive lands," says Zenón, an Iquicha farmer, while overlooking the rubble and brush that was once his village. "This is where we will start over."

Notes

1   Jürgen Golte and Norma Adams, *Los caballos de Troya de los invasores* (Lima: Instituto de Estudios Peruanos, 1990).
2   On December 26, 1982, President Fernando Belaúnde placed nine provinces in the states of Ayacucho, Apurímac, and Huancavelica in a state of emergency, ceding control to the military, in an effort to improve the efficiency of the fight against the Maoist Communist Party of Peru–Shining Path. A political-military command was established at the Los Cabitos army base in Huamanga, Ayacucho.

3   Isabel Coral, "Ayacuchanos: ¿Migrantes o refugiados de guerra?" in *Los caminos del labe-rinto* (Lima: CEDAP, 1986).

4   OXFAM, untitled report (Lima: OXFAM, 1985).

5   *Sinchis* are specialized antiterrorism police. The word comes from the Inca term for warrior-chief.

6   Nelson Manrique, "Sierra Central: La batalla decisiva," *Quehacer* (August–September 1989), 62–71.

7   Some names have been changed for security reasons.

HUAMANGUINO

Ranulfo Fuentes

One of Ayacucho's premier balladeers, Ranulfo Fuentes here turns his eye to the "dirty war" and the tactic of "disappearance" used by the security forces to instill terror. Here suspected guerrillas would be kidnapped never to reappear. Fuentes, a high school teacher who wrote "Huamanguino," after Ayacucho's capital, in collaboration with a student workshop, often writes in Quechua. Since many Quechua-speaking families cannot afford to buy the scarce newspapers or books written in that language, songs like these, sung in bars and broadcast over local radio stations, have served as an underground medium for protest and lament.

I

Huamanguinos chinkarqun ¿imay hora?
chawpi tuta chaychaytas
wasinmanta
allin puñuykuy horatas
urqurunku, aparunku

II

Maqasqa qapariptinsi
mama allwan
makinta chaqnaykuspankus
pasachinku
ñawinta vendaykuspankus
aysarunku, pusarunku

Figure 38. Songwriter Ranulfo Fuentes in the high school where he teaches in Huamanga, Ayacucho. Photograph by Robin Kirk.

III

Killapas, watapas pasanñam
¿maypiñaraq?
ranrapa ukupinñachu
allpayachkan
kichkapa chawpinpiñachu
qurayachkan, qurayachkan

IV

(Qawachan)
Kutirqamunqañam, chayarqamunqañam
tarpuy para hina muqullay wiñarichiq
akchiriq inti hina

sisalla, sisarichiq
rurulla panchirichiq

I

Someone from Huamanga has disappeared!
At what time?
About midnight
from his house,
at the hour of deepest sleep
they have taken and kidnapped him.

II

When he screamed after being hit
his mother protested, crying
Hands bound tightly
they took him
covering his eyes
they dragged him away.

III

Months and years have passed
Where could he be?
Perhaps under the stony ground
becoming earth
or among the thorns
budding like wild flowers.

(Coda)
IV

Soon he will return, he will come back
like rain for the crops
to make the seeds sprout
like the sun at dawn
that makes flowers bloom.

"THERE HAVE BEEN THREATS"

María Elena Moyano

An original settler of Villa El Salvador and vice mayor of that municipality, one of Lima's largest, María Elena Moyano was a grassroots leader and an articulate proponent of a nonviolent path between state and guerrilla terror. Villa El Salvador, Huaycán, San Juan de Lurigancho, and other poor neighborhoods have always been far more divided by personal infighting and political factionalism than might be supposed from romantic claims about "urban self-determination" and "popular unity." However, Moyano represented a new kind of leader emerging in the pueblos jóvenes, or "new towns": young, feminist, nonwhite (she was African-Peruvian), progressive but not tied to any major political party. This interview by journalist Mariella Balbi was published in 1991, just five months before Moyano was murdered by a Shining Path assassination squad to silence her criticism of their terror tactics.

Q: Mrs. Moyano, a week ago the Shining Path bombed a food warehouse in Villa. Did you see this coming?

María Elena Moyano (MEM): Yes. I felt it when they attacked Juana López, a "Glass of Milk" program [groups formed to serve free breakfasts to poor children] leader, fifteen days ago.

Q: And before this?

MEM: There have been threats. About a year ago, they attacked me and the Women's Federation through *El Diario*.[1] They said we were a mattress for the system, that we don't value or empower women because they are emancipated only through war. That we practice only charity. That [I] am a revisionist and manipulate women. They have taken pictures of the Women's Center and published them in *El Diario*. It's a permanent threat. It seems to me that their prime objective has been to discredit the

Figure 39. María Elena Moyano, 1992. (Courtesy of *La República*)

Women's Federation in preparation for an attack. I believe this is a tactic of theirs.

Q: Did you think they would make themselves known with so much violence?

MEM: The truth is that I didn't. Until a while ago, I thought the Shining Path was wrong-headed but that they in some way wanted to fight for some sort of justice. But when they murdered [a workers' rights activist], although I was horrified by the act, I didn't go so far as to condemn the Shining Path's terrorist attitude. Now they have touched grassroots organizations, made up of the poorest people. Who participates in the soup kitchens and the "Glass of Milk" program? People who can't afford to eat in their houses, so I don't understand this unbalanced group. They want to snuff out survival organizations so that levels of malnutrition and death rise.

Q: Was this initial attitude of a certain tolerance for the Shining Path an error shared by the left?

MEM: I believe so. If the left had wanted, it could have defeated the Shining Path. In this country, it is the only movement capable of defeating the Shining Path.

Q: Why is that?

MEM: Because in the face of the ideas put forward by the right, which the poor cannot identify with, the only alternative is the left. Before it divided, of course. They are the ones who have associated themselves most with the neediest, poorest people. In the wake of the left's division, the Shining Path has advanced. Many people felt tricked, disillusioned, and they haven't found another alternative. Some in poor neighborhoods look at the Shining Path from afar and see them as something mythical, fighting for justice. Few see them well from close up. I believe the left bears a serious responsibility for not educating people about the Shining Path. We all know each other. Shining Path militants were among those who renounced their memberships in leftist parties. When the left had an opportunity, its most radical wing didn't want to draw distinctions either. And right now, what left-wing party has made a statement on what happened in Villa? Not one, not one political leader has come to see what is happening with these organizations or to find out how the mothers are, if they want to continue working in the soup kitchens. I don't know what they are doing in their commissions, clowning around. People laugh a little at this posing, but not for long. What we need to do is strengthen grassroots organizations.

Q: You and the Women's Federation leaders are strong and courageous, but many of your neighbors are not as convinced that they should do something.

MEM: If I have courage, it's because the Federation women have given it to me. On the same day that [the Shining Path] put a bomb in our offices, we met. We reacted rapidly. This gave me strength and a sense of worthiness. There, the women agreed to reject and repudiate the Shining Path and even publicly name them. Also, inspired by the example of Villa El Salvador, the metropolitan association of soup kitchens agreed to sponsor a march against hunger and terror.

Q: In Puno, in Ayacucho, grassroots organizations have been weakened by terror, murder. . . .

MEM: In Ayacucho, there were no solid, strong organizations. In Puno, although they were strong, there was a political problem. The Unified Mariátegui Party (PUM) divided. That opened the way for the Shining Path to enter. When the organizations are solid, cohesive, it is very difficult.

Q: Why do you think the subversives' argument mainly attracts young people?

MEM: It's because they make a big show of the mysticism, total dedication. Young people are rebels, impulsive, vehement. To a degree, the Shining Path speaks to their doubts and frustrations. Before, the left was like that: we organized things, we protested. Now, everything is paralyzed. But the majority of young people don't favor their argument. In fact, the majority bet on development, generating their own income. In Villa El Salvador, there are small businesses run by young people. But it's true that the poorest are most receptive to the Shining Path's argument.

Q: The Shining Path is attempting to create a ring of hunger in the "human settlements" that surround Lima. How will the soup kitchens and the "Glass of Milk" committees combat terror?

MEM: If the Shining Path believes the soup kitchens will close, they are wrong. Where will a mother go to eat if not there? That's why when I hear that they will close the kitchens, I reply that it is impossible. People go there in order to survive. Those that don't eat there starve to death.

Q: How can the Shining Path be fought?

MEM: I believe that we women have a lot of strength. If we believe in what we are building, there's no reason to be afraid. We are working for the well-being of our people, solidarity, justice. I believe it's necessary for us to debate Shining Path members. I have done it. I say to them, "If you are ready to give up your lives, many other people also are and in this way fight for development and justice, but without terror and murder." That's why I no longer consider the Shining Path a revolutionary group, but just a terrorist group.

Q: Have you organized urban patrols?

MEM: Yes. We are organizing neighborhood watch committees. We are also taking measures within our organizations—we know each other.

Q: These organizations will serve in an intelligence capacity to later press charges through the police. . . .

MEM: There is no trust in the police in this country. They use violence and very often murder. . . . They have much yet to do to gain the confidence of the people. Let them give justice to the "disappeared" and murdered. Then we would be able to believe in these forces of order. Since the Shining Path murders grassroots leaders, the people themselves can teach them a lesson without killing them. But the defeat of the Shining Path must be political and ideological. They are not just fighting militarily. A distinct alternative has to emerge in the face of the Shining Path's political proposal. That's why I say it's necessary to galvanize the left.

Q: The Shining Path has infiltrated some grassroots organizations. . . .

MEM: But it's minimal. For a while, they may not be identified, but once they enter the debate, one can rapidly identify them. In addition, they have been defeated politically in many areas. I invite them to reflect on their position. They are bearing the country toward more misery. If there is a Shining Path member who believes in equality, in a better world, I ask him or her to think more. I don't believe they all are murderers.

Q: Haven't we already spent eleven years on this plan? This argument is too altruistic and doesn't work with the Shining Path. Aren't you being too impractical?

MEM: We must continue to combat the Shining Path, reject their terrorist acts. But one cannot combat terror with terror. We must also call for dialogue and reflection. Political parties are not monolithic and impenetrable—this is for outside consumption. Within the Shining Path, there are currents and factions, and this is something we can take advantage of.

Q: Does the municipality of Villa El Salvador coordinate with the ministries of defense and the interior?

MEM: No. It is necessary to reorganize the police force and make it more effective. We don't trust it or believe in it. Within the municipality, we are organizing a defense committee for life and peace. We are going to hold a forum. What is important is that all the sectors in Villa realize right now what violence is. The municipality is working well in this respect.

Q: Have you been threatened by the Shining Path?

MEM: I am under permanent attack by *El Diario*. The mayor and former mayor, Michel Azcueta, are also under attack.[2]

Q: How have political parties failed to confront subversion?

MEM: It is not their priority. They are more worried about their speeches, their personal lives, the official scene. Problems as serious as the economic situation and terror are blocked out by commissions, which I don't condemn, but it's a question of priorities. They are completely separated from the popular movement.

Q: There are some who think that the Shining Path will continue murdering grassroots leaders. Is this opinion too pessimistic?

MEM: Since they have murdered peasants and activists in the past, I believe that this has become part of their way of behaving. As they say, it's a tactic. Yes, I believe they will continue. In order to take Lima, they must murder leaders.

Q: Would you leave your position?

MEM: Absolutely not, it's part of my life. Some people ask me if I am afraid. Sometimes I am, but I have a lot of strength and moral force. I have always been ready to give my life. I have faith. If women are responding to this call in Lima, something can be done. If people organize, pool their efforts, we can defeat the Shining Path. It won't be easy, but neither is it impossible.

Notes

1 *El Diario* was a newspaper, published clandestinely, that functioned as the official voice of the Shining Path.
2 A year after Moyano's murder, her replacement as vice mayor was also killed by Shining Path militants. In 1993, militants attacked and wounded Azcueta, who survived and continues to work in Villa.

PEASANTS AT WAR

Ponciano del Pino

One of the key developments of the early 1990s was the rise in the southern Andes of rural militias to combat the Shining Path. Originally known as Comités de Defensa Civil, or Civil Defense Committees—and later as rondas campesinas *after the very different peasant patrols organized against thievery in the north—the first of these groups was started in 1983 by the military, which often forced reluctant peasants to fight. By the early 1990s, the patrols had taken on a substantial degree of autonomy, particularly in the Apurímac, the subtropical Ayacucho valley populated by poor Andean migrants over the past twenty years. In the eyes of historian Ponciano del Pino, these militias imposed a hard-won peace against the dramatic background of drug trafficking, evangelical Protestantism, desperate poverty, and terror by both the Shining Path and the military.*

Judgment Day shall come. And then, all who invoke the name of the Lord shall be saved.
—Acts 2:21, inscription over the door of the Presbyterian church in Quimbiri, Apurímac Valley

During 1983 and 1984, terror dominated the Apurímac valley. Bodies in varying states of decay floated daily down the river. When fishermen ran into them, they simply let them drift by, without any interest or curiosity. "*Todos se acostumbraban,*" everyone was used to it, recall many inhabitants of this coffee- and then coca-growing valley in the jungle foothills 250 miles southwest of Lima.

Although few had any love for the Shining Path guerrillas, many began to refer to army and navy troops as "mercenaries," like men in the *Rambo*-style movies they saw in *videocines* [makeshift movie theaters, often the front room of a house, where videos are shown] in the town of San Francisco, as if it were impossible for Peruvian soldiers to be so cruel and

Figure 40. Patrollers from a civil defense committee in the foothills
of the Apurímac Valley. Photograph by Orin Starn.

bloodthirsty, committing massacres like those in Sivia and Llochegua in
1984. The brutality of what historian Alberto Flores Galindo called this
"colonial military" was compounded by their racism toward the dark-
skinned locals, most of whom were poor migrants from the highlands of
Ayacucho and Junín to this frontier valley on the eastern Andean slope.[1]

More than a thousand died in these two years alone. The toll was compounded by epidemics aggravated by a scarcity of money, food, and medicine. Children were especially devastated by tuberculosis, malaria, and
typhoid fever. Peasants tell of days when three or even five children perished. Nostalgia for the past and fatalism about the future gripped the
valley. The years ahead seemed to augur only war without end.

Over the next four years, however, the Apurímac witnessed a remarkable transformation. Civilian militias called Comités de Defensa Civil, or
Civil Defense Committees (cdcs), grew into a powerful force in the valley, propelled by an explosion of disenchantment with the Shining Path
and frustration with the inability of the state to put down the Maoists.
By 1990, there would be cdcs, armed with homemade guns called *hechi-
zos* as well as FALS, Kalashnikovs, Winchesters, and shotguns donated by

the government, in 280 villages. Comandos Especiales, or Special Commands, were established in some parts of the valley, permanent armies of local youth paid by merchants, state employees, peasants, traders, and even drug traffickers. Between civilians and the Special Commands, twenty thousand were armed to fight, and the Shining Path was expelled from most of the valley. In this jungle region, one of the most devastated by Peru's fourteen-year civil war, a fragile peace prevailed.

Although the rise of the CDCs is a complicated story, most remarkable, perhaps, is the protagonism of evangelical churches, what Peruvians call Protestant denominations, as diverse as Presbyterians and Pentecostals. Roughly half of the valley's peasants are evangelicals. They were the first to refuse to collaborate with the guerrillas in a struggle that became a holy war against the Antichrist, defined in the Apurímac as the Shining Path.

When the Shining Path arrived in the early 1980s, cadres ordered evangelicals to abandon their faith. Local youths had to go away with the Maoists to carry out "actions": assisting in propaganda meetings or assassinating suspected "stool pigeons," "exploiters," community leaders, and government authorities who, the guerrillas said, stood in the way of their conquest of power.

One of the first reactions of the *hermanos*, or "brothers," as the Protestant faithful called themselves, was to tell the Shining Path they had no right to take human life. Killing was not necessary for salvation. Christ died for us all on the cross. Some even prayed to the Holy Spirit for the *senderistas'* souls, that they might leave the "path of evil."

There was a fundamental contradiction between allegiance to Christ and God and to Gonzalo and Revolution, and it was sharpened by the killing of evangelicals who dared resist. In the village of Quisto, for instance, the Shining Path arrived and commanded everyone, without exception, to join the armed struggle. As Vidal Trujillano, a Presbyterian who had spread the gospel in Ayacucho's jungles since 1957, remembers: "A brother came forward and told them: 'I am an evangelical. I only believe in God, and I refuse to accept your doctrines.' He was executed with a single shot before the crowd. This should be an example, they said."

Stories of martyrdom were common. One could give up the body, because the soul belonged to God. Evangelical Protestantism turned out to be a faith even stronger than faith in the Shining Path. Intimidation and terror were not as effective with the evangelicals as with other peasants, who could be coerced into collaborating out of fear.

The final decision to fight, however, was difficult for many evangelicals. How could they take up arms without disobeying the gospel? "Thou shalt not kill," commanded the Bible. Yet the Maoists had by 1984 already closed five Presbyterian churches in the Ayna–San Francisco area and nine in Unión-Pichari, often attacking the temples in the middle of services with machine guns and hand grenades. In the context of constant attacks, the pastor in Anchihuay's Pentecostal church found another message from the Bible, God's word in the face of the Shining Path's massacres. He told his flock of the war between David and the Philistines. The Philistines persecuted and killed thousands of Israelites. Ordered by God, David organized a small army to fight the heathen enemy. This message was soon adopted by almost all of the evangelical churches: in times of war, violence in the defense of the faith is not a sin. The brothers could take the offensive, organize, respond to the enemy.

Depicting the *senderistas* as worse than the Philistines, the words of Juan Reynoso, an early CDC organizer and the Pentecostal pastor in San Agustín, reflect the ferocity of the subsequent fight: "The Shining Path is like a demon, worse than a devil. They are worse. There is no name for them, because they eat human flesh, the liver. . . . They suck blood." Vidal Trujillano concurs: "The *senderista* is diabolical. He is no longer a real man. He is like a dog, that's how he is. Like an animal. They do not care whether they live or die, it's all the same to them."

By 1984, the evangelicals had turned the Shining Path's own tactics against them. "For every Christian, one hundred *terrucos* will die," became their motto. Crystallized was the belief that the struggle was in God's name, to defend the gospel and Christianity. In the words of one *rondero*, or patroller: "I was no longer a simple fighter, but a fighter for God, under God's protection." There are innumerable stories about God's protection in the war, like this one from a peasant in the village of Anchihuay: "The Shining Path arrived at a brother's house, they surrounded it. But this brother had a foreboding. Inside his house, he began to pray, and the *senderistas* all of a sudden seemed to see armed soldiers in the house and fled at the sight of them. That was God's protection. In truth, they weren't soldiers. They were heavenly armies protecting those who fear God." In this view, the rebels shriveled before the Lord's wrath, and faith spurred the evangelicals to wage their crusade against the Shining Path, God's enemy.

Evangelicals were pivotal in the CDCs not just in Anchihuay and San Francisco, but also in Llochegua, Sivia, Boca Mantaro, Santa Rosa, and Miraflores, among other places. They could be found among both the

Figure 41. Evangelicals mourn a pastor murdered by the Shining Path, 1985.
(Courtesy of Jesus Quispe, *Caretas*)

rank and file and the leadership. A Catholic storekeeper from San Francisco remembers that "the evangelicals were ready to die whenever and wherever they had to. Their souls were with God, and they were with God."

Realizing the threat to their cause, the Shining Path vowed to "finish off the evangelicals." In one of many confrontations, some sixty *senderistas* descended upon the Pentecostal church of Qano on July 27, 1984. Shirtless, their bodies and faces were painted with *achiote* and shoeblack.[2] Surrounding the church, they threw dynamite at the door and opened fire on the parishioners with pistols, shotguns, and submachine guns. "This is how the miserable traitors of the people die," read a sign left by the rebels. Six evangelicals and a Catholic died. Seven were left wounded, including Alfredo Vásquez, the pastor. Several of the parishioners remember Vásquez shouting at the Shining Path in the middle of the attack: "We serve God. We don't want two masters."

Even at the decade's end, after the CDCs had expelled the Shining Path from much of the valley, the danger did not end. In 1990, for instance, the rebels attacked the Presbyterian church in the village of Teresa, setting it afire with a parishioner inside. By this time, however, attacks were less frequent, and the death toll from the war in the entire valley dropped from 569 in 1985 to 95 in 1992. Against the odds, the evangelicals had spearheaded a powerful crusade against the Maoists. People in the Apurímac began to speak of a new tranquility instead of referring in biblical terms to the apocalypse and the Last Judgment as just a few years earlier.

Before the war, the largest organization in the valley was the Peasant Federation of the Apurímac River Valley (FECVRA). Unlike the FECVRA, which represented only peasants, the CDCs have drawn together a variety of interests and classes. Evangelicals. Priests. Coca farmers. Truckers. Merchants. Shopowners. It may seem a fragile coalition, and some observers have predicted that the CDCs will dissolve when the Shining Path is finally defeated.

But this view underestimates the CDCs. Over these years of war, they have expanded beyond their initial military role. Leaders were elected in local assemblies and arbitrate family and land disputes as well as supervise small public works projects. In April 1992, cholera broke out in Palmapampa, killing ten people. The CDC president traveled to Lima to request medicine and rehydration salts. That same month, the CDC of Pichiwillca, with no funds from the state, organized the construction of a health clinic. This is not to say, of course, that the CDCs did not have an array of problems, from the marginalization of women from leadership positions to the conversion of CDC chiefs into ambitious and sometimes violent *caudillos*, or bosses. Clearly, however, they became a rallying point for identity and pride, and a vehicle for autonomy and self-government in the valley.

As part of the transformations of the war years, the armed forces developed a better relationship with valley inhabitants. Although there continued to be cases of torture and "disappearance," the indiscriminate terror of the first years ceased. For their part, most civilians recognized that these were not the same killers of 1983 and 1984, or the ones who fled in 1986 and 1987 in the face of a guerrilla counteroffensive.

In the meantime, however, relations with the police worsened. Perhaps because they never fought directly in the war, they did not learn from it, and their conduct remained marked by corruption and lawlessness. Most policemen simply wanted the CDCs to disappear. Jealous of their own authority, they did not recognize that the organizations were becoming a fixture of valley life, fueled by the *ronderos*' secret knowledge of the price they paid for victory: the lives of hundreds of relatives and friends, a struggle they waged on their own, orphaned by the state that was chartered to protect them.

Although it would be hard to overestimate the role of the evangelicals, the consolidation of the CDCs points to another thread in their complicated history: the coca trade. In the early 1980s, illegal coca cultivation began to spread in the valley. Production was triggered by growing demand abroad and an assured market for coca paste. This demand was in stark contrast to the miserable prices for coffee, cacao, and peanuts, older valley exports. Also, coca is easy to grow, allowing peasants to spend more time patrolling in the CDCs. Ironically, the very logic of the war encouraged the expansion of coca production. Although precise figures are unavailable, more than half of the valley's economy rested on coca as of 1990. Marintaria, Iribamba, and Palmapampa, among other places, turned into drug centers, where farmers came to sell the leaf and traders dealt in coca paste. As of 1992, at least five Cessna flights a month flew from the valley to Colombia, each carrying between 1,200 and 2,000 pounds of paste, worth between $50,000 and $85,000.

Drug dollars helped to buy the weapons used by the CDCs to drive out the Shining Path. Automatic rifles and submachine guns were essential for the *ronderos*, who fought well-armed rebels. Some were purchased through impromptu schemes. The CDCs in Qano, for instance, cleared the dirt highway into town of rock falls and mudslides. Truck drivers then paid a toll, which was invested in two Kalashnikovs. Other weapons were bankrolled by the more prosperous drug growers and traffickers in Palmapampa and Sivia. In exchange, they counted on CDC protection. As one of the employees at Sivia's health clinic summed up this quid pro quo, "When *ronderos* ask for arms, food, rope, or whatever, the narcos give it to them right away."

In Palmapampa, every Cessna that landed in 1993 reportedly paid the CDCs $5,000. The money was invested in munitions, food, and trips to Ayacucho and Lima to ask for government support. The equation in the Apurímac valley turns out to be exactly the opposite of that in the Huallaga valley, where the Shining Path milked the drug economy for its own ends. In the Apurímac, by contrast, drug money financed the war against the Maoists, and the alliance between the *ronderos* and the traffickers flourished all the more in the absence of viable development plans from the state. When the Fujimori government signed an antinarcotics treaty with the United States in 1991, the vast majority of the inhabitants of the valley opposed it. They would defend their economic privileges, some said, "to the death." Coca had brought a measure of income to the valley and financed the war against the Shining Path, and few wanted to return to those worst of times of the early 1980s.

Perhaps the final irony of the nexus between CDCs and coca is that not everyone benefited equally. A new drug class equipped with Toyotas and high-tech communications equipment emerged in the newly peaceful climate. Most profits were invested in Ayacucho or Lima, though, leaving the valley just as poor in appearance as before the drug boom, mostly without decent highways, electricity, running water, or other basic services.

The evangelicals, who led the resistance against the Maoists, largely shunned the coca economy and its rewards. Though a few cultivated the leaf, many believed it was a sin and refused to plant it, even though their congregations, full of Quechua-speaking migrants, remained among the valley's poorest residents. The reasoning mirrors the reasoning that led them to resist the guerrillas' message in the first place: their reward lay in heaven, not in earthly revolution or wealth. As two young Pentecostals explained it, the Bible teaches, "Ye shall not reap riches on earth, where urine and termites corrupt, but reach salvation in heaven."

It is impossible to predict whether the CDCs will continue to function with the apparent defeat of the Shining Path. But given the unlikely series of events that led to their growth in the first place—Maoists bent on converting Peru into a kind of Chinese utopia paired with the almost total retreat of the state—it shouldn't surprise anyone to see the CDCs survive beyond the war, perhaps reinventing themselves in some new form still not yet clear.

Notes

Many of the places and names in this essay have been changed for reasons of security.

1 Alberto Flores Galindo, *Buscando un Inca* (Lima: Instituto de Apoyo Agrario, 1987), p. 395.
2 *Achiote* is a red-colored dye made of the plant of the same name.

TIME OF RECKONING

Salomón Lerner

The unexpected fall of President Alberto Fujimori followed by the election of former shoeshine boy Alejandro Toledo in 2001 brought a fresh look at the forces that had torn Peru apart. That year, Peru established a government-appointed Truth and Reconciliation Commission to investigate the "time of fear." In April 2001, its seven commissioners began holding public hearings in the cities and towns that had experienced the worst violence. Unlike a similar commission in South Africa, which explicitly linked truth telling to justice, Peru's commission was limited to collecting accounts and making recommendations for future change. But the response was massive and emotional. Often in Quechua and with pain still fresh, thousands of Peruvians spoke, sometimes for the first time, about what had happened. Based on these testimonies and other information, the commission concluded in 2003 that more than sixty-nine thousand people had perished, a number that shocked even the most attentive observers of the war. In this emotional 2003 speech before an overflow crowd including Peru's top military and political leaders, commission president Salomón Lerner formally delivered the final report to Alejandro Toledo, Peru's president.

Ladies and Gentlemen:

The history of Peru contains more than its fair share of crisis and sorrow, of real national humiliation. As documented in the report we present today to our fellow Peruvians, the events of the last two decades of the twentieth century were among the most shameful and horrifying of all. They are a black badge of horror and disgrace for the government and this country as a whole.

Two years ago, when the Truth and Reconciliation Commission was established, we faced a vast and difficult task: to investigate and to make public the truth about the mass violence of the two decades beginning

Figure 42. Mothers protest the disappearance of loved ones, Ayacucho, 1985.
(Courtesy of Ernesto Jiménez)

in 1980, when the Communist Party of Peru–Shining Path launched its war to overthrow the government. Now, at our labor's end, the commission has concluded that the death toll in those twenty years was at least sixty-nine thousand Peruvians, between those killed by rebel groups and government forces. It has been our task, Mr. President, to record, one by one, the names of those thousands of vanished Peruvians, our brothers and sisters. This list, which we give to the country today, is too long for anyone in Peru to continue talking about "mistakes" or "excesses" on the part of those who committed the crimes. And the truth and scale of what we have uncovered is also simply too stark and overwhelming for any government official or person in the street to continue to deny.

These statistics are horrifying. But they do not convey the whole truth. We have learned that three out of every four victims were peasants whose native tongue was Quechua. As we Peruvians know, these are the people in our society who have been for centuries ignored by the government and urban society, the powerful and privileged in our nation. The intense violence in the Andes was fueled by a profound contempt for the poor and for dark-skinned Peruvians that is shared by members of both the Communist Party of Peru–Shining Path and the police and military. It was, in this sense, part of the pattern of the dehumanization of the marginalized that has for so long been woven into the fabric of daily life in this country. Much has been written about racism and discrimination in Peru. Little have government officials or any of us done to fight this plague. Our report shows the country and the world that it is impossible to live with hatred, that this is a sickness carrying unspeakable costs. From today, the names of the dead and disappeared will be here, in these pages, to remind us of this.

Who Was to Blame?

We must be the first to admit a collective blame shared by all of us who did not ask enough questions in the years of violence. The commission has nonetheless named many specific people, both guerrillas and members of government forces, responsible for crimes and violations of human rights. We want our countrymen to know that we are passing on these names to the proper authorities, in each case following the procedures laid down by the law for criminal prosecution. The commission demands that the justice system act immediately to prosecute these cases, free of vengeance, but with energy and purpose. Peru—like any society emerging from a period of political violence and the abuse of human rights—cannot allow impunity. Impunity is incompatible with the dignity of any democratic nation.

At the same time, the crimes committed were not the acts of a deviant few acting outside the will of their organizations. Our investigation shows that the Communist Party of Peru–Shining Path foresaw village massacres as part of its strategy to achieving a single objective—power—that the rebels considered more important than the life of any single human being. What the Shining Path called "strategic reason"—and its will to kill and destroy in the service of revolution—was a death sentence for thousands of innocents. The will to destroy was rooted deeply in the ideology of the Communist Party of Peru–Shining Path, in the very nature of the organization. In interviews with us, imprisoned Shining Path leaders have unapologetically described their readiness to kill and even commit acts of the most extreme cruelty as weapons for achieving their revolutionary aims. Because of its inherently criminal and totalitarian character, and contempt for even the most basic humanitarian standards, the Communist Party of Peru–Shining Path has no place in a democratic and civilized nation like the Peru we wish to build.

Faced with this violent insurgency, the government was bound to protect the population—its most elemental duty—with the force of the law. No democracy wants torture and concentration camps; instead, democracies should endeavor to craft measures that maintain order while ensuring the right to life and dignity of every citizen. But this is not how our security forces saw it. We have arrived at the conviction that the police and military committed systematic, widespread violations of human rights—and that evidence exists showing that crimes against humanity as well as violations of international humanitarian law also took place. Extrajudicial executions, disappearances, torture, massacres, rape, and other equally horrible atrocities constitute a pattern of human rights violations. The Peruvian government and its representatives must recognize this in order to make amends.

So much death and suffering cannot be explained as the action of a police and military force acting alone. One must have, in addition, the complicity or at least the consent of those with the power to prevent such crimes. Investigation has convinced us that much violence could have been prevented had it not been for the indifference, passivity, or simple ineptitude of those who occupied the highest public offices in this land. Those who swore to uphold the Constitution chose with too much frequency to cede control of the counterinsurgency to the armed forces. Exceptional emergency was transformed into a permanent norm; unfathomable abuses became commonplace; the innocent were imprisoned; and finally, killing became confused with peace. When the victims of human rights violations protested, the politicians of that time reverted to the old custom of relegating petitions and demands for justice to the same place that the pleas of humble people have always been sent: to the place of forgetting.

In a country like ours, fighting the tendency to forget is a powerful way of serving justice. We are convinced that recovering the truth about the past—even a truth as difficult to acknowledge as the one we were charged to investigate—is a way of moving closer to those democratic ideals that we Peruvians assert with such vehemence and practice with such inconsistency. A democracy not practiced with stubborn regularity loses meaning for its citizens and disappears without tears.

The report that we present to you has been prepared from the thousands of testimonies we gathered across the country, predominantly from poor men and women who opened their doors and hearts to us, who agreed to remember—for the benefit of their fellow citizens—a set of events that anyone would wish to forget. They had the courage to identify those responsible for serious crimes, the integrity to share their pain, and, also, the stubborn desire to insist on, someday, being recognized as Peruvians by their own people. The politicians who lead us would do

Figure 43. Ceremony mourning the dead at a Truth and Reconciliation Commission hearing, 2001. (Courtesy of Luis Gonzáles, *Caretas*)

poorly, we would all do poorly, to pretend that these voices do not exist, to shrug off the demands that they make on us. We must ensure that justice is done in the paired sense of reparations for damages suffered and fair punishment, not revenge, against those responsible. We must also transform our government and society to prevent the repetition of the horror that we have lived through.

By giving this report to you, Mr. President, we trust that we leave it in good hands. It is the truth as far as we have been able to determine it from the understanding and reflection of our fellow citizens. Embracing the moral obligations emanating from this report is a job for a statesman, that is, for a man or woman dedicated to governing for the good of others.

The history recorded here belongs to all of us, and it speaks of what we have been and what we should become.

It is a history that obliges us to move forward with the tasks ahead of us.

This history begins today.

VIII · THE COCAINE ECONOMY

I t is an unassuming bush, with green, elongated leaves and slender branches, a miniature of the northern bay tree. In the subtropical valleys of the eastern Andes, where it flourishes, other plants, like orchids and banana trees, are more lush and eye-catching. Yet for millennia, coca (*Erythroxylum coca*) has been among the most prized of crops by indigenous Peruvians, central to religious rituals and daily life. Chewed with a pinch of lime, called *cal*, the leaf releases a mild dose of cocaine alkaloid, numbing sensory nerves, dulling hunger, and providing a small dose of vitamins absent in a starch-heavy diet.

Ethnobotanists estimate that coca was cultivated as far back as 6000 B.C. Some civilizations buried their dead with a woven bag filled with coca leaves. Under the Incas, coca was considered a privilege and was somewhat restricted. After the conquest, its role in indigenous religion and divination provoked Catholic authorities to ban it as "a plant that the devil invented for the total destruction of the natives." Yet Spanish planters promoted the crop for sale to highland natives, forcing them to work lowland plantations despite high mortality rates because of the lucrative market among the half-starved conscripts in the mines of Huancavelica and Potosí.[1]

By the seventeenth century, coca use was no longer considered an upper-class custom, but a vice to be avoided by anyone claiming to be civilized. As anthropologist Catherine J. Allen has noted, coca chewing marked "the developing boundary between *runa* and *misti*," which remains to this day.[2] Subsequent attempts to limit or ban coca use in Peru have ended in standoffs. Whereas some medical professionals argue that coca is addictive and produces lethargy, others claim that its effects are benign and the leaf an integral part of Andean culture.

It took the West much longer to discover coca, as journalist Jo Ann

Kawell points out in "The Cocaine Economy," reproduced here. Only in 1860 did a German chemist refine pure cocaine, later marketed as a wonder cure for opium addiction, a general anesthetic, an energy tonic, and a headache remedy (a claim of the newly concocted soft drink Coca-Cola). Injected (as done by Arthur Conan Doyle's supersleuth Sherlock Holmes), it produced a burst of clear-headed energy. Although cocaine was officially banned by the U.S. Congress in 1922, its physiological effects were already well established (as Billie Holiday's version of "I Get a Kick Out of You" shows).

But it wasn't until the 1970s, with the drug's growing popularity in the United States as providing a supposedly nonaddictive high, that it became an issue of international importance. Colombian former car thief and grave robber Pablo Escobar turned his criminal genius to building a cartel that linked Peruvian farmers to American trendsetters, flooding Wall Street parties and Hollywood nightclubs with the white powder. At $1,700 a wholesale ounce in 1981, cocaine was too expensive for the poor and middle class until some unknown chemist first cooked "crack," a derivative that stretches cocaine powder into cheap and highly addictive "rocks."[3] Drugs and the violence and crime associated with them became a leading concern of U.S. voters, prompting President Ronald Reagan to declare drugs a "national security threat" in 1986. But the measures adopted to eradicate or suppress drug production and sales have been ineffective—and even comically counterproductive.[4] After all, it was Vladimiro Montesinos, a former Central Intelligence Agency asset and Peruvian President Alberto Fujimori's devious advisor, who himself arranged the 1999 drugs-for-guns swap with Colombia's guerrillas.

Both President Bill Clinton and his successor, George W. Bush, amplified the role of Latin militaries in the drug fight. By the decade's end, the United States had devoted millions of dollars and increasing amounts of weaponry and military might to stop cocaine production "at the source": Peru's Huallaga valley and the Bolivian and Colombian lowlands. But demand in the United States remains robust. In 2004, Peruvian officials admitted that coca production was once again on the increase, and that Colombian traffickers were enticing farmers to diversify to opium poppy to supply American users.

Few of the peasant families who cultivate Peru's crop are ever made wealthy.[5] Yet the drug continues to dramatically affect entire generations, from urban crack babies in the United States to Huallaga families whose farms were converted into Peru's most violent war zone. Although thousands of miles apart in distance as well as culture, south-central Los Angeles and the Huallaga remain tightly bound by a bush: Andean treasure and international villain housed in the same green sheath.

Notes

1 John Hemming, *The Conquest of the Incas* (New York: Harcourt, Brace, Jovanovich, 1970), pp. 367–368.
2 Catherine Allen, *The Hold Life Has* (Washington, D.C.: Smithsonian Institution, 1988), p. 35. In Quechuan, *runa* means the people or indigenous Peruvians and *misti* means Spaniard or white.
3 José María Salcedo, "La coca en su laberinto," *Quehacer*, no. 59 (June–July 1989): 42.
4 See, for instance, "The Drug War: U.S. Programs in Peru Face Serious Obstacles," a report to the U.S. Congress by the General Accounting Office, GAO/NSIAD-92-36, October 1991.
5 Ibán de Rementería, "Tráfico de drogas psicoactivas, crisis cocalera y desarollo alternativo," unpublished paper written for the Andean Commission of Jurists–Peruvian Section, April 4, 1991.

THE HOLD LIFE HAS

Catherine J. Allen

The highland ritual of coca chewing is as old—and intricate—as a Japanese tea ceremony. As anthropologist Catherine Allen recounts, in Sonqo, a Cuzco village, the ritual begins with the careful preparation of the k'intu, *or coca bundle, and involves not only an often elaborate invocation to local spirits but also a nuts-and-bolts understanding of social hierarchies, so that leaves are extended to kin or guests in the proper order. In sharp contrast to coca's image as a leaf that causes chaos— when it is refined into cocaine—in Sonqo, it is part of the fabric that binds society together.*

At five A.M. one March morning in 1976, I left Sonqo to return to the United States. Don Luis was accompanying me to Cuzco, but he sent me on ahead of him. He walked faster than I and would easily overtake me on the muddy paths, which were drenched after three months of heavy rain. The sun had not yet fully risen, and a heavy fog was rising out of the valley. As I walked over the now familiar footpath, wondering when and if I would return there again, I felt as though I were saying good-bye to the *Tirakuna*, whose names I had come to know and who had tolerated my intrusion.

But in the fog the *Tirakuna* had changed entirely, or so it seemed to me. I could hardly see my feet in front of me and slipped off the path several times. The hills and ridges loomed and dipped around me strangely, and for a while I got completely lost. As the fog lifted I found myself on a path below the one I had intended to follow and had to scramble up a long way to get onto the muddy highway where I was to meet Luis. (Actually, "highway" is a misnomer, for the road was completely impassable to motor vehicles, scored as it was with ruts and washouts.)

Luis caught up with me, marveling at my slow progress, and I commented in relief how good it was to be walking on the road. He looked at me with his characteristic deadpan irony.

"It's a wonderful road," he replied. "Just wonderful. Especially now."

We were clambering through a rut so deep we had to climb in and out of it while the mud came almost to our knees.

It was hardly a propitious leave-taking. Later in Cuzco, I asked Don Luis why the fog had come up and confused me like that. Were the *Tirakuna* displeased with me?

"You still don't blow your coca *k'intus* properly," Luis answered. And again, he showed me how to do a proper *phukuy* (ritual blowing). Let me pass on what I learned from him.

To make the *k'intu* you choose three or more of the best leaves from your coca bundle. If your leaves are broken and ragged, you make do with them the best you can, but if they are moldy you throw them out. You place the leaves, shiny side up, one on top of the other and hold the little bundle between your thumb and forefinger. If you offer the *k'intu* to a companion, you present the shiny side. If you consume it yourself, you hold the shiny side toward yourself.

You wave the *k'intu* a few inches from your mouth and blow on it softly. This is *phukuy*, ritual blowing. As you blow, you make your invocation. Actually, "invocation" is not quite accurate; your words are more like the address on a letter, for they identify the recipients of the coca's fortifying essence.

Your *phukuy* should always include the Earth (*Pacha, Pacha Mama, Santa Tira, Pacha Tira,* etc.); the Sacred Places (*Tirakuna, Apukuna, Rugrarkuna,* etc., or as specific named Places); and your *ayllu*, either the neighborhood or the community. The *Machula Aulanchis* and *chullpas* can stand in for the *ayllu* to fulfill the last rule.

"*Pacha Mama, Tirakuna, Sonqo*" is a good basic *phukuy*.

You can add a request as you direct the *sami* to its powerful recipients: "Let me have a good trip," or "Please make it stop raining." I long failed to realize how much concentration is needed when an important request is at hand, for you must focus single-mindedly on what is being asked while directing the request via the coca's *sami*. Erasmo prides himself on the effectiveness of his *phukuy* and has pointed out instances when his request was quickly granted. Before I left Cuzco in 1984, he offered to do *phukuy* for my trip and asked me for the exact time my plane was scheduled to leave.

Figure 44. During the Feast of St. John, Serafeo (center left) and Valentina (center right) share coca *k'intus* and *trago* with their grown son Santos (left). (Courtesy of Catherine J. Allen)

"*Noqaqa yachani allinta*" ("I know how to do it very well"), he said with the pleased air of one who can offer a significant favor.

Luis instructed me that in Cuzco I should blow to the local *Tirakuna*: to the ancient fortress of Sacsahuamán and to Calle Sapphi, the street where my room was located. "*Santa Tira, Apu Sacsahuaman, Calle Sapphi*" was a respectable Cuzco *phukuy* and would ensure that my immediate environment would feel kindly toward me.

"We do this for our well-being" ("*Hina ruwanchis allin kawsayninchispaq*"), Luis commented as he blew on his coca *k'intu*.

The Etiquette of Coca Chewing

Hallpay provides a frame within which peaceful and constructive social interaction takes place. An invitation to chew coca is an invitation to social intercourse. Friends who meet on the road pause to chat and to chew coca; men gathering to work in a field settle down to chew coca beforehand. When serious or troubling problems are at hand, *hallpakuy*, or the shared chewing of coca leaves, expresses the participants' commitment to rational and peaceful discourse. For the solitary individual, the brief *hallpay* break provides a meditative interlude in which to gather stray thoughts and prepare mentally for the task ahead.

Coca's uses are hedged about with ceremony. The exact etiquette for chewing coca varies from region to region, but whatever the specific social forms, coca is always shared. Among the Quechua-speaking Qollahuaya of northern Bolivia, for example, men exchange coca bags with one another while women chew from a common pile. In the Cuzco region, both men and women exchange coca *k'intus* with prescribed phrases of invitation and thanks.

For example, let's say that you and I sit down to chew coca. We first each make a *k'intu* and perform the ritual *phukuy* before chewing it. Then we make *k'intus* for each other. I offer my *k'intu* to you by saying, "*Hallpakusunchis.*" ("Let's chew coca together.") You receive the *k'intu* with thanks and do *phukuy* again with this *k'intu* before chewing it. While chewing, you prepare a *k'intu* for me. Ideally, all *k'intus* are reciprocated.

We both gradually add leaves to the wads in our cheeks, and after a while we add a tiny bit of *llipt'a*, hard compressed ash resembling a charcoal briquette, to activate the coca's stimulating alkaloids. After twenty to thirty minutes a good-sized wad has been built up, and if there is work to be done, we thank each other and get on with the job. The wads stay in our mouths for about forty-five minutes, after which we carefully remove them and gently throw them away on the ground. One never spits coca. *Runakuna* find this unthinkable. Neither should coca be swallowed. For me this is the hard part. Julian likes to tease me by demanding that I display my coca wad and then scolding me for having inadvertently swallowed most of it—like an adolescent not yet *santuyuq* (possessing skill) in coca chewing.

Hallpay is performed approximately five times daily as part of the normal routine. *Runakuna* chew coca after their three daily meals and pause for a coca break in midmorning and midafternoon. Although these coca breaks function much like our coffee breaks, the ceremony surrounding them has social and religious dimensions that the coffee break lacks. If we said grace over our coffee and exchanged cups the similarity would be stronger. Coca chewers share *k'intus* with each other in a tangible expression of their social and moral relationship, while simultaneously sharing the leaf's *sami* with the Earth and the Sacred Places.

The social group is defined and organized by the *k'intu* exchanges, for social ranking is implied by the order in which *k'intus* are offered. High-status individuals should receive *k'intus* before those of lower status. In practice, the relative status of participants is seldom clear-cut. Men rank higher than women, but age ranks higher than youth. A respected old lady may receive *k'intu* before a callow young man (who may or may not feel slighted by the action). Guests rank higher than coresidents, and the passing of many *cargos* [ritual duties] ranks higher than marginal participation in the *cargo* system. Wealth itself confers high status only indirectly, by facilitating the passage of many *cargos*. The size of the gathering and the distance the participants are seated from one another are complicating factors. One should rise and carry *k'intu* to a very high status person, whereas companions of equal status who sit at a distance may be politely bypassed.

Any actual coca-chewing session calls for a complicated spur-of-the-moment combination of various criteria, forcing each participant to organize the situation in hierarchical terms. Conversely, each person is put in his place by his companions. *K'intu* exchanges therefore define a gathering of individuals as a social group; they commit each individual—for the duration of the *hallpay*, at least—to group membership, and they situate him or her relative to other participants.

In Sonqo a respected *kuraq tayta* (community elder) like Don Inocencio Quispe can expect to join a gathering and receive *k'intus* from all of the coca-chewing adults, even when they have to rise to bring the *k'intus* to him. Inocencio has long passed the essential *cargos*, including those of *alcalde* [mayor] and Corpus Christi sponsor. He is a hardworking, vigorous man in late middle age, strong-minded, pious, and well-to-do. He is reputed to have seen the cathedral submerged in Lake Q'eskay, a sight vouchsafed only to the virtuous. His attendance at the ceremonial table at all public occasions is taken for granted.

If more than one elder is present, one tries to prepare their *k'intus* at the same time and present the first to the elder sitting nearest. These elders may precede community officials with the exception of the *alcalde*, who, when he is present in his official capacity, always takes precedence.

I found that I was ranked in various ways: as the person of highest status in the group; as the woman of highest status (that is, on the border between men and women), or occasionally as the person of lowest status. The older, more traditionally minded men consistently ranked me with the women even when, as a trouser-clad guest, I was seated with the men. Don Francisco Quispe used to pass me by with a significant glance, and once when I got up and sat on the ground next to his daughter he muttered his audible approval. Women often preferred to treat me as the highest-ranking woman rather than as a man. *Runakuna* who did not like my being there shared their *k'intus* with me last, usually only in response to my offering one first. A *k'intu* does not go unreciprocated, even from persons one dislikes.

All this changed when I switched from blue jeans to the traditional black *pollera* (skirt). Suddenly everyone ranked me as a woman—usually as a young, low-ranking woman. By putting aside my Westernized man's clothing I lost my senior status, a move that was met with universal approval (among *runakuna*, that is; the schoolteachers were horrified). The lower status was, in its way, a compliment and a mark of acceptance.

Since it is important that a coca-chewing session be respectful, relaxed, amicable, and meditative, *runakuna* rarely use coca-chewing etiquette to harass one another. Occasionally it seemed to me that one individual, with malice of forethought, presented a companion with *k'intu* after *k'intu*, forcing the recipient to spend the whole session composing and offering *k'intus* in return. Such villainy is easily thwarted when the teaser is of lower status, as the victim can simply stop reciprocating. Sometimes I felt put upon when a group of three or four chewers showered *k'intus* upon me at the same time, forcing me (1) to decide from whom to accept the first *k'intus*; (2) to receive the *k'intus*, complete with *phukuy*, in rapid succession; not to mention (3) to set to work composing and offering *k'intus* as fast as possible, surely a comical sight. Nevertheless, I am not sure my companions intended to torment me. I have seen elders join a group and receive the same treatment, simply by virtue of their late arrival.

Orientation in Space and Time

K'intu sharing cements a relationship with the fellow members of one's group, whereas *phukuy* draws the human actor into a relationship with the Earth and the Sacred Places. The invocation of animated geography provides a particular kind of orientation in space. The "grammar" of *phukuy* requires that one call upon the vast, generalized Earth, upon local Places, and upon more distant regional Places. *Runakuna* orient themselves within a nested, hierarchical sense of space as they direct their attention to local Places who punctuate their landscape as well as to the high *Apus* who overlook a larger region.

When *runakuna* travel they approach unfamiliar *Tirakuna* in other localities with a mixture of interest and apprehension. They know these Places are likely to look upon outsiders with hostility, or at best with indifference. They assiduously blow their *k'intus* to the new locality by way of introducing themselves. Basilia was doing me a favor when she instructed me to blow my coca to Antaqaqa as I first entered Sonqo. On another occasion, I upset my companions by wandering off while they were doing *phukuy* in the high *puna* before crossing a bad-tempered mountain pass named Panapunku. My disregard for the placation of important and hostile powers could have gotten us all in trouble.

In contrast, when *runakuna* chew coca during their routine activities, with familiar *Tirakuna* around them, their *phukuys* are brief and pro forma. A chewer simply whispers under his breath while blowing the leaves, without calling attention to the words. A loud, elaborate *phukuy* is likely to be directed as much to one's companions as to the *Tirakuna*. The invocation provides a way to confide anxieties without having to admit them directly. For example, the night before he was to travel to Cuzco for a confrontation with a mestizo official, Don Luis blew over his *k'intu*, asking that he might have a good trip. This expressed his nervousness and opened the way for supportive behavior on our part without his having to come out and say, "I'm scared." In other contexts, one may find a whole group of chewers passionately, if quietly, asking the *Tirakuna* to make it stop raining, to help them find their lost animal, and so forth. In this way, they commiserate over their troubles, create an atmosphere of mutual support, and assure each other of their goodwill.

Phukuy provides a good opportunity to show off rhetorical prowess (Rufina used to giggle appreciatively when Luis launched into a long-winded *phukuy*). The best invocations, however, use verbal artistry to impress one's companions while, at a deeper level, communicating precise information to the *Tirakuna*. The following poetic invocation by Erasmo reveals a dense semantic structure:

> *Pacha Tira Mama, Machula Aulanchis, Aukikuna. Manan para paramanchu tarpunaypaq.* (*Pacha Tira Mama, Machula Aulanchis, Aukikuna.* Don't let it rain on my potato planting.)

Every word of this invocation expresses Erasmo's preoccupation with planting. The word order is significant as well. "*Pacha Tira*" shows his awareness that the Earth may be dangerous during planting time, and he placates her with the addition of "*Mama*." He then calls on *Machula Aulanchis*, who as fertilizing ancestors concerned with the potato crop are particularly important to Erasmo at the moment. He calls on the

Sacred Places last, using a generic title, *Aukikuna*, which is occasionally applied to the ancestors as well as to the local Places. The invocation orients Erasmo to his current activities by communicating his intentions and needs to the categories of deities most important to him at that moment.

The *runakuna* orient themselves similarly each time they chew coca before beginning work. Coca chewing focuses their minds on the task and helps them articulate its nature. Coca chewing also marks off the passage of time. The length of a chew, about forty-five minutes, can be used as a temporal unit. The sequence of coca-chewing sessions—after breakfast, in midmorning, after the midday meal, in midafternoon, and at night after dinner—divides the day into longer intervals.

On a more distant, or greater, dimension of time, the invocation of the *ayllu* directs the chewer to ancestral and parental-like figures such as *Machula Aulanchis* and Antaqaqa. Moreover, the act of chewing coca declares the chewer's cultural loyalty to and identification with traditions handed down from the Incas, beings of the past and future, who are hidden from the present.

In *phukuy*, *runakuna* orient themselves to local and distant geography by entering into a personal relationship with Sacred Places. Since space and time are isomorphic for them, *runakuna* orient themselves in local (or immediate) time and in distant time as well. Through these actions they are also oriented relative to their fellows.

The Contract

The *ayllu*, in its most general definition, is a group of individuals cohering as a social body around a place, ancestor, or task that provides a unifying focus. The ceremony of *hallpay*, in which participants exchange *k'intus* and share the coca's *sami* with Sacred Places, provides the framework within which this social cohering takes place.

All reciprocity has a symbolic aspect; an exchange of any kind expresses a relationship between the people involved. *K'intu* exchanges carry a particularly heavy symbolic load. In economic terms the value of the exchanged leaves is negligible. But while the economic aspect of the exchange is minimized, the symbolic aspect is maximized, for the exchange seals a social contract.

A request to do *ayni* is accompanied by a handful of coca, and once the coca is accepted, refusing the job is unthinkable. Similarly, a man chosen for a *cargo* signifies his agreement to serve when he accepts the coca bundle offered by the *alcalde*. A marriage contract is sealed when the groom's parents visit the bride's with presents of coca and alcohol.

In these contexts, refusal of the proffered coca signifies refusal of the contract. When Alcides refused the *alcalde*'s coca bundle during the Eustaquio crisis, his *ayllu*-mates understood that he wanted to withhold acceptance of the *cargo* until he was sure Eustaquio would not take on the *alcalde*ship. But to refuse coca in routine *hallpay* is to deny human inter- course—or at least to reject interaction with the other on an equal and amicable footing as comembers of a group.

When Luis vehemently insisted that the school was no longer an *ayllu* because mestizo schoolteachers lived there, I asked him about myself and Rick. Did we belong to an *ayllu*? Luis replied that we were members of Pillikunka *ayllu* because we lived like *runakuna* and chewed coca.

Three characteristics—to live as a *Runa*, to belong to an *ayllu*, and to chew coca—are intrinsically connected, for it is through coca that the relationship between people and their locality is maintained. It is under- standable, therefore, that Sonqo *runakuna* find the increasing shortage and high price of coca a great hardship. To be without coca is, for them, inconceivable.

Among *runakuna* the social contract is continually resealed, since adults chew coca several times a day in various contexts. *Hallpay* is a deeper contract than that expressed by the greetings, farewells, thank- yous, and expressions of esteem that frame virtually every encounter. It is deeper because coca itself is a sacred substance with a powerful *sami*, whose consumption creates communion among human beings and be- tween humans and deities. Sonqueños explicitly point out this aspect of coca chewing. Coca is the quintessential Andean sacrament; they call it *hostia*, the host, in an explicit analogy with the Catholic communion ser- vice.

"Sacraments are not only signs, but essentially different from other signs, being instruments." Mary Douglas's statement certainly holds true for the coca leaf as well as for the wine and the wafer of Christianity. From the perspective of the participants in *hallpay*, coca plays both symbolic and instrumental functions. Coca chewing is not only a sign of orderly social relations; it is also an instrument through which these relations are defined, created, and maintained. Through coca's *sami* the Earth, the Places, and the Ancestors are included in society.

As a channel for communication with the powers that be, coca has far-reaching pragmatic effects on existence. *Runakuna* monitor their relationship with the Sacred Places through the vicissitudes of fortune: tripping, losing a sheep, getting caught in the rain, getting lost in the fog—all are signs of something amiss in the relationship. To avoid such an unbalance, *runakuna* blow on their *k'intus*. It is not surprising that my first and longest stay in Sonqo began and ended with lessons in *phukuy*.

Coca, the Transmitter

Pacha and the *Tirakuna* communicate with human beings via coca, but not everyone knows how to interpret the messages encoded in the leaves. *Coca qhaway* ("looking at coca," the art of coca divination) takes years of study and practice, as well as a lot of inspiration.

Most Sonqueños know the rudiments of coca divination, but in serious matters—like severe illness or plotting the course of an important action—they turn to a specialist. Unlike *hallpay*, a ceremony carried out by all adults as part of their routine, *coca qhaway* is an extremely serious act that is performed in secret. In 1984, nine years after I first came to Sonqo, Erasmo offered to teach me about coca divination with the admonishment that knowing a little about *coca qhaway* is worse than knowing nothing at all. Some people, he remarked, think they know more than they really do and divine badly. They take advantage of people and pronounce falsehoods.

I asked Erasmo whether he objected to my writing down what I learned from him. To the contrary, he rather liked having his instruction written down—as long as I wrote it in English and published it in my country, where Sonqo *runakuna* would not know about it. My fellow gringos could not misuse it, Erasmo said, since they don't have coca anyway.

Erasmo showed me two kinds of *coca qhaway*: one to determine the cause of illness and the other to determine the nature of events distant in space and time. This second type of *qhaway* predicts how one's luck will hold, reveals the causes of past events (the identities of thieves, for example), and tells how distant loved ones are doing.

Both types of *qhaway* are preceded by an invocation. The *paqo* (diviner) calls on *Pacha Mama* and on the *hatun Rurgrarkuna* (the great Places) of his client's locality. Erasmo insisted that I tell him the names of Places where I lived in the United States, explaining that without them the coca would not "know" the answers to his questions. He explained that the *qhaway* process was the reverse of *phukuy*: in *phukuy*, human beings send messages to the Places via coca's *sami*; in *qhaway*, the Places send messages to humans via configurations of coca leaves.

The opening invocation may be long and poetic, praising the Earth and the Places, explaining the client's problem, and asking for their advice. The invocation invariably ends with the cry "*Sut'ita willaway!*" ("Tell me clearly!") as the diviner dramatically throws down his coca bundle or handful of coca, depending on the type of divination.

In both types of *qhaway*, the coca-carrying cloth (*unkhuña*) serves as a field against which the diviner interprets configurations of leaves. To divine distant events, he spreads the cloth before he begins and places a coin in its center. This is the *ñawin* (eye). Taking a handful of leaves with his right hand, the diviner lets the coca run through his fingers onto the coin. Then he studies the configurations carefully to understand their meaning. Leaves landing right side up or pointing to the right are good signs; those falling upside down or pointing to the left are bad. The diviner picks out certain leaves as significant, as standing for particular individuals or objects. A large leaf with a small leaf on top of it, for example, was me with my "cargo" of stories to carry back to the States.

The *paqo* divining *unqoqpaq* (for a sick person) invokes the deities while holding the filled coca-carrying cloth folded first in half and then in thirds. As he cries "*Sut'ita willaway!*" he pulls forcefully on the ends three times, with a cracking noise and a puff of dust. Then he throws down the bundle and opens it to reveal a configuration of leaves explaining the nature of the illness and its prognosis. Again, leaves shiny side up and pointing to the right are good signs, whereas those upside down and pointing leftward are bad. A large leaf sitting apart from the others can indicate the patient. If it points away from the diviner the patient "is going away" ("*ripushan*") and will die; if it points toward the diviner the patient "is turning back" ("*kutimushan*") and will recover. A leaf folded over at both ends shows that the patient is "*Tira hap'isqan*" ("seized by the Earth") and should make a *despacho* (burnt offering). Leaves falling perpendicularly in a cross are very good signs. Irregularly folded leaves indicate great sickness, whereas leaves folded neatly along the middle indicate health.

There are other signs I have not learned, some of which concern sorcery, but in general the code is fairly limited in terms of its repertoire of signs. The difficulty of *qhaway* lies in learning how to interpret the configurations of leaf signs *within the context of the given situation*. This is where the diviner's inspiration and experience come into play, and why it is easy to read coca badly (for the basic vocabulary of signs is easily learned) and extremely hard to read coca well. Since coca reading is context-dependent, the meaning of any given configuration will vary according to the person for whom it is read and his or her situation. The *paqo* must astutely apply all his knowledge and insight concerning his client if he is to interpret successfully what the coca has to tell him.

Obviously, coca reading provides great opportunities for quackery; but a quack *paqo*—who simply takes his clients' money to tell them what they want to hear—will eventually fall into disrepute as his diagnoses are recognized as mistaken or unhelpful. A diviner can encourage his client in the course of a reading, but he may also force the recognition of unpleasant truths and prescribe difficult changes in behavior. A good diviner studies a situation before he agrees even to go ahead with a reading.

In 1984 a mestizo official from Colquepata sought out Erasmo's services. The official's wife was refusing to cook for him, and he believed her to be *layqasqa* (bewitched). He wanted Erasmo to divine the source of the spell. Erasmo talked to the official for a long time and finally refused to do the reading, explaining that he did not think sorcery was involved and suggesting that the official try treating his wife better. The man went off annoyed to find another *paqo*. In the short run Erasmo's response resulted in the official's antipathy, but in the long run it may be recognized as the more helpful insight.

The fact that Erasmo draws on his own knowledge of the client and his problem to interpret the coca leaves does not mean that a genuine *paqo* cynically uses the *qhaway* as a kind of mumbo-jumbo to validate his own guesses. As far as a diviner and his client are concerned, coca always knows the answers. In other words, the configurations of leaves are always meaningful; the *paqo*'s problem is to focus all his knowledge and insight in order to perceive what the meaning is.

Learning to Be a Runa

All adult skills are said to have been invented by specific saints. *Hallpay*, one of the most significant of these skills, was invented by one of the greatest saints, Mamacha Santísima María (Holy Mother Mary). The person who is *santuyuq* (skillful, possessed of the saint) in coca chewing has established contact with the *mamacha*'s creative virtue and her consoling power. Properly chewed, the leaves absorb grief and pain and comfort the chewer like a mother.

As with other skills, one becomes *santuyuq* in coca chewing through a long if playful process of trial and error. Although children are excluded from routine *hallpay* until well into their teens, they enjoy helping their parents share *k'intus* by carrying the leaves proudly and carefully from one adult to the other. Sometimes children sit next to an open coca bundle, trying with great concentration to put the leaves together into a respectable *k'intu*. Parents criticize their children's handiwork and usually reject the *k'intus*, showing them leaves they have placed wrong side up or pointing out that they have used brown and broken leaves while better ones were left in the bundle.

Children are often included in the preparation of the ritual offering bundles burned on the eve of certain festivals. Brimming with excitement, they gingerly chew the leaves and prepare *k'intus* to be offered to *Pacha* and the *Tirakuna*. Thus, their first full participation in coca chewing begins not with routine *hallpay*, but in the intensified context of family ritual. Later, as adolescents, they will be included in routine *hallpay* as they begin working with adults on grown-up tasks. Boys are invited to chew as they participate in work parties on an equal footing with men; likewise, girls are offered *k'intus* as they take on adult responsibilities among women cooking for a festival or a work party.

Hallpay and *hallpay* manners suffuse the atmosphere in which *runakuna* grow up and in which they absorb their culture. *Hallpay*'s dense symbolism unifies diverse dimensions of a *runa*'s physical, mental, and emotional experience. Since the symbols are actions, an individual is put in the position of "acting out" basic cultural principles, of entering several times a day into a contract to participate in Quechua tradition. Coca-chewing etiquette, a set of collectively held rules of conduct, reveals a process of self-definition on the part of *runakuna*.

"How can we know the dancer from the dance?" The *runa* self is formulated in and through the "dance" of *hallpay*. When a *runa* decides to become a *misti*, he turns from coca chewing to new cultural dances and a different definition of self.

Note

For complete references and footnotes, see the original version of this piece in Catherine J. Allen, *The Hold Life Has* (Washington, D.C.: Smithsonian Institution Press, 1988), pp. 125–136.

MY LITTLE COCA, LET ME CHEW YOU!

Anonymous

Between coca's centuries-old importance in Andean ritual and the contemporary violence associated with its refining for First World drug markets lies a universe of other meanings and appropriations, one on display in this wicked lyric from the province of Angaraes, Huancavelica. Here, coca and the cal, *or lime, needed to release the mildly narcotic effect of the cocaine alkaloid embedded in the leaf stand in for female sexuality and male infidelity, a favorite theme of mountain balladeers.*

My little coca with the round leaf, it's me, let me chew you.
My lime, my little lime, it's me,
let me bite you.

How could I chew the *cal* of another?
How gross it would be
to have to chew the wad of another!

People are talking because
last night I went out to have fun.
People are whispering because last night I went out for a stroll,
"He's partying forgetting about his wife," they say.
"He's partying forgetting his beloved mother-in-law," they say.
"That's how it is," they say.

THE COCAINE ECONOMY

Jo Ann Kawell

Short memories in the United States often fix the beginning of coca cultivation in Peru in the 1970s, when North American consumption blossomed among white-collar professionals and in the inner cities. But as journalist Jo Ann Kawell points out in this overview, not only has coca been a Huallaga valley staple for centuries, but U.S. intervention there has contributed to the boom-and-bust economic cycles that have converted the bush into a survival crop for poor farmers. By the end of the 1980s, U.S. antidrug efforts paired with guerrilla insurgencies, ruthless transnational drug mafias, rampant corruption, and persistent poverty had converted this once promising agricultural valley into one of Peru's most violent regions. In the 1990s, interdiction efforts paired with a blight ruined Peru's crop and prompted investors to move to Colombia. But the cycle was already moving back to Peru in the first years of the twenty-first century, demonstrating that the stability of the U.S. and European markets remains the real engine of coca production.

Before the mid-1970s, most outsiders knew of Peru's Huallaga, if they had heard of it at all, only as a picturesque but drowsy jungle valley whose main town, Tingo María, was nicknamed "La Bella Durmiente" (Sleeping Beauty) for the profile of a reclining woman suggested by the surrounding hills. A handful of adventurers, naturalists, and tourists had long been attracted to the valley with its green, lush hills and plentiful wildlife.[1] There were also a few settlers and investors, Peruvian and foreign, who had seen limitless economic promise there. Orchids thrive in the moist heat. So do coffee, tea, and cacao. Most important of all for the valley's history, so does coca, the plant used to fabricate cocaine.

In the 1970s, the first ripples of a global increase in cocaine use awakened the "Sleeping Beauty." International drug buyers moved to Tingo

María. Its image changed to that of a violent frontier town where U.S. dollars and the white powdered drug flowed freely. Tingo took on a new nickname: Snow City.

By the end of the 1980s, the region was still notorious, but its image had changed again. It was a war zone. Helicopters, many piloted by Americans, brought troops into and out of local bases. Truckloads of camouflage-garbed soldiers and police rumbled past automatic weapon–toting sentries. On the veranda of a local hotel frequented once by tourists and later by drug dealers, U.S. officials quaffed beer with their Peruvian counterparts, planning operations and discussing how to "harden" a downriver base against enemy attack.[2]

At the time, the Huallaga valley was the most important coca-growing zone in the world. According to U.S. officials, 200,000 acres of coca were under cultivation in the Huallaga in 1990, almost 40 percent of the world coca crop.[3] Tingo María used to be the center of the business, but in the wake of the U.S.-sponsored eradication program of the 1980s and early 1990s, coca farming moved north, to the towns of Uchiza, Tocache, and Juanjuí. Intediction efforts then forced cultivation downriver around Tarapoto, the northern valley's major town. Coca replaced fields of rice and corn.

Most Huallaga coca farmers, many poor migrants from the Andean highlands, owned small plots of only a few acres or less. They sold their coca harvests to wholesale buyers, who in turn processed the leaves into *pasta*, or cocaine paste, a semirefined form of the drug. This simple, low-tech process calls for mixing leaves, kerosene, and other inexpensive chemicals in pits lined with plastic sheeting. Hired laborers then stamp the mixture into a murky brown soup.

The final refining, which turns *pasta* into the commercial product cocaine hydrochloride, requires more sophisticated equipment. In the early 1990s, a few labs had reportedly been set up in the Huallaga, though earlier almost all the *pasta* was flown to large plants in Colombia or even more remote parts of the Peruvian jungle. During the 1980s, many of the "narcos" who organized and supervised cocaine-related businesses in the Huallaga were Colombians, representatives of the big-name traffickers like the Escobars and the Ochoas who ran the international trade. But by the early 1990s, more Peruvians, including some members of the security forces, had become active at the highest levels of the Huallaga cocaine business.[4]

As a matter of fact, coca production and processing involved almost everyone in the valley, not just a few criminals. Tens of thousands of farmers grow the hardy bush. Thousands more were employed stomping coca in the paste pits, transporting coca or processed paste, or bringing chemicals and other paste-making supplies from Lima. Those who didn't directly participate—from shopkeepers to schoolteachers—benefited as so-called coca dollars were spent.[5]

But cocaine was not an unmitigated boon for the Huallaga. Violence became an integral part of the valley's daily life: bullet-ridden, mangled bodies were often found floating in the Huallaga River or lying near the roadside. Many of these deaths were the work of drug traffickers or their underlings, the result of vendettas or rivalries between narco groups.

In addition, the Maoist Communist Party of Peru–Shining Path movement had sent its first organizers to the Huallaga by 1982. The Movimiento Revolucionario Túpac Amaru (MRTA), a Cuban-style group with ties to the radical left, got its start soon afterward.[6] Following bloody battles between the two as they competed for dominance of the central Huallaga, the Shining Path established its control in the southern and central valley, while the MRTA was more active in the north.

To fight the guerrillas, the Peruvian government placed parts of the Huallaga valley under a state of emergency in 1984, suspending constitutional guarantees and placing military authorities in charge of many aspects of civil government. Nevertheless, both insurgent groups continued to carry out sizable armed operations. In 1987, for example, three hundred Shining Path guerrillas attacked and completely destroyed the Uchiza police post. Later the same year, an MRTA column, with a television news reporter in tow, briefly occupied the town of Juanjuí.[7]

Most insurgent activity was less spectacular but more threatening to the central government's authority. The Shining Path frequently expelled town officials, many of them appointed by Lima, and installed its own representatives as the local government. In some areas, the group took complete control of the main highway. The insurgents also imposed what could well be called "taxes" on the Huallaga's main productive activity, coca paste manufacture. Researcher Raúl González estimated that the Shining Path took in $30 to $40 million a year in the late 1980s by "taxing" valley paste production.[8]

Military and police forces were usually able to retake guerrilla-held areas eventually, at least as long as they remained massed in the area. But human rights groups charged that officers were responsible for a heavy toll of deaths and "disappearances."[9] There were also fierce turf battles between some army officers responsible for the "antisubversive" campaign and some police officials leading the antidrug effort. Some corrupt

Figure 45. Police arrest suspected drug dealer, Uchiza, 1986.
(Courtesy of Alejandro Balaguer)

officers competed for lucrative narco payoffs and even to run the business themselves.

In the face of growing violence, some valley residents sided with the insurgents, who brought their own brand of law and order. In April 1987, for instance, the Shining Path took on the drug mafia in the town of Tocache. At least thirty people died in one battle won by the Shining Path, which declared Tocache a "liberated zone." The Shining Path executed local officials and residents who refused to cooperate or who were suspected of collaboration with the security forces. But the narcos were allowed to keep their businesses as long as they paid "taxes" to the insurgents.[10] Armed guerrillas patrolled the streets. Every day, Shining Path cadres "made the entire population line up double file, and masked guerrillas gave speeches," a town resident told a reporter. But "the people liked the *terrucos* [guerrillas] better than the police, because [the Shining Path] let them work their coca."[11]

Both the Shining Path and the MRTA won support in the valley by serving as "union representatives" or "bargaining agents" when area coca growers negotiated with wholesalers. The insurgents forced buyers to pay good prices for coca leaf, punishing paste producers who abused their workers and merchants who abused customers. The Shining Path was especially effective, in part because of their brutal methods, seldom hesitating to back their threats by public executions.[12]

Both insurgent groups also tried to shield valley farmers from U.S.-sponsored eradication operations. The Shining Path made the United States a primary focus of its local propaganda efforts: "Down with the imperialist coca eradication plan!" read many Shining Path graffiti along the road outside Tingo María in the late 1980s.

Huallaga History: A Shining Path Paved with Good Intentions

Since they began in 1979, U.S. drug control programs in the Huallaga were based on the idea that coca production is an aberration in local history and that coca appeared to feed the cocaine boom of the 1970s. It is true that, since the 1970s, world demand for cocaine had stimulated a steady increase in coca production. But the structure of the coca economy has its foundation in centuries-old local and regional custom.

An estimated 4 million Peruvians, most from the highlands, use coca leaves medicinally or in social and ritual events.[13] They also chew coca as a mild labor-enhancing stimulant. Despite pressure from the United States and international agencies, Peru has never outlawed coca production entirely. The government still licenses some farmers to grow and some merchants to sell moderate quantities in leaf form. The state-run National Coca Company (ENACO) makes and sells a coca tea popular throughout Peru.

Some ethnobotanists maintain that the Huallaga valley is the place where coca was first domesticated some eight to ten thousand years ago. There is clear archaeological evidence that coca has been an important economic resource for valley dwellers since long before the Inca empire.[14] In pre-Inca and Inca times, during Spanish rule, and into the republican era, coca was a key crop in trade and tribute, especially in the highlands.[15]

A German chemist first extracted the cocaine alkaloid from coca leaves in 1860.[16] Cocaine became a staple of U.S. and European medical practice in the 1880s, touching off the first cocaine "boom."[17] Before, Peruvian coca had never been an overseas export. At first, Peruvian authorities welcomed the creation of an international market for coca and even encouraged local cocaine production. In 1905, Peru's development minister reported proudly that twelve cocaine "factories" were functioning in the Huallaga valley region around the city of Huánuco.[18]

But if coca has always provided a base for the Huallaga valley economy, other local products have periodically, if temporarily, overtaken it in profitability. Thus the region's economic history, like that of much of the rest of Latin America, is one of boom-and-bust cycles tied to changes in world demand for regionally produced commodities like rubber, coffee, and barbasco, a plant whose roots are used in making the pesticide rotenone. International booms contributed to upswings in the valley's population. Busts forced this new population to turn to coca farming for survival.[19]

The 1930s marked the initiation of a national push to colonize Peru's jungle frontier. Unlike previous attempts, aimed at attracting foreign settlers, including Germans and Italians, these plans emphasized the resettlement of Peruvians from other parts of the country. The strategy had the support of coastal plantation owners, who faced an increasingly militant peasantry bent on land reform. Jungle settlement was seen as a way of diverting such pressure. At the same time, old plans for a road connecting Lima to the Amazon region were revived. Tingo María was chosen as the site of the main construction camp and quickly became a typical boom town.[20]

As the United States was drawn into World War II, North American interest grew in obtaining "strategic" jungle products: rubber, medicinals like quinine, and insecticides, particularly rotenone. To encourage Peruivan industry, the United States agreed in 1942 to provide half the funding and all of the experts for a major tropical research station in Tingo María.[21] Later studies showed that the station played a major role in drawing settlers to the area—as would extensions of the highway paid for by the United States.[22]

After the war, military demand for rubber and quinine plummeted. Synthetic pesticides like DDT wiped out demand for barbasco. U.S. experts at the Tingo María station began promoting products believed to have a domestic market, such as beef and dairy cattle and tea. These products, however, were profitable only if produced on a large scale. Smaller growers, the majority of valley residents, continued to rely on coca as their cash-producing mainstay. In the 1950s, as in the 1940s, coca ranked as one of the region's most valuable crops.[23]

Coca farming in the Huallaga continued with minimal government regulation until 1961, when the United States began pressing the Peruvian government to sign a United Nations drug control treaty pledging to eradicate the country's entire coca crop—including leaves for chewing and other traditional uses—within twenty years. But after the Peruvians signed the accord, it was largely ignored by both Peruvian and U.S. officials until the mid-1970s, when U.S. drug warriors declared cocaine their number one problem.

The U.S. Drug War in Peru

In 1974, the U.S. Drug Enforcement Administration (DEA) announced that cocaine seizures in the United States had surpassed heroin for the first time and warned ominously that cocaine use was on the rise. Although some officials in the Ford and Carter administrations believed that cocaine use was not a social problem, leading members of Congress began to demand strict controls on cocaine production "at the source," the Andean coca fields.[24]

Under growing pressure from the United States, the Peruvian government began a series of U.S.-funded coca eradication operations in the Huallaga valley in 1979. In March of the following year, more than a thousand police descended on Tingo María to carry out an eradication project known as Verde Mar—Green Sea—a reference to the perception that the Huallaga was nothing more than a sea of coca. Officials calculated valley coca production at the time to be 30,000 acres.[25]

Operation Green Sea destroyed only 150 acres of coca,[26] but it had far-

Figure 46. Although the United States has spent millions of dollars on coca eradication, the bush remains a much planted crop in Peru's jungles. (Courtesy of Herman Schwarz)

reaching and destructive effects on local social and political life. During the operations, a professor from the university in Tingo María explained to reporters that 95 percent of the area's residents depended on coca for their livelihood. Because of coca's long history as a cultural and economic staple, growers viewed themselves not as criminals but as farmers with valid interests to protect despite a changed international view of their crop.

Farmers complained that Operation Green Sea had targeted only the most accessible farms along the highway outside Tingo María. Many considered their coca production to be completely legal. They had licenses to grow coca and sold it to ENACO. Farmer Eduardo de la Cruz Ramírez, whose family had cultivated a hundred-acre plot outside Tingo María since 1935, told me in 1988 that his crop had been uprooted and he had been arrested during Operation Green Sea despite his ENACO licenses.

By defining coca growing as a crime, the government soon made it impossible for farmers to lobby legally against forced eradication or to negotiate a viable plan for switching to other crops. According to Abram Ramos, a leader of the Aucayacu branch of the Confederación Nacional Agraria (CNA),[27] he and other local coca growers created a local defense committee in 1978 and were soon joined by others in neighboring communities. These growers' committees held a series of talks with central government representatives. The farmers believed they had reached an agreement to eradicate their coca fields gradually in return for some financial compensation and aid in planting alternative crops, but they were soon surprised by Operation Green Sea.

Ramos said in a 1988 interview that, although some of the old growers' groups continue to exist, local farmers quickly lost interest in joining since the groups had been ineffective in protecting farmers' interests. In the course of enforcing U.S.-mandated coca laws, the Peruvian government delegitimated the most important institutions representing the interests of local residents—the growers' associations and unions—and thus provided an opening for the still-embryonic guerrilla insurgencies.

At the same time, the U.S. Agency for International Development (USAID) drew up plans for a $167 million, five-year valley development project. This project was supposed to provide farmers with alternatives to coca, but it did not formally involve the growers or their organizations in planning, and it was not designed to break the economic stranglehold of the local merchants and middlemen. Although the Reagan administration, which took office in January 1981, signed off on the development plan, it was never fully implemented.

The plan failed, mostly because many farmers discovered another option: flight. Small producers had little to lose by packing up and moving on, clearing a new plot in the vast expanse of virgin forest. During the 1980s and into the 1990s, a steady stream of new migrants joined them, clearing coca plots on the steepest and most inaccessible (and, not coincidentally, most ecologically fragile) slopes in the valley. These new farmers found that they, too, needed protection against exploitative, dishonest coca buyers and against eradication. Insurgents were happy to comply.

The decade following Operation Green Sea saw the increased importance of four phenomena in the valley: coca production, insurgent influence, police and military presence, and direct involvement by U.S. personnel. All of these were closely interrelated, although the relations of cause and effect were not always as simple as drug control strategists portrayed them to be.

U.S. drug policymakers and politicians often claimed that the overall escalation of the U.S. "War on Drugs" during this period was simply a response to the increased threat posed by what they called the "international drug mafia." First Reagan and then George H. W. Bush declared that drug trafficking was not simply a domestic social or health problem, but a threat to national security. Both pressed the U.S. military to take a more active role in drug control, a task traditionally restricted to civilian law enforcement agencies like the DEA. Similarly, they characterized the escalation of the U.S. role in the Huallaga as inevitable given Peru's inability to stop the drug business.

This logic was superficially appealing. Despite ongoing eradication operations, valley coca production expanded from 30,000 acres in 1979 to about 260,000 acres in 1986.[28] And the traffickers used more force to protect their investments. Nineteen eradication workers were murdered in 1984. By 1987 the number had risen to thirty.[29] Starting in November 1987, U.S. helicopters, piloted by American civilians contracted by the State Department, airlifted Peruvian eradication teams and Peruvian police guards to their work sites. The United States also tested chemical herbicides, applied from the air from armored crop dusters, as a potential replacement for manual eradication. But the herbicide program and the presence of American pilots—called *los vietnamitas* by locals because the pilots were rumored to be veterans of the Vietnam War—fueled valley resentments against the United States along with sympathy for the insurgents, reinforcing the old cycle of militarization and violence in the Huallaga.

Despite demands from the Reagan administration, the Pentagon was initially reluctant to fight drug trafficking. Many military analysts saw the "drug war" as unwinnable and the situation in Peru's Huallaga valley as particularly murky. As the military itself hesitated, U.S.-supported operations in the Huallaga took on a distinctly paramilitary air. Agents of the DEA received jungle warfare training before being sent to Peru. In turn, agents trained Peruvian police in the same techniques. With the end of the cold war, however, the Pentagon, in search of new budget-justifying missions, became more enthusiastic about the "War on Drugs." Soon, the Mazamari police base, built by the United States in the 1960s to train Peruvian counterinsurgency police, was refurbished, and Green Beret trainers once again set up shop, this time training Peru's antidrug police.

At heart, the official U.S. vision of the relation between traffickers and insurgents in Peru was curious and contradictory. While administration analysts contended that the two groups had the same overall goal— the destruction of U.S. society—and were inextricably woven together as "narcoterrorists" or "narcoguerrillas,"[30] policymakers were careful to specify that drug traffickers were the *only* target of U.S. operations in Peru. Officially, counterinsurgency remained a Peruvian problem. Though Peru received some low-key U.S. help in this matter—the Green

Berets at Mazamari, for instance, enrolled some counterinsurgency police in their training sessions—the main U.S. mission continued to be phrased as drug control. On paper, if not always in practice, U.S. "rules of engagement" kept U.S. personnel away from armed confrontations with guerrillas. U.S. officials contended that this was simply an appropriate division of labor and that the Peruvian fight against the Shining Path and the antidrug war were mutually compatible.

This view clashed with a growing conviction within the Peruvian government that the drug war, especially eradication, undermined their primary goal of combating guerrillas. President Alan García and his successor, Alberto Fujimori, promoted the idea that the government had to win over valley coca growers in order to stem the guerrillas' appeal. This meant recognizing the coca farmers' organizations and concerns as legitimate and allowing them to continue cultivating coca until alternative sources of income were in place. When Peruvian Army General Alberto Arciniega tried to implement this policy in the Huallaga, García was barraged with U.S. protests and charges that the general was in the pay of the drug mafia. General Arciniega was replaced.[31]

In the end, any program realistically aimed at "going to the source" of drugs and guerrilla movements in the Huallaga required the direct participation of Huallaga residents. It entailed talking with, rather than trying to jail, coca farmers. It also required some larger-scale changes not only in Peru, where the legal economy provided few jobs and the majority remained locked out of political power, but also in the United States, where racism and joblessness fueled domestic demand for drugs. Finally, the United States failed to take into account Peru's own special needs and circumstances.

Yet over two decades after "Operation Green Sea," no U.S. president has addressed the dramatic failure of the war on drugs. To the contrary, both President Bill Clinton and President George W. Bush intensified involvement of the U.S. and Latin American militaries. Coca remains as abundant as ever, and as yet there are no effective trade, aid, or major economic programs to assist farmers willing to switch to legal crops. Who knows what kind of monster the once-Sleeping Beauty will become in its next incarnation?

Notes

1   Noted nineteenth-century naturalists J. J. Tschudi, Richard Spruce, and Eduardo Poeppig all wrote extensively about the Huallaga's natural splendors, as did their twentieth-

century counterpart Alex Shoumatoff in *The Rivers Amazon* (San Francisco: Sierra Club, 1986). Armando Robles Godoy's 1970 film *The Green Wall* is an autobiographical glimpse of a Huallaga settler's life at midcentury.

2   Jo Ann Kawell, "Under the Flag of Law Enforcement" and "Going to the Source," NACLA *Report on the Americas* 22, no. 6 (March 1989): 13–21; Robin Kirk, "Sowing Violence in Peru," *The Progressive*, July 1991, pp. 30–32.

3   U.S. State Department, *International Narcotics Control Strategy Report*, March 1, 1991, p. 113. Peru's total coca production was put at 303,000 acres, or about two-thirds of world production. Official Peruvian figures are, in general, about double the U.S. numbers.

4   "Peru's Deadly Drug Habit: Behind the Fujimori Front, Corruption and Cocaine Trafficking Are Booming," *Washington Post*, February 28, 1993; *Andean Newsletter/Drug Trafficking Update* (Lima), no. 33, November 9, 1992.

5   As does the rest of Peru. In 1988, the Peruvian Central Bank estimated cocaine income at $1.2 billion, which at that time would have made it the source of a third of Peru's foreign exchange earnings. As Peru's legal economy has declined, this proportion has undoubtedly increased. It is difficult to estimate what proportion of this income remains in the valley.

6   Raúl González, "Coca's Shining Path," NACLA *Report on the Americas* 22, no. 6 (March 1989): 22–24.

7   *Sí* (Lima), November 16, 1987; *Caretas* (Lima), November 9 and 16, 1987. In 1991, the MRTA made simultaneous incursions into San Martín's five largest cities (GAP *Informativo*, no. 14 [New York, undated]: 6), though by mid-1993 the group had reportedly been wiped out nationwide (*Andean Newsletter*, no. 78 [May 19, 1993]: 7).

8   González, "Coca's Shining Path."

9   Bulletins of the Peruvian Pro–Human Rights Association have periodically documented the Huallaga situation since 1987. GAP *Informativo*, no. 14, summarized recent abuses in San Martín.

10 *La República* (Lima), April 30, 1987; *El Diario* (Lima), June 21, 1987; *Sí*, June 1, 1987.

11 *Caretas*, July 20, 1987.

12 González, "Coca's Shining Path," p. 22.

13 *Boletín Internacional Acción Andina* (Cochabamba/Lima), November 1992, p. 28.

14 Timothy Plowman, "The Ethnobotany of Coca," *Advances in Economic Botany* 1 (1984): 62–111.

15 Ibid., pp. 72–77; John V. Murra, "La visita de los chupachu como fuente etnológica," *Documentos para la historia y etnología de Huánuco y la Selva Central*, vol. 1 (Huánuco, Peru: Universidad Nacional Hermilio Valdizán, 1967); Edmundo Morales, *Cocaine: White Gold Rush in Peru* (Tucson: University of Arizona Press, 1989), chapters 1 and 3.

16 In 1855 a different German chemist had extracted a substance he called "erithroxylin" from coca. This may have been identical to the alkaloid we now call cocaine, but colleagues were unable to use his method to duplicate his results.

17 For the history of cocaine's rise and the eventual reaction against it, see David F. Musto, *The American Disease: Origins of Narcotics Control* (New York: Oxford University Press, 1987), chapters 1–3; Arnold H. Taylor, *American Diplomacy and the Narcotics Traffic, 1900–1939* (Durham, N.C.: Duke University Press, 1969); William O. Walker, *Drug Control in the Americas* (Albuquerque: University of New Mexico Press, 1989), chapters 1–4.

18 Alejandro Garland, *Reseña industrial del Perú* (Lima: Ministerio de Fomento del Perú,

1905), p. 143. The Peruvian "factories" produced what would today be called cocaine paste. Most of this paste was shipped to pharmaceutical companies in Germany and the United States for the final refining. Peruvian law freely permitted the licensing of private cocaine producers until 1939.

19 Centro Nacional de Capacitación e Investigación para la Reforma Agraria, *Diagnóstico socio-económico de la colonización Tingo María–Tocache–Campanilla* (Lima: Centro Nacional de Capacitación e Investigación para la Reforma Agraria, 1974), vol. 1, pp. 78–82; Carlos Peñaherrera del Aguila, *Estudio ambiental del área del proyecto especial Alto Huallaga* (report for USAID, IRI Research Institute, 1985), pp. 4–5; Kathleen Foote Durham, "Expansion of Agricultural Settlement in the Peruvian Rainforest: The Role of the Market and the Role of the State" (ms. prepared for LASA/ASA meeting, November 1977); Wolfram Drewes, *The Economic Development of the Western Montaña of Central Peru as Related to Transportation* (Lima: Peruvian Times, 1958), pp. 26, 28.

20 Peñaherrera, *Estudio ambiental*, p. 92; Drewes, *The Economic Development of the Western Montaña*, p. 22.

21 Drewes, *The Economic Development of the Western Montaña*, p. 23; U.S. State Department, "Agricultural Experiment Station at Tingo María," agreements signed April 1942, April 1952; *Peruvian Times Yearbook*, 1941, p. 57; Arthur T. Mosher, *Technical Co-operation in Latin American Agriculture* (Chicago: University of Chicago Press, 1957), pp. 18–19, 71.

22 Drewes, *The Economic Development of the Western Montaña*, p. 36; Durham, "Chronology."

23 George A. Woolley, "Boomtown South America: The Story of Tingo María" (Washington, D.C.: Institute of Inter-American Affairs, 1952), pp. 6–7; Drewes, *The Economic Development of the Western Montaña*, p. 26.

24 Musto, *The American Disease*, pp. 263–265; *La Crónica* (Lima), August 14, 1977; *El Comercio* (Lima), August 16, 1977, pp. 1, 4.

25 *Caretas*, no. 581 (December 10, 1979); no. 592 (March 17, 1980); no. 594 (March 31, 1980); no. 595 (April 14, 1980); no. 604 (June 23, 1980); USAID, *Peru Project Paper, Upper Huallaga Agricultural Development* (Washington, D.C., August 1981), p. 60.

26 Bruno Lesevic, "Dinámica demográfica y colonización en la Selva Alta Peruana: 1940–1981," in *Población y colonización en la Alta Amazonia Peruana* (Lima: Consejo Nacional de Población Centro de Investigación y Promoción Amazónica, 1984), p. 31.

27 The CNA is a peasant federation formed under the Velasco regime.

28 U.S. State Department, *Peru: Status of Illicit Narcotics Production and Trafficking*, 1987.

29 U.S. State Department, *International Narcotics Control Strategy Report*, 1988.

30 Merrill Collett, "The Myth of the 'Narco Guerrilla,'" *The Nation* 247, no. 4 (August 13–20, 1988), pp. 113–117.

31 Robin Kirk, "Sowing Violence," *The Progressive*, July 1989, pp. 30–32; "Peru's Rebels' Muddy Drug Drive," *Washington Post*, November 3, 1989.

DRUGS, SOLDIERS, AND GUERRILLAS

"Chanamé"

"Chanamé" was the pseudonym used by an army officer sent to the upper Huallaga valley in 1991 to survey guerrilla activity and official involvement in the drug trade, estimated to net $700 million annually in Peru alone. The dry, matter-of-fact tone of this confidential report only heightens the surreal quality of the land-scape he surveys, where Maoist guerrillas guard coca plantings, young men called "kangaroos" keep raw cocaine in school-style backpacks, and Colombian hired killers carrying machine guns lounge under the nose of the local army commander, paid by gangster bosses like "The Vatican" and "The Minister" for each drug flight in and out of town.

Lima, 22 November 1991
Report No. 016/91
To: Mr. Brigadier General, Director of Army Intelligence
Re: Information obtained in Mariscal Cáceres Province

I have the honor of addressing myself to you to convey the information about narcoterrorism obtained on my trip to Mariscal Cáceres Province in the Department of San Martín.

1. During my stay, I learned that the subversive revolutionary groups (Shining Path and MRTA) operate in these places:

a. On the Jungle Highway: on the part from Sacanche to Punta Arenas, about eighty miles. There are small settlements along the road, where most of the inhabitants are involved in drug trafficking, permanently pro-tected by the criminal terrorists of the Shining Path and in some cases with the support and/or permission of the official forces, including the military at Antisubversive Base No. 30 in Campanilla.

b. On the Huallaga River: in little villages along the banks between

Juanjuí and Campanilla, about two hours by boat. Here drug traffickers and the general population use motorboats to transport coca paste, bringing it to Campanilla to sell, and transporting it to Colombia. The Shining Path appears to have a camp in Pajillal, where Shitari Creek runs into the Huallaga River.

2. In Campanilla district, approximately 90 percent of the population comes from out of town, especially from the central highlands. They dedicate themselves openly to drug trafficking without the least fear of the army, apparently because of an "understanding." There are four "firms" in the district. The Peruvian citizen Demetrio Chávez Peñaherrera runs the most respected and the best known. It enjoys a popularity among the locals for having financed the beautification of the main square. Chavez goes by the alias "The Minister" and likes to pass himself off as Colombian (having fled the law to live for a number of years in that country). In fact, this criminal was born in Campanilla, the third of seven children, all drug traffickers. In this area, drug traffickers parade around the town in pickup trucks with their hired killers [sicarios] and bodyguards. Because of the tropical heat, the guards wear light clothes and short-sleeved shirts. It is easy to see the outline of their holstered revolvers and automatic pistols. Some have machine guns slung over their shoulder. With the blessings of the army, they go back and forth between their labs and storehouses, which are right in the middle of the town. One is just two blocks from the army base. On the streets, one [also] sees hordes of teenagers with backpacks. They are the *traqueteros*, or messengers. They sit around on the curbs as if at a street fair or on a picket line, waiting to be paid for drugs delivered to one of the "firms" or for the arrival of some scheduled flight [from Colombia]. Walking around the town, it is also common to overhear the radios of the "firms," buzzing with communications to Colombian buyers to confirm flights and other details of this illegal business. On November 9, 1991, at about 3:00 P.M., a small plane from Colombia landed on part of the highway that "The Minister" has fixed to double as a runway. The unloading of the dollars and the loading of drugs lasted about three or four minutes. Because of the "understanding" between the "firms" and the military, the base commander gets between $3,000 and $4,000 per flight, arriving three or four times a week, except during thunderstorms. The army always closes off the streets [when the planes are scheduled to arrive], allowing access only to the lords of the "firms," their *sicarios*, and those in charge of securing the perimeters of the airstrip.

This is all that I have the honor to inform you of at this time, putting this information at your disposition for whatever ends you may deem appropriate.

Chanamé

IX · THE STRUGGLE FOR SURVIVAL

Hope raised by the country's return to democracy in 1980 was short-lived. Political corruption, violence, a dive in real wages, hyperinflation, drugs, crime, and disastrous flooding augured ill for civilian leaders. The so-called Lost Decade of the 1980s brought debt and International Monetary Fund–imposed austerity programs to much of Latin America. Yet no country shared Peru's sheer quantity of calamity, recorded in line graphs of health, social welfare, and productivity indicators pitched as steeply downward as the Andes themselves.

Neither the technocrats under Fernando Belaúnde (1980–1985) nor Alan García's populism (1985–1990) effectively confronted these problems. To the contrary, ineptitude and graft stained the record of all branches of government, including Congress and the judiciary. The number of poor exploded, while roads, hospitals, and communications systems fell into ruin, prompting the shrinking middle class to remember the midcentury as a golden age.

To be sure, such times also breed alternatives and new forms of social mobilization. The tremendous ability to organize in the face of what appeared to be certain defeat was surely the decade's greatest achievement. Soup kitchens, peasant patrols, mothers' clubs, street vendors' associations, agrarian leagues, internal refugee organizations, and the families of the "disappeared" belied the images of chaos and helplessness so often invoked in the media. Much of the Peruvian economy was driven by the rise of the so-called informal sector, made up of street sellers and small businesspeople who rejected Shining Path guerrillas for what economist Hernando de Soto dubbed the "other path" of entrepreneurship.

By 1990, two extremes squared off over Peru's future: a right-wing coalition led by novelist–turned–presidential candidate Mario Vargas

Llosa and the Marxist Shining Path. Vargas Llosa billed himself as the realist who would reduce government and unlock Peru's entrepreneurial spirit with a free market key. Yet voters found it difficult to believe that this white sophisticate, surrounded by the sleek industrialists and bankers of Peru's plutocracy, would look out for the poor majorities. For its part, the Shining Path moved its war increasingly to the capital. Few were won over by its call for total destruction or shared Vargas Llosa's dream of Peru as a Latin Switzerland. Yet guerrilla assassinations, bombings, and blackouts held the population in paralyzed thrall, ready to believe that terror might eventually prevail.

Into this vacuum stepped a political unknown: Alberto Fujimori, an agronomist by trade whose career was in university administration. A nisei, Fujimori upset the heavily favored Vargas Llosa in the 1990 presidential election by appealing to voters as an ethnic minority, who, with the brown-skinned *cholos*, would defeat the white elites, symbolized by Vargas Llosa. No one guessed that *el chino*, as Peruvians called Fujimori, would become Peru's most powerful and longest-serving modern president, ruling the country for the next ten years.

Fujimori's record was mixed and controversial. Following the recipe of the International Monetary Fund and international lenders, his neoliberal free market economics brought hyperinflation under control, but sent unemployment soaring and cut into already precarious family budgets. In 1993, an independent survey registered never-before-seen levels of poverty in the states of Amazonas, Apurímac, and Huancavelica, where 76 percent of the boys and 68 percent of the girls suffered chronic malnutrition. The tough-minded Fujimori simultaneously led the defeat of the violent, tyrannical Shining Path, and a welcome end to political violence. But, with military support, he claimed quasi-dictatorial powers of his own in 1992. His right-hand man was Vladimiro Montesinos, who ran a shadowy government within the government as chief of the Military Intelligence Service. Montesinos used bribery, fraud, and thuggery to ensure Fujimori's election to a second and then third term. Peru was a democracy only in name by the turn of the new century.

In 2000, the wheels came off for Fujimori and Montesinos. The last straw was the release of secret videos, including one transcribed here, that showed Montesinos bribing an opposition congressman to become a Fujimori supporter. Fujimori was forced into exile in Japan; Montesinos, extradited from Venezuela despite plastic surgery to escape detection, is serving a long sentence in the same high-security prison as Abimael

Guzmán. Amid resurgent optimism about democracy and change, Alejandro Toledo won a new presidential election and become Peru's first humbly born, brown-skinned president in modern times. Toledo raised the multicolored Inca flag over the presidential palace to declare Indian pride. His Stanford degree seemed to offer bona fides for his capacity to manage the economy as well.

Although the economy grew under Toledo, he failed to deliver on his promise of good jobs. Many Peruvians had written him off as a weak, ineffective leader by the end of his term. Like Fujimori, Toledo encouraged foreign investment. Now those with the money can choose between KFC, McDonald's, and T.G.I. Friday's in Lima's wealthier neighborhoods, or have Domino's deliver a pizza. In the Andes near the city of Cajamarca, where Atahualpa and Pizzaro had their fateful encounter in 1532, the Denver-based Newmont Mining Corporation runs the gigantic Yanacocha strip mine, spewing smoke and polluting village water supplies for miles around. No matter who won the presidency, the Peru of the new millennium was linked more than ever before to the global economy.

For all the changes, the country remains marred by the realities of racism and an astonishing gap between rich and poor. To be Indian is still more often considered a stigma than a point of pride in Peru. In this country where the overwhelming majority has Indian and sometimes black blood, the smiling faces on the billboards and in the soap operas are typically white, as if Peru was somehow ashamed of the truth and vibrancy of its mixed roots. The Andean heartland of the Inca empire is today Peru's poorest region. Almost three-quarters of highland villagers live on less than $1.00 a day.[1]

Frustration sometimes boils over. A mob of Aymara Indians in 2004 lynched a local mayor, an Aymara himself, on charges of stealing government money. Striking schoolteachers turned to the desperate tactic of *desangreandose*, or opening a vein to bleed bright red onto a white banner to dramatize their plight before the television cameras. Although such protests continue in Peru today, they are scattered and without any central direction. The hardships of these past decades have bred cynicism and mistrust, leading many Peruvians to feel that everyone is on his or her own.

Film director Francisco Lombardi captures the sense of failed expectations in his aptly named *Caídos del cielo* (Fallen from Heaven), whose most poignant scenes involve an elderly couple who have lost their fortune yet sink their retirement savings into marble for a mausoleum they can no longer afford to complete. The empty shell stands not only for a vanished class, but for the realization that progress over time is not a natural law, but a luxury Peruvians can no longer afford to believe in.

Note

1   These and other statistics about poverty in Peru can be found at the Web site of the World Bank, htttp://web.worldbank.org.

SOUP OF THE DAY

Family Kitchen No. 79

Without soup kitchens, formed by poor women who cannot feed their families on their own, mass starvation would be a real possibility in Peru, especially with cuts in social spending. With them, tens of thousands just manage, filling their battered pots with rations that are divided frugally between the hungry mouths at home. More than 2,500 soup kitchens have been formed in Peru, serving as many as a million people a day. This is the menu served in a Lima kitchen in Santa Anita for the week of May 31 to June 4, 1993. There, three hundred rations are sold daily for the equivalent of 15 cents apiece. To save money, Monday's fish are served without the heads, which are saved for Friday's soup, and the beef head is bought without its expensive tongue.

Monday
Beef Head Noodle Soup/*Sopa de Fideos con Cabeza de Res*
Fried Fish with Rice, Lentils, and Mixed Salad/*Pescado Frito con Arroz, Lentejas, y Ensalada Mixta*
Sweetened Yerbaluisa Herb Tea/*Agua de Yerbaluisa*

Tuesday
Cream of Green Pea and Egg Soup/*Crema de Arveja con Huevo*
Beef Intestine Stew with Rice and Mixed Salad/*Cau Cau con Ensalada Mixta*
Sweetened Manzanilla Herb Tea/*Agua de Manzanilla*

Wednesday
Polenta and Chicken Giblet Soup/*Sopa de Polenta con Menudencia de Pollo*
Chicken and Fried Rice with Chopped Beets/*Arroz con Pollo con Ensalada de Betarraga*
Sweetened Yerbaluisa Herb Tea/*Agua de Yerbaluisa*

Figure 47. Soup kitchens, like this one in Lima, are key to the survival of many poor Peruvian families. (Courtesy of Yolanda Crucinata)

Thursday
Beef Head Cream of Wheat Soup/*Sopa de Morón con Cabeza de Res*
Noodles in Red Sauce with Tomato, Carrot, and Tuna/*Tallarín Rojo con Tomate, Zanahoria, y Atún*
Sweetened Manzanilla Herb Tea/*Agua de Manzanilla*

Friday
Fishhead and Mussel Noodle Soup/*Sopa de Fideos con Cabeza de Pescado y Choros*
Fish with Beans and Rice/*Arroz con Frejoles y Pescado*
Sweetened Yerbaluisa Herb Tea/*Agua de yerbaluisa*

Saturday
Rice Soup with Cabbage, Corn, and Chicken Giblets/*Sopa de Arroz con Col, Choclo, y Menudencia de Pollo*
Sauteed Fish with Fried Potatoes/*Saltado de Pescado con Papa Frita*
Sweetened Manzanilla Herb Tea/*Agua de Manzanilla*

NIGHTWATCH

Orin Starn

Rondas campesinas, or peasant patrols, began in 1976 to combat thieves in the northern mountains of Cajamarca. By the early 1980s, they had taken over much of the work of the official courts by resolving disputes over land or family arguments, and they supervised small public works projects, becoming a major rallying point for peasant pride. The original rondas campesinas *in northern Peru are often confused with the quite different organizations of the same name in Ayacucho and the southern highlands, which formed a decade later to combat the Shining Path. Still, the northern* rondas *were one of the largest Latin American social movements of the late twentieth century, as Orin Starn explains in this essay, originally published in the Peruvian newsmonthly* Quehacer. *Many villages in northern Peru maintain their* rondas *even today.*

Give me your little heart,
I'll pack it away,
if I lose it on my journey
I'll search for it with the ronda.
—*Los Obreritos de Santa Rosa,*
Hualgayoc, Cajamarca, 1987

I don't agree with this at all," laments the skinny, pleasant-faced *ronda* activist Dionisio Ramos.[1]

The dilapidated, cavernous movie theater in the small mountain town of Cutervo smells of sweat, chewed coca, and Premiere brand cigarettes. Ramos and I are surrounded by three hundred delegates to the Third Congress of the Cajamarca Peasant Patrol Federation. Brown mud spatters the polyester pants and Ecuadorian rubber boots of the many peasants who have come on foot or by truck from Chota, Jaén, and even

Celendín. One after another, delegates take the stage to launch fiery accusations of corruption against local authorities and praise for the patrols into the dank, smoke-filled air. They wave their arms like karate fighters to applause and whistles. Representatives from Lima-based development groups as well as a sprinkling of gringos—with our notebooks, tape recorders, cameras, and video recorders, we are a familiar part of the scenery of any peasant event—circulate among the crowd. There is no shortage of politicians, either. The Federation is closely linked to the Communist Party of Peru–Red Homeland. Senator Jorge "Ludovico" Hurtado—tall, silent, and a little Rasputinish—watches everything from the dark theater's depths. He wears an expensive leather jacket, the unofficial uniform for leftist parliamentarians. Completing the scene— peasant congress as postmodern pastiche—on the concrete benches of the mezzanine, an acupuncturist with a Fu Manchu moustache runs thin copper needles through the ears, arms, and knees of peasant patients in their ponchos, "Beverly Hills Cop" T-shirts, *polleras, ojotas,* and Power sneakers.[2]

Ramos is looking at a *La República* photograph showing him on night patrol in his cold and misty community of Lingán Grande, in the Andean heights above Chota.[3] The patrollers glare sternly at the camera and wear the standard garb of the *rondas*: straw hat, poncho, *ojotas,* and a stout stick.

What bothers Ramos is the headline: "Patrollers kill eight Shining Path members." The newspaper has published an article about the anti-guerrilla patrols of the south-central highlands, originally formed by the military in the counterinsurgency campaign against the Maoists. But the article is accompanied by a photograph of the northern patrols of Caja-marca and Piura, begun seven years before at the initiative of peasants tired of thievery and official corruption. The transposition reflects a general confusion about peasant patrols both in Peru and abroad, exacerbated by their common name of *rondas campesinas.*

The northern patrols deserve better. Whereas many of the grassroots initiatives of the 1980s have weakened or dissolved, these organizations continue with a unique force and scope. As of 1993, there were about 3,435 patrols in an area covering 40,000 square miles in the northern mountains of Amazonas, Ancash, La Libertad, Cajamarca, Huánuco, Piura, and Lambayeque. "This," concludes Francisco Chuquihuanga, president of the Ambulco patrols, which operate in the stony heights above Ayabaca, Piura, "is something new, justice we didn't have before."

Origins

Although their precise origin is a matter of fierce debate, the first patrol began on December 29, 1976, in Cuyumalca, Cajamarca, after a village assembly attended by four policemen, schoolteachers, and more than 150 local residents. The motive was a rise in cattle rustling and a series of robberies from the school, constructed by the parents' association from wattle, daub, and tile. A principal organizer was Régulo Oblitas, the lieutenant governor of Cuyumalca and a farmer of modest means with only a couple of acres and nine children. He had returned to the mountains of Cuyumalca at the end of the 1960s, after cutting sugarcane for seventeen years on the Pucalá and Tumán plantations near the coastal city of Chiclayo.

"At the beginning, many were against forming the patrol," Oblitas, now fifty-one, remembers of his fellow Cuyumalcans, who scratch a precarious living from small plots and the occasional trip to the coast and jungle to work as day laborers. "Some were scared of the rustlers and others were involved with the robbery."

Red Homeland, Ludovico's party, got involved in the patrols only a month later. The key protagonist was Daniel Idrogo, born to one of Cuyumalca's five hundred peasant families and two years into law studies at Trujillo University. The Red Homeland's Maoist ideology placed a priority on converting peasants to the cause of revolution. Idrogo saw the newly formed patrols as a way to expand the party's influence while propelling them beyond their role as what he called "cow keepers."

Idrogo was only twenty-two years old in 1976. But a combination of advanced studies, knowledge of the countryside, political vision, and personal charisma made him a powerful organizer. He worked in semiclandestinity, afraid of arrest by the military government. Legend holds that the Chota Investigative Police put a bounty of 2 million *soles* ($200) on his head and that the skinny, baby-faced youth walked the hills disguised as a woman to avoid capture. He was elected to congress in 1985 with the highest number of votes in Cajamarca, becoming one of the first peasant-born legislators in Peru's history.

As for so many of Peru's popular organizations, often riven by personal jealousies and political infighting, the 1980s brought bitter division. Early in the decade, Pedro Risco, a merchant and a member of the American Popular Revolutionary Alliance (APRA), began to form what he baptized as "Pacific Patrols," like the other night patrols but meant to work in close cooperation with police and authorities. "The authorities must be respected and one must not go against the Constitution," I was told by Risco, the former mayor of Chota who now runs the Pacific Patrols from his store near Chota's central square. Mixing *aprista* populism with attacks against what he gleefully satanized as the "terrorist communists" and "failed plotters" of Red Homeland, Risco took advantage of his government connections to convince several nearby villages to distance themselves from the rival Red Homeland Patrol Federation. He also traveled to Puno and Cuzco to spread the news of the APRA Pacific Patrols. Never modest, Risco crowned himself "the President of the presidents of the Pacific Patrols."

Despite these partisan battles, the 1980s brought a major geographical expansion of the patrols. In part, growth followed a political logic. Activists from leftist parties as well as the APRA spread out to form patrols, hoping to convert them into party strongholds. Mostly, however, they multiplied because of a reputation for efficiency. The loss of a goat or a cow was a hard blow for a peasant family, all the more so with the deepening of economic crisis in the 1970s and 1980s. The police were understaffed and often indifferent to poor villagers—or simply corrupt. The patrols emerged as the best way to stop crime. "We formed our patrol after hearing that in Chota they had completely eradicated cattle rustling," concludes Roberto Cruz, one of the founders of the Huancacarpa Alto patrol near Huancabamba, where he sows potatoes and raises sheep in the lunar landscape of the frozen moors and the lakes known as Las Huaringas.

Village Justice

As the patrols spread, their duties also multiplied. In some villages, they organized small public works projects, for example, cleaning irrigation canals or constructing health posts and meeting halls. Most extraordinary in the patrols' development, however, is their role in administering justice. More important than patrolling, throughout the north their principal activity now consists of *arreglos*, or village-based trials. At assemblies attended by the entire village and presided over by the elected patrol steering committee, small yet often bitter disputes—property disagreements, inheritances, water rights, and intrigues—are settled. These are problems that abound in rural communities: "small town, big hell," as they say in the mountains. Resolution comes after long hours of often contentious debate by the light of a Coleman lantern or a kerosene lamp made from a can of Gloria brand evaporated milk. At times, the final

Figure 48. Patroller in Lingán Pata, Cajamarca, with a cow recovered from rustlers. (Courtesy of ILLA)

settlement includes a fine or whipstrokes. In addition, the litigants almost always sign a "trial record."

Far from an expression of "pure" or "autochthonous" Andean values, many of the rules have been adapted by patrollers from the formal justice system, with its apparatus of seals, record books, fingerprints, and the byzantine bureaucratic language of "commissions," "memorials," and "investigations." Yet it would be a mistake to assume that peasants simply imitate bureaucracy. To the contrary, they incorporate these conventions into an original and in many ways more democratic system. Steering committees are elected at well-attended assemblies, and leadership usually changes every couple of years. In the old days, to patrol for the hated estates was a resented obligation. To do it for the *ronda*, however, is a matter of pride. "You go back to bed," goes the bravado of one ballad. "I'm going out to *rondar*."

This "informal" patrol justice competes with—if not replaces—the state's inefficient and corrupt formal system. As one *huayno* (ballad) from Hualgayoc goes:

> With the peasant patrols,
> the justice you awaited.

The little bribes are finished and the money you had to spend.
The authorities are putting on
their mourning clothes
their salaries no longer keep them
sleeping all day long.

According to anthropologists Karin Apel and Ludwig Huber, more than 85 percent of those interviewed in the Ayabaca district of Frías said they had more confidence in the patrols than in government authorities for the resolution of disagreements, robbery, public drunkenness, and injuries.[4] This confidence is visible in the rapid decrease in the number of cases brought by peasants to the state. "Since 1984," says Teófilo Rivera, secretary to the judge in charge of land disputes, from his empty Chota office, "we have registered a 90 percent decrease in the number of cases."

Some government officials sympathize with the patrols. But like many bureaucrats, Benjamín Vílchez, Chota's district attorney, can hardly contain his fury, fed by the old presumption of the supremacy of the urban over the rural, the Western over the Andean, the official over the informal, the state over the peasantry. "Peasants think they can resolve any sort of problem . . . and they get drunk and stoned on coca and have protest meetings and marches where they challenge constituted authority."

Until the mid-1980s, judicial authorities, especially the police, tried to repress the patrols with constant threats and arrest warrants. "I was called to the Paimas police station twelve times, and once I was threatened with death by the sergeant," recounts Víctor Córdova, at forty-three the president of the Tunnel Six Central Committee. There is still intimidation, including the 1992 arrests of several Chota patrol leaders, charged under draconian antiterrorist laws imposed by the Fujimori government. But a certain modus vivendi has been achieved over recent years. A 1986 law gave the patrols legal recognition and a new legitimacy. The authorities have realized that, after fourteen years, they are simply not able to get rid of them. Instead of repression, they opt for attempting to exert control and talk incessantly of the need for the patrols to "collaborate" with the authorities.

Pride and Fights

Patrol customs—like customs throughout Peru—vary from region to region. On the moors of San Miguel, where eagles and hawks circle the desolate spaces that extend for miles between each house, patrolling is done on horseback. A patroller is called a "soldier" in Hualgayoc, while in Chota he "does a turn of duty." The preferred weapon of an Ayabacan patroller is a leather whip. In Chota, Cutervo, and Hualgayoc, it is the walking stick.

What they share is pride in the patrols. Organizations have so much legitimacy that when a northern peasant speaks of the "president," normally he is referring not to a national elected official or the Shining Path's "Gonzalo," but to the man who presides over the local patrol committee. The patrol *huayno* is its own genre, part of the identity politics that flourish around the new organizations. These songs tell of clashes with cattle rustlers and hostile authorities. They celebrate the end of robbery and the beginnings of peasant strength:

> Little animals and fields were saved with the patrols
> when the thieves ruled they left us nothing.
> The town authorities didn't want to help us
> but we peasants said we must organize ourselves.

The date of each patrol's founding has become a key celebration day in the ritual calendar of many villages. Speeches, parades, theater, poetry, and school anthems to the patrols along with patrol music and an open kitchen—punctuated by an act of national affirmation, the raising of the Peruvian flag and intonation of the national anthem—all underscore the importance of having sacrificed rest to long nights on the trail and at assemblies. Far from "losing" a sense of identity in the face of the homogenization of coastal modernity, with its Natacha,[5] New Kids on the Block, and Ninja Turtles, northern peasants have built an original form of political culture. An "alternative modernity," a new way of being Andean, has coalesced out of this rural response to difficult circumstances through the new cultural politics of the patrols.

There are serious limitations to the success of the patrols, as in other so-called new social movements in Latin America. The most obvious are political rivalries. The APRA and leftist parties have competing federations, each publishing their own literature (for instance, Red Homeland's "Moral Guidelines for the Revolutionary Patroller" quotes the six exhortations and six prohibitions of Ho Chi Minh, the Sandinista oath, and the three cardinal rules and eight warnings of Mao).

The involvement of political parties does not reduce to manipulation of the peasants by the "external forces" of city activists, however. Northern peasants are not prepolitical innocents, but rather take an active and

Figure 49. Patrollers from Bambamarca, Cajamarca, celebrate the election of a new president. Photograph by Orin Starn.

often well-informed interest in municipal and national elections. Moreover, a good number of political activists who have pursued advanced studies and now work in the city were born in peasant homes.

With fewer political squabbles in the 1980s, the patrol movement would have had more power to advance demands of broad interest to peasants—more peasant representation in government, more rural investment by the state, better prices. Indeed, over the past few years, there have been clear signs of a growing rejection of attempts to link the patrols to political parties, reflecting the general disillusionment with traditional politics that culminated with Fujimori's election. "We are tired of the politicians," says Flavio Meléndez, president of the Quispampa, Huancabamba, Central Committee of Peasant Patrols, "and we don't want more 'orientations' and 'training sessions' that in the end only serve political campaigns."

Another problem relates to *caudillismo*, "bossism." In Cajamarca, for example, the number of federations claiming to represent the true Cajamarcan patroller has multiplied, each under the stewardship of a boss. Many Cajamarcans dismiss these federations as simply "Eriberto's" or "Quiroz's." Although an extreme case, Cajamarca illustrates how the

familiar specters of clientelism and hierarchy can reappear with an ostensibly "new" and "democratic" movement.

Finally, women remain on the margins, a measure of the challenges
they face in northern peasant culture and indeed in much of Peru. Patrolling is considered men's work. The woman who talks too much in an assembly—unless she is a principal litigant—risks being accused of being a
"*machona*" or "bossy." No woman has ever been elected patrol president.
Anthropologist Marisol de la Cadena has argued that women's subordination in the Andean countryside is reflected in their tendency to be regarded as "more Indian" than men by virtue of their lesser involvement in
political affairs and their more "traditional" dress and duties, like weaving and herding.[6] Although women were among the first to support the
patrols and may use assemblies to pursue charges of wife beatings against
abusive husbands, the organizations have not broken away from the ideology of the second-class status of women in Andean society.

Patrol Abuses?

An aura of intimidation is part of the patrols' public culture. There are
whips, walking sticks, and stories of having administered "whacks" or
"firecrackers" to thieves. This reputation for tough justice, as sociologists John Gitlitz and Telmo Rojas write, "contributes to popular enthusiasm and social solidarity, while at the same time undoubtedly frightens
[cattle] rustlers."[7]

On visits to villages during assemblies, I've witnessed "baths" of freez-
ing water and rougher methods, like the "little bird," in which a suspect is
hung from a tree with arms tied behind the back. Ironically, these techniques—like the seals and record book—come from the official system.
"We became familiar with the little bird because they always did it in the
Ayabaca Investigative Police station," explains one local patroller. In this
case, syncretism and recombination have reinscribed the logic of force
and terror, underscoring the dangers as well as the joys and pleasures of
the "hybrid cultures" that have proliferated in Latin America in this century.[8]

It would be wrong to ignore the occasional violence in the patrols. At
the same time, it is important to remember the years of abuse suffered
by peasants at the hands of thieves and the new security brought by the
patrols. A series of developments have decreased abuses. One is a sharp
reduction in robberies, moderating the patrols' initial spirit of warlike
confrontation with rustlers. Another is the influence of department fed-

eration activists. Anxious to protect the patrols' positive image and influenced by growing talk about human rights in Peru, they counsel moderation to followers.

Religion also plays a role. Many patrol leaders at the village level—in
general, measured, honest men—are at the same time catechists or local
coordinators for a Protestant church. Not a few see in severe punishment
an affront to Christian morality. Although the patrols' tough ethos will
likely continue to ignite occasional abuse against suspected thieves, most
patrollers share the opinion of Eladio Idrogo, a catechist and president
of the Cuyumalca Central Committee of Peasant Patrols: "We had to be
tough at the beginning, but now it's time to moderate and not punish so
much."

A Positive Balance

Despite their limitations, the patrols have brought peasants impressive
benefits. Cattle rustling has practically disappeared. In Tunnel Six, where
I lived in 1986–87, thieves stole 561 animals between 1980 and 1983.
As happened in many villages, the "fingernails"—as peasants call them—
were a mix of "fruit birds" (neighbors who rob every once in a while) and
"big magnates" (professional rustlers who belong to organized bands).
The rise of the patrols caused a precipitous decline in robbery. The best-
known thief was hung by a rope and dunked head first in the rushing
water filling a cement canal. While I was there, only three hens, four
ducks, and a pig were lost. This experience is echoed across the northern mountains. Most peasants have only a few hectares of land and small
herds. Given the precarious economics of survival in Peru, the patrols
have provided a vital margin of security.

Moreover, peasants in search of justice have an efficient forum for dispute resolution. Villagers not only avoid small bribes and fees, but also
save time and money that would otherwise be spent in traveling to city
courtrooms and police stations. "We solve in a night," says Oscar Sánchez,
"problems that lasted for years with the authorities."

The Shining Path and the Patrols

Another payoff of the patrols was claimed frequently in the 1980s: they
stopped the Shining Path's advance. The theory is simple. The Shining
Path's difficulty in moving into Cajamarca and Puno was thought to be
due to autonomous peasant organizations—the northern patrols and

southern peasant communities—that rejected the Shining Path's vertical authoritarianism.

Several concrete examples exist. In 1984, the charismatic Félix Calderón, one of the Shining Path's most important leaders in the north, introduced himself in a meeting in the village of Morán Lirio, four hours uphill by foot from Bambamarca. But the patrollers, partly due to the presence of Red Homeland activists, rivals of the Shining Path, rejected his invitation to join the armed struggle. They asked Calderón to leave before police arrived. The Shining Path militants had to move north, where they were captured on the highway between Cutervo and Sócota. Calderón died in the 1986 Lima prison uprising.

But the relationship between the Shining Path and the patrols cannot be reduced to a mere rejection. Peasant mobility—youths who migrate constantly from their mountain provinces to Lima, Chiclayo, Trujillo, and other urban centers and also to temporary jobs on African palm and coca farms in the jungle's "red zones"—makes proselytizing easier for both the Shining Path and MRTA. One morning in 1990, after I spent a night in the home of a *ronda* leader near Chota, we woke to discover that the local school was painted with Shining Path threats against voting in upcoming elections. "These are kids who come back from the jungle," my friend explained to me. "They aren't really organized, but they like to paint to screw around."

What does the Shining Path think about the northern patrols? Flor, age twenty, is in the Chiclayo prison accused of having participated in a series of dynamite attacks in Cutervo, where she was studying nursing. Her parents are Chota peasants. She dresses like any other poor woman living on the coast: flip-flops, a cheap blouse, and a stained polyester skirt. "The patrols are all right," she tells me in the jail's dark waiting room, "but they need the leadership of a party." In other words, the Shining Path.

Evidence suggests that the Shining Path considers the patrols' methods too soft. One patrol leader from San Marcos told sociologist Nora Bonifaz in 1989 that Shining Path militants "say that in the patrols we try to correct people's behavior and that we are wasting time pleading with them. . . . Bad weeds must be eradicated."[9]

But it's another matter in areas where the Shining Path has the necessary force. There, the Maoists have proved themselves ready to take apart patrols and impose themselves using their familiar strategy of terror. The macabre murder of eleven patrollers in the central square of Choras, Huánuco, occurred on June 27, 1990. Organized by Red Homeland, Choras was the first district with a patrol in Huánuco. When the

Shining Path began to extend its influence to the Huánuco mountains from Tingo María in 1988, it considered Choras an obstacle. A group of over one hundred militants rang the church bell to call the population to the square. They pulled out the main leaders, then stabbed them to death in front of the horrified crowd. When Daniel Idrogo and another Red Homeland activist arrived a week later, they had to take down the flag bearing the hammer and sickle.

During the 1980s, however, the Shining Path's weakness in the north meant that the patrols didn't have to confront guerrillas directly. Then and now, the patrollers' daily worries revolve around how to solve disputes, deal with government repression, and prevent a resurgence of cattle rustling, something that occurred in Cutervo, for example, when some patrols disbanded.

The immediate future appears relatively stable. On the one hand, it appears clear that the patrols will never be the "seeds of a new grassroots power," as Red Homeland once dreamed. Some leftist activists now talk of their concern that the patrols not fall into what Daniel Idrogo calls "patrolism": "There is that chance that peasant justice would spend so much energy on resolving small disputes that they would forget about the larger problem of agricultural policy and social change."

But it's also impossible to assert that the patrols have been or will be domesticated. An attitude of cooperation and even respect for the authorities and the constitution coexists with a vigorous independence. At the same time, pragmatism pairs with fragments of a utopian vision. "Perhaps if the police, the judges, and the bureaucrats have caused us so many problems," Víctor Córdova slyly smiles, "it's because they think that some day we'll no longer want authorities."

Notes

1   *Rondas campesinas* literally means "peasant rounds," referring to the nighttime patrols that were the original task of these peasant justice organizations.
2   A *pollera* is the thick wool skirt, often finely embroidered and worn several at a time, used as traditional dress by peasant women. *Ojotas*, also called *llanques*, are open sandals generally made of tire rubber.
3   *La República* is Peru's second-largest daily newspaper.
4   Ludwig Huber and Karin Appel, "Comunidades y rondas campesinas en Piura," *Bulletin de l'Institut français d'études andines* 19, no. 1 (1992): 165–182.
5   *Natacha* was a popular soap opera broadcast in 1991 that featured Peruvian and Venezuelan actors. The story followed a mountain girl who moved to Lima to work as a maid and ended up marrying the son of her wealthy patrons.

6   Marisol de la Cadena, "'Women Are More Indian: Ethnicity and Gender in a Community Near Cuzco," in *Ethnicity, Markets, and Migration in the Andes: At the Crossroads of History and Anthropology*, edited by Brooke Larson, Olivia Harris, and Enrique Tandeter (Durham, N.C.: Duke University Press, 1995).

7   John Gitlitz and Telmo Rojas, "Peasant Vigilante Committees in Northern Peru," *Journal of Latin American Studies* 15, no. 1 (1983): 188.

8   The term "hybrid cultures" comes from the title of literary theorist Nestor García Canclini's *Culturas híbridas: Estrategias para entrar y salir de la modernidad* (Mexico City: Horizonte, 1990).

9   Nora Bonifaz, personal communication, August 12, 1991.

"A MOMENTOUS DECISION"

Alberto Fujimori

When he stepped to the podium of the Democratic Constituent Congress on July 28, 1993, Peruvian Independence Day, Alberto Fujimori was both one of the most popular Latin American presidents ever and one of the most vilified. A year earlier, he had suspended the constitution and abolished Congress in a bloodless coup backed by the military. His rationale, reviewed here, was that economic collapse and a Shining Path victory were imminent and drastic measures to end a deadlock perpetuated by traditional political parties were inevitable. Pundits baptized it a dictablanda, *soft dictatorship, combining press freedom and the election of a pro-Fujimori legislature with, among other repressive measures, a refusal to punish human rights abuses, the restriction of due process in the courts, and the concentration of power in the hands of the executive. This speech is infused by Fujimori's almost religious belief in the healing power of a* mano dura, *a firm hand, dispensing efficiency, modern technology, and the allure of the international marketplace.*

It has been sixteen months since the day when, under my full responsibility, I adopted a decision of an exceptional nature in order to correct the dangerous deficiencies and vacuums of our political system and thus be able to cope with the serious problems of the country.

My speech before this illustrious body is a reencounter with the true democratic system that I respect and a reason for addressing the entire nation with the purpose of reporting on what I have done since then as well as to establish a necessary contrast between the Peru that we found and the one that we begin to build with the efforts of all Peruvians.

On that day, 5 April 1992, I faced a predicament: either Peru continued walking, quickly heading to the abyss of anarchy and chaos, pushed by terrorism and before the passiveness of the state organization, or I took the risk of providing the state with the necessary instruments for putting an end to that threat.

It was not an easy decision, as you may well imagine. With violence and terror embedded into our daily activities, the economic crisis worsened and brought about greater poverty. We were on the road to national collapse. In economic terms, we were doing the right thing. There was no other solution. However, what we patiently did during the day, the terrorists mercilessly destroyed at night.

The isolation we wanted to overcome when Peru rejoined the international financial community was being prolonged because no foreign investors or capital dared to come to a country where there was not the slightest security for investments or even their lives.

Tourism, the second most important source of foreign currency for the country, languished. Before April 5, the state and its institutions—despite having been somewhat reformed and modernized—continued to lose prestige as they proved unable to end the terrorist criminal wave. Until April 5 we had a national government and a criminal force that was challenging it in an increasingly evident balance of armed power that we could not allow. Within that context, the previous judicial branch was unable to mete out justice to the terrorist criminals. Following legal proceedings that were a farce, the terrorists returned to the streets to rejoin annihilation cells. For over a decade prisons stopped performing their fundamental duty of confining criminals to protect society. Terrorists enjoyed unbelievable opportunities in jail that allowed them not only to train their cadres but also to coordinate from there attacks and other criminal operations because of the submissiveness and inaction of the authorities.

What seemed like a daring attempt now looms as a reality. Now, we are establishing realistic deadlines to finish once and for all with the MRTA [Túpac Amaru Revolutionary Movement] and the Shining Path.

History is based on momentous decisions. One day Abimael Guzmán crossed the river that separates us from the dark side of history, and he sowed destruction and death in Peru to impose a ferocious and inhuman regime. Compelled by the circumstances and my profound conviction that I was fundamentally loyal to a nation that hopes to achieve peace and progress, I, too, had to cross the river—but in the opposite direction. I do not regret this now that I see Peru can recover from its wounds and become strong. I realize that I did the right thing in assuming my responsibility as a leader, come what may.

It is necessary and befitting to mention the work carried out by our armed forces and members of our national police. They were able to defeat the most fanatic and perverse enemy under the most difficult circumstances we can imagine. The armed forces and national police have fought terrorism and sacrificed the lives of their members amid a critical economic situation. This has prevented us from providing them with adequate salaries, but they have fulfilled their duty nevertheless. They have fought, and continue to fight, intrepidly so that Peru is progressively rid of the threat of Pol Pot terrorism. The military has been supported by the people organized in peasant self-defense groups, which have played a historic role in the struggle. Glory and honor to all these brave Peruvians!

This year human rights have been the topic of headlines. No one denies that we must all defend and promote those rights. This government in particular has a policy that clearly defends human rights. There is no other way to explain that today the jails are filled to the brim with terrorists. Isolated cases of human rights violations, which I firmly condemn, cannot be attributed to a systematic and official policy. No one can deny that we are winning the war against terror with intelligence and with the people's participation.

In a little over one year, one of the most violent nations, the most violent in the region, has begun little by little to transform into a safe and stable nation. We are now a nation that has its affairs in order. Our country is starting to gain the admiration and respect of citizens in other nations that have similar problems. In three years we have gone from international isolation to a position of hope, not only in Latin America but in the world.

For investors, the previously valuable mineral, hydrobiologic, agro-industrial, and tourism resources in such a rich nation as Peru were worthless. To invest here was sheer madness, but that is no longer true. In three years, a group of reforms have been applied, the sole purpose of which is to lay the foundations for a new society, that is, a society that is socially and economically democratic, because our goal is to end all privileges and install efficiency and healthy competition. In sum, we want opportunities for everyone. We have gone from a gigantic state apparatus, oversized with ministries that occupied enormous buildings—all the result of political influence peddling—to a completely different situation.

We arrived at this point by implementing a firm policy that encompasses the most basic principles of soundness, austerity, and efficiency. My government has been labeled authoritarian for this, but exercising order and authority should be normal in a civilized society, in a society

Figure 50. Alberto Fujimori combined populism with a belief that authoritarian rule would solve Peru's problems. (Courtesy of *Quehacer*)

Figure 51. Cartoonist Alfredo is skeptical about the claimed success of neoliberal economics. The cartoon reads: "The economic program is on its feet." (Courtesy of *La República*)

that wants to advance. It is abnormal for disorder and anarchy to prevail. The absence of a modicum of respect for the law is unacceptable. It is condemnable that people take advantage of this state of affairs to profit or maintain prerogatives at the people's expense.

My government's structural reforms posit a modern state. In the new structure, the prefects need not exist because the municipalities, police, and judicial authorities will implement government acts and exercise authority.

The economic program has sought to achieve its objectives through two basic mechanisms: fiscal and monetary policies. The first is based on the strict management of our fiscal accounts. We only spend in accordance with the taxes collected and what we obtain through foreign financing. We have managed to reduce the inflation rate in the past years by exercising strict fiscal discipline and adequate monetary and foreign exchange management. Therefore, it is important to reiterate that the government will continue to implement this policy, which has allowed us to continue to bring down the inflation rate.

In order to give the recovery process a firm base, it was necessary to establish a whole range of structural reforms and seek a new pattern of economic development based on efficiency, modernization, and international competitiveness, gradually eliminating foreign trade difficulties as a mechanism to encourage economic competitiveness. The government has established rules prohibiting unfair competition in international trade, dumping, and direct export subsidies in accordance with international standards.

Reentry into the international financial community has allowed our country once again to be eligible for credit and able to receive foreign financing to boost and support the economic growth outlined in the program. The recovery of our image and credibility abroad has helped generate investments, jobs, and growth.

Transportation, perhaps unlike any other sector, has faced disaster. A national road infrastructure has been affected as if Peru had been at war. The traditional isolation of many peoples of Peru has increased for this reason. The goal of the government-designed program is to complete reconstruction work on 1,800 kilometers of roads this year in various parts of the country and completely repair 2,000 kilometers of the Pan-American highway from Tacna to Tumbes and the central highway between Lima and Huánuco. These roads will be completely paved.

To promote small businesses and microbusinesses, we have channeled the increase in social expenditure to purchasing school bags, jogging suits, shoes, school books, and foods prepared with local products. The idea is to give support to the community through an emergency program that at the same time will stimulate local industrial and agricultural production.

Within the program of structural reforms, privatization is a fundamental component. Privatization is a means to redefine the state's role; in practice it is to reduce the enormous $2.5 billion gap accumulated year after year. The state must provide economic guidance, not implement productive activities.

What percentage of state resources destined for education have truly reached the students rather than being used to pay the immense administrative bureaucracy? The university park building was a great monument to the use of influential people's personal cards to obtain privileges and favors in the education sector. The ministry now operates modestly as befits a country where resources must be used rationally and with fairness.

With more bureaucracy, inefficiency, and confusion, the educational product was extremely poor. Of course, I prefer not to talk about the strikes of the Trade Union of Education Workers, which made the school year seem like a joke. Now, we must turn the page and use the resources the state assigns for students.

I emphatically maintain that anyone who says we had free education is mocking the Peruvian people. Because of populist statism and its pseudo–free education, there are millions of youths with deficient education.

Some of the country's most important state universities had become, quite simply, true trenches of terrorism. How did this happen? It is very simple. In an effort to defend an alleged constitutional principle, that of university autonomy—a pseudo-autonomy, truthfully speaking—the right to defend life itself was violated.

Demagoguery allowed terrorists to take advantage of these so-called democratic principles to destroy democracy and the democrats.

Now, we have rescued the true principle of autonomy. Autonomy meaning a self-government and not a puppet government. As former president of the Assembly of Rectors I ask: Where was the authority back then?

It is also amazing that a few of our state universities were training professors under the teachings and pressures of the Shining Path and the MRTA. This is incredible. Later on, these professors used teachers unions to use other teachers for their own objectives.

Building schools has obviously been the area where we have focused our efforts. Let us not forget that our deficit is 30,000 classrooms throughout the country. Consequently, the pace for the inauguration of schools is not the result of any personal political campaign. It is based on a need, the need to give millions of Peruvian children a decent structure. It is a decent structure that was promised a million times, but a promise that was never kept. . . .

Is there a Peruvian who does not want to end poverty, for God's sake? To be sure, it is not possible for a government that is overcoming a crisis of the scope we inherited to eliminate in three years a centuries-old problem. Please, let us not confuse the people! Let us not politicize the matter of poverty with seemingly innocent demands!

The impoverishment and exploitation of millions of Peruvians throughout five centuries has accomplices known to all. That poverty has worsened in the past decade owing to misgovernment and terrorism. Let us work in an orderly and responsible fashion to eliminate terrorism and for the first time create objective conditions to uproot the problem of poverty. Terrorists must repent, surrender to justice, and serve a life sentence, or they go to hell!

My government policies have been described as liberal [i.e., free market] by certain individuals who like to label reality. I am sorry but you have the wrong label. My government and I are simply pragmatic. This means that I do not pay homage to theories, dogmas, or myths.

I am an agronomist, but I do not breed cows and I do not believe in sacred cows.

The past three years—can there be any doubt?—have been the most intense of recent times. I am sure that, as time passes and passions cool, my adversaries will examine with greater objectivity the set of political decisions that I believe have been essential to the guaranteed existence of the Peruvian state and nation. Despite a well-conducted campaign against the emergency measures imposed on April 5, I am convinced that even my opponents now feel safer in this country where yesterday their own lives were worth nothing because they were on the selective extermination list prepared by the Shining Path and MRTA.

With all due respect, if the government and the state failed in the battle against terrorism, perhaps some of our supporters, as well as some of our opponents, would not be here, but instead be enjoying the perpetual peace of a cemetery.

Yesterday's huge and impressive military parade in Lima and the parades throughout the republic are the best proof that the objectives sought by those enemies of Peru have not been fulfilled. Yesterday, university students, police officers, and soldiers mixed with enthusiastic people to offer a beautiful lesson of national unity for peace and progress in the hopes of a better future. Today, we can say that Peru is no longer the country of lost opportunity. Today, Peru is a feasible and possible country.

Long live Peru!

CHOLERIC OUTBREAK

Caretas

Crafted in the style of a theater script, this journalistic gem from leading newsweekly Caretas *takes a bitingly satirical look at how the cholera outbreak in 1991 was at first avoided, then grossly mishandled by the government, particularly ministries whose portfolios were most affected: Fisheries and Agriculture. Within a year, the disease, unknown in South America since the 1800s, had spread to neighboring Ecuador and Bolivia, with new cases to come in Brazil, Chile, and Argentina. However, its effects remained most dramatic in Peru, where the lack of adequate sewage systems, potable water, and health care produced by economic crisis paired with mixed messages from the government meant that many preventable cases ended in tragedy.*

A Tragedy of Errors

The drama called "Tragedy" takes place in Peru in the year 1991, at a time when this South American country is experiencing the worst economic crisis of its history. Of its 22 million inhabitants, the World Health Organization estimates that 13 million live in extreme poverty. The leading characters are these: Alberto Fujimori Fujimori, enigmatic and authoritarian constitutional president of the republic; Carlos Vidal Layseca, robust and hard-nosed health minister; and *Vibrium cholerae*, the malevolent bacillus that causes cholera. Supporting cast: medical authorities, investigative institutes, street vendors, fishermen, the press, and the marine species that inhabit the 200 miles of Peru's territorial ocean, the time-honored "Grau's Sea."

Peru's bad situation becomes worse when in late January a disturbing series of deaths is detected in Chimbote, one of the country's northern cities. All the cases present the same symptoms: diarrhea and vomiting. In addition, almost all of those affected say they ate fish before getting sick. This unknown evil begins its rapid march down the coast, heading south. Soon, it arrives in Lima. But not until February 2 is the first alarm sounded in the press: a cholera epidemic. What is cholera? Only then is the first official voice heard. The curtain rises.

Thursday, February 7
Health Minister Vidal advises the population to take preventive measures: avoid eating *cebiche*,[1] fish, and shellfish; boil drinking water; and stop going to the beach. He announces that scientists from the Health Ministry and the Atlanta Center for Disease Control (CDC) have begun an exhaustive investigation into the epidemic's origins and how it spread. At the same time, he adds that he will ask President Fujimori to declare a national health emergency.

For its part, Agence France Presse, quoting former health minister Uriel García Cáceres, reports that in Lima alone, about 2 million people eat from the carts of street vendors. The epidemic has claimed 25 lives and infected 730 people so far.

Friday, February 8
Carley Guerra de Macedo, director of the Pan-American Health Organization, confirms that cholera can be prevented by avoiding the consumption of raw food and water that hasn't been boiled.

At midday, the Lima Municipality begins to seize trays of *cebiche* and fish dishes sold by street vendors. Vice-Mayor Juan Ortega announces that two and a half tons of Chimbote fish have been incinerated. Since some people have stopped eating seafood, fishermen and market vendors must throw out 190 tons of fish and shellfish. There are already 42 dead.

Sunday, February 10
María Alina Ratto, director of the National University of San Marcos (UNMSM) Latin American Center for the Teaching and Investigation of Food Bacteria, begins a radio program on how to avoid cholera with proper hygiene: cook raw foods and avoid at all costs eating from the carts of street vendors.

—The CDC releases its first test results: the cholera bacillus lashing Peru is identified as 01 INABATOR, a strain considered among the most dangerous because of its ability to adapt to different climates.
—A rumor circulates that the lime juice used to make *cebiche* "kills the bacillus."

—The health minister releases a statement dated February 9. In point 3, he states: "The biological characteristics of this germ permit it to multiply in microplankton and through it in shellfish and fish, where it lodges and infects people, producing massive diarrhea with severe dehydration."

—President Alberto Fujimori, accompanied by his wife, Susana, and their four children, goes to the beach at the Navy Recreational Center in Huarmey.

Tuesday, February 12
Dr. Abad Flores, coordinator of the UNMSM laboratory of environmental microbiology and biotechnology, says it cannot yet be determined whether or not our coast's fish, mollusks, or crustaceans directly transmit cholera. He adds that this will be known when they finish analyzing three hundred water and fish samples.

—Some Lima *cebicherías* go bankrupt.[2] Others change their menus. New summer dishes include chicken *cebiche*, stew, and *anticuchos*.[3]

—Audberto Morales, a United Nations engineer, assures people that they can eat marine species from the high seas that inhabit depths of over 30 feet, like mackerel and cod. He recommends that people avoid *lorna*, mullet, and *pejerrey*, although he adds the proviso that frying or boiling sterilizes the meat. Nevertheless, he emphasizes that consuming *cebiche* or sashimi, a Japanese dish using raw fish, constitutes a risk.

—Lima beaches are semideserted even on the weekends.

Saturday, February 16
In a display of public epicureanism worthy of the title "The Last Supper," the health minister, health authorities, doctors, and journalists consume several dishes made of cooked fish: tripe stew, fish stew, baked fish in tomato sauce, and deep-fried fish. The minister says: "I have not said that cooked fish cannot be eaten. What I have said is that, for the time being, we must forget about *cebiche*."

Cholera statistics: 90 dead, 13,768 cases. Nevertheless, thanks to the health minister's preventive campaign, the death rate drops from 1 percent to 0.6 percent.

Tuesday, February 19
During a new spate of epicurean sampling of "hydrobiologic products" (a bit of scientific mumbo jumbo used by reporters instead of "fish") in

the Fish Terminal in Villa María del Triunfo, Miguel Arca, health director for southern Lima, says that boiled or fried fish can be eaten. Francisco Peña González, president of the National Federation of Peruvian Fish and Shellfish Vendors, is present. He describes the current situation of fishermen as a "trail of tears."

— Former ministers Hurtado Miller and Pennano are feted at a dinner in the Government Palace. The entire cabinet attends, including the ministers' wives. There is astonishment when it is noticed that the menu features cooked fish. "It does no harm well cooked," the president explains.

Friday, February 22

The president of the Peruvian Sea Institute (IMARPE), Admiral Ricardo Zevallos Newton, soothes public opinion by announcing that the high saline content of Peru's sea does not favor the survival of cholera. He says: "Fish don't pollute people. To the contrary, people pollute the sea."

Sunday, February 24

President Alberto Fujimori visits Pisco's San Andrés Cove and eats *cebiche* and sashimi in front of news photographers and television cameras in a dim-witted and dangerous attempt to eradicate the fear of fish created in the wake of the Health Ministry's intense campaign. As justification for his act, he cites the IMARPE report, repeating that fish caught on the high seas are healthy, that one must not fear eating fish but only a lack of hygiene, and that his family never stopped eating fish during the epidemic. The president does not mention that the optimal hygienic conditions surrounding the preparation of the presidential *cebiche* are not those of the majority of the population. On the same day, the Health Ministry's public education advertisement cautioning people not to eat *cebiche* is broadcast nationally.

Tuesday, February 26

After the intense media coverage of the president eating *cebiche*, the number of cholera cases reported in Lima's Cayetano Heredia and Loayza hospitals increases.

Wednesday, February 27

Faced with what the Health Ministry terms elegantly "recent events that throw doubt on the hygienic measures" recommended to combat cholera, an announcement is released: "The Ministry recommends prevention and control measures, including boiling water, personal hygiene, and proper food handling. At the same time, we recommend that people avoid the beach since it is polluted with fecal material from sewage pipes that dump into the sea. In addition, the ministry invokes community solidarity and responsibility and suggests that we guide ourselves by the scientific and technical criteria that exist to control cholera and avoid the uncontrolled spread of this disease, which could lead to its becoming endemic, bringing serious consequences for the country's health and economy."

— Fishing Minister Felix Canal Torres, imitating the president's show, although taking a much higher risk, eats a plate of *cebiche* in the Aurora Market in Lima's Cercado municipality. With his mouth still full, he declares that this raw fish dish is "pleasant and nutritious." The vendors applaud.
— The Health Ministry continues to run ads that recommend Peruvians not eat *cebiche*.
— A rumor circulates that the health minister may resign.

Thursday, February 28
— The Gulf War ends, but the *cebiche* war is declared in Peru.
— In a press conference, Health Minister Vidal, accompanied by a group of North American gastroenterologists from New York's Mayo Clinic, insists that it is right to recommend against eating *cebiche*. Then comes the following question: But if the president of the republic has eaten it in front of television cameras, with the sea behind him, in Pisco?

One of the doctors responds: "This is not a meeting of politicians, but of scientists, and I recommend to you that you eat well-cooked or boiled fish."

Minister Vidal adds: "As a precaution, I believe it is necessary for people not to consume raw fish and to eat fish only well cooked or well fried." He then made it clear that this recommendation did not mean a confrontation with the president of the republic.
— Inaugurating what could be deemed the "Fruit Front" of the *cebiche* war, the agriculture minister visits a market and eats unwashed grapes in front of television cameras. When their poor hygienic state is pointed out to him, the minister responds: "At times, eating a bit of dirt is good for the digestion."

—Meanwhile, the latest studies on cholera's advance reveal the following: 45,446 infected, 10,017 hospitalized, and 193 dead.

Friday, March 1
Dramatic finale. The nightly news programs announce the foreseeable consequences of the president's irresponsibility, imitated by some ministers: 509 cases in Chimbote herald a new cholera outbreak in the city where the epidemic began.

Notes

1 *Cebiche* is a salad made of raw seafood marinated in lime juice and tossed with onion, hot pepper, and spices.
2 A *cebichería* is a restaurant specializing in *cebiche*.
3 *Anticuchos* are pieces of beef heart marinated and grilled on skewers over charcoal braziers, found throughout Peru.

BRIBING A CONGRESSMAN

Alberto Kouri and Vladimiro Montesinos

The shady spy-master Vladimiro Montesinos may have been Peru's most powerful man in the last years of the twentieth century. As head of the Army Intelligence Service and chief advisor to President Alberto Fujimori, Montesinos doled out patronage, controlled major television stations, and amassed a personal fortune of over $100 million. In this secretly videotaped conversation from May 5, 2000, Montesinos bribes an opposition congressman, Alberto Kouri, to switch over to the ruling party to consolidate Fujimori's majority. The release of this and other so-called "Vladivideos" later that year precipitated the fall of the Fujimori government and the once formidable Montesinos's own ignominious flight to Venezuela.

MONTESINOS: We want to arrange this for you in a personal way, tailored for you individually, for your own peace of mind.

KOURI: Thank you for that.

MONTESINOS: It's better that it look like an individual decision [in other words, Kouri himself should formally announce his switchover to the government party]. It's better that way.

KOURI: If I need to write a letter, I'd like to propose a date . . . for example, October 1st.

MONTESINOS: Well, I don't think October will work. We need to have things in order by August. Image is everything. We're concerned with the international image of the country. And how do you produce a positive image? With a strong Congress, a solid majority, a thoughtful majority. We already have a majority, but we don't just want a narrow majority. I want it to be 70 or 75 percent.

KOURI: Well, how about September? Or does it really have to be in August?

MONTESINOS: It has to be August. It really has to be August. If you

Figure 52. Artist Miguel Det depicts the bribing of Alberto Kouri by Vladimiro Montesinos in a style echoing the famous seventeenth-century drawings of Guamán Poma de Ayala. (Courtesy of Miguel Det)

want, at the end of August. Whatever you want. But it needs to be August, because that's when there'll be the vote for the President of the Congress. The President of Congress, and the other leadership positions. . . . Here's a letter with an open date for your switch. That's what one does formally. Nothing more, and we're done. Okay, here's the letter [they both look at a letter produced by Montesinos].

KOURI: How about September 25th?

MONTESINOS: Let's not date it now. I trust people. I have good relations with people. . . .

KOURI: What are the possibilities [in other words, for being paid to switch over to the government party]?

MONTESINOS: You can negotiate.

KOURI: Well, I'd like to . . .

MONTESINOS: How much? How much? Here's ten [thousand dollars] [pulling out an envelope of money from his left pocket]. You tell me.

KOURI: No, let's say fifteen or twenty.

MONTESINOS: Fine.

KOURI: Let's say fifteen.

MONTESINOS: Ten plus five, fifteen [pulling out another envelope of money from his right pocket].

KOURI: And what about getting some help with my campaign debts from the last election? I spent sixty thousand or so dollars . . . and it would be good to have some help.

MONTESINOS: Sure, of course. I'll talk to some friends right away. Then we'll talk. But it will be important for you to send that letter, I think. We all need to work together on this.

SIMPLY PASCUALA

José María Salcedo

With their reliance on statistics and numerical trends, economic studies can lose sight of the human lives involved in the unlicensed, or "informal," sector, which now sustains more Peruvians than the formal economy and its legal employment. Pascuala Alvarado Huallpa's story is one among many. She was a shepherdess from the southern altiplano *who, if not for a childhood weakness for sweets, might never have left her peasant home. Unlike the all-too-frequent tales of misfortune and failure, this one contains a healthy dose of good luck, as Alvarado's ingenuity and stubbornness convert her into a Peruvian Horatio Alger for the 1990s.*

One August afternoon in 1983, Pascuala Alvarado Huallpa, dazzled by so many stairs, climbed up to one of the shops in the Santa Lucía shopping center and bought a spool of thread and two yards of pique cloth to sew a girl's dress.

Pascuala Alvarado Huallpa was born thirty-two years before in Desaguadero in the Department of Puno. The day she went to buy the material for that little dress she was already living on Juan Velasco Alvarado Avenue, Sector 2, Group 24, Block N, Lot 9, in Villa El Salvador.

Her parents, Luis Alvarado Sarmiento and María Huallpa Ponce, had twelve children. The father traded cattle between Bolivia and Arequipa. He was illiterate, able only to sign his name in big, slow letters. Puno's traditional droughts left the family with a taste for water boiled with potatoes and corn. This stew took on a greenish color until it turned into a smooth mush. With a bit of imagination, one could call it spinach.

Little Pascuala only went to school until the first grade. She flunked it three years in a row. Her father gave her a choice: study harder or herd the family's sheep, llamas, alpacas, pigs, and cows. Pascuala became a shepherdess. Her skill surprised her own father. On her eleventh birthday, Luis gave her the incredible sum of 500 *soles*. She was supposed to start her own business with the money. But Pascuala spent it on candies and trinkets, perhaps trying to hold on to a childhood that was slipping through her hands.

Fear and shame kept Pascuala from returning home on the day she spent the last penny of that small fortune. In the Desaguadero bus station, she met a woman who was going to Bolivia and wanted a girl as a maid. She lived for a year in La Paz. Although never able to save enough to replace the lost capital, she returned home to Desaguadero and felt her father had forgiven her.

At fifteen, she embarked on the forty-eight-hour bus trip to the house of an uncle who was a jeweler in Lima. She lived in the Barrios Altos neighborhood and missed her home and the food she grew up with terribly that first year. In Lima there was no *timpo*: mutton with dried potatoes and hot peppers. No *chayro*: soup with ground dried potatoes and strips of mutton and greens. But she was exposed to new flavors in exchange for these losses: the perfumes, the brilliantine her uncle used to try to tame his bristly Andean hair. She was fascinated by the sound of cars and the cries of the buyers of old bottles and newspapers, slowly pedaling their tricycles through the city.

The uncle's jewelry business did not attract her. She headed instead for the wealthy neighborhoods of Miraflores and San Isidro and found a job as a maid. Her mistress was obsessed about keeping up with the latest fashions. Young Pascuala was in charge of taking chic fabrics to the seamstress to make dresses according to the styles from a big collection of foreign magazines. Fascinated by the seamstress's skills, Pascuala begged her mistress to enroll her in a sewing and fashion school. She became one of the best students in the Manuela Felisa Gómez National Industrial Institute Number Two.

Shortly afterwards, the same thing happened to Pascuala as to many other young domestics in Lima. She fell in love with a man who promptly abandoned her, leaving her with a baby son just a few months old. Son in arms, Pascuala swore to have revenge and to earn more than that no-good employee of a foreign company who belonged to what he himself called "the decent middle class."

Revenge was rapid. Pascuala decided to leave her uncle's house when Lima's newspapers announced that thousands of people had invaded a stretch of desert to the south of the city. Heading right away for what would soon be known as Villa El Salvador, she sweltered in a long line under the hot sun and registered for a piece of land.

Figure 53. A seamstress and her baby look over material in a Lima store. (Courtesy of *Quehacer*)

Carrying her year-old son, she found a shop in the Surquillo district that gave her piecework to do at home. She didn't realize it then, but she was part of an immense web of seamstresses. Since Villa El Salvador still did not have electricity, she rented a manual sewing machine and a kerosene lamp. She began sewing garrison caps for the army. A little later, the shop owner proposed to pay her for her sewing with a more sophisticated machine. She doubled her nighttime work, making caps by the light of the kerosene lamp, and earned her first machine. About the time electricity arrived at Villa El Salvador, the owner of the Surquillo shop told her there was no more work. But now she had a machine and electric light.

She sewed her first girl's dress with the cloth from the shopping center on Gamarra Street. She took it to the Caquetá market and sold it quickly. After that, her visits to Gamarra Street became more frequent, and she started to multiply her sales at the market. The woman who bought Pascuala's dresses to sell in her stall at Caquetá belonged to an evangelical church. Business and faith led Pascuala to join that same church, and she discovered that religious connections also expanded her clientele. Pascuala began a feverish campaign to make not only girls' dresses, but also aprons, shirts, pullovers, and all kinds of garments. As her commitments grew, she found herself obligated to set up her own network of seam-stresses, and as it grew she began to buy mechanical looms.

She returned to the Gamarra Street shopping center, but this time to rent a combination workshop–retail outlet, where she stayed for two years. There she specialized in sports uniforms for schoolchildren. Then she moved to another shopping center on nearby Antonio Bazo Street and began to discover just how many of her seamstress colleagues spoke Aymara and came from Puno. She started to make thick jackets for the cold of the *altiplano*, or high moors. The jackets were sold back in her native Desaguadero.

Contemplating the array of mending and cutting machines in her new shop, Pascuala knows that she will never go back to Desaguadero, except to visit, perhaps at the steering wheel of the shiny car she just bought. But sending those jackets back to her hometown, she also feels that her father, if he were still alive today, might say that those 500 *soles* from her childhood were at last well spent.

X · CULTURE(S) REDEFINED

On one's first arrival, cultural diversity and creativity may be hard to spot in grimy, poverty-stricken Lima, prone beneath a lead-colored sky that lifts for only a few fleeting summer weeks. "In Lima," poet Carmen Ollé writes, "beauty is a steel corset." Yet even the worst poverty and terror have not prevented the forging of alternative identities and visions, part of what Mariátegui called "society's will not to petrify itself in a particular moment, not to freeze in a single position."

Symbol and meaning have always mattered in Peru. One reason for the left's failure in recent decades has been its inability to forge a "politics of meaning" that speaks to the *cholo* majorities. Alberto Fujimori identified skillfully with the underclasses through his folksy campaign style, using a tractor to symbolize his slogan of "Honesty, Technology, and Hard Work" (not to mention his canny strategy of appealing to evangelicals and informal business, invisible to traditional parties). As the forms through which people make sense of their lives, culture defines the contours of the everyday and the esoteric, the mundane and the elevated, the artistic and the political.[1]

To be sure, "culture" is a tricky word. It conjures up an image of wholeness and timelessness, or even an immutable link between identity and place. Such a view cannot convey the intermixture and fluidity that defined Peru's traditions even in ancient times, as when the Incas ceaselessly remade their pantheon to incorporate the local deities of those they conquered. One does not have to look far for Indian tradition, as in the stately masonry of the Temple of the Sun in downtown Cuzco; yet Santo Domingo Church stands on top, a symbol not only of conquest but of plural traditions. In a photograph from the Workshop on Social Photography (TAFOS), a vendor hawks polyester socks in front of Inca walls, reflecting the collapse of divisions between old and new, non-Western and Western, traditional and modern. Whether destructive or fertile, the interplay of continuity, imposition, and invention molds the topography of the country's cultural landscape.

Painters like Fernando de Syszlo and writers Mario Vargas Llosa and Alfredo Bryce Echenique have built international reputations in the toniest galleries and journals of New York and Paris. More often, however, Peruvian artists and writers straddle the line between "high" and "low," "art" and "politics." Thus, popular experience inspires novels like Eduardo González Viaña's *Sarita Colonia Comes Flying*, about the folk saint of migrants and bus drivers. Once the imported was associated with the lofty aesthetics of the European Enlightenment or Romanticism. Now, Peruvians may be just as likely to borrow from Motown or Hollywood, like Barranco's Nosequién y los nosecuantos, whose rock and hip-hop address the contemporary themes of migration to the United States, and the *apagones*, or blackouts, that sometimes throw the capital into darkness. Instead of tidy distinctions of style and place, culture develops in the busy and sometimes conflictual crossroads that break apart the expectation of wholeness, continuity, or essence.[2]

A prime example is the department of Ayacucho, where, despite political violence, art has flourished. Ballads, weavings, ceramics, and *retablos* respond to and expound on themes of loss and terror, flight and urban decay.[3] To earn precious dollars from North American and European consumers, drawing on their own everyday lives, refugee women in one of Lima's poorest shantytowns have turned the *arpillera*, the quilted wall-hanging first crafted in Chile, into a vehicle of cultural expression as gripping as the musket-bearing baroque angels of seventeenth-century Cuzco or the nineteenth-century textiles from Lake Titicaca islands. Although artistry abounds in Peru's National Museum, where Paracas weavings hang near the paintings of the Liman Julia Codesido and the Cajamarcan José Sabogal, it also exists on the street, at the church altar, and, for those who see the artistic in the everyday, in the tight weave of a Cajamarcan straw hat and the elaborate pyramids of cans and boxes in a vendor's stall at an Arequipan market.

Culture is inevitably contested terrain. Some of today's most powerful movements seek to shift the very terms of spiritual identity, like the Pentecostal churches that have grown explosively in some of the country's poorest neighborhoods and rural backwaters. Others strive to redefine the terms of gender and sexuality, as in the case of fledgling gay and lesbian journals and the feminist movement, linking figures like Ollé with activist María Elena Moyano. It would be wrong to assume that the pro-liferation of new initiatives is essentially good, "subversive," or politically progressive. Witness, for instance, the explosion of fan clubs for prepack-aged teen stars, like the Mexican Gloria Trevi. But even the most seem-ingly banal kinds of cultural expression can sometimes be multivalent, as in the mild antiracism of the hit soap opera *Natacha*, underscoring that even commercial culture can contain what critic Stuart Hall asserts are "elements of recognition and identification to which people are respond-ing."[4]

Nowhere is Peru's talent for cultural reconfiguration more on display than during carnival, those February days when people gather to sing, dance, drink, and celebrate having survived another year. Although these have been difficult years for Peru, carnival has not lost its relevance. Dra-matized in skits featuring abusive policemen and lecherous priests, young lovers and aged spinsters, are not only violence and disorder, but life's pleasures. Above all, perhaps, the mix of tennis shoes and *ojotas*, hot dogs and *cuy*, *salsa* and *huayno* encapsulates the spliced yet no less vigorous quality of Peruvian traditions, even as the crowd's wild energy reaffirms the Arguedas poem *kachkaniraqmi*, "I still exist."[5] "This is to make Peru," bellows the master of ceremonies over the makeshift sound system at one Lima coliseum packed with *comparsas*.[6] "This is to make a nation."

Notes

1 We borrow some of this phrasing from Renato Rosaldo, *Culture and Truth: The Remaking of Social Analysis* (Boston: Beacon Press, 1989), p. 26.

2 We draw this wording in part from James Clifford, *The Predicament of Culture* (Cam-bridge, Mass.: Harvard University Press, 1988), p. 233.

3 *Retablos* are wooden boxes filled with plaster of paris or potato flour figurines, originally used as home altars.

4 Stuart Hall, talk given in 1989 at the Institute of Contemporary Art, London, and quoted in Allen Pred and Michael Watts, *Reworking Modernity: Capitalisms and Symbolic Discontent* (New Brunswick, N.J.: Rutgers University Press, 1992), p. 193.

5 *Ojotas* are sandals made of leather and tire rubber. *Cuy* is guinea pig. A *huayno* is a moun-tain ballad.

6 A *comparsa* is a group of dancers and musicians, usually from the same village or neigh-borhood.

CHAYRAQ!

Carlos Iván Degregori

Half a century of migration has remade Lima into an Andean city, with the world's single largest population of Quechua speakers. New arrivals have redefined identities and cultures, maneuvering to forge a popular culture at the fraught intersection of the autochthonous and the imported, the past and the present, the indigenous and the Western. One of the most vibrant of their transplanted traditions is chay-raq, or carnival. In this spectacle of cultural catharsis and regeneration, Carlos Iván Degregori finds that everything—politics, local disputes, even poverty and hardship—is material for play, invention, parody, and denunciation.

It's the last Sunday in March, late summer, but a leaden sky hangs over the three or four thousand Ayacuchans who fill the Yuli Recreation Center in Lima's Vitarte district. Guitarists tune and dancers tug last ribbons into place. From the stage of the cement amphitheater, the master of ceremonies pleads for order from the crowd, made up of maids on their day off, artisans, wealthy merchants, workers, housewives, schoolchildren, babies, the underemployed, and momentary visitors to the capital. The grand parade of *comparsas* competing for the Gold Tambourine is about to begin.

More than fifteen minutes go by before the organizers from the Federation of Ayacucho Migrants impose a precarious order. "Beer, *chicha de jora*, and mouth-watering *pukapicante*," touts one of the organizers from the stage, as a phalanx of young spectators with cassette players, boom boxes, and even a few video cameras push forward to record the event.[1]

Santiago de Pischa district opens the competition. At the head goes a flashy green standard with gold flecks and a coat of arms with a fish and a key. One bearer features a Penn State University T-shirt, yet others wear ponchos and felt hats, reflecting the cultural hybridity that has always characterized Andean traditions. Paraders follow as overloaded as *eqeqos*, adorned with prickly pear, corn cobs, grenadines, and sugarcane.[2] Women boast black Huancayan shawls and skirts embroidered with flowers, and offer *chicha* from clay jars to fellow revelers. In addition to the usual chorus of tambourines, whistles, and flutes, many of plastic or aluminum, the Santiago de Pischans play other instruments: guitars, mandolins, violins, ringers, cowbells, and burro jaws.

Others follow across the stage. Ocros. Quinua. Acocro. Each carries a *quille*, a long plank dangling with flowers, streamers, grapes, apples, corn, potatoes, bananas, flour pastries. Behind, the costumes overflow with imagination and symbolism. There are wizened elders, fat merchants, and some dancers, animal-like, have even donned deer heads with flowery horns. Others wear thick lambskins as wool wigs, or blackface. For wild unorthodoxy, all would be the envy of any Liverpool punk.

Indeed, during carnival, identities change, order inverts, hierarchies collapse. It's supremely democratic, as the world turns upside down. Mercilessly satirized are the macho father and the priest, traditional power symbols in a patriarchal society. And so, a gyrating priest leads San Juan Bautista *comparsa*. He is a mock Franciscan with frog-eyed glasses, face whitened with talcum and crude cross in hand. He sprinkles holy water with a little bundle of grass, pronouncing solemn blessings. Suddenly, he drops the cross, chases after a pretty dancing girl, and wrestles for a kiss. At last he throws the girl over his shoulder and carries her away, then whips her until she kneels to kiss the cross. "*Qarqacha cura*—son-of-a-bitch priest," the crowd laughs and yells.

In Acocro's *comparsa*, the eventual winner according to the panel of judges, two men stand out. They are the tallest and most muscular, yet dressed and made up as women, as *comadres*. One fusses over the simulated baby on her back, a little blonde doll that she now and then favors with a nip of cane liquor. The other flirts with the crowd, hitching her skirt to the highest allowable level, in gender bending that exuberantly transgresses expected norms.

Throughout, the masculine and the feminine grapple with each other in unexpected ways. Men and then women from the upper, or *hanan*, and lower, or *hurin*, neighborhoods of Ticllas square off in a kind of Greco-Roman wrestling, where the first to fall loses. Then, a man takes on a woman. The woman wins, this ritual violence a burlesque inversion of everyday life where the feminine so often loses. The crowd roars, as the old mountain themes of women warriors, "effeminate" men, upper and lower reappear and reembody the tensions of division, domination, and union between the sexes in Andean history.

It is those from Ocros who begin throwing things at the crowd. Their captain, in a rabbit-skin hat, flings baby powder, which floats in the air like silver. Then an older woman reaches for apples slung over her back in a carrying blanket, launching them from the stage. Subsequent *comparsas* throw not only itching powder, but also an avalanche of fruit: corn, custard apples, and prickly pears fly over the crowd. A papaya explodes on the head of a young spectator. Susa flings a duck, Acocro a chicken. The only nonhuman not thrown into the crowd is the colorfully harnessed Ticlla burro.

Acocro are deserving winners. Their organization is old, a mutual society founded in 1967. Along with Quinua, the winner of the first Gold Tambourine, they are also the largest delegation. Muleteers and transvestites, besides men disguised in corn, a ghost spirit of the mine in a hard hat, old folks, and effigies to burn. Acocro does everything: inviting the judges to a plate of *pukapicante*, as well as first-row spectators, lucky them. An oldster tries to whip one of the transvestites, who fends him off with her purse. They unleash a real bombardment of fruit on the crowd. A big apple gets me on the arm. During it all, the music and dancers twirl tirelessly around the stage, leaving a trail of streamers, impudence, talc, and happiness. The crowd surrenders, and the master of ceremonies screams, "We can't abandon these customs, Peru's pride."

"*Kachkaniraqmi*—I still exist," goes a poem by José María Arguedas. Ayacuchans say something similar with this festival. With all its latent violence and stiff contradictions, it reflects an unbearable desire to be, in the wake of a war that claimed so many loved ones and the persistent grind of want and racism in the big city.

Dusk falls. We get ready to leave and, moving away from the stage, enter the kingdom of beer. Drinking is by the case, the pilsener on the ground in the middle of groups that surely will drink to the end. Meanwhile, the children of migrants parade between the carnivalesque circles of those who have already taken the stage, young blades carrying Walkmans, with unlighted cigarettes dangling from their lips, and teenage girls in shorts and blouses, hatching plans for the night. An old woman out of a Breughel painting tries to smear my face with a sticky green liquid.

"*Huamanga llaccta, ancha sumac llacta*—City of Huamanga, what a beautiful city," comes the master of ceremonies' voice from far away. And so it is.

Notes

1   *Chicha de jora* is a fermented corn beer, and *pukapicante*, an Ayacucho specialty, is a stew of beets, potatoes, garlic, peanuts, and pork.
2   *Eqeqos* are good-luck dolls, laden with miniature replicas of houses, shoes, money, and other desired goods.

THE CHONCHOLÍ CHEWING GUM RAP

Nosequién y los nosecuantos

Most tourists associate Peruvian music with the breathy strains of pan pipes, but in Lima music subcultures fed on American rock-and-roll and hip-hop, Colombian cumbia, English acid house, Dominican merengue, and Jamaican reggae flourish. One group, Nosequién y los nosecuantos ("Whoever and the what do you call thems"), stands out for lyrics that address contemporary issues like political violence, migration, urban decay, and corruption. In this song, Cousin Antonia, who has moved to the United States, figures out how to beat poverty by fabricating a new kind of chewing gum for gringos made out of the chewy beef intestines Peruvians call choncholí.

I just got a letter from Cousin Antonia
who packed her bags and left for California
she sent money to her mom [in Lima] and before
much time had passed they both moved to Miami.
In her letter she tells me that they sacked her from her job
for not having a visa they told her to go to hell.
But you know, friend, how we Peruvians are
if our stomach is growling we do something or other.
Pay attention to what I'm telling you
because it's no lie even if that's what it sounds like.
Antonia went around hopelessly with nothing in her pockets
asking for handouts as little kids do in Lima
a stingy gringo approached in a Mickey Mouse T-shirt
looking at her contemptuously, he gave her only a stick of gum.
Antonia walked back to her house,
thinking whatever could she do with that
and all of a sudden her face turned blissful

a marvelous idea had occurred,
and enough crying! enough suffering!
because she had just invented *choncholí* chewing gum.
Take four sticks of gum and put them in a pot
add parsley, pepper, garlic, and two onions
throw in a tomato, salt, and carrots:
creole ingredients and you'll see it tastes like Glory.
She went out into the cold night with one hundred sticks in hand
and all the Cubans bought them up without complaint.
Today *choncholí* chewing gum is on sale in New York
and also in Tennessee and Antonia does her driving
in a Rolls Royce.

SARITA COLONIA COMES FLYING

Eduardo González Viaña

Although there are other folk saints in Peru—individuals who after their deaths are said to perform miracles but who have not been sanctified by the Catholic Church— none have gained the fame of Sarita Colonia, whose shrine sits in a corner of the Callao's Baquíjano Cemetery. Nothing about her life was remarkable. Born in the provinces, in 1926 she moved with her family to Lima, where she worked as a maid until her death from malaria at age twenty-six, when she was buried in a mass grave. Yet by the 1980s popular imagination made of her the saint of the street vendors, taxi and bus drivers, maids, job seekers, homosexuals, migrants, and, as author Eduardo González Viaña writes, "the timid, the offended, the shamed, the suspicious, and the unhappy." In this excerpt from his magic-realist novel-cum-meditation on Sarita Colonia and her place in contemporary Peru, the narrator, a devotee of Sarita's, possesses, as he here explains to others in line at her shrine, a special "double vision" that allows him to see the ghosts that plague the poor and are capable of killing a police sergeant searching for the treasure left by ancient peoples.

Be careful, friends! Don't look straight at him, or better yet don't look at him at all. Excuse me for interrupting, for jolting you from your memories, but I only want to warn you not to keep staring at that man, because he's cursed, and I don't know why Sarita Colonia allows somebody like that, haunted by a shadow, to come to her as a pilgrim.

And, besides, what is he going to find here when he knows perfectly well that his sickness has no cure? As if he didn't know what he had! Listen, please! This guy is coming to ask the little saint to free him from the shadow that persecutes him, or at least to help him to die. That's where he goes wrong, because Sarita may be a little saint, but she doesn't traffic in death.

So you can't see the shadow. Right? True, he has left it at the cemetery gate, but he is still tied to it, still tied to it, and you can even see the rope. Anyone can see that this man has gone to all the healers there are, the good ones and evil ones, first the evil ones; he wants them, of course, to untie him. But this is impossible. Already the sorcerers have told him what any honest sorcerer would say under the circumstances. An honest sorcerer first communicates with the ancient ones, his advisers, and they respond: this job can be done, this one no. The latter is what all of them must have told him, including the healer in that northern port city that you've come from.

Isn't life strange! I thought that you all had double vision just because I have it, just like the thief believes that everyone is a crook like him. But don't think that I'm very proud or very happy about my double vision. No way, friends. This double vision is a sickness that is attacking me and all my family, and that's why I have come to see Sarita, to ask her to intercede so that we will be cured.

The illness called "the boy" has got us, though some also call it "the grandfather." I don't know what they call it in your town, but in mine, and I'm from Jauja, they call it "the boy," and it presents itself in the shape of a snake, invisible until it bites you. The bad part is that it does not kill you, but charms you and infects you with snake dreams and snake eyes, which, as you know, can see the spirits. Right now, even as we speak, all of you should make the sign of the cross, because a curious spirit is wandering nearby.

(To the spirit:) Go away in peace, brother. If you are one of the good ones, my prayers will make you feel better. If you are one of the others, go, too, because one can't read fortunes among the gypsies, amen.

As I was saying, the snake does it at the command of an evil sorcerer or just because it feels like it, and with us I think it just felt like it. And one day, all of a sudden, you have it in your house and it may be with you for months without your realizing it. With us, it so happened that the miserable snake got into the corral, and it slept there for ten years. In the tenth year, it awoke, and at first, we didn't even feel anything. The ones who saw it were the chickens and ducks, and they were in a panic, fluttering around and honking and crowing morning, afternoon, and night, as if they wanted to tell us something. The poor rooster seemed to have gone crazy, and who can stand a crazy rooster? He woke up the whole neighborhood at midnight, or crowed at midday, and also some chickens suddenly died, with no visible wound, as if somebody had eaten out their hearts without cutting their throats.

Later, we started to see snake tracks on the sand and on a rock. They

Figure 54. A street vendor outside the shrine to Sarita Colonia displays
the folk saint's image. Photograph by Robin Kirk.

were very clear. It must be "the grandfather," we joked. But I think we
just laughed from pure fear. At night, a giant rooster the size of a house
danced on our roof. Forget "the grandfather," we said hopefully; do you
think a snake is going to be flying around at night, heavy sleepers that
they are?

My aunt Angélica, who passed away to sainthood some years ago, consulted a priest, and she brought us a little stamp of Saint George and the
dragon to put on the door of our house, saying we should not let the
snake pass and that if it tried we should say an Our Father and whisper:
stop, ferocious animal, because God is more ferocious than you. But this
didn't work at all because snakes don't knock on doors. Besides, snakes
are not dragons, and, lastly, dragons do not exist.

Around this time, most of our kids had fallen ill with the same sickness
and now we are all suffering, but we didn't believe them. They said they
saw "the grandfather" everywhere and even played with him, and "the
grandfather" taught them to talk with the frogs and owls. But we didn't
believe them, and instead we told them absolutely not to talk to owls.
One never knows what those nightbirds may know.

Finally the thing started to scare us when the neighbors stopped visiting and preferred to cut a wide detour around the house. Imagine, they even crossed themselves as they went by. That's when I said it would be good to consult a healer, but no one paid any attention to me.

And that was when Sergeant Rosendo Valdivia, the police commander of the Civil Guard, arrived at our house.

"They tell me strange things are happening," he said. "Maybe you've discovered an ancient tomb? Because you know that the state should take charge of these matters. Here I am, as a representative of the state, to claim the part that belongs to me."

"We haven't found anything, boss," I told him. But he didn't believe me.

"In any case, we can look together for the tomb and each one will have his part," he whispered.

But I saved him the bother, answering, "Look, esteemed Sergeant, you can have the treasure. As far as we are concerned, we were born poor and that's how we'll die. Search wherever you want and, if you find a tomb, it's all yours. As I told you, our problem is that 'the grandfather' is frightening us."

You must have known Sergeant Rosendo Valdivia and be aware of his money lust. I didn't have to tell him twice that he could look for the tomb himself, and it didn't even occur to him to find a helper, because from pure greed he wanted the tomb all to himself.

"What's happening," he yelled, "is that all of you here are a bunch of idiots, going around believing in 'the grandfather.' What you call 'the grandfather' is the rainbow snake, and any educated person knows there's always a treasure at the end of the snake's tail, and what must be done is to find it."

And that was how the sergeant started to look for the snake's tail. While we worked by day, the sergeant worked by night, and by the next morning he had found only a few needles here and there, but nothing of the treasure or the serpent, which perhaps was making fun of the sergeant, who in the end decided to look for the treasure in the lake.

The poor guy didn't pay any attention to us, didn't pay attention to us because of our ignorance, and one fine day he just vanished. When they came to look for him, we said that he was looking for treasure in the lake. They searched for him there and found him dead. The strangest thing of all was that his body was intact and dry. Dry. Without a drop of water on it and no signs of having drowned.

How horribly strange! This showed us that "the grandfather" was living in our lands and that we had to look for the best way to beg him to go trouble someone else, and if he couldn't, then just go sleep in hell for a while. The first person we consulted was Don Guillermo Tornique, who, as you know, is an evangelical. The bad thing about Don Guillermo is that he told us that we shouldn't go to a sorcerer and that he would be angry with us if we used supernatural remedies, because he favors only cures authorized in the Bible.

Don Guillermo's remedy for scaring away the snake consisted of boiling heavily salted water in twenty cans. To know if there was enough salt, one had to put a potato in the water and see if it floated. Then we were supposed to dump the salty water on the land around the house. That way, the snake would think he was at sea. Being a land animal, he would never return.

I guess the snake didn't buy this little ruse, maybe because he already knew about the trick. As you know, Don Guillermo is a journalist in Huancayo and writes a famous column on home remedies. I'm not trying to say that snakes can read, but that at least some of them know how to float.

And now we're all floating. Between life and death, land and sky, the visible and the invisible. That's where we are. Or rather, that's where we were until a sorcerer from Paca Lake, Master Dimas Fernández, advised us to go to find a snake egg.

"Don't think that I'm telling you to go find a snake egg just to screw you up. No, not at all, this is the way to go," he said, telling us a trick to find an egg that I can't tell you about now because we're just about to get our turn in line to see Sarita.

What I can tell you is that the trick worked, and we really did find some eggs, and we took them to Master Dimas.

"Now you have to find out which of the eggs will hatch into male and which into female snakes. If it's a female egg and you burn it, then you will kill 'the grandfather.' But if it is a male egg, all of you will turn into snakes. And how to find out whether they are male or female? Well, that's your problem."

And that's why I'm here, so that Sarita will cure us once and for all, or so that she will tell me which of the eggs is female.

IS PERU TURNING PROTESTANT?

Luis Minaya

Although Protestant missionaries first arrived in Peru in the 1800s, it wasn't until the 1980s that Peruvians began converting in large numbers. By 1990, Protestants numbered more than 1 million people in at least twenty-seven different denominations, including Assembly of God, Baptist, Presbyterian, and Pentecostal. For the first time that same year, seventeen professed Protestants, called "evangelicals" in Peru, won seats in congress, and although many rallied behind President Fujimori, others were sharply critical of his policies, including second vice president Carlos García, a Baptist. In this interview with journalist Lucien Chauvin, Pastor Luis Minaya Ballón, general secretary of the Evangelical Church of Peru (IEP), discusses the history of Protestantism in Peru and the unique perspective of the IEP, Peru's only autonomous Protestant denomination and currently its largest.

Q: What are the roots of the Peruvian Evangelical Church?

Luis Minaya (LM): In the early decades of the last century, a new wave of immigrants made its way to Latin America as a result of the political independence sweeping the region. Anglo-Saxon businessmen arrived to take advantage of new markets. With them came their religion. The Protestant missionaries were soon to follow.

In 1821, the same year [José] San Martín declared Peru's independence, Diego Thompson, a Church of Scotland minister, landed in Peru. From the moment Thompson arrived, his presence could be called "revolutionary." He began his mission with an analysis of Peru's social conditions and concluded that an educational campaign, especially in the Andean region, was needed.

This first Protestant experience was also an ecumenical breakthrough, because Thompson joined together with some Catholic clerics to pro-

Figure 55. An evangelical sings in Quechua to a rapt congregation.
(Courtesy of Eusebio Quispe)

mote education. In the end, however, Thompson's efforts were doomed
to fail, given the political instability during the process of independence.

Q: When was the IEP established?

LM: Toward the end of the last century, John Ritchie, a Scottish minister, came to Peru as part of a faith mission. Ritchie, however, had radical
ideas that questioned even the mission group that sent him to Peru.

He was a natural and charismatic leader with his own ideas on the role
of mission. He tried to move the Presbyterian Church away from the
model of implanting a European-style church structure toward one that
allowed a Peruvian church to develop according to the country's particular situation. When the Presbyterian leadership refused, Ritchie broke
with them and set out to form his own church.

At the turn of the century, this was a very revolutionary move. Ritchie's
ideas led to the formation of an autonomous church that cultivated its
own theology based on Peru's reality. It was a church that identified with
the indigenous populations.

Q: What makes you describe it as "revolutionary?"

LM: Ritchie's proposal broke completely with the position fostered by all the other missionary churches. When these missionaries arrived, they saw a poor country where they wanted to work. And what did they see as a means of doing something for everyone? Working with the dominant classes. The idea was that by changing the ruling classes you could change the country. The Methodists and Presbyterians, for example, set up schools for the children of the rich and made inroads in the intellectual community.

But not Ritchie. He went to the highlands, to the jungle. No one understood what he was doing. This is why today the IEP has a presence in Lima's shantytowns and in the highlands that no other Protestant church can equal.

Q: Did the IEP encounter many problems organizing a church based solely on the Peruvian experience?

LM: One of the major deficiencies was formulating a theological process that was our own. Many of the people who followed Ritchie did not embrace his idea of developing a new way of approaching theology. They had their own theological formation and incorporated their ideas into the church.

One of the reasons behind this lack of theological preparation had to do with the region where we were working and the level of education. Many of our early pastoral agents and church members were highland peasants who were illiterate. Before we were able to think about developing our own theology, we had to teach people how to read.

It wasn't until the 1970s that we began our own brand of theology and theological formation. Our pastors began to attend nondenominational seminaries in order to gain a broader knowledge of theology.

We are pioneers in our efforts to develop a theology that has its roots in the Peruvian reality. We are also criticized for this because many people do not consider our theological approach valid—some even go as far as to say the seminaries we attend are satanic.

Q: Does this independent theological approach include allowing women to become ministers?

LM: The IEP's position on the role of women is a holdover from our past that we are slowly trying to change. The presence of women in leadership positions within the church is strong. Officially, there is no recognition of women's leadership, but unofficially women play an important role in the life of the church.

There are new openings for women to develop their ministry. Their voices are being heard and their issues are being taken seriously. This new openness will be extremely beneficial. Women are very involved in our human rights commissions and in many of the committees organized to benefit the communities served by each congregation.

There is still a long way to go in recognizing the work done by women, but I think that we are moving in the right direction.

Q: What is the relationship between the IEP and the Catholic Church?

LM: I think the Catholic Church missed an opportunity, with the celebration of the five hundredth anniversary of the arrival of Christianity in the Americas, to critically examine its role in the history of the region.

All churches have historically responded to the interests of the dominant system, and so it is with the Catholic Church. The Catholic Church arrived as part of the Spanish empire's expansion: the cross arrived with the sword. After centuries of cooperation between ecclesiastical power and political power, the Catholic Church needs to examine its history in a critical manner. It can no longer continue to cover up the past and say, "We have been at the side of the people," because it isn't true. The Catholic Church continues to be identified with the status quo, which will not benefit it in the future.

The official religion is absent in many of the country's highland and jungle towns.[1] You can travel to any Andean village, and you won't find a priest, a nun, or a pastoral worker. But you will find an IEP pastor.

We have more than 1,500 congregations in the Andean region alone. Many of the other churches criticize the IEP for the number and size of our congregations because they don't understand the concept of community.

Our congregations are small because we respect the traditional idea of *ayllu*, the Andean community. The *ayllu* is like a family, though it may have thirty to forty members. Our churches aren't based on the concept of numbers, where the individual gets lost. In our congregations all the people know each other. They share many things in common.

The concept of community is absent from the Catholic Church. The IEP pastor is part of the community. He works, eats, sleeps like everyone else and endures the hardships that everyone else has to endure. This hasn't been the case with the Catholic clergy, and the people know it.

Q: Because of its presence in the highlands and the jungle, areas where political violence is an everyday reality, has the IEP run into any problems?

LM: The truth is that we have problems with all sides. We are caught in the crossfire.

Because we don't accept the status quo, the army sees us as an enemy.

The army doesn't have a problem with the Pentecostals, because they go by the book and do everything they are told. Members of the IEP, in contrast, challenge the army. We know our rights and we ask questions when we see something that doesn't seem right. So, we are seen as possible enemies. They say that we've been infiltrated.

I've seen documents drafted by the state's security forces that say the IEP has been infiltrated and needs to be watched. We are the only church that has had members of the security forces visit our congregations on a regular basis to see what is going on inside. Our members, especially our young people, are often abused by the state's agents.

We are also threatened by the Shining Path, which sees us as a potential alternative to its political project. The Shining Path wants all the power. When its members look at us, they see a group of people with its own ideas and project—we are a threat to their order.

Since the early 1980s, more than four hundred members of the IEP, many of whom were pastors, have been killed as a result of political violence. Many others have "disappeared," such as Manuel Meneses, who was arrested by the army while he was waiting outside one of our churches in Junín [a state in the central highlands]. Meneses's case has become a rallying point for many of the young people in our church.

Q: Where is the IEP headed?

LM: Since the 1970s, immigration to the cities from the highlands—one of the trends that has always existed in Peru—has become even more pronounced. These highland immigrants, many of whom are illiterate, follow early migrants to the poverty belts that surround Lima. Among these new immigrants are many members of the IEP. We are going through a process of change as the church expands in the cities.

For many years the IEP had only one congregation in Lima, which in many ways was alienated. It was part of the IEP but didn't represent what the church was about. In the past twenty years, more than seventy IEP congregations have been formed in Lima, especially in the shantytowns.

What makes us different is our approach to Peruvian reality. Our pastors and members are aware of the economic, political, and social conditions in which they live and try to improve the situation instead of escaping from it.

Many people in the shantytowns are attracted to the IEP because our pastors are like them and preach to their reality, not to some distant theology coming out of Europe or the United States. When people attend an IEP church, they hear the pastor talk about the Bible, but also about life in the shantytowns, about hardships. Like me, most of our ministers live in the shantytowns where we work as pastors. We are like everyone else.

Note

1 Although not called the official religion, Catholicism is recognized in the 1979 Peruvian Constitution as having played a major role in the country's history.

INTERVIEW WITH A GAY ACTIVIST

Enrique Bossio

The youngest member of the group that founded the Lima Homosexual Movement (MHOL) in 1985, Enrique Bossio became well-known in Peru through frequent appearances on television and in radio and press interviews. He has tried to educate the public about homosexuality, which is still believed by many to be prostitution or a disease treatable by psychotherapy. In this interview with prominent journalist Lucien Chauvin, Bossio notes that among his greatest challenges is finding a way to live outside Peru's family-oriented culture without experiencing a crushing loneliness or losing a sense of identity as a Peruvian. Like homosexuals in other countries, Peruvian gays and lesbians have also been leaders in the fight against AIDS, which has already claimed more than a thousand lives.

Q: What was your role in organizing the Homosexual Movement of Lima?

Enrique Bossio (EB): I was going through many personal changes at the time. It was 1984. I had just left the Catholic University of Peru and had enrolled in San Marcos National University, and I was coming out as a gay man. I was searching, without much luck, for a way in which I could live as a homosexual person. In our society, words such as "homosexual," "lesbian," or "gay" are not used as adjectives but as nouns. Homosexuality is not seen as just another component of a person, but as a self-sufficient condition that constitutes the very nature of the person and is commonly associated with vice, illness, sin, crime, and loneliness.

Toward the end of the year, I met a group of people who would eventually organize MHOL. One of the people in the group invited me to an informal discussion session where we shared our experiences as gay and lesbian people. Although the group had been organizing theatrical and social events for more than two years, it wasn't until we began to asso-

Figure 56. Gay rights
activist Enrique Bossio.
(Courtesy of Lucien
Chauvin)

ciate with gay and lesbian groups in Europe and the United States that we
began to believe it was possible to organize the kind of group we wanted.

For me, it was a time of incredible personal growth and reaffirmation.
For the first time I had an opportunity to talk about my fears, myths, and
feelings of love toward other men without feeling criticized or ridiculed.
It was a chance to develop a healthy awareness of what it is to be a gay man.

Q: What are some of these fears or myths you mention?

EB: Although Lima is a city of more than seven million people, it continues to maintain a very rural and colonial mentality in many ways. The
only way a child can leave his or her parents' house is by getting married,
and, at times, this isn't even the case. For gay and lesbian people this is
like a life sentence in the paternal jail.

Loneliness is one of the greatest fears that preoccupies gay men and
women. Since we are not going to start families, and our own families are
usually not willing to accept us for who we are—gay men and lesbians—
it is not unusual to find homosexual men and women struggling to evade
their sexual orientation. It's as if the loneliness we are hoping to avoid is
an inherent condition of homosexuality.

Q: What are some of the ways society shows intolerance?

EB: One of the first experiences of rejection, and probably one of the
strongest, occurs at school. If you don't adopt the same attitudes and behavior patterns as the rest of the students, you will be pointed out as the
weird one, the butch, or the fag.

It is very important to note that even before you understand the role sexuality will play in your life, you are taught to reject your feelings of emotional and physical attraction to members of the same sex and also to incorporate feelings of hatred and rejection of people who demonstrate these associations.

Several years ago, for example, I was on an elevator with a young mother and her daughter. Although the little girl was just beginning to talk, she had already internalized a rejection of any sort of gender transgression. She pointed to my earrings and, with a new tone of voice, said to her mother: "Mommy, look. He has earrings. He is a woman." I couldn't hold back from saying to the girl's mother: "Those kinds of jokes only serve to perpetuate the idea that feminine qualities somehow 'diminish' the status of men."

Q: In 1993, the Peruvian government fired 117 diplomats, offering as a reason, among other things, homosexual behavior. Is the government's action indicative of the way gays and lesbians are treated in Peru?

EB: The discrimination against gay and lesbian people in Peru is not legal, but social. Some people will always see homosexuality as something scandalous. Because of this, we need to openly discuss what homosexuality is and what it means in the life of a gay person. Many people in Peru think being a gay man means dressing up as a woman and working as a prostitute. I believe prostitution is more of a social and economic phenomenon than a demonstration of sexual identity. If we look at the question of transvestite prostitution from a different angle, we find one of the many hypocrisies of Peru. I see the problems of sexual identity exhibited more by the clients of homosexual prostitutes than by the transvestites themselves. The men who decide to pay for sex with transvestite prostitutes obviously know they are picking up a man and not a woman, but they do not see themselves as homosexuals.

The homosexual is always considered "the other." Not only do these men reject their homosexuality, but their families deny that there might be a gay man among them. Peru is a macho country that applauds the image of a strongman. The television programs with the highest ratings are those based on jokes that denigrate people based on sexual orientation, ethnic background, or physical challenges.

For me the problem wasn't only the firing of the diplomats, but that the decision was supported by a majority of the population. Popular support shows that homosexuality continues to be viewed negatively in Peruvian society.

Q: What can be done to change this attitude?

EB: Gays and lesbians in Peru have historically been marginalized and characterized as transvestites, prostitutes, or butches. MHOL has been successful in portraying a new image of gay men and women and offering homosexuality as a viable and positive lifestyle for certain social groups.

What I fear is that in our efforts to fit into the mainstream we were not successful in changing the opinion people have of most gay men and women. In Peru today everyone knows that there are a few homosexual men and women who go to the university and who appear on TV and radio talk shows to defend their rights. Eventually there will be a certain level of respect for these people. But the transvestites and the hair stylists—the most visible part of the homosexual community—will continue to be discriminated against and marginalized.

Q: What has been the impact of AIDS in Peru?

EB: The first cases of AIDS were detected in the mid-1980s almost exclusively among the gay male population. We began AIDS prevention programs shortly after MHOL was founded in 1985 and almost immediately after the first cases of the virus were diagnosed.

Official statistics put the number of AIDS cases today at close to one thousand, but there are several reasons to believe that this number doesn't reflect the true dimensions of AIDS in Peru.

First, there is an underreporting of cases. The Health Ministry's statistics do not include people who are rejected by hospitals, those who die at home because they don't have the money to receive medical attention, or those who ask their doctors not to report their cases because of the stigma associated with AIDS. One out of three of my friends who currently have AIDS or have died of the disease fall into this last category.

Unfortunately, the success of education has been overshadowed by the rise in AIDS cases among heterosexual men and women. In the past four years the rate of new infection among gay men has fallen dramatically, only to be replaced by new cases among heterosexuals, especially women. The lack of prevention programs for women has meant the number of women with the virus has increased at a rapid pace.

AIDS tended to be seen as a disease associated with sex among men. Homosexuality in Peru, as I've said, is still taboo, and many gay men continue to live out their homosexuality where no one can see them. Our programs were successful because they were designed to function at this "underground" level. Our pamphlets, which contained basic information about AIDS and referred to our hotline and safe sex workshops, were regularly distributed at more than a hundred places in Lima, such as adult movie houses, parks, and bars, where men go to meet other men for sex. The majority of Peruvians, however, depend on the media for information, and the self-censorship of these outlets basically ensures that no one receives accurate information on how AIDS is spread and how to prevent it. The media also continue to perpetuate the myth that women need to be subservient to their husbands, which translates into few women having the courage to ask their partners to use condoms, for example.

In addition, the Catholic Church's fervent opposition to birth control has led to a "demonization" of condoms. Conservative Catholic groups have been successful in blocking government attempts to promote condom use as an effective way of preventing the spread of AIDS.

Q: What has been the government's role in the fight against AIDS?

EB: In 1986, the government established a commission to control the spread of HIV. Among the decisions made by the commission was the mandatory testing of prostitutes, homosexual men, and tourists. Only a handful of people, all in the first two groups, were subjected to the tests.

Little by little, medical professionals began to familiarize themselves with the disease and to develop programs that were increasingly more efficient. Unfortunately, these programs were almost all individual efforts. The government has been lax at best and criminally negligent at worst in developing an effective and realistic AIDS prevention program.

The government's economic program, which has weakened Peru's already precarious social programs, has put health care and medicines out of reach for most Peruvians. A government that neglects its citizens' basic health care needs obviously cannot be expected to put too many resources into AIDS prevention.

ADRENALINE NIGHTS

Carmen Ollé

Many poets of the 1960s and 1970s experimented with rebellion against the status quo. In the context of social upheaval, a group of female poets challenged traditional expectations of womanly passivity and subservience. Among the most influential of these new voices was Carmen Ollé. Her book Adrenaline Nights *(1980) embraced a forthrightly feminist yet unabashedly erotic brand of verse. Although married to Enrique Verástegui, a member of the group known as the Zero Hour poets, and borrowing some of their convictions about the need to challenge preconceptions, Carmen Ollé stands apart in her focus on the female body not as object but as point of view.*

Snap
30 irreversible years
2 or 3 decades of memories like rock islands
the age at which if we don't advance or move toward a
goal, the generations will devour us.
Given over to desperate chores or in search of the
ideal lover
I decide to take off without goals
there is no Where To
only Where?
And why must I annihilate my sweet, spontaneous experience
because of the future's uncertainty?

Last night, I was kissing my man, begging him for a new position
apart from my excitement I lacked a little air because of
a certain contrariness in the nose from keeping myself flat
on my back

the position is the diagram that translates
the way to make oneself into "those from above" or "those from below"
shoulders—hump—pendulous breasts—dental orifices
am I that old lady at less than 40?
my grandmother approached 80 with resignation without fury
without mourning, she had time to recognize herself in the change
and she was owed no rebellion.
The Mona Lisa's smile points out the way of aging
detained by creams
the lips of the libertine and the matron stain
the sheet's edge purple and also translate
laughter—volcano—wear and tear versus economy—sensuality in doses
with their grins or murmurs.
I hear the neighbor's laughter on the upper floor
from the cot moaning noises frozen by boredom
that fall to the sea
the naked, splendid swimmers slip by the
shore between the beacons they walk hand in hand
and they return to the sea mysterious and simple
I admire their broad shoulder blades in the night
and remember my timidity
in Lima beauty is a steel corset.

REENCOUNTER

Giovanna Pollarolo

Although her work is different in tone from that of Carmen Ollé, Giovanna Polla-
rolo draws on the direct, confessional style pioneered by Ollé, in this case to chart
the changing relationships between middle-class women. Although known for her
poetry, the Tacna-born Pollarolo is also a busy screenwriter and has collaborated
in the writing of three of Peru's most interesting recent films: La boca del lobo
(The Lion's Den), about an army atrocity in the southern highlands, Caídos del
cielo *(Fallen from Heaven), and* Todos somos estrellas *(We're All Stars), about*
contemporary Lima.

You haven't changed a bit, she tells me.
The years have passed right by you, I lie back.
I married, I have two children, the two of us say at once.
I'm well, yes, very well.
We must see each other more often.
Yes, we must.
What did we talk about before, I ask myself?
Of what, when we had no children, husband, or maid?
when it wasn't necessary to cover up or embellish
a well-applied mask, almost a face.
Then, we spoke of the future
each dreaming of what is now not
or what is now, but different
to marry, have children
to leave the house that seemed a prison
to say good-bye forever to the nuns
a postcard life, without dirty clothes
or dishes to wash

these things are not dreamed in dreams.
With so many smiling masks we make
the first toast
the second and third
someone has brought photos from back then
we read the signatures
we laugh the same as always, the teachers
who were younger then than we are now
once again seem to be the boring old ones. The women
hysterical spinsters, the bitter old
we remember the great loves
that did not end in marriage
single, married, widow, divorced, nun
childless, with children, one, two, three
once the rope game is announced
we are astonished by a list of dead companions
remembering, we are saddened
drinking, smoking
telling our miseries, we are friends
for an afternoon
we compare our husbands' penis size
their skill or awkwardness in bed
the lovers.
No Mother Superior Giusseppina spying from behind the door
father who sends us to bed, or upcoming exams.
Days marked by the bells between gym and class
they remind us now of happiness. It was there
and we didn't know it.
How could we know that twenty years later
we would be dreaming backwards
and give everything to start afresh
when the cards were not already on the table.
We eat and we drink
we give an accounting of our lives
so many surprises, we say
the afternoon is not enough
to tell each other what we are
so many years is a lot of time
we have so much to talk about.

I AM THE BAD GIRL OF THE STORY

María Emilia Cornejo

The literary contribution of María Emilia Cornejo, a university student who committed suicide in 1972, was brief but intense. In its rhetorical bite and relentless self-examination, her work, published posthumously by her family in Halfway Down the Traveled Road *(1989), resembles that of the North American poet Sylvia Plath, who also took her life. Here, the political is consumed by the personal. Easy notions of good and bad break apart in the explosive play of preconception and sexuality.*

I am
the bad girl of the story,
the one who fornicated with three men
and cuckolded her husband.

I am the woman
who tricked him every day
for a miserable plate of lentils,
who took from him slowly his clothing of goodness
until he became a black
and sterile stone,
I am the woman who castrated him
with infinite gestures of tenderness
and fake moans in bed.

I am
the bad girl of the story.

CONVERSATION IN THE CATHEDRAL

Mario Vargas Llosa

Mario Vargas Llosa became best known in Peru for his unsuccessful 1990 run for the presidency. However, he remains one of the world's premier writers, and Conversation in the Cathedral *is considered one of his best novels. The story begins with a chance meeting between Santiago Zavala, a newspaper editor from a wealthy Miraflores family, and Ambrosio, his father's former chauffeur, and their conversation in a rundown restaurant known as La Catedral. A journey through the backroom scheming of the Odría dictatorship, the novel captures a Peru poised between the power of old families like the Zavalas and the cunning of newcomers symbolized by Odría's ruthless security chief, whose web of political intrigue binds the Zavalas with Ambrosio in a tragic denouement. Above all, perhaps, the novel stands out as one of the sharpest evocations of the vitality and decay of Peru's capital, Lima.*

From the doorway of *La Crónica* Santiago looks at the Avenida Tacna without love: cars, uneven and faded buildings, the gaudy skeletons of posters floating in the mist, the gray midday. At what precise moment had Peru fucked itself up? The newsboys weave in and out among the vehicles halted by the red light on Wilson, hawking the afternoon papers, and he starts to walk slowly toward Colmena. His hands in his pockets, head down, he goes along escorted by people who are also going in the direction of the Plaza San Martín. He was like Peru, Zavalita was, he'd fucked himself up somewhere along the line. He thinks: when? Across from the Hotel Crillón a dog comes over to lick his feet: don't get your rabies on me, get away. Peru all fucked up, Carlitos[1] all fucked up, everybody all fucked up. He thinks: there's no solution. He sees a long line at the taxi stop for Miraflores, he crosses the square, and there's Norwin, hello, at a table in the Zela Bar, have a seat, Zavalita, fondling a *chilcano*[2] and having his shoes shined, he invites him to have a drink. He doesn't look drunk yet and Santiago sits down, tells the bootblack to shine his shoes too. Yes, sir, boss, right away, boss, they'll look like a mirror, boss.

"No one's seen you for ages, Mr. Editorial Writer," Norwin says. "Are you happier on the editorial page than with the local news?"

"There's less work." He shrugs his shoulders, it was probably that day when the editor called him in, he orders a cold Cristal, did he want to take Orgambide's place, Zavalita? He thinks: that's when I fucked myself up. "I get in early, they give me my topic, I hold my nose, and in two or three hours all set, I unbuckle my chains and that's it."

"I wouldn't write editorials for all the money in the world," Norwin says. "It's too far removed from the news, and journalism is news, Zavalita, believe me. I'll end my days on the police beat, that's all. By the way, did Carlitos die yet?"

"He's still in the hospital, but they're going to let him out soon," Santiago says. "He swears he's off the bottle this time."

"Is it true that one night he saw cockroaches and spiders when he went to bed?" Norwin asks.

"He lifted up the sheet and thousands of tarantulas and mice came at him," Santiago says. "He ran out into the street bare-ass and hollering."

Norwin laughs and Santiago closes his eyes: the houses in Chorrillos are cubes with gratings on them, caves cracked by earthquakes, inside there's a traffic of utensils and reeking little old women with slippers and varicose legs. A small figure runs among the cubes, his shrieks make the oily predawn shudder and infuriate the ants and scorpions that pursue him. Consolation through alcohol, he thinks, against the slow death of the blue devils of hallucination. He was all right, Carlitos was, you had to defend yourself against Peru as best you could.

"One of these days I'm going to come across the creatures too." Norwin contemplates his *chilcano* with curiosity, half smiles. "But there's no such thing as a teetotaling newspaperman, Zavalita. Drinking gives you inspiration, believe me."

The bootblack is through with Norwin and now he's putting polish on Santiago's shoes, whistling. How were things at *Ultima Hora*, what were the scoundrels there saying? They were complaining about your ingratitude, Zavalita, that you should stop by and see them sometime, the way you used to. But since you have lots of free time now, Zavalita, did you take a second job?

"I read, I take naps," Santiago says. "Maybe I'll go back to law school."

"You get away from the news and now you want a degree." Norwin looks at him sadly. "The editorial page is the end of the road, Zavalita. You'll get a job as a lawyer, you'll leave the newspaper business. I can already see you as a proper bourgeois."

"I've just turned thirty," Santiago says. "That's kind of late for me to start being a bourgeois."

"Thirty, is that all?" Norwin is thoughtful. "I'm thirty-six and I could pass for your father. The police page puts you through the grinder, believe me."

Male faces, dull and defeated eyes at the tables of the Zela Bar, hands that reach for ashtrays and glasses of beer. How ugly people are here, Carlitos is right. He thinks: what's come over me today? The bootblack cuffs away two dogs that are panting among the tables.

"How long is the campaign against rabies in *La Crónica* going to last?" Norwin asks. "It's getting boring, another whole page on it this morning."

"I wrote all the editorials against rabies," Santiago says. "Hell, that doesn't bother me as much as writing on Cuba or Vietnam. Well, the line's gone now. I'm going to catch a taxi."

"Let's have lunch, I'm inviting," Norwin says. "Forget about your wife, Zavalita. Let's bring back the good old days."

Hot coney and cold beer, the Rinconcito Cajamarquino in the Bajo el Puente district and a view of the vague waters of the Rímac River slipping along over snot-colored rocks, the muddy Haitian coffee, gambling at Milton's place, *chilcanos* and a shower at Norwin's, the midnight apotheosis at the whorehouse with Becerrita, which brought on deflation, the acid sleep, the nausea and the doubts of dawn. The good old days, maybe it had been then.

"Ana's made some shrimp soup and I wouldn't want to miss that," Santiago says. "Some other time."

"You're afraid of your wife," Norwin says. "Boy, you really are fucked up, Zavalita."

Not because of what you thought, brother. Norwin insists on paying for the beer, the shine, and they shake hands. Santiago goes back to the taxi stop, the car he takes is a Chevrolet and the radio is on, Inca Cola refreshed the best, then a waltz, rivers, canyons, the veteran voice of Jesús Vásquez, it was my Peru. There were still some jams downtown, but República and Arequipa were empty and the car was able to move along, another waltz, Lima women had traditional souls. Why are all Peruvian waltzes so goddamned stupid? He thinks: what's come over me today? He has his chin on his chest and his eyes are half closed, as if he's spying on his belly: God, Zavalita, every time you sit down you get that bulge in your

jacket. Was it the first time he'd drunk beer? Fifteen, twenty years ago?
Four weeks without seeing his mother, Teté. Who would have thought that
Popeye would become an architect, Zavalita, who would have thought
that you'd end up writing editorials against the dogs of Lima? He thinks:
I'll be potbellied in a little while. He'd go to the Turkish baths, play tennis at the Terrazas, in six months the fat would burn away and he'd have a
flat belly again the way he did when he was fifteen years old. Get moving,
break the inertia, shake himself up. He thinks: sports, that's the answer.
Miraflores Park already, Quebrada, the Malecón, the corner of Benavides, driver. He gets out, walks toward Porta, his hands in his pockets,
his head down, what's come over me today? The sky is still cloudy, the
atmosphere is even grayer and the light drizzle has begun: mosquito legs
on his skin, the caress of a cobweb. Not even that, a more furtive and disagreeable feeling. Even the rain is fucked up in this country. He thinks:
if at least there were a heavy rain. What were they showing at the Colina,
the Montecarlo, the Marsano? He'd have lunch, a chapter of *Point Counter
Point*, which would drag and carry him in its arms to the sticky sleep of
siesta time, maybe they were showing a crime movie, like *Rififi*, a cowboy
picture like *Rio Grande*. But Ana would have her tear-jerker all checked off
in the newspaper, what's come over me today? He thinks: if the censors
would only ban all Mexican films he'd fight less with Ana. And after the
movies, what then? They'd take a walk along the Malecón, smoke under
the cement shelters in Necochea Park listening to the sea roaring in the
darkness, they would return to the elf houses, we fight a lot, love, we argue a lot, love, and between yawns, Huxley. The two rooms would fill up
with smoke and the smell of oil, was he very hungry, love? The morning
alarm clock, the cold water in the shower, the taxi, walking among office
workers along Colmena, the voice of the editor, would he rather have the
bank strike, the fishing crisis, or Israel? Maybe it would be worth putting
out a little effort and getting a degree. He thinks: going backward. He sees
the harsh orange walls, the red tiles, the small barred windows of the elf
houses. The apartment door is open but Rowdy doesn't appear, mongrel,
leaping, noisy and effusive. Why do you leave the door open when you go
to the Chinaman's, dear? But no, there's Ana, what's the matter, her eyes
are puffy and weepy, her hair disheveled: they took Rowdy away, love.

"They pulled him out of my hands," Ana sobs. "Some dirty niggers,
love. They put him in the truck. They stole him, they stole him."

The kiss on the temple, calm down, love, he caresses her face, how did
it happen, he leads her to the house by the shoulder, don't cry, silly.

"I called you at *La Crónica* and you weren't there." Ana pouts. "Bandits, Negroes with the faces of criminals. I had him on the leash and everything. They grabbed him, put him in the truck, they stole him."

"I'll have lunch and go to the pound and get him out." Santiago kisses her again. "Nothing will happen to him, don't be silly."

"He started to kick his legs, wag his tail." She wipes her eyes with the apron, sighs. "He seemed to understand, love. Poor thing, poor little thing."

"Did they grab him out of your arms?" Santiago asks. "What a bunch. I'm going to raise hell."

He picks up the jacket he threw onto a chair and takes a step toward the door, but Ana holds him back: he should eat first, quickly, love. Her voice is soft, dimples on her cheeks, her eyes sad, she's pale.

"The soup must be cold by now." She smiles, her lips trembling. "I forgot about everything with what happened, sweet. Poor little Rowdy."

They eat lunch without talking, at the small table against the window that looks out on the courtyard of the houses: earth the color of brick, like the tennis courts at the Terrazas, a twisting gravel path with geranium pots on the side. The soup has grown cold, a film of grease tints the edges of the plate, the shrimp look like tin. She was on her way to the Chinaman's on San Martín to buy a bottle of vinegar, love, and all of a sudden a truck put on its brakes beside her and two Negroes with criminal faces got out, the worst kind of bandits, one of them gave her a shove and the other one grabbed the leash and before she knew what was happening they'd put him in the cage and had gone. Poor thing, poor little creature. Santiago gets up: they'd hear from him about an abuse like that. Did he see, did he see? Ana is sobbing again; he too was afraid they were going to kill him, love.

"They won't do anything to him, sweet." He kisses Ana on the cheek, a momentary taste of raw meat and salt. "I'll bring him right back, you'll see."

He jogs to the pharmacy on Porta and San Martín, asks to use the telephone and calls *La Crónica.* Solórzano the court reporter answers: how in hell would he know where the dog pound was, Zavalita.

"Did they take your dog away?" The druggist puts his solicitous head forward. "The pound's by the Puente del Ejército. You'd better hurry, they killed my brother-in-law's Chihuahua, a very expensive animal."

He jogs to Larco, takes a group taxi, how much would the trip from the Paseo Colón to the Puente del Ejército cost? he counts a hundred eighty soles in his wallet. On Sunday they wouldn't have a cent left, too bad Ana had left the hospital, they'd better not go to the movies that night, poor Rowdy, no more editorials against rabies. He gets out on the Paseo Colón, on the Plaza Bolognesi he finds a taxi, the driver doesn't know where the pound is, sir. An ice cream vendor on the Plaza Dos de Mayo gives them directions: farther on a small sign near the river, Municipal Dog Pound, there it was. A broad yard surrounded by a run-down, shit-colored adobe wall—the color of Lima, he thinks, the color of Peru—flanked by shacks that mix and thicken in the distance until they turn into a labyrinth of straw mats, poles, tiles, zinc plates. Muffled, remote whining. A squalid structure stands beside the entrance, a plaque says Office. In shirtsleeves, wearing glasses, a bald man is dozing by a desk covered with papers and Santiago raps on the table: they'd stolen his dog, they'd snatched it out of his wife's hands, the man sits up, startled, by God, he wasn't going to leave it at that.

"What do you mean coming into this office spouting goddamns?" The bald man rubs his stupefied eyes and makes a face. "Show some respect."

"If anything's happened to my dog I'm not going to leave it at that." He takes out his press card, pounds the table again. "And the characters who attacked my wife are going to be sorry, I can assure you."

"Calm down." He looks the card over, yawns, the displeasure on his face dissolves into beatific weariness. "Did they pick up your dog a couple of hours ago? Then he must be with the ones the truck brought in just now."

He shouldn't get that way, my newspaper friend, it wasn't anyone's fault. His voice is bland, dreamy, like his eyes, bitter, like the folds of his mouth: fucked up too. The dogcatchers were paid by the number of animals, sometimes they committed abuses, what could you do, it was all part of the struggle to buy a little something to eat. Some muffled blows in the yard, whines that seemed filtered through cork walls. The bald man half smiles and, gracelessly, lazily, gets to his feet, goes out of the office muttering. They cross an open stretch, go into a shed that smells of urine. Parallel cages, crammed with animals who push against each other and jump in place, sniff the wire, growl. Santiago leans over each cage, not there, he explores the promiscuous surface of snouts, rumps, tails stiff and quivering, not there either. The bald man walks beside him, his look far away, dragging his feet.

"Take a look, there's no more room to keep them," he protests suddenly. "Then your newspaper attacks us, it's not fair. The city gives us almost nothing, we have to perform miracles."

"God damn it," Santiago says, "not here either."

"Be patient," the bald man sighs. "We've got four more sheds."

They go outside again. Earth that had been dug up, weeds, excrement, stinking puddles. In the second shed one cage moves more than the others, the wires shake and something white and woolly bounces, comes up and sinks back into the wave: that's more like it, that's more like it. Take a snout, a piece of tail, two red and weepy eyes: Rowdy. He still has his leash on, they had no right, a hell of a thing, but the bald man calm down, calm down, he'd have them get him out. He goes off with sluggish steps and a moment later comes back followed by a Negro-Indian half-breed in blue overalls: let's see, he was to get that little whitish one out, Pancras. The half-breed opens the cage, pushes the animals apart, grabs Rowdy by the scruff of the neck, hands him to Santiago. Poor thing, he was trembling, but he turns him loose and he takes a step back, shaking himself.

"They always shit." The half-breed laughs. "It's their way of saying we're glad to be out of jail."

Santiago kneels down beside Rowdy, scratches his head, lets him lick his hands. He trembles, dribbles urine, staggers drunkenly, and only outside does he start to leap and scratch the ground, to run.

"Come with me, take a look at the conditions we work under." He takes Santiago by the arm, smiles at him acidly. "Write something for your paper, ask the city to increase our budget."

Sheds that were foul-smelling and falling apart, a gray steel roof, gusts of damp air. Fifteen feet from them a dark silhouette stands next to a sack and is struggling with a dachshund who protests in a voice too fierce for his minimal body as he twists hysterically: help him, Pancras. The short half-breed runs, opens the sack, the other slips the dachshund inside. They close the sack with a cord, put it on the ground, and Rowdy starts to growl, pulling on his leash, whining, what's the matter, he watches, frightened, barks hoarsely. The men already have the clubs in their hands, are already beginning, one-two, to beat and grunt, and the sack dances, leaps, howls madly, one-two, the men grunt and beat. Santiago closes his eyes, upset.

"In Peru we're still living in the stone age, friend." A bittersweet smile awakens the bald man's face. "Look at the conditions we work under, tell me if it's right."

The sack is quiet, the men beat it a little more, throw their clubs onto the ground, wipe their faces, rub their hands.

"We used to kill them the way God wanted, now there isn't enough money," the bald man complains. "You tell him, the gentleman's a reporter, he can make a protest in his paper."

He's taller, younger than Pancras. He takes a few steps toward them and Santiago finally sees his face: oh my God! He releases the chain and Rowdy starts to run and bark and he opens and closes his mouth: oh my God!

"One sol for each animal, mister," the half-breed says. "And besides, we have to take them to the dump to be burned. Only one sol, mister."

It wasn't him, all Negroes look alike, it couldn't be him. He thinks: why can't it be him? The half-breed bends down, picks up the sack, yes, it was him, carries it to a corner of the yard, throws it among other bloody sacks, comes back swaying on his long legs and drying his forehead. It was him, it was him. Hey, buddy, Pancras nudges him, go get yourself some lunch.

"You complain here, but when you go out in the truck to make pick-ups you have a great time," the bald man grumbles. "This morning you picked up this gentleman's dog, which was on a leash and with its mistress, you nitwits."

The half-breed shrugs his shoulders, it was him: they hadn't gone out on the truck that morning, boss, they'd spent it with their clubs. He thinks: him. The voice, the body are his, but he looks thirty years older. The same thin lips, the same flat nose, the same kinky hair. But now, in addition, there are purple bags on his eyelids, wrinkles on his neck, a greenish-yellow crust on his horse teeth. He thinks: they used to be so white. What a change, what a ruin of a man. He's thinner, dirtier, so much older, but that's his big, slow walk, those are his spider legs. His big hands have a knotty bark on them now and there's a rim of saliva around his mouth. They've come in from the yard, they're in the office, Rowdy rubs against Santiago's feet. He thinks: he doesn't know who I am. He wasn't going to tell him, he wasn't going to talk to him. Who would ever recognize you, Zavalita, were you sixteen? eighteen? and now you're an old man of thirty. The bald man puts a piece of carbon paper between two sheets, scrawls a few lines in a cramped and stingy hand. Leaning against the doorjamb, the half-breed licks his lips.

"Just a little signature here, friend; and seriously, do us a small favor, write something in *La Crónica* asking them to raise our budget." The bald man looks at the half-breed. "Weren't you going to lunch?"

"Could I have an advance?" He takes a step forward and explains in a natural way: "I'm low in funds, boss."

"Half a pound." The bald man yawns. "That's all I've got."

He accepts the banknote without looking at it and goes out with Santiago. A stream of trucks, buses and cars is crossing the Puente del Ejército, what kind of a face would he put on it? in the mist the earthen-colored hulks of the shacks of Fray Martín de Porres, would he start to run? seem to be part of a dream. He looks the half-breed in the eyes and the other one looks at him.

"If you'd killed my dog I think I would have killed all of you," and he tries to smile.

No, Zavalita, he doesn't recognize you. He listens attentively and his look is muddled, distant and respectful. Besides getting old, he's most likely turned into a dumb animal too. He thinks: fucked up too.

"Did they pick this woolly one up this morning?" An unexpected glow breaks out in his eyes for an instant. "It must have been black Céspedes, that guy doesn't care about anything. He goes into backyards, breaks locks, anything just so he can earn his sol."

They're at the bottom of the stairs that lead up to Alfonso Ugarte; Rowdy rolls on the ground and barks at the ash-gray sky.

"Ambrosio?" He smiles, hesitates, smiles. "Aren't you Ambrosio?"

He doesn't start to run, he doesn't say anything. He looks with a dumb-founded and stupid expression and suddenly there's a kind of vertigo in his eyes.

"Don't you remember me?" He hesitates, smiles, hesitates. "I'm Santiago, Don Fermín's boy."

The big hands go up into the air, young Santiago, mister? they hang in the air as if trying to decide whether to strangle or embrace him, Don Fermín's boy? His voice cracks with surprise or emotion and he blinks, blinded. Of course, man, didn't he recognize him? Santiago, on the other hand, had recognized him the minute he saw him in the yard: what did he have to say? The big hands become active, I'll be goddamned, they travel through the air again, how he'd grown, good Lord, they pat Santiago on the shoulders and back, and his eyes are laughing at last: I'm so happy, son.

"I can't believe you've grown into a man." He feels him, looks at him, smiles at him. "I look at you and I can't believe it, child. Of course I recognize you now. You look like your papa; a little bit of Señora Zoila too."

What about little Teté? and the big hands come and go, with feeling? with surprise? and Mr. Sparky? from Santiago's arms to his shoulders to his back, and the eyes look tender and reminiscent as the voice tries hard to be natural. Weren't coincidences strange? Who would have thought they'd ever meet again! And after such a long time, I'll be goddamned.

"This whole business has made me thirsty," Santiago says. "Come on, let's go have a drink. Do you know someplace around here?"

"I know the place where I eat," Ambrosio says. "La Catedral, a place for poor people, I don't know if you'll like it."

"As long as they have cold beer I'll like it," Santiago says. "Let's go, Ambrosio."

It seemed impossible that little Santiago was drinking beer now, and Ambrosio smiles, his strong greenish-yellow teeth exposed to the air: time did fly, by golly. They go up the stairs, between the vacant lots on the first block of Alfonso Ugarte there's a white Ford garage, and at the corner on the left, faded by the inexorable grayness, the warehouses of the Central Railroad appear. A truck loaded with crates hides the door of La Catedral. Inside, under the zinc roof, crowded on rough benches and around crude tables, a noisy voracious crowd. Two Chinese in shirt-sleeves behind the bar watch the copper faces, the angular features that are chewing and drinking, and a frantic little man from the Andes in a shabby apron serves steaming bowls of soup, bottles, platters of rice. Plenty of feeling, plenty of kisses, plenty of love boom from a multi-colored jukebox and in the back, behind the smoke, the noise, the solid smell of food and liquor, the dancing swarms of flies, there is a punctured wall—stones, shacks, a strip of river, the leaden sky—and an ample woman bathed in sweat manipulates pots and pans surrounded by the sputter of a grill. There's an empty table beside the jukebox and among the scars on the wood one can make out a heart pierced by an arrow, a woman's name: Saturnina.

"I had lunch already, but you have something to eat," Santiago says.

"Two bottles of Cristal, good and cold," Ambrosio shouts, cupping his hands to his mouth. "A bowl of fish soup, bread and stewed vegetables with rice."

You shouldn't have come, you shouldn't have spoken to him, Zavalita, you're not fucked up, you're crazy. He thinks: the nightmare will come back. It'll be your fault, Zavalita, poor papa, poor old man.

"Taxi drivers, workers from the small factories in the neighborhood." Ambrosio points around them as if excusing himself. "They come all the way from the Avenida Argentina because the food is passable and, most important, cheap."

The Andean brings the beers, Santiago fills the glasses and they drink to your health, boy, to yours, Ambrosio, and there's a compact, undecipherable smell that weakens, nauseates and wipes the head clean of memories.

"What a stinking job you've got for yourself, Ambrosio. Have you been at the dog pound a long time?"

"A month, son, and I got the job thanks to the rabies, because there hadn't been any openings. It certainly is stinking, it squeezes you dry. The only relief is when you go out on the truck to make pickups."

It smells of sweat, chili and onions, urine and accumulated garbage and the music from the jukebox mingles with the collective voice, the growl of motors and horns, and it comes to one's ears deformed and thick. Singed faces, prominent cheekbones, eyes made drowsy by routine or indolence wander among the tables, form clusters at the bar, block the entrance. Ambrosio accepts the cigarette that Santiago offers him, smokes, throws the butt on the floor and buries it under his foot. He slurps the soup noisily, nibbles on the pieces of fish, picks up the bones and sucks them, leaves them all shiny, listening or answering or asking a question, and he swallows pieces of bread, takes long swigs of beer and wipes the sweat off with his hand: time swallows a person up before he realizes it, child. He thinks: why don't I leave? He thinks: I have to go and he orders more beer. He fills the glasses, clutches his and, while he talks, remembers, dreams, or thinks he watches the circle of foam sprinkled with craters, mouths that silently open up, vomiting golden bubbles and disappearing into the yellow liquid that his hand warms. He drinks without closing his eyes, belches, takes out cigarettes and lights them, leans over to pet Rowdy: the things that have happened, Jesus. He talks and Ambrosio talks, the pouches on his eyelids are bluish, the openings in his nose vibrate as if he'd been running, as if he were drowning, and after each sip he spits, looks nostalgically at the flies, listens, smiles, or grows sad or confused, and his eyes seem to grow furious sometimes or frightened or go away; sometimes he has a coughing spell. There are gray hairs in his kinky mat, on top of his overalls he wears a jacket that must have been blue once too and had buttons, and a shirt with a high collar that is wrapped around his neck like a rope. Santiago looks at his enormous shoes: muddy, twisted, fucked up by the weather. His voice comes to him in a stammer, fearful, is lost, cautious, imploring, returns, respectful or anxious or constrained, always defeated: not thirty, forty, a hundred, more. Not only had he fallen apart, grown old, become brutalized; he probably was tubercular as well. A thousand times more fucked up than Carlitos or you, Zavalita. He was leaving, he had to go and he orders more beer. You're drunk, Zavalita, you were about to cry. Life doesn't treat people well in this country, son, since he'd left their house he'd gone through a thousand movie adventures. Life hadn't treated him well either, Ambrosio, and he orders more beer. Was he going to throw up? The smell of frying, feet and armpits swirls about, biting and enveloping, over the straight-haired or bushy heads, over the gummy crests and the flat necks with mange and brilliantine, the music on the jukebox grows quiet and revives, grows quiet and revives, and now, more intense and irrevocable than the sated faces and square mouths and dark beardless cheeks, the abject images of memory are also there: more beer. Wasn't this country a can of worms, boy, wasn't Peru a brain-twister? Could you believe it, Odriístas and Apristas, who used to hate each other so much, all buddy-buddy now? What would his father have said about all this, boy? They talk and sometimes he listens timidly, respectfully to Ambrosio, who dares protest: he had to go, boy. He's small and inoffensive there in the distance, behind the long table that's a raft of bottles and his eyes are drunken and afraid. Rowdy barks once, barks a hundred times. An inner whirlwind, an effervescence in the heart of his heart, a feeling of suspended time and bad breath. Are they talking? The jukebox stops blasting, blasts again. The thick river of smells seems to break up into tributaries of tobacco, beer, human skin and the remains of meals that circulate warmly through the heavy air of La Catedral, and suddenly they're absorbed by an invincible higher stench: neither you nor I was right, papa, it's the smell of defeat, papa. People who come in, eat, laugh, roar, people who leave and the eternal pale profile of the Chinese at the bar. They speak, they grow silent, they drink, they smoke, and when the Andean appears, bending over the tabletop bristling with bottles, the other tables are empty and the jukebox and the crackling of the grill can no longer be heard, only Rowdy barking, Saturnina. The Andean counts on his darkened fingers and he sees Ambrosio's urgent face coming toward him: did he feel bad, boy? A little headache, it would go away. You're acting ridiculous, he thinks, I've had a lot to drink, Huxley, here's Rowdy, safe and sound, I took so long because I ran into a friend. He thinks: love. He thinks: stop it, Zavalita, that's enough. Ambrosio puts his hand into his pocket and Santiago puts out his arms: don't be foolish, man, he was paying. He staggers and Ambrosio and the Andean support him: let me go, he could walk by himself, he felt all right. By God, boy, it was to be expected, he'd had a lot to drink. He goes forward step by step through the empty tables and the crippled chairs of La Catedral, staring at the chancrous floor: O.K., it's all gone. His brain is clearing, the weakness in his legs is going away, his eyes are clearing up. But the images are still there. Getting tangled in his feet, Rowdy barks impatiently.

"It's good you had enough money, boy. Are you really feeling better?"

"My stomach's a little queasy, but I'm not drunk, the drinks didn't do anything to me. My head's spinning from thinking so much."

"It's four o'clock, I don't know what kind of story I can make up. I could lose my job, you don't realize that. But thanks in any case. For the beer, for the lunch, for the conversation. I hope I can make it up to you some-day, son."

They're on the sidewalk. The Andean has just closed the big wooden door, the truck that hid the entrance has left, the mist wipes out the build-ing fronts and in the steel-colored light of the afternoon, oppressive and identical, the stream of cars, trucks and buses flows over the Puente del Ejército. There's no one nearby, the distant pedestrians are faceless sil-houettes that slip along through smoky veils. We say good-bye and that's it, he thinks, you'll never see him again. He thinks: I never saw him, I never spoke to him, a shower, a nap and that's it.

"Do you really feel all right, son? Do you want me to go with you?"

"The one who doesn't feel well is you," he says without moving his lips. "All afternoon, four hours of this, it's made you feel bad."

"Don't you believe it, I've got a good head for drinking," Ambrosio says, and, for an instant, he laughs. He stands there with his mouth ajar, his hand petrified on his chin. He's motionless, three feet from Santiago, his lapels turned up, and Rowdy, his ears stiff, his teeth showing, looks at Santiago, looks at Ambrosio, and scratches the ground, startled or rest-less or frightened. Inside La Catedral they're dragging chairs and seem to be mopping the floor.

"You know damned well what I'm talking about," Santiago says. "Please don't play dumb with me."

He doesn't want to or he can't understand, Zavalita: he hasn't moved and in his eyes there's still the same blind challenge, that terrible dark tenacity.

"If you don't want me to go with you, son," he stammers and lowers his eyes, his voice, "do you want me to get you a taxi then?"

"They need a janitor at *La Crónica*," and he lowers his voice too. "It's not as nasty a job as the one at the pound. I'll see that they hire you with-out any papers. You'd be a lot better off. But please, stop playing dumb for a little while."

"All right, all right." There's a growing uneasiness in his eyes, it's as if his voice were going to break up into shreds. "What's the matter, boy, why do you act like this?"

"I'll give you my whole month's pay," and his voice suddenly becomes thick, but he doesn't weep; he's rigid, his eyes opened very wide. "Three thousand five hundred soles. Couldn't you get along with that money?"

He's silent, he lowers his head and automatically, as if the silence had loosened an inflexible mechanism, Ambrosio's body takes a step backward and he shrugs his shoulders and his hands come forward at the level of his stomach as if to defend himself or attack. Rowdy growls.

"Have the drinks gone to your head?" he snorts, his voice upset. "What's the matter, what is it you want?"

"For you to stop playing dumb." He closes his eyes and breathes in some air. "For us to talk frankly about the Muse, about my father. Did he order you? It doesn't matter anymore, I just want to know. Was it my father?"

His voice is cut off and Ambrosio takes another step backward and Santiago sees him crouched and tense, his eyes open wide with fear or rage: don't leave, come here. He hasn't become brutalized, you're not a boob, he thinks, come on, come on. Ambrosio wavers with his body, waves a fist, as if threatening or saying good-bye.

"I'm leaving so that you won't be sorry for what you've said," he growls, his voice painful. "I don't need work, I want you to know that I won't take any favors from you, least of all your money. I want you to know that you don't deserve the father you had, I want you to know that. You can go straight to shit hell, boy."

"All right, all right, I don't care," Santiago says. "Come on, don't leave, come back."

There is a short growl by his feet, Rowdy is looking too: the small dark figure is going off clinging to the fences of the vacant lots, standing out against the gleaming windows of the Ford garage, sinking into the stairway by the bridge.

"All right," Santiago sobs, leaning over, petting the stiff little tail, the anxious snout. "We're going now, Rowdy."

He straightens up, sobs again, takes out a handkerchief and wipes his eyes. For a few seconds he doesn't move, his back against the door of La Catedral, getting the drizzle in his face full of tears once more. Rowdy rubs against his ankles, licks his shoes, whimpers softly, looking at him. He starts walking slowly, his hands in his pockets, toward the Plaza Dos de Mayo and Rowdy trots alongside. People are collapsed at the base of the monument and around them a dung heap of cigarette butts, peels and paper; on the corner people are storming the run-down buses that become lost in dust clouds as they head to the shantytowns; a policeman is arguing with a street vendor and the faces of both are hateful and discouraged and their voices seem to be curled by a hollow exasperation. He walks around the square, going into Colmena he hails a taxi: wouldn't his dog dirty the seat? No, driver, he wouldn't dirty it: Miraflores, the Calle Porta. He gets in, puts Rowdy on his lap, that bulge in his jacket. Play tennis, swim, lift weights, get mixed up, become alcoholic like Carlitos.

He closes his eyes, leans his head against the back of the seat, his hand strokes the back, the ears, the cold nose, the trembling belly. You were saved from the pound, Rowdy, but no one's ever going to get you out of the pound you're in, Zavalita, tomorrow he'd visit Carlitos in the hospital and bring him a book, not Huxley. The taxi goes along through blind noisy streets, in the darkness he hears engines, whistles, fleeting voices. Too bad you didn't take Norwin up on lunch, Zavalita. He thinks: he kills them with a club and you with editorials. He was better off than you, Zavalita. He'd paid more, he'd fucked himself up more. He thinks: poor papa. The taxi slows down and he opens his eyes: the Diagonal is there, caught in the headlights of the cab, oblique, silvery, boiling with cars, its lighted ads quivering already. The mist whitens the trees in the park, the church steeples drift off in the grayness, the tops of the ficus trees waver: stop here. He pays the fare and Rowdy starts to bark. He turns him loose, sees him go into the entrance to the elf houses like a rocket. Inside he hears the barking, straightens his jacket, his tie, hears Ana's shout, imagines her face. He goes into the courtyard, the elf houses have their windows lighted, Ana's silhouette as she hugs Rowdy and comes toward him, what took you so long, love, I was nervous, so frightened, love.

"Let's get this animal inside, he'll drive the whole street crazy," and he barely kisses her. "Quiet, Rowdy."

He goes to the bathroom and while he urinates and washes his face he listens to Ana, what happened, sweet, what took you so long, playing with Rowdy, at least you found him, love, and he hears the happy barking. He comes out and Ana is sitting in the small living room, Rowdy in her arms. He sits down beside her, kisses her on the temple.

"You've been drinking." She holds him by the jacket, looks at him, half merry, half annoyed. "You smell of beer, love. Don't tell me you haven't been drinking, right?"

"I met a fellow I haven't seen in a hundred years. We went to have a drink. I couldn't get away, sweet."

"And me here half crazy with worry." He hears her plaintive, caressing, loving voice. "And you drinking beer with the boys. Why didn't you at least call me at the German woman's?"

"There wasn't any phone, we went to a dive." Yawning, stretching, smiling. "Besides, I don't like to keep bothering that crazy German all the time. I feel lousy, I've got an awful headache."

You deserved it, having kept her nerves on edge all afternoon, and she runs her hand over his forehead and looks at him and smiles at him and speaks to him softly and pinches one ear: you deserve to have a headache, love, and he kisses her. Would he like to sleep a little, should she draw the curtains, love? Yes, he gets up, just for a bit, falls onto the bed, and the shadows of Ana and Rowdy busying themselves about him, looking for himself.

"The worst is that I spent all my money, love. I don't know how we'll get by till Monday."

"Oh, that's all right. It's good that the Chinaman on San Martín always trusts me, it's good that he's the nicest Chinaman in the world."

"The worst is that we'll miss our movies. Was there anything good showing today?"

"One with Marlon Brando at the Colina," and Ana's voice, far, far away, arrives as if through water. "One of those detective movies you like, sweet. If you want I can borrow some money from the German woman."

She's happy, Zavalita, she forgives you for everything because you brought Rowdy back to her. He thinks: at this moment she's happy.

"I'll borrow some and we'll go to the movies, but promise me that you won't ever have a few beers with your buddies without telling me." Ana laughs, farther and farther away.

He thinks: I promise. The curtain has one corner folded over and Santiago can see a chunk of almost dark sky, and imagine, outside, up above, falling down onto the houses and their elves, Miraflores, Lima, the same miserable drizzle as always.

Notes

1   Carlitos is a fellow newspaperman of Santiago Zavala, the main character in *Conversation in the Cathedral*.
2   A *chilcano* is a cocktail made with orange brandy.

THE SLAVE

Jaime Bayly

The precocious, outspoken Jaime Bayly was already a prominent television commentator by his early twenties. No one suspected that he was also a talented writer. His 1995 novel No Se Lo Digas a Nadie, *or* Don't Tell Anyone, *became a national bestseller. By turns sad, sexy, and hilarious, the novel is a supremely entertaining, no-holds-barred exploration of family life, race and racism, and homophobia and desire among Lima's moneyed elite. In this first chapter, Bayly's semiautobiographical protagonist, Joaquín, begins a journey that will take him to Miami and Madrid and a struggle to come to terms with his own sexuality and the paradoxes of Peru today.*

When Joaquín finished fifth grade, his mother, Maricucha, decided to move him to a new school. One summer day, she told him that she had taken him out of Sacred Heart and enrolled him at Markham. He started crying.

"Don't cry, my little prince, it's for your own good," she said, hugging him.

"I don't want to go to a new school, Mommy," he said.

"You'll love your new school, my sweetheart," she said. "It's the best in Lima."

"But I don't understand why you're taking me out of Sacred Heart when I was getting the best grades in my class, Mommy."

"Sacred Heart wasn't good enough for you, darling," she said, kissing him on the cheek. "That school has gone downhill. You got the best grades without even trying, sweetie."

"But you didn't even ask if I wanted to go to a new school, Mommy. It's not fair."

"You're still a child, my love. Your Mommy knows what's best for you."

"I'm telling you that if you put me in a new school, I'm never going to get the best grades in my class again."

"Don't be silly, my little darling. You were born to be the best at everything."

Joaquín ran to his room, slammed the door, and ripped up all the diplomas he'd received at Sacred Heart.

On the first day of class at Markham, Maricucha woke up Joaquín earlier than usual. It was still dark. Joaquín got out of bed and hugged his mother.

"Say your prayers, darling," she said.

Joaquín kneeled on the floor, crossed himself, closed his eyes, and prayed: Lord, I am in your hands. Then he stood up.

"How do you like your new uniform?" Maricucha asked, showing him the Markham uniform: brown jacket, short pants, striped tie, and brown hat.

"The Sacred Heart uniforms were a lot better."

"Don't be silly, honey," she said, smiling. "Besides, you look cute in brown. It matches your complexion."

Maricucha and Joaquín went into the bathroom. She helped him change and showed him how to knot his tie. Then she combed his hair with plenty of hair gel.

"Your hair has to be nice so all your new friends will think that you're a real little English lord," she said.

"Don't put that greasy stuff on my hair," he said, hating the hair gel.

"It's so you look even more handsome, my little prince," she said, combing in more gel.

She finished dressing him, and the two of them went to the dining room. Joaquín ate his breakfast quickly.

"I'm never going to forgive you for taking me out of Sacred Heart, Mommy," he whispered, without looking at his mother.

"Don't be bitter, honey," she said, caressing him. "In time, you'll understand that I'll do anything to make you happy."

"I don't know what you want from me, Mommy."

"You know exactly what I want from you, my little Joaquín. That you always be the best."

"I know what you want, Mommy. You want me to be a priest."

"No, my darling, I just want you to be happy, happy as a clam. But, yes, if the Lord blesses me with a son who's a priest, I'd consider myself very lucky."

"I'm telling you, Mommy, I'm not going to be a priest. You should forget the idea that I'm ever going to be a priest."

"One never knows what the Lord will want for us, my darling."

As soon as Joaquín finished breakfast, Maricucha got up, went to her room, and came back with a camera.

"I'm going to take a few pictures of you, darling," she said, smiling.

"I don't want to, Mommy," he said. "I hate it when you take my picture."

"Don't be difficult, sweetie," she said. "Let me take some pictures so that when you're big you'll remember your first day at Markham."

He picked up his book bag, put on his hat, and stood by the front door.

"Take off the hat, honey," his mother said. "A real gentlemen always takes his hat off for pictures."

He took off his hat.

"Cheese," she said. "Smile, my little honeypot."

He smiled unenthusiastically. She took a few pictures.

"Now wait for your Daddy by the car. I don't want you to be late for school," she said, hugging him.

He started crying.

"That's life, love," she told him. "Little birds have to leave their nests and learn to fly."

Ten minutes later, Luis Felipe, Joaquín's father, came out of the house and got into the car. He was a tall, stocky man. He'd just grown a moustache. He put his briefcase in the back seat, closed the door, and saw that Joaquín was crying.

"Stop crying, goddammit," he said in a threatening voice. "Men don't cry."

Then he started the car, turned on the radio news station, and drove off to the highway. The sun had come up. Old trucks rumbled toward Lima. Luis Felipe drove fast and silently. Like most mornings, he was in a bad mood. After passing Chaclacayo, he had to slow down behind a truck. "The Lone Avenger of Jauja" it said on the back bumper.[1] There was also a picture of Che Guevara. Luis Felipe honked his horn.

"Fucking Indian, move your goddam ox-cart," he yelled, still honking the horn.

A little farther on, the trucker let them pass. As they went by, Luis Felipe rolled down his window.

"Shitty Indian, go drive a fucking llama," he yelled.

Then he accelerated, giving the trucker the finger.

"They should shoot all the Indians once and for all and dump them in Rímac River, goddamit," he said. "That's how Peru will get ahead."

Half an hour later, Luis Felipe and Joaquín arrived at Markham. They hadn't spoken at all.

"I'm going to give you some advice, man to man," Luis Felipe said to his son, as soon as he'd parked in front of the school.

"Tell me, Daddy," Joaquín said.

"If some little prick tries to fuck with you, don't let him, okay?"

"Yes, Daddy."

"Punch him in the face a couple of times, kick him in the balls, and beat the shit out of him until he says uncle. That's the only way to make people respect you. If not, they're going to get on you from the start and you'll be fucked, son."

"Thanks, Daddy." Joaquín kissed his father on the cheek.

"Now you know," Luis Felipe told him, "Beat the shit out of the first little fuck who bothers you."

Joaquín got out of the car and walked away quickly. Before going into the school, he turned around and waved to his father. Luis Felipe replied by throwing a few shadow punches.

That morning, after singing the national anthem and listening to the welcome from Markham's principal, Joaquín went to his new classroom, the sixth grade. Entering the room, he greeted his teacher, Mr. MacAlpine, a young, thin, and somewhat pale man. MacAlpine wished him luck and showed him his desk. It was a desk for two children, like all the others in the room. Joaquín sat down and looked at the boy sitting next to him.

"Hi," the boy said. "My name is Jorge."

Jorge was short and a bit chubby. He had a restless look.

"I'm Joaquín."

They shook hands and put their notebooks in the desk. MacAlpine took attendance.

"What school were you in before?" Jorge asked.

"Sacred Heart."

They were whispering so MacAlpine wouldn't notice them.

"What happened?" Jorge asked. "Did they kick you out?"

"No, nothing like that," said Joaquín. "I had really good grades."

"Then why did you leave?"

"Because my Mom didn't like Sacred Heart."

Just then, MacAlpine called Jorge Bermúdez. The boy next to Joaquín raised his hand and said, "Present."

"Do you like soccer?" Joaquín asked.

"Pretty much," said Jorge.

"What's your favorite team?"

"The U of course. All us whites root for the U."[2]

Then MacAlpine called Joaquín Camino. Joaquín raised his hand and said, "Present."

"Have you been to Miami?" Jorge asked.

"No, but my Dad promised to take me for July vacation," said Joaquín.

"Miami is incredible. I went last summer."

"You're lucky. My Dad says that there's no thieves in Miami or little kids asking for money in the streets."

"What does your Dad do?"

"He's a manager."

"Oh yeah? Mine's a chief executive. Chief executive is higher than manager. It's the highest there is."

"Jeez, that's really cool."

"Is your dad a millionaire?"

"I don't know. I don't think so. I'll ask him."

"Mine is."

"Really?"

"He's not a millionaire. He's a multimillionaire."

"Boy, you've got all the luck."

MacAlpine called for silence and began to teach the year's first lesson.

That afternoon, at 3 P.M. sharp, Joaquín came out of the school together with the other Markham students. His mother was waiting for him at the door. They hugged, gave each other a kiss, and got into the car.

"How was your first day of school?" she asked him.

"Great," he said.

"Oh, that's wonderful. Are you happy at Markham, darling?"

"Yes, Mommy. I liked it a lot. Thanks for changing my school."

"I told you to trust me, my little Joaquín. I knew it was for your own good."

Just then, Jorge walked by Maricucha's side of the car and waved goodbye to Joaquín, who smiled and waved back.

"Who's that nice-looking boy?" Maricucha asked.

"My friend Jorge," Joaquín said.

"Just look at my little Joaquín, what a little Mr. Popularity he's become," said Maricucha, smiling and caressing her son's head.

"Jorge is a great guy, Mommy," Joaquín said. "We sit at the same desk."

"Jorge what?"

"Jorge Bermúdez."

"Rosa and Cucho's son?"

"I don't know. If you want, I'll ask him tomorrow."

"Yes, ask. I was good friends with Rosita Bermúdez in school. Wouldn't it be divine if your little friend Jorge was her son?"

"You know what, Mommy? There wasn't any boy as great as Jorge at Sacred Heart."

"How lucky, precious. But if you think about it, it's not luck, my darling; it's that the Lord has put him in your path as a reward for being an obedient son."

Joaquín smiled. Maricucha started the car.

"Do you know if Jorge goes to mass every Sunday?" she asked.

"No idea," he said.

"Ask him, okay? Because it's very important that your little friends have the right moral values, my little Joaquín. And also ask him if he prays every day."

"Why do I have to ask him so many things? Don't be so nosy, Mommy."

"It's your Christian duty to try to save the souls of your little friends, Joaquín. Or don't you want to meet Jorge up in the sky someday?"

"Yes, I want to, Mommy. Of course I want to. Jorge is a great guy."

"Then take an interest in his spiritual training and try to put him on the path of holiness, my love."

"But Mommy, if I say anything about religion, maybe he'll get mad and not want to be my friend ever again."

"Don't be afraid of criticism, my darling. Don't be afraid of what other people say. You're a leader. A born leader. You were born to be president or a cardinal. And maybe more than that. Sometimes I even think you'll end up in the Vatican, my Joaquín."

Maricucha stopped at a light and looked at her son. Her eyes were filled with tenderness.

"Let's play a game," said Jorge.

"Great," said Joaquín.

They were in math class. It was only a few days after the start of school. Jorge was the only friend Joaquín had made at Markham.

"It's a really easy game," said Jorge. "You're my slave and you do everything I say."

"Everything?" asked Joaquín, surprised.

"Everything. Because you're my slave. I'm your master."

"Okay, fine."

They were whispering while Mr. Tamayo did equations on the board.

"Now, say: You're my master and I'm you're slave," said Jorge.

"You're my master and I'm you're slave," Joaquín repeated.

"I like it like that, slave. Now I want you to take the eraser out of my pants pocket."

"Okay, but it's only a game, right?"

Joaquín didn't mind the game. He thought it was fun to be Jorge's slave.

"You have to say: At your service, master," said Jorge.

"At your service, master," Joaquín repeated.

"Now take out my eraser, slave."

Joaquín put one hand in Jorge's pocket. He tried to find the eraser. He felt a hole in the pocket. He touched something soft, warm.

"There's no eraser," he said, taking his hand out quickly.

"Sure there is," said Jorge, smiling. "You just touched it."

"That wasn't an eraser."

"Touch it again, slave."

Again, Joaquín put a hand into Jorge's pocket.

"Now play with my eraser, slave," said Jorge.

Joaquín caressed Jorge's penis. He knew very well that it wasn't an eraser.

One night, Joaquín went in his pajamas to the living room and sat down to watch TV with his father.

"So? Have you picked a fight with someone at your school?" Luis Felipe asked him.

"No, Daddy, not yet," Joaquín said.

Luis Felipe was having a drink and smoking a cigarette.

"What are you waiting for?" he asked.

"Well, I haven't had a chance, Daddy," Joaquín said.

"Hasn't anybody tried to fuck with you?"

"Nobody, Daddy. Everyone's been nice to me so far."

"That's strange, because school is usually full of little assholes. You're not fucking with me, are you?"

"No, Daddy, how could you think that?"

Luis Felipe had a drink.

"You know what you're going to do, then?" he said. "You're going to watch and see who the bullies are in your class, and you're going to grab one of those dickheads during recess and beat the shit out of him."

"But why, Daddy? Why should I fight someone if they haven't done anything to me?"

"So they respect you straight off, dickhead. So they know not to mess with you."

"But Daddy, I don't like fighting for no reason."

"What's wrong, Joaquín? Are you scared?"

Joaquín didn't say anything.

"Are you afraid to fight?" Luis Felipe asked, raising his voice. "Does my son piss in his pants because he's scared to slug some little prick?"

"It's that I'm not a good fighter, Daddy," Joaquín said.

"What? Speak up, goddammit. We men should talk with balls. You sound like you're talking with your asshole, boy."

"It's that I'm not good at fighting," Joaquín yelled.

"You don't know how to fight?" said Luis Felipe, smiling. "Is that your problem? I'll show you how to mix it up, boy. Your old man is going to teach you a thing or two."

He got up from the sofa and put out his cigarette.

"Wait here," he said. "I'll be right back."

Luis Felipe went off to his room. Joaquín kept watching TV. He was sorry he'd come in to watch with his father. Before long, Luis Felipe came back with a pair of boxing gloves.

"Put them on," he said, giving Joaquín the gloves.

"What for?" Joaquín asked, surprised.

"I'm going to teach you to fight."

Joaquín laughed nervously.

"Don't worry about it, Daddy," he said. "It's not worth the trouble."

"Put them on, goddammit," said Luis Felipe, raising his voice.

Resigned, Joaquín put on the gloves. Luis Felipe moved the table and the chairs, leaving an open space in the middle of the living room.

"Now we're going to get it on," he said. "You can hit me anywhere from the belt up."

"Better just your stomach, Daddy. I don't want to hit you in the face."

"Hit me where you want, boy, as long as you don't hit me in the balls."

Joaquín laughed. He didn't know what to do. His legs were trembling.

"Okay, move, get going," said Luis Felipe. "Imagine that I'm one of those little assholes in your school."

Joaquín put up his gloves. Luis Felipe began to dance around him. Joaquín got up the courage to throw a few punches at his stomach. His father blocked them with his hands.

"Too slow," he said, circling Joaquín. "Harder. Faster. Faster."

Joaquín tried to hit him hard in the stomach, but his father blocked the punch and slapped him. Joaquín laughed nervously.

"Don't laugh," said Luis Felipe. "Keep fighting. Concentrate."

"But you said you weren't going to hit me, Daddy."

"Just fight. Don't waste your breath."

Joaquín threw a couple of hard punches. Luis Felipe blocked them easily and replied with a pair of slaps. Again, Joaquín's face stung, feeling hot.

"I don't want to fight anymore," he said.

"It's no good to throw in the towel. Don't play the faggot with me, boy. I'm teaching you to fight like a man."

Suddenly, Luis Felipe slapped him again. Joaquín went into a rage and hit him twice in the stomach.

"Shit, you're getting tough with me," said Luis Felipe, smiling.

Then he slapped Joaquín two more times, harder than before. Joaquín turned his back on him, took off the gloves, and threw them down.

"No fair, Daddy," he said.

He was crying. He couldn't help it.

"Put on your gloves, goddammit," said Luis Felipe. "Don't pull that faggot crap with me."

"I don't want to," Joaquín said. "I don't like this game."

"Fight, boy," said Luis Felipe, slapping him again. "Come on, concentrate. We're still fighting."

"You're a big jerk," Joaquín yelled, running to his room.

Joaquín locked the door, and looked at his face in the mirror. His face was red. He wept with anger, clenching his teeth. He looked for his photo album. He opened it. He ripped up a pair of pictures of his father. He kept crying. Then Luis Felipe knocked on the door.

"Son, open the door," he said.

Joaquín didn't answer. Luis Felipe kicked the door.

"Open, goddammit," he yelled.

Joaquín put his head under the pillow.

"I hope they kick the shit out of you in school," said Luis Felipe.

Joaquín heard his father's footsteps walking away. I hate him, he thought.

A few days later, one Saturday afternoon, Joaquín went for the weekend to Jorge's house. After lunch, Jorge and Joaquín went up the stairs to Jorge's bedroom.

"I'm going to show you a secret thing," said Jorge.

"What?" Joaquín asked.

Jorge locked the door. Then he opened his closet, looked under his clothes, and took out a magazine.

"A magazine with naked ladies," he said, smiling, showing Joaquín the copy of *Playboy*.

"How did you get it?" Joaquín asked.

"I stole it from my Uncle Augusto's house," said Jorge. "That stud has a bunch of *Playboys*."

They sat on the bed and looked at the magazine. It was the first time Joaquín had seen a magazine with naked women.

"I like that one," said Jorge, pointing to the photo of a blonde woman who was on a swing with her legs spread open.

"Yes, it's a nice photo," said Joaquín, not knowing what else to say.

"I've looked at it so much that sometimes I dream about her," said Jorge. "The other night I dreamed that we were swinging face-to-face, and I stuck my cock in her when we got to the top. Look, I'll show you how I stained my bed."

Jorge pulled back his bed sheets and showed Joaquín some stains.

"It looks like butter," said Joaquín.

Jorge laughed.

"When you dream about women, you make these stains," he said.

They were quiet. They continued looking at the magazine.

"We can play a game that's really good," said Jorge.

"How do you play?" Joaquín asked.

"We rub our cocks looking at these photos and we see who can shoot the farthest."

"What are we going to shoot?"

"The white stuff that comes out when you rub yourself."

Joaquín looked down, embarrassed.

"Haven't you ever jerked off?" asked Jorge.

"Never," said Joaquín. "It's a mortal sin. And you go to hell for a mortal sin."

"Yeah, sure, but we're not going to die yet."

Jorge got up, put the magazine on the rug, and opened it to his favorite page.

"Now come over here, stand next to me," he said.

Joaquín stood up next to Jorge.

"The game goes like this: we both pull down our pants and jerk off," said Jorge. "Whoever shoots off first wins."

"I've never jerked off, Jorge. Maybe I can't shoot it out."

"All penises can shoot, stupid."

Jorge raised his hands to his belt.

"One, two, three," he said.

Then he pulled down his pants and started masturbating. Joaquín watched with curiosity.

"You can't watch," said Jorge.

"It was so I can learn how," said Joaquín, pulling down his pants.

"I'm shooting," said Jorge.

Joaquín started masturbating.

"I'm going to give it to her, I'm going to give it to her," said Jorge, closing his eyes.

Then he ejaculated.

"I won, I won," he yelled.

That night, Jorge and Joaquín put on their pajamas and went to bed. Jorge got in his bed, and Joaquín squeezed into a sleeping bag on the rug.

"Have you ever been hypnotized?" asked Jorge.

"Never," said Joaquín.

The room was dark. They could hear the traffic on Coronel Portillo Street.

"I've got a record that teaches you how to hypnotize yourself that I bought in Miami," said Jorge. "I haven't listened to it yet because I'm scared to alone."

"I think hypnotizing yourself is a mortal sin," said Joaquín.

"Maybe, but we've already committed a mortal sin by jerking off, so it doesn't matter if we commit another one."

"Well, yeah, you're right."

Jorge got out of bed, went out of the room, and came back with a record player. He put the record player on the rug and took a record from his closet.

"Maybe it's dangerous to hypnotize yourself," said Joaquín.

Jorge cued up the record.

"Don't be afraid," he said. "Nothing's going to happen."

Then he lay down next to Joaquín.

"Concentrate hard," he whispered. "If you get scared, tell me."

A voice in English began the instructions. Following the instructions, Jorge and Joaquín closed their eyes, opened their palms, took deep breaths and tried to clear their minds. The voice told them they were on a deserted beach. The record played sea noises, the whistling wind, and the cry of a few seagulls.

"Now you're hypnotized, slave," whispered Jorge.

Joaquín yawned.

"I'm not hypnotized," he said. "I'm dead tired."

"I'm telling you, you're hypnotized, slave."

"Okay, master."

"That's the way I like it, slave. Now concentrate and imagine you're a woman. You are hypnotized and you're a woman, a woman, a woman."

Joaquín smiled.

"Tell me that you're a woman," said Jorge.

"I'm a woman," said Joaquín.

"I'm a woman, *master*," Jorge corrected.

"I'm a woman, *master*," Joaquín repeated.

"Very good, very good. Now I want you to be the woman in the magazine, the woman on the swing."

"I'm the woman in the magazine, master. I'm the woman on the swing."

"Now turn around. Don't open your eyes. You're hypnotized. You're a woman."

Joaquín lay down on his stomach. Jorge pulled down his pajama pants. Joaquín opened his eyes, surprised.

"I don't want to play anymore," he said.

"Hey, shut up, don't ruin the game," said Jorge. "Close your eyes, dammit. You're hypnotized."

Joaquín closed his eyes. Jorge climbed onto him.

"I'll put it in you first and then you can put it in me, okay?" he whispered, pushing his penis between Joaquín's butt cheeks.

"It hurts a lot," Joaquín complained.

"Just at the beginning, then it doesn't hurt anymore."

Jorge put a lot of saliva on the tip of his penis and put it into Joaquín.

"Tell me that you're the woman in the magazine, please," he whispered, moving faster each time.

"I'm the woman in the magazine, master," said Joaquín, putting up with the pain.

Jorge finished and lay there on top of Joaquín.

"Doing it in the ass is a thousand times better than jerking off," he said.

"Good, now it's my turn," said Joaquín.

"No, it's too late," Jorge said. "Better some other time."

Then he went back to his bed and slipped between his Batman and Robin sheets.

A few weeks later, Joaquín was reading the newspaper in the living room when his mother yelled at him to come. Frightened, he jumped up and ran to his mother's room.

"May I ask why this garbage was in your room?" she asked, showing him the *Playboy*.

Jorge had lent the magazine to Joaquín, who had hidden it behind one of the pictures on the wall of his room.

"I don't know, Mommy," said Joaquín.

"What do you mean you don't know?" Maricucha asked. "Irma says she was cleaning your room and all of a sudden found this trash."

He looked down, ashamed.

"I can't believe that my sweet little boy has his head filled with smut," she said.

"I'm sorry, Mommy," he said. "I won't do it again."

"You're still a boy and you're already defiling your soul, Joaquín," she said. "If at your age you're already reading these sick magazines, what's going to happen to you when you're big, my poor son?"

Then she threw down the magazine, sat on her bed, and started crying. "I must have been a very bad mother to have such a twisted son."

Joaquín didn't like seeing his mother cry.

"It's the first time I've looked at a nude magazine, Mommy," he said. "I promise I'll never do it again."

"And I had so many hopes for you, my beloved darling," she said, weeping. "I can't believe that you've turned into a pervert. What a disappointment."

Then Luis Felipe came into the room. He saw his wife crying, the magazine on the floor.

"What the hell's going on here?" he yelled.

"Our son is a pervert," said Maricucha.

Luis Felipe bent over, picked up the magazine, and looked at it with a little smile.

"Well, goddammit, you little prick," he said to Joaquín.

"Luis Felipe, please, don't talk like that to the child," said Maricucha.

"Shut up, Maricucha. This is men's business, I'll take care of it."

Luis Felipe looked sternly at Joaquín.

"Where did you get that magazine?" he asked.

"I don't know, Daddy," said Joaquín.

"Don't fuck with me," yelled Luis Felipe, and smacked Joaquín in the face with the magazine.

Maricucha hugged her son.

"Luis Felipe, please, don't hit the child," she yelled.

"That's why our boy is a little princess," yelled Luis Felipe. "Because you spoil him, you treat him like a doll."

"Don't say that, you're going to give him a complex," yelled Maricucha.

"Goddammit, where did you get this magazine?" Luis Felipe asked Joaquín.

"I got it at Cristian's newsstand," said Joaquín.

Cristian was a pleasant, quiet man who had a newsstand a few blocks from their house.

"That faggot *cholo* is fucked with me," said Luis Felipe.[3]

"We're going to get rid of that piece of garbage right now," said Maricucha, grabbing the magazine from her husband. "We're going to burn that horrid thing before the devil enters our house."

"Mommy, please don't burn it," said Joaquín. "That magazine isn't mine. I have to give it back."

Luis Felipe grabbed Joaquín by the neck and shook him violently.

"Listen, devil boy, don't get fresh with your mother," he yelled.

"We're going to burn that disgusting smut right this minute," said Maricucha, leaving the room with the magazine.

Joaquín ran after his mother.

"I have to give it back, Mommy," he yelled. "Cristian loaned it to me."

"You're not giving anything back, goddamit," yelled Luis Felipe. "I'm going to talk to Cristian and I'm going to kick the crap out of that *cholo* faggot."

Maricucha, Luis Felipe, and Joaquín went out on the terrace.

"Marcelo, Marcelo," yelled Maricucha.

Marcelo was the gardener. He was a short, half-hunchbacked man. The servants in the house called him "Hawaii Five-O" because he looked like one of the detectives on the program.

"I'm right here, Ma'am," yelled Marcelo. "Over here, by the duck pen."

Luis Felipe, Maricucha, and Joaquín went out to the duck pen where

Maricucha had ordered Marcelo to raise ducks, chickens, and rabbits ("because my Christian home should be like an earthly paradise, Marcelo," she had said).

"Marcelo, build a fire right now," said Maricucha.

"Right away, Ma'am," said Marcelo, looking scared.

Then he piled up some dry leaves and old newspapers, took out a box of matches, and lit a fire.

"We've found a nudie magazine in Joaquín's room," said Maricucha.

"How can that be, little Joaquín?" said Marcelo.

"It's that ungrateful Indian Cristian's fault," said Luis Felipe. "I'm going to tear down his newsstand with my bare hands."

"That Cristian is one crafty *cholo*," said Marcelo.

Maricucha went up to the fire, glanced at the magazine, grimaced in disgust, and threw the magazine into the flames.

"May those shameless women roast in hell," she whispered.

The next day, on the way to school with his son, Luis Felipe stopped at Cristian's newsstand, belched, and got out of the car.

"Is the little girlie afraid to get out?" he mocked Joaquín.

Joaquín got out of the car and walked in back of his father.

"Good morning, Mr. Luis Felipe, what a surprise to see you here," said a smiling Cristian, taking a bite of biscuit.

"Don't play the fool with me, you *cholo* faggot," yelled Luis Felipe, grabbing Cristian by the neck. "Listen to me, you fucking Indian. Give another adult magazine to my son, and I'll turn this hovel to shit. I'll rip it up with my bare hands, and I'll set a match to it myself. Do you understand?"

"Yes, Mr. Luis Felipe," stammered Cristian.

He was pale, terrified.

"Besides, my police friends tell me that you rent this newsstand at night as a quickie whorehouse," said Luis Felipe. "Don't think you're so fucking smart, you *cholo* asshole. I know that there's more fucking going on in this newsstand than in the Five and a Half Club."[4]

"Lies, Mr. Luis Felipe, lies," said Cristian.

"One more fuck-up and I'm burning down your newsstand, don't forget it," said Luis Felipe, letting him go.

"Thanks, Mr. Luis Felipe," said Cristian, bowing his head.

Luis Felipe went back to his car, walking fast.

"I'm sorry, Cristian, it's all my fault," said Joaquín, in a low voice.

"Give these to your Daddy so he'll forgive me, little Joaquín," said Cristian, giving him a pack of cigarettes.

Joaquín ran to the car and got in as fast as he could.

"All *cholos* are the same," said Luis Felipe. "You fuck with them a bit and they piss in their pants."

Then he started the car and pulled out. Joaquín gave him the cigarettes.

"Cristian says to forgive him," he said.

Luis Felipe opened the pack, took out a cigarette, and lit it.

"Did you see how fucking scared that Indian looked when I grabbed him by the neck?" he said, smiling. "Learn from your father, Joaquín. If you want to get ahead in Peru, you have to learn how to shit on the *cholos*."

That morning, when he went into the classroom, Joaquín felt his hands sweating. He was nervous.

"I lost your magazine," he told Jorge, as soon as they sat down at their shared desk.

"How did you lose it?" asked Jorge, surprised.

"My parents took it," said Joaquín, looking at the ground.

Jorge slammed the desk with his hand.

"Shit, you asshole," he said. "I never should have lent it to you. You have to make them give it back to you."

"That's impossible," said Joaquín. "They already burned it."

"They burned it? How did they burn it?"

"My Mom went crazy and threw it in a bonfire in the garden."

Jorge kicked Joaquín's lunchbox.

"Son of a bitch, why did I ever give the magazine to an idiot like you?" he said.

"I'm sorry, Jorge."

"Dumbshit. You knew that magazine wasn't mine, that I'd stolen it from my uncle."

"I'll do whatever you want so you'll forgive me," said Joaquín.

"Let me think about your punishment, slave," said Jorge.

A few hours later, Jorge and Joaquín had recess and walked to the jungle gym.

"I've decided on your punishment," Jorge said. "I want you to let the air out of the tires of Moulbright's car."

Harry Moulbright was the Markham principal. He was a plump, bald man. He was rumored to be an alcoholic. A story had also gotten around the school that he was a Nazi spy and that he'd come to Peru under a false name, escaping the law.

"Moulbright's tires?" asked Joaquín, surprised.

"Yes," said Jorge. "The four tires."

"And why Moulbright?"

"Because he's a jerk, a son of a bitch. Last year, he took me to his office and smacked me twenty times on the hand with a ruler. That piece of shit has a metal ruler that hurts like hell. My hand got red and swelled up like a yam. He's a sadist, that fucking limey."

"And what did you do for him to smack you twenty times with the ruler?"

"Nothing, it was bullshit. During recess, I stayed in the classroom, opened the lunchboxes of some other kids, and ate the best things. Those were some great lunches, Joaquín. They had Sublimes, Doña Pepas, Coronitas, piononos, everything.[5] I wiped out those lunchboxes. Those kids were such dumbshits they didn't even notice. But one day that little shit Fisher fingered me to Moulbright."

Joaquín smiled.

"I don't know if I can do it," he said.

"Don't be a faggot," said Jorge. "You have to."

"But if somebody catches me, I might get expelled."

"No one's going to catch you, Joaquín. Now when we get out look for Moulbright's car and take down his tires fast."

"There's tons of people around when we get out, Jorge. Somebody's going to see me."

"If you still want to be my friend, you have to do it. If you don't, I'll never talk to you again."

Joaquín had grown very fond of Jorge. He didn't want to lose their friendship.

"Okay, I'll try," he said.

Jorge smiled and slapped Joaquín on the back.

"When we get out today, then?" he asked him.

"When we get out today," said Joaquín.

They shook hands, smiling.

That afternoon, as always, the Markham bell rang at exactly three. Jorge and Joaquín left the school together. Jorge left his book bag in his driver's pickup and went with Joaquín over to Moulbright's car, a green Volkswagen parked in front of the school office.

"I can't do it," said Joaquín. "There's too many people."

There were dozens of students in their brown uniforms milling around in front of the school's main door, impatient drivers honking their horns, ice cream vendors selling more loose cigarettes than ice cream, and a couple of teachers from England who stood out because they wore suit-coats and tennis shoes to school.

"Well then, just let the air out of a couple of the tires," said Jorge. "Sit on the sidewalk and stick a pen point in the valve. No one will notice."

"Okay, I'll try," said Joaquín, feelings his legs tremble.

"Hurry up! Moulbright will be out any minute," said Jorge, and walked away towards his driver's pickup.

Joaquín crouched next to Moulbright's car, took out a pen, stuck the point into the valve of one of the front tires, and let the air out. When he finished, he started with the back wheel on the same side.

"Hey, young man, what the hell are you doing there?" he heard sud-denly.

Joaquín looked up and saw Mr. Pérez-Mejía, the head of school disci-pline, watching him from a second-floor window. Pérez-Mejía was a thin, dark-skinned man. Students at the school called him Lizard, Tadpole, or The Boa.

"Nothing, sir," said Joaquín. "I was tying my shoes."

"Don't move," yelled Pérez-Mejía.

Frightened, Joaquín stood up and looked around for Jorge, but couldn't find him. Pérez-Mejía came running out of the school. Seeing the flat tire on Moulbright's car, he grabbed Joaquín by the hair.

"You've been caught committing an act of vandalism against Mr. Moul-bright's property," he said.

"I didn't do anything, sir, the tires were like that," said Joaquín.

Yanking him by the hair, Pérez-Mejía took Joaquín back into the school.

"I'm going to turn you over to Mr. Moulbright," he said, smiling. "He'll be very pleased to know that you were letting the air out of his tires."

"Please, sir, don't tell anyone, I beg you," said Joaquín.

"In this school, you pay a high price for breaking the rules," said Pérez-Mejía. "There's no place in Markham for little shitheads."

When they got to the principal's office, Pérez-Mejía knocked three times. Moulbright opened the door right away. He was wearing a shirt and tie. He had on glasses with thick lenses.

"I caught this student trying to take the air out of your tires, sir," said Pérez-Mejía. "I'm leaving him for you to apply the appropriate punish-ment."

"Thanks, Mr. Pérez-Mejía," said Moulbright, looking at Joaquín over his glasses. "You may go."

Péréz-Mejía nodded and left.

"Come in, please," said Moulbright.

Joaquín went into the office. Moulbright closed the door, sat at his desk chair, crossed his legs, and took out a whiskey bottle. Then he took a drink from the bottle, looked at Joaquín, and smiled. He had a round face, as if inflated, and almost no hair on his head.

"Name and section?" he asked.

"Joaquín Camino, A First."

Moulbright wrote it down.

"Now tell me what you were doing to my car," he said, smiling.

"Nothing, Mr. Moulbright," said Joaquín. "I wasn't doing anything."

"Don't lie to me."

"I swear I didn't do anything."

Moulbright got up and took another drink.

"*These Peruvians are such liars,*" he murmured in English.

Then he opened a drawer in his desk and took out a metal ruler.

"You're going to tell me why you were letting the air out of my tires or I leave your hands swollen," he said.

Joaquín didn't say anything.

"Right hand," said Moulbright.

Joaquín put out his right hand. Moulbright hit him on the hand ten times in a row with the metal ruler. Each time he hit, he smiled, and a little thread of drool dribbled from the corner of his mouth.

"Why did you do it?" he asked.

"I wasn't doing anything," said Joaquín, crying.

"Left hand," ordered Moulbright.

Then the ruler came down ten more times on the palm of Joaquín's left hand.

"Are you going to confess why you wanted me to take a taxi home?"

Joaquín looked at his red, swollen hands, and kept crying. Moulbright took another swig from his whiskey bottle.

"Turn around and pull down your pants," he ordered.

Joaquín silently obeyed. Moulbright began to hit him on the butt with the metal ruler.

"I'm not going to stop until you tell," he said, continuing to hit Joaquín.

"I did it for a friend," said Joaquín. "A friend asked me to do it."

Moulbright stopped.

"His name," he said.

"Jorge Bermúdez."

Moulbright smiled.

"Poor little thing, his teensey little butt is red," he said, slapping Joaquín's butt a couple times. "Now pull up your pants and go home."

The next day, Jorge and Joaquín met on the playground. It was a gray morning, as usual in Lima.

"What happened yesterday?" asked Jorge.

"Nothing," said Joaquín, putting his hands in his pockets so Jorge wouldn't see them.

"Don't play dumb. I saw when the Lizard caught you."

"Yeah, he caught me, but I didn't tell him anything."

"What did he say?"

"Nothing, Jorge. Nothing happened."

"Don't lie, Joaquín. Tell me what happened. If you're lying, you're fucked with me forever."

Joaquín looked down.

"Lizard took me to Moulbright's office, and Moulbright hit me a bunch of times with the ruler," he said.

"Did you tell him my name?" Jorge asked.

"Are you crazy? I didn't say a word about you."

"Then why are you turning red?"

"I'm not turning red."

"You're as red as a tomato, asshole."

"I swear I didn't tell on you, Jorge. I took all the blame."

"I hope so, Joaquín. If you fingered me, you're fucked with me."

At that moment, the bell rang. Jorge and Joaquín entered the classroom and sat down at their desk.

"How many tires did you let the air out of?" asked Jorge.

"Two," said Joaquín. "I left two of his tires flat as a pancake."

"Well done. That fucking limey. Did he hit you hard?"

"Really hard. He made me cry."

Joaquín showed him his hands. They were still red and swollen.

"That limey is a sadist," said Jorge. "He likes hitting kids."

A little later, Mr. Candelares entered the classroom and asked for silence. Candelares taught chemistry. He had black hair, slicked back with gel, and big, round eyes, like an owl. Candelares liked to joke with his students. He was very popular in the school.

"My name is Napoleón Candelares," he said, at the beginning of class. "I didn't fight at Waterloo, but I fight every day in the bathroom because I have a constipation problem."

The students had a big laugh.

Halfway through chemistry, one of Moulbright's assistants, Mr. Tapia, came into the room, said a few words to Mr. Candelares, and then said:

"Jorge Bermúdez, please come with me."

The class rustled. Everyone knew that a trip to Moulbright's office was bad news. Before getting up, Jorge looked threateningly at Joaquín.

"I swear I didn't tell him anything about you," whispered Joaquín.

"You're fucked with me," whispered Jorge.

Then Jorge left the classroom with Mr. Tapia. Joaquín was very nervous. Unable to concentrate, he opened his notebook and wrote: "Jorge, I'm sorry. What I did was wrong. I swear I'm sorry. I've never had a friend who was as great a guy as you. I don't want to lose your friendship. I'll do whatever you tell me to keep being your friend. Please, forgive me and give me one more chance, Joaquín (your slave)." Then he tore out the sheet and put it in Jorge's desk.

A bit later, Mr. Tapia came into the class again.

"Joaquín Camino, please come with me," he said.

Joaquín got up and left the classroom. His face felt hot. He was afraid.

"It looks like you've gotten in big trouble, young man," Tapia told him, as they walked to the principal's office.

"Do you think they'll expel me, Mr. Tapia?" asked Joaquín.

"I don't know, but that limey is plenty nasty," said Tapia.

They entered the main office, climbed the stairs, and walked through a hallway lined with pictures of Markham's graduating classes.

"I'd advise you to go along with whatever he wants, because that limey breathes fire when you contradict him," said Tapia, lowering his voice. "You have to agree with everything baldie says."

"Thanks, Mr. Tapia," said Joaquín.

Tapia knocked on the door of Moulbright's office and left quickly.

"Come in," yelled Moulbright.

Joaquín opened the door and went into the office. Jorge was sitting in front of Moulbright's desk.

"Have a seat," said Moulbright.

Joaquín sat next to Jorge.

"One of you two has lied to me," said Moulbright. "And I want to know which one is the liar."

Jorge and Joaquín didn't say anything.

"Joaquín Camino told me yesterday that it was Jorge Bermúdez's idea to let the air out of my tires, and Jorge Bermúdez just told me that he didn't have anything to do with it," said Moulbright.

"That's right, Camino made the story up," said Jorge, staring vengefully at Joaquín.

"Which of the two of you is lying, Mr. Camino?" asked Moulbright.

Joaquín didn't want to get Jorge in any more trouble.

"Me," he said. "It was all my idea."

"And may I ask why you told me yesterday that you were letting the air out of the tires because Jorge Bermúdez asked you to?" asked Moulbright.

"I lied because I'm a coward, Mr. Moulbright," said Joaquín. "I lied to put the blame on someone else."

"The problem is that Camino is a faggot, Mr. Moulbright," said Jorge.

Moulbright smiled, as if he'd received good news.

"Is that right?" he said. "How so?"

"Camino has tried to touch me sometimes in class," said Jorge. "Once in the bathroom, he told me to do something dirty."

"What dirty thing was that?" asked Moulbright.

"Camino told me he'd suck me off in the bathroom, I didn't let him," said Jorge, speaking rapidly. "And as I said, Mr. Moulbright, several times Camino has tried to touch me in the classroom."

"Is that true, Mr. Camino?" asked Moulbright. "Are you a degenerate?"

"It's true that I've touched Bermúdez, Mr. Moulbright, but it was because he asked me to," said Joaquín.

"That's a lie," yelled Jorge. "I never let him."

"In other words, Mr. Camino, we have a faggot problem in the sixth grade?" asked Moulbright. "Are you a fucking queer?"

Joaquín didn't know what to say. It was the first time anyone had asked him that question.

"I think so," he said.

"Dear me, dear me, that's very serious," said Moulbright, touching a finger to his nose. "And you, Mr. Bermúdez?"

"Not me, Mr. Moulbright," said Jorge. "I hate queers."

"Very good, very good, because faggots aren't allowed in this school," said Moulbright. "You can go back to your class, Mr. Bermúdez. And I don't want to see you in any more trouble. Next time, I'll suspend you, don't forget."

Jorge got up.

"Thanks, Mr. Moulbright," he said. "The only thing I ask is to be moved to another desk, because I can't stand Camino anymore."

"I'll take the appropriate measures," said Moulbright.

Jorge looked at Joaquín contemptuously and left the office. Moulbright got out a whiskey bottle, took a swig, and burped.

"This is a very delicate matter, Mr. Camino," he said. "I'm going to have to suspend you for two weeks."

Jorge didn't say anything.

"Faggotry is punished very severely in this school," Moulbright continued. "There's no worse crime a student can commit than homosexual degeneracy. If you want to stay in this school, things can't continue this way."

"I understand, Mr. Moulbright. I promise it won't happen again."

Moulbright smiled.

"Promises, promises," he said.

Then he opened one of his drawers, took out a notebook, and filled in Joaquín's suspension sheet.

"You're suspended for two weeks for immoral conduct," he said. "Now get your things while I call your parents."

"Please, Mr. Moulbright, don't call them," said Joaquín.

"I'm sorry, Mr. Camino, but those are the rules."

"Couldn't you make an exception, Mr. Moulbright? My parents are very strict. My father will beat me if he finds out about this."

"Your father will find out anyway, Mr. Camino. You're already suspended."

"But please, only tell them about the tires, not what I did with Jorge."

Moulbright loosened the knot on his tie.

"All right, all right, I won't call them," he said, smiling. "But then I'll have to spank you a few times on your bottom. Does that seem fair, Mr. Camino?"

"Sure, fine, Mr. Moulbright. Whatever you want."

"Come here. Turn around and pull down your pants."

Joaquín turned his back to Moulbright and pulled down his pants. Moulbright started spanking him on the behind. Suddenly, Joaquín turned around.

"Don't look at me, you brat," yelled Moulbright.

He had unzipped his fly. He was masturbating. Joaquín turned back around. Moulbright kept spanking him. When he finished, he told Joaquín he could go.

"Thanks, Mr. Moulbright," said Joaquín.

Then he left the office and returned to his classroom. Mr. Candelares was still there when he came in.

"What's wrong with you young people, all these long faces?" said Candelares, seeing Joaquín.

"Good, that's what you get for being a fag," whispered Jorge, as Candelares continued with the chemistry lesson.

"I just wanted to still be your friend," whispered Joaquín.

"Shut up," whispered Jorge. "We'll never be friends again."

Joaquín picked up his book bag, showed the suspension sheet to Mr. Candelares, and left the classroom clenching his teeth, trying not to cry.

Jorge and Joaquín didn't speak to each other again until the end of high school.

On prom night, Joaquín and Claudia, the girl he'd invited, were sitting at a table talking and having a drink when Jorge came up to them.

"Great party, isn't it?" said Joaquín.

Those were the first words he'd spoken to Jorge after years of silence between them.

"Great, great," said Jorge.

His eyes were shining. He seemed a bit drunk. He was still a bit chubby, with fat cheeks and a restless look.

"What happened to your date, handsome?" Claudia asked him.

"I had to take her home," said Jorge. "Her parents only let her stay until 2 in the morning."

"Jeez, what a drag," said Joaquín.

"Well, that's the problem when you go out with little girls," said Claudia.

Claudia was twenty-two, six years older than Joaquín and Jorge. Joaquín knew her because she was a friend of his sister, Ximena.

"A toast," said Joaquín.

"Good idea," said Claudia. "Let's all three of us toast."

"To certain friendships that never die," said Joaquín, and he looked at Jorge, smiling.

They clinked glasses.

"Can I tell your date a secret?" Jorge asked Joaquín.

"Sure, if she doesn't mind," said Joaquín.

"I love men who whisper in my ear," said Claudia, smiling flirtatiously.

Jorge whispered something in Claudia's ear. She smiled and slapped his leg.

"You bandit," she said.

Then Claudia held Joaquín's hand.

"I'll be back right away. I have to go to the bathroom," she told him.

"I have to go to the bathroom, too," said Jorge.

Claudia and Jorge got up from the table, walked across the garden, and went together into the house. A few minutes later, impatient because Claudia hadn't returned, Joaquín got up to look for her. He found her in the living room, talking to Jorge.

"What are you doing here?" he asked her, surprised.

"Chatting," said Claudia. "Gossiping about this and that."

"Do you want to dance?" Joaquín asked her.

"Oh, I just promised Jorge I'd dance with him," said Claudia.

"Sure, no problem," said Joaquín.

Claudia and Jorge went to dance. They held each other close, and Jorge whispered things in her ear. She laughed. When they finished, they went up to Joaquín.

"Joaquín, darling, forgive me, but Jorge asked me to give him a quick ride home," said Claudia.

"Sure, that's fine," said Joaquín. "I'll go with you."

"Why don't you just stay?" said Claudia. "I'll be right back."

"Fine, whatever you want," said Joaquín.

"I'll be right back, it'll be quick," said Claudia, and she gave him a kiss.

She grabbed her purse and went over to the next table to say goodbye to some friends. Then Jorge bent over and whispered in Joaquín's ear.

"You're still my slave," he said, and then left with Claudia.

At dawn, Joaquín was still waiting for her.

Notes

1   Jauja is a town in the central Andes.

2   The "U" stands for Club Universitario de Deportes, a famous Lima soccer team; their historical rival is Alianza Lima, a team that has traditionally included many black players.

3   *Cholo* refers to brown-skinned Peruvians of Indian descent.

4   The Five and Half Club is a famous brothel at the 5.5 kilometer mark out of Lima on the Central Highway to the Andes.

5   These are favorite candies and chocolates.

AGUARUNA ADVENTURES

Anonymous

*For Peru's 200,000 indigenous people of the Amazon, survival has been a diffi-
cult and sometimes losing battle for rights to land, health, language, and culture.
Successive booms—rubber, timber, petroleum, coca—have enriched outsiders and
left native communities with a shrinking margin of livelihood. Today, one of the
largest groups is the Aguaruna (literally, "the people of the water"), who occupy the
humid valleys of the Marañón and Mayo rivers. Despite massive colonization by
poor Andean settlers, the Aguaruna have adapted to changing conditions, learning Spanish and fighting for land titles, yet persisting in a way of life grounded
in hunting, fishing, jungle farming, and village autonomy. The magical realism
of Aguaruna mythology, like this tale collected by local schoolteacher José Luis Jordana, reflects the permeable boundaries between the human, the natural, and the
sacred that characterize much Amazonian cosmology. The continuing popularity
of these often humorous and engaging tales—sometimes featuring characters or
themes woven in from Bible stories or even TV programs—sums up the ability of
this indigenous group to maintain a distinctive sense of humor and history even
in the face of outside pressure.*

S úwa and Ipák were two single women in the old days. They didn't
have a house of their own and went looking for a place to live. On
the path, they met Nayáp, and he asked where they were going:

"We're looking for a house, because we don't have anywhere to take
shelter from the night's cold or the rain."

So Nayáp said they should stay with him and come at nightfall: "The
path is easy, because it's marked by *tucán* and *guacamayo* feathers all the
way.[1] When you get there, help my mother make *masato*.[2] I'll come later."

But Tsuna was hidden nearby, listening. He set out ahead, dropping

Figure 57. Making *masato* in an Aguaruna village.
(Courtesy of Margaret VanBolt)

feathers along the path that led to his house. So Súwa and Ipák, following the feathers, arrived at Tsuna's house. There, they were received by his mother, who was grinding corn for the chickens.

That night, Tsuna returned. He asked his mother: "Where did those two women come from?"

His mother replied: "I don't know. They came alone, without husbands."

That night, Tsuna hopped into bed with the two women. He left the house before they awoke, saying he was going to hunt. He returned late in the evening. From then on, Tsuna slept with Súwa and Ipák every night. Every day before dawn, he left the house, saying he was off to hunt. And he only returned at dusk. Súwa and Ipák were very puzzled at his behavior.

So they decided to find out why Tsuna avoided being seen during the day. One night, they rubbed nettles all over themselves before going to bed, to keep themselves awake. Then, they passed the whole night frolicking with Tsuna and tickling him. Finally, he fell fast asleep. Súwa and Ipák examined his naked body and were amazed by his crooked penis.

When Tsuna's mother awoke, she saw the two women snickering and laughing at her sleeping son's strange penis.

She said: "My son, you're embarrassing me."

Then Tsuna woke up. Ashamed, he grabbed his blowgun and ran for the forest.

He went to find Tseje, the spider, and said: "Weave me a palm rope, because I'm going to kill Súwa and Ipák. I want to hang up their innards and make *patarashca*."[3]

Tseje started spinning palm for rope. He was in the middle of this when Súwa and Ipák arrived.

They asked: "Why are you weaving palm thread?"

"I can't tell you," Tseje replied, to spark their curiosity.

"Please tell us, Tseje, why you're weaving palm! If you tell, we'll come to live with you," said the two women.

Tseje replied: "First I'll have to test the two of you. Then I'll tell you why I'm weaving the rope."

Súwa and Ipák agreed. Tseje slept first with Súwa, then with Ipák. They let Tseje have them as much as he wanted.

Then Tseje said: "Women, escape! Tsuna's going to kill you if you don't run far away. He told me he's having the rope made to hang your innards and make *patarashca*. Run far away!"

The women escaped. They ran to a big river, called Kanús, which is now known as the Santiago River. It was too wide to cross.

But Súwa and Ipák saw Taátanch, another spider, and called him: "Taátanch! Taátanch! Please carry us across! Tsuna is following to kill us!"

Taátanch agreed. He carried the two women on his back and plunged into the water. But they were heavy, and he tired halfway across. He returned because he was sinking.

Then Wijisám, a small frog, came by and sang:

"Tue-tuó! Tue-tuó! Tue-tuó!"

The women yelled at him: "Wijisám, get us to the other side. We'll give you anything you want!"

Wijisám was carrying a spear and was dressed in black. He replied: "Okay, here I come."

And saying this, he disappeared underwater and then came up next to Súwa and Ipák. He grabbed them by their long hair and dived again. The women held their breath. They arrived at the other side. Wijisám said: "Now wash your clothes. You stink of Tsuna."

While Súwa and Ipák were washing their clothes, Tsuna appeared, chasing them. Angry at seeing them on the other side, he yelled: "Who took you across? Taátanch, you were the one, right?"

And he squashed Taátanch with a rock. That's why, ever since, Taátanch has been a squished spider, almost flat, who glides across the water as if floating. Angrily, Tsuna returned to his house.

The women, with clothes washed and dried in the sun, went to the house of the frog Wijisám and said: "Wijisám, we want to live with you. We'll take good care of you."

Wijisám replied: "No, I live in a burrow. My brother-in-law Nayáp has a nice house and plenty of food. Better for you to go with him. With me, you'll only suffer."

So the women continued on their way and finally came to Nayáp's house. They lived there for a long time, eating the fish Nayáp caught every day.

One day, as Nayáp was leaving, he said: "I'm going to fish for *bocachicas* and *palometas*.[4] Meanwhile, give my mother a bath with clean water, warmed up a bit. She's old, and it's hard for her to bathe alone. When I get back, we'll all eat fish together. See you soon!"

When Nayáp left, Súwa and Ipák whispered to each other: "When Nayáp returns with the fish, he'll give his mother the biggest *bocachicas* and us the little ones. That's how men are. Better we should kill his mother. If we're left alone with him, we'll be able to eat the best fish."

So they got the water ready for the old woman's bath, bringing it to a boil. Then they poured it over Nayáp's mother. As if made of tar, the old woman melted, disintegrating in their hands as they bathed her. Just a bit of her remained under the bench.

Súwa and Ipák said: "When Nayáp returns, we'll tell him that his mother went to the fields."

A little later, Nayáp came back with plenty of fish. He asked: "I don't see my mother here. Where is she?"

"Oh, she went to the fields to dig yucca. She said she'd return right away," chorused the women.

Nayáp answered: "Yes, my mother will return soon, because too much sun is bad for her."

And he shouted for his mother: "Mother! Mother! Mother!"

Since no one answered, Nayáp asked: "You haven't killed my mother, have you?"

They replied: "No. What's the matter with you? Why do you ask?"

And again he began to shout for his mother: "Mother! Mother! Mother!"

Underneath the bench, a little voice said: "Son, they've killed me!"

Nayáp screamed at Súwa and Ipák: "Get out of my house immediately! Out, evil women!"

Súwa and Ipák left. They walked hard until they came to another house. It was Nantatáy's. He lived with his mother.

Nantatáy was ugly and deformed. His penis was very long. So no one would see, his mother always hid him in a big clay jar.

On arriving, Súwa and Ipák talked on and on about how much they wanted to live with his mother and help with her chores in the house and fields. Nantatáy's mother agreed to have them stay and even promised her son as a husband.

"My son Nantatáy is very handsome. And he's still young. He has a beautiful *tawas* that he wove himself.[5] He's not here now, because he went to war. My son is very brave, and he always wins in fights. When he returns, you can be his wives."

In fact, her son Nantatáy was not at war, because he was hidden in the jar, listening to his mother. But Súwa and Ipák believed the old woman. They decided to stay.

One night, the two women were asleep, when the old woman called her son: "Nantatáy! tay! tay! tay!"

She helped him out of the jar. He didn't walk well, half dragging himself across the floor. His mother gave him yucca she had chewed beforehand and said: "Son, go see the two women. Enjoy them."

Nantatáy went to their bed. Because his penis was so long, it scratched the sleeping women. They awoke, saying: "Sister, did you feel something slippery moving over us? I think someone was trying to do something bad to us."

"I felt the same thing. What can it have been? Tomorrow night, we'll have to pretend to be asleep to see what it is."

Night fell. Once more, the old woman helped her son get out of the jar, gave him chewed yucca, and sent him to enjoy the two women. Meanwhile, Súwa and Ipák were pinching each other constantly to keep from falling asleep. Suddenly, they felt something slippery on their thighs. They give it a big kick. Nantatáy fell into the red-hot coals of the cooking fire. Nantatáy shrieked: "Mother! They're still not asleep! They got mad and kicked me!"

His mother answered: "Wait until they're in a heavier sleep."

She hid Nantatáy in the jar again. The next day, Súwa and Ipák told the old woman: "We dreamed about your son. We think he'll return today. Your son is tall, brave, and young. We dreamed that your son is coming with blood on his spear and *tsantsas* in his hand."[6]

They continued: "My sister and I are going to fish, so your son will have something to eat when he gets back. You, little mother, should go to the fields to dig yucca to serve with the fish."

So the two women left the house. But they hid nearby in the bushes. A bit later, the old woman went out to the fields. Súwa and Ipák returned to the house. They asked each other: "Where can Nantatáy be? He bothered us very much last night. Let's look for him!"

"Nantatáy! tay! tay! tay!"

They called just like his mother. Nantatáy answered from inside the jar. They found him and took off the cover. Nantatáy was seated inside. They were horrified at his long penis. They said to each other: "That's what he was bothering us with so much last night. Let's kill him!"

So they poured boiling water into the jar, scalding Nantatáy. Then they put it back where it was and went out fishing as if nothing had happened.

Súwa and Ipák dug some *barbasco* to fish in a stream. They ground the poisonous roots on a rock. The water turned murky, and many fish suffocated. They scooped them into their baskets and returned to the house. From far away, they heard the cries of Nantatáy.

The old woman had come back from the fields and called her son. When he didn't respond as usual, she uncovered the jar and found him dead. When Súwa and Ipák returned, they asked her: "Mother, why are you crying? What's happened?"

The old woman wept: "I just received bad news, that my son Nantatáy was killed at war."

The women tried to cry. But they couldn't fake it, chuckling because they knew who had killed Nantatáy. The old woman told them: "Leave my house, my son is dead! You bring bad luck!"

Súwa and Ipák walked and walked, not knowing where to go. They arrived at Kunám's house. They talked with him for a long time. Kunám liked them. He begged them to stay with him. They accepted happily.

One day, Kunám sent the women to his fields. He told them: "When you arrive, break off just one corn plant and put it in your basket. Then walk all the way around the field and, when you arrive, the basket will be full of corn."

The women went to the field. They found the corn. There were only four stalks, and they said to each other: "How are we going to fill the basket if there are only four corn plants? Let's cut the four plants and take everything at once."

That's what they did, disobeying Kunám's instructions. They cut all the corn plants, stripped the husks, and put the ears in the basket. Then they walked once around the field. When they got back to the basket, they were amazed to see it overflowing with corn. Also, all around were thousands of kernels, strewn over the ground.

Súwa and Ipák said: "Sister, where can so much corn have come from? We can't waste it. We'll have to gather it all and take it home!"

They filled the basket and even used their *tarachis* to avoid leaving any behind.[7] But when they hoisted the basket, the rope broke, and everything fell out.

Súwa and Ipák began to insult Kunám: "How does that ugly guy do any carrying, with his ground-down teeth? That stub-toothed old man doesn't even know how to weave baskets! He's good for nothing!"

Kunám was hidden, listening. He returned home very sad at the insults.

When night fell, Kunám took apart his house, while Súwa and Ipák were sleeping. He took it piece by piece to the other side of the river, rebuilding it there.

The women awoke when it started raining. One said to the other: "Sister, get up and stoke the fire. It's cold. A storm's coming."

She got up. But there were nettles all around. When they moved just a bit, the nettles stung them. It rained hard, storm winds blew, and lightning and thunder crashed. When the storm passed, they could hear Kunám on the other side of the river, singing: "They called me stub-tooth! tum! tum! tum! . . . They called me stub-tooth! tum! tum! tum! . . . They called me stub-tooth! tum! tum! tum!"

The women said to each other: "Dear sister, how can he have heard us insulting him? He's taken away the house. That miserable wretch!"

By dawn, they were half-dead from cold, and their legs were covered with spider bites. They despaired: "Sister, what are we going to do? Are we going to spend our whole lives wandering like this from one place to another? We suffer too much."

They felt very sad, a big emptiness. So they thought hard that day. At last, Súwa said: "Sister, let's change ourselves into two giant stones."

But Ipák replied: "No, because when people go by, they'll say that these two stones were human beings. Because they didn't want to live, they turned themselves into stones. We'll be horribly embarrassed when they say that."

After thinking some more, Súwa said: "Then sister, why don't we turn ourselves into high hills?"

Ipák replied: "No, because when young hunters have to climb those hills after a monkey, wildcat, or peccary, they'll get tired, and they'll curse us."

Súwa kept thinking. Then she said: "Sister, let's make ourselves into flat valleys."

But Ipák replied: "No, sister, no. Because someday people will come to those valleys. Tired of walking, they'll say, 'What a huge plain!' Then they will curse us, and we'll be very embarrassed."

So Súwa said: "I know what I'm going to do. I'm going to turn into *huito*. When men get sick, they will come to look for my fruit, and they'll paint their bodies black with my seeds. And when they want to blacken their teeth or dye their hair, they will come to me and use my seeds. That's it! I'll turn into *huito*. Ipák, you could become *achiote*."

And Ipák liked the idea. She exclaimed: "Yes, sister. I'll turn into *achiote*. So when men celebrate a successful fishing expedition or hunt, or some good news, they'll come to me and paint their faces and breasts red with my fruit. And when they want to redden their skin when they feel weak and anemic, they'll come to me and eat my seeds, and their skin will turn a healthy color."

Contented, the sisters exclaimed: "*Nú atí*—Let it be so!"

Then Súwa got on her feet. She made a huge jump and turned into a small *huito* tree. It grew rapidly, becoming full of branches. It filled completely with ripe fruit. Then she said to Ipák: "Sister, get on your knees so you can turn into an *achiote* tree. Standing, on your feet, you may be afraid."

"Okay," Ipák replied. She knelt and began to grow quickly. She turned into an *achiote*, laden with ripe red fruit.

Such were the adventures and misadventures of Súwa and Ipák, the two single sisters. To this day, the Aguaruna and the Huambisa, the inhabitants of the upper Marañón, go to the *huito* and *achiote* trees for black and red paint to paint their pots and plates, dye their hair and teeth, heal sores, and paint tattoos on their faces and chests for *masato* drinking and big parties, and many other uses.

Notes

1   Two birds found in the Peruvian jungle.
2   A fermented beverage made of chewed yucca, drunk by many indigenous groups in the Amazon.
3   Food wrapped in leaves and roasted on coals.
4   Two common fish in the Amazon and its tributaries.
5   A *tawas* is a crown of colored feathers.
6   *Tsantsas* are shrunken heads, formerly made by Aguarunas as war trophies.
7   *Tarachis* are the cloth wraps that Aguaruna women wear.

SELF-IMAGES

Workshop for Social Photography

Apart from family snapshots, most photographs of Peru are taken by "outsiders" looking in—tourists, journalists, anthropologists, aid workers. But the Lima-based Social Photography Workshops (TAFOS) has put Yashica T3 cameras loaded with T-MAX film in the hands of "insiders," with dramatic results. Not only is their relation to their subjects unique (they are members of the communities they photograph); they also capture moments invisible to most outsiders, like the lonely protest march of peasants across a Puno moor or the street vendor hawking his wares against an ancient Inca wall. These five photographs are taken by five different photographers: two in Lima, one in Cuzco, one in Morococha, and one in Puno.

Figure 58. Miners entering the shaft, Morococha.
(Courtesy of Máximo Palomino)

Figure 59. Playing music on a bus to earn a little money, Lima.
(Courtesy of Víctor Bustamante)

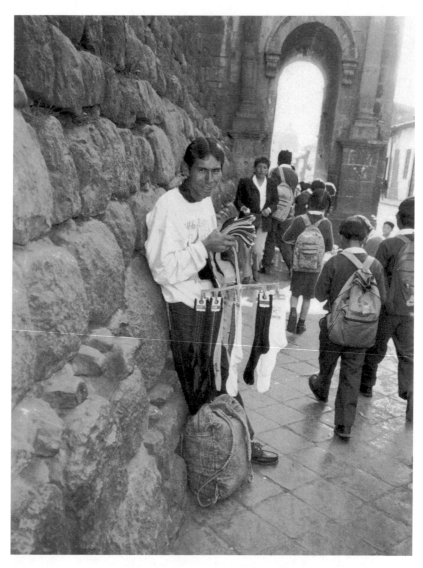

Figure 60. Street seller leaning on an Incan wall near the
San Pedro Market, Cuzco. (Courtesy of Mario Cutipa)

Figure 61. Takeover of unused government cooperative land, Ayaviri, Puno. (Courtesy of Melchor Lima)

Figure 62. Party, San Martín de Porres, Lima. (Courtesy of Daniel Pajuelo)

SUGGESTIONS FOR FURTHER READING

The amount of good writing on Peru is huge. We have no pretensions to complete coverage in these suggestions. The following articles and books, however, all offer important views of major themes. Where one exists, we list the English translation of works first published in Spanish, although we encourage those who can to go to the original.

The Ancient Civilizations

Lumbreras, Luis. *The Peoples and Cultures of Ancient Peru.* Translated by Betty Meggers. Washington, D.C.: Smithsonian Institution, 1974.

MacCormack, Sabine. *Religion in the Andes.* Princeton, N.J.: Princeton University Press, 1992.

Moseley, Michael. *The Incas and Their Ancestors.* New York: Thames and Hudson, 1992.

Murra, John. *Formaciones económicas y políticas del mundo andino.* Lima: Instituto de Estudios Peruanos, 1975.

Rostworowski, María. *Historia del Tahuantinsuyu.* Lima: Instituto de Estudios Peruanos, 1988.

Zuidema, R. T. *Reyes y guerreros: Ensayos de cultura andina.* Lima: Fomiciencias, 1990.

Conquest and Colonial Rule

Glave, Luis Miguel. *Trajinantes: Caminos indígenas en la sociedad colonial, siglo XVI–XVII.* Lima: Instituto de Apoyo Agrario, 1989.

Gutiérrez, Gustavo. *Las Casas: In Search of the Poor of Jesus Christ.* Maryknoll, N.Y.: Orbis, 1993.

Noble, David Cook, and Alexandra Parma Cook. *Good Faith and Truthful Ignorance: A Case of Transatlantic Bigamy.* Durham, N.C.: Duke University Press, 1991. 1993.

Spalding, Karen. *Huarochirí: An Andean Society under Inca and Spanish Rule.* Stanford: Stanford University Press, 1984.

Stern, Steve J., ed. *Resistance, Rebellion, and Consciousness in the Andean Peasant World, 16th–19th Century.* Madison: University of Wisconsin Press, 1989.

Varese, Stefano. *La sal de los cerros.* Lima: Universidad Peruana de Ciencias y Tecnología, 1968.

Republican Peru

Bonilla, Heraclio, ed. *La independencia en el Perú*. Lima: Instituto de Estudios Peruanos, 1981.

Gootenberg, Paul. *Imagining Development: Economic Ideas in Peru's "Fictitious Prosperity" of Guano, 1840–1880*. Berkeley: University of California Press, 1993.

Kristal, Efraín. *The Andes Viewed from the City: History and Political Discourse on the Indian in Peru, 1848–1930*. New York: Peter Lang, 1987.

Manrique, Nelson. *Campesinado y nación: Las guerrillas indígenas en la guerra con Chile*. Lima: Centro de Investigación y Capacitación, 1981.

Taylor, Lewis. *Bandits and Politics in Peru: Landlord and Peasant Violence in Hualgayoc, 1900–1930*. Cambridge, England: Centre for Latin American Studies, 1987.

Thurner, Mark. *From Two Republics to One Divided: The Contradictions of Postcolonial Nation-Making in Andean Peru*. Durham, N.C.: Duke University Press, 1992.

The Advent of Modern Politics

Cotler, Julio. *Clase, estado, y nación en el Perú*. Lima: Instituto de Estudios Peruanos, 1978.

De la Cadena, Marisol. *Indigenous Mestizos: The Politics of Race and Culture in Cuzco, 1919–1991*. Durham, N.C.: Duke University Press.

Flores Galindo, Alberto. *La agonía de Mariátegui*. Lima: Instituto de Apoyo Agrario, 1989.

Klarén, Peter. *Modernization, Dislocation, and Aprismo: The Origins of Peru's Aprista Party, 1870–1932*. Austin: University of Texas Press, 1973.

Mariátegui, José Carlos. *Seven Interpretive Essays on Peruvian Reality*. Austin: University of Texas Press, 1971.

Stein, Steve. *Populism in Peru: The Emergence of the Masses and the Politics of Social Control*. Madison: University of Wisconsin Press, 1980.

The Breakup of the Old Order

Alegría, Ciro. *The World Is Broad and Alien*. Translated by Harriet de Onis. London: Merlin Press, 1973.

Arguedas, José María. *Deep Rivers*. Austin: University of Texas Press, 1978.

——. *Yawar Fiesta*. Austin: University of Texas Press, 1985.

Brown, Michael, and Eduardo Fernández. *War of Shadows: The Struggle for Utopia in the Peruvian Amazon*. Berkeley: University of California Press, 1991.

Lowenthal, Abraham, ed. *The Peruvian Experiment*. Princeton, N.J.: Princeton University Press, 1975.

Matos Mar, José, and José Carlos Mejía. *La reforma agraria en el Perú*. Lima: Instituto de Estudios Peruanos, 1980.

McClintock, Cynthia, and Abraham Lowenthal, eds. *The Peruvian Experiment Reconsidered*. Princeton, N.J.: Princeton University Press, 1983.

Thorndike, Guillermo. *No, mi general*. Lima: Mosca Azul, 1976.

The Shining Path

Degregori, Carlos Iván. *Ayacucho 1969–1979: El surgimiento de Sendero Luminoso*. Lima: Instituto de Estudios Peruanos, 1990.

DESCO. *Violencía Política en el Perú.* Lima: DESCO, 1989.

Gorriti, Gustavo. *Shining Path: A History of the Millenarian War in Peru.* Chapel Hill: University of North Carolina Press, 1999.

Stern, Steve J. ed. *Shining and Other Paths: War and Society in Peru, 1980–1995.* Durham, N.C.: Duke University Press, 1998.

Manchay Tiempo

Americas Watch. *Untold Terror: Violence against Women in Peru's Armed Conflict.* New York: Human Rights Watch, 1992.

Degregori, Carlos Iván, José Coronel, Ponciano del Pino, and Orin Starn. *Las rondas campesinas y la derrota de Sendero Luminoso.* Lima: Instituto de Estudios Peruanos, 1996.

Gamboa, Jeremías, ed. *Yuyanapaq: Relato visual del conflicto armado en el Perú.* Lima: Comisión de la Verdad y Reconciliación, 2003.

Kirk, Robin. *The Monkey's Paw: New Chronicles from Peru.* Amherst: University of Massachusetts Press, 1997.

Truth and Reconciliation Commission. *Final Report.* Lima: Truth and Reconciliation Commission, 2003. Available at http://www.cverdad.org.pe/ingles/ifinal/index.php.

Youngers, Coletta. *Violencia política y sociedad civil en el Perú: Historia de la Coordinadora Nacional de Derechos Humanos.* Lima: IEP, 2003.

The Cocaine Economy

Carpenter, Ted Galen. *Bad Neighbor Policy: Washington's Futile War on Drugs in Latin America.* London: Palgrave Macmillan, 2003.

Cultural Survival. "Coca and Cocaine: Effects on People and Policy in Latin America." Report no. 23. Boston: Cultural Survival, 1986.

Kennedy, Joseph, *Coca Exótica.* Rutherford, N.J.: Fairleigh Dickinson University Press, 1985.

Morales, Edmundo. *Cocaine: White Gold Rush in Peru.* Tucson: University of Arizona Press, 1989.

The Struggle for Survival

De Soto, Hernando. *The Other Path: The Invisible Revolution in the Third World.* New York: Harper and Row, 1989.

García, María Elena. *Making Indigenous Citizens: Identities, Education, and Multicultural Development in Peru.* Stanford: Stanford University Press, 2005.

Golte, Jürgen, and Norma Adams. *Los caballos de Troya de los invasores: Estrategias campesinas en la conquista de Gran Lima.* Lima: Instituto de Estudios Peruanos, 1987.

Klarén, Peter. *Peru: Society and Nationhood in the Andes.* New York: Oxford University Press, 2000.

Starn, Orin. *Nightwatch: The Politics of Protest in the Andes.* Durham, N.C.: Duke University Press, 1999.

Wise, Carol. *Reinventing the State: Economic Strategy and Institutional Change in Peru.* Ann Arbor: University of Michigan Press, 2002.

Culture(s) Redefined

Cornejo Polar, Antonio Vidal, and Luis Fernando Vidal, eds. *Nuevo Cuento Peruano.* Lima: Mosca Azul, 1986.

Degregori, Carlos Iván, Cecilia Blondet, and Nicolás Lynch. *Conquistadores de un nuevo mundo: De invasores a ciudadanos en San Martin de Porres.* Lima: Instituto de Estudios Peruanos, 1986.

Silva-Santiesteban, Ricardo, ed. *Poesía Peruana, Antología General.* Lima: Ediciones Edubanco, 1984.

Vargas Llosa, Mario. *A Fish in the Water: A Memoir.* Translated by Helen Lane. New York: Farrar, Straus and Giroux, 1994.

Vásquez, Chalena, and Abilio Vergara. *Chayraq! Carnaval Ayacuchano.* Lima: Centro de Desarollo Agropecuario, 1988.

ACKNOWLEDGMENTS

There are many people to whom we owe our gratitude. This book is in large measure the fruit of their generosity and patience in sharing with us their ideas, passion, and personal lists of must-reads. Special thanks are due to Susan Ackerman, Alexandra Balaguer, Jaime Bayly, Michael Brown, Leigh Campoamor, the Committee of the Families of the Detained and Disappeared (COFADER), Julia Chambi, Teo Allaín Chambi, Arturo Escobar, Jorge Frisancho, Paul Gelles, Luis Miguel Glave, Jürgen Golte, Juan Larco, Florencia Mallon, Mónica Newton, Angel Páez, Jaime Regan, Francisco Reyes, Irene Silverblatt, Steve J. Stern, Frances Starn, Randolph Starn, Margaret VanBolt, Carol Wise and Caroline Yezer. Lucien Chauvin and Lewis Taylor were of huge help at every step of the way.

We are also indebted to Richard Collier, Jackie Love, Vivian Scales, Ajantha Subramanian, Clare Talwalker, Ruth Camacho, Patricia Van Norman, and María Angélica Velásquez, all of whom provided invaluable assistance. For financial and moral support, we are grateful to the Duke-UNC Latin American Studies Consortium and to the Duke University Department of Cultural Anthropology, especially William O'Barr, and Naomi Quinn. Iván Rivasplata of the Institute of Peruvian Studies tracked down material in Peru and made wise suggestions about how to organize the book. Ken Wissoker at Duke University Press guided *The Peru Reader* into print, and we thank him for his patience, skill, and friendship. Valerie Millholland has been a wonderful editor for this new edition of *The Peru Reader* and of the Latin America Readers Series.

ACKNOWLEDGMENT OF COPYRIGHTS

INDEX

Acevedo, Juan, 310
acllas, 70, 106
African-Peruvians, 95, 287; music of, 7, 263, 305; in shantytowns, 387. *See also* María Elena Moyano; San Martín de Porres; slavery
agrarian reform, 270, 279–284, 285–286
Aguaruna Indians, 553–561
AIDS, 505–506
Alfredo, 357–464
Allen, Catherine J., 411
Allpachaka, 343, 345–347
Alvarado Huallpa, Pascuala, 477–480
Amazon: colonization of, 553, indigenous life in, 215–216, 553–561
Ancash, 14
Ancón: Treaty of, 197
Andes, 230, 231–234, 263; and the Andean "reconquest," 293; and modernity, 273; and ways of being of Andean, 453. *See also* agrarian reform; culture; Incas; Indians; peasants; Quechua; *rondas campesinas*
anti-imperialism: of Víctor Raúl Haya de la Torre, 253; José Carlos Mariátegui's view of, 240, 243–245
Apasa, Julián (Túpac Katari), 160
Appadurai, Arjun, 6
APRA: founding of, 229; principles of, 253–257; uprising of 1932, 258, 260–261. *See also* Alan García; Víctor Raúl Haya de la Torre
Apurímac Valley, 393–400
Arciniega, Alberto, 435
Arguedas, José María, 269–270, 273, 483, 487; concept of "all the bloods," 7; con-cept of "Andean reconquest," 293; and Quechua modernity, 273
art, 482; in pre-Columbian society, 14–16, 25–27; and war, 458. *See also* culture
asentamientos humanos. See shantytowns
Atahualpa, 50–51, 71; capture of, 93, 97–118
Atahualpa, Juan Santos, 94
Ayacucho: and the Shining Path, 319, 325, 343–350; artistic traditions, 384, 482; battle of, 179–180; carnival in, 487; refugees from, 371–372; in wartime, 357–363. *See also* Huamanga; military; Shining Path
ayllu, 21–22, 38–49, 94, 234, 418, 499; and colonialism, 125–126, 128–138; and gender, 43–45

Bambarén, Luis, 291
Basadre, Jorge, 175
Bastidas, Micaela, 164, 169
Bayly, Jaime, 528
Beals, Carleton, 257
Belaúnde, Fernando, 270, 353–354, 362, 441
Belaúnde, Víctor Andrés, 227
Benavides, Oscar, 230
Bingham, Hiram, 1, 14, 82
Bird, Junius, 56–57
black. *See* African-Peruvians
Blondet, Cecilia, 287
Bolivar, Simón, 175
Bolognesi, Francisco, 199, 205
Bossio, Enrique, 502
Bryce Echenique, Alfredo, 270, 313
Burger, Richard, 22, 27

cabildo, 94

Cáceres, Andres Avelino, 177, 182–188, 190–198

Cajamarca, 63–64, 193; capture of Atahualpa in, 103–106, 111–113, 116; and *rondas campesinas*, 447

Callao, 357, 491

carnival, 483, 485–488

Castro Pozo, Hildebrando, 228

Catholicism, 491, 501 n.1; and colonialism, 80–81, 119–122, 124–143, 153; and homosexuality, 506; and Inca religion, 50–51; and liberation theology, 270, 309–312; and Protestantism, 499; and shantytowns, 291–292. *See also* Bartolomé de las Casas; Gustavo Gutiérrez; Martín de Porres; Sarita Colonia

caudillos, 176, 183, 184–85, 202–205, 206; and *rondas campesinas*, 454–455

Caui Llaca, 30–35

Chalcuchima, 103

Chambi, Martín, 231, 233, 276

Chan Chan, 258–262

chaqwa, 370

Charles I, 99–100

Charles III, 161

chasqui, 76–77

Chauvin, Lucien, 496, 502

Chavín de Huántar, 14, 17–27

chicha 40, 109; drinking rules, 264; music, 8, 365

Chimú, 257–261

Chinese: labor by, 175–176

cholera, 468–473

cholos, 7, 288–289, 442, 481; racism against, 361

Cisneros, Antonio, 179

civil defense committees. See *rondas campesinas*

Civilista Party, 183

Cobo, Bernabe, 37, 43, 57–58, 60

coca, 160; and Andean culture, 411–423, 424; and cocaine, 425–436; in pre-Columbian times, 74, 407; Spanish promotion of, 407

cocaine, 411; trafficking, 425–436; invention of, 407. *See also* drugs

Colonia, Sarita, 288–289, 292, 482, 491–495

colonialism, 93–95; social relations under, 124–148, 149, 153, 161–163. *See also* Incas; Spanish

Comas, 177, 185, 187–198

comedores populares. See soup kitchens

Communist Party of Peru-Red Homeland. *See* Red Homeland

Communist Party of Peru-Shining Path. *See* Shining Path

Condorcanqui, José Gabriel (Túpac Amaru II), 8; rebellion of, 159–168; sentence against, 169–173

conquest, 93–122; and concept of "Andean reconquest," 293. *See also* Atahualpa; Incas; Francisco Pizarro; Spain

Córdova, Manuel, 215

Córdova, Víctor, 458

Cornejo, María Emilia, 511

corregidor, 130, 136, 147, 159, 161

Cortés, Hernán, 98, 100, 103

cotton: in pre-Columbian society, 19–21, 58–70. *See also* textiles

criollos: 96, 160, 161, 203, 241, 243, 360; music of, 305. *See also* elites; whites

Cuban Revolution, 307

culture: and the "heterodoxy of tradition," 240–241; and "hybrid cultures," 455, 459 n.8; in Lima, 489; problems with concept of, 481–482; repression of Inca, 166, 169, 170–172

Cuni Raya, 30–34

curaca, 39, 41, 48, 61–62, 67–68, 124–146, 161

Cuzco: 77, 93, 273, 285, 411, 450; and the Inca empire, 71; *indigenismo* in, 231; origins of, 50, 53–55

de Almagro, Diego, 84, 98, 100

de Areche, José Antonio, 166, 169, 173

de Avila, Francisco, 30

de Benalcázar, Sebastián, 65, 101, 110–111

de Cieza de León, Pedro, 1, 3–4, 13, 58, 63–64; and Inca taxation, 71–74

de la Puente Uceda, Luis, 307

de la Riva Agüero, José, 269

de las Casas, Bartolomé: and Indians, 119–122; and liberation theology, 309, 311

de la Vega, Garcilaso, 1, 13, 42, 50, 57, 69

del Pino, Ponciano, 393

de Mena, Cristóbal, 13

de Mugaburu y Honton, Josephe, 149

de Piérola, Nicolás, 183, 194
de Soto, Hernando, 101, 107, 110
desplazados. *See* refugees
de Sucre, José Antonio, 179
Deustua, Alejandro, 269
de Valdivia, Pedro, 65
de Valverde, Vicente, 113–114
drugs, 425–440; and military, 357, 360,
    438–440; policy of Fujimori toward,
    435; and *rondas campesinas*, 393, 399–
    400. *See also* Apurímac Valley; cocaine;
    Pablo Escobar; Huallaga Valley; military;
    Shining Path; United States

elites: and "gentlemen's clubs," 230; life of,
    313–318; in War of the Pacific, 187–188,
    192–193, 196. See also *Criollos*; whites
El Niño, 19
El Paraíso, 22–23, 25
encomiendas, 94, 148 n.2
Escobar, Pablo, 408
evangelicals. *See* Protestantism

feminism, 482; concept of "feminitopia,"
    207; and Flora Tristán, 175, 207; and
    poetry, 507. *See also* gender; women
Flores Galindo, Alberto, 159; concept of
    "colonial military" of, 394
Fuentes, Ranulfo, 355, 384
Fujimori, Alberto, 9, 481; and cholera,
    468, 470, 471–472; drug policy of, 435;
    economic policy of, 6–7, 442, 462–
    467; election of, 442; and evangelicals,
    496; government by *dictablanda* of, 460;
    and human rights, 6, 462; "self-coup"
    by, 460; and Shining Path, 442–461;
    Vladimiro Montesinos, 9, 442, 474

García, Alan, 354, 373, 375, 435
García Calderón, Francisco, 227
gays and lesbians. *See* sexuality
gender: inversion of, 486; "parallelism" in
    Andean society, 36–49; redefinition of,
    482; in Republican Peru, 175. *See also*
    feminism; women
Ginés de Sepúlveda, Juan, 119
Gitlitz, John, 455
Glave, Luis Miguel, 95
González, Raúl, 427
González Prada, Manuel, 9, 199; and the
    Church, 199–202; and heroes, 203–206;

and Indians, 202–203; and the military,
    199–202
González Viaña, Eduardo, 491
Gorriti, Gustavo, 331, 353
Grau, Miguel, 199, 203–206
guano, 175
Gutiérrez, Gustavo, 270–271, 309
Guzmán, Abimael, 319–321, 325; cap-
    ture of, 321; and the "Myth of Gonzalo"
    about, 321; and "the quota," 331–334,
    337–341. *See also* Shining Path

Hacas Poma, 39, 41
haciendas: abolition of, 279–286; mobiliza-
    tion against, 235–239, social relations
    on, 273–278; in War of the Pacific,
    181–198
Hall, Stuart, 483
Haya de la Torre, Víctor Raúl, 228, 229,
    240, 253, 260
Heraud, Javier, 307
huacas, 141–143, 146, 261, 264
Huallaga Valley, 425–435
Huamanga: carnival in, 487; colonial his-
    tory of, 124; university of, 343–347. *See
    also* Ayacucho
Huancabamba, 263, 450
Huancavelica, 353, 424
Huancayo, 181–198
Huanta, 354
huaqueros, 14
Huáscar: and Incan civil war, 69, 102
Huáscar (ship): sinking of, 203–206
Huaychao, 353
Huayna Capac, 1, 64–65, 68, 102
human rights: and "Anti-Terrorism Laws,"
    381; and "dirty war," 384; and "disap-
    pearance," 349, 354, 384, 391; and
    women, 366

Ica, 235
Idrogo, Daniel, 449, 458
Iglesias, Miguel, 193
Ilapa, 37–40, 46
Incas: and coca, 407; conquest of, 97–118;
    gender relations under, 37; and "Inca
    nationalism," 94; and *indigenismo*, 231–
    234; military expansion of, 14; origins
    of, 50–55; and Peruvian tradition, 241;
    redistributive policy, 68; religion of,
    50–55, 67–68; roads and bridges of, 77–

Incas (*continued*)
    78; royal marriages of, 66–67; sources
    of information about, 13; taxation by,
    71–75
Independence War (1820–1824), 175, 179
Indians: and colonialism, 124–148, 167;
    criticism of subjugation of, 119–122,
    202–203; and *indigenismo*, 228, 231–
    234; mobilizations by, 234; mythology
    of, 215–226, 553; "Republic of," 124–
    125, 148; and rubber boom, 215–226,
    273–278; and socialism, 228, 229. *See
    also* Amazon; Andes; Incas; peasants;
    Quechua
Inkarrí myth, 93–94, 169, 273
Iquicha, 9–10, 382

Jauja, 64–65
Jordana, José Luis, 553
Junín, 181–198

Kawell, Jo Ann, 425

La Breña: campaign of, 183–198
Lagos, Edith, 320
Lamb, Bruce, 215
Lathrap, Donald, 23
Leguía, Augusto, 229, 260
Lewin, Boleslao, 160
liberation theology. *See* Catholicism
Lima, 8, 481, 508, 527; colonial life in,
    149–155; elites of, 313–318; and evan-
    gelical churches, 498–501; gay and
    lesbian life in, 503; racism in, 350; refu-
    gees in, 370–383; shantytown life in,
    287, 293–294; women in, 207–214
llamas, 56
Lombardi, Francisco, 296, 444
Lumbreras, Luis, 14
Lynch, John, 162

Machu Picchu, 1, 4, 82–91
Mallon, Florencia E., 181
mamaconas, 106
Manco Inca, 7
Manrique, Nelson, 374
Maoism. *See* Red Homeland; Shining Path
Mariátegui, José Carlos, 7, 229, 240, 481;
    and the "heterodoxy of tradition" of,
    240–241; and revolution, 242
Martín de Mejía, Raquel, 366

Martín de Porres, San, 154–158, 292
Martos, Marco, 123
Marxism, 299, 244, 307. *See also* socialism;
    Red Homeland; Shining Path
Mendoza, Angélica, 381
mestizos, 50, 202–203, 231, 241, 243, 420;
    creation of category of, 161
migration: to Amazon, 431; to cities, 269;
    history of, 370–371; and popular cul-
    ture, 485; to the United States, 6,
    489–490
military: in the Apurímac Valley, 393–400;
    criticism of, 199–202; and drug trade,
    426–440; and emergency zones, 353–
    354; government by, 270–271; praise
    for, 462; and Shining Path, 349–350,
    353–363
Minguet, Charles, 167
mining, 127, 227, 563
mita, 58, 62, 69, 94, 125, 131–132
mitmaq, 57
Moche: ancient civilization of, 13–15, 65;
    town of, 258, 262–263
Mochica. *See Moche*
modernity, 12, 270, 273; and concept of
    "alternative modernity," 453; and "mod-
    ernization," 227, 269; and "tradition,"
    481–482
Montesinos, Vladimiro, 9, 442, 474–476
montoneras, 177, 181–198
Moro, César, 5, 265
Morote, Osmán, 323
Morse, Richard, 161
Movement of the Revolutionary Left
    (MIR), 307
Moyano, María Elena, 387
MRTA, 427, 438
Murra, John: and "verticality," 56

nationalism, 9, 177–180, 215; as "imagined
    community," 164; and "Inca national-
    ism," 82; and land invasions, 272, 278;
    and "New Fatherland," 217; of peas-
    ants, 170; and revolution, 231, 292; and
    rondas campesinas, 432
Nazca, 13, 15, 28

Oblitas, Régulo, 449
Odría, Manuel, 313, 512
Ollé, Carmen, 481, 507
orejones, 72, 74

Pachamama, 60, 412, 421; and gender norms, 36–43
Palma, Ricardo, 154
panacas, 66
peasant patrols. See *rondas campesinas*
peasants: movements of, 235; position on *haciendas* of, 273–278. *See also* agrarian reform, Indians, *rondas campesinas*
Pévez, Juan, 235
Piura, 101, 448
Pizarro, Francisco, 93, 123; and the conquest, 97–118; as founder of Lima, 149
Pizarro, Gonzalo, 100
Pizarro, Hernando, 100, 105, 107–111
Pizarro, Pedro, 112
police: mistrust of, 390; praise for, 462; and *rondas campesinas*, 398; repression by, 288; and Shining Path, 377–379
politics, 5, 227–230, 253–257; disenchantment with, 9; and the "politics of meaning," 481; and stereotype of peasants as "prepolitical," 453–454. *See also* APRA; Fernando Belaúnde; Alberto Fujimori; Alan García; Red Homeland; Shining Path
Pollarolo, Giovanna, 509
Polo de Ondegardo, Juan, 37, 39, 59
Poma de Ayala, Guamán, 2, 57, 137; view of Inca bureaucracy, 76–81
Popular Revolutionary Alliance of America. *See* APRA
poverty: and agrarian reform, 279; and cholera, 468–473; persistence of, 5, 441–444; and refugees, 370–383; and religion, 309–312, 496–501; responses to, 441–459, 477–480; stereotypes about, 296; and women, 445
Pratt, Mary, 207
Protestants, 479; and military, 499–500; and *rondas campesinas*, 393–400, 456; and Shining Path, 499–500; in shantytowns, 498–501; and women, 498–499
pueblos jóvenes. *See* shantytowns
Puno, 477

Quechua, 269, 285, 357, 384, 485; and national culture, 273. *See also* Andes; Indians; peasants
quinoa, 40, 42, 56, 73, 78
Quinua, 179–180

quipus, 13, 72
Quispez Asín, Alfredo. *See* César Moro
Quisquis, 65, 102
Quito, 102

racism, 7–8, 394; in the counterinsurgency, 361
reciprocity: in the Andes, 367
Red Homeland, 449, 453
refugees, 353–356, 370–383
religion. *See* Catholicism; colonialism; culture; Incas; Protestantism
revolution: and Mariátegui, 239; and poetry, 307. *See also* Red Homeland; Shining Path
Reyes, Lucha, 305
Ribeyro, Julio Ramón, 296
Risco, Pedro, 449–450
Rojas, Telmo, 455
rondas campesinas: and drug trafficking, 393–400; and evangelicals, 393–400; in northern mountains, 447–459; in the north versus the south, 393, 448; and the Shining Path, 393–400, 456–458
Rosaldo, Renato, 5, 169
Rostworowski, María, 13
Rowe, John, 94
rubber: boom in, 215; tapping and trade, 216–223
Rumiñavi, 65, 102

Sabogal, José, 361–262, 482
Salcedo, José María, 477
Sánchez Cerro, Luis, 230, 235, 260–261
San Martín, José, 175, 496
Santa Cruz, Nicomedes, 305
Sendero Luminoso. *See* Shining Path
sexuality: in carnival, 487; in feminist poetry, 507; and gay and lesbian rights, 502–506; preconceptions about, 511; redefinition of, 482–483
shantytowns, 287; founding of, 293–295; popular culture in, 482, 485–488; and refugees, 375–377; and Shining Path, 364–365; and soup kitchens, 445–446
Shining Path: cult to "President Gonzalo" of, 351–352; and drug trafficking, 320, 425–439; and Maoism, 319–321, 325–342; and Marxism, 331–342; origins of, 319–321; "poeticization of death" by, 320; and "the quota," 331; and refugees,

Shining Path (*continued*)
379; and *rondas campesinas*, 393–400,
456–458; the "Sacred Families" of, 323;
in shantytowns, 364, 387–392; and
villagers, 343–350, 354. *See also* Abimael Guzmán; military; police; Osmán
Morote
Silverblatt, Irene, 36
slavery, 175, 305–306. *See also* African-Peruvians
socialism, 228–229
Sologuren, Javier, 17, 30
Sonqo, 411
soup kitchens: 377, 391, 445–446
Spain: abuses of Indians by, 79–81, 119–123, 282; and colonial rule, 159–168;
conquest of Incas by, 97–118; Independence Wars against, 175, 179–180;
negative influence of, 202–203; nostalgia for, 154; and Peruvian culture, 241;
promotion of coca by, 407; and reforms
by Bourbon dynasty of, 161–163; in
sixteenth century, 98
Stern, Steve J., 94, 124
surrealism, 265

Taki Onqoy, 124–125, 134, 141
Tandeter, Enrique, 163
tapadas, 2, 210
Tello, Julio C., 14, 23–25
textiles, 56–70. *See also* cotton
Tiahuanaco, 14
Tingo María, 425–437
Tinta, 159, 169
Toldeo, Alejandro, 9, 443
Toledo, Francisco, 94–96, 125
Torribio, Mercedes, 293
Tristán, Flora, 175, 207
Tumbes, 99–100
Túpac Amaru, 93
Túpac Amaru II. *See* José Gabriel Condorcanqui

Túpac Amaru Revolutionary Movement.
See MRTA
Túpac Katari. *See* Julián Apasa

Uchuraccay, 353
United States, 229, 243–244, 313, 345;
drug policy of, 7, 319, 399, 408, 425–436; migration to, 6, 489–490
Urrutia, Jaime, 372
Urton, Gary, 18

Valcárcel, Luis, 228, 230–231
Vallejo, César, 7, 246
varayoq, 47
Vargas Llosa, Mario, 266, 512; campaign
of, 442; and Uchuraccay report, 10, 353;
view of the conquest of, 93; view of Lima
of, 512–527
Velasco, Juan, 279–280, 286, 289
Villa El Salvador, 387–392, 479; founding
of, 287–292
Vitarte, 485–488
von Humboldt, Alexander, 167

Wachtel, Nathan, 163
War of the Pacific (1879–1883), 175, 181–198; disenchantment after, 199; recovery
from, 227; and social divisions, 176–177
Wari, 14
whites, 227, 231, 243; description of, 313–318, 442; and 1992 election, 442. See
also *Criollos*; elites
women, 76; before the Spanish, 36–48, 58; and the "informal economy,"
477–480; in the middle-classes, 509;
and misogyny, 76, 240; in nineteenth-century Lima, 207–214; and poetry,
507; and political violence, 361, 366–369; and religion, 498–499; in shanty-towns, 293–295, 387–392, 445. *See also*
feminism; gender

Orin Starn is Professor of Cultural Anthropology at Duke University.
Carlos Iván Degregori is Professor of Anthropology at the National University
of San Marcos in Lima.
Robin Kirk is Co-director of the Human Rights Initiative at Duke University.

Library of Congress Cataloging-in-Publication Data
The Peru reader : history, culture, politics / edited by
Orin Starn, Carlos Iván Degregori, and Robin Kirk. — 2nd ed.,
rev. and expanded.
p. cm. — (The Latin America Readers)
Includes bibliographical references and index.
ISBN 0-8223-3655-3 (cloth : alk. paper)
ISBN 0-8223-3649-9 (pbk. : alk. paper)
1. Peru — History. 2. Peru — Social conditions. 3. Peru — Economic
conditions. I. Starn, Orin. II. Degregori, Carlos Iván. III. Kirk,
Robin. IV. Series.
F3431.P478 2005   985—dc22   2005011391